Yorkshire Quarter

Widow Greene	Thomas Yale	John Sanderson	John Jansen	Will. Thorp	Jeremiah Dixon	Edw. Tench
T. Powell		Thomas Fugill		Robt Hill		
Edward Wigglesworth			Abra Bell	Wid. Williams		Mrs Higginson
	Mrs Constable	Mr. Mayes	John Evance	Andr. Low	Fra. Browne David Atwater	John Evance Francis Newman Henry Rutherford
John Cockerell				Mr Lines		
Joshua Atwater						

			Francis Brewster	Mark Mow Goods to picke	George man Lamberton James Laybart
			Mrs Eldred		Robert Newman
			Mr. Marshall	Richard Beckley	William Andrews
					John Cooper

Mr Goodyear's Quarter

Matthew Gilbert	Owen River	An Elder	Richard Perry 2½ acres	Nathaniel Turner	Ezekiel Cheevers	
Thomas Kimberley		Jasper Crane		David Yale		
		Richard Hulse	Theophilus Eaton	Mr. Eaton		
John Benham	Edward Banks John Davenport		Samuel Eaton	William Tuttle		

Mr Herriman Quarter

Mr Davenport's Quarter

The Governor's Quarter

History
of
The Colony of New Haven
to Its Absorption into
Connecticut

by
Edward E. Atwater

with
Supplementary History and Personnel
of the
Towns of Branford, Guilford, Milford, Stratford, Norwalk, Southold, Etc.

Compiled by
Robert Atwater Smith

Assisted by
Bessie E. Beach and Lucy M. Hewitt

— *Second Edition* —

HERITAGE BOOKS
2009

HERITAGE BOOKS
AN IMPRINT OF HERITAGE BOOKS, INC.

Books, CDs, and more—Worldwide

For our listing of thousands of titles see our website
at
www.HeritageBooks.com

A Facsimile Reprint
Published 2009 by
HERITAGE BOOKS, INC.
Publishing Division
100 Railroad Ave. #104
Westminster, Maryland 21157

Originally published
Meriden, Conn.:
The Journal Publishing Company
1902

— Publisher's Notice —
In reprints such as this, it is often not possible to remove blemishes from the original. We feel the contents of this book warrant its reissue despite these blemishes and hope you will agree and read it with pleasure.

International Standard Book Numbers
Paperbound: 978-1-55613-224-7
Clothbound: 978-0-7884-4929-1

THE first edition of the History of the Colony of New Haven having been exhausted, and there still existing a demand for additional copies, the entire book is hereby reproduced, with considerable additional matter that has been laboriously compiled by the three interested parties mentioned on the title page.

Their work is a matter of love, possessing as they do the high ideal of each contributing his or her share toward perpetuating the history of the forefathers of the towns comprising New Haven Colony.

The undersigned has undertaken the publication, agreeing that all moneys beyond its cost shall go to the widow of the author who first published the work, and to whom the copyright was issued. We trust the subscriptions will be liberal.

FRANCIS ATWATER.

MERIDEN, CONN., July 1, 1902.

PREFACE.

THE author cannot better express the feelings which have prompted him to study and write the history of the Colony of New Haven, than by appropriating the following words of Dr. Trumbull:—

"No man of genius and curiosity can read accounts of the origin of nations, the discovery, settlement, and progress of new countries, without a high degree of entertainment. But in the settlement of his own country, in the lives of his ancestors, in their adventures, morals, jurisprudence, and heroism, he feels himself particularly interested. He at once becomes a party in their affairs, and travels and converses with them with a kind of filial delight. While he beholds them braving the horrors of the desert, the terrors of the savage, the distresses of famine and war, he admires their courage, and is pleased with all their escapes from danger, and all their progress in settlement, population, opulence, literature, and happiness."

Deeply interested in the early history of New Haven, he thought that by imparting the information which many desire, but few have leisure to glean from the wide field over which it is scattered, he might do some service to the community in which he lives. He feels assured that many descendants of the Christian Englishmen, who first brought the light of civilization to these shores, will be interested in his work. He hopes that some whose ancestors came hither at a later period, and others who, though born in foreign lands, have chosen New Haven as their home, and learned to love it, will gladly acquaint themselves with the men by whose toil and heroism this goodly heritage was cut out of a wilderness.

The fullness of the records, both of the town and of the colony of New Haven, makes it possible to present the first planters as, in large measure, the narrators of their own history. The author, preferring that they should speak for themselves, has made large extracts from their records and from other contemporary writings. The town records of New Haven for the first ten years are in print, and the manuscript records of the next sixteen years have been carefully read. The records of other towns within the colony, being less accessible to the author, have not been so thoroughly examined; they are, however, but meagre as compared with those of New Haven. Ralph D. Smith diligently searched those of Guilford, and Lambert those of Milford; and their histories have been freely used.

Introducing the fathers of the New Haven Colony, and forbearing for the most part both eulogy and censure, the author has left them to make, with their own words, such impression as they may. He does not conceal his admiration of them; he does not claim that they were faultless; he desires to present them just as they were.

His first thought was to allow every person to appear in his own orthography; but on further reflection, he concluded to give a few specimens of the phonetic spelling of the seventeenth century, and then, by reducing all quotations to present usage, to deliver his readers from the difficulty of interpreting incident to the ancient lawlessness. Accordingly the certificate of conformity which Davenport received the first Sunday after his induction at St. Stephen's is printed on page 30 as it was written; as are also the first two documents in the Appendix.

PREFACE.

In recording an event which took place between the first day of January and the twenty-fifth day of March, the year has been written according to New Style, or else both styles are given; but the days in a month are in all cases numbered according to the ancient computation. The use of Old Style as applied to days will occasion little if any trouble to the reader. Even if he forgets that, according to our way of reckoning, the event took place ten days later, his misconception will not be very important. But to record in Old Style an event which happened in the early part of the modern year, without intimating that the year needed correction, might seriously mislead.

Reference has not always been made to the original authority, in confirmation of a particular statement. Such references may be useful to the specialist, but when frequent are annoying to most readers. Public records have been sufficiently indicated as authority for information derived from that source, and any item acquired by gleaning from the collections of Historical Societies is definitely referred to the volume from which it was taken. But references to Winthrop's Journal, Hubbard's History of New England, Mather's Magnalia, and Hutchinson's History of the Colony of Massachusetts Bay, have been for the most part omitted, for the reason that the specialist can readily find whatever these writers have transmitted to us concerning any particular event.

To all who in answer to his inquiries have aided the author in the compilation of this history, he presents his grateful acknowledgments. A special tribute is due to one who has passed suddenly and peacefully into the invisible world since this preface was begun. Henry White was, of all men, the most learned in antiquarian lore pertaining to New Haven. Other occupations obliged him to relinquish his long-cherished design of writing a topographical history of his native town; but historical inquiries were to the last his recreation and delight. He took a deep interest in the author's work as soon as he knew that it had been undertaken, encouraged him to believe that it would be a pleasure to converse frequently concerning it, and on one occasion spent days in such a search of the land-records as only he was competent to make. In the last interview which the author had with him, he gave vocal expression to a desire already evident, exclaiming with animation, "I wish I could help you more."

NEW HAVEN, October, 1880.

TABLE OF CONTENTS.

CHAPTER I.
CONDITION OF ENGLAND IN THE SEVENTEENTH CENTURY, AS IT AFFECTED THE PURITAN EMIGRATION IN GENERAL . 1

CHAPTER II.
EVENTS WHICH INFLUENCED SOME OF THE FIRST PLANTERS OF NEW HAVEN TO REMOVE FROM THEIR NATIVE LAND TO NEW ENGLAND 28

CHAPTER III.
THE VOYAGE OF THE HECTOR 45

CHAPTER IV.
THE WINTER SPENT IN MASSACHUSETTS 58

CHAPTER V.
THE FIRST YEAR AT QUINNIPIAC 69

CHAPTER VI.
FOUNDATIONS LAID IN CHURCH AND STATE 93

CHAPTER VII.
DIVISION OF LAND 104

CHAPTER VIII.
PERSONNEL OF THE PLANTATION 112

CHAPTER IX.
Milford.— Guilford.— Southold.— Stamford . . 155

CHAPTER X.
Establishment of a Colonial Government . . . 177

CHAPTER XI.
Industrial Pursuits 189

CHAPTER XII.
Religion and Morals 225

CHAPTER XIII.
Learning 261

CHAPTER XIV.
Military Affairs 293

CHAPTER XV.
The Aborigines 316

CHAPTER XVI.
Domestic and Social Life 348

CHAPTER XVII.
History of the Colonial Government to the Restoration of the Stuarts . . , ... 385

CHAPTER XVIII.
The Stuarts and the Regicides 419

CHAPTER XIX.
Connecticut procures a Charter which covers the Territory of New Haven 445

CHAPTER XX.
CONTROVERSY WITH CONNECTICUT 463

CHAPTER XXI.
NEW HAVEN SUBMITS 509

APPENDIX.

		PAGE.
I.	AUTOBIOGRAPHY OF MICHAEL WIGGLESWORTH	531
II.	NATHANAEL ROWE'S LETTER TO WINTHROP	535
III.	LAMBERTON'S SHIP	537
IV.	NAMES OF PEOPLE AS THEY WERE SEATED IN THE NEW HAVEN MEETING HOUSE IN 1647, 1656, AND 1662	542
V.	HOPKINS GRAMMAR SCHOOL	555
VI.	NEW HAVEN'S REMONSTRANCE	561
VII.	NEW HAVEN'S CASE STATED	565

SUPPLEMENTARY HISTORY.

	PAGE.
BRANFORD	595
BRANFORD—PERSONAL SKETCHES	603
PERSONNEL OF GUILFORD	626
PERSONNEL OF MILFORD	639
PERSONNEL OF STRATFORD	657
PERSONNEL OF FAIRFIELD	664
PERSONNEL OF SOUTHOLD	673
PERSONNEL OF NORWALK	679
PERSONNEL OF STAMFORD	684
PERSONNEL OF NEW LONDON	691
PERSONNEL OF SAYBROOK	698a
RESIDENTS OF NEW HAVEN, 1640 TO 1650	699
CATALOGUE OF REV. ROGER NEWTON'S BOOKS	705

xii TABLE OF CONTENTS.

ALPHABETICAL LIST OF THE SEATING OF THE MEETING-
    HOUSE 711
LIST OF OFFICERS OF MILITIA COMPANIES 718
NAMES OF NEW HAVEN RESIDENTS BEFORE 1640 . . . 728

ILLUSTRATIONS.

1. NEW HAVEN IN 1641 . . . . Faces title-page.
2. A BARQUE OF THE SEVENTEENTH CENTURY . . . 55
3. AUTOGRAPHS OF DAVENPORT AND EATON . . 67
4. MEDAL COMMEMORATING THE SETTLEMENT OF NEW HAVEN 74
5. AUTOGRAPHS OF MOMAUGIN AND HIS COUNCIL . . 88
6. AUTOGRAPHS OF MONTOWESE AND SAWSEUNCK . . 89
7. A PORTRAIT WHICH BELONGED TO THE EATON FAMILY 115
8. PORTRAIT OF JOHN DAVENPORT 123
9. MILFORD IN 1646 . . . . . Faces page 155
10. TOWN SEAL OF MILFORD 157
11. A MEETING-HOUSE OF THE SEVENTEENTH CENTURY . 246
12. GROUND PLAN OF A MEETING-HOUSE 249
13. WHITFIELD'S HOUSE AS SEEN FROM THE SOUTH . . 349
14. WHITFIELD'S HOUSE AS SEEN FROM THE WEST . . 349
15. FIRST FLOOR OF WHITFIELD'S HOUSE 351
16. SECOND FLOOR OF WHITFIELD'S HOUSE 351
17. ATTIC FLOOR OF WHITFIELD'S HOUSE 351

HISTORY OF NEW HAVEN COLONY.

CHAPTER I.

CONDITION OF ENGLAND IN THE SEVENTEENTH CENTURY, AS IT AFFECTED THE PURITAN EMIGRATION IN GENERAL.

EMIGRATION to New England in the seventeenth century is to be attributed to the discomfort experienced by the English Puritans in their native land, rather than to any attractiveness in this transatlantic wilderness. It is difficult for those who from their earliest remembrance have been surrounded with the security, beauty, and plenty enjoyed by the posterity of these colonists, to conceive of the same territory as it was seen by their ancestors when they arrived, or as it presented itself to the eye of imagination when they decided to emigrate. New England is to its present inhabitants their pleasant home; but the Englishmen, who in the seventeenth century were uncomfortable in England, loved England as their dear native land, and thought of America as a foreign country, and as such, destitute of the attraction and charm which appertain to the idea of home.

Moreover, emigration to the New World was not merely exile from a land they were reluctant to leave; it was exposure to suffering by cold and hunger, to peril of death by shipwreck, by wild beasts, and by treacherous savages. Such liabilities are, indeed, not unattractive to men in whom the love of adventure predominates; but the English Puritans were in general as free from that restlessness of mind which seeks relief in excitement as any people in the world. Their theology furnishing a central Being whom they acknowledged as infinitely their superior, they were content to rest in him, and so had inward peace. Religion, inclining them to sobriety and industry, fostered the love of home, of security, and of comfort. Individuals among them may have been susceptible to the love of adventure; but, as a class, the planters of New England were not men naturally inclined to desert their homes, and expose themselves to hardships and perils on the ocean and in the wilderness. On the contrary, their training had been such as inclined them to remain in their native land. This is true, even of the unmarried men; but the reluctance to emigrate was, of course, far greater when one must expose wife and children to hardships they were less able than himself to endure.

If the settlement of New England had been the result of mere adventure, its history would have had so little connection with that of the mother-country, that its relation might properly commence with the first arrival of colonists: but actually there is such a continuity of history between the emigration and the influences which led to it as requires the historian of a New England colony to discourse of England more than the mere title of his work would seem to justify. To relate the history of New Haven, therefore, one must go back to an earlier date than its actual settlement.

The contest between arbitrary and constitutional government, which had never ceased in England after King John signed the *Magna Charta*, raged with unusual violence while the throne was occupied by the Stuarts. The reign of the Tudors had been a period of comparative rest; the Wars of the Roses having so weakened the great barons, who in earlier times made and deposed kings at their pleasure, and the introduction of artillery having so strengthened the monarch against an enemy destitute of these engines of destruction, that, from Henry the Seventh to Elizabeth, there was but faint resistance to the will of the sovereign by the hereditary lords who sat in the upper house of Parliament. By the transfer of the supremacy of the Church, another check on the royal prerogative had been removed; so that the lords spiritual, who in the olden time had been as little dependent on the king as the lords temporal, were now subservient to the power which placed them in office. The Tudors, therefore, transmitted to their successors a more arbitrary sceptre than had been wielded by earlier kings.

But the time of the Stuarts was less favorable than that of the Tudors for maintaining a theory and practice of government which contravened the rights of the subject. Formerly the great barons had come to Parliament followed by hundreds of archers and spearmen ready to back their lords in any contest which might occur; but the barons only, and not their retainers, had presumed to put to question the conduct of the overlord. Out of the decay of this feudal baronage, there had gradually grown up a new antagonist to despotism, which, exhibiting considerable power in the reign of Elizabeth, vigorously encountered the house of Stuart at its accession, and suffered no permanent defeat till it had brought a king of England to the scaffold.

The change in the tenure of land whereby the vassal had become a farmer and in some instances a freeholder; the growth of towns by the increase of manufactures and of commerce; the intellectual activity awakened by the revival of learning, by the new art of printing, by the reform in theology, and by the revolutionary transfer of the supremacy of the Church,—had conspired to lift the common people into a higher position. With this elevation of the common people, the House of Commons rose in importance. The shires and towns, which originally were invited to send representatives to Parliament, that through them they might give consent to taxes which the king wished to levy not only upon the greater lords, but upon the whole population, at first sent men, who, having no ambition to figure as legislators, gladly retired to their homes as soon as they had voted the supplies required. But consent to taxation was sometimes accompanied with a statement of grievances; and afterward, when the Commons had grown in power and courage, was withholden till a promise of redress had been obtained. At first the Commons were content if laws were enacted by the royal authority in accordance with their petitions, but afterward required that the order of proceeding should be reversed, so that all legislation must originate and receive its final shape in Parliament.

Whatever resistance had been offered to arbitrary government during the reign of the Tudors, had proceeded, not chiefly, as in earlier times, from the House of Lords, but chiefly from the House of Commons, representing a power already great and constantly increasing. There had been a change, moreover, in the mode in which acts of despotism were resisted; for the king no longer found his subjects arrayed in arms against him, but meeting him, whenever he asked for another supply of money, with a demand for further restriction on his prerogative. Elizabeth, the last of the Tudors, found this disposition of the Commons so annoying, that she avoided, as much as possible, giving occasion for such conflicts; well knowing that the Crown, if dependent on Parliament for supplies, could obtain them only by concession. By avoiding as much as possible the waste of war, by conducting into her exchequer every stream of tribute which could be controlled without the aid of the Commons, she hoped to render herself independent of Parliaments, and would probably have succeeded but for the wars forced upon her, in the last half of her reign, by Mary of Scotland and Philip of Spain.

This new antagonist to arbitrary government, which had become somewhat formidable to the last of the Tudors, continued to increase in courage and strength under her successor. But not only was the age in which the Stuarts reigned less favorable than that of the

Tudors to the theory and practice of arbitrary government, but the two families differed in their ability to cope with this new antagonist as much as their respective eras differed in the kind of ability required. If the two families could have changed places, the Stuarts might perhaps have been competent to deal with such Parliaments as assembled in the reign of Henry the Seventh; and the Tudors would certainly have shown more tact than the Stuarts did in contending against the English people of the seventeenth century.

This contest between the Stuarts and the English people, on account of its bearing on emigration to New England and the commencement of a new colony at New Haven, we shall briefly review.

James the First ascended the throne of Elizabeth in the belief that by the ordinance of God he was entitled to govern without regard to the will of his subjects. He had already declared, in his work on "The True Law of Free Monarchy," that, "although a good king will frame his actions to be according to law, yet he is not bound thereto but of his own will and for example-giving to his subjects." At a later date, he said in a speech in the Star-Chamber, "As it is atheism and blasphemy to dispute what God can do, so it is presumption and a high contempt in a subject, to dispute what a king can do, or to say that a king cannot do this or that." Some writers attribute to him, and some to his son Charles, the saying, "I will govern according to the common weal, but not according to the common will." If James did not originate, he would doubtless have been willing to adopt, this form of words.

But, though the new king was known to entertain such a theory of kingship, he was received by those of his subjects who held the opposite sentiments with joy and hope; for he was no more objectionable in this respect than Elizabeth, and they confidently expected that he would so exercise his prerogative as to relieve them from one of the most galling of their burdens. The Tudors had transferred the supremacy of the Church from the pope to the king, but had shown themselves as arbitrary in their ecclesiastical as in their civil supremacy, legislating without the concurrence of clergy or laity, and enforcing the strictest conformity to the established ritual. The spirit in which Elizabeth ruled the Church may be inferred from the note she sent to the Bishop of Ely, when he demurred to a proposal that he should surrender a portion of his garden because a favorite of the queen desired that site for a new palace. "Proud prelate," she wrote, "you know what you were before I made you what you are. If you do not immediately comply with my request, by God, I will unfrock you." With similar tyranny she had refused every application for the relief of persons who had scruples in regard to some of the ceremonies prescribed in the ritual of the Church. These Puritans hoped, that as James had been educated in Scotland, where the Church itself had controlled its own reformation, and had carried the reform farther than the Tudors had been willing to carry it in the Church of England, they should find the new king friendly to their wish for further progress in the work of amendment. Possibly, if they had been of the same political principles with the king, they might have obtained some concessions.

But he well knew that the Puritans were to a man of the popular party, and constituted its strength, and that on the other hand the opponents of further reform in the Church were supporters of the royal prerogative. His choice between the parties was soon made, and at the Hampton Court Conference, in the first year of his reign, was fully declared. In his journey from Scotland, a petition signed by eight hundred and twenty-five English clergymen from twenty-five counties had been presented to him, asking for a *conference* in regard to ecclesiastical abuses. In response to this petition, four of the leading Puritan divines, selected by the king, were invited to meet some dignitaries of the Church opposed to all change, in a conference before the king as moderator. But the conference was so conducted as to show that the king had already decided the matter adversely to the Puritans. The first day they were not admitted to his presence, the time being spent in preliminary consultation between the king and the bishops. On the second day, after the Puritans had stated their case, and their opponents had replied, the king, forgetting his position as moderator, took up the argument for conformity, and so "peppered" the Puritans, to use his own expression, that they were dismayed and put to silence.

All that the petitioners could obtain, as the result of this conference, was that candidates for confirmation should be previously instructed by means of a catechism to be prepared for that purpose, that a new translation of the Scriptures should be provided, that the Apocrypha should be distinguished from the canonical Scriptures, that a few explanatory words should be inserted in the Articles of Religion, and that the enforcement of uniformity might be delayed to give time for the resolution of doubt and the settlement of conviction.

In his interview with the bishops, previous to the admission of the Puritan clergymen, the king had propounded the prejudice he himself entertained against private baptism by persons not in orders, and the Churchmen had consented that it should be restricted to cases of necessity. His own objection to conformity to the Church of England being thus taken away, he had no regard to the scruples of others. As between the two Churches of England and of Scotland, he avowed his preference for the former, naïvely admitting that the preference issued from his political principles, rather than from his religious convictions. "No bishop," said he, "no king." "A Scottish presbytery agreeth as well with monarchy as God with the devil."

But James had no occasion for instituting such a comparison in reply to the petitioners; for the petition expressly disavowed a wish for "parity," and asked only for changes not affecting the constitution of the Church. The Puritans had not yet become disaffected toward episcopacy; and, if James had granted them relief from the grievances mentioned in their petition, there would have been less of extravagance in the flattery of the courtiers who styled him the Scottish Solomon. As it was, he resembled Rehoboam rather than Solomon; driving the Puritans into such hostility to prerogative, both royal and episcopal, that nothing less would content them than "a church without a bishop, and a state without a king." It appears from

"Certain Considerations Touching the Better Pacification and Edification of the Church of England," written by Lord Bacon, and "dedicated to his most excellent majesty," that James, like Rehoboam, came to his decision in opposition to wise counsel. Bacon says, "These ecclesiastical matters are things not properly appertaining to my profession; but finding that it is in many things seen that a man that standeth off and somewhat removed from a plot of ground doth better survey it and discover it than those which are upon it, I thought it not impossible, but that I, as a looker-on, might cast mine eyes upon some things which the actors themselves, especially some being interested, some being led and addicted, some declared and engaged, did not or would not see." He inquires, "Why the civil state should be purged and restored by good and wholesome laws made every third or fourth year in parliament assembled, devising remedies as fast as time breedeth mischief; and contrariwise the ecclesiastical state should still continue upon the dregs of time, and receive no alteration now for these five and forty years or more. But if it be said to me that there is a difference between civil causes and ecclesiastical, they may as well tell me that churches and chapels need no reparations, though castles and houses do: whereas, commonly, to speak truth, dilapidations of the inward and spiritual edifications of the church of God are in all times as great as the outward and material."

The first parliament in the reign of the new king met a few weeks after the conference at Hampton Court. A majority of the lower house were in full sympathy with the Puritan clergy in desiring further reformation of the Church; and some who were personally indifferent to the ceremonies and other matters in controversy were disposed to side with the aggrieved party, either on the ground that rings, surplices, and crosses *were important* to those who esteemed them important, or that, by favoring the Puritans, they might obtain from them more aid in the impending contest between the Crown and the Commons. The speaker, in his first address to the king, took occasion to affirm that "by the power of your majesty's great and high court of parliament only, new laws are to be instituted, imperfect laws reformed, and inconvenient laws abrogated;" that "no such law can be instituted, reformed, or abrogated, but by the unity of the Commons' agreement, the Lords' accord, and your majesty's royal and regal assent;" that "this court standeth compounded of two powers; the one ordinary, the other absolute: ordinary in the Lords' and Commons' proceedings, but in your highness absolute, either negatively to frustrate or affirmatively to confirm, but not to institute."

In making up the roll of the house, it was found that the king had already decided that one of the persons returned as elected was ineligible, and had ordered a new election, so that there were two claimants of the seat. The House insisted on its privilege of determining its own membership in all cases of contested elections, but compromised with the king by excluding both claimants with the consent of the first chosen, and ordering a third election. With great copiousness of courteous speech they established so firmly the privilege of the House to determine contested elections, that it has never since been brought in question.

On the 13th of June, a committee reported a form for a petition to his majesty, in which they say, "We have thought it expedient, rather by this our humble petition to recommend to your majesty's godly consideration certain matters of grievance resting in your royal power and princely zeal, either to abrogate or moderate, than to take the public discussing of the same unto ourselves; to the end (if it so seem good to your highness) we may from the sacred fountain of your majesty's most royal and religious heart, wholly and only derive such convenient remedy and relief therein as to your princely wisdom may seem most meet. The matters of grievance (that we be not troublesome to your majesty) are these: the pressing the use of certain rites and ceremonies in this Church, as the cross in baptism, the wearing of the surplice in ordinary parish churches, and the subscription required of the ministers further than is commanded by the laws of the realm; things which, by long experience, have been found to be the occasion of such difference, trouble, and contention in this Church, as thereby divers profitable and painful ministers, not in contempt of authority or desire of novelty, as they sincerely profess and we are verily persuaded, but upon conscience toward God, refusing the same, some of good desert have been deprived, others of good expectation withheld from entering into the ministry." It is not certain that this petition was ever presented to the king; but he must have known that it was on the way, when, on the 26th of the same month, he sent a letter to the House declining to receive a subsidy, which all the world knew would be granted only in return for the redress of grievances.

Meantime the House had sent to the king a letter styled "An Apology Touching Their Privileges," in which they complain, with great copiousness of respectful language, of the wrong which had been done to his majesty by misinformation, touching the estate of his subjects and the privileges of the House, and "disclosing unto your majesty the truth of such matters as hitherto by misinformation hath been suppressed or perverted."

On the 7th of July the House was prorogued; and when it again assembled in November, 1605, the discovery of the gunpowder-plot had hushed the strife between the Puritans and the king, uniting all Protesants in a common enmity against Papists. But in subsequent sessions the Commons found so many grievances to be redressed before supplies could be granted, that the king preferred to dissolve the Parliament in February, 1611, rather than fill his exchequer by further sacrifices of his prerogative.

In April, 1614, having first by private negotiation secured a promise of aid from some who had been leaders of the popular party, the king ventured to call his second Parliament, but the experiment proved a failure; the Commons, even after the king had sent a message requesting that a supply might be granted and threatening to dissolve the Parliament if they refused, voting to postpone supply till their grievances were redressed. The Parliament was accordingly dissolved just two months after it began to sit.

The Parliament which assembled in January, 1621, was at first on good terms with the monarch, who in the opening speech, acknowledging that he had been misled by evil counsellors, made fair promises for the future. The two parties were drawn together by their common sympathy with the king's son-in-law, the Elector Palatine, involved in a quarrel with the German emperor, which threatened to deprive him of his hereditary dominions. The king naturally desired to assist the husband of his daughter and the father of her children to preserve his patrimony; and the people sympathized with the elector as the champion of Protestantism, overborne by the combined forces of Romanism. The Commons at once voted supplies for carrying on war in aid of the elector. But, before the expiration of the year, the king and the Commons were again at variance; he rebuking them for meddling with matters of state which did not concern them, and declaring himself "very free and able to punish any man's misdemeanors in Parliament, as well during their sitting as after;" and they responding with a formal protest as follows: viz., "That the liberties, franchises, privileges, and jurisdictions of Parliament are the ancient and undoubted birthright and inheritance of the subjects of England; and that the arduous and urgent affairs concerning the king, state, and the defence of the realm and of the Church of England, and the making and maintenance of laws and redress of mischiefs and grievances which daily happen within this realm, are proper subjects and matter of counsel and debate in Parliament; and that, in the handling and proceeding of those businesses, every member of the House hath, and of right ought to have, freedom of speech to propound, treat, reason, and bring to conclusion the same; that the Commons in Parliament have like liberty and freedom to treat of these matters in such order as in their judgments shall seem fittest; and that every such member of the said House hath like freedom from all impeachment, imprisonment, and molestation (other than by the censure of the house itself), for or concerning any bill, speaking, reasoning, or declaring of any matter or matters touching the Parliament or Parliament business; and that, if any of the said members be complained of and questioned for anything said or done in Parliament, the same is to be showed to the king, by the advice and assent of all the Commons, before the king give credence to any private informations."

This formal protest having been recorded in the journal of the House, the king erased it with his own hand, and a few days afterward dissolved the Parliament.

The next Parliament met in February, 1624, was prorogued in May, and did not again assemble, being dissolved by the king's death on the 27th of March, 1625. During its brief session, unusual concord prevailed between the king and the Commons, by reason of war with Spain, which religious animosity rendered popular; and the more so, that the war had been preceded by an apprehension that a Spanish princess would become the wife of the heir to the British crown. The Commons voted large supplies for carrying on the war, and with the more alacrity, because the king had himself proposed that the money should be put into the hands of a committee of Parliament, to be expended by them, and not into the royal exchequer.

Charles the First was constrained by his need of money to call a Parliament immediately upon his accession, but soon quarreled with the Commons, as his father had done, about his prerogative and their privileges. Putting an end to their sessions, he called another Parliament in the succeeding year, but with no improvement in the state of feeling between the king and the Commons; and in a few months the second Parliament of this reign came to an end. The king, left without revenue by the refusal of Parliament to vote supplies, not only laid and collected arbitrary taxes, but exacted from the nobility, the gentry, the clergy, and the merchants, forced loans. Those who refused to lend were imprisoned, and, when they claimed their liberty by *habeas corpus*, found that *Magna Charta* was of no avail against the will of the king.

In this state of things, Charles called his third Parliament in 1628; being constrained to such a course by the insufficiency of the revenue collected by illegal means. When the Commons assembled on the 17th of March, they came with the determination not to vote supplies unless the king would promise to put an end to his arbitrary measures. Early in the session, they passed the following resolutions, without a dissenting voice:—

"1. That no freeman ought to be committed or detained in prison, or otherwise restrained, by command of the king, or the Privy Council, or any other, unless some cause of the commitment, detainer, or restraint be expressed, for which by law he ought to be committed, detained, or restrained. 2. That the writ of *habeas corpus* cannot be denied, but ought to be granted to every man that is committed or detained in prison or otherwise restrained by command of the king, Privy Council, or any other; he praying the same. 3. That if a freeman be committed, or detained in prison, or otherwise restrained, by command of the king, Privy Council, or any other, no cause of such commitment, &c., being expressed, and thè same be returned upon an *habeas corpus* granted for the said party, that then he ought to be delivered, or bailed. 4. That the ancient and undoubted right of every freeman is, that he hath a full and absolute property in his goods and estate; and that no tax, tallage, loan, benevolence, or other like charges, ought to be commanded or levied by the king, or his ministers, without common assent of Parliament."

A few days after this declaration of the right of English subjects, they presented a petition to the king, in which they showed how all these rights of the subject had been recognized in *Magna Charta*, and in acts of Parliament subscribed by his majesty's royal predecessors; declared that they had all been violated of late by forced loans, by imprisonment without cause shown, by disregard of the writ of *habeas corpus*, by billeting soldiers and mariners in private houses, and by the unnecessary establishment of martial law. The petition closed with a prayer that such illegalities and wrongs might cease.

The answer of the king was regarded as evasive; and both houses of Parliament joined in a request that his majesty would return a more explicit reply to the Petition of Right. Charles, thus harassed, came into the House of Lords, commanded the Commons to attend upon him there, and gave his assent to the petition in the customary form, declaring that in his former answer he had had no intention of withholding any thing conceded in the latter. Three days later, to accelerate a vote of supplies, he expressed his willingness that the Petition of Right should be recorded, not only in both houses of Parliament, but in all the courts of Westminster, and that it should be printed for his honor, and the content and satisfaction of his subjects.

The Commons, pleased with such a triumph of law over autocracy, immediately voted a liberal sum for supplying the king's necessities, and were proceeding to pass an act for a further supply by a grant of tonnage and poundage, when the incorrigible Stuart, learning that the grant was to be accompanied by a remonstrance against the illegal collection of the tax before it had been granted, prorogued the Parliament in a speech in which he denied that in giving assent to the Petition of Right he had debarred himself from exacting tonnage and poundage by virtue of his royal prerogative, and commanded all present to take notice, that the interpretation he was giving to the instrument was its true meaning and intent; adding, "But especially you, my lords the judges, for to you only, under me, belongs the interpretation of laws." After the prorogation this violent speech was, by the king's command, entered on the journal of the House; and by the same authority it was printed along with the Petition of Right and the unsatisfactory answer it had at first received, no mention being made of the explicit assent afterward given in the customary formula of royal ratification.

When the Parliament again assembled on the 20th of January, 1629, the nation was greatly irritated, not only by the collection of tonnage and poundage and other illegal taxes, but by the excessive and cruel punishments unjustly, and without warrant of law, inflicted by the Star-Chamber and the High Commission. Hitherto the questions at issue between the king and the Commons had pertained chiefly to civil rights: but, during the contest, the assertors of civil rights and the advocates of further reform in the Church had more and more coalesced; the Puritans being to a man opposed to despotism, and the leaders of the popular party, if they had no positive and earnest convictions in regard to the religious questions at issue, taking sides with the Puritans because the Puritans had taken sides with them.

Similar reasons had drawn the king into a closer connection with those Churchmen who insisted on the retention of the ceremonies obnoxious to Puritans, and on the enforcement of an absolute conformity. The king favored such men as Laud and his coadjutors in their churchmanship, because they supported him in his attempt to trample upon the constitution and the laws. Through Laud, who since the death of the Duke of Buckingham had become his principal adviser, Charles enjoined upon the clergy to preach the merit of paying taxes and making loans not authorized by Parliament. When Archbishop Abbot refused to license the printing of one of the sermons thus originated, he was suspended from the functions of his office, and his authority was transferred to a commission over which Laud presided.

The two parties being thus at variance on ecclesiastical as well as on political questions, Parliament had no sooner assembled than the Commons began to seek the redress of grievances relating to religion, as well as of such as related to person and property. It had been discovered that in the negotiations for the marriage of Charles with Henrietta Maria, both he and his father had secretly signed a promise that not only the queen and her attendants, but all Englishmen as well, should be exempt from the operation of the laws of England which prohibited the exercise of the Roman Catholic worship. It was seen that the Church of England, under the direction of Laud, was drifting toward the Church of Rome, and thus becoming more unsatisfactory to Puritans than it had been under the administration of Abbot. The latter prelate had been lenient toward those who had conscientious scruples about ceremonies; Laud, on the other hand, not only exacted the most rigid conformity to the ceremonies legally required, but procured an order of the king's privy council, ordaining changes in the position and furniture of the communion-table, exceedingly unpalatable to those who already experienced sufficient difficulty in overcoming their scruples and persuading themselves to conform.

On the 25th of February a committee previously appointed for the purpose made a report on religious grievances. They complained, among other things, that books in favor of popery were licensed by the bishops, and books against popery were suppressed; that candlesticks were placed on the communion-table, which they said was now wickedly called a high altar; that pictures, images, and lights were used in the worship of the Church; that clergymen celebrating divine service crossed themselves at every change of posture, and in time of prayer turned their backs toward the people, as if the eastward position were essential; that, these rituralistic practices being enjoined upon them by their bishops, learned, orthodox, and pious ministers, who could not in conscience obey the injunction, were brought to grief for disobedience.

The king, enraged at this attack upon his hierarchical allies, endeavored to prevent action on the report by ordering the speaker to pronounce the House adjourned. But, the House claiming that it could be adjourned only by its own act, some of the members held the speaker in the chair, while others locked the door, and brought the keys to the table. The speaker declaring that he dare not and would not put to vote any motion, seeing that the House was adjourned by the king's command, one of the members read a protest to which others assented, and the House then adjourned itself to the 10th of March. On the 10th of March the king dissolved the Parliament, in a speech in which he threatened with his vengeance, those *vipers*, as he called them, who had been most active in resisting his adjournment of the House of Commons.

His third Parliament being thus brought to an end, Charles was by this time so disgusted, that in a proclamation issued twelve days afterward he said, "We have showed, by our frequent meeting our people, our love to the use of Parliaments; yet, the late abuse having for the present driven us unwillingly out of that course, we shall account it presumption for any to prescribe any time unto us for Parliaments, the calling, continuing, and dissolving of which is always in our power." So deep-rooted was his dislike, that eleven years intervened between his third and his fourth Parliaments, during which time he levied taxes, and exacted benevolences and loans at his pleasure, punishing with imprisonment and heavy fines those who refused to open their purses at his arbitrary demand.

The Puritan emigration from England, for which we are endeavoring to account, commenced while Charles was holding his third Parliament. Plymouth had, indeed, been settled before this time, and before Charles came to the throne; but the Pilgrims who planted that colony had been already exiles from their native land for twelve years before they crossed the ocean. The successful prosecution of that enterprise for eight years had now demonstrated the feasibility of establishing such plantations on the American coast, and had suggested to the Puritans of England that by emigrating to America they might not only escape from their foes, but establish, in a new world, those principles of civil freedom and pure worship for which they were contending with little success in their native land.

The first company who left their homes in the mother-country to establish a Puritan plantation in New England sailed in 1628, and, under the leadership of Endicott, established themselves in Salem. They had been twice re-enforced, when a much larger company came with Winthrop in 1630, and settled first at Charlestown, and afterward at Boston. To induce Winthrop and other gentlemen of capacity and wealth to engage personally in this enterprise, the Company of Massachusetts Bay generously offered to transfer to New England the government of the plantations which had been or might be formed there, by electing a majority of its directors and its governor from among those who would engage to emigrate with their families and estates.

From this time onward the current of emigration was broad and rapid, stimulated as well by the descriptions of the New World which the first adventurers sent back as by the troubles in the mother-country. So general was the interest in these reports that three editions of "New England's Plantation" by Rev. Francis Higginson, who arrived in Salem in 1629, were printed during the following year. The stream thus set in motion did not cease to flow till the civil war had given the Puritans hope of relief without exile from their native land.

The project which resulted in the establishment of a colony in New Haven was undertaken in 1636. Seven years had then elapsed without a parliament; the king was evidently determined not to call another: without a parliament no check could be put on arbitrary government. To all other illegal methods of replenishing the exchequer, including the sale of monopolies, the demand of loans and benevolences, the collection of tonnage and poundage, the imposition of arbitrary and excessive fines, another had now been added called ship-money: the first writ for levying it in London being issued in 1634, and the exaction being extended to the whole country in the following year. The tax was small in amount; for John Hampden (who, having already suffered imprisonment for not submitting to a forced loan, now refused to pay ship-money) was a man of large wealth, and yet was assessed at only twenty shillings. But, though small in amount, this new tax excited earnest indignation in the minds of thoughtful patriots, because it was laid without the consent of those who were to pay it.

The Star-Chamber, instead of relaxing its severity, had of late in numerous instances punished with ruinous fines, and with imprisonment of which no one could foresee the end, those who resisted the exactions of the government, or even ventured to speak of them with too strong disapproval. Thus in 1630, Richard Chambers, a merchant of London, smarting under a sense of the wrong he suffered in having a bale of silk confiscated because he would not pay the duty illegally demanded, was heard to say that merchants had more encouragement, and were less screwed and wrung, in Turkey than in England. For this ebullition of temper he was fined two thousand pounds. In the same year Alexander Leighton, a Scotch clergyman, was sentenced, for publishing a book entitled, "An Appeal to the Parliament; or, Sion's Plea against Popery," to be twice publicly whipped, to stand two hours in the pillory, to have his ears cut off, to have his nostrils slit, to be branded in the cheek with the letters S. S. to denote a sower of sedition, and to be imprisoned for life. He lay in prison ten years, and until he was released by the Long Parliament. In 1634 Prynne, a Puritan lawyer, being prosecuted before the same tribunal for publishing a book against plays, masquerades, &c., which was thought to reflect severely upon the royal court where such amusements were in vogue, was sentenced to pay a fine of five thousand pounds, to stand twice in the pillory, to lose his ears, and to remain a prisoner for life. He employed the leisure of his prison in writing another book, for which he suffered, by decree of the Star-Chamber, another mutilation. This second punishment, however, did not take place till after the company, which planted the colony of New Haven, had left behind them the shores of England.

The High Commission, which had cognizance of ecclesiastical offences, punished the Puritans for disobedience to bishops, as the Star-Chamber did for offences against the royal prerogative. This tribunal did not, indeed, mutilate its victims, and so far forth was less inhuman than the Star-Chamber. The fines which it exacted from non-conformists for their irregularities were not so large as the fines imposed by the other court, or by this same court in cases of immorality committed by rich men; but the reason doubtless was, that the non-conformists were men of moderate means. Those who suffered for non-conformity were, in many cases, clergymen without income save what they derived from their benefices. To such a man, the sentence of the ecclesiastical court, ejecting him from his living, was as severe as a ruinous fine would be upon a merchant. But, in truth, fines and imprisonment were often added to the sentence of deprivation which took from the clergyman and his family their daily bread. For example, Peter Smart, a prebendary of Durham, having inveighed in a sermon against innovations recently made in his cathedral, such as the change of the communion-table into an altar, and the restoration of some images and pictures which had been removed in the reign of Elizabeth, was fined five hundred pounds, committed to prison, and ordered to recant. For neglecting to recant, he was fined again, deprived of his prebend, degraded from orders, and excommunicated.[1] He was at last released by the Long Parliament, after eleven years confinement.

[1] Fuller's Church History.

The elevation of Laud to the primacy, in 1633, increased the troubles of the Puritans. Abbot had shielded them in his own diocese, and had encouraged, at least indirectly, other bishops to do likewise. But now there was no such shield in any diocese from the fury with which Laud assailed, not only all who deviated in any particular from the ceremonies prescribed by law, but even those who, being careful to conform in all things legally required, opposed the changes in the furniture and services of the church, ordained by the Privy Council at the instigation of Laud. Puritan clergymen in larger numbers than before were imprisoned. Some, having reason to expect a similar fate, concealed themselves and, when opportunity offered, secretly embarked for New England. It was under pressure of this kind that most of the ministers who came over between 1628 and 1640 decided to leave their native land.

Though the clergy were more exposed than the laity to the storm of persecution, the latter were not exempt. If the spies of the High Commission discovered a conventicle,—as a worshiping assembly in which the ceremonies did not conform to those of the Church of England was called,—not only the officiating minister, but all who were present, were seized, and imprisoned till on their oaths they had purged themselves of all non-conformity, or till the court was pleased to release them.

Snch was the condition of England which induced the Puritan emigrants to exile themselves from their native country, and encounter the perils of the sea and of the wilderness. Colonization produced by such causes peopled New England with a superior population. The colonists were, as a class, intelligent, moral, religious, heroic. "God sifted a whole nation, that he might send choice grain over into this wilderness."[1]

[1] William Stoughton, Election Sermon, 1668.

CHAPTER II.

EVENTS WHICH INFLUENCED SOME OF THE FIRST PLANTERS OF NEW HAVEN TO REMOVE FROM THEIR NATIVE LAND TO NEW ENGLAND.

ON the sixth day of October, 1624, a general vestry was holden in St. Stephen's Church, Coleman Street, London, for the election of a new incumbent; this being one of the few parishes in England where the right of presentation is vested in the parishioners. Of seventy-three votes, John Davenport, a curate in a contiguous parish, received all but three or four. He had held this curacy about six years, and was now regarded as one of the ablest preachers in the city. "He was reported," says the Bishop of London, in reply to a letter in which Sir Richard Conway interceded for Davenport's induction, "to be factious and popular,[1] and to draw after him great congregations and assemblies of common and mean people." Endowed with imagination, earnest in his piety, Calvanistic in his theology, possessing the full strength of manhood with no abatement of the fervor of youth, he was a great favorite with the merchants, tradesfolk, and artisans, whose dwellings were in Coleman Street and other

[1] The bishop meant that Davenport did not stand for the king's prerogative.

streets since surrendered entirely to business. His admirers were almost universally of that class of Englishmen whose representatives in Parliament so much displeased King James by presenting a list of grievances whenever he asked for money. Therefore to be popular, whether it means to be on the side of the people or to be regarded by the people with favor, was to be suspected at court.

It was soon found that something stood in the way of Davenport's induction. The young preacher had been traduced to the king as a Puritan, or as puritanically affected; and the king had spoken of him to the Bishop of London in such terms that the bishop was unwilling to induct him into the benefice to which he had been elected. The charge of puritanism, if it meant that Davenport did not conform to all the prescribed ceremonies of the Church, had no foundation at this early date. The accusation had probably proceeded from one of the king's pages, who, having been reproved by Davenport for profane swearing, either innocently adjudged him for that reason to be a Puritan, or revengefully applied an opprobrious epithet to prejudice his reprover in the king's esteem.

Davenport's friends, however, were not all "common and mean people." At his solicitation, seconded by that of Lady Mary Vere, his cause was undertaken by her brother-in-law, Sir Richard Conway, principal secretary to his majesty, who conciliated the king and persuaded the bishop to proceed to the induction, which took place before the date of the following certificate, indorsed in the handwriting of Davenport on a copy of "The Thirty-Nine Articles," now in the library of the American Antiquarian Society at Worcester:—

Novemb. 7th 1624.

"John Davenporte, Clerk, Vicar of St. Stephen's in Coleman Street, London, did, this day above written, being Sunday, publiquely read this booke of Articles herein Contayned, being in number 39 besides the ratificacion, and declared his full and unfeigned assent and consent thereunto in the tyme of morning Prayer, next after the Second Lesson, before the whole Congregacion. As also the sayd John did, the same day, administer the Holy Communion in the sayd parish, in his surplis, according to ye order prescribed by ye Church of England; in the presence of these whose names are here underwritten."

The certificate is signed by one of the church-wardens and seven other parishioners, and was doubtless given on the first Sunday after his induction.

The first two or three years of Davenport's incumbency were prosperous and comparatively peaceful. So far as can be ascertained, he conformed as faultlessly as in his curacy at St. Lawrence's, where, as he declares in a letter to Secretary Conway, he "baptized many, but never without the sign of the cross; monthly administered the sacrament of the Lord's Supper, but at no time without the surplice, nor to any but those that kneeled."

In 1627 he brought himself into trouble by uniting with other ministers in a circular letter soliciting contributions for the oppressed Protestants of the Upper Palatinate. Laud, who was now the principal adviser of the king, was displeased with the signers of the letter for such sympathy with Presbyterians, and caused them to be reprimanded in the Star-Chamber.

The translation of Laud in 1628, to the see of London, brought greater peril of collision between him and the Calvanistic vicar of St. Stephen's. What was Davenport's first offence, is not known; but how soon he was summoned before the High Commission, appears from the following extract from one of his letters to Lady Vere:—

"LONDON, June 30, 1628.

"MADAM,—Since my recovery out of a dangerous sickness, which held me for a week or a fortnight before Shrovetide to as long after Easter, for which I return most humble thanks to the God of my life, the Father of mercies, I have had divers purposes of writing to your honor, only I delayed in hope to write somewhat concerning the event and success of our High Commission troubles; but I have hoped in vain: for to this day we are in the same condition as before,—delayed till the finishing of this session in Parliament, which now is unhappily concluded without any satfying contentment to the king or commonwealth. Threatenings were speedily revived against us by the new Bishop of London, Dr. Laud, even the next day after the conclusion of their session. We expect a fierce storm from the enraged spirit of the two bishops. Ours, as I am informed, hath a particular aim at me upon a former quarrel: so that I expect ere long to be deprived of my pastoral charge in Coleman Street. But I am in God's hands, not in theirs; to whose good pleasure I do contentedly and cheerfully commit myself.[1]"

In January, 1631, he was required to answer certain charges brought against him by Timothy Hood, some time his curate. Hood had been dismissed for not complying with the requirement that he should reside within the parish, and, according to Davenport's relation of the case, had become incensed against him for that reason. One of the charges was, that the vicar had sometimes administered the sacrament to communicants who did not kneel, and the accusation was brought to a fine edge by the specification of Mrs. Davenport as one of the said communicants.

[1] Birch MSS., 4275.

The vicar replied to this objection against him, that the parish contained about fourteen hundred communicants, and that the chancel being small, it was a matter of necessity to administer to the communicants from pew to pew, and that the pews were sometimes so filled that it was impossible to kneel; that when he had observed some to sit, that might conveniently kneel, he had advised them to kneel; that, in case of refusal to kneel, he had refused to administer the sacrament to the party so refusing. The specification concerning his wife, he meets by testifying that she had received the sacrament at his hand, kneeling, many times, and that the curate had "not acquainted him, the said John Davenport, that he observed any such thing concerning his wife" as was charged.

It is evident from this disingenuous but doubtless literally true statement, that some of Davenport's parishioners, including his own wife, were at this time non-conformists, and that he had winked at their irregularity. It does not appear, however, that he himself had any scruple about kneeling, or had personally omitted any required ceremony.

The complaint seems to have resulted in nothing worse than a private admonition from his bishop. It was probably the conference between Laud and Davenport in reference to this complaint to which the prelate referred, when, in his report of the diocese of London for that part of the year 1633 which elapsed before his elevation to the primacy, he said, "Since my return from Scotland, Mr. John Davenport, vicar of St. Stephen's in Coleman Street (whom I used with all moderation, and about two years since thought I had settled his judgment, having him then at advantage enough to have put extremity upon him, but forebore it), hath now resigned his vicarage, declared his judgment against conformity with the Church of England, and is since gone (as I hear) to Amsterdam." To his moderation with Davenport in reference to the complaint of Hood, the prelate again referred in his defence, when on trial for his life, before the Long Parliament. One charge being, that he had forced Davenport to flee from his parish and from the country, he said in reply: "The truth is, my lords, and 'tis well known, and to some of his best friends, that I preserved him once before, and my Lord Vere came, and gave me thanks for it."

About one year after Davenport had escaped from this danger, Laud discovered the existence of a company, whose design was to purchase such advowsons as, having been impropriated to laymen in the time of Henry the Eighth, were now for sale, in order that the trustees, or, as they were styled, *feoffees*, of the company might present for induction men whom they regarded as orthodox, that is, as Calvinists. The company had been in operation for some years, and had already purchased several impropriations with money contributed for that purpose. The discovery of the project excited Laud vehemently. He hated Calvinists, whether conforming or non-conforming; partly for their theology, and partly for their almost invariable adhesion to the popular side in the contest between the Commons and the king. It was part of his plan of administration to exclude them from preferment; so that this company was, in his estimation, an organized attempt to frustrate his plans. Davenport was one of the *feoffees* of this company, and, as such, participated in the heavy displeasure of the man who in the king's name ruled both Church and State. He and his associates were apprehensive that they might be proceeded against in the Star-Chamber, and punished with ruinous fines; but Laud, having caused the corporation to be dissolved and its property to be confiscated, abstained from further vengeance. When the prosecution was brought to an end, Davenport recorded in his Bible his thanks to God for deliverance from the thing he feared.

The policy of excluding Calvinists from church preferment, even if faultless in their conformity, naturally forced conforming clergymen of that school of theology into closer sympathy with non-conformists, and into a wider estrangement from Laud and his associates. Doctrinal Puritans, as Calvinists were now called, finding themselves proscribed by their ecclesiastical superiors, began to feel the force of the reasons which the ceremonial Puritans alleged for not conforming. Perhaps the suppression of the company of which he had been a trustee, and the confiscation of its property, turned the scales with which Davenport weighed these reasons. However this may be, it appears from his own testimony that he was "first staggered in his conformity, and afterward fully taken off, by set conferences and debates, which himself and sundry other ministers obtained with Mr. John Cotton, then driven from Boston [in Lincolnshire] on account of his non-conformity."

For several months he absented himself from the communion-service celebrated monthly in his church, but might perhaps in time have relapsed into conformity. The tidings which came on Sunday, Aug. 4, 1633, that the old Calvinistic Archbishop of Canterbury, George Abbot, was dead, seem to have brought him to a decision. Abbot had been decidedly friendly to Calvinists who conformed, and not very severe against those who were guilty of some slight aberrations from the ritual. His brother, Sir Maurice Abbot, afterward lord mayor, was a parishioner of St. Stephen's, and had sometimes spread over Davenport the shield of the archbishop's protection. But the primate was now dead, and the succession of Laud cast its shadow before. On Monday Davenport left the city; and on Tuesday Laud, returning from his missionary tour to Scotland, was saluted by the king as "my Lord of Canterbury." Davenport, after lying in concealment for about three months, escaped to Holland "disguised in a gray suit and an overgrown beard.[1]"

We learn from one of his letters to the representative of the king of Great Britain, resident at the Hague, that when he went into that country he intended to remain only three or four months and then return to his native land. He cannot have expected that the storm which had driven him into exile would so soon subside entirely, or even sufficiently to permit him to resume his work as a Puritan preacher in England. Some thoughts may have been in his mind of undertaking in 1634 what he accomplished in 1637. He had been interested in the Massachusetts Bay Company as early certainly as 1629, having contributed money to procure the charter which the king signed in that year, and had continued from

[1] Letter of Stephen Goffe, dated 1633, Dec. $\frac{18}{28}$.

that time to meet with its directors and to act on its committees. A short absence might be considered expedient to allow the vigilance of his enemies to abate before he should organize an expedition. Nevertheless any project of leading a colony from England to America, which he may have entertained when he landed in Holland, was so vague that he listened to a proposal to settle permanently in Amsterdam.

If for a time he cherished the thought of finding a home in Holland, he had doubtless relinquished it as early as 1635, for in that year his family returned to England. He followed them, probably in the summer or autumn of 1636; for the organization of a company of emigrants was so far forwarded in January of the following year that they had chartered a vessel, "made ready all their provisions and passengers, fitting both for the said voyage and plantation, and most of them thereupon engaged their whole estates.[1]"

While these preparations were in progress, Davenport doubtless kept himself out of sight as much as he conveniently could, both on his own account, and for the sake of the expedition. Years afterward, Laud, alluding to him and his escape to New England, exclaimed, "My arm shall reach him even there." If it had been known that those who had chartered "the good ship Hector," to carry them to New England, and had engaged their whole estates in preparing for the voyage, were to have the former vicar of St. Stephen's as their leader, their undertaking might have been extinguished with as little regard to the rights of property

---

[1] Petition of the Owners and Freighters of the Good Ship called the Hector of London. State Papers: Colonial.

as that of the *feoffees* had been. It did, indeed, become known at last that Davenport had returned. The vicar-general of the Bishop of London, reporting his visitation of the diocese, writes from Braintree, March 6, " Mr. Davenport hath lately been in these parts, and at Hackney, not long since. I am told that he goeth in gray, like a country gentleman." We may infer from what this reporter relates, that Davenport had not shown himself much in public, and, from his silence in reference to the expedition to New England, that he had heard nothing of Davenport's connection with it.

About twelve months before Davenport fled from London, Samuel Eaton and John Lathrop,[1] two non-conforming clergymen, were imprisoned by the High Commission for holding conventicles. With the connivance of the jailer, Eaton continued to hold conventicles after his incarceration, as appears from a document preserved among the English State Papers, and here subjoined:—

" *To the most Reverend Father in God, William, Lord Archbishop of Canterbury, his grace, Primate and Metropolitan of all England :—*
"Humbly sheweth:—The most humble petition of Francis Tucker, Bachelor of Divinity, and prisoner in Newgate for debt. That whereas there is one Samuel Eaton, prisoner in Newgate, committed by your grace for a schismatical and dangerous fellow; that the said Eaton hath held divers conventicles within the said gaol, some whereof hath been to the number of seventy persons or more, and that he was permitted by the said keeper openly and publicly to preach unto them; and that the said Eaton hath often

[1] Lathrop had formerly been vicar of Egerton in Kent, but now was the teacher of a congregation of Separatists in London. Egerton had become a stronghold of Puritanism.

times affirmed in his said sermons that baptism was the doctrine of devils, and its original was an institution from the devil; and oftentimes he would rail against your grace, affirming that all bishops were heretics, blasphemers, and antichristian. That the said keeper, having notice hereof by the petitioner, who desired him to be a means that these great resorts and conventicles might be prevented, and that he would reprove the said Eaton for the same, and remove him to some other place of the prison. That hereupon the said keeper, in a disdainful manner, replied that the petitioner should meddle with what he had to do; and if he did dislike the said Eaton and his conventicles, he would remove the petitioner into some worse place of the prison. That at this time there was a conventicle of sixty persons or more; that the said keeper coming into the room where the conventicle was, and the said Eaton preaching unto them and maintaining dangerous opinions, having viewed the said assembly, he said there was a very fair and goodly company; and staying there some season, departed without any distaste thereat, to the great encouragement of the said Eaton and the said persons to frequent the said place. That the said keeper had a strict charge from the said commission to have a special care of the said Eaton; and that since, the said keeper hath several times permitted him to go abroad to preach to conventicles appointed by him, the said Eaton. That daily there doth resort to the said Eaton much people to hear him preach. That the said petitioner reproving the said keeper for the said contempt, he thereupon abused him with uncivil language, and further, caused the said Eaton to abuse the petitioner, not only with most abusive words, but also with blows."

Eaton and Lathrop were probably released on bail, for the court, after calling them several times, finally decreed, Feb. 19, 1635, that for their contempt in not appearing to answer charges touching their holding conventicles, their bonds should be certified, and they attached and committed. Lathrop, fortunately for him, was already in New England, having arrived at Boston with thirty-two of his congregation Sept. 18, 1634.

Eaton, having lain in concealment till the return of Davenport from Holland, became his associate in the voyage to America. Perhaps he was drawn into such association by personal friendship, as well as by the peril to which they were exposed in common; for both were natives of Coventry, where Eaton's father, a beneficed clergyman, had been the religious teacher and guide of Davenport's childhood and youth.

Theophilus Eaton, an older brother of Samuel Eaton, was so nearly of the age of Davenport that they had been schoolmates and intimate friends in Coventry. Intended by his parents for the church, he had become a merchant in London. Respected for his character and for his success in business, he was elected at an early age Deputy Governor of the Fellowship of Eastland Merchants, and sent by them, as their agent, to superintend their affairs and promote their interests in the countries bordering on the Baltic. Returning after an absence of three years, he became a parishioner of his friend, the vicar of St. Stephen's. Already so much a Puritan that he had scrupled when abroad at the lawfulness of drinking toasts, he was probably, when Davenport resigned his vicarage, as far advanced as he in nonconformity. The idea of expatriation had, perhaps, become less repulsive to his mind by reason of his long connection with the company of Massachusetts Bay, of which he was one of the original patentees, and to which he, like Davenport, had liberally given time and money. The acquaintance he had made with the court of High Commission through the recent experience of his brother Samuel, and perhaps through personal experience as his brother's bondsman, would naturally incline him to put himself and his children beyond its jurisdiction. He not only joined the expedition, but acted so important a part in its history, that he and Davenport have been styled its Moses and Aaron.

Theophilus Eaton was living at this time with his second wife, whose daughter by a former husband was married to Edward Hopkins, a Puritan merchant of London. Hopkins much esteemed his wife's stepfather, and resolved to accompany him to America. Two young men, David Yale and Thomas Yale, sons of Mrs. Eaton, were also of the company.

John Evance, a London merchant and a parishioner of St. Stephen's, was present at the general vestry when Davenport was elected vicar in October, 1624. He had been married in May of the same year to Anne Young. It has been assumed by some writers that many of the New Haven planters had been parishioners of Davenport in London. He was so popular and prominent a preacher, that probably all of the company who had lived in London had heard him preach; but of the seventy-three persons present at the general vestry in October, 1624, only one is known to have come with Davenport to New Haven. Theophilus Eaton may have been a parishioner thus early; but, even if so, was probably absent at that time in the East countries. Other New Haven names than those of Evance and Eaton are found on the parish register of St. Stephen's; but the names are such as might be found elsewhere in England, and most of the persons who brought them to America are known to have crossed the Atlantic at an earlier or a later date than Eaton, Evance, and Davenport.

Besides these who were related to Davenport, as his former parishioners, or to Theophilus Eaton by family ties, several citizens of London joined the company. Not all of them can now be distinguished from those who came from other parts of the kingdom, but there is more or less authority for including in such a list the names of Stephen Goodyear, Richard Malbon, Thomas Gregson, William Peck, Robert Newman, Francis Newman, and Ezekiel Cheever.

The London men with their families forming the nucleus of the company, other families or companies from the rural counties became united with it. One group of families came from Kent, or, in other words, from the diocese of Canterbury, which, three years before, by the death of Archbishop Abbot, had fallen under the immediate administration of Laud. Abbot was, like the Puritans, a Calvinist in his theology; like them he was in sympathy with the reformed churches of the Continent, continuing to tolerate the French refugees, who from the time of Elizabeth had maintained worship according to the forms of their own church within his diocese and even in the basement of his cathedral; like them he believed in the sanctification of the Lord's day, preventing the reading, in the parish church of Croydon where he was residing at the time, of King James's proclamation which allowed and encouraged athletic games on the afternoon of Sunday. It was natural that a man so much in sympathy with the Puritans should deal leniently with them in regard to their deviations from ritual regularity. He was loath to deprive the Church of its most instructive and influential preachers, and hoped by mild treatment to bring them back to conformity.

Upon the accession of Laud, there was an immediate and radical change in the administration of the diocese. In the reports which he rendered annually to the king, the primate complains, both in 1634 and 1635, of a part of Kent around Ashford, as specially infected with distemper against the Church. In his account for 1636, he said:—

"I have every year acquainted your majesty, and so must do now, that there are still about Ashford and Egerton divers Brownists and other Separatists. But they are so very mean and poor people, that we know not what to do with them. They are said to be the disciples of one Turner and Fenner, who were long since apprehended by order of your Majesty's High Commission Court. But how this part came to be so infected with such a humor of separation, I know not, unless it were by too much connivance at their first beginning. Neither do I see any remedy like to be, unless some of their chief seducers be driven to abjure the kingdom; which must be done by the judges at the common law, but is not in our power."

On the margin of the paper containing this account the king wrote, "Inform me of the particulars, and I shall command the judges to make them abjure." Among the English State Papers is a "Book of Rough Notes" by the king's secretary, containing these and other memoranda:—

"163⅞ JAN. 6.—Proceedings of the Council at their several meetings during this month beginning this day.

"JAN 21.—A catalogue of books written by anabaptists.

"That the statute of abjuration may be put in execution against some principal men. That the judges be spoken with against Fenner and Turner.

"Speak with Lord Keeper and Mr. Attorney to draw a proclamation for altering the style or date of the year to begin in January.

"JAN. 25.—To mind the Lords and Lord Keeper to speak with the judges and Mr. Attorney about altering the date of year [of] our Lord; that it may begin the first of January as in other kingdoms.

"And about putting the statute of abjuration; to be put in execution against Fenner and Turner.

"Mr. Attorney is to speak with the judges about the date [of] beginning the new year."

From these documents it is evident that the attention of Laud was turned in 1636, and the beginning of the following year, to the Separatists about Ashford and Egerton in Kent, and that he attempted to have the statute of abjuration put in execution against them. Such a movement of one so powerful and so relentless accounts for the emigration of the Kentish men, who, according to tradition, came with Davenport, or two years later with Whitfield, bringing so many family names identical with the names inscribed in the churchyards of Kent.[1]

Another company came from Hereford, a shire in the West of England, bordering on Wales. The particular events which moved them to leave their homes at that time are yet to seek; but it is known that they left

[1] The writer may be excused for specifying two brothers of his own name, whose ancestral home, though in another parish, was less than two miles from Egerton Church and in full view of its massive tower. Joshua Atwater, the elder of the two, had established himself as "a mercer" at Ashford. David Atwater, from whom all in America who bear that family name are descended, had not completed his twenty-second year when he landed in America. They had buried their father in November, 1636, and their mother in the following January; and, being thus liberated from filial duties, joined the expedition with their sister, the only surviving member of the family besides themselves.

under the influence and guidance of Peter Prudden, a clergyman of Hereford, well known to all of them by reputation, if not by personal knowledge of him as a preacher and pastor. Probably they learned through him of the expedition originated by Davenport and his friends, and became, through his agency, members of the association which, leaving London in April, 1637, founded New Haven in April, 1638. The fact that after they had belonged to the association more than two years, after they had resided some months in the new plantation, after some of them had built for themselves houses, and had left behind them the hardest of the hardships incident to such an enterprise, they separated themselves from their associates, removed to Milford, and settled in a town by themselves, with Prudden for their minister, evinces the strength and permanence of their attachment to the man whom they followed in leaving their homes in England. The Herefordshire people, for reasons which will appear hereafter, can be with more certainty distinguished from their fellow-passengers, and grouped together, than those from Kent or those from London.

CHAPTER III.

THE VOYAGE OF THE HECTOR.

IT was a great undertaking for the company which gradually gathered around Davenport and the Eatons, to prepare for a voyage across the Atlantic, and a permanent residence in the New World. The ministers could perhaps embark, with their books and household-stuff, in a few days; but merchants engaged in foreign commerce needed several months, after deciding to emigrate, for the conversion of their capital into money, or into merchandise suitable for the adventure in which they were engaging.

But this company projected something more than emigration. They were not to scatter themselves, when they disembarked, among the different settlements already established in New England, but to remain together, and lay the foundation of a new and isolated community. For this reason a more comprehensive outfit was necessary than if they had expected to become incorporated, individually or collectively, in communities already planted. In addition to the stores shipped by individuals, there must be many things provided for the common good, by persons acting in behalf of the whole company. There is evidence, that, after the expedition arrived at New Haven, its affairs were managed like those of a joint-stock association, and therefore some ground for believing, that, from the beginning, those who agreed to emigrate in this company, or at least some of them, associated themselves together as partners in the profit and loss of the adventure.

Higginson, some years before, had advised emigrants that "it were a wise course for those that are of abilities to join together and buy a ship for the voyage;" alleging as a reason, that transportation was so dear as five pounds a man, and ten pounds a horse, and commonly three pounds for every ton of goods. "All that come," he says, "must have victuals with them for a twelvemonth." Still earlier, Winslow had written from Plymouth, "Bring good store of clothes and bedding with you. Bring paper and linseed-oil for your windows, with cotton yarn for your lamps."

These directions, intended in both cases for emigrants coming to join communities already established, illustrate the need of studious foresight and careful co-operation in a company of persons proposing not only to remove to New England, but to begin a new and independent plantation.

Davenport and Eaton had learned by experience, in fitting out vessels for the Massachusetts Bay Company, what would be needed in a new settlement, and were as well qualified, perhaps, as any could be, to prepare a list of necessary articles. The Abigail, the first ship which came to Salem, brought ten thousand bricks as ballast; and bricks with "London" stamped on them were found at the demolition of a very ancient house in

New Haven.[1] It is not certain that the vessel in which Davenport and Eaton embarked, was, like the Abigail, ballasted with bricks; but the fact that bricks were sometimes brought from England illustrates the care with which emigrant ships were fitted out. The Abigail brought also sea-coals, but all freighters must have soon learned that it was useless to carry fuel to a country so well timbered as New England. An emigrant-ship was further ballasted with iron, steel, lead, nails, and other heavy articles of utility. The bulk of the cargo consisted of apparel, bedding, food, tools, arms, ammunition, and seeds. Neat-cattle and goats were usually taken, and sometimes horses. The Massachusetts Bay Company had a rule, that a ship of two hundred tons should not carry above one hundred passengers, and other ships were limited after the same proportion.

In the summer of 1636, several vessels recently arrived from England being in the harbor of Boston, Thomas Miller, the master's mate of one of them, was apprehended and brought before the Governor and Council, for saying, to some who came on board, that the colonists were traitors and rebels because they did not display the king's colors at the fort. The ship on which this insufferable speech was spoken was the Hector of London, William Fernes, master. Sailing from Boston in July, she was chartered after her arrival

[1] The writer remembers to have seen some of these bricks taken from the Atwater house of which Dr. Dana in his Century Sermon speaks as built by Joshua Atwater, one of the emigrants. I think, however, that the house was built by a nephew of Joshua Atwater. Certainly Thomas Attwater (as he chose to write his name), who in Dr. Dana's time occupied the house, was not descended from Joshua Atwater, but from his brother David.

in London by the company whose origin has been related in the preceding chapter. While they were preparing her for another voyage to Boston, she was seized by the Lords of the Admiralty for the king's service, as will appear from the following petition without date, but indorsed, "Received January, 1637:"—

"*To the Right Honorable the Lords and other Commissioners of his Majesty's High Court of Admiralty:*—

"The humble petition of the Owners and Freighters of the good ship called the Hector of London,

"Humbly showeth unto your honors that your petitioners having contracted for a voyage with the said ship from here to New England for a plantation there, and from there to divers parts in the Streights, the freighters have made ready all their provisions and passengers, fitting both for the said voyage and plantation, and most of them thereupon engaged their whole estates and paid part of their moneys. Since which agreement and preparation made, the said ship is impressed for his Majesty's service whereby she is hindered from proceeding on the said intended voyage.

"Their most humble suit therefore is that in respect of the petitioners' great charges already arisen before the impressing of the ship, and her not proceeding on her voyage will tend to the great loss, if not utter undoing of divers of your honors' suppliants, and for that, if it pleased God the ship do safely returne, the Custom to his Majesty of the goods to be imported in her from the Streights hither will amount to £3000 at the least, your Lordships would be pleased to give order and warrant for the release of the said ship from her impression that so she may proceed on her said voyage,

"And they as in duty bound shall daily pray."

This petition was supported by the following certificate, signed by Samuel Hutchinson, Richard Hutchinson, and Arthur Hollingworth, who were perhaps the owners of the Hector:—

"We whose names are hereunto subscribed do hereby certify that the good ship called the Hector of London was contracted for,

THE VOYAGE OF THE HECTOR. 49

for a voyage, and that provision was made and provided before the said ship was impressed for the king's Majesty's service. In testimony whereof we have hereunder set our names the nineteenth of January A. D. 1637."

On the 23d of the same month the Secretary of the Admiralty wrote to Sir William Russell, through whom the petition, with others of like import, had reached them, as follows:—

"SIR,—The Lords Commissioners for the Admiralty (having perused your letter of the 21st of this month touching the merchant ships ordered to be taken up for his Majesty's service) have commanded me to signify to you that they think it not fit to release any of the said ships upon the pretences expressed in your letter (albeit the same may be true) in regard they perceive by your letter that there are not at present any merchant ships in the Thames fit to send in their places. But when you shall certify their Lordships that there are other merchant ships in the river of the like burden and force, fit for his Majesty's service that may be completely fitted and ready by the 20th of April next, their Lordships will consider further of the allegations of the owners of the four ships mentioned in your said letter and declare their further pleasure thereupon."

Not entirely discouraged by this reply, the captain of the Hector presented another petition without date, but indorsed, " 1637, February 14:"—

"*To the Right Honorable the Lords and other Commissioners of the Admiralty:—*
" The humble petition of William Fernes, master of the ship called the Hector,
" Humbly showeth that whereas the petitioner hath been an humble suitor to your honors for the releasing of the said ship; for that there was a contract and provision was made for a voyage long before, which tends to the ruin of many, except your honors be pleased to give orders for her discharge; for that there are

divers ships come in more fit and able for his Majesty's service, viz., the Vinty about 300 tons and 22 pieces of ordnance; the Royal Defence 300 tons and upwards, with 22 pieces of ordnance; the Pleiades 350 tons, 26 ordnance; Prudence 370 tons, 28 pieces ordnance; one whereof Mr. Wise is Master, 350 tons and 24 pieces of ordnance;

"His humble suit therefore is that your honors will please to give order that the said ship called the Hector may be discharged for the reasons aforesaid, that she may go on in her intended voyage,

"And the petitioner with many others shall pray."

Ultimately, the Hector was released; and from an order of the king in council, that the Pleiades, with other impressed vessels, should be ready for sea on the 25th of April, it may be inferred that she was substituted for the Hector. The reader will have noticed that the names of the freighters are withheld in all these negotiations for the release of their ship. It is alleged that many will suffer, and perhaps be undone, but there is nothing to call attention to any individuals as engaged in the enterprise.

The lords of the council were not ignorant that considerable emigration to New England had already taken place, or that the exodus still continued; but they believed that those who went were for the most part poor and mean people, who would be of little advantage at home and might, if colonized, be of use by increasing foreign commerce. Moreover they were unaware how strongly this emigration was leavened with Puritanism. If they had known that several wealthy merchants of London, inclined to non-conformity, had embarked their whole estates in the Hector, and were intending to go to New England with their families to find there a permanent residence, they would have found means to frustrate the undertaking. On the 30th of April proclamation was made, "that the king—being informed that great numbers of his subjects are yearly transported into those parts of America which have been granted by patent to several persons, and there settle themselves, some of them with their families and whole estates, amongst whom are many idle and refractory humors, whose only or principal end is to live without the reach of authority—doth command his officers and ministers of the ports, not to suffer any persons, being subsidy men or of their value, to pass to any of those plantations without a license from his Majesty's commissioners for plantations first obtained; nor any under the degree of subsidy men, without a certificate from two justices of the peace where they lived, that they have taken the oaths of allegiance and supremacy, and a testimony from the minister of the parish, of their conformity to the orders and discipline of the Church of England." As the Hector arrived in Boston on the 26th of June, we may infer from the date of this proclamation that it was issued immediately after she had sailed, and that it was occasioned by the discovery of the true nature of an expedition in which several persons, being subsidy men, or of their value, had clandestinely left the kingdom and carried away their estates.

If the ship was chartered by a joint-stock association, it does not follow that the shareholders took passage in her. The Massachusetts Bay Company had a regular tariff of rates at which they received all freight that was offered, and all passengers who were approved. Theophilus Eaton owned a sixteenth of the Arbella, which had been purchased expressly for that company's service; and both he and Davenport, as directors of the company, had become familiar with its methods. The rates of that company were five pounds for the passage of an adult, and four pounds for a ton of goods. The association of adventurers which chartered the Hector would naturally adopt similar methods and similar rates. Having secured accommodation for themselves and their families, and for the freight which belonged to the association and to the individuals composing it, they would receive persons not shareholders, at the regular rates. Some of the emigrants may have been precluded from taking stock in the association by the expenses of emigration; but the originators of the enterprise would naturally desire that all who were of sufficient ability should have a pecuniary interest in its welfare. There was at least one passenger who did not come as an emigrant. Winthrop writes in his journal, "In the Hector came also the Lord Leigh, son and heir of the Earl of Marlborough, being about nineteen years of age, who came only to see the country. He was of very sober carriage, especially in the ship, where he was much disrespected and unworthily used by the master, one Fernes, and some of the passengers; yet he bore it meekly and silently.[1]"

Before the Hector sailed, the company which chartered her had so increased that it became necessary to hire another vessel to accompany her on the voyage; but the name of the vessel has not been preserved to us. This unexpected increase was due to the accession

[1] Winthrop perhaps changed his mind about Lord Leigh, when that youth, having accepted the governor's invitation to a dinner-party made expressly to honor him, was persuaded by Harry Vane to absent himself.

of those who have been mentioned as coming from Kent and from Herefordshire. Concerning the latter, we have no means of determining when Prudden began to negotiate with Davenport; but the men of Kent appear to have joined the expedition after the Hector was engaged for the voyage. Their departure was so hasty that many who wished to go were forced to wait for another opportunity. and came out two years afterward in the first ship which sailed from England direct to the harbor of New Haven.

No documents have yet been found which indicate the day when the Hector and her consort sailed from London,[1] or the manner in which the officers of the port discharged their official duty in examining the certificates of the passengers. Similar requirements to those prescribed by the proclamation of April 30 had been made by a proclamation issued more than two years earlier, but were nevertheless insufficient to prevent the emigration of Puritans. Many found no difficulty in obtaining a *bona-fide* certificate of conformity, and it does not appear that any objected to the oaths of allegiance and supremacy. If unable to obtain a certificate from the minister of the parish where they had lived, they came, some clandestinely, and some under borrowed names and corresponding passports. It is said that John Aylmer, Bishop of London in Queen Elizabeth's time, and an exile for religion in Queen

[1] Sir Matthew Boynton, who had previously sent out some cattle, and some servants to care for them, in a letter dated "London, April 12, 1637," writes to John Winthrop, jun., "I have sent either of my servants half a year's wages by Mr. Hopkins, which, I pray you, deliver to them." Probably this letter came in the Hector with Mr. Hopkins. If so, she sailed after the 12th of April.

Mary's reign, was so small of stature, that, when the searchers were clearing the ship in which he made his escape, the merchant put him into a great wine-butt that had a partition in the middle, so that Aylmer was enclosed in the hinder part while the searchers drank of the wine which they saw drawn out of the head on the other part.[1] The Puritans of the seventeenth century were capable of exercising equal ingenuity when necessary; but, in a ship full of his friends, a person obnoxious to the government might be secreted for an hour without so much trouble, even if the searching officer were in sympathy with the lords of the Privy Council. In many cases, however, the searcher discharged his duty perfunctorilly, and with no earnest desire to discover and arrest those who embarked without the required certificates. If ever lists of the passengers in the Hector and her consort should be discovered, they will probably not contain the name of John Davenport or of Samuel Eaton.

Two months was perhaps the average time consumed in sailing from London to Boston in the vessels of that day. The Arbella, when she brought Winthrop and his company, was a little more than two months from Yarmouth to Salem; and there is no intimation in his journal that the voyage was unexpectedly long. Higginson says, "Our passage was short and speedy; for whereas we had three thousand miles English to sail from Old to New England, we performed the same in six weeks and three days." A passage was indeed sometimes made in less time, but in other instances was protracted to three months. A vessel made but one round

---

[1] Fuller's Worthies, B. II., 248.

trip in a year, leaving England in the spring and arriving home in the autumn. Crowded cabins rendered the passage uncomfortable, even when speedy; but a protracted voyage often induced not only discomfort, but disease.

None of the passengers in the Hector, or in the vessel which accompanied her, having supplied us with his journal, we must avail ourselves of diaries of contemporary voyages if we would see them in imagination pursuing their way down the Thames, through the

A BARQUE OF THE SEVENTEENTH CENTURY.

Channel, and over the Atlantic. Sea-sickness reigned supreme as they passed along the southern coast of their native island; but in the first pleasant weather after they had gained the open sea, they "fetched out the children and others, that were sick and lay groaning in the cabins, and, having stretched a rope from the steerage to the mainmast, made them stand, some on one side and some on the other, and sway it up and down till they were warm. By this means they soon grew well and merry." Afterward, "when the ship

heaved and set more than usual, a few were sick, but of
these such as came upon deck and stirred themselves
were presently well again, therefore, our captain set
our children and young men to some harmless exercises
in which the seamen were very active, and did our people much good, though they would sometimes play the
wags with them.¹" Once or twice during the voyage
the wind blew a gale; and the passengers being confined
to the cabin united in the observance of a fast with a
protracted service of prayer, which, when the wind sub-
sided, was followed by a service of thanksgiving. "We
constantly served God morning and evening, by reading
and expounding a chapter, singing, and prayer; and
the sabbath was solemnly kept by adding to the former,
preaching twice, and catechising. Besides, the ship-
master and his company used every night to set their
eight and twelve o'clock watches by singing a psalm,
and prayer that was not read out of a book.²" Sometimes one vessel so far outsailed her consort, that she
must take in some sail, and stay for her, lest the two
should be entirely separated for the remainder of the
voyage. "Our captain, supposing us now to be near
the coast, fitted on a new mainsail, that was very strong
and double, and would not adventure with his old sails as
before, when he had sea-room enough." "This evening
we saw the new moon more than half an hour after
sunset, being much smaller than it is at any time in
England." "About four this morning, we sounded,
and had ground at thirty fathom; and, it being somewhat calm, we put our ship a-stays, and took, in less
than two hours, with a few hooks, sixty-seven codfish,

¹ Winthrop. ² Higginson.

most of them very great fish. This came very seasonably, for our salt fish was now spent, and we were taking care for victuals this day, being a fish day." "We had now fair sunshine weather, and there came a smell off the shore like the smell of a garden." Four days later, both the ships lay at anchor, and the weary voyagers were on shore, some gathering store of fine strawberries, and others entertained in the houses of friends, who feasted them with "good venison pasty, and good beer."

CHAPTER IV.

THE WINTER SPENT IN MASSACHUSETTS.

BOSTON in its infancy welcomed all Puritan immigrants. Its inhabitants rejoiced in the growth of their town and of their colony; they were pleased to find a market for the products of their gardens; they enjoyed the society of those through whom they could receive tidings from the mother-country, and with whom they could fraternize in religious worship. In many cases they found among the new-comers old acquaintances, the sight of whom awakened memories of the past and the absent, in which, after so long an exile from home, they experienced unspeakable pleasure. But the immigrants who landed in Boston on the 26th of June, 1637, received a warmer welcome than ordinary. The eminence of "the famous Mr. Davenport," and the opulence of the merchants who accompanied him, gave to this company, in the estimation of the colonists, an unusual value. Not only Boston, but the whole colony of Massachusetts, was desirous that they should settle within that Commonwealth. "Great pains were taken, not only by particular persons and towns, but by the General Court, to fix them in the colony. Charlestown made them large offers; and Newbury proposed to give up the whole town to them. The

General Court offered them any place which they should choose.[1]"

The arrival of Davenport was considered especially opportune because of the influence he might exert in bringing to an end the controversy which then divided the churches in Massachusetts in regard to Ann Hutchinson and the doctrines which she preached. "There are certain opinions which always come forth, under one form or another, in times of great religious excitement, to dishonor the truths which they stimulate, and to defeat the work of God by heating the minds of men to enthusiasm, and thus leading them into licentiousness of conduct. These opinions, essentially the same under many modifications, have been known in various ages by various names, as Antinomianism, Familism, and—in our day—Perfectionism. Persons falling into these errors commonly begin by talking mystically and extravagantly about grace, the indwelling of the Spirit, the identity of believers with the person of Christ, or of the Holy Ghost, or of God. As they proceed, they learn to despise all ordinances and means of grace; they put contempt upon the Bible as a mere dead letter, worth nothing in comparison with their inspiration; they reject and revile all civil government and order; and not unfrequently they end in denying theoretically all the differences between right and wrong so far as their conduct is concerned, and in rushing to the shameless perpetration of the most loathsome wickedness. This intellectual and spiritual disease had broken out in Massachusetts, and threatened to become epidemic. An artful, enthusiastic, and eloquent

[1] Trumbull.

woman, forgetting the modesty of her sex, had set herself up for a preacher; and by the adroitness with which she addressed herself to the weaknesses and prejudices of individuals and drew to her side the authority of some of the most honored names in the colony, she seemed likely, not only to lead her own blind followers to the wildest extravagance, but to spread division through all the churches. In this crisis, a man so eminent as Davenport, so much respected by all parties, so exempt from any participation in the controversy, so learned in the Scriptures, so skilled in the great art of marking distinctions and detecting fallacies, could not but be welcomed by all.[1]"

A synod of "all the teaching elders in the country" was called to discuss the questions at issue, and discriminate between truth and error. Of this assembly, which began its sessions Aug. 30, and continued to sit for three weeks, Davenport was one of the most influential members. "The wisdom and learning of this worthy man," says Mather, "did contribute more than a little to dispel the fascinating mists which had suddenly disordered our affairs." A few days after the adjournment, Davenport, by request of the synod, preached a sermon in which, "with much wisdom and sound argument, he persuaded to unity.[2]"

Meantime it had become evident that the people who had come from the mother-country with Davenport, and acknowledged him as a leader, were not content to settle in the vicinity of Boston. Trumbull suggests that the Antinomian controversy was one reason why they wished to remove to a distance. But the same

[1] Bacon: Historical Discourses.   [2] Winthrop.

writer says, "It is probable that the motive which had the greatest influence with the principal men was the desire of being at the head of a new government, modelled, both in civil and religious matters, agreeable to their own apprehensions. In laying the foundations of a new colony, there was a fair probability that they might accommodate all matters of church and commonwealth to their own feelings and sentiments. But in Massachusetts the principal men were fixed in the chief seats of government, which they were likely to keep, and their civil and religious polity was already formed."

The day after the synod assembled, Theophilus Eaton started with a considerable party on a tour of exploration. The Pequot war had made the English acquainted with the country west of the Connecticut River and bordering on Long Island Sound. The Indians fled westward after the destruction of their fort at Mystic, and the English pursued them as far as Fairfield, where on the 13th of July, seven weeks before Eaton started, so many of the Pequots were slain, that the few survivors ceased to maintain a tribal organization, and became incorporated with other tribes. In this pursuit, the troops marching on the land, and their vessels holding a parallel course on the water, the English came to a harbor, which the Indians called by a name variously written in that age, but known in modern orthography as Quinnipiac, where they staid several days. They were charmed with the country. Capt. Stoughton, in a letter to Gov. Winthrop, speaks of it as preferable to Pequot as a place for a settlement. He says, "The providence of God guided us to so excellent a country at Quellipioak river, and so all along the coast as we traveled, as I am confident we have not the like as yet."

In another letter "from Pequot, the 2nd day of the 6th week of our warfare," he says, "For this place is scarce worthy much cost. But if you will enlarge the state and provide for the poor servants of Christ that are yet unprovided (which I esteem a worthy work), I must speak my conscience. I confess, the place and places whither God's providence carried us, that is, to Quillepiage River, and so beyond to the Dutch, is before this, or the Bay either (so far as I can judge), abundantly."

This was probably written Aug. 14; and the gallant captain reached Boston on the 26th of the same month, when he had opportunity to give more copious description of what he had seen.

Capt. Underhill doubtless made report answerable to what he has written in his "History of the Pequot War," of that famous place called Queenapiok. "It hath a fair river, fit for harboring of ships, and abounds with rich and goodly meadows."

Moved by such tidings, Eaton went immediately to view the place; and so well did he like it, that, when he set out on his return to Boston, he left seven of his men to remain through the winter and make preparation for the arrival of the rest of the company. It was September when he and his followers first saw Quinnipiac; and they doubtless spent some weeks in the neighborhood, skirting the shore with their pinnace to examine harbors and rivers. There can be no doubt that Eaton, when he returned to Boston, was fully persuaded in his own mind, that Quinnipiac was preferable to any

THE WINTER SPENT IN MASSACHUSETTS. 63

other available place for the projected plantation. Indeed, Winthrop speaks as if he thought the question already settled when Eaton started on his tour of exploration. Under date of Aug. 31, he says, "Mr. Eaton and some others of Mr. Davenport's company went to view Quinnipiac with intent to begin a plantation there. They had many offers here, and at Plymouth, and they had viewed many places, but none would content." But in a matter of so great importance it was necessary to proceed slowly. The exploring party must report to those who had remained in Massachusetts, and all the shareholders must have a voice in selecting a place for their plantation. Perhaps it was already too late in the year to build houses that would sufficiently shelter women and children from the rigor of the approaching winter, even if the work were commenced immediately. Certainly it was deemed expedient to remain in Massachusetts till the opening of spring; and this was the expectation when Eaton leaving seven men at Quinnipiac, returned to Boston to make his report.

Joshua Atwater, Francis Brown, John Beecher, Robert Pigg, and Thomas Hogg were of the seven. The names of the others have not been preserved. One of the seven died during the winter; and his bones were found in the year 1750, in digging the cellar of the stone house at the corner of George and Meadow Streets.[1] The hut which sheltered these adventurous

[1] I think that the man who died was John Beecher, as his name does not occur on the earlier records, and there was a widow Beecher whose son Isaac was old enough in 1644 to take the oath of fidelity. Dr. Dana has preserved the tradition that Joshua Atwater was one of the seven who remained at Quinnipiac during the winter: Lambert mentions the four other names.

men was near the creek, and about fifty yards west of the place where the survivors buried the body of their comrade. A copious spring which once issued from the bank between George Street and the creek, and was covered when the creek was converted into a sewer, may have determined the location of the hut. We may imagine that they spent their time in hewing, cleaving, and sawing, in hunting and trapping, and in collecting, by means of barter with the natives, beaver and other furs for the European market. If, like their brethren at Saybrook, they had dogs, they might, by enclosing their house with palisades, lie down to sleep with as little danger of being surprised by an enemy, as if they had been in Boston. Whatever communication they had with their friends during the winter must have been by means of special messengers. Indian runners were easily found to perform such a service.[1] We shall presently see, that before the 12th of March, letters had been sent by their friends in Massachusetts, directing them to transact with the natives for the purchase of land. Doubtless the same letters instructed them to build huts, and make all possible provision for the comfort of those who were to arrive.

With the exception of these seven, the people who crossed the Atlantic in the Hector and her consort remained in Boston or in the vicinity during the winter, many of them having found employment suitable to their several vocations. Though somewhat scattered, some finding lodgings and employment in one place and some in another, they were still an organized com-

[1] Trumbull quotes Roger Williams as saying, "I have known them run between eighty and a hundred miles in a summer's day."

pany, and as such were required by the government of Massachusetts to pay taxes as if they had already settled as a town in that Commonwealth. A tax was levied by the General Court, in November after their arrival, to pay the expenses of the Pequot war. The sum required was a thousand pounds, of which nine hundred and eighty pounds was assessed upon the several towns; the name of Mr. Eaton being added to the list of towns, with the minute, "Mr. Eaton is left out of this rate, leaving it to his discretion what he will freely give toward these charges." The difference between the amount required, and the amount of the assessments, indicates what sum it was desired that Mr. Eaton should "freely give;" and the discretion allowed him was probably due to the fact that these expenses had been for the most part incurred before he and his party arrived in the country; the destruction of the fort at Mystic, which was the great event of the war, having taken place on the 26th of May, a full month before the Hector cast anchor in the harbor of Boston. But when another rate was levied, on the twelfth day of March of the following year, amounting to fifteen hundred pounds, Mr. Eaton's name was again appended to the list of towns with an assessment of twenty pounds, and without intimation that payment was optional.

It is a noteworthy coincidence that this second tax is of the same date with the following letter:—

"It may please the worthy and much honored Governor, Deputy, and Assistants, and with them the present Court, to take knowledge, that our desire of staying within this patent was real and strong, if the eye of God's providence (to whom we have committed our ways, especially in so important an enterprise as this, which, we confess, is far above our capacities) has guided us to a place convenient for our families and friends. Which, as our words have often expressed, so, we hope, the truth thereof is sufficiently declared by our almost nine months' patient waiting in expectation of some opportunity to be offered us, for that end, to our great charge and hindrance many ways. In all which time we have, in many prayers, commended the guidance of our apprehensions, judgments, spirits, resolutions, and ways into the good hand of the only wise God, whose prerogative it is to determine the bounds of our habitations, according to the ends for which he hath brought us into these countries; and we have considered, as we were able, by his help, whatsoever place hath been propounded to us, being ready to have with contentment accepted (if by our stay any public good might be promoted) smaller accommodations and upon dearer terms (if they might be moderately commodious) than, we believe, most men, in the same case with us in all respects, would have done. And whereas a place for an inland plantation, beyond Watertown, was propounded to us, and pressed with much importunity by some, whose words have the power of a law with us, in any way of God, we did speedily and seriously deliberate thereupon, it being the subject of the greatest part of a day's discourse. The conclusion was that, if the upland should answer the meadow ground in goodness and desirableness (whereof yet there is some cause of doubting), yet, considering that a boat cannot pass from the bay thither, nearer than eight or ten miles distance, and that it is so remote from the bay, and from any town, we could not see how our dwelling there would be advantageous to these plantations or compatible with our conditions or commodious for our families or for our friends. Nor can we satisfy ourselves that it is expedient for ourselves, or for our friends, that we choose such a condition, wherein we must be compelled to have our dwelling houses so far distant from our farms as Boston or Charlestown is from that place, few of our friends being able to bear the charge thereof (whose cases, nevertheless, we are bound to consider), and some of them, that are able, not being persuaded that it is lawful for them to live continually from the greatest part of their families, as in this case they would be necessitated to do. The season of the year, and other weighty considerations, compelled us to hasten to a full and final conclusion, which we are at last come unto, by God's appointment and direction, we hope, in mercy, and have sent letters to Connecticut for a speedy transacting the purchase of the parts about Quillypiac from the natives which may pretend title thereunto. By which act we absolutely and irrevocably engaged that way; and we are persuaded that God will order it for good unto these plantations, whose love so abundantly above our deserts or expectations, expressed in your desire of our abode, in these parts, as we shall ever retain in thankful memory, so we shall account ourselves thereby obliged to be any way instrumental and serviceable for the common good of these plantations as well as of those; which the divine providence hath combined together in as strong a bond of brotherly affection, by the sameness of their condition, as Joab and Abishai were, whose several armies did mutually strengthen them both against their several enemies, ii. Sam. x. 9, 10, 11; or rather they are joined together, as Hippocrates his twins, to stand and fall, to grow and decay, to flourish and wither, to live and die, together. In witness of the premises we subscribe our names,

"The 12th day of the 1st month, 1638."

This letter, which is still preserved, is in the handwriting of Davenport, but is superscribed as follows in the handwriting of Eaton: "To the much honored, the Governor, Deputy, and Assistants." From this communication it appears that even if Eaton had returned from his tour of exploration fully expecting that he and his company would settle at Quinnipiac, he had not so fully expressed his determination as to preclude further effort to persuade him to remain in Massachusetts. It further appears that before the date of this communication the company had formally decided to fix their plantation at Quinnipiac, and had sent notice thereof to those who were already on the ground. Eighteen days afterward, that is, on the 30th of March, the leaders of the company and most of their followers embarked at Boston. After a tedious voyage of "about a fortnight they arrived at their desired port.[1]" Winthrop thus narrates their departure: "Mr. Davenport and Mr. Prudden and a brother of Mr. Eaton (being ministers also), went by water to Quinnipiac; and with them many families removed out of this jurisdiction to plant in those parts, being much taken with the opinion of the fruitfulness of that place and more safety (as they conceived) from danger of a general governor, who was feared to be sent this summer; which though it were a great weakening to these parts, yet we expected to see a good providence of God in it (for all possible means had been used to accommodate them here; Charlestown offered them largely, Newbury their whole town, the court any place which was free), both for possessing those parts which lay open for an enemy, and for strengthening our friends at Connecticut, and for making room here for many, who were expected out of England this year, and for diverting the thoughts and intentions of such in England as intended evil against us, whose designs might be frustrate by our scattering so far; and such as were now gone that way were as much in the eye of the state of England as we here."

[1] Trumbull.

CHAPTER V.

THE FIRST YEAR AT QUINNIPIAC.

THE company which came from London in the Hector and her consort, numbered about fifty adult men; or, including women, children, and servants, about two hundred and fifty persons. But so great was the enthusiasm excited by the report which the soldiers brought of Quinnipiac, and so strong the confidence felt in the leaders of the expedition, that when the company left Boston in the spring of 1638 its number was considerably increased by accessions from Massachusetts. Skirting the coast, and perhaps calling at Saybrook fort where Lion Gardiner, an old acquaintance of Davenport, commanded,[1] they at last reached the harbor of Quinnipiac. West of the river of that name, they saw two smaller streams pouring into the harbor, each sufficient to float such a vessel as theirs. The mouth of the East Creek was where the railway now crosses East Water Street, and vessels entering it could be floated up, over what is now the bed of the rail-

[1] Gardiner, in his relation of the Pequot wars, says that it was "through the persuasion of Mr. John Davenport and Mr. Hugh Peters, with some other well-affected Englishmen of Rotterdam," that he left the service of the Prince of Orange in Holland to serve the patentees of Connecticut.—*Mass. Hist. Coll. XXIII.*, p. 136.

way, as far as Chapel Street.[1] The West Creek emptied its waters where the sewer now crosses West Water Street. Still farther westward, beyond Oyster Point, the West River also emptied its waters into the harbor. Up the West Creek sailed Davenport and his companions, gazing with interest on the wilderness which was to be their home. They saw a plain extending inland about two miles, at which distance stood basaltic rocks colored with iron, and so prominent in the landscape that the Dutch had called the place Rodenbergh or Red Mount. It was well supplied with timber, but there were spaces where the natives had raised successive harvests of maize. A dense forest covered a small tract where the "spruce masts" grew; but the larger portion was an open forest, promising to supply sufficient timber for building houses and fences, with perhaps a little surplus for exportation in the form of clapboards and shingles. The tree under which they held their service of worship on the first Sabbath after their arrival was a spreading oak which had not lacked room for development. Before the expiration of the second year it was ordered by the General Court that "no man shall cut any timber down, but where he shall be assigned by the magistrate, except on his own ground." Such an enactment implies that there was no superabundance of timber in the vicinity of the settlement.

On the west side of this plain were broad salt meadows, bordering the West River on either bank, and extending inland almost to the Red Hill which the planters called the West Rock. On the east side of the plain were

[1] N. H. Col. Rec. I. 143.

still more extensive salt meadows spread out on both sides of the Quinnipiac, or East River, and also on both sides of a stream flowing into it a short distance above its outlet, which the settlers named Mill River as soon as they were able to erect a mill. The meadows on the Quinnipiac extended northward much farther than those on West River. These salt meadows on both sides of the plain, yielding abundant provender without delay and without labor, had greatly influenced the company in choosing this place for their plantation. Invisible from the deck of the pinnace, they were doubtless eagerly inquired for by those who had not been of the exploring party. But, though rendered invisible by the intervention of higher ground, they so much widened the view, that on one side the eye could reach the hills beyond the West River, and, on the other, the highlands beyond the Quinnipiac.

The temporary shelters, which the first planters of New England provided for their families till they could erect permanent dwellings, were of different kinds. Some planters carried tents with them to the place chosen for a new home; some built wigwams like those of the natives. Either species would suffice in summer; but for winter they usually built huts, as they called them, similar to the modern log-cabins in the forests of the West, though in some instances if not in most, they were roofed, after the English fashion, with thatch. It was perhaps a peculiarity of New Haven, that cellars were used for temporary habitations. They were, as the name suggests, partially under ground, and perhaps in most cases on a hillside. If built on the bank between the West Creek and George Street, with apertures opening to the south, they would be open to the sun and sheltered from the northern winds. Rev. Michael Wigglesworth,[1] who came to Quinnipiac with his parents in October, 1638, when he was about seven years old, describes the cellar in which the family spent the first winter, as covered with earth on the roof. Such a covering might be effectual to exclude the cold winds of winter, but, as the boy's experience proves, it was a poor protection from a' heavy rain. When he was an old man he remembered how he had been, while asleep, drenched with water permeating the muddy roof, and had been afflicted in consequence with a dangerous illness. Doubtless the party which had wintered at the place had made ready not only a public storehouse, but several huts or cellars in which their friends who were to arrive might temporarily shelter their familes. These would be visible to the new-comers as they approached the shore and ascended the creek.

The pinnace in which they had made the voyage was perhaps the property of some of the company, for such a vessel would be constantly in requisition for various services to the inhabitants of a new plantation. But, even if owned in Boston, she would remain for some days till accommodations on shore could be provided for all.

It was Friday when they left Boston; and, as they are said to have spent about a fortnight on the voyage, it was the latter part of the week when they arrived. On the Sabbath they worshiped under an oak-tree near the landing: and Mr. Davenport, in a sermon on Matt. iv. 1, "insisted on the temptations of the wilderness, made such observations, and gave such directions and

[1] See his autobiographical paper in Appendix I.

exhortations, as were pertinent to the then present condition of his hearers." He left this remark, that he "enjoyed a good day.¹" Lambert says that Mr. Prudden preached in the afternoon, but does not give his authority. It was perhaps a Milford tradition, and it has inherent probability.

In the valedictory letter of Davenport and Eaton to the General Court of Massachusetts they say, "We have sent letters to Connecticut for a speedy transacting the purchase of the parts about Quinnipiac from the natives." The purchase had probably been effected before their arrival in April, though no written deed was signed till the following November. The natives, therefore, were expecting the large re-enforcement received by the six Englishmen with whom they were now well acquainted. They welcomed the new-comers, and were pleased to have in their neighborhood a plantation of Englishmen, to which they might retreat when molested by their enemies, and where they might barter their venison, pelts, and furs, for the much-admired tools and trinkets of the English. They now for the first time saw English women and children; and their curiosity, which, in respect to the little company left by Eaton in the preceding autumn, had waned, again drew them to the border of the West Creek. The medal

¹ Trumbull, i. 96. It is apparent that Trumbull had access to some diary or other written statement of Davenport. The oak-tree was about twenty feet north of George Street, and about forty-five feet east of College Street. It is said that a section of the tree afterward supported the anvil on which two stalwart generations of Beechers hammered, before Lyman Beecher transferred the rôle of the family from the anvil to the pulpit. Their shop was in College Street, near the place where the tree had stood.

struck two centuries afterward, in commemoration of the settlement of the town, very properly represents some of them sitting near the company assembled on Sunday under the oak-tree. Here they witnessed the worship which the English rendered to the Great Spirit. Here they began to be acquainted with the preacher whom afterward they characterized as "so-big-study man."

MEDAL.

The English soon after their arrival at Quinnipiac observed a day of extraordinary humiliation, when they formed a social compact, mutually promising "that as in matters that concern the gathering and ordering of a church, so likewise in all public offices, which concern civil order, as choice of magistrates and officers, making and repealing of laws, dividing allotments of inheritance, and all things of like nature," they would all of them be ordered by those rules which the Scripture holds forth. For more than a year they had no other civil or ecclesiastical organization. There were doubless frequent meetings for the transaction of business, and, if we may judge of that year by the years that followed, there were penalties inflicted on evil-doers. But, if any individuals were authorized to act as magistrates, the record of their appointment has not been preserved. The plantation covenant, like the compact signed in the cabin of the Mayflower, was a provisional arrangement of men, who, finding themselves beyond the actual jurisdiction of any earthly government, attempted to govern themselves according to the law of God.

The first care of the planters was to choose a site for their future town; the next to lay out streets and house-lots, so that each family might as soon as possible make preparations for gardening and building. Tradition reports that they would have chosen Oyster Point but for the difficulty of digging wells, water being obtained in that neighborhood only at great depth. They decided, however, to locate the principal part of their town on the north side of the West Creek, rather than on the south side, and to make a line parallel with that stream and near its border, the base-line of the town plot.

Accordingly George Street was laid out half a mile in length and upon it as a base, a square was described. The half-mile square not being sufficient, two suburbs were added. One consisted of a four-sided piece whose shape and dimensions were determined by the two creeks as the water ran when nearing the harbor. It was bounded by George, Water, Meadow, and State Streets. The other was on the west side of the West Creek. Changes since made in the highways render difficult the task of defining it; but Hill Street was its eastern, or more properly northeastern boundary.

The square described on George Street was divided by two parallel streets running east and west, and by two parallel streets running north and south, into nine equal squares; of which the square in the center was sequestered as a market-place. The remaining eight squares and the suburbs were divided into house-lots, and assigned to the planters severally, who seem to have grouped themselves, to some extent, according to personal acquaintance and friendship in the old country. The Herefordshire men, for example, had their lots on the southwest and south-center squares, or quarters, as they were then called. The eight squares were for a long time distinguished one from another by the names of some prominent persons who lived on the quarters to which their names were respectively applied. The northeast square was called Mr. Eaton's quarter, or in later years the Governor's quarter. The north-center was Mr. Robert Newman's quarter. The northwest was Mr. Tench's quarter. The west-centre was Mr. Evance's quarter, or, for a reason which will be explained hereafter, the Yorkshire quarter. The southwest was Mr. Fowler's, or the Herefordshire quarter. Mr. Gregson's name was applied to the south-center, Mr. Lamberton's to the southeast, and Mr. Davenport's to the east-center. The suburbs were sufficiently indicated by that appellation without attaching the name of an inhabitant. In the division of out-lands the two suburbs were united together as one society or quarter. Four lots situated on East Water Street were included with Mr. Davenport's quarter, as one of the nine quarters or societies into which the town was divided for the allotment of out-lands.

John Brockett seems to have been the chief surveyor; and he doubtless is responsible for the accuracy of angles, and the equality of the nine equal sections into which he was required to cut the larger square first laid out. The dimensions of the town plot may have been determined by the course of the creeks; for George Street, if it had been continued a few rods farther west, would have crossed the West Creek, which in its course made an angle of about ninety degrees near that point.

The town-plot having been laid out, the sections into which it was cut by its streets were assigned to groups of families drawn together by social affinity, and were severally divided among those families in house-lots differing in dimensions according to a ratio depending partly on the number of persons in the family, and partly on the amount the family had invested in the common stock of the proprietors. Among the minor benefits secured by this elective grouping, was delay in building division fences. Each quarter, being immediately enclosed by a fence separating it from the highway, was ready for tillage. These fences were sometimes of pickets and sometimes of rails. In June, 1640, prices for both kinds were established by law. Fencing with pales must be "not above two shillings a rod for felling and cleaving posts and rails, cross-cutting, hewing, mortising, digging holes, setting up and nailing on the pales, the work being in all the parts well wrought and finished; but, in this price, pales and carting of the stuff not included." "Fencing with five rails, substantial posts, good rails, well wrought, set up, and rammed, that pigs, swine, goats, and other cattle may be kept out, not above two shillings a rod." A year later these rates were reduced twenty-five per cent, the reduction being probably due to the ebbing of that tide of emigration which, till the civil war in the mother-country commenced, had constantly supplied New England with money, and a market for labor as well as for cattle and other products of husbandry.

There was time for building all these fences before the season had sufficiently advanced to justify the colonists in planting gardens or driving cattle across the country from Massachusetts. The cold, which had been unusually severe during the winter, was protracted into the months of spring. Winthrop records on the twenty-third day of April, "This was a very hard winter. The snow lay, from November 4th to March 23d, half a yard deep about the Massachusetts, and a yard deep beyond the Merrimac, and so the more north, the deeper; and the spring was very backward. This day it did snow two hours together (after much rain from the northeast) with flakes as great as shillings." Again he writes on the 2d of May, "The spring was so cold, that men were forced to plant their corn two or three times, for it rotted in the ground." But notwithstanding this unpropitious beginning, which threatened a dearth through all New England, warm weather afterward brought on corn beyond expectation; and Quinnipiac seems to have shared in the blessing of a good harvest, so that there was no such scarcity of bread as there had been at Hartford the preceding winter, when the price of Indian corn rose to twelve shillings per bushel, which was five or six times its usual value.

THE FIRST YEAR AT QUINNIPIAC. 79

While some were planting and fencing, others were preparing lumber for the erection of permanent dwellings. Having no mill for sawing, they were obliged to slit the logs by hand; and the tariff of prices prescribes how much more the "top-man, or he that guides the work and perhaps finds the tools," shall receive than "the pit-man, whose skill and charge is less." The log was first hewn square, and then placed on a frame over a pit, so that a man could stand beneath and assist in moving the saw. This department of industry demanded their earliest attention; so that the boards, being exposed to the winds of spring and the heat of summer might be ready for the carpenter as soon as possible. The price of inch boards must not exceed five shillings and ninepence per hundred feet if sold in the woods, or seven shillings and ninepence if sold in the town. But, as the tariff was established in 1640, prices may have been somewhat less in 1638, when the town-plot furnished all the lumber required for immediate use. Indeed, the price of lumber had fallen considerably in 1641, when inch boards must not be sold above four shillings and eightpence per hundred in the woods, or above six shillings in the town.

Before winter most of the colonists who had arrived in April were living on their house-lots, leaving their cellars or other temporary shelters for new-comers. Some of the houses, being occupied by persons of small estates, were presumably such as a Dutch traveler saw at Plymouth, and describes as block-houses built of hewn logs. Such a presumption explains an item in a bill of sale by which one of the first planters alienated his house and house-lot and "two loads of clay brought home." The clay was doubtless to be "daubed" between the logs. From the mention of thatchers, and the precautions taken against fire, it may be inferred that these humbler tenements were roofed with thatch. Many of the houses, however, were of framed timber, and were covered with shingles or clapboards on the sides, and with shingles on the roof. Quinnipiac had a larger proportion of wealthy men than any other of the New England colonies. Some of them, having been accustomed to live in large and elegant houses in London, expended liberally in providing new homes. It was but natural that they should wish to maintain a style not much inferior to the style in which they had formerly lived; and as they confidently thought they were founding a commercial town in a country so rich in resources that on a single cargo exported to England they could afford to pay duties to the amount of three thousand pounds, they justified themselves in a liberal expenditure in building their houses. If they had foreseen the political changes in England which after a few years turned the flow of emigration backward toward the mother-country,—even if they had known that their plantation must depend on husbandry more than on commerce,—they might have been content with less expensive dwellings. As it was they drew upon themselves the criticism of brethren in the other colonies. Hubbard the historian, who in 1638 was seventeen years old, speaks of their "error in great buildings," and afterward says, "they laid out too much of their stocks and estates in building of fair and stately houses, wherein they at the first outdid the rest of the country." Tradition reports that the house of Theophilus Eaton was so large as to have nineteen fireplaces, and that it was lofty as well as large. Davenport's house, on the opposite side of the street, is said to have had thirteen fireplaces.[1]

It is not necessary to believe that any of the "fair and stately" houses in Quinnipiac were finished in 1638. If the frame were set up and covered, and a few rooms were made ready to be occupied by the family, the remainder of the work might be postponed till the next summer.

In October the planters welcomed an accession to their number which they regarded as an earnest of still greater enlargement. Ezekiel Rogers, a minister of high standing in Yorkshire, having embarked at Hull on the Humber, with a company who personally knew him and desired to enjoy his ministry, arrived in Boston late in the summer. Such representations were made to him by Davenport and Eaton or their agents, that he engaged to come with his followers to Quinnipiac; and within eight weeks after his arrival in Massachusetts a portion of his people came by water to the new settlement, encountering on the voyage a storm which drove them upon a beach of sand where they lay rocking till another tide floated them off. Rogers, expecting to be joined in a year or two by some persons of rank and wealth who had been providentially thwarted in their desire to embark with him, had inserted in his engagement to take stock in the Quinnipiac company,

[1] Stiles' History of the Judges. President Stiles had been, when a boy, personally familiar with the interior of the Davenport house.

certain stipulations referring to these friends for whom he was authorized to act. The nature of the stipulations cannot now be known; but, whatever they were, Rogers, who did not come to Quinnipiac with the first instalment of his company, became convinced that they would not be fulfilled to his satisfaction, and laid the matter as a case of conscience before the Massachusetts elders, who advised him that he was released from his engagement. He thereupon decided to remain in Massachusetts, and sent a pinnace to bring back those of his company who had left him in October.

Davenport and Eaton, being less willing than the Massachusetts elders to release Rogers from his engagement, detained the pinnace, and by a special messenger despatched letters of remonstrance which seem to have staggered him, till the elders again assembling and examining all the correspondence between the parties, confirmed their former judgment. He accordingly began a plantation in Massachusetts, which received the name of Rowley, from the place where he had exercised his ministry in the mother-country. But some of his Yorkshire friends, who had gone to Quinnipiac expecting that he would follow, did not return in the pinnace he sent for them. It was now winter, and perhaps the inclemency of the season disinclined them to leave the cellars in which they were sheltered. Perhaps the storm they encountered in coming, inspired them with dread of the sea. Perhaps they were pleased with the new plantation, admiring its leaders, enjoying intercourse with its people, and participating with them in sanguine expectation of its future. For some reason several of the Yorkshire families remained, and became permanently incorporated in the new community.

Rogers in the course of the next two years mentions several times, in letters to Gov. Winthrop, the losses sustained by the people of Rowley in consequence of coming back to Massachusetts. He says, "None do know (or few) what we are impoverished by this purchase, and Quinnipiac, and the failing of some expected friends." Again, "I suppose you hear of a new sad cross from Quinnipiac in Jo. Hardy's pinnace, wherein may be much of my estate for aught I know." And still later: "It hath been a trouble of late to my poor neighbors to hear of this" (that a part of Rowley was claimed by others) "after their purchase, and building, and return from Quinnipiac." These hints were preparatory to a claim which he formally made in the autumn of 1640, that this land claimed by another party as previously granted, should be confirmed to Rowley. Appearing before the court over which Winthrop was presiding, he "pleaded justice, upon some promises of large accommodations, &c., when we desired his sitting down with us." The scene that ensued when the request was refused on the ground that the land had already been granted, is in several respects instructive. The elder lost his temper, and by that means gained his cause; for the court, after disciplining him for contempt, "freely granted what he formerly desired.[1]"

[1] In one of the letters from Rogers to Winthrop cited above, he speaks of one of the New Haven planters as follows: "Sir: Mr. Lamberton did us much wrong. I expected his coming to the Bay: but it seems he sits down at Quinnipiac: yet he hath a house in Boston: I would humbly crave

The next event after the arrival of the Yorkshire company, which deserves notice, is the formal purchase of land from the Indians. The terms had been agreed upon in the winter, but no written title had been given, formalities being postponed perhaps till a more competent interpreter than any of the planters could be obtained. Thomas Stanton, of high repute for knowledge of the Indian tongue, having been employed to come from Hartford and explain the written deed to the Indian sachem and his council, it was signed by them on the 24th of November.[1] Its full text is as follows, with the exception of two hiatuses where the record-book has been torn:—

"Articles of agreement between Theophilus Eaton and John Davenport and others, English planters at Quinnipiac on the one party, and Momaugin the Indian Sachem of Quinnipiac and Sugcogisin, Quesaquaush, Carroughood, Weesaucuck and others of his council on the other party, made and concluded the 24th of November 1638; Thomas Stanton being interpreter.

"That he the said sachem, his council, and company do jointly profess, affirm and covenant that he the said Momaugin is the sole sachem of Quinnipiac, and hath an absolute and independent power to give, alien, dispose or sell, all or any part of the lands in Quinnipiac and that though he have a son now absent, yet neither his said son, nor any other person whatsoever hath any right, title or

your advice to Mr. Will Bellingham about it, whether we might not enter an action against him and upon proof get help by that house." This evidently refers to Rogers' disappointment in not receiving back those of his flock who staid in New Haven, and reads as if Lamberton were to be counted among them.

[1] In "New Haven's Case Stated" it is claimed that Stanton, at the request of the New Haven people, was sent by their friends in Connecticut to assist in this purchase, and that Connecticut had thus consented to the transaction.

interest in any part of the said lands, so that whatsoever be, the forenamed sachem, his council and the rest of the Indians present do and conclude, shall stand firm and inviolable against all claims and persons whatsoever.

"Secondly, the said sachem, his council, and company, amongst which there was a squaw sachem called Shaumpishuh, sister to the sachem, who either had or pretended some interest in some part of the land, remembering and acknowledging the heavy taxes and eminent dangers which they lately felt and feared from the Pequots, Mohawks, and other Indians, in regard of which they durst not stay in their country, but were forced to fly and to seek shelter under the English at Connecticut, and observing the safety and ease that other Indians enjoy near the English, of which benefit they have had a comfortable taste already, since the English began to build and plant at Quinnipiac, which with all thankfulness they now acknowledged, they jointly and freely gave and yielded up all their right, title and interest to all the land, rivers, ponds, and trees with all the liberties and appurtenances belonging unto the same in Quinnipiac to the utmost of their bounds east, west, north, south, unto Theophilus Eaton, John Davenport and others, the present English planters there and to their heirs and assigns forever, desiring from them the said English planters to receive such a portion of ground on the East side of the harbor, towards the fort at the mouth of the river of Connecticut as might be sufficient for them, being but few in number, to plant in; and yet within these limits to be hereafter assigned to them, they did covenant and freely yield up unto the said English all the meadow ground lying therein, with full liberty to choose and cut down what timber they please, for any use whatsoever, without any question, license or consent to be asked from them the said Indians, and if, after their portion and place be limited and set out by the English as above, they the said Indians shall desire to remove to any other place within Quinnipiac bounds, but without the limits assigned them, that they do it not without leave, neither setting up any wigwam, nor breaking up any ground to plant corn, till first it be set out and appointed by the forenamed English planters for them.

"Thirdly, the said sachem, his council, and company, desiring liberty to hunt and fish within the bounds of Quinnipiac now given

and granted to the English as before, do hereby jointly covenant and bind themselves to set no traps near any place where the . . . . whether horses, oxen, kine, calves, sheep, goats, hogs or any sort . . . .
. . . to take any fish out of any wier belonging to any English, nor to do any thing near any such wier as to disturb or affright away any fish to the prejudice of such wier or wiers, and that upon discovery of any inconveniency growing to the English by the Indians disorderly hunting, their hunting shall be regulated and limited for the preventing of any inconvenience and yet with as little damage to the Indians in their hunting as may be.

"Fourthly, the said sachem, his council, and company do hereby covenant and bind themselves that none of them shall henceforth hanker about any of the English houses at any time when the English use to meet about the public worship of God; nor on the Lord's day henceforward be seen within the compass of the English town, bearing any burdens, or offering to truck with the English for any commodity whatsoever, and that none of them henceforward without leave, open any latch belonging to any Englishman's door, nor stay in any English house after warning that he should leave the same, nor do any violence, wrong, or injury to the person of the English, whether man, woman or child, upon any pretence whatsoever, and if the English of this plantation, by themselves or cattle, do any wrong or damage to the Indians, upon complaint, just recompense shall be made by the English; and that none of them henceforward use or take any Englishman's boat or canoe of what kind soever, from the place where it was fastened or laid, without leave from the owner first had and obtained, nor that they come into the English town with bows and arrows or any other weapons whatsoever in number above six Indians so armed at a time.

"Fifthly, the said sachem, his council, and company do truly covenant and bind themselves that if any of them shall hereafter kill or hurt any English cattle of what sort soever, though casually or negligently, they shall give full satisfaction for the loss or damage as the English shall judge equal: but if any of them for any respect, wilfully do kill or hurt any of the English cattle; upon proof, they shall pay the double value: and if, at any time, any of them find any of the English cattle straying or lost in the woods, they shall bring them back to the English plantation and a moderate price or recompense shall be allowed for their pains: provided if it can be proved that any of them drove away any of the English cattle wheresoever they find them, further from the English plantation to make an increase or advantage or recompense for his pains finding or bringing them back, they shall in any such case pay damages for such dealings.

"Sixthly, the number of the Quinnipiac Indians, men or youth grown to stature fit for service, being forty-seven at present, they do covenant and bind themselves not to receive or admit any other Indians amongst them without leave first had and obtained from the English, and that they will not, at any time hereafter, entertain or harbor any that are enemies to the English, but will presently apprehend such and deliver them to the English, and if they know or hear of any plot by the Indians or others against the English, they will forthwith discover and make the same known to them, and in case they do not, to be accounted as parties in the plot and to be proceeded against as such.

"Lastly, the said sachem, his council, and company do hereby promise truly and carefully to observe and keep all and every one of these articles of agreement; and if any of them offend in any of the promises, they jointly hereby subject and submit such offender or offenders to the consideration, censure, and punishment of the English magistrate or officers appointed among them for government, without expecting that the English should first advise with them about it: yet in any such case of punishment, if the said sachem shall desire to know the reason and equity of said proceedings, he shall truly be informed of the same.

"The former articles being read and interpreted to them, they by way of exposition desired that in the sixth article it might be added, that if any of the English cattle be killed or hurt casually, or negligently, and proof made it was done by some of the Quinnipiac Indians, they will make satisfaction, or if done by any other Indians in their sight, if they do not discover it and, if able, bring the offender to the English, they will be accounted and dealt with as guilty.

"In consideration of all which, they desire from the English, that, if at any time hereafter they be affrighted in their dwellings assigned by the English unto them as before, they may repair to the English plantation for shelter and that the English will then in a just cause endeavor to defend them from wrong. But in any quarrel or wars which they shall undertake or have with other Indians, upon any occasion whatsoever, they will manage their affairs by themselves without expecting any aid from the English.

"And the English planters before mentioned accepting and granting according to the tenor of the premises do further of their own accord, by way of free and thankful retribution, give unto the said sachem, council, and company of the Quinnipiac Indians, twelve coats of English trucking cloth, twelve alchemy spoons, twelve hatchets, twelve hoes, two dozen of knives, twelve porringers, and four cases of French knives and scissors. All which being thankfully accepted by the aforesaid and the agreements in all points perfected, for ratification and full confirmation of the same, the sachem, his council, and sister, to these presents have set to their hand or marks the day and year above written.

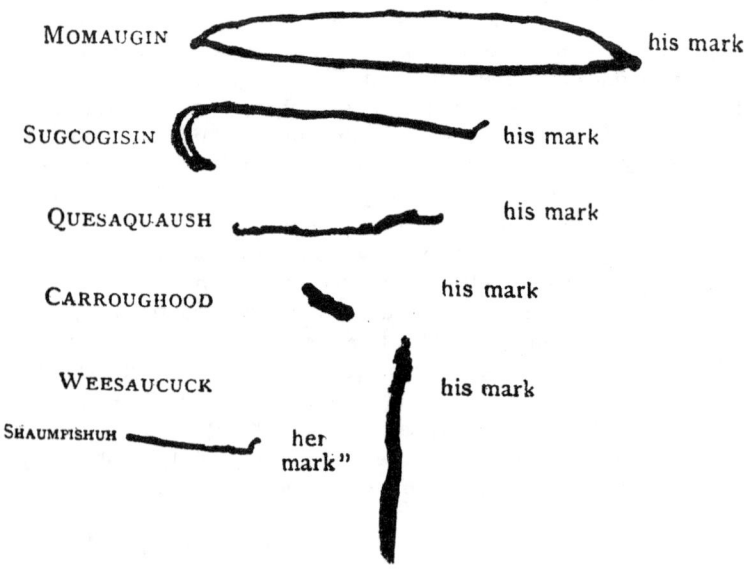

THE FIRST YEAR AT QUINNIPIAC. 89

"I, Thomas Stanton, being interpreter in this treaty, do hereby profess in the presence of God that I have fully acquainted the Indians with the substance of every article and truly returned their answer and consent to the same, according to the tenor of the foregoing writing, the truth of which, if lawfully called, I shall readily confirm by my oath at any time.

THOMAS STANTON."

On the 11th of December, Montowese, sachem of another tribe, "in presence and with allowance and consent of Sawseunck, an Indian who came in company with him," sold to the English a tract of land lying north of that sold by Momaugin, and described as "extending about ten miles in length from north to south, eight miles easterly from the river of Quinnipiac toward the river of Connecticut and five miles westerly toward Hudson's river." Montowese, reserving a piece of land near the village which now bears his name, "for his men which are ten, and many squaws, to plant in," received "eleven coats of trucking cloth, and one coat of English cloth made up after the English manner," in payment for the territory thus alienated.

The attesting marks of Montowese and Sawseunck are as follows:—

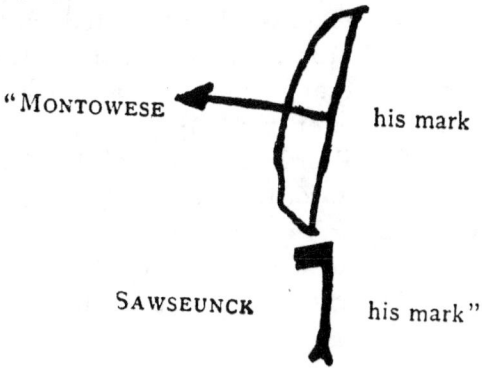

At the present day we are apt to think that the sachems sold their land for a ridiculously low price; but one who attentively considers all the circumstances of the case, the reservations they made; the protection they secured, and the opportunity for trade afforded by the English settlement, will perhaps conclude that what they received was of greater value to them than what they sold. It does not appear that the Indians were afterward dissatisfied with the terms of sale.

Contemporaneously with the excitement among the Yorkshire people about returning to Massachusetts, there was conference among those who had come with Prudden from Hereford, tending toward a removal from Quinnipiac to a separate plantation, in which they might enjoy his ministry. What the understanding had been between his Herefordshire flock and the London men in reference to a church and church-officers at Quinnipiac, it is impossible to determine with certainty; but, as the latter party had brought with them two ministers in whom they were interested, we may conjecture that if they encouraged the Hereford men to believe that Prudden should be their minister, they did so in expectation that he would be united with Davenport and Samuel Eaton in the eldership of the church.

Trumbull relates that Prudden preached at Wethersfield during the summer of 1638; and, as a part of the first planters of Milford came from Wethersfield on account of their regard for him and some disagreement in their church, it is probable that the project of a settlement at Milford grew out of Prudden's visit to Wethersfield. Ascertaining that by uniting his friends in Wethersfield with those who had followed him across the sea, he could become the minister of a new plantation, and stand foremost if not alone in the eldership of its church, he naturally preferred such a position to that of a colleagueship with Davenport.

Prudden's friends having determined to commence a new plantation at Wepowaug, land was formally conveyed to them by a written deed subscribed by Ansantaway, the sachem of the place, and by his council, Feb. 12, 1639. Lambert relates that "a twig and a piece of turf being brought to the sagamore, he placed the end of the branch in the clod, and then gave it to the English as a token that he hereby surrendered to them the soil, with all the trees and appurtenances." But, though the land was bought in February, the projected plantation was not commenced till autumn, so that those who intended to remove from Quinnipiac remained in their houses through the summer, and cultivated their fields as they had done the previous year.

We find nothing more on record concerning the first winter at Quinnipiac, except that two vessels, bound thither from Boston, were cast away in December, there being, says Winthrop, "so great a tempest of wind and snow, all the night and the next day, as had not been since our time." We may conjecture that the work of removal was not yet entirely accomplished;—that some who had come from Massachusetts in the preceding spring, and had spent the summer and autumn in the erection of houses, were now transporting to their new homes comforts for which there had been no place in their summer habitations.

CHAPTER VI.

FOUNDATIONS LAID IN CHURCH AND STATE.

THE spring of 1639 found the plantation in Quinnipiac no farther advanced in its ecclesiastical or its civil organization than on the morrow after its "first day of extraordinary humiliation." Its public property was still managed by the members, or in ordinary cases, by the officers, of the joint-stock association. Civil government was administered, if at all, by a democracy acknowledging no authority but that of God, and no constitution but God's word as contained in the Scriptures. Public worship was regularly offered, but no church had been instituted and no sacraments had been celebrated.

Several reasons may be suggested for the slowness with which the planters came to the work of organization. They had much to occupy their minds and hands during the first summer, in providing for the approaching winter. During the winter the Yorkshire people were exercised in mind with the question, whether they should remain, or go back to Massachusetts, and, till this question was decided, were not ready to unite with any church. The leading men in the plantation would naturally prefer to wait for their decision, rather than to proceed immediately with an organization which did not include so desirable an addition.

The Hereford men began in the autumn, and perhaps late in the summer, to think of removing, and by midwinter had purchased land at Milford, and thus were fully committed. So long as they were hesitating, their brethren would wait for their decision as they had done for that of the Yorkshire people, though with a different feeling toward their proposal to remove. There is no reason to believe that the people of Quinnipiac were unwilling that a new plantation should be established a few miles west of their own; for, if their population should be thereby somewhat diminished, those who removed would still be near them, and would draw to the neighborhood a considerable accession of planters. So far as appears, Prudden and Davenport were as much at one in their plans after the former had decided to establish a new plantation, as before.

We may find another reason for the slowness with which the planters came to the work of laying foundations of Church and State, in the difference of opinion which prevailed among them in regard to such foundations. Some had been non-conforming members of the Church of England; others had separated themselves from the national church while still residing in the mother-country. In other words, there were in the colony both Puritans and Separatists. But, so far as concerns church organization, these two classes were practically agreed. As the Puritans of Massachusetts felt themselves obliged to follow the example of the Separatists at Plymouth in organizing their churches, so at Quinnipiac those who had never yet belonged to a Congregational church saw that such a church was the only ecclesiastical organization possible to them in their circumstances. There was a difference of opinion, however, in the colony, on the question whether civil authority should be confined to men who were in communion with the church; and this difference was to a great extent coincident with the division into the two classes of Puritans and Separatists. The Puritan planters of Massachusetts relinquished episcopacy because they did not see their way clear to retain it; but they would not relinquish the old English idea that the State should be governed by Christians only, and that the Christian character thus required should be certified by the Church. Following the Separatists at Plymouth in organizing their churches, they would not follow them in admitting to the elective franchise planters who were not church-members. The English idea long prevailed in Massachusetts; but the Plymouth or Separatist belief that church-membership is not an essential qualification of free burgesses gradually gained adherents. When the river-towns in Connecticut were planted by emigrants from Massachusetts, so much progress had been made from the Puritan toward the Separatist theory, that church-membership was never required in the colony of Connecticut as a qualification for the elective franchise.

There being in the colony at Quinnipiac some who belonged to Congregational churches, and some who had never separated from the Church of England, there was a tendency in these two classes to divide on the question whether civil authority should be confined to members of the church. The Separatists desired to lay the foundations of both Church and State in accordance with the Plymouth model. Their leader, Samuel Eaton, stood up for the principle that all free planters, that is, proprietors in the plantation, however they might delegate authority, should have power to resume it into their own hands. But Davenport, who had never been a Separatist, and would have been content to remain in the Establishment if only his party had been in the ascendant, stoutly defended with Scriptural arguments the position that the power of choosing magistrates, of making and repealing laws, of dividing inheritances, and of deciding differences, should be vested in church-members. In the course of the debate between them Davenport wrote a treatise, afterward printed and still extant, entitled, "A Discourse about Civil Government in a New Plantation whose Design is Religion." Ultimately the views of Davenport prevailed over all opposition, but not till a long time had been consumed in the discussion.

On the fourth day of June, 1639, a meeting of all the proprietors, or free planters as they were called, was held in the barn of Mr Robert Newman, "to consult about settling civil government according to God, and about the nomination of persons that might be found by consent of all, fittest in all respects for the foundation work of a church." In reporting this meeting we shall chiefly use the language of the contemporary record:—

" For the better enabling them to discern the mind of God and to agree accordingly concerning the establishment of civil order, Mr. John Davenport propounded divers queries to them, publicly praying them to consider seriously in the presence and fear of God the weight of the business they met about, and not to be rash or slight in giving their votes to things they understood not, but to digest fully and thoroughly what should be propounded to them, and without respect to men, as they should be satisfied and persuaded in their own minds, to give their answers in such sort as they would be willing they should stand upon record for posterity."

At the earnest request of Mr. Davenport,—

"Mr. Robert Newman was entreated to write in characters and to read distinctly and audibly in the hearing of all the people what was propounded and accorded on, that it might appear that all consented to matters propounded, according to words written by him."

Mr. Davenport then proposed his queries as follows:—

"QUERY 1.—Whether the Scriptures do hold forth a perfect rule for the direction and government of all men in all duties which they are to perform to God and men as well in the government of families and commonwealths as in matters of the church.

"This was assented unto by all, no man dissenting, as was expressed by holding up of hands. Afterward it was read over to them that they might see in what words their vote was expressed. They again expressed their consent thereto by holding up their hands, no man dissenting.

"QUERY 2.—Whereas there was a covenant solemnly made by the whole assembly of free planters of this plantation the first day of extraordinary humiliation which we had after we came together, that as in matters that concern the gathering and ordering of a church, so likewise in all public offices which concern civil order, as choice of magistrates and officers, making and repealing of laws, dividing allotments of inheritance, and all things of like nature, we would all of us be ordered by those rules which the Scripture holds forth to us (this covenant was called a plantation covenant to distinguish it from a church covenant which could not at that time be made, a church not being then gathered, but was deferred till a church might be gathered according to God); it was demanded whether all the free planters do hold themselves bound by that covenant in all business of that nature which are expressed in the covenant to submit themselves to be ordered by the rules held forth in the Scripture.

"This also was assented to by all, and no man gainsaid it, and they did testify the same by holding up their hands, both when it was first propounded, and confirmed the same by holding up their hands when it was read unto them in public. John Clark, being absent when the covenant was made, doth now manifest his consent to it; also Richard Beach, Andrew Low, Goodman Banister, Arthur Halbidge, John Potter, Robert Hill, John Brockett, and John Johnson, being not admitted planters when the covenant was made, do now express their consent to it.

"QUERY 3.—Those who have been received as free planters and are settled in the plantation with a purpose, resolution and desire that they may be admitted into church fellowship according to Christ as soon as God shall fit them thereunto, were desired to express it by holding up of hands: accordingly all did express this to be their desire and purpose by holding up their hands twice, viz., both at the proposal of it, and after when these written words were read unto them."

The response to this question is instructive, as it shows that all the proprietors were earnestly religious men, were desirous of being admitted to the communion of the church, and, if they had not already become conscious of spiritual enlightenment wrought in them by the Spirit of God, were hoping for such an experience to qualify them for such admission. The "purpose, resolution, and desire" to be admitted into church-fellowship thus unanimously declared, prepare us to learn with less astonishment that in response to the fifth query, to which those that preceded logically conducted, they voted to confine the elective franchise to church-members.

"QUERY 4.—All the free planters were called upon to express whether they held themselves bound to establish such civil order as might best conduce to the securing of the purity and peace of the ordinances to themselves and their posterity according to God. In answer hereunto they expressed by holding up their hands twice as before, that they held themselves bound to establish such as might best conduce to the ends aforesaid."

After some remarks by Mr. Davenport, the fifth query was propounded as follows:—

"QUERY 5.—Whether free burgesses shall be chosen out of church members, they that are in the foundation work of the church being actually free burgesses and to choose to themselves out of the like estate of church fellowship: and the power of choosing magistrates and officers from among themselves, and the power of making and repealing laws according to the word, and the dividing of inheritances, and deciding of differences that may arise, and all the businesses of like nature are to be transacted by those free burgesses.

"This was put to vote and agreed unto by the lifting up of hands twice as in the former it was done. Then one man stood up after the vote was past, expressing his dissent from the rest in part, yet granting 1st, That magistrates should be men fearing God; 2d, That the church is the company whence ordinarily such men may be expected; 3d, That they that choose them ought to be men fearing God: only at this he stuck that free planters ought not to give this power out of their hands. Another stood up and answered that in this case nothing was done but with their consent. The former answered that all the free planters ought to resume this power into their own hands again if things were not orderly carried. Mr. Theophilus Eaton answered that in all places they choose committees; in like manner the companies of London choose the liveries by whom the public magistrates are chosen. In this the rest are not wronged, because they expect in time to be of the livery themselves and to have the same power. Some others entreated the former to give his arguments and reasons whereupon he dissented. He refused to do it, and said they might not rationally demand it, seeing he let the vote pass on freely and did not speak till after it was past, because he would not hinder what they agreed upon. Then Mr. Davenport, after a short relation of some former passages between them two [1] about this question, prayed the company that nothing might be concluded by them in this mighty question but what themselves were persuaded to be agreeing with the mind of God, and [as] they had heard what had been said since the voting, entreated them again to consider of it and put it again to vote as before."

The assembly having again unanimously assented, and some who had previously leaned to the opposite side, or halted between the two opinions, having given vocal expression to their confidence that the action taken was "according to the mind of God revealed in the Scriptures:—"

"Mr. Robert Newman was desired to write it as an order, whereunto every one that hereafter should be admitted here as planters should submit and testify the same by subscribing their name to the order, namely, that church-members only shall be free burgesses, and that they only shall choose magistrates and officers among themselves."

The elective franchise being thus limited to church-members, the assembly proceeded to consider and determine what method they should pursue in organizing their church:—

"Mr. Davenport advised that the names of such as were to be admitted might be publicly propounded, to the end that they who

[1] Although the name of the "one man" who dissented is not given in the record, there can be no doubt that it was Samuel Eaton. Mather records the tradition that it was he; and the treatise of Davenport bears internal evidence that it was addressed to one of his clerical friends in the plantation, that is to Eaton or Prudden. But Prudden could not have been the dissentient speaker to the assembly in Mr. Newman's barn; for he and his company, having resolved to remove, took no part in laying the foundation of civil order in Quinnipiac.

were most approved might be chosen; for the town being cast into several private meetings, wherein they that dwelt nearest together gave their accounts one to another of God's gracious work upon them, and prayed together and conferred to their mutual edification, sundry of them had knowledge one of another, and in every meeting some one was more approved of all than any other. For this reason and to avoid scandals, the whole company was entreated to consider whom they found fittest to nominate for this work."

The sixth query was then read in these words, viz. :—

"Whether are you all willing and do agree in this, that twelve men be chosen that their fitness for the foundation work may be tried; however there may be more named, yet it may be in their power who are chosen to reduce them to twelve, and it be in the power of those twelve to choose out of themselves seven that shall be most approved of the major part to begin the church.

"This was agreed upon by consent of all, as was expressed by holding up of hands, and that so many as should be thought fit for the foundation work of the church shall be propounded by the plantation and written down and pass without exception unless they had given public scandal or offence; yet so as in case of public scandal or offence, every one should have liberty to propound their exceptions at that time publicly against any man that should be nominated when all their names should be written down; but if the offence were private, that men's names might be tendered, so many as were offended were entreated to deal with the offender privately, and if he gave not satisfaction, to bring the matter to the twelve that they might consider of it impartially and in the fear of God. The names of the persons nominated and agreed upon were Mr. Theophilus Eaton, Mr. John Davenport, Mr. Robert Newman, Mr. Matthew Gilbert, Mr. Richard Malbon, Mr. Nathanael Turner, Ezekiel Cheever, Thomas Fugill, John Punderson, William Andrews and Jeremiah Dixon.[1] No exception was brought against any of those in public, except one about taking an excessive rate for meal

---

[1] The registrar omitted one of the twelve names. Was the name of the penitent extortioner designedly dropped, or was the omission accidental?

which he sold to one of Pequonock in his need, which he confessed with grief, and declared that having been smitten in heart and troubled in his conscience, he restored such a part of the price back again with confession of his sin to the party as he thought himself bound to do. And it being feared that the report of the sin was heard farther than the report of his satisfaction, a course was concluded on to make the satisfaction known to as many as heard of the sin. It was also agreed upon at the said meeting that if the persons above named did find themselves straitened in the number of fit men for the seven, that it should be free for them to take into trial of fitness such other as they should think meet, provided that it should be signified to the town, upon the Lord's day, whom they so take in, that every man may be satisfied of them according to the course formerly taken."

In due time the twelve thus appointed chose out of their own number the following seven, as "most approved of the major part, to begin the church," namely, Theophilus Eaton, John Davenport, Robert Newman, Matthew Gilbert, Thomas Fugill, John Punderson and Jeremiah Dixon. "By these seven persons, covenanting together, and then receiving others into their fellowship, the first church of Christ in New Haven was gathered and constituted on the 22d of August, 1639.[1]"

On the 25th of October these seven proceeded to organize themselves as a civil court, proceeding as follows, "after solemn prayer unto God:"—

"First: All former power or trust for managing any public affairs in this plantation, into whose hands soever formerly committed, was now abrogated and from henceforward utterly to cease.

[1] Bacon's Hist. Dis., p. 24. Dr. Bacon ascertains the date from the records of the First Church in Milford, which was gathered in New Haven, where its members still resided, and, as the local tradition says on the same day with the New Haven church. Mather (Mag., Book III., ch. 6) records the tradition somewhat differently, giving to each church one of two consecutive days employed in the formalities of institution.

"Secondly: All those that have been received into the fellowship of this church since the gathering of it, or who, being members of other approved churches, offered themselves, were admitted as members of this court: namely, Mr. Nathanael Turner, William Andrews and Mr. Cheever, members of this church; Mr. Samuel Eaton, John Clark, Lieutenant Seeley, John Chapman, Thomas Jeffrey and Richard Hull, members of other approved churches."

The court then proceeded to choose Theophilus Eaton "magistrate for the term of one whole year;" and Robert Newman, Matthew Gilbert, Nathanael Turner and Thomas Fugill, "deputies to assist the magistrate in all courts called by him for the occasions of the plantation for the same term of one whole year."

Thomas Fugill was chosen clerk, and Robert Seeley marshal.

"It was further agreed that there should be a renewing of the choice of all officers every year at a general court to be held for this plantation the last week in October yearly; and that the word of God shall be the only rule to be attended unto in ordering the affairs of government in this plantation."

The formal institution of civil authority may have been hastened by foresight of an event which immediately followed; for, the next day after the magistrate had been clothed with power, an Indian named Nepaupuck was brought before him upon his warrant, charged with the murder of an Englishman at Wethersfield. A few days afterward a general court was assembled, and the prisoner was brought before it for trial. Being found guilty upon evidence so clear that he confessed his guilt, he was condemned to death. "Accordingly his head was cut off the next day, and pitched upon a pole in the market-place."

CHAPTER VII.

DIVISION OF LAND.

WE have already seen that immediately after the town-plot was laid out, a house-lot was assigned to every free planter; by which appellation a person who had invested in the common property of the plantation was distinguished from other inhabitants. These house-lots were so large as to require, in most cases, all the labor their owners could give to husbandry during the first two summers. The few who needed more land for cultivation were allowed to plant in "the neck" between Mill River and Quinnipiac River. So desirable did the proprietors regard the increase of population, that they not only made the quantity of land thus assigned to a free planter to depend partly on the number of persons in his family, but also freely assigned a small lot on the outside of the town-plot to every householder in the plantation who desired to become a permanent resident, but was unable to purchase a share in the common property. The number of householders thus gratuitously supplied with house-lots was in the beginning thirty-two. Others were afterward added.

In January, 1640, arrangements were made for the division of the neck, the salt meadows, and a tract which, extending in every direction about a mile from the town, was called the two-miles-square. The division was so arranged that every free planter should have some land in the neck, some in the meadows, and some in the upland of the two-miles-square.

Out of the last-mentioned tract certain reservations were made; and the remainder was divided into nine parts, one for each of the nine quarters into which the town was divided, each quarter in the town having its out-lands as nearly as possible contiguous to itself. In consequence of this arrangement, these sections of out-lands were also called quarters; and, there being more occasion for using the term in connection with the out-lands than the home-lots, it came by degrees to be applied almost exclusively to them in later records.

Commencing with the east-center, or Mr. Davenport's quarter, let us connect the nine quarters with out-lands assigned to them respectively in the first division. The out-lands of Mr. Davenport's quarter were bounded by Chapel Street, Grand Street, a line about three hundred feet east of State Street, and Mill River. Mr. Eaton's quarter was bounded by Grand Street, State Street (or, as it was called, Neck Lane), a line in continuation of that just mentioned, described as three hundred feet east of State Street, and the meadows bordering on Mill River. Mr. Newman's quarter was bounded by Neck Lane, Mill Lane (as Orange Street was called), Grove Street, and the meadows bordering on Mill River. Mr. Tench's quarter, lying between Mill Lane and Prospect Street, extended outward from Grove Street so far as was necessary to furnish every planter in the quarter with his proportionate allotment.

It will be seen, that, while Mr. Davenport's quarter

had their out-lands near their home-lots, Mr. Tench's out-land quarter only touched his town quarter, and that, if the out-lands of the next quarter had been assigned so as to be contiguous to those of Mr. Tench's quarter, they would have been far distant from the home-lots to which they belonged. This difficulty was solved by the sequestration of land lying west of Prospect Street, for common use. This tract included the cow-pasture, the ox-pasture, the Beaver-pond meadows, and a field farther west than these, which remained unfenced, and was called the Common.

By means of this sequestration, the out-lands of the Yorkshire quarter were so assigned that they were immediately contiguous to the house-lots to which they belonged, lying between the common land on the north and Chapel Street on the south, and extending from York Street westward to or beyond West River. The Herefordshire quarter lying between Chapel Street and Oak Street, extended from York Street to or beyond the river. Mr. Gregson's out-land quarter lay south of the Herefordshire quarter, and was bounded on the east by the road to Milford, which passed through Broad Street and Davenport Avenue, as they are now named. Next was the suburbs quarter, between Milford Road and Washington Street. Last in our enumeration, Mr. Lamberton's quarter covered all the land between Washington Street and the harbor.

There still remained within the two-miles-square four reservations besides those which have been mentioned: viz., one called the market-place; another containing so much of the land bordering on the West Creek as had not been allotted to persons who were not proprietors;

a third containing the land bordering on the East Creek; a fourth called Oyster-shell Field, east of the East Creek reservation, and comprehended between Chapel Street and a line about three hundred feet north of East Water Street. The last-named tract was leased from year to year to persons who desired to cultivate more land than they owned. The reserved land on both sides of the two creeks was either allotted in small parcels to persons who were not proprietors, or was reserved to be so disposed of when there should be occasion.

In the first division of out-lands, no provision was made for those who had been gratuitously supplied with house-lots; but in the second division the rule was adopted to allot "six acres for a single person, eight acres for a man and his wife, with an acre added for every child they have at present." If they accepted these out-lands, they were to pay taxes on them as other planters did, at the rate of twopence per acre; and "if any of them, satisfied with their trades, or not liking the place of their allotment, shall refuse or neglect to take up the land, yet every one admitted to be a planter shall pay twelvepence a year to the treasurer toward public charges."

The out-lands thus assigned to each of the nine quarters were subdivided according to the same rule of division which had obtained in the division of the town quarters; every planter having "a proportion of land according to the proportion of estate which he hath given in, and number of heads in his family." Five acres were allowed for every hundred pounds of estate, and an equal quantity for every two heads. These subdivisions, however, were not separated one from another by division fences; but each quarter was enclosed by a common fence, for his proportion of which every proprietor was responsible. As might be expected, much legislation and frequent fines were necessary to keep these fences sufficient for the protection of the enclosures from the forays of hungry cattle.

The meadows were sufficient to afford five acres for every hundred pounds of estate and half an acre for every head, and an addition in quantity to some allotments where the quality was inferior. The neck was divided so as to give one acre for every hundred pounds, and half an acre for every head.

Some months after this division was ordered, and, as it would seem, before it was consummated, a second allotment was made, disposing of those portions of the common property which lay outside of the two-miles-square. At a general court held the 23d of October, 1640, it was "ordered that in the second division every planter in the town shall have for every hundred pounds of estate given in, twenty acres of upland, and for every head two acres and a half."

The sequestered lands were held as common property for many years, but were ultimately divided, one portion after another, till, with some unimportant exceptions, only the market-place was held in common. After the second division of lands, and probably in fulfillment of an order passed at the general court mentioned above, that "all the upland in the first division, with all the meadows in the plantation, shall pay fourpence an acre yearly; and all the land in the second division shall pay twopence an acre yearly, at two several days of payment, viz., the one in April, and the other in October, to raise a common stock or public treasury," the following schedule was prepared, exhibiting the name of every proprietor, the number of persons in his family, the amount of his estate, and the number of acres belonging to him in each of four classes of land; viz., the first division of upland, the neck, the meadows, and the second division of upland. The eighth and last column shows the amount of his annual tax. The schedule, though prepared before April, 1641, is found in the record-book amid the records of 1643. It is not easy to determine whether it was copied into the record-book in 1643, after some changes had been made corresponding with changes of title; or was recorded when first prepared, the secretary reserving for his report of the court's proceedings the thirty pages which precede it.[1]

The schedule furnishes important aid in determining who were proprietors of the town in the first years of its history, the social importance of each so far as the measure of his wealth determined it, and, when studied in connection with the land-records of the town, the location of his house-lot. The schedule disposes the proprietors into eleven groups; eight of which occupied the eight squares surrounding the market-place; another group, consisting of only four, had their dwellings on East Water Street, fronting the harbor; the remaining two inhabited the two blocks of land of irregular shape, called suburbs.

[1] "Mr. Crane resigned Mr. Hickock's lot into the town's hand," Sept. 30, 1641; yet the lot stands in Mr. Hickock's name. There is so much probability that the schedule was recorded before the collection of the rate due in April, 1641, that it will be designated as the schedule of 1641.

Names of the Planters.	Persons Numbered.	Estates.	Land in the First Division.	In the Neck.	Meadow.	Land in the Second Division.	Rates yearly paid for Land.
Mr. Theophilus Eaton	6	3,000	165	33	153	612	£10 13 00
Mr. Samuel Eaton	2	800	45	9	41	164	2 19 00
Mrs. Eaton	1	150	10	2	8	32	0 12 00
David Yale	1	300	17½	3½	15½	62	1 02 06
William Tuttle	7	450	37½	7½	26	107	2 01 06
Ezekiel Cheever	3	20	8½	1½ ,, 32	2½	10	0 5 11
Capt. Turner	7	800	57½	11½	43½	174	3 06 06
Richard Perry	3	260	20½	4½ ,, 16	14½	58	1 02 08
Mr. Davenport	3	1,000	57½	11½	51½	206	–
Richard Malbon	7	500	42½	8½	28½	114	2 05 06
Thomas Nash	7	110	23	4½ ,, 16	9	36	0 18 02
John Benham	5	70	16	3 ,, 32	6	24	0 12 04 *ob.*
Thomas Kimberley	7	12	18 ,, 16	3½ ,, 19	4 ,, 16	16½ ,, 24	0 11 02
John Chapman	2	300	20	4	16	64	1 04 00
Matthew Gilbert	2	600	35	7	31	124	2 05 00
Jasper Crane	3	480	16½	3¼ ,, 8	25½	120	1 15 01
Mr. Rowe	6	1,000	65	13	53	212	–
An Elder	4	500	35	7	27	108	2 01 00
George Lamberton	6	1,000	65	13	53	212	3 19 00
William Wilkes	2	150	12½	2½	8½	34	0 13 06
Thomas Jeffries	2	100	10	2	6	24	0 10 00
Robert Seeley	4	179	18¾ ,, 32	3¾ ,, 8	10¾ ,, 32	43	0 18 05
Nicholas Elsey	2	30	6½	1¼ ,, 8	2½	10	0 5 01
John Budd	6	450	31½	7½	25½	102	2 00 06
Richard Hull	4	19	11	2 ,, 30	3	11¾ ,, 4	0 7 04
William Preston	10	40	27	5¼ ,, 24	7	28	0 17 09
Benjamin Fenn	2	80	9	1¾ ,, 8	5	20	0 8 07
William Jeanes	5	150	20	4	10	40	0 18 00
John Brockett	1	15	3¼	½ ,, 24	1¼	5	0 2 06 *ob.*
Roger Alling	1	40	4½	¾ ,, 24	2½	10	0 4 03 *ob.*
Mr. Hickock	6	1,000	65	13	53	212	3 19 00
Mr. Mansfield	4	400	30	6	22	88	–
Thomas Gregson	6	600	45	9	33	133	–
Stephen Goodyear	9	1,000	72½	14½	54½	218	9 19 02
William Hawkins	2	1,000	55	11	51	204	–
Jeremiah Whitnell	2	50	7½	1½	3½	14	0 6 06
Samuel Bailey	1	250	15	3	13	52	0 19 00
Thomas Buckingham	4	60	13	2½ ,, 16	5	20	0 10 02
Richard Miles	7	400	37½	7½	23½	94	1 18 06
Thomas Welch	1	250	15	3	13	25	0 19 00
Nathanael Axtell	1	500	27½	6	25½	101	1 16 07
Henry Stonell	1	300	17½	3½	15½	62	1 02 06
William Fowler	3	800	47	9½	41½	166	3 06 06
Peter Prudden	4	500	35	7	27	108	2 01 00
James Prudden	3	10	8	1½ ,, 16	2	8	0 5 02

Names of the Planters.	Persons Numbered.	Estates.	Land in the First Division.	In the Neck.	Meadow.	Land in the Second Division.	Rates yearly paid for Land.
Edmund Tapp	7	800	52½	11½	43½	174	3 06 06
Widow Baldwin	5	800	52½	10½	42½	170	3 03 06
An Elder	6	500	40	8	28	112	-
Richard Platt	4	200	20	4	12	48	1 00 00
Zachariah Whitman	2	800	45	9	41	164	2 19 00
Thomas Osborne	6	300	30	6	18	72	1 10 00
Henry Rutherford	2	100	10	2	6	24	0 10 00
Thomas Trowbridge	5	500	37½	7½	27½	110	2 02 06
Widow Potter	2	30	6½	1¼	2½	10	0 5 01
John Potter	4	25	11¼	2¼	3¼	13	0 7 09
Samuel Whitehead	2	60	8	1½ ,, 16	4	16	0 6 06
John Clark	3	240	19½	3¾ ,, 24	13½	54	1 11 00 *ob.*
Luke Atkinson	4	50	10	2 ,, 16	4½	18	0 9 06
Arthur Halbidge	4	20	11	2 ,, 32	3	12	0 7 04
Edward Bannister	3	10	8	1½ ,, 16	2	8	0 5 02
William Peck	4	12	10½ ,, 16	2 ,, 16	1½ ,, 16	10¼	0 6 10
John Moss	3	10	8	1½ ,, 16	2	8	0 5 02
John Charles	4	50	12½	2½	4½	18	0 9 06
Richard Beach	1	20	3½	½ ,, 32	1½	6	0 2 10
Timothy Ford	2	10	5½	1 ,, 16	1½	6	0 3 08
Peter Brown	3	30	9	1¾ ,, 8	3	12	0 6 07
Daniel Paul	1	100	7½	1½	5½	22	0 8 06
John Livermore	4	100	15	3	7	28	0 13 00
Anthony Thompson	4	150	17½	3½	9½	38	0 16 06
John Reeder	2	140	12	2¼ ,, 24	8	32	0 12 10
Robert Cogswell	4	60	13	1½ ,, 16	5	20	0 10 02
Matthias Hitchcock	3	50	10	2	4	16	0 8 00
Francis Hall	3	10	8	1½ ,, 16	2	8	0 5 02
Richard Osborne	3	10	8	1½ ,, 16	2	8	0 5 02
William Potter	4	40	12	2¼ ,, 24	4	16	0 8 09 *ob.*
James Clark	4	50	12½	2½	4½	18	0 9 06
Edward Patteson	1	40	4½	¾ ,, 24	2½	10	0 4 03 *ob.*
Andrew Hull	4	40	12	2¼ ,, 24	4	16	0 8 09 *ob.*
William Ives	2	25	6¼	11¼	2¼	9	0 4 09
George Smith	1	50	5	1	3	12	0 5 00
Widow Sherman	2	50	7½	1½	3½	14	0 6 06
Matthew Moulthrop	-	-	-	-	-	-	-
Thomas James, sen.	5	200	22½	4½	12½	50	-
Widow Greene	3	80	11½	2¼ ,, 24	5½	22	0 10 02
Thomas Yale	1	100	7½	1½	5½	22	0 8 06
Thomas Fugill	2	100	10	2	6	24	0 10 08
John Punderson	2	180	14	2½ ,, 32	10	40	0 15 06
John Johnson	5	150	20	4	10	40	0 18 00
Abraham Bell	1	10	3	½ ,, 16	1	4½	0 2 02 *ob.*
John Evance	1	500	27½	5½	25½	102	1 16 06
Mr. Mayres	2	800	45	9	41	164	2 19 00
Mrs. Constable	3	150	15	3	9	36	0 15 00

DIVISION OF LAND.

Names of the Planters.	Persons Numbered.	Estates.	Land in the First Division.	In the Neck.	Meadow.	Land in the Second Division.	Rates yearly paid for Land.
Joshua Atwater .	2	300	20	4	16	64	1 11 06
Thomas Fugill . .	1	400	22½	4½	20½	82	1 09 06
Edward Wigglesworth	3	300	22½	4½	16½	66	1 05 06
Thomas Powell	1	100	7½	4½	5½	22	0 08 06
Henry Browning .	8	340	37	7½ ,, 24	21	84	1 15 09
Mrs. Higginson .	8	250	32½	6½	16½	66	1 08 06
Edward Tench .	3	400	27½	5½	21½	86	1 12 10
Jeremiah Dixon .	1	300	11	2½	15½	62	1 01 04
William Thorp .	3	10	8	1½ ,, 16	2	8	0 5 02
Robert Hill .	1	10	3	½ ,, 16	1	4	0 2 02
Widow Williams	2	60	8	1½ ,, 16	4	16	0 7 02
Andrew Low .	3	10	8	1½ ,, 16	2	8	0 5 02
Francis Newman	2	160	13	2½ ,, 16	9	36	0 14 02
John Caffinch .	2	500	67½	13½	29¼	73	2 08 06
David Atwater	1	400	—	—	24¼	141	1 11 04
—— Lucas .	6	400	35	7	23	92	—
—— Dearmer	1	300	17½	3½	15½	62	
Benjamin Ling .	2	320	21	4 ,, 32	17	68	1 05 04
Robert Newman .	2	700	40	8	36	144	2 12 00
William Andrews .	8	150	27½	5½	11½	46	1 02 06
John Cooper .	3	30	9	1¾ ,, 8	3	12	0 6 07
Richard Beckley	4	20	11	2 ,, 32	3	12	0 7 04
Mr. Marshall.	5	1,000	62½	12½	52½	210	3 17 06
Mrs. Eldred .	5	1,000	62½	12½	52½	210	3 17 06
Francis Brewster	9	1,000	35	7	54½	263	3 15 10
Mark Pearce .	2	150	12½	2½	8½	34	0 13 06
Jarvis Boykin .	2	40	7	1¼ ,, 24	3	12	0 5 09
James Russell .	2	20	6	1 ,, 32	2	8	0 4 04
George Ward .	6	10	15	3 ,, 16	3½	14	0 9 08
Lawrence Ward .	2	30	6½	1½ ,, 8	2½	10	0 4 09
Moses Wheeler .	2	50	7½	1½	3½	14	0 6 06

Commencing with this distribution of the proprietors into groups, and studying the land-records of the town, one may assign to almost every proprietor his house-lot in respect of location and, approximately, of measure, The map opposite the title-page was drawn with these aids.¹ It locates the house-lots of all the proprietors except eleven. Of the thirty-two non-proprietors, seven had "small lots" given them on East Water Street, east of the lots of the four proprietors who lived on that street, and twenty-five were accommodated between George Street and the West Creek.

While the division of lands was in progress, the name of the plantation was changed, by order of a general court held on the first day of September, 1640, from Quinnipiac to New Haven. There is no reason for believing that any of the planters came from the port of that name on the southern shore of England, and the record gives no clew to the reasons which influenced the court in

---

¹ The author of this history is alone responsibie for the map; but he thankfully acknowledges his obligation to Henry White, Esq., for the use of manuscript volumes which trace the land-titles from the original to the present proprietors, and for assistance in the solution of difficult problems. He feels some degree of confidence in regard to all the eleven groups, except that occupying the suburb on the west side of West Creek. Several transfers of title occurred in this group before the recording of alienations was imperative, and the shape of the quarter has been so changed that its original boundaries have not been ascertained. Only three, therefore, of the proprietors in this quarter have been located on the map; namely, William Ives, George Smith, and Widow Sherman.

The dotted lines on the map represent fences of uncertain location. A street, cut from the corner of George and York Streets through to Oak Street, would be in line with Oak Street, and I am credibly informed that there was such a street; but how Mr. Gregson's quarter was bounded on the side toward the town, I cannot determine. The dotted lines on one side of the suburb lying west of West Creek are nearly coincident with the lines of Lafayette Street; but I am told that Lafayette is a modern street. There must have been an ancient lane nearly coincident with it, since one of the lots is described in 1679 as bounded east by the street (Hill Street), and "west by the way that goeth down to Jonathan Lamson's lot on the bankside."

naming their plantation. In dropping the aboriginal designation, and adopting one familiar to Englishmen, they followed the custom of their time. They did it perhaps partly for their own pleasure, but more for the gratification of friends; for in the course of two years, use must have greatly diminished the uncouthness, to English ears, of the Indian name. A letter of Davenport to his early friend and patron, Lady Vere, is extant, in which he speaks of the arrival, in the summer of 1639, of the first ship from England; and in it he says, "The sight of the harbor did so please the captain of the ship, and all the passengers, that he called it the Fair Haven." Perhaps this attempt of the English captain to give an English name occasioned the formal action of the court a twelvemonth afterward, which is thus recorded, "This town now called New Haven." Perhaps, also, this ship which first cast anchor in the harbor of New Haven, bringing passengers from Kent, Surrey, and Sussex, had weighed anchor in the port of that name on the coast of Sussex.

CHAPTER VIII.

THE PERSONNEL OF THE PLANTATION.

WITH the map in hand, let us survey the town, and review the list of proprietors. As we pass around the several quarters, perhaps no time will be more suitable for such information in regard to the colonists as is obtainable and of sufficient importance to be recorded.

Commencing with the northeast quarter, we find a large part of it owned by Gov. Eaton and his relations. The governor's homestead was on Elm Street, about equidistant from the corners of the square. Here he lived with his wife, his mother, his four children, and the two sons of his wife by her first husband. In later years Mrs. Hopkins, wife of Edward Hopkins, the governor of Hartford, having become incurably insane, spent much time in the family under the care of her mother.[1] Several young persons of both sexes, wards

---

[1] Winthrop writes in his diary April 13, 1645: "Mr. Hopkins, the governor of Hartford upon Connecticut, came to Boston and brought his wife with him (a godly young woman and of special parts), who was fallen into a sad infirmity, the loss of her understanding and reason, which had been growing upon her divers years, by occasion of her giving herself wholly to reading and writing, and had written many books. Her husband, being very loving and tender of her, was loath to grieve her; but he

of Eaton, also found a home under his roof. In addition, there was, as appears from the records, a numerous retinue of servants for the work of the house and of the field. Mather says that the family sometimes consisted of not less than thirty persons.

The New Haven Colony Historical Society has in its possession a portrait said to have belonged to the Eaton family. It was painted in 1635, and in the

A PORTRAIT WHICH BELONGED TO THE EATON FAMILY.

twenty-fifth year of the age of the lady whom it pictures. In one corner is a coat of arms, which, in connection with the dates, may determine whether it represents Mrs. Hopkins, the daughter of Mrs. Eaton by her first husband, or Mary, the daughter of Gov. Eaton by his

saw his error when it was too late. For if she had attended her household affairs and such things as belong to women, and not gone out of her way and calling to meddle in such things as are proper for men, whose minds are stronger, &c., she had kept her wits, and might have improved them usefully and honorably in the place God had set her."

first wife, or some other lady. At present the question is in suspense.

The principal apartment of the dwelling-house, denominated, as in the mother-country, the hall, was the first to be entered. It was sufficiently spacious to accommodate the whole family when assembled at meals and at prayers. It contained, according to the inventory taken after the governor's decease, "a drawing-table," "a round table," "green cushions," "a great chair with needlework," "high chairs," "high stools," "low chairs," "low stools," "Turkey carpets," "high wine stools," and "great brass andirons."

"The parlor," probably adjoining the hall and having windows opening upon the street, served as a withdrawing-room, to which the elder members of the family and their guests retired from the crowd and bustle of the hall. But, according to the fashion of the time, the parlor contained the furniture of a bedroom, and was occasionally used as the sleeping apartment of a guest.

Mather, speaking of Eaton's manner of life, says that "it was his custom when he first rose in the morning to repair unto his *study;*" and again, that, "being a great reader, all the time he could spare from company and business, he commonly spent in his beloved *study.*" There is no mention in the inventory of "the study," but perhaps the apartment referred to by Mather was described by the appraisers as "the counting-house," the two names denoting that it was used both as a library and as an office.

If these three rooms filled the front of the mansion the reader may locate behind them at his own discretion the winter-kitchen, the summer-kitchen, the buttery, the pantry,—offices necessarily implied, even if not mentioned as connected with an extensive homestead of the seventeenth century,—and then add the brew-house and the warehouse, both mentioned in the inventory.

Of the sleeping apartments in the second story, the green chamber, so called from the color of its drapery, was chief in the expensiveness and elegance of its furniture, and presumably in its size, situation, and wainscoting. The walls of the blue chamber were hung with tapestry, but the green drapery was of better quality than the blue. The blue chamber had a Turkey carpet, but the appraisers set a higher value on the carpet in the green chamber. All the other sleeping-rooms were furnished each with a feather-bed of greater or less value, but the green chamber had a bed of down. In this chamber, probably, was displayed the silver basin and ewer, double gilt, and curiously wrought with gold, which the Fellowship of Eastland Merchants had presented to Mrs. Eaton, in acknowledgement of her husband's services as their agent in the countries about the Baltic. The appraisers valued it at forty pounds sterling, but did not put it in the inventory because Mrs. Eaton claimed it as "her proper estate."

There was in the house, in addition to the bowl and ewer, plate to the value of one hundred and seven pounds, eleven shillings, sterling. Taking into consideration all that we know of the house and furniture, we must conclude with Hubbard, that the governor "maintained a port in some measure answerable to his place."

Samuel Eaton, who owned and occupied the land between his brother's premises and State Street, obtaining in 1640 from the court a grant of Totoket, "for such friends as he shall bring over from old England, and upon such terms as shall be agreed betwixt himself and the committee chosen to that purpose," sailed for the mother-country, to return with a band of colonists and settle a new plantation at Branford. But he found his friends well pleased with the new condition of affairs in England, and unwilling to emigrate. He himself, preferring to remain in his native land, sent a power-of-attorney to his brother; by whom the corner-lot, which had been Samuel Eaton's, was sold in 1649 to Francis Newman. It afterward became the property of James Bishop, and remained in his family more than two centuries.

Edward Hopkins, though he settled in Hartford, was one of the first proprietors of Quinnipiac. At a court held the third day of November, 1639, the town ordered "that Mr. Hopkins shall have two hogsheads of lime for his present use, and as much more as will finish his house as he now intends it, he thinking that two hogsheads more will serve." One can scarcely doubt that Mr. Hopkins's house was in the same quarter with that of his beloved father-in-law; but the tax-schedule of 1641 does not contain his name, and there is no existing record of the alienation of the house and land. The order concerning the lime seems to imply that he had made some changes in his intentions, and we may infer that his determination to settle in Hartford was formed after the house was begun and before it was finished. Having spent some time in Connecticut, while his fellow-passengers in the Hector were sojourning in Massachusetts, he did not rejoin them when they removed to Quinnipiac, though he retained his interest as a joint-proprietor in their plantation. Becoming gradually adherent to Connecticut, where he sat as a deputy in the General Court as early as March, 1638, and was chosen to assist in the magistracy in April, 1639, he probably sold his estate in New Haven before the tax-schedule of 1641 was written; but which of the proprietors in the governor's quarter succeeded him, cannot be determined. Though removed from daily intercourse with Eaton, he cherished such love for him to the end of life, that, as he lay on his death-bed in England, he said, "How often have I pleased myself with thoughts of a joyful meeting with my father Eaton! I remember with what pleasure he would come down the street, that he might meet me when I came from Hartford to New Haven; but with how much greater pleasure shall we shortly meet one another in heaven!" In his will, after providing for his "poor distressed wife," and giving to friends tokens of his affection, he bequeathed his estate to trustees for the promotion of liberal education in New England. The Hopkins Grammar School in New Haven owes its existence to this bequest.

Although we cannot determine with certainty where Mr. Hopkins's house was situated, it is a plausible conjecture that he alienated his land and buildings to William Tuttle, who, in 1641, owned the lot on the corner of Grove and State Streets. Mr. Tuttle, who came over in the Planter in 1635, was, in April, 1639, still a resident of Boston, as appears from the baptism of one of his children there on the seventh day of that month; but some time in the same year he removed to

Quinnipiac, for he signed the fundamental agreement before it was copied into the record-book. Although not a member of the court, he was active and influential in public affairs. His daughter Elizabeth became the wife of Richard Edwards of Hartford, and the mother of Rev. Timothy Edwards of East Windsor, who numbered among his children the greatest of American metaphysicians and ten daughters, "every one of which has been said to be six feet tall, making sixty feet of daughters, all of them strong in mind.[1]"

The lot on Grove Street, adjoining Mr. Tuttle's, belonged to the mother of Theophilus and Samuel Eaton; but, as she was an inmate of the governor's family, probably no buildings were erected while it was in her possession. She sold it, in 1646, to Richard Perry.

West of Mrs. Eaton's land was that of David Yale, who, when the schedule of 1641 was written, was still unmarried. In 1645 he purchased a house in Boston, where his second child was born the same year. While residing in Boston he distinguished himself as a friend of the Church of England, joining with a few others in a petition for liberty to use its liturgy. A few years later he returned to the mother-country, where he remained to the end of life. To his care his still insane sister was committed by Gov. Hopkins, when he died in 1657. He was the father of Elihu Yale, for whom Yale College was named.

Ezekiel Cheever, who lived at the corner of Grove and Church Streets, came in the Hector from London, where he was born, Jan. 25, 1615. He opened a school in his own house a few months after he arrived

---

[1] Semi-centennial sermon of Rev. Joab Brace, D. D.

at Quinnipiac with the main company of planters, and was thenceforth the schoolmaster of the plantation, receiving for some time a yearly stipend of twenty pounds, which in 1644, was increased to thirty pounds. He was one of the twelve chosen for the foundation work of the Church and State, and, though never ordained to the ministry, occasionally preached. Both in the field of education and in the field of theology he was an author, having written "A Short Introduction to the Latin Tongue," which he called an "Accidence," and a book on the millennium, under the title "Scripture Prophecies Explained." He was chosen a member of the Court for the plantation at its first session, when it was instituted by the seven appointed for that purpose, and, in 1646, was one of the deputies to the General Court of the Jurisdiction. Dissenting from the judgment of the church and its elders, in respect to some cases of discipline, he commented on their action with such severity that he was himself censured in 1649.[1] Soon after this, and perhaps on account of it, he removed from New Haven, and, according to Mather, "died in Boston, August 21, 1708, in the ninety-fourth year of his age, after he had been a skillful, painful, faithful schoolmaster for seventy years." President Stiles mentions two aged clergymen of his acquaintance who had been pupils of Cheever, one of whom said, "that he wore a long white beard, terminating in a point; that, when he stroked his beard to the point, it was a sign to the boys to stand clear."

Nathanael Turner, whose home-lot was on Church

[1] In Conn. Hist. Soc., Coll. I., may be seen the "Trial of Ezekiel Cheever, before the Church at New Haven."

Street, next south of Mr. Cheever's, came from England with Winthrop in 1630, and was one of the most considerable citizens of Lynn, representing the town in the first General Court of Massachusetts. In January, 1637, his house was destroyed by fire, "with all that was in it save the persons;" and this event happening the same year that tidings came of "that famous place called Quinnipiac," with "a fair river, fit for harboring of ships," and "rich and goodly meadows," may have occasioned his removal from Lynn. Having had military experience as an officer in the Pequot war, he was from the beginning intrusted with "the command and ordering of all martial affairs" in the new plantation. To facilitate the performance of this trust it was ordered by the Court "that Capt. Turner shall have his lot of meadow and upland where he shall choose it for his own convenience, that he may attend the service of the town which his place requires." He accordingly located a farm about three miles from the market-place, between East Rock and Quinnipiac River. After his death, if not before, his family resided at the farm. He was lost at sea in "the great ship" which sailed from New Haven in January, 1646.

Richard Perry, the only proprietor in Mr. Eaton's quarter who has not been mentioned, lived at the corner of Church and Elm Streets. Having married Mary, the daughter of Richard Malbon, in the old country, he accompanied his father-in-law from London to New Haven. He took an active part in the public affairs of the plantation, and in 1646, when Fugill, the secretary of the court, had fallen into disgrace, was chosen to succeed him in that office. He sold his house to

Thomas Kimberly in 1649, and after that date his name does not occur in the records.

Passing from the northeast square to the east-center square, we find Mr. Davenport's lot on the corner of Elm and State Streets, and his house on Elm Street, nearly opposite Mr. Eaton's. Here the pastor and his wife received their only child after a separation from him of

JOHN DAVENPORT.
[From a portrait in possession of Yale College.]

more than two years; the child having been left in England, and brought over by a maid-servant in a ship, which, in the summer of 1639, sailed from England direct for the harbor of Quinnipiac.

Richard Malbon lived on State Street, his lot being next south of Mr. Davenport's. He was one of the London merchants who came with Eaton and Davenport, was one of the twelve chosen for the foundation of Church and State, and one of the five whom the twelve sifted out of that number by their own action before the foundation was laid. For some reason, probably for want of church-membership, he was not admitted a member of the court till February, 1642; but only two months after he was made a freeman, he was chosen one of four deputies for the half-year ensuing to assist the magistrates " by way of advice, but not to have any power by way of sentence," and was the first-named of the four. Such a limitation was expressly put upon the deputies in the October election of that year, and was probably implied in the election six months before. In this office he was continued for a long time by re-election, and, after the organization of the Colonial Government, was often a deputy to represent the plantation in the General Court of the Jurisdiction. In 1646 he was appointed by that body one of its magistrates in New Haven. The town manifested its confidence in him as a military officer by appointing him "to order the watches and all the martial affairs of this plantation," during Capt. Turner's absence at the Delaware Bay in 1642; and again, when Turner was about to embark in the ill-fated ship of 1646, by choosing Malbon "captain, with liberty to resign his place to Capt. Turner at his return." Mr. Malbon was an enterprising merchant, trading coast-wise and in the West Indies. He was also one of "the company of merchants of New Haven," who chartered for a voyage to England the ship in which the town lost so much property and so many valuable lives.

Next south of the Malbon house was that of Thomas Nash, formerly a member of the church in Leyden, Holland, and one of the five who wrote from that city in

1625, to their brethren in Plymouth, informing them of the death of John Robinson, pastor of the church which included in its membership the planters of Plymouth, as well as the brethren still sojourning in Leyden. Mr. Nash came from England to New Haven with Mr. Whitfield and his company, and was one of the signers of the agreement which that company made on shipboard to remain together. But being not only a smith, but a gunsmith, it was for the common welfare as well as his own, that he should have his shop in the largest and most central plantation. His change of purpose was probably after the fundamental agreement was made, as he had not signed his name to it when it was copied into the record-book. He must have been advanced beyond the zenith of life, for his eldest son became a proprietor and a freeman not long after his father.

John Benham probably came from England in 1630, and had been a freeman in Dorchester, Mass. Removing to New Haven, he wrought as a brickmaker. As late as 1651 he petitioned for compensation for time spent at the first settlement in searching for clay suitable for making brick, and his claim was allowed. He was also, by appointment, town-crier. Although himself a freeman, he was at one time implicated in what the General Court of the Jurisdiction regarded as "a factious, if not seditious," opposition to the "fundamental law" which limited the right of suffrage.

John Chapman had also been a freeman of Massachusetts before he came to New Haven. He removed to Fairfield in 1647, and thence to Stamford, where he made his will, 1665.

Thomas Kimberly removed from Dorchester, Mass.,

to New Haven, where he was admitted a freeman in November, 1639. It is said that his son Eleazar, baptized the same month, was the first child born of English parents in Quinnipiac. Mr. Kimberly was one of two pound-keepers appointed by the town in January, 1643; and the pound of which he had charge was situated on the east side of State Street, opposite the house of Thomas Nash. Mr. Kimberly had only a small estate when he came to New Haven, but his five children entitled him under the rule of allotment to a much larger acreage than he could draw from his estate. After the removal of Seeley, the first marshal, Kimberly was appointed to that office.

Matthew Gilbert, who lived at the corner of Chapel and Church Streets, in a house fronting toward the market-place, doubtless came with Eaton and Davenport from England, for there is no record of him in Massachusetts; but whether he had been a citizen of London, or had come from some other part of the kingdom, is not known. His election to be one of the seven founders of the theocracy shows that he was, even in the beginning of the settlement, held in high estimation; and the appointment of him as a deacon shows that he retained the confidence of the church in subsequent years. He was honored with political as well as ecclesiastical office, being first an assistant magistrate of the jurisdiction, and afterward deputy-governor. A rough stone still standing on the green, marked "M. G. 80," marks the place of his burial. President Stiles conjectured that the M was a W inverted for the purpose of concealing from his enemies the last resting-place of William Goffe, the regicide; but acknowledged that he had not found the least tradition or surmise that Goffe was buried in New Haven till he himself conjectured it. The initials are those of Matthew Gilbert; and, if the Arabic numerals were designed (as Stiles supposed) to express that the person buried beneath died in 1680, they give correctly the date of Gilbert's death. More probably they were meant to indicate the number of years he had lived.

Owen Rowe, a citizen of London, took stock in the plantation company, but could not leave home when the Hector sailed. He, however, sent his son Nathanael, a boy in his teens, under the care of Davenport and the Eatons. The youth was left behind in Massachusetts in the spring of 1638, that he might pursue his studies under the care of Nathanael Eaton, the brother of Theophilus and Samuel Eaton, who about that time commenced his extraordinary and disgraceful career as master of the school afterward called Harvard College.[1] There is extant a pathetic letter from young Rowe to Gov. Winthrop, complaining that Eaton had never given him any instruction. and soliciting the governor to advise him how he may return to his father.[2] Owen Rowe, delaying to come till the civil war broke out, became a colonel in the Parliamentary army, and, when King Charles was tried for treason, was one of the judges who condemned him to death. It appears from the records, that, like other wealthy friends of New

---

[1] The coincidence in time between the arrival of the Hector, and the appearance of Nathanael Eaton as an educator, suggests that he may have come in the same ship with his brothers. Winthrop in his Journal, and Savage in his Notes thereupon, have jointly given a graphic picture of him and of his wife, the housekeeper of the college.

[2] This letter may be found in Appendix II.

England who did not emigrate, he sent over, as an adventure, some cattle. These were regarded as security for the expense of fencing, and for the rates to be paid "in consideration of his lot and estate here given in." His town-lot was on Church Street, next north of Mr. Gilbert's. As it touched Mr. Davenport's lot in the rear, it was ordered by the town (doubtless at the pastor's suggestion), "that when Mr. Rowe's lot shall be fenced in, our pastor shall have a way or passage eight feet broad betwixt it and Mr. Crane's lot, that he may go out of his own garden to the meeting-house." Mr. Rowe not making his appearance, the lot was, after some years, divided and granted on certain conditions to Mr. Davenport, Mr. Gilbert, and Mr. Crane, the adjoining proprietors.

The lot on the corner of Church and Elm Streets was at first reserved by the proprietors as a parsonage, if at Mr. Davenport's death or removal it should be needed, but afterward was granted to Nicholas Augur, a practitioner of medicine. This grant had not been made when the schedule of 1641 was written, and the earliest mention of Mr. Augur is in 1644. Some relation of Mr. Augur's troubles as a practitioner of medicine, and of the wretchedness of his death, will be given in subsequent chapters.

Jasper Crane, the only remaining occupant of the east-center square, was presumably from London, as he was much connected with the London men in various ways. He first put in his estate at one hundred and eighty pounds, and land was assigned him according in amount with that appraisal; but before the meadows and the out-lands of the third division were allotted, he was permitted to increase his appraisal to four hundred and eighty pounds, and receive thereafter corresponding allotments of land. He afterward removed to Branford; represented that town in the General Court of the Jurisdiction in 1653, and was afterward chosen to be a magistrate.

Four lots on East Water Street, fronting the harbor, were, for the allotment of out-lands, attached to Mr. Davenport's quarter. Their proprietors were James Russell, George Ward, Lawrence Ward, and Moses Wheeler.

Commencing the survey of the southeast square at the corner of Chapel and State Streets, we find the house of William Preston, a Yorkshireman, who died in 1647, leaving a large family, and a small estate here, which was supplemented by his right in a house, land, and other goods, "in Yorkshire, in a town called Giglesweke, in Craven." He and his wife had the care of the meeting-house, which she was to "sweep and dress" every week, having one shilling a week for her pains. He was at one time under the censure of the church, but in his will describes himself as "a member of the church of New Haven.[1]"

Next to the premises of Mr. Preston were those of Richard Mansfield, who came to Quinnipiac with the other planters as a steward for Mr. Marshall, who was perhaps of London when he engaged in the enterprise,

[1] Mr. Malbon, Mr. Lamberton, and Mr. Evance contracted with the town in 1644, to "dig a channel which shall bring boats, at least, to the end of the street beside William Preston's house, at any time of the tide, except they meet with some invincible difficulty, which may hinder their digging the channel so deep."

but afterward of Exeter. There was presumably no house on Mr. Mansfield's lot; for he was at first in the service of Mr. Marshall, and afterward, when Mr. Marshall had abandoned the idea of coming, bought of him his lot at the corner of Elm and Church Streets. This became the Mansfield homestead, and a part of the land remained in possession of the family for several generations. It seems, however, from Mr. Mansfield's will, which was nuncupative, and declared by two of his neighbors, that at the time of his decease he was residing at his farm between East Rock and Qunnipiac River. Being asked if, according to English custom, he would give more to his elder than to his younger son, he replied in the negative, alleging that the former "was a wild boy, and the younger was of a better spirit."

Thomas Jeffrey, who lived next south of Mr. Mansfield's lot, was by trade a tanner, and doubtless had reference to his trade in choosing his home-lot; for a stream of water flowed through his land at that time, though it has long since disappeared. At an early day he relinquished his trade, to become a mariner. In 1647, "Capt. Malbon propounded that the town hath been ill provided of sergeants, in regard that Sergeant Jeffrey is abroad much by reason of his occasions at sea, therefore whether the town will not see cause to appoint another sergeant in his room, and the rather seeing Sergeant Jeffrey hath earnestly desired it, as Lieut. Seeley and Sergeant Munson did testify in court. The captain also affirmed the same, and that he was unwilling to move for a change till that now he understandeth Sergeant Jeffrey proposeth to employ himself more fully in sea affairs."

George Lamberton, who lived next south of Sergeant Jeffrey, was one of the nine proprietors, who, in the schedule of 1641, are rated at one thousand pounds. Of these nine, however, five were non-resident, and soon ceased to pay rates. So that Lamberton was one of four planters who were excelled only by Theophilus Eaton in the amount of their estates. He was from his first appearance in the plantation a mariner, and lost his life in the ship which, under his command, left the harbor of New Haven in January, 1646, and was never afterward heard from. He is mentioned by Ezekiel Rogers in a letter to Gov. Winthrop, in a manner which suggests that he had been one of Rogers's flock. His influence as a man of mind and of substance may have principally occasioned the large secession of Yorkshiremen who refused to return to the Bay when sent for by Rogers.[1]

William Wilkes, who lived at the corner of State and George Streets, removed to Quinnipiac from Boston, where he had resided since 1633. He went to England in 1644, intending to return; but, instead of returning, he sent for his wife to join him in England. She, embarking in Lamberton's ship, was lost at sea. News of Mr. Wilkes's decease was probably received soon after; for a will made by his wife was admitted to probate, which disposed of their whole estate. The house and orchard were sold for forty pounds; the house being appraised at thirty pounds, and the land at ten pounds.

Benjamin Fenn, proprietor of the lot on George Street, adjoining the premises of William Wilkes, removed to Milford with the other first planters of that

[1] See page 83.

town. At this time he had but a small estate, and was in no way prominent; but afterward he became one of the leading men in the colony.

Robert Seeley, the next grantee, sold, in 1646, "his house and house-lot" to John Basset, with two acres of upland out of his first division, and afterward resided on the west side of West Creek, as appears from a deed of gift which he made of "his dwelling-house with his orchard" to his son Nathaniel. He had removed from Watertown, now called Cambridge, Mass., with the first planters of Connecticut, and had been Captain Mason's lieutenant in the attack on the Pequot fort at Mystic. Removing again, he came to Quinnipiac before its planters had established their fundamental agreement, and was admitted a freeman on the day the court was organized. He was by trade a shoemaker; but being marshal of the court, lieutenant of the train-band, and captain of the artillery company, much of his time was employed in public affairs. In the autumn of 1646, about the time he sold his house in Mr. Lamberton's quarter, he had "liberty of the court to go for England, although a public officer." It appears, however, that he did not immediately use his liberty, for he was here in the following February. In 1649 he was minded to remove from the town, and offered his resignation; but the court refused to receive it as long as he remained, and "the four sergeants were desired to take some pains to see what men would underwrite" for the encouragement of Lieut. Seeley to remain. At a subsequent meeting, the sergeants having accomplished but little, sixteen or seventeen pounds were pledged by those present, and "the sergeants were desired to speak with those that are not present, to see what they will do." In 1659 appears the alienation of another house, after which his name disappears for a time from the records, as if he were absent. In 1662 he had "returned from England;" and "a motion was made in his behalf for some encouragement for his settling among us," which, however, was ineffectual.

Roger Alling came to New Haven with Capt. Lamberton, acting as steward during the last half of the voyage, the former steward having died. Judging from the wages allowed, viz., five pounds ten shillings for the whole voyage, one would conclude that the vessel came from a greater distance than the Bay. He was at this time unmarried, and of small estate. At an early date he became a member of the church and of the court. In 1661 he was chosen treasurer of the jurisdiction, and afterward a deacon of the church.

John Brockett was also, in 1643, unmarried, and of even smaller estate than his neighbor, Roger Alling. Like him he early became a member of the church and of the court. He was much employed by the court, as well as by individuals, in his profession as a surveyor.

Mr. Hickock's lot probably lay next to that of Brockett. Mr. Crane, his agent, surrendered it to the town in 1641, the proprietor having relinquished his intention of coming here to reside.

John Budd, the next proprietor, signed the fundamental agreement before it was copied into the book, and remained here till he removed, about 1646, to Southold, L. I., where he acted a more prominent part than at New Haven. Soon after his removal he was appointed a lieutenant, and afterwards represented his town in the General Court of the jurisdiction. During his absence in England another person was allowed and desired to exercise the company; the General Court "understanding that he is a member of the church of Salem, and, had he letters of recommendation, might be admitted a freeman as others are." But he must take the oath of fidelity to the jurisdiction: otherwise the command must vest in the corporal of the company. Mr. Budd sold his house and lot, in New Haven, for a hogshead of sugar.

William Jeanes, who lived at the corner of Church and Chapel Streets, had been one of the first planters, but was not admitted a freeman till 1648. He sold this corner-lot the same year to John Meggs.[1] Some years afterward he was at Northampton, whence he removed to Northfield with its first planters, and, though not an ordained minister, conducted the first public Christian worship in that town, preaching under an oak-tree.

Nicholas Elsey, who received his allotment on Chapel Street, adjoining that of Mr. Jeanes, was a cooper by trade. He was present at the ratification of the fundamental agreement in Mr. Newman's barn, and a few years afterward was admitted a freeman.

Richard Hull, who lived on Chapel Street, between Nicholas Elsey and William Preston, signed the fundamental agreement at the time when it was established, and at the first meeting of the court was admitted a

---

[1] See History of the Cutler Corner, by Henry White, in N. H. Col. Hist. Soc. Coll., vol. i. Mr. White illustrates the relative inferiority in early times of that part of Chapel Street which lies between Church Street and State Street, by a quotation from the records in which it is called "the lane that leadeth to Zuriel Kimberley's house."

freeman, as a member of some other church than that of New Haven.

Commencing the survey of the south-center square, we find at its northeast corner, where the Glebe building now is, the house of Thomas Gregson. President Stiles records the tradition that Gregson's house was one of four which excelled in stateliness all other houses erected in New Haven by the first generation of its inhabitants; the three which he groups with Gregson's belonging respectively to Mr. Theophilus Eaton, Mr. John Davenport, and Mr. Isaac Allerton.[1] Gregson was one of the most honored men in the community, intrusted with office continuously from 1640 till he embarked in 1646, with a commission from the colony of New Haven to obtain, if possible, a charter from Parliament. Having been a merchant in London, he engaged in commerce after his arrival at Quinnipiac; and the voyage in which he lost his life was primarily undertaken for commercial ends.

Next west of Mr. Gregson lived Stephen Goodyear, another of the London merchants originally associated together for the commencement of a plantation in New England. Here he was engaged in foreign commerce, sometimes in company with Eaton, Malbon, and Gregson, and sometimes adventuring largely on his individ-

---

[1] As Isaac Allerton was not here at the time of which we are discoursing, it may be appropriate to say that he was one of the voyagers in the Mayflower, and, that having fallen under censure at Plymouth, on account of some commercial transactions in which he was the agent of the colony, he removed first to Marblehead, then a part of Salem, and afterward to New Haven. A lot was granted him on the east side of Union Street, near Fair Street, where he built a "grand house with four porches."

ual responsibility. Having lost his first wife in Lamberton's ship, he married the widow of Lamberton, thus uniting two families in one home with advantage to the children of each. Second only to Eaton in the colonial government, his absence in England when Eaton died was a sufficient reason why he was not then advanced to the chief magistracy; and his death in London not long afterward brought his useful and honorable career to an end.

The lot next west of that occupied by Mr. Goodyear extended to College Street, and had been assigned to Mr. Hawkins, one of the non-resident proprietors. He seems to have been a friend of Mr. Goodyear, into whose possession the land afterward passed when its first proprietor had relinquished his intention of residing in New Haven.

Fronting on College Street was a lot assigned to Samuel Bailey, who did not long remain in New Haven. His allotment was purchased by William Davis.

Fronting on George Street were six lots belonging to Thomas Buckingham, Thomas Welch, Jeremiah Whitnell, Richard Miles, Nathanael Axtell, and Henry Stonhill, respectively. Axtell, "intending to go home, died in a few weeks before embarking, at Boston." Of the remaining five, four, namely, Buckingham, Welch, Miles, and Stonhill, removed to Milford with the first planters of that town, leaving only Whitnell on that side of the square. Deacon Richard Miles, however, returned to New Haven in 1641.

According to the schedule of 1641, the proprietors of the southwest square were, at that time, William

Fowler, Peter Prudden, James Prudden, Edmond Tapp, Widow Baldwin, An Elder, Richard Platt, Zachariah Whitman, and Thomas Osborne. The town records show that the lot reserved for an elder had been originally assigned to Timothy Baldwin, who, removing to Milford, sold his allotment to the town. As no land within this square has been traced to Thomas Osborne, it may be inferred that he sold to Mr. Fowler at an early date, and before a record of alienation was required. Mr. Osborne owned and occupied a house and tanyard on the south side of George Street, between Broad and Factory Streets, doubtless preferring this location to his original allotment because of the facilities it afforded for his vocation as a tanner. He afterward became one of the first planters of Easthampton on Long Island; but this property, being given to one of his sons, remained in the name of Osborne far into the nineteenth century. With the exception of Osborne, the original grantees of this square removed to Milford. As they had all emigrated from Herefordshire, or its vicinity, the square was for some years designated as the Herefordshire quarter.

The square next north of that occupied exclusively by Prudden and his friends from Hereford, had been assigned for the most part, if not wholly, to the Yorkshiremen who came with Ezekiel Rogers.

At the corner of Chapel and York Streets, a lot surrendered by Francis Parrot, one of the Yorkshiremen who returned to Massachusetts and settled at Rowley, was assigned by vote of the town, Nov. 3, 1639, to Thomas James, who, having been pastor of the church in Charlestown, Mass., had resigned his charge and come hither to reside. In 1642, in response to a call from Virginia for ministers from New England, Mr. James went with two of his clerical brethren to Virginia. The mission was unsuccessful, not however for want of "loving and liberal entertainment" but because the colonial government would not allow them to remain unless they would conform to the Church of England. Mr. James afterward returned to the mother-country, and was a beneficed clergyman in Needham, county of Suffolk, till ejected in 1662 by the Act of Uniformity.

Widow Greene, who owned the lot on York Street, next north of the corner-lot of Mr. James, probably did not long remain at New Haven, as the name does not continue to appear on the records.

Thomas Yale, step-son of Gov. Eaton, owned the next lot, but probably never lived on it. Marrying a daughter of Capt. Turner, he engaged in husbandry, and appears to have made his home at a farm some miles north of the town-plot.[1]

Thomas Fugill, a Yorkshireman, and, as we learn from the autobiography of Rev. Thomas Shepard, a member, before his emigration, of the family of Sir Richard Darley at Buttercrambe, was one of the seven men selected by the planters of New Haven for their "foundation work." He was also "notary public" or secretary of the plantation, and when a colonial government was instituted by the union of New Haven, Mil-

---

[1] Thomas Yale has usually been reputed to be the father of Elihu Yale, the benefactor of Yale College; but Professor Dexter has conclusively proved that Elihu Yale was son of David Yale, a brother of Thomas.

ford, and Guilford, was appointed secretary of the jurisdiction. He wrote a neat, legible hand, and so far forth performed the work of his office well; but the town, becoming suspicious of the records, appointed a committee "to view all those orders which are of a lasting nature, and where they are defective, to mend them and then let them be read in the court that the court may confirm or alter them as they see cause." The summary thus prepared is on record in the book kept by Fugill. Meanwhile another committee was investigating the result of a false entry by means of which Fugill had possessed himself of fifty-two acres and thirteen rods in the second division of lands, "instead of twenty-four acres, his full proportion." When this committee reported, "some of the court and town propounded whether it were not requisite and necessary to choose another secretary, who might more faithfully enter and keep the town's records. The secretary confessed his unfitness for the place by reason of a low voice, a dull ear, and slow apprehensions. He was answered, the court had long taken notice of sundry miscarriages through weakness or neglect, yet in tender respect to himself and his family, they had continued him in the place (though with trouble to others); a review of orders, before these offences brake out, being upon that consideration thought necessary and ordered. But upon this discovery of unfaithfulness and falsifying of orders and records, they were called to lay aside those private respects for the public safety. By the court, therefore he was presently put out of his office of secretary for this plantation." Unable to sustain himself under the weight of this punishment and of the censure of the church which followed it, he sold his estate, left the town, and probably returned to England.

John Punderson, another of the Yorkshire company, and also one of the seven chosen for "foundation work," was Fugill's nearest neighbor on the north. Few men of that generation were so faithful in all public duties as entirely to avoid pecuniary mulct; but there is no record of a fine imposed on John Punderson. A son and a grandson, both bearing the name of John, were deacons in the church which he helped to institute. Another grandson, Rev. Ebenezer Punderson, was one of the fathers of the Episcopal church in Connecticut.

On the corner of York and Elm Streets lived John Johnson, also of the Yorkshire company, who after a few years removed to Rowley, selling his house to his brother Robert, from whom was descended Rev. Samuel Johnson, two years younger than Ebenezer Punderson, but earlier than he in the ministry of the Episcopal Church.

Corporal Abraham Bell lived on Elm Street, next east from Mr. Johnson's corner. In 1647 he sold his estate in New Haven to Job Hall, and removed to Charlestown, Mass.

John Evance, who had been a London merchant and a parishioner of Mr. Davenport at St. Stephen's, had a large lot on the corner of Elm and College Streets, part of it being held by him for his brother-in-law, Mr. Mayer, who had not yet emigrated, and, as it proved, never came. Mr. Evance, though less active and conspicuous in civil affairs than some others, was inferior to few or none in commercial enterprise, drawing bills of exchange on Mr. Eldred for beaver and hides shipped to London, and sending shingles and clapboards to Barbadoes in vessels to be freighted with sugar in return.

The lot on College Street, next south of that occupied by Mr. Evance, was owned by a widow bearing the Yorkshire name of Constable. The question has been raised whether the husband of this woman were the Sir William Constable, who, according to Mather, proposed to follow Ezekiel Rogers to New England. This woman was plainly a widow, but not the widow of Sir William. Her husband was styled Mr.; her estate was small; she emigrated apparently as early as Rogers, and probably in his company; while Sir William did not sail with Rogers, and could not have come afterward without impressing on the page of history some notice of his arrival. Both the name and the location of this family suggest that they belonged to Rogers's company, and they may have been related to the knight who bore their family name. Mrs. Constable afterward became the wife of Deacon Richard Miles.

On the corner of College and Chapel Streets lived Joshua Atwater. He was born at Lenham, County of Kent, where he was baptized June 2, 1612. Having been a merchant in Ashford, in the same county, he emigrated in the company of Davenport and Eaton, and engaged in mercantile pursuits, first at New Haven, then at Milford, and afterward at Boston, where he died in 1676. He was treasurer of the jurisdiction till he removed out of its bounds.

The lot on Chapel Street, next west of Mr. Atwater's, was assigned to John Cockerill, probably a Yorkshireman, who built a house thereon, but shortly after removed, leaving his house and lands in charge of Thomas

Fugill. The estate stands in the name of Fugill in the schedule; but when after Fugill's departure the fences decayed, and the rates remained unpaid, it was ascertained that Cockerill had never alienated and still claimed it. Allen Ball, a brother-in-law of Fugill, and perhaps also related to Cockerill, was requested by the town to "take the house and land and improve them for defraying charges of rates and fencings;" but he declined, saying "that the house was uncomfortable to live in." A curious record in regard to this property was made more than sixty years after Cockerill left it in the hands of Fugill; viz.,—

"June 20, 1710. Capt. Nathan Andrews and Mr. John Todd, both of New Haven, testify and say that upon their certain knowledge, they formerly knew one Mr. John Fugill to be at New Haven above forty years since, who was reputed to be the son of Mr. Thomas Fugill formerly of New Haven, and that he did not, as they know of, lay any claim to the land in New Haven that was his father's."

Edward Wigglesworth, whose tombstone, marked E. W. 1653, was for a time supposed to distinguish the grave of Edward Whalley, one of the regicide judges; lived on the lot next west of Mr. Cockerill's. An autobiographical paper by his son, Rev. Michael Wigglesworth, printed in the appendix to this volume, gives a more distinct view of Quinnipiac and of one of its families than any other single document.

Thomas Powell lived to old age on the only remaining lot in the Yorkshire quarter.

Commencing the survey of the northwest square at

its northwest corner, we find the corner occupied by Edward Tench, whose name was at first given to the quarter. He died in February, 16$\frac{38}{40}$. His wife, of whom he speaks in his will as "lying in the house with me, dangerously sick and near to death by a consumption, so that in the judgment of man she draweth near her change," probably survived him for some time, as his will was presented to the court nearly seven years afterward.

The lot on Grove Street, next east from Mr. Tench's corner, still remained, when the schedule was written, in the name of Mrs. Higginson, though thst lady had died a few weeks before her neighbor, Mr. Tench. She was the widow of Rev. Francis Higginson, the first minister of Salem, and probably a kinswoman of the Eatons, as the names Theophilus and Samuel had been given to two of her children, and one of the children was taken by the governor into his family after the death of Mrs. Higginson. In the settlement of the estate, no mention is made of any house on the home-lot; but in 1647 Theophilus Higginson sold to "Christopher Todd his house and home-lot in New Haven lying betwixt the lot now William Judson's and Mr. Tench's." The inference is, that when Mrs. Higginson died, the family were still occupying a temporary habitation.

Henry Browning lived on the corner of Grove and College Streets. He does not appear to have been a freeman. In 1647 he "sold to Goodman William Judson all his real estate and commonage, together with a bedstead and trundle-bed, a pair of valance and a piece of blue darnix, a malt mill, a well bucket and chain, two loads of clay brought home, and the fence about the lot repaired." His name does not occur afterward on the records.

Francis Newman, the owner of the next lot, was admitted a freeman in 1640, chosen ensign of the train-band in 1642, lieutenant of the artillery company upon its formation in 1645, secretary of the plantation in 1647, and was finally advanced to the highest office in the jurisdiction, being chosen governor after Eaton's death.

John Caffinch, whose lot lay next south of Francis Newman's, probably sailed direct from England to Quinnipiac, arriving in 1639 with the first planters of Guilford, though not in the same ship with Whitfield. He was one of the six principal men chosen to receive from the aboriginal proprietors of Guilford a deed in trust for the whole company of planters. For some reason he concluded to live at New Haven rather than at Guilford. He does not appear to have been a freeman.

David Atwater, a younger brother of Joshua Atwater, had a lot adjoining that of Mr. Caffinch, but never lived on it. He seems to have become a proprietor at a late date, and to have received his whole allotment, with the exception of this town-lot, in the third division. It is conjectured, that, before he became a proprietor at New Haven, he may have had some thought of joining the Kentish colony at Guilford. His residence in New Haven was at his farm between East Rock and Quinnipiac River, where his neighbors were Capt. Turner, Richard Mansfield, and William Potter. His town-plot had been previously assigned to John

Pocock, who became one of the first planters of Milford. Mr. Atwater died in 1692, having outlived most of the first planters,

Two lots, extending from Mr. Atwater's to the corner of College and Elm Streets, were reserved for non-residents named respectively Dearmer and Lucas.

On Elm Street, between Mr. Lucas's corner and the corner of Elm and York Streets, lived Andrew Low, widow Williams, Robert Hill, and William Thorpe.

On York Street, between Mr. Thorpe's corner and Mr. Tench's corner, was a lot belonging to Jeremiah Dixon, one of the seven men chosen for foundation work. He early removed from the plantation; and, as he was unmarried, there was probably no house upon his lot.

The only remaining square of the eight which surrounded the market-place was occupied on Elm Street by the lots of two non-residents, Mr. Marshall and Mrs. Eldred, and by the lot of Francis Brewster. Mr. Marshall has already been mentioned in connection with Richard Mansfield, who was his representative and agent. Mrs. Eldred was apparently a widow in London, and perhaps the mother of a Mr. Eldred with whom some of the colonists had commercial correspondence. As the name occurs on the parish-register of St. Stephen's, it may be that the family had been parishioners of Mr. Davenport in Coleman Street.

Francis Brewster was from London, and one of the company which came with Davenport. He does not appear to have been a freeman. Mr. Brewster having been lost in Lamberton's ship, and his widow having married Mr. Pell and removed to New Jersey, the house and home-lot were sold to Mr. Goodenhouse, a Dutchman, who had married the widow of Capt. Turner.

Mark Pearce, whose lot was on College Street north of Brewster's corner, had lived at Cambridge, Mass., and removed to New Haven as late as 1642. At a general court held Feb. 24, 164⅘, "Mr. Pearce desired the plantation to take notice, that if any will send their children to him he will instruct them in writing or arithmetic." This was several years before Mr. Cheever removed, so that Mr. Pearce's school, if his offer was accepted, must have been additional to that of Cheever.

Jarvis Boykin, a carpenter by trade, was the next proprietor on College Street. He came from the town of Charing in Kent, and had resided two or three years in Charlestown, Mass., before he joined the company which settled at Quinnipiac.

Benjamin Ling occupied the corner of College and Grove Streets. He had removed from Charlestown, Mass., and was present at the formation of the fundamental agreement in 1639. He died in 1673, commending his wife to the care of James Davids, who for some years had been an inmate of his house. Mr. Davids married the widow, who, dying not long after the marriage, left the homestead to him. It was known to some of the inhabitants of New Haven that James Davids was an *alias* for John Dixwell, and that this man was one of the regicide judges. Marrying a second wife, he became the father of a family, and resided here many years, not only unbetrayed, but much revered and beloved. Here he died in old age; and his grave on the green is marked, not only by the rude stone bearing his initials which his contemporaries placed there, but by a marble monument erected in later times.

On Grove Street, next east from Mr. Ling's corner, was the lot of Robert Newman. In his barn was held the meeting of planters at which the fundamental agreement was adopted, Mr. Newman himself being the secretary of the meeting. He was elected ruling elder of the church, and continued in that office till his return to England. The latest mention of him as a resident of New Haven is on the eighth day of October, 1649.

On the east side of Elder Newman's lot was the lot of William Andrews, a member of the church and of the court from the first. He was a carpenter by trade, but found time to keep "an ordinary" or house of entertainment for strangers.

John Cooper lived at the corner of Grove and Church Streets. He was present at the adoption of the fundamental agreement, and became a freeman in October, 1645, his name being the last but one on the list made by Secretary Fugill. "John Cooper took oath to be faithful to the trust committed to him in viewing fences and pounding cattle, according to the court's order, without partiality or respect of persons." In the execution of this trust, he was to inspect all the fences within the two miles "once every week if no extraordinary providence hinder."

Sergeant Richard Beckley, whose lot lay between that of Mr. Cooper and that of Mr. Marshall, was present when the fundamental agreement was adopted, and, as his military title implies, was a member of the court.

Having now surveyed the eight squares which lay around the market-place, let us proceed to the two suburbs, and first to that which lay between the two creeks.

Sergeant Samuel Whitehead lived at the corner of George and Meadow Streets. Previous to his residence in New Haven, he had spent some years in Massachusetts and at Hartford. By the marriage of his granddaughter his homestead passed into the family of Hubbard, and so continued for nearly two centuries.

John Clark, who lived on Meadow Street, next south of Mr. Whitehead, was interpreter when the Montowese Indians sold their land to the English. He had lived about four years in Massachusetts before he came to Quinnipiac with its first planters.

Of Luke Atkinson, the next proprietor on Meadow Street, little is known but that he dared to quarrel with Mr. Davenport, and, being charged with slander, was fined forty pounds. He removed from New Haven in 1656.

Edward Bannister died in 1649, and his lot passed into other hands. Another lot which lay between State Street and the East Creek was granted to his widow by the town, on which she built a house.

John Moss, though by no means a wealthy man, gave his son Joseph a liberal education, and had the pleasure of seeing him settled in the ministry at Derby. In his old age John Moss removed to Wallingford, where he died in 1707, aged one hundred and three years.

John Charles, a brother-in-law of John Moss, had lived some years in Massachusetts. He was a seafaring man, and removed first to Branford and afterward to Saybrook.

Richard Beach removed to New London.

Arthur Halbidge came from England to Boston in 1635. He died in 1648.

William Peck crossed the Atlantic with Davenport and Eaton. He is said to have been a merchant in London; but the tradition is not easily reconciled with his estimate of his estate, which he put into the list at twelve pounds. Though not wealthy he was much respected in the plantation, as appears from his election as a deacon of the church.

Timothy Ford, whose lot was at the corner of Meadow and Water Streets, had lived in Massachusetts.

Peter Brown, at a court holden Feb. 5, $16\frac{39}{40}$, was "licensed to bake to sell, so long as he gives no offence in it justly." He afterward removed to Stamford.

Daniel Paul, whose lot was at the corner of Water and State Streets, soon disappeared from the plantation; and his lot came into the possession of William Westerhouse, a Dutch merchant. July 3, 1655, John Thompson "bought, at an outcry, the house and lot, and lands which belong to it, which was Mr. Westerhouse's, for £40.05, which was thus sold by order of the court." About a month afterward the purchaser sold to John Hodson "the house he bought of the court, which was Mr. Westerhouse's, and the land which belongs to it, and Mr. Hodson is to pay the court for it, £40.05."

John Livermore, who lived on State Street, next north of Goodman Paul's corner, came to Massachusetts from Ipswich, England, in 1634. He signed the fundamental agreement after it had been copied into the record-book.

Henry Rutherford died in 1668: his widow married William Leete, Governor of the Colony of New Haven and afterwards Governor of the Colony of Connecticut.

Thomas Trowbridge was from Taunton or its vicinity, in the county of Somerset. He was a merchant, trading to Barbadoes.

The lots of widow Potter and John Potter passed at an early date into the possession of Allen Ball, though there is no record of the transfer.

Passing now to the suburb on the west side of West Creek, we find, on the corner made by the streets now named Hill Street and Congress Avenue, the lot of William Ives. He died in 1648, leaving a wife and four children. William Basset married the widow; and the family continued to reside in the house till it was sold, in 1652, to the widow of Anthony Thompson.

The next lot fronting on Hill Street was assigned to George Smith, who in 1655 sold his house and home-lot to Timothy Ford. He describes the premises as lying between the house that was Matthew Canfield's and that which was William Ives's.

The lot thus described as having belonged to Matthew Canfield must have been, if the order of the schedule is to be followed, the property of Widow Sherman before Matthew Canfield acquired it. "An inventory and will of old father Sherman was delivered into the court" in May, 1641, and soon afterward the name of (Campfield) Canfield first appears.

THE PERSONNEL OF THE PLANTATION. 151

These three are all of the lots in the suburb on the west side of the West Creek that can be located. The other proprietors in this suburb were Matthew Moulthrop, Anthony Thompson, John Reeder, Robert Cogswell, Matthias Hitchcock, Francis Hall, Richard Osborne, William Potter, James Clark, Edward Patteson, and Andrew Hull.

As the schedule assigns nothing to Matthew Moulthrop, it is doubtful whether he ever acquired a complete title to a lot in this quarter.

Anthony Thompson died about ten years after the first settlement of the town. His widow married Nicholas Camp of Milford. As one of his two brothers was childless, and the other had only daughters, he is probably the ancestor of all, or nearly all, in New Haven who bear the name of Thompson.[1]

The name of John Reeder is not found in any record later than the schedule of 1641. The name of Robert Cogswell disappears about the same time. At that early day alienations were not always recorded; and, unless it has escaped a very close scrutiny, there is no record of the sale of their lots by these two proprietors.

The names of Matthias Hitchcock, Francis Hall, and Richard Osborne follow next in the schedule. They all remained long in the town, and probably died here. "Matthias Hitchcock passeth over to John Wakefield his house and home-lot on the other side of the West

---

[1] There was another Thompson at Fairfield, contemporary with Anthony of New Haven. Possibly, from that source or some other, Thompsons may have removed to New Haven, and become undistinguishably mixed with the descendants of Anthony.

Creek," Feb. 6, 1655. Richard Osborne was a tanner by trade, and the coincidence of name and occupation suggests that he was a brother of Thomas Osborne.

William Potter removed from his town-lot, if he ever built a house on it, to his farm on the west side of Quinnipiac River. After having been for many years a church-member, he was accused of bestiality, and upon his own confession was condemned to death and executed.

James Clark removed to the north part of the town, and afterward to Stratford.

The name of Edward Patteson does not occur after 1646.

Andrew Hull died in 1643, and his widow became the wife of Richard Beach.

Besides the home-lots assigned to proprietors, thirty-two "small lots" had been freely given to as many householders, before the second division of out-lands was made. The records furnish a list of these householders having no right of commonage, in the order in which they were drawn by lot for the choice of the out-lands allowed them in the second division. Seven of them dwelt on "the bank-side," that is, on East Water Street and east of the four proprietors whose land extended from Union Street to Chestnut Street; the other twenty-five had their homes between George Street and the West Creek. The seven on the bank-side were William Russell, Francis Brown, Thomas Morris, Nathaniel Merriman, Robert Pigg, Thomas Beamont, and William Gibbons.

THE PERSONNEL OF THE PLANTATION. 153

The whole catalogue reads thus, viz.,—

1. Stephen Metcalf.
2. Adam Nicolls.
3. Nathaniel Merriman.
4. John Thompson.
5. Brother Kimberly's brother.
6. John Nash.
7. Mrs. Swinerton.
8. Goodman Davis.
9. Richard Newman.
   Thomas Mitchel.
   Thomas Morris.
   Goodman Peck.
   Another lot.
   Goodman Hames.
   Goodman Dayton.
   Goodman Pigg.

17. Francis Brown.
    George Larrymore.
    Thomas Beamont.
    Thomas Leaver.
    John Vincent.
    John Hall.
    William Russell.
    Christopher Todd.
    Thomas Munson.
    Benjamin Wilmot.
    John Walker.
    Benjamin Pauling.
    A brickmaker.
    Obadiah Barnes.
    Elizabeth, the washer.
    William Gibbons.

In estimating the population of New Haven at this period, one must take into account not only proprietors and householders, but indentured and hired servants. The records show that both these classes were numerous. The families of the proprietors contained four hundred and twenty souls, counting only their wives and children with themselves. Deducting those who never left England, and those who removed to Milford, and adding the families to which lots had been freely given, we have by equal ratio a population of about four hundred and sixty. But the houses of the Milford people were not all empty. Some of them were hired and occupied by persons who did not care to become proprietors. The number of dependents of one kind and another attached to all these families must have nearly equalled, and perhaps it exceeded, the census returned by the proprietors. Gov. Eaton returns only six; but his family is said to have contained thirty persons. In no other family was there so large a proportion of servants; but there was scarcely a householder whose family was limited to himself, his wife, and his children. Artisans and farmers had young men and boys in their employ, and maid-servants were to be found in almost every household.

If on the basis of these facts we estimate the whole number of souls in the plantation at eight hundred, confirmation of such an estimate is found in the military census, which after the elders, deacons, magistrates, deputies, physicians, military officers of a higher grade than sergeants, the schoolmaster, the miller, and masters of vessels carrying more than fifteen tons were exempted, provided thirty-one watches, each consisting of seven men, out of the male population between sixteen and sixty years of age. If there were two hundred and seventeen men liable to this duty, and thirty more who were exempt, the entire population could not have been much less than eight hundred.[1]

---

[1] The Dutch authorities at New Amsterdam reported to their superiors in Holland that Rodenbergh, or New Haven, contained, eleven years after it was founded, about 1,340 families. But, though affirmed of New Haven town, it must have been, I think, their informant's estimate of the population of the colony.

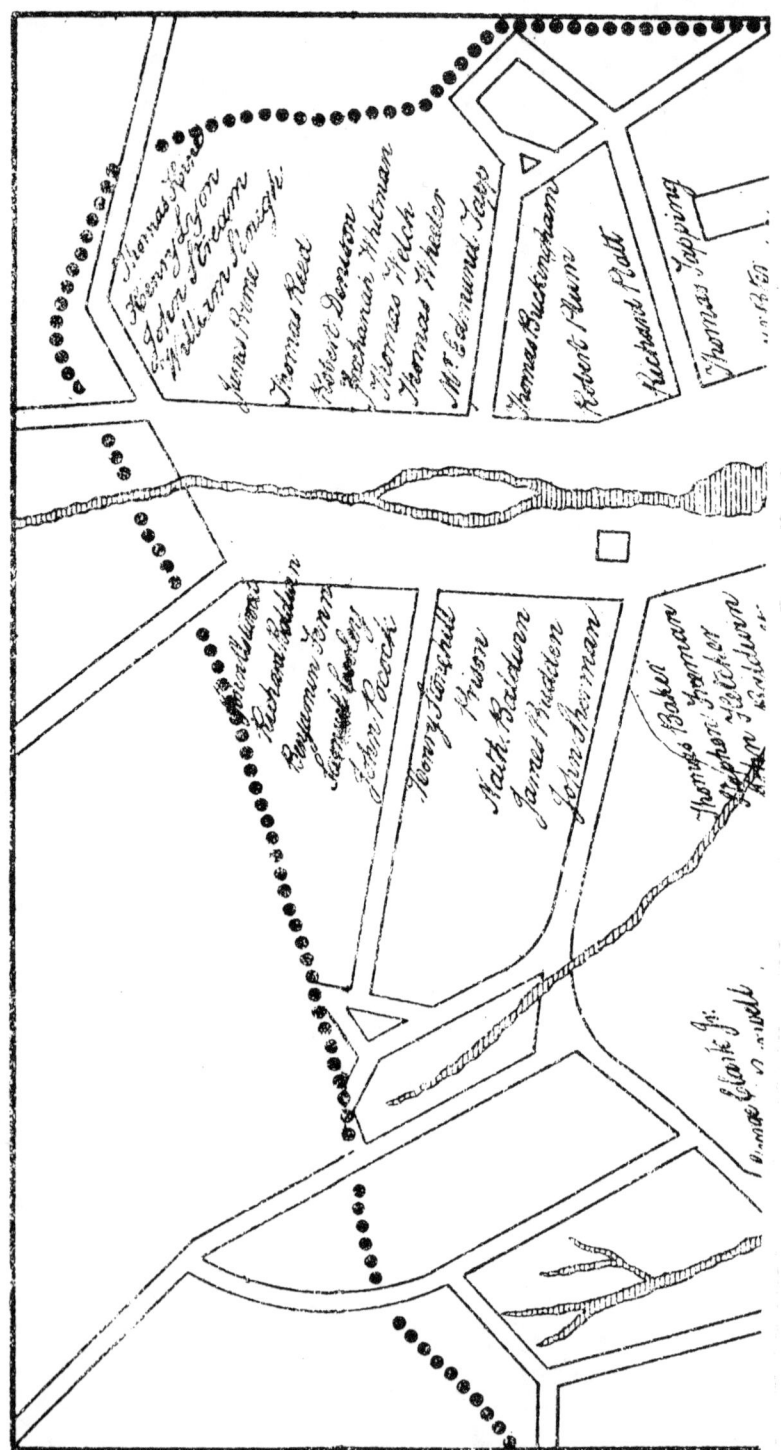

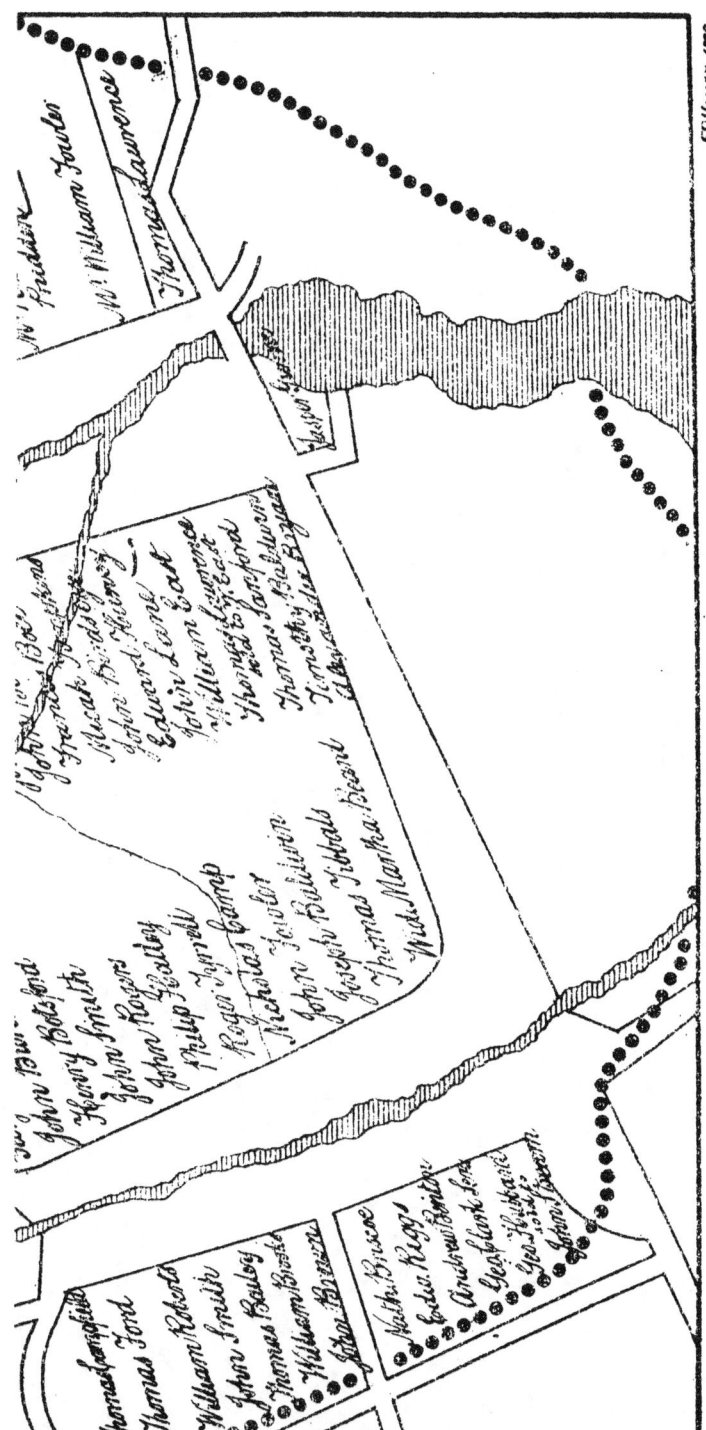

CHAPTER IX..

MILFORD.—GUILFORD.—SOUTHOLD.—STAMFORD.

BENJAMIN FENN, Thomas Buckingham, Thomas Welch, Richard Miles, Henry Stonhill, William Fowler, Peter Prudden, James Prudden, Edmund Tapp, Timothy Baldwin, Richard Platt, and Zachariah Whitman were mentioned in the last chapter as having removed to Milford. Other persons from New Haven who engaged with them in commencing a new plantation were John Pocock, Thomas Tibbals, John Fowler, Richard Baldwin, Nathanael Baldwin, Joseph Baldwin, and John Baldwin. The four last named were perhaps sons of the widow Baldwin, who was one of the proprietors in the Herefordshire quarter at New Haven. To these was added a company from Wethersfield, who, with perhaps a few from other places, increased the number of planters commencing the settlement at Milford to fifty-four.

Before their removal to Milford, a church had been organized by them at New Haven on the twenty-second day of August, 1639, the day when the New Haven church was constituted, or, as Mather reports it, one day later. The same method of organization was adopted by the people who were to remove to Milford as by their brethren who were to remain at New Haven.

They chose seven men for the foundation, and these admitted others. The names of the seven were Peter Prudden, William Fowler, Edmund Tapp, Zachariah Whitman, John Astwood, Thomas Buckingham, and Thomas Welch. Six of them had been resident at New Haven; and one, viz., John Astwood, had resided at Wethersfield.

The town records begin with a list of forty-four persons "allowed to be free planters, having for the present, liberty to act in the choice of public officers for carrying on of public affairs in this plantation." The list was prepared in accordance with an order passed at the first general court of the planters held in Milford on the 20th of November, 1639, at which it was "voted and agreed that the power of electing officers and persons to divide the land into lots, to take order for the timber, and to manage the common interests of the plantation, should be in the church only, and that the persons so chosen should be only from among themselves."

At the same court other orders were passed, as follows: viz.,—

That they would guide themselves in all their doings by the written word of God, till such time as a body of laws should be established;

That five men should be chosen for judges in all civil affairs, to try all causes between man and man, and as a court to punish any offence and misdemeanor;

That the persons invested with the magistracy should have power to call a general court whenever they might see cause, or the public good require;

That they should hold particular courts once in six

weeks, wherein should be tried such causes as might be brought before them, they to examine witnesses upon oath as need should require;

That, according to the sum of money which each person paid toward the public charges, in such proportion should he receive or be repaid in lands, and that all planters who might come after should pay their share equally for some other public use;

That the town seal should be the letters M and F joined thus:

The court then proceeded to choose for judges, William Fowler, Edmund Tapp, Zachariah Whitman, John Astwood, and Richard Miles, to continue in office till the next court of election, to be holden the first week in October.

It appears from this action taken at their first general court, that the planters of Milford, like those of New Haven, allowed the right of suffrage to church-members only, and that forty-four of them out of fifty-four were at first possessed of this qualification. This was a much larger proportion than at New Haven, where a great majority of the planters not possessing this qualification, though "having a purpose, resolution, and desire that they may be admitted into church-fellowship according to Christ as soon as God shall fit them thereunto," voluntarily deprived themselves of the right of suffrage till they should become thus qualified. One might easily believe that Milford, where so great a majority of the planters were church-members, would adhere to the rule once established, longer than New Haven; but in truth Milford within three years, and perhaps in much less time, admitted six of the ten who had been excluded, to be free burgesses while they were not church-members. On second thought one will conclude that the smallness of the minority was in itself a reason why the rule was changed. Perhaps, when four of the ten had become members of the church and of the court, the absurdity of apprehending any evil from the admission of the remaining six to equal political rights was an irresistible appeal to the majority to change the rule. There may have been less objection to the change for the reason that the rule was not, as at New Haven, a fundamental law, but subject to repeal by a majority of votes, like the common orders of the court. Indeed, the heading of the list of the forty-four reads as if there were some doubt at the time whether the exclusion of the ten would be permanent. It is a list of persons "having *for the present*, liberty to act in the choice of public officers."

At the second general court, held March 9, 1640, "it was agreed between William Fowler and the brethren (the five judges), that he should build a mill, and have her going by the last of September, when the town were to take it off his hands, if they saw proper, for one hundred and eighty pounds; or else the brethren were to appoint what toll he should take." "It was (says Lambert) the first mill erected in New Haven colony." The high estimation in which it was held by the planters is evident from the fact that when it had been injured by a freshet, they voted in a general court held in December, 1645, that all the town should help Mr. Fowler repair the mill, and he was to call for them, each man a day, till he should have gone through the town, whenever he needed help. "If he went not through the town in one year, the same liberty was granted till he had gone through."

Until this time the plantation had been called by its Indian name of Wepowaug; but at a general court held Nov. 24, 1640, "with common consent and general vote of the freemen, the plantation was named Milford." The letters in the town seal indicate, however, that the name of Milford had been chosen at an earlier date, and that this formal action was taken for the purpose of superseding the Indian name.

A record of home-lots was made in 1646, from which a map of the town-plot can be drawn, showing the names of all who were proprietors at that time, and the relative position of their dwellings; for as every planter was required to erect a good house within three years, or forfeit his lot, it may be presumed that nearly all to whom home-lots were recorded in 1646 had complied with this condition. The number of proprietors had by this time increased to sixty-six. The map opposite page 155 was enlarged from Lambert's History of the Colony of New Haven. It exhibits the line of palisades which enclosed the whole settlement, and the arrangement of the home-lots on both sides of Mill River and of West End Brook. A footway across the field, such as is often seen in England, led from the West End to the meeting-house, "the stiles to be maintained by brother Nicholas Camp at the West End and by brother Thomas Baker at the meeting-house (for the outside stiles); and for the inner fences, each man shall maintain his stile in the most convenient place; and the passage over Little Dreadful Swamp in John Fletcher's lot, shall be by a long log hewed on the upper side."

In the allotment of out-lands, a course was taken similar to that taken at New Haven. "In the first division abroad" a tract lying south of the town and east of Mill River was assigned to the planters whose home-lots fronted on that river, and was called Eastfield. Another tract west of the same river was allotted to the planters whose houses fronted on West End Brook, and was called Westfield. Each of these fields, or quarters as they would have been called in New Haven, being subdivided among the proprietors according to the estates they had respectively reported for taxation, was enclosed with a fence, to the expense of which each proprietor contributed in proportion to the number of his acres. Meadow-land was also allotted to each planter in proportion to his estate. Several divisions of upland subsequently made, were conducted according to the same rule.

We have already observed that a few families from Kent, moved by the change which took place in ecclesiastical administration when Laud succeeded Abbot, had emigrated in the company of Mr. Davenport. These were the earnest of a company from Kent, Surrey, and Sussex, which came two years later, and settled in Guilford. That the two companies were connected, and that they were in communication after the arrival of Mr. Davenport at Quinnipiac, appears from the fact that Mr. Whitfield sailed direct for Quinnipiac, and that Mr. Davenport's only child, whom his parents had left behind on account of his tender years, came with his nurse in the same ship, as also from the covenant which Mr. Whitfield's company made and signed on shipboard.¹ The covenant was as follows:—

"We, whose names are hereunder written, intending by God's gracious permission to plant ourselves in New England, and, if it may be, in the southerly part, about Quinnipiac: We do faithfully promise each to each, for ourselves and families, and those that belong to us; that we will, the Lord assisting us, sit down and join ourselves together in one entire plantation; and to be helpful each to the other in every common work, according to every man's ability and as need shall require; and we promise not to desert or leave each other or the plantation, but with the consent of the rest or the greater part of the company who have entered into this engagement.

"As for our gathering together in a church way, and the choice of officers and members to be joined together in that way, we do refer ourselves until such time as it shall please God to settle us in our plantation.

"In witness whereof we subscribe our hands the first day of June, 1639.

"ROBERT KITCHEL.	WM. DUDLEY.
JOHN BISHOP.	JOHN PARMELIN.
FRANCIS BUSHNELL.	JOHN MEPHAM.
WILLIAM CHITTENDEN.	HENRY WHITFIELD.
WILLIAM LEETE.	THOMAS NORTON.
THOMAS JONES.	ABRAHAM CRUTTENDEN.
JOHN JORDAN.	FRANCIS CHATFIELD.
WILLIAM STONE.	WILLIAM HALL.
JOHN HOADLEY.	THOMAS NASH.
JOHN STONE.	HENRY KINGSNORTH.
WILLIAM PLANE.	·HENRY DOWD.
RICHARD GUTRIDGE.	THOMAS COOK."
JOHN HUGHES.	

The exact time when Mr. Whitfield and his fellow-voyagers arrived in the harbor of Quinnipiac cannot be

¹ Inquiry for the autograph of this covenant has been unsuccessful.

ascertained; but there is reason to believe they were near the end of their voyage when they signed the above agreement, three days previous to the meeting of the New Haven planters in Mr. Newman's barn, when permanent foundations of ecclesiastical and civil order were laid. It is here given as found in the "History of Guilford" by Ralph D. Smith. Under date of "Quinnipiac, July 28, 1639," Mr. Davenport writes to his friend Lady Vere:—

"MADAM,—By the good hand of our God upon us, my dear child is safely arrived with sundry desirable friends, as Mr. Fenwick and his lady, Mr. Whitfield, &c., to our great comfort.

"Their passage was so ordered, as it appeared that prayers were accepted. For they had no sickness in the ship except a little sea-sickness; not one died, but they brought to shore one more than was known to be in the vessel at their coming forth, for a woman was safely delivered of a child, and both were alive and well. They attained to the haven where they would be, in seven weeks. There provisions at sea held good to the last. About the time when we guessed they might approach near us, we set a day apart for public extraordinary humiliation by fasting and prayer, in which we commended them into the hands of our God whom winds and seas obey, and shortly after sent out a pinnace to pilot them to our harbor: for it was the first ship that ever cast anchor in this place. But our pilot, having waited for them a fortnight, grew weary and returned home; and the very next night after, the ship came in, guided by God's own hand to our town. The sight of the harbor did so please the captain of the ship and all the passengers, that he called it the Fair Haven. Since that, another ship hath brought sundry passengers, and a third is expected daily."

It appears from this letter that Mr. Whitfield's company did not all come in one ship. The signers of the agreement are twenty-five in number, of whom one, and perhaps two, did not settle at Guilford. Thomas Nash, being a smith competent to repair guns as well as to do general work in the line of his trade, became a planter at New Haven, and is third in the list of those who signed the fundamental agreement after it was copied into the record-book. The reasons why he should reside in the larger plantation were so weighty that his fellow-passengers doubtless released him from his agreement. The name of John Hughes not appearing on the earliest record of planters in Guilford, it may be conjectured that he died at an early date, or was diverted from that to some other plantation.

As the first ship brought only twenty-three of the first planters of Guilford, we must conclude that the others arrived in the second or in the second and third ships mentioned in Mr. Davenport's letter. If the first ship arrived in June, the second early in July, and the third [1] soon after the date of the letter, we may conclude that only preliminary steps were taken for selecting a site previous to the arrival of the last division of their company. Soon after all had arrived, a meeting was held in Mr. Newman's barn, which is thus alluded to in the "Guilford Book of the more fixed Orders for the Plantation."

"JANUARY 31st, 1649 (N. S. 1650).

"Upon a review of the more fixed agreements, laws and orders formerly and from time to time made, The General Court here held the day and year aforesaid thought fit, agreed and established them

---

[1] It is a reasonable conjecture that the third ship brought the company which settled Southold on Long Island. As the first vessel is known to have brought about half of the Guilford families, the second would probably be sufficient for the transportation of the remainder. The third vessel sufficiently accounts for the presence at New Haven of the Southold Company, a problem which, so far as the writer is aware, no one has attempted to solve.

according to the ensuing draft, as followeth, viz.,—first we do acknowledge, ratify, confirm and allow the agreement made in Mr. Newman's barn[1] at Quillipeack, now called New Haven, that the whole lands called Menunkatuck should be purchased for us and our heirs, but the deed-writings thereabouts to be made and drawn (from the Indians) in the name of these six planters in our steads, viz., Henry Whitfield, Robert Kitchel, William Leete, William Chittenden, John Bishop and John Caffinge; notwithstanding all and every planter shall pay his proportionable part or share towards all the charges and expenses for purchasing, selling, securing or carrying on the necessary public affairs of this plantation according to such rule and manner of rating as shall be from time to time agreed on in this plantation."

According to this agreement made in Mr. Newman's barn, a purchase was made from Shaumpishuh, the sachem squaw of Menunkatuck, which is defined in the following deed:—

"Articles of agreement made and agreed on the 29th of September, 1639, between Henry Whitfield, Robert Kitchel, William Chittenden, Wm. Leete, John Bishop and Jno. Caffinch, English planters of Menunkatuck, and the sachem squaw of Menunkatuck together with the Indian inhabitants of Menunkatuck as followeth:

"First that the sachem squaw is the sole owner, possessor and inheritor of all the lands lying between Ruttawoo and Ajicomick river.

"Secondly, that the said sachem squaw with the consent of the Indians there inhabiting (who are all, together with herself, to remove from thence) doth sell unto the foresaid English planters all the lands lying within the aforesaid limits of Ruttawoo and Ajicomick river.

"Thirdly, that the said sachem squaw having received twelve

---

[1] This was a meeting of the newly arrived Guilford planters, and should not be confounded with the earlier meeting of New Haven planters on the fourth day of June.

coats, twelve fathom of wampum, twelve glasses, twelve pairs of shoes, twelve hatchets, twelve pairs of stockings, twelve hoes, four kettles, twelve knives, twelve hats, twelve porringers, twelve spoons, two English coats, professeth herself to be fully paid and satisfied."

"JOHN HIGGINSON
ROBT. NEWMAN } *Witnesses.* { SACHEM SQUAW, her mark.
HENRY WHITFIELD, *in the name of the rest.*"

Additional territory was afterward purchased of other Indians; but the aforesaid deed covers all the land within the present limits of Guilford.

At the time when the deed was written, the purchasers must have been already resident on the land purchased, as they are described as " English planters of Menunkatuck." Probably those who arrived in the first ship had visited the place, and prepared the way by negotiating with the Indians, so that, soon after the others came to land, all went together to their new home. If this be true, the deed was signed at Menunkatuck, though there is no proof of this in the writing itself. The presence of John Higginson, one of the witnesses, is worthy of notice. This young gentleman, now in the twenty-fourth year of his age, may have stopped at the new settlement merely for needful refreshment as he journeyed from Saybrook Fort, where he was chaplain, to visit his mother at Quinnipiac. But, if this was his first introduction to the planters of Menunkatuck, we may conclude from his subsequent history that he soon repeated his visit; for within two years he married a daughter of Mr. Whitfield, and fixed his residence at Guilford.

Trumbull says of the founders of this plantation:—

"As they were from Kent and Surrey, they took much pains to find a tract of land resembling that from which they had removed. They therefore finally pitched upon Guilford, which, toward the sea, where they made the principal settlement, was low, moist, rich land, liberal indeed to the husbandman, especially the great plain south of the town. This had been already cleared and enriched by the natives. The vast quantities of shells and manure, which in a course of ages they had brought upon it from the sea, had contributed much to the natural richness of the soil. There were also nearly adjoining to this several necks, or points of land, near the sea, clear, rich, and fertile, prepared for immediate improvement."

No list of planters is extant bearing an earlier date than 1650. About that time a catalogue of the freemen was recorded, to which were appended the names of planters not yet admitted to the right of suffrage. Two or three names of each of these classes appear to have been added as late as 1652. The freemen of the plantation were:—

Henry Whitfield.	Thomas Jones.
Jno. Higginson.	William Hall.
George Hubbard.	Thomas Betts.
Mr. Samuel Desborough.	John Parmelin, sen.
Mr. Robert Kitchel.	Henry Kingsnorth,
Mr. Wm. Chittenden.	Thomas Cook.
Mr. William Leete.	Richard Bristow.
Thomas Jordan.	John Parmelin, Jr.
John Hoadley.	John Fowler,
John Scranton.	Wm. Dudley.
George Bartlett.	Richard Gutridge.
Jasper Stillwell.	Abraham Cruttenden, sen.
Alexander Chalker.	Edward Benton.
John Stone	John Evarts.

The planters who had not been admitted as freemen were:—

John Bishop, sen.	John Johnson.
Thomas Chatfield.	John Sheader.
Francis Bushnell.	Samuel Blachley.
Henry Dowd.	Thomas French.
Richard Hughes.	Stephen Bishop.
George Chatfield.	Thomas Stevens.
William Stone.	William Boreman.
John Stevens.	Edward Seward.
Benjamin Wright.	George Highland.
John Linsley.	Abraham Cruttenden, Jr.

The planters of both these classes were at that time forty-eight in number; of whom four, namely, John Higginson, George Hubbard, John Fowler, and Thomas Betts, had not been of the company of original planters. Higginson came from Saybrook, where he had been chaplain for four years; and the three others removed from Milford. But the plantation had lost as many or more by removals from it as it had gained by removals to it from other places; and at least seven proprietors are known to have died before 1650. We have seen how Thomas Nash, who came in the same ship with Whitfield, was detached from the company. John Caffinge, or Caffinch, one of the six trustees for purchasing and holding land, and the only one of them who did not come in the same ship with Whitfield, became a planter at New Haven within two or three years after the deeds were signed in which he is named as grantee. Thomas Relf and Thomas Dunk had also removed. In the list of the dead were Thomas Norton, Thomas Mills, John Mepham, John Jordan, William Somers, William Plane, and Francis Austin.

The catalogue of planters in 1650 doubtless contains some names of young men, who, coming with their parents in 1639, had since become proprietors. If these amounted to seven, the number of planters in 1639 was the same as in 1650. Comparing Guilford with other plantations in New England during these eleven years, we must conclude that if it had neither gained nor lost in population, it had been comparatively prosperous. England, which had sent so many Puritans to America, was now governed by Puritans, and emigration had consequently ceased. Many plantations were losing from year to year more families by the removal of those who were "going home" and by deaths than they gained by marriages. The people of Guilford, depending entirely on agriculture for subsistence, and having abundance of fertile land, though they suffered in the general depression, were not so much impoverished as the merchants of New Haven.

From the commencement of the plantation till the gathering of a church in 1643, the undivided lands were held in trust by the six planters in whose names the deed was originally taken. Four of the six were early designated as a provisional committee in whom all civil power was vested. At a meeting of the planters held Feb. 2, 1642, it was "agreed that the civil power for administration of justice and preservation of peace shall remain in the hands of Robert Kitchel, William Chittenden, John Bishop, and William Leete, formerly chosen for that work, until some may be chosen out of the church that shall be gathered here." Mr. Whitfield was doubtless excused from acting in this provisional magistracy on account of his pastoral relation, and Mr. Caffinch had removed to New Haven. When the church had been formed, civil government was instituted by the members of it; and the record of its institution is preceded by the following minute concerning the provisional committee of four: viz.,—

"Into their hands we did put full power and authority to act, order, and despatch all matters respecting the public weal and civil government of the plantation till a church was gathered among us, which the Lord in mercy having now done according to the desire of our hearts; the said four men at the public meeting having resigned up their trust as most safe and suitable for securing of those main ends for which we came hither," &c.

What the *main ends* thus alluded to were, may be learned from the following extract:—

"The main ends which we propounded to ourselves in our coming hither were that we may settle and uphold the ordinances of God in an explicit Congregational church way with most purity, peace, and liberty, for the benefit both of ourselves and our posterities after us."

Their ideal church, for the realization of which they had been willing to make so great sacrifices, was instituted June 19, 1643, after the example of New Haven and Milford, by choosing seven men who might admit other approved persons. The seven who were chosen were Henry Whitfield, John Higginson, Samuel Desborough, William Leete, Jacob Sheafe, John Mepham, and John Hoadley.

The settlement of their ecclesiastical and civil polity may have been hastened by events taking place beyond the precincts of Guilford. Commissioners from the four colonies of Massachusetts, Plymouth, Connecticut, and New Haven had agreed on articles of Confederation; and these articles had been signed at Boston on the nineteenth day of May, just one month before the church of Guilford was instituted. This confederation of colonies was formed for mutual assistance and defence, and was deemed especially necessary in view of the distracted condition of England, which forbade them to expect help from the mother country in any quarrel that might arise with the colonies of Holland or Sweden, or against any combination of savages to extirpate the white people.

Such a confederation of the four New England colonies made it necessary that the plantations about New Haven, if they would reap the expected advantages of the confederation, should be combined into one colonial government. The plantations at Stamford and at Southold on Long Island were already united with the plantation at New Haven in one jurisdiction. Guilford accordingly qualified itself to be admitted, by organizing its plantation government after the pattern set by New Haven, and proposed by that plantation as a condition of union with it in one colonial government.

The planters of Guilford who were not church-members were not inferior in magnanimous self-abnegation to those of New Haven, who for the public weal and in allegiance to principle had relinquished the right of suffrage. So far as is known, none objected to the fundamental agreement thus expressed: "We do now therefore, all and every of us, agree, order and conclude that only such planters as are also members of the church here shall be and be called freemen, and that such freemen only shall have power to elect magistrates, deputies, and other officers of public interest or authority in matters of importance concerning either the civil affairs or government here, from amongst themselves and not elsewhere; and to take an account of all such officers for the honest and faithful discharge of their several places respectively."

It will be observed that by this agreement civil power is restricted to members of the church in Guilford; while at New Haven church-membership in general was the required qualification, and members of "other approved churches" were admitted freemen, as well as members of the church in New Haven. But this divergence from the New Haven rule was probably owing to the fact that all church-members at Guilford entered at once into the new ecclesiastical organization.

Southold on Long Island was settled by a company emigrating from Norfolkshire, England, under the guidance of Rev. John Youngs. As they sailed direct for New Haven, it may be inferred that their leader was in communication with Mr. Davenport, and had heard from him since his arrival at Quinnipiac. There is no documentary testimony in regard to the time of their arrival. The common opinion is, that they came over in 1640; and this opinion seems to be founded on the testimony of Trumbull, that Mr. Youngs gathered his church anew on the 21st of October, 1640. But, if they arrived in New Haven in the summer of 1640, we should hardly expect, in view of what the planters at New Haven, Milford and Guilford did, that they would be prepared for the formal organization of a church the same year. That they had been some time on the ground when the church was instituted, appears from the record "that one man sold his house only four days afterward.[1]" If Mr. Youngs conferred with Mr. Davenport in the spring of 1637, and waited to hear that the latter had found "accommodations" sufficiently ample for himself and for his friends, he needed not to wait longer than 1639. Moreover, tradition says that Mr. Youngs' company staid some time at New Haven. For these reasons it is not improbable that they landed at New Haven in 1639, and that they came in the vessel mentioned in Mr. Davenport's letter to Lady Vere, "as expected daily." Be this as it may, they not only shaped their institutions according to the pattern set by the planters of New Haven, but placed themselves from the first under the same jurisdiction. Milford and Guilford, though using the mould fashioned by Davenport and Eaton, had established each a jurisdiction entirely independent. But Southold, or Yennicot (as it was for a time called), was a part of the jurisdiction of New Haven. Hubbard says, "This came to pass by reason of the purchase of the land by some of New Haven, who disposed of it to the inhabitants upon condition of their union." Perhaps it would be more accurate to say that, Mr. Youngs' company having been persuaded to unite their plantation with that at New Haven under one jurisdiction, the magistrates assisted them in their negotiations, and took the deed in their own name as officers of the jurisdiction. That the conveyance was made to the jurisdiction, and not to the plantation of Southold, is evident from the petition of the freemen of Southold at a general court held at New Haven for the jurisdiction, the 30th of May,

[1] History of Southold, by Rev. Epher Whitaker, in New Haven Colony Historical Society Coll., Vol. II.

1649, "that the purchase of their plantation might be made over to them." But, though Yennicot was nominally a part of the jurisdiction of New Haven, it does not appear that it was represented in any court at New Haven, or that any legislative action was taken in regard to it at New Haven for several years. Stamford appears on the record earlier than Southold, as a plantation combined with that at New Haven. The freemen of Southold were for the time being, left to manage their own affairs, and no sufficiently cogent reason urged them to send deputies to the court at New Haven.

"Among the early settlers," says Rev. Epher Whitaker, "were Rev. John Youngs, William Wells, Esq., Barnabas Horton, Peter Hallock, John Tuthill, Richard Terry, Thomas Mapes, Matthias Corwin, Robert Akerly, John Corey, John Conklyne, John Budd, Thomas Moore, Richard Benjamin, Philemon Dickerson, Barnabas Wines, James Reeve, William Purrier, John Tucker, Jeremiah Vail, Henry Case, John Swazey, Charles Glover, Robert Smyth, Richard Skidmore, John Elton, Thomas Benedict, John Booth, Richard Brown, Ralph Goldsmith, Simon Grover, Thomas Cooper, Caleb Curtis, Thomas Dimon, James Haines, John Herbert, Peter Paine, and Samuel King." But some of these did not come from England with Mr. Youngs' company, and did not become planters at Southold when it was first settled. Lieut. John Budd removed from New Haven, and probably others from other plantations. Trumbull mentions Mr. Youngs, Mr. William Wells, Mr. Barnabas Horton, Thomas Mapes, John Tuthill, and Matthias Corwin as "some of the principal men."

When Trumbull speaks of Mr. Youngs as gathering his church anew, he seems to intimate that some of his company had been under his pastoral care in England. Youngs had probably been the pastor of a separate or Congregational church in Hingham, Norfolkshire, and, like John Lothrop, had brought his church with him. Though Trumbull says nothing of gathering the church upon a foundation-work of seven men chosen for that purpose, there can be no doubt, considering the close union between New Haven and Southold, that the church was gathered in that way, or that the seven thus chosen were the foundation and beginning of the general court, as well as of the church.

Stamford was purchased of the Indians by Capt. Turner, as agent for the people of New Haven, July 1, 1640. New Haven doubtless purchased the territory for the sake of securing it for planters who would establish institutions like her own. On the fourth day of November in the same year, the General Court of New Haven sold the territory to Andrew Ward and Robert Coe, the representatives of about twenty-two families wishing to leave Wethersfield, and establish a new plantation after the pattern set by New Haven, and under its jurisdiction. The terms of the sale were:—

"First, that they shall repay unto the said town of New Haven all the charges which they have disbursed about it, which comes to £33, as appears by a note or schedule hereunto annexed. Secondly, that they reserve a fifth part of the said plantation to be disposed of at the appointment of this court to such desirable persons as may be expected, or as God shall send hither; provided, that, if within one whole year such persons do not come to fill up those lots so reserved, that then it shall be free for the said people to nominate and present to this court some persons of their own choice who may fill up some of those lots so reserved if this court should approve of them. Thirdly, that they join in all points with this plantation in the form of government here settled."

Trumbull says that the whole number for whom the purchase was made, obliged themselves to remove with their families the next year before the last of November, and that the settlement commenced in the spring of 1641. He mentions as the principal planters, Rev. Richard Denton, Mr. Matthew Mitchel, Mr. Thurston Raynor, Mr. Andrew Ward, Mr. Robert Coe, and Mr. Richard Gildersleeve. He might have added the name of Francis Bell, who, with Andrew Ward, was present at a general court of election held at New Haven the 27th of October, 1641, where they were admitted members of the court, and received the charge of freemen. Their presence as members of the court is the first intimation in the records that that assembly had become a court for the plantations combined in the jurisdiction of New Haven. At the same court "Thurston Raynor (was) chosen constable for Rippowams, to order such business as may fall in that town, according to God, for the ensuing year; but is not to be established in his office till he have received his charge from this court, and signified his acceptance thereof to this court."

On the 6th of April, 1642, Matthew Mitchell and John Whitmore of Rippowams were admitted members of the court, and accepted the charge of freemen. On the same day "the plantation of Rippowams is named Stamford." The record styles Mitchell and Whitmore "deputies for Stamford," as if they had been appointed by the freemen of that plantation to attend as their deputies. Doubtless Andrew Ward and Francis Bell had received a similar appointment in the preceding autumn.

At the same court John Tuthill of Southold was appointed "constable to order the affairs of that plantation, the time being, till some further course be taken by this court for the settling a magistracy there according to God."

The court, having thus assumed to legislate for other plantations than New Haven, "ordered that every first Wednesday in April, and every Wednesday in the last whole week in October, shall be a general court held at New Haven for *the plantations in combination with this town.*"

This may be regarded as the first formal institution of colonial government at New Haven. The General Court, so far as appears from the records, had confined its legislation to the affairs of the New Haven plantation till October, 1641. At its next semi-annual meeting, it declares itself to be, in all its regular semi-annual meetings, a colonial legislature, having jurisdiction over the combined plantations of New Haven, Southold, and Stamford.

In the next chapter we have to relate how Guilford and Milford, which, though organized after the pattern of New Haven, were entirely independent, became united with the three plantations mentioned above as already combined in one jurisdiction, and how the colony which included these five plantations united with other colonies in a federation which they called "THE UNITED COLONIES OF NEW ENGLAND."

CHAPTER X.

ESTABLISHMENT OF A COLONIAL GOVERNMENT.

IN narrating the settlement of Stamford, we showed that its freemen were received as members of the General Court at New Haven. The court by so receiving them became a court for the jurisdiction. Six months afterward, when Stamford again made its appearance, the court formally declared that in its regular April and October meetings it was "a General Court held at New Haven for the plantations in combination with this town." Its records, however, were made in the same book and by the same secretary as before, and are intermingled with those of the New Haven plantation courts, both general and particular. The general courts for the jurisdiction are not distinguished from the general courts previously held in April and October by any different title, till the secretary styles it on the 26th of October, 1643, "a General Court of Election held at New Haven for this jurisdiction;" and on the following day, "a General Court held at New Haven for the jurisdiction." Thereafter, as long as its proceedings were recorded in the same book, this colonial assembly is distinguished by this title from an assembly of the freemen resident at New Haven, which was sometimes but not always contradistinguished as "a General Court held at New Haven for the plantation." The record-book of the New Haven plantation records only two courts for the jurisdiction later than April, 1644,—one a court of magistrates held June 14, 1646, and the other a court of election held Oct. 27 in the same year. Plainly some other book was ordinarily used; and probably some other secretary had been appointed in place of Fugill, who acted as secretary for the jurisdiction till April, 1644. Unfortunately the first record-book belonging to the jurisdiction has been lost; and there is consequently, with the exception mentioned, a hiatus in the records of the jurisdiction extending from April, 1644, to May, 1653. The history of the colony during this period of nine years must be gleaned from the records of the towns and of the United Colonies. After May, 1653, the records are complete, and furnish more copious information. At a general court held at New Haven on the 5th of April, 1643, the transaction of business, both for the jurisdiction and for the town, shows that the court itself, as well as its secretary, had not quite learned to discriminate between the local and the colonial government. Besides calling Goodman Osborne to account for spoiling divers hides in the tanning, and ordering "that sister Preston shall sweep and dress the meeting-house every week, and have one shilling a week for her pains," the court appointed Thurston Raynor "magistrate to execute that office at Stamford until the next general court of election at New Haven, which will be in October next," and "ordered that those four men already employed in the town's occasions there, namely, Capt. John Underhill, Mr. Mitchell, Andrew Ward, and Robert Coe, shall assist as the deputies at New Haven in counsel and advice for the more comely carrying on of public affairs."

Thus Stamford, like New Haven, had its magistrate and its four deputies. The meaning of the specification that the deputies should assist the magistrate in counsel and advice will be seen by referring to the order appointing "the deputies at New Haven" six months before, which reads thus: "Mr. Malbon, Mr. Gregson, Mr. Gilbert, and Mr. Wakeman are chosen deputies for this ensuing year to assist in the courts by way of advice, but not to have any power by way of sentence."

There is no evidence that a magistracy had been at this time set up at Southold. The freemen there held general courts in which the affairs of the plantation were ordered; and these assemblies were convened by persons commissioned to do so, and to act for the freemen in the intervals between the courts as the selectmen of a town now are. Besides these plantation officers, there was a constable at Southold appointed by the jurisdiction to be its representative and functionary till a magistracy should be settled.

Such was the condition of the colonial government when it entered into federation with the colonies of Massachusetts, Plymouth, and Connecticut, in 1643. A confederation of colonies had been proposed, and articles of union had been drawn, before any government had been established at Quinnipiac. Gov. Haynes and Rev. Mr. Hooker of Connecticut had spent nearly a month in Massachusetts in 1639, endeavoring to carry the project into effect. Various obstacles had retarded the desired union. Massachusetts, being much more populous and powerful than the other colonies, was not favorable to union on equal terms. The other colonies were still more averse to terms which implied inferiority. Besides, there were questions at issue between Massachusetts and Connecticut in regard to the Pequot country, Massachusetts claiming a part of it for the assistance she rendered in the Pequot war; and in regard to the boundary between the two colonies, Connecticut claiming the towns of Springfield and Westfield.

The union was finally consummated, notwithstanding the difficulties in the way. Their Dutch neighbors were troublesome to the planters of Connecticut and New Haven, and the Indians in various places throughout New England were hostile. The triumph of the Puritan party in the mother-country had brought to an end the large accessions of strength from that source, which till recently the colonies had annually received. Each of the parties needed, or might at any moment need, help from the others.

At a general court, the 6th of April, 1643, "it was ordered that Mr. Eaton and Mr. Gregson, as commissioners from this jurisdiction of New Haven, shall go with other commissioners for other plantations into the Bay of Massachusetts, to treat about a general combination for all the plantations in New England, and to conclude and determine the same, as in their wisdom they shall see cause, for the exalting of Christ's ends, and advancing the public good in all the plantations."

These commissioners met similar appointees from

Connecticut, Plymouth, and Massachusetts at Boston; and, on the 19th of May, articles of union were completed and signed by the representatives of Connecticut, New Haven, and Massachusetts. The commissioners of Plymouth approved the articles, but were not authorized to sign them. But, being afterward empowered to do so, they signed them in the following September.

These articles declare in substance :—

I. That the four colonies agree to be and to be called, THE UNITED COLONIES OF NEW ENGLAND.

II. That they enter into a league of amity for offence and defence, mutual advice and succor.

III. That each colony shall have peculiar jurisdiction and government within its own limits; that without consent of all, no two members shall be united in one, and no new members shall be received.

IV. That the expense of wars shall be borne in proportion to the number of male inhabitants between sixteen and sixty years of age.

V. That its confederates shall aid any colony invaded by an enemy in the proportion, of one hundred men for Massachusetts, and forty-five for each of the other colonies.

VI. That each of the four colonies shall choose two commissioners, "being all in church fellowship with us, who shall bring full power from their several general courts respectively, to hear, examine, weigh, and determine all affairs of war and peace, leagues, aids, charges, and number of men for war, division of spoils, or whatsoever is gotten by conquest, receiving of more confederates or plantations into combination with any of these confederates, and all things of like nature which are the proper concomitants or consequents of such a confederation for amity, offence, and defence, not intermeddling with the government of any of the jurisdictions, which by the third article is preserved entirely to themselves;" and that, if these eight do not agree, then any six agreeing shall have power to determine the business in question.

VII. That the eight commissioners at each meeting may choose a president by the concurrence of all or of six.

VIII. That the commissioners shall frame and establish such orders as may preserve friendship between the members of the union, and prevent occasions of war with others. Under this head are specified, the free and speedy passage of justice in each jurisdiction to all the confederates equally as to their own; not receiving those that remove from one plantation to another without due certificates; how all the jurisdictions may carry it toward the Indians; and the surrender of fugitive servants and fugitive criminals.

IX. That no colony may engage in war without the consent of all, unless upon some exigency.

X. That in extraordinary occasions, four commissioners, if more are not present, may direct a war which cannot be delayed, sending for due proportion of men out of each jurisdiction; but that the expense of a war thus begun may not be levied till at least six commissioners have approved of their action.

XI. That if any colony shall break any article of the confederation, or injure one of the other colonies, such breach or injury shall be considered and ordered by the commissioners of the three other confederates.

XII. That this confederation and the several articles and agreements thereof were freely allowed and confirmed by Massachusetts, Connecticut, and New Haven, and, if Plymouth consents, the whole treaty, as it stands, is and shall continue firm and stable without alteration; but, if Plymouth consents not, then the other three confederates confirm the confederation and all its articles, except that new consideration may be taken of the sixth article which determines the number of commissioners for meeting and determining the affairs of this confederation.

When the colony of New Haven entered into this confederation, it consisted only of the plantations of New Haven, Southold, and Stamford; but Guilford, establishing a plantation government in the following month, was ready to become incorporated into the colony as soon thereafter as the consent of the confederated colonies could be obtained. Such consent was obtained in the following September, at the first meeting of the commissioners held under the articles. At the same meeting, "upon a motion made by the commissioners for New Haven jurisdiction, it was granted and ordered that the town of Milford may be received into combination and as a member of the jurisdiction of New Haven, if New Haven and Milford agree upon the terms and conditions among themselves."

The obstacle which had delayed the entrance of Milford into the combination will be sufficiently displayed by the record of the action taken at New Haven for its admission. We transcribe, therefore, without abridgment, the proceedings at a general court held at New Haven, the 23d of October, 1643:—

"Whereas this plantation at first with general and full consent laid their foundations that none but members of approved churches should be accounted free burgesses, nor should any else have any vote in any election, or power or trust in ordering of civil affairs, in which way we have constantly proceeded hitherto in our whole court with much comfortable fruit through God's blessing; and whereas Stamford, Guilford, and Yennicock have, upon the same foundations and engagements, entered into combination with us: this court was now informed that of late there have been some meetings and entreaties between some of Milford and Mr. Eaton, about a combination, by which it appeareth that Milford hath formally taken in as free burgesses, six planters who are not in church-fellowship, which hath bred some difficulty in the passages of this treaty, but at present it stands thus: the deputies for Milford have offered, in the name both of the church and the town, First, that the present six free burgesses who are not church-members shall not at any time hereafter be chosen, either deputies or into any public trust for the combination; Secondly, that they shall neither personally, nor by proxy, vote at any time in the election of magistrates; and, Thirdly, that none shall be admitted freemen or free burgesses hereafter at Milford, but church-members according to the practice at New Haven. Thus far they granted, but in two particulars they and their said six freemen desire liberty: First, that the said six freemen, being already admitted by them, may continue to act in all proper particular town business wherein the combination is not interested; and, Secondly, that they may vote in the election of deputies to be sent to the general courts for the combination or jurisdiction, which deputies so to be chosen and sent shall always be church-members."

"The premises being seriously considered by the whole court, the brethren did express themselves as one man, clearly and fully, that in the foundation laid for civil government they have attended their light, and should have failed in their duty, had they done otherwise, and professed themselves careful and resolved not to shake the said groundworks by any change for any respect, and ordered that this their understanding of this their way and resolution to maintain it should be entered with their vote in this business, as a lasting record. But not foreseeing any danger in yielding to Milford with the forementioned cautions, it was by general consent and vote, ordered that the consociation proceed in all things according to the premises."

The action taken above was the action of the town (as a plantation about that time began to be called) of New Haven: but it seems to have determined the question respecting the admission of Milford. Three days afterward a general court of election for the jurisdiction was held at New Haven, at which two magistrates were chosen for Milford; and on the next day after the election a general court for the jurisdiction was held, at which the two magistrates for Milford were present, as were also two deputies appointed by that town. At this general court a constitution for the colonial government was adopted, the provisions of which were as follows:—

1. "It was agreed and concluded as a fundamental order, not to be disputed or questioned hereafter, that none shall be admitted to be free burgesses in any of the plantations within this jurisdiction for the future, but such planters as are members of some or other of the approved churches of New England; nor shall any but such free burgesses have any vote in any election (the six present freemen at Milford enjoying the liberty with the cautions agreed); nor shall any power or trust in the ordering of any civil affairs be at any time put into the hands of any other than such church-members, though, as free planters, all have rights to their inheritance and to commerce, according to such grants, orders, and laws as shall be made concerning the same."

2. "All such free burgesses shall have power in each town or plantation within this jurisdiction to choose fit and able men from amongst themselves, being church-members as before, to be the ordinary judges to hear and determine all inferior causes, whether civil or criminal, provided that no civil cause to be tried in any of these Plantation Courts in value exceed twenty pounds sterling, and that the punishment in such criminals, according to the mind of God revealed in his word, touching such offences, do not exceed stocking and whipping, or if the fine be pecuniary, that it exceed not five pounds. In which court the magistrate or magistrates, if any be chosen by the free burgesses of the jurisdiction for that plantation, shall sit and assist with due respect to their place, and sentence thall pass according to the vote of the major part of each such court; only, if the parties or any of them be not satisfied with the justice of such sentences or executions. appeals or complaints may be made from and against these courts to the court of magistrates for the whole jurisdiction."

3. "All such free burgesses through the whole jurisdiction, shall have vote in the election of all magistrates, whether governor, deputy-governor, or other magistrates, with a treasurer, a secretry, and a marshal, &c., for the jurisdiction. And for the ease of those free burgesses, especially in the more remote plantations, they may by proxy vote in these elections, though absent, their votes being sealed up in the presence of the free burgesses themselves. that their several liberties may be preserved, and their votes directed according to their own particular light; and these

free burgesses may, at every election, choose so many magistrates for each plantation, as the weight of affairs may require, and as they find fit men for that trust. But it is provided and agreed, that no plantation shall at any election be left destitute of a magistrate if they desire one to be chosen out of those in church fellowship with them."

4. "All the magistrates for the whole jurisdiction shall meet twice a year at New Haven, namely, the Monday immediately before the sitting of the two fixed general courts hereafter mentioned, to keep a court called the Court of Magistrates, for the trial of weighty and capital cases, whether civil or criminal, above those limited to the ordinary judges in the particular plantations, and to receive and try all appeals brought unto them from the aforesaid Plantation Courts, and to call all the inhabitants, whether free burgesses, free planters, or others, to account for the breach of any laws established, and for other misdemeanors, and to censure them according to the quality of the offence, in which meetings of magistrates, less than four shall not be accounted a court, nor shall they carry on any business as a court; but it is expected and required that all the magistrates in this jurisdiction do constantly attend the public service at the times before mentioned, and if any of them be absent at one of the clock in the afternoon on Monday aforesaid, when the court shall sit, or if any of them depart the town without leave, while the court sits, he or they shall pay for any such default, twenty shillings fine, unless some providence of God occasion the same, which the Court of Magistrates shall judge of from time to time, and all sentences in this court shall pass by the vote of the major part of magistrates therein; but from this Court of Magistrates appeals and complaints may be made and brought to the General Court as the last and highest for this jurisdiction; but in all appeals or complaints from or to what courts soever, due costs and damages shall be paid by him or them that make appeal or complaint without just cause."

5. "Besides the Plantation Courts, and Courts of Magistrates, there shall be a General Court for the jurisdiction, which shall consist of the governor, deputy-governor, and all the magistrates within the jurisdiction, and two deputies for every plantation in the jurisdiction, which deputies shall from time to time be chosen against

the approach of any such general court by the aforesaid free burgesses, and sent with due certificate to assist in the same, all which, both governor and deputy-governor, magistrates, and deputies, shall have their vote in the said court. This general court shall always sit at New Haven (unless upon weighty occasions the general court see cause for a time to sit elsewhere), and shall assemble twice every year; namely, the first Wednesday in April and the last Wednesday in October, in the latter of which courts the governor, the deputy-governor, and all the magistrates for the whole jurisdiction, with a treasurer, a secretary, and a marshal, shall yearly be chosen by all the free burgesses before mentioned, besides which two fixed courts, the governor, or in his absence the deputy-governor, shall have power to summon a general court at any other time, as the urgent and extraordinary occasions of the jurisdiction may require; and at all general courts, whether ordinary or extraordinary, the governor and deputy-governor, and all the rest of the magistrates for the jurisdiction, with the deputies for the several plantations, shall sit together till the affairs of the jurisdiction be despatched or may safely be respited; and if any of the said magistrates or deputies shall either be absent at the first sitting of the said general court (unless some providence of God hinder, which the said court shall judge of), or depart, or absent themselves disorderly before the court be finished, he or they shall each of them pay twenty shillings fine, with due consideration of further aggravations, if there shall be cause; which general court shall, with all care and diligence, provide for the maintenance of the purity of religion, and shall suppress the contrary, according to their best light from the word of God and all wholesome and sound advice which shall be given by the elders and churches of the jurisdiction, so far as may concern their civil power to deal therein."

" Secondly, they shall have power to make and repeal laws, and while they are in force, to require execution of them in all the several plantations."

"Thirdly, to impose an oath upon all the magistrates for the faithful discharge of the trust committed to them, according to their best abilities, and to call them to account for the breach of any laws established, or for other misdemeanors, and to censure them as the quality of the offence shall require."

"Fourthly, to impose an oath of fidelity and due subjection to the laws upon all the free burgesses, free planters, and other inhabitants within the whole jurisdiction."

"Fifthly, to settle and levy rates and contributions upon all the several plantations, for the public service of the plantation."

"Sixthly, to hear and determine all causes, whether civil or criminal, which by appeal or complaint shall be orderly brought unto them from any of the other courts, or from any of the other plantations. In all which, with whatsoever else shall fall within their cognizance or judicature, they shall proceed according to the Scriptures, which is the rule of all righteous laws and sentences; and nothing shall pass as an act of the general court, but by the consent of the major part of magistrates and the greater part of deputies."

The adoption of this constitution seems to have put an end to that confusion of ideas which had sometimes allowed the administration of both plantation and colonial affairs in the same court. The written constitution may have helped the New Haven men to discriminate; and the presence in the court of members from Guilford and Milford, hitherto independent plantations, necessarily tended strongly in the same direction. The colonial constitution remained substantially the same from this time till the colony was absorbed into Connecticut, more than twenty years afterward. The union of these plantations in a colonial government, and the confederation of the colony with the other colonies of New England, were auxiliary to security and peace.

CHAPTER XI.

INDUSTRIAL PURSUITS.

FROM the establishment of the New Haven colonial government, to its extinction by the absorption of the colony into Connecticut, there was a period of twenty-two years. Before proceeding to narrate the political history of the colony during this period, we propose to give some account of the various industries in which its people were employed; of its institutions for the maintenance of intelligence, morality, and religion; of its military organization and achievements; of the aboriginal inhabitants with whom its people had intercourse; and of the domestic and social life which resulted from these concurrent influences.

The leading men at Quinnipiac, having been engaged in commerce before their emigration, endeavored to make their new plantation a commercial town. Trade was soon established with Boston, New Amsterdam,— as New York was then called,— Delaware Bay, Virginia, Barbadoes, and England.

Supplies from the mother-country came chiefly by way of Boston; for the three ships which in 1639 sailed direct from England to Quinnipiac were exceptions to the custom that emigrants into New England landed in

Massachusetts. If the tide of emigration had not ebbed soon after the settlement was made at Quinnipiac, ships from England might have cast anchor in its "fair haven" with such frequency as to render the plantations in the neighborhood independent of Boston as a base of supplies. But, as it happened, small vessels owned in New Haven, and navigated by her seamen, sailed frequently to and fro between the two ports. Doubtless they sometimes returned home freighted with merchandise purchased of Massachusetts men; but there is evidence that New Haven merchants exported and imported by way of Boston, sending their beaver and other furs to be transferred to the ships which had brought them English goods.

The diary of Winthrop records several such voyages that were disastrous, and others that were dangerous, though without fatal results. Nicholas Augur, one of the earliest physicians at New Haven, occupied himself to some extent, as did also his colleagues in the practice of medicine, in commercial adventures. In 1669, "being about to sail for Boston," he made his will, as if he regarded the voyage as exposing him to unusual peril of his life. In 1676 he made another voyage to the same port; and on his return, setting sail from Boston on the tenth of September, he was shipwrecked on an uninhabited island off Cape Sable, where he and all his fellow-voyagers died except Ephraim Howe, the captain of the ketch, who, having endured great hardship during the winter, was taken off by a vessel in the following summer and carried to Salem, whence he returned to his family at New Haven after an absence of nearly eleven months. The pinnaces, shallops, and ketches employed in this coasting-trade, carried letters and packages from friend to friend; seamen and passengers rendering such service as is now performed by express-companies and by the postmen of the government.[1]

The trade with Manhattan, as Fort Amsterdam is at first named in the records, did not apparently include any great amount of European supplies: otherwise it was in general of similar character to that maintained with Massachusetts Bay. The Dutch however, being exempt from the prejudice against tobacco manifested by the good people of Boston, the merchants of New Haven, when they anchored at Fort Amsterdam on their return from a southern voyage, carried on shore many hogsheads of this Virginia product.[2] To the same market they conveyed their imports from the West Indies, such as cotton, sugar, molasses, and "strong water;" completing a cargo with such products of their own neighborhood as wheat, biscuit, beef,

---

[1] The germ of a post-office appears in an order of the General Court of Massachusetts passed Nov. 5, 1639: "For preventing the miscarriage of letters, it is ordered, that notice be given that Richard Fairbanks's house in Boston is the place appointed for all letters which are brought from beyond the seas, or are to be sent thither, to be brought unto; and he is to take care that they be delivered or sent according to their directions; and he is allowed for every such letter one penny, and must answer all miscarriages through his own neglect in this kind; provided that no man shall be compelled to bring his letters thither, except he please."

[2] Sumptuary laws were early enacted in Massachusetts, prohibiting the use of and the traffic in tobacco. These laws were repealed, in 1637, while the New Haven company were sojourning in Massachusetts; but, though the prohibitory laws were repealed, some of the prejudice which led to their enactment must have remained. The only law regulating the use of tobacco, at New Haven, was one passed by the general court for the jurisdiction in reference to danger from fire.

pork, hides, and furs. It is not so evident what they received in return; but probably the trade between the two towns was chiefly an exchange of merchandise for the supply of whatever articles might be temporarily scarce and dear in either market. The Dutch at one time attempted to discriminate between their own shipping and that of their English neighbors, requiring the latter to anchor under "an erected hand," and to pay an *ad valorem* duty of ten per cent. on all imports and exports; but were shamed into reciprocity by the sharp pen of Gov. Eaton, backed by the commissioners of the United Colonies.

Stephen Goodyear, who in the prosecution of this commerce between the towns often visited Fort Amsterdam, purchased there of the Dutch governor a ship called the Zwoll, to be delivered in the harbor of New Haven. Under pretext of conveying the ship in safety, the Dutch put soldiers on board, who on a Sunday boarded and seized the St. Beninio, a Dutch vessel lying in the harbor of New Haven, and carried her away to Fort Amsterdam, where the vessel was confiscated as a smuggler, the owner having evaded payment of certain duties or "recognitions" claimed by his government. William Westerhouse, who owned the vessel, and Samuel Goodenhouse, another Dutch merchant in some way implicated in the business, were then sojourning at New Haven, and, finding it more agreeable to remain than to follow the vessel which had been seized, placed themselves under the protection of the court, and became permanent residents. The settlement at New Haven of these strangers served to abate somewhat the commercial discouragement consequent on a succession of losses. The acquisition of Westerhouse was additionally pleasing, because he was not only a merchant, but a practitioner of medicine. Not long after he became a citizen, he intrusted a cask of liquor to John Lawrencson to be retailed. Some disorder having attracted attention, a fine was imposed upon Lawrencson for "selling strong waters by small quantities," contrary to an order of the court. Westerhouse hearing of it, "acquainted the court through Mr. Evance, his interpreter, that he knew it not to be an offence to the court that he employed any to sell his strong water, but seeing he had done it he justified the court in the fine they had laid, and he came to tender the payment. The court told him they looked not upon it as *his* fault, for they intended not to fine *him*; but, seeing he would pay it, the court considering how useful he had been in the town by giving physic to many persons, and to some of them freely, the court agreed not to take the fine, but returned it to him again."

Within three years after the foundations of government had been laid at New Haven, "there was a purchase made by some particular persons of sundry plantations in Delaware Bay, at their own charge, for the advancement of public good, as in a way of trade, so also for the settling of churches and plantations in those parts in combination with this. And thereupon it was propounded to the general court, whether plantations should be settled in Delaware Bay in combination with this town,—yea or nay; and, upon consideration and debate, it was assented unto by the court, and expressed by holding up of hands." This attempt to establish an English settlement in Delaware Bay encountered opposition from the Dutch and from the Swedes, both of whom claimed exclusive jurisdiction in those waters, and, though contending one with the other, united in resisting the English. In 1642 the governor of New Amsterdam "despatched an armed force, and with great hostility burned the English trading-houses, violently seized and for a time detained their goods, and would not give them time to take an inventory of them. The Dutch also took the company's boat, and a number of the English planters whom they kept as prisoners. The damages done to the English at Delaware were estimated at a thousand pounds sterling.[1]"

The same year the Swedish governor seized and imprisoned George Lamberton, "master of the pinnace called the Cock," and some of his seamen, on a false charge of inciting the Indians to rise against the Swedes. Finding himself unable to support the charge, he improved the opportunity to impose a fine for trading at Delaware, though within the limits of the New Haven purchase. Not long after, Mr. Lamberton, happening to be at New Amsterdam, was compelled by the Dutch governor to give an account of all the beaver he had purchased at the New Haven trading-post in Delaware Bay, and to pay an impost upon the whole.

The next year, New Haven becoming confederate with the other New England colonies, the commissioners of the United Colonies sent letters of remonstrance to the Dutch and the Swedes, and gave Lamberton a commission to treat with the Swedish

[1] Trumbull.

governor in their name about satisfaction for the injuries done him, and about the settlement of an English plantation in Delaware Bay.

The settlement of a plantation was delayed, however, from one year to another, till, in 1651, a company of about fifty men, chiefly from New Haven and Totoket, afterwards called Branford, started on a voyage for Delaware Bay with the intention of beginning the plantation so long kept in abeyance. Bearing a commission from Gov. Eaton, and letters from him and from the governor of Massachusetts to the Dutch governor, explaining their intention, and assuring him that they would settle upon their own lands only and give no disturbance to their neighbors, they came to anchor at New Amsterdam, and sent their letters on shore. "But no sooner had Gov. Stuyvesant received the letters than he arrested the bearers, and committed them close prisoners under guard. Then sending for the master of the vessel to come on shore, that he might speak with him, he arrested and committed him. Others, as they came on shore to visit and assist their neighbors, were confined with them. The Dutch governor desired to see their commission, promising it should be returned when he had taken a copy. But, when it was demanded of him, he would not return it to them. Nor would he release the men from confinement until he had forced them to give it under their hands that they would not prosecute their voyage, but, without loss of time, return to New Haven. He threatened, that, if he should afterwards find any of them at Delaware, he would not only seize their goods, but send them prisoners into Holland.[1] "

[1] Trumbull.

Three years later, as appears from the following extract from the records, another attempt was made:—

"At a general court for the town of New Haven, Nov. 2, 1654, the governor read a letter he wrote on the 6th of July, by order of the general court, to the Swedish governor, with his answer in Latin, dated Aug. 1, and the answer of the commissioners to that, dated Sept. 23. At the same time he informed them, that, while attending the meeting of the commissioners at Hartford, several had spoken with him in reference to settling at Delaware Bay, if it might be planted. The town was desired to consider which way it may be carried on. After much debate about it, and scarce any manifesting their willingness to go at present, a committee was chosen; viz., Robert Seeley, William Davis, Thomas Munson, and Thomas Jeffrey, to whom any that are willing to go may repair to be taken notice of, and that, if there be cause, they treat with those of New Haven who have purchased those lands, to know what consideration they expect for them."

"On the 27th of November the committee reported that they had spoken with sundry persons in the town, but that not answering expectation, they got a meeting of the brethren and neighbors, and for the most part they were willing to help forward the work, some in person, others in estate, so the work might be carried on and foundations laid according to God; and at that meeting they desired that the governor and one of the magistrates, with one or both the elders, might by their persons help forward that work, whereupon they had a church-meeting, and propounded their desire. The elders declared they were willing to further the work, and glad it was in hand; but Mr. Davenport said in reference to his health, he sees not his way clear to engage in it in person; nor Mr. Hooke, because his wife is gone for England, and he knows not how God will dispose of her. The governor gave no positive answer, but said it was worthy of consideration."

"They further informed that some from other plantations see a need of the work, and are willing to engage in it, and the rather if it be begun by New Haven, and foundations laid as here, and government so carried on, thinking it will be for the good of them and their posterity."

" They also declared that they had treated with the proprietors about the purchase of the land, and understand that they are out about six hundred pounds, but are willing to take three hundred pounds to be paid in four years."

Mr. Samuel Eaton[1] and Mr. Francis Newman, being invited to go with the company as magistrates, took the matter into consideration, and on the 4th of December signified their conditional assent. At a general court for the jurisdiction, on the thirtieth day of the following January, a petition was presented on behalf of a company of persons intending to remove to Delaware Bay, wherein they propounded that the court " would afford some encouragement to help forward so public a work." The Court returned answer:—

"1. That they are willing so far to deny themselves for the furtherance of that work in order to the ends propounded, as to grant liberty to one or both of those magistrates mentioned to go along with them, who, with such other fit persons as this court shall see meet to join with them, may be empowered for managing of all matters of civil government there, according to such commission as shall be given them by this court."

"2. That they will either take the propriety of all the purchased lands into their own hands, or leave it to such as shall undertake the planting of it, provided that it be and remain a part or member of this jurisdiction. And for their encouragement they purpose

[1] The person here intended was a son of Theophilus Eaton by his first wife. He graduated at Harvard College in 1649. In April, 1654, the people of New Haven, " hearing that Mr. Samuel Eaton, son of our governor, is now sent for into the Bay, which, if attended to, they feared they may be deprived, not only for the present, but for the future, of the helpfulness which they have hoped for from him, and considering the small number of first able helps here for the work of magistracy for the present, who also by age are wearing away," induced him to remain with them by offering to elect him magistrate. He was accordingly elected, and had now been in office about six months.

when God shall so enlarge the English plantations in Delaware as that they shall grow the greater part of the jurisdiction, that then due consideration shall be taken for the ease and conveniency of both parts, as that the governor may be one year in one part and the next year in another, and the deputy-governor to be in that part where the governor is not, and that general courts for making laws may be ordinarily but once a year, and where the governor resides; and if God much increase plantations in Delaware, and diminish them in these parts, then possibly they may see cause that the governor may be constantly there and the deputy-governor here, but that the lesser part of the jurisdiction be protected and eased by the greater part, both in rates and otherwise, which they conceive will be both acceptable to God and (as appears by the conclusions of the commissioners *anno* 1651) most satisfying to the rest of the United Colonies."

"3. That for the matters of charge propounded for encouragement to be given or lent, to help on their first beginnings, they will propound the things to the several particular plantations, and promote the business for procuring something that way, and shall return their answer with all convenient speed."

A special messenger was sent to Massachusetts in hope of securing recruits from that colony; for at a general court for the town of New Haven held on the 16th of the following March:—

"The town was informed that the occasion of this meeting is to let them understand how things are at present concerning Delaware now John Cooper is returned. He finds little encouragement in the Bay, few being willing to engage in it at present, and therefore they may consider whether to carry it on themselves or to let it fall. Mr. Goodyear said, notwithstanding the discouragements from the Bay, if a considerable company appear that will go, he will adventure his person and estate to go with them in that design; but a report of three ships being come to the Swedes, seems to make the business more difficult. After much debate about it, it was voted by the town in this case, that they will be at twenty or thirty pounds charge; that Mr. Goodyear, Sergeant Jeffrey, and such other as they may think fit to take with them, may go to Delaware, and carry the commissioners' letter, and treat with the Swedes about a peaceable settlement of the English upon their own right; and then after harvest, if things be cleared the company may resort thither for the planting of it."

On the 9th of April (1655):—

" The town was informed that there were several who have purposes to go, but they conceive they want number of men and estate to carry it on; now if any be willing to further it in person or estate, they may do well to declare it. It having been first made known to them, that, though they may go free and not engaged to be a part of this jurisdiction, yet they and all such as come after must engage upon the same foundations of government as were at first laid at New Haven, which were now read unto them, and though some objections were made, yet notwithstanding the business proceeded, and divers declared themselves willing to further it."

"And for their further encouragement the town granted, if any go and leave none in their family fit to watch, their wives shall not be put upon the trouble and charge to hire a watchman, the persons only which are present being to carry on that service. They also further agreed to lend the company the two small guns which are the town's, or else one of them and one of the bigger, if they can procure leave of the jurisdiction for it, with at least half a hundred of shot for that bigger gun if they have it, and a meet proportion of musket bullets, according to what the town hath, and also a barrel of that powder which the town bought of Mr. Evance. And concerning their houses and lands which they leave, what of them lieth unimproved shall be freed from all rates one year and a half from the time they leave them, paying as now they do for what they improve. Then they shall have one year's time more, that they shall pay but one penny an acre for fenced land and meadow as they do at present."

The project for establishing a plantation at Delaware Bay was never carried into execution; but the agitation of it for fourteen years not only evinces great interest in that particular region, springing out of and nurtured by the voyages of New Haven merchants, but illustrates the extent to which the commercial spirit ruled in New Haven. It shows us a people, who, having become satisfied that they could never in their present home see their wishes fulfilled, were looking for new shores, where, "foundations being laid as here, and government so carried on," the younger plantation might become "the greater part of the jurisdiction."

It is not impertinent here to observe that during this agitation of the people of New Haven about a removal to Delaware, two attempts were made by Cromwell to divert their attention to other places. Hutchinson says, "Cromwell had been very desirous of drawing off the New Englanders to people Ireland after his successes there; and the inhabitants of New Haven had serious thoughts of removing, but did not carry their design into execution." In another place he says, of the New Haven people, "They had offers from Ireland after the wars were over, and were in treaty for the purchase of lands there for a small distinct province by themselves." Mather says, "They entered into some treaties about the city of Galway, which they were to have had as a small province to themselves." If any formal action was taken at New Haven on the proposal of Cromwell, it was probably taken by the jurisdiction, whose records from 1644 to 1653 have been lost.[1] Five years afterward the Lord Protector, having taken the

---

[1] In Ellis's Collection of Original Letters Illustrative of English History is a letter of certain ministers and others in New England replying to and entertaining Cromwell's proposal. None of the signers are New Haven men. Its date is Dec. 31, 1650.

island of Jamaica from the Spaniards, offered a portion of it to the people of New Haven. A letter of instructions for Daniel Gookin, bound for New England, is still extant in the State Paper Office at London, dated Sept. 26, 1655. According to the epitome prepared for the calendar published by authority, he is instructed:—

"To acquaint the governors and inhabitants in New England that the English army took possession of Jamaica on the 10th of May last: to describe the situation and goodness of the island, the plenty of horses and cattle, and the convenience of the harbors, which are now being fortified by the English: that there are about seven thousand well armed men there, besides eight hundred more lately sent over with Major Robert Sedgwick, a commissioner in the civil affairs of the island; and that it is intended to defend the place against all attempts, and to have a good fleet always in those seas: to offer to the people of New England to remove to Jamaica, in convenient numbers, for certain specified reasons, viz., to enlighten those parts (a chief end of our undertaking the design) by people who know and fear the Lord, and that those of New England, driven from the land of their nativity into that desert and barren wilderness for conscience' sake, may remove to a land of plenty: to make these propositions to the people of New Haven, who have thoughts of removing to Delaware Bay, viz., that a part of the island next to some good harbor will be granted to them and their heirs forever without payment of rent for seven years, and then one penny an acre; their goods of the growth and manufacturer of the island shall be three years free from customs; one of their number to be from time to time appointed governor and commander-in-chief with persons to assist in the management of affairs; six ships will be sent for their transportation; twenty acres granted to every male above twelve years old, and ten to every other male or female, six weeks after the agreement is concluded; the whole number of males to be transported within two years."

It does not appear from the records whether the project of removing to Delaware Bay had been abandoned before this offer of Cromwell reached New Haven, or whether it gave place to his proposal of Jamaica; but his offer was at first favorably entertained. When it had been before the people for consideration about three weeks, the governor desiring the town at a meeting held May 19, 1656, to give an answer:—

"Lieut. John Nash spoke what he conceived to be the mind of the generality of the town, viz., That they conceive it is a work of God, and that it should be encouraged, and if they see meet persons go before them, that is, engage in the design to go with them, or quickly after, fit to carry on the work of Christ in commonwealth and also in church affairs, they are free, and will attend the providence of God in it; provided that they have further encouragement, both of the healthfulness of the place and a prosperous going on of the war, that other places thereabouts be taken, with what also Richard Miles may bring from Capt. Martin. And that this was the town's mind, they all declared by vote."

On the 28th of the same month the matter was brought before the General Court for the jurisdiction, where a copy of the instructions given by his Highness the Lord Protector to Capt. Gookin was read, with letters from Capt. Gookin and letters from Major Sedgwick from Jamaica, and the intelligence which Richard Miles (who by this time had arrived home) "brought from Capt. Martin, to whom he was sent to inquire." "The deputies from the several plantations were desired to let the Court understand what is the mind of their towns in this business." "Much debate there was about this thing, and a serious weighing and considering thereof." The proposal received less favor in this assembly than it had in the town-meeting at New Haven. Perhaps the other plantations, where husbandry was the principal occupation, did not feel so much need of a change as New Haven felt: perhaps the intelligence which Deacon Miles brought, had affected unfavorably even the New Haven people. The conclusion to which the General Court of the jurisdiction came was: "Though they cannot but acknowledge the great love, care, and tender respect of his Highness the Lord Protector to New England in general, and to this colony in particular, yet for divers reasons they cannot conclude that God calls them to a present remove."

The disposition to find a place more favorably situated for commerce, seems from this time to have yielded to a purpose to make the best of the opportunities afforded by New Haven, and to a willingness so to modify the original intention of the planters that the town should be less dependent on commerce, and give more attention to agriculture, than was at first expected.

In the attempt to write the history of commerce with Delaware Bay, we have been led into a history of the efforts to connect with that commerce the establishment there, of a plantation under the New Haven colonial government. Such a relation is, however, pertinent to the subject, for these efforts grew out of the commerce which New Haven merchants prosecuted between the two places.

Of the commerce itself there is much less to record than we have written of these futile attempts to establish at Delaware Bay the jurisdiction of New Haven and of England. The traffic was carried on by a corporation which owned two large tracts of land lying— one on each side of the bay—above the Swedish forts. On one of these parcels of land was a trading-house where agents of the company remained to traffic with the Indians, and collect beaver and other pelts to be sent home by the vessels which from time to time came into the bay.

In their traffic with Virginia the New Haven merchants traded with the English planters, and not with the aborigines as at Delaware. Tobacco was the staple export of Virginia, but they brought away in addition, store of beaver which the planters had purchased of the Indians. In exchange for these commodities they left with the Virginians supplies brought from England and from Barbadoes, as well as from home. The following extract from the record of a general court for the jurisdiction is illustrative:—

"Mr. Allerton, Ensign Bryan, and Mr. Augur appeared and informed the court, that, by reason of bad biscuit and flour they have had from James Rogers of Milford, they have suffered much damage, and likewise the place lies under reproach at Virginia and Barbadoes, so as when other men from other places can have a ready market for their goods, that from hence lies by and will not sell, or if it do, it is for little above half so much as others sell for; they desire, therefore, that some course may be taken to remedy this grievance. The court approved of their proposition, and thought it a thing very just and necessary to be done, and sent for the baker and miller from Milford, who also appeared, and, after some debate, did confess there had been formerly some miscarriages. The baker imputed it, or a greater part of it, to the miller's grinding his corn so badly, which the miller now acknowledgeth might be through want of skill, but he hopes now it is and will be better, which the baker owned; and, as Mr. Allerton now informed his bread is at present better, after much debate about this business. James Rogers was told, that if, after this warning, his flour or bread prove bad, he must expect that the damage will fall upon him, unless it may be proved that the defectiveness of it came by some other means."

The first mention of commerce between New Haven and Barbadoes occurs in a letter written by Deputy-Gov. Goodyear, advising Gov. Stuyvesant of the delivery of beef, which Goodyear had contracted to deliver upon demand, probably in payment for the ship which the Dutch governor had sent to him at New Haven. The Dutch commissary having come for the beef at a time inopportune for Goodyear, the latter writes: "I was necessitated to furnish a great part out of what I had provided for the Bardadoes; but my endeavors are and shall be to my utmost to perform my covenants in all things. I desire we may attend peace and neighborly love and correspondency one with another." This letter dated Nov. 22, 1647, must have been written at a very early period in the history of the trade with Barbadoes; for sugar, the principal product of that island, began to be exported to England in 1646. At a court held Dec. 7, 1647, "Stephen Reekes, master of a vessel that came from the Barbadoes, was called before the court to answer for some miscarriages of his on the Sabbath day, viz., that he, the said Stephen, did, contrary to the law of God, and of this place, haul up his ship to or towards the neck-bridge upon the Sabbath, which is a labor proper for the six days, and not to be undertaken on the Lord's day." As Mr. Reekes was excused on the ground that he was a stranger, and "did not do it out of contempt but ignorantly," it is evident that vessels not owned in New Haven participated thus early in transporting hither the products of Barbadoes. In 1651 Mr. Goodyear sold Shelter Island, which he had owned about ten years, for "sixteen hun-

dred pounds of good, merchantable, muscovado sugar.[1]"
One of the purchasers certainly was a resident of Barbadoes, and apparently two others; so that it may be presumed that the sugar was delivered in the West Indies, and brought away by Goodyear in his own ship. To illustrate further the use made of this product of Barbadoes as a medium of exchange, reference is made to the fact already mentioned, that Lieut. Budd sold his house in New Haven for a hogshead of sugar.

A more interesting illustration is that which Dr. Bacon thus records in his Historical Discourses: "In the year 1665, on the day of the anniversary thanksgiving, a contribution was 'given in' for 'the saints that were in want in England.' This was at the time when, in that country, so many ministers, ejected from their places of settlement, were, by a succession of enactments, studiously cut off from all means of obtaining bread for themselves, their wives, and their children. The contribution was made, as almost all payments of debts or of taxes were made at that period, in grain and other commodities; their being no money in circulation, and no banks by which credit could be converted into currency. It was paid over to the deacons in the February following. We, to whom it is so easy, in the present state of commerce, to remit the value of any contribution to almost any part of the world, cannot easily imagine the circuitous process by which that contribution reached the 'poor saints' whom it was intended to relieve. By the deacons, the articles contributed were probably first exchanged to some extent

---

[1] " Muscovado. The name given to unrefined or moist sugar."—*Brande's Dictionary.*

for other commodities more suitable for exportation. Then, the amount was sent to Barbadoes, with which island the merchants of this place had intercourse, and was exchanged for sugars, which were thence sent to England, to the care of four individuals, two of whom were Mr. Hooke the former teacher, and Mr. Newman the ruling elder, of this church. In 1671, Mr. Hooke, in a letter to the church, said, ' Mr. Caryl, Mr. Barker, Mr. Newman, and myself have received sugars from Barbadoes to the value of about ninety pounds, and have disposed of it to several poor ministers, and ministers' widows. And this fruit of your bounty is very thankfully received and acknowledged by us.'"

Commerce between New Haven and the mother-country was chiefly carried on by way of Boston and Barbadoes. Bills of exchange on London were purchased with beaver-skins and other products of New England exported from Boston, or with sugar procured by barter in Barbadoes. The funds thus obtained were invested in English goods, sometimes by the New Haven merchants in person when visiting their native land, but usually by their correspondents residing in London. These English goods were sent out in the ships which sailed every spring for Massachusetts Bay, and at Boston were re-shipped to New Haven.

Allusion has been made to three vessels, which in 1639 came to New Haven direct from England. We have now to speak of an attempt made at New Haven to establish at a later date a direct trade with the mother-country. Such an achievement was regarded as beyond the ability of any individual, and yet so desirable as to demand a general combination of effort. A company was formed, in which apparently all who were able to help, took more or less stock. This company, called "The Ship Fellowship," bought or built a ship which they made ready for sea in January, 1646. She was chartered for a voyage to London, by another association called "The Company of Merchants of New Haven." The feoffees of the ship-fellowship were "Mr. Wakeman, Mr. Atwater, Mr. Crane, and Goodman Miles." The company of merchants consisted of "Mr. Theophilus Eaton (now governor), Mr. Stephen Goodyear, Mr. Richard Malbon, and Mr. Thomas Gregson." Winthrop says, "She was laden with pease and some wheat, all in bulk, with about two hundred West India hides, and store of beaver and plate, so as it was estimated in all at five thousand pounds." Seventy persons embarked in her, some of whom were counted among the most valued inhabitants of New Haven. Dr. Bacon has graphically depicted the departure of the vessel, and the solicitude felt for her safety by those whom she left behind. "In the month of January, 1646, the harbor being frozen over, a passage is cut through the ice, with saws, for three miles; and 'the great ship' on which so much depends is out upon the waters and ready to begin her voyage. Mr. Davenport and a great company of the people go out upon the ice, to give the last farewell to their friends. The pastor in solemn prayer commends them to the protection of God, and they depart. The winter passes away; the ice-bound harbor breaks into ripples before the soft breezes of the spring.

Vessels from England arrive on the coast; but they bring no tidings of the New Haven ship. Vain is the solicitude of wives and children, of kindred and friends. Vain are all inquiries.

> 'They ask the waves, and ask the felon winds,
> And question every gust of rugged wings
> That blows from off each beaked promontory.'

"Month after month, hope waits for tidings. Affection, unwilling to believe the worst, frames one conjecture and another to account for the delay. Perhaps they have been blown out of their track upon some undiscovered shore, from which they will by and by return, to surprise us with their safety: perhaps they have been captured, and are now in confinement. How many prayers are offered for the return of that ship, with its priceless treasures of life and affection! At last anxiety gradually settles down into despair. Gradually they learn to speak of the wise and public-spirited Gregson, the brave and soldier-like Turner, the adventurous Lamberton, that 'right godly woman' the wife of Mr. Goodyear, and the others, as friends whose faces are never more to be seen among the living. In November, 1647, their estates are settled, and they are put upon record as deceased.[1]"

Besides its commerce with the places which have been indicated, New Haven made occasional ventures out of the usual channels, as opportunity offered. Boston had considerable trade with the Canary Islands,

[1] Of this ship, and of the strange atmospheric phenomenon which the people of New Haven regarded as a miraculous tableau of her fate, some further account may be found in Appendix III.

and Winthrop has put on record an attempt which New Haven made to share in it. We copy from his journal under the date of July 2, 1643:—

"Here arrived one Mr. Carman, master of the ship called (blank), of one hundred and eighty tons. He went from New Haven in December last, laden with clapboards for the Canaries, being earnestly commended to the Lord's protection by the church there. At the island of Palma he was set upon by a Turkish pirate of three hundred tons, twenty-six pieces of ordnance, and two hundred men. He fought with her three hours, having but twenty men and but seven pieces of ordnance that he could use, and his muskets were unserviceable with rust. The Turk lay across his hawse, so as he was forced to shoot through his own hoodings, and by these shot killed many Turks. Then the Turk lay by his side, and boarded him with near one hundred men, and cut all his ropes, &c.; but his shot having killed the captain of the Turkish ship, and broken her tiller, the Turk took in his own ensign, and fell off from him, but in such haste as he left about fifty of his men aboard him. Then the master and some of his men came up, and fought with those fifty, hand to hand, and slew so many of them as the rest leaped overboard. The master had many wounds on his head and body, and divers of his men were wounded, yet but one slain. So with much difficulty he got to the island (being in view thereof), where he was very courteously entertained, and supplied with whatever he wanted."

Besides merchants engaged in coasting and foreign trade, there were shopkeepers in New Haven who kept for sale an assortment of such goods as were required by the people of the town and of the other plantations. One of these was a widow named Stolyon, living in the Herefordshire quarter, in a house which Richard Platt of Milford built and still continued to own. A disagreement between her and Capt. Turner concerning a bargain in which he was to buy cloth of her, and she to buy cows of him, served to put on record specifications in a charge of extortion, from which one may glean some knowledge of prices, and of the methods in which trade was carried on :—

"1. The captain complained that she sold some cloth to William Bradley, at 20 shillings per yard, that cost her about 12 shillings, for which she received wheat at 3 shillings 6 pence per bushel, and sold it presently to the baker at 5 shillings per bushel, who received it of William Bradley, only she forbearing her money six months. 2. That the cloth which Lieutenant Seeley bought of her for 20 shillings per yard last year, she hath sold this year for seven bushels of wheat a yard, to be delivered in her chamber, which she confest. 3. That she would not take wampum for commodities at six a penny, though it were the same she had paid to others at six, but she would have seven a penny. Thomas Robinson testified that his wife gave her 8 pence in wampum at seven a penny, though she had but newly received the same wampum of Mrs. Stolyon at six. 4. That she sold primers at 9 pence apiece which cost but 4 pence here in New England. 5. That she would not take beaver which was merchantable with others, at 8 shillings a pound, but she said she would have it at 7 shillings, and well dried in the sun or in an oven. Lieutenant Seeley, the marshal, and Isaac Mould testified it. John Dillingham by that means lost 5 shillings in a skin (that cost him twenty shillings of Mr. Evance, and sold to her), viz., 2 shillings 6 pence in the weight and 2 shillings 6 pence in the price. 6. She sold a piece of cloth to the two Mecars at 23 shillings 4 pence per yard in wampum; the cloth cost her about 12 shillings per yard, and sold when wampum was in great request. 7. That she sold a yard of the same cloth to a man of Connecticut at 22 shillings per yard, to be delivered in Indian corn at 2 shillings per bushel at home. 8. She sold English mohair at 6 shillings per yard, which Mr. Goodyear and Mr. Atwater affirmed might be bought in England for 3 shillings 2 pence per yard at the utmost. 9. She sold thread after the rate of 12 shillings per pound, which cost not above 2 shillings 2 pence in Old England. 10. That she sold needles at one a penny which might be bought in Old England at 12 pence or 18 pence per hundred, as Mr. Francis Newman affirmeth."

These specifications will give the reader some idea not only of prices, but of that scarcity of money which the records everywhere make apparent. Dr. Bacon has taken notice of the fact that when Gov. Eaton died, "the richest man in New Haven, with something like seven hundred dollars' worth of plate in his house, had only about ten dollars in money." The inventories of the time seldom mentioned gold or silver coin. Rates were collected in wheat, rye, pease, or maize, at a price fixed by the court. These grains and beaver-skins being always marketable, were much used in trade. Wampum, or Indian money, consisted, says Trumbull, of "small beads, most curiously wrought out of shells, and perforated in the centre, so that they might be strung on belts, in chains and bracelets. These were of several sorts. The Indians in Connecticut, and in New England in general, made black, blue, and white wampum. Six of the white beads passed for a penny, and three of the black or blue for the same." In December, 1645, "it was ordered that wampum shall go for current pay in this plantation in any payment under twenty shillings, if half be black and half be white; and, in case any question shall arise about the badness of any wampum, Mr. Goodyear shall judge if they repair to him." The scarcity of money naturally occasioned much use of credit; the probate-records showing lists of small debts, some of them less than a shilling, due to and by the estate inventoried. The town-records also bear witness to the same fact, allowing us to see that when A owed B, and B owed C, arrangements were made for A to deliver to C some commodity which he required, and thus to cancel both debts.

Although the leading planters of Quinnipiac relied on commerce as the chief means of prosperity to themselves and to their town, they all engaged from the first to some extent in husbandry. As the years advanced and they found themselves disappointed in their town as a seat of commerce, and unable to remove to a place more opportune to their pursuits, they set a relatively greater, if not an absolutely greater, value on husbandry. For the first year or two, tillage was confined to the home-lots; then it was extended to the fields in the first division of upland. Afterward farmsteads were established in the second division; some occupied by the owners themselves, and some by tenants, or by bailiffs as agents for the proprietors. At East Farms, a neighborhood on the west side of the Quinnipiac, were the allotments of David Atwater, Nathanael Turner, William Potter, Richard Mansfield, Francis Brewster, and Gov. Eaton. The governor had another farm at Stoney River, in East Haven, consisting of fifty acres of meadow, "with upland anwering that proportion." Mr. Brewster must also have had land of the second division elsewhere than at East Farms, as that farm contained only one hundred and fifty-four acres of upland, and thirty-three of meadow. This land of Mr. Brewster soon passed into the possession of William Bradley; and Gov. Eaton's farm, "by the brick-kilns," was, by his children, transferred to their half-brother, Thomas Yale. The four families of Atwater, Turner,

Potter, and Mansfield have never enterely disappeared from that neighborhood. Mr. Davenport's farm was on the opposite side of the Quinnipiac. A portion of it remained in the family for six generations.[1] Mr. Gregson had a farm in East Haven, near Morris Cove, or, as it was then called, Solitary Cove. Dodd says, in his East Haven Register, that Gregson placed his family there before embarking for England in "the great ship;" but there is no sufficient evidence that the family vacated their stately house in the town, or that Gregson ever intended to give to the cultivation of the farm his personal attention. Mr. Goodyear's farm was north of the town, and in the neighborhood of Pine Rock.

The planters brought with them, or procured from Massachusetts, plants and seeds which soon yielded the vegetables and fruits they had been accustomed to enjoy in England. On the first day of July, 1640, a naughty boy was, by order of the court, "whipped for running from his master, and stealing fruit out of Goodman Ward's lot or garden." Goodman Ward must have given early attention to the planting of his currant-bushes, to have fruit in the third summer of the plantation's history. The English grains, especially wheat, rye, and pease, were sown, and seem to have rewarded the labor of the husbandman more bountifully than in our time, producing a supply for the home

---

[1] A diagram of Mr. Davenport's farm, as surveyed by Mark Pearce in 1646 may be seen in the Town Records, Vol. III. p. 296. "The general total of the lands belonging to this farm is seven hundred eighty-three acres and two rods." The diagram and survey were recorded by Rev. John Davenport of Stamford, grandson of Rev. John Davenport of New Haven.

market, and some surplus for export. From the aborigines the English learned to plant Indian corn, and to stimulate its growth with fish. Cattle — such as swine, goats, oxen, and horses — were suffered to pasture on unenclosed lands, and increased in number from year to year. Cows — when the public cow-pasture did not furnish sufficient grass — were driven abroad under the care of herdsmen, whose active aid they sometimes needed in leaving the soft, treacherous swamps where the feed was most luxuriant.

In the other plantations of the jurisdiction, husbandry occupied the time and attention of a much larger part of the people than at New Haven. At Milford, a few planters were engaged in commerce; and some who were artisans worked at their trades, but the population was not sufficiently numerous to support many kinds of handicraft. Guilford was even more closely limited to tillage as an occupation. In consequence of the decision of Thomas Nash to settle at New Haven, serious inconvenience was experienced for want of a smith, till, in 1652, Thomas Smith came from Fairfield on the invitation of the planters, who gave him a considerable tract of land, "on condition of serving the town in the trade of a smith, upon just and moderate terms, for the space of five years."

The annals of husbandry are not eventful, and the records afford but little information upon that subject which would interest the general reader. There were pounds and pound-keepers, defective fences, unruly cattle, fines, and awards for damages. We read in the town-records of New Haven: "It is ordered, that, for what blackbirds John Brocket or others kill, he or they applying themselves thereto shall receive from the treasurer after the rate of ten shillings a thousand." At first a considerable bounty was offered for heads of foxes and wolves; but in 1645, "the court, being informed that no man attends this service as his employment and business, but improves opportunity as he finds it occasionally, ordered that the treasurer henceforward pay only two pounds of powder and four pounds of bullets or shot, or the value thereof, for every wolf's head, and one shilling for every old fox's head, and sixpence for every young one, to such of this plantation as within New Haven limits kill and so bring them."

The great variety of useful arts practiced in New Haven obviated, in some degree, the inconvenience which the smaller plantations in the neighborhood must otherwise have experienced. Few instances occur in the history of colonization, where within ten years from the commencement there was such fullness of equipment for producing at home the requirements of civilized life, as at New Haven. The records do not enable us to make a complete list of its artisans, or of the crafts at which they wrought, and the writer has never made a systematic attempt to collect the names of such trades as are incidentally mentioned; but these are some which he has remembered, or with but little search has collected: viz., sawyers, carpenters, ship-carpenters, joiners, thatchers, chimney-sweepers, brick-makers, bricklayers, plasterers, tanners, shoemakers, saddlers, weavers, tailors, hatters, blacksmiths, gunsmiths, cutlers, nailers, millers, bakers, coopers, and potters. Of these handicrafts some are so nearly related that a workman easily passed from one to another. Accordingly we find the same person appearing as a carpenter, a ship-carpenter, and a joiner; and his neighbor described at one time as a shoemaker, and at another as a tanner. So that, with more than the usual variety of a new settlement, there was something of the versatility commonly developed by emigration.

We have already had occasion to speak of the now obsolete handicraft by which logs were sawn into the boards and planks necessary for the buildings and palings of the planters. It may seem to us a slow process; but, as sawmills had not at that time been introduced into the mother-country, it did not seem so to them. "The first recorded attempt to establish a sawmill in Great Britain was made near London, in 1663, by a Dutchman, in whose native country they had long been in use; but the enterprise was abandoned on account of the opposition of hand-sawyers.[1]" A tree having been felled and cross-cut, one of the logs was rolled upon a frame over a pit. Then, the master-workman or "top-man" standing above to guide the work, and the "pit-man" or assistant standing beneath, they pulled the saw up and down, — briskly if at work by the piece, patiently if by the day. The maximum price of sawing by the hundred, as determined by the General Court in 1640, being four and sixpence for boards, five shillings for planks, and five and sixpence for slit work, and the wages of the two men who wrought at a saw-pit amounting, according to the same tariff, to four and sixpence for a day's work, we may conclude that at least one hundred feet of lumber was produced per day by each pair of workmen.

[1] Appleton's New American Cyclopædia, art. "Saw."

The trade of carpentry had many followers in a place where dwellings were to be erected within a short period for more than a hundred families. William Andrews appears to have stood at the head of this guild. He contracted in 1639 to build the meeting-house, but let out some parts of the work to Thomas Munson and Jarvis Boykin, who, with the consent of Andrews, transferred some part of their contract to Thomas Saul and William Gibbons. The two carpenters last named did not fulfill their engagement "to make the roof of the tower and turret tight, to keep out wet," and were probably absent, at least temporarily, when the defect was discovered; for a question arose between Andrews and the two who had contracted with him, which party should make the work good. "Because there was a defect of testimony on all sides, the Court advised them to consult together, and do it amongst them, so as the meeting-house may be kept dry without delay." The name of Thomas Saul does not appear after this transaction, but William Gibbons was some years later a resident of the town. The meeting-house needing further repairs a few years afterward, a large committee of carpenters was appointed to "consider whether the house may stay safely another year without repairs; if not, then how it may be best done for most safety to the town, and least charge; also, whether the tower and turret may safely stand, and will not in a short time decay the house; and, if taken down, then what will be the charge of that, and to make the roof tight and comely again." The committee consisted of William Andrews, Thomas Munson, Jarvis Boykin, John Bassett, Robert

Bassett, George Larrymore, Jonathan Marsh, and Thomas Morris. These were, doubtless, master-workmen, having under them journeymen and apprentices. The last named wrought as a ship-carpenter, but his appointment on this committee indicates that he did not confine himself to ship-building.

Some of the ship-carpenters in the plantation, besides Morris, were James Russell, William Russell, George Ward, Lawrence Ward, and Daniel Paul. The building of a ship of large size brought in workmen from other colonies. It is impossible to determine conclusively whether the New Haven artisans were responsible for the fatal crankness which Winthrop attributes to the vessel in which so many of their townsmen lost their lives in 1646. Rev. James Pierpont, in his letter to Mather, testifies that she was built in Rhode Island, and nothing appears to invalidate his testimony. The only occasion for doubt is found in the improbability that the feoffees would purchase rather than build; but perhaps the business required a ship sooner than one could be produced in a port where nothing larger than a shallop or a pinnace had ever been launched. If Pierpont was correct in his apprehension that she came from Rhode Island, the first large ship was built at New Haven immediately after the Rhode Island vessel sailed, and by the same "ship-fellowship" to which that vessel belonged. In August, 1646, one of the feoffees desired the justice of the court about some nails that a workman had stolen from the ship. In October "it was propounded that help might be afforded to launch the ship, for Goodman Paul informed the governor that the keel would rot if it were not launched before winter.

Brother Leeke had liberty to draw wine for them that work at the ship." In the following January there was a lawsuit in which the plaintiff, accounting for the fact that Sergt. Jeffrey did not go as master of a shallop on "a voyage to Guilford, Saybrook, and back to New Haven," affirmed that "Mr. Crane, Mr. Wakeman, and Mr. Atwater, intrusted as feoffees *for the building of a ship at New Haven*, desired Sergeant Jeffrey might be spared to go to the Massachusetts about rigging and other occasions concerning the said ship."

In 1648 another vessel was built at New Haven, and the interest felt in it was so general that one can hardly believe it was the adventure of an individual; though there is no definite information that it belonged to the ship-fellowship whose feoffees had purchased a vessel in Rhode Island, and in 1646 were building one at New Haven.

The production of leather and the manufacture of shoes increased so rapidly, that, within nine years after the commencement of the plantation at New Haven, shoes were made for exportation. At first the tanners spoiled many hides through ignorance, as they alleged, of the tan of the country; but, even after they had professedly acquired skill in the use of the native bark, poor leather was sometimes produced. There was a lawsuit in 1647, in which John Meigs, a shoemaker, sued Henry Gregory of the same trade for damage suffered from the unworkmanlike manner in which thirteen dozen pairs of shoes had been made. It appears that Meigs furnished the leather and the thread, and carried them to Gregory "ready cut out," agreeing to pay him one shilling per pair for making them. Abundant testimony was borne by persons who had bought some of the shoes, that they were worthless, coming to pieces in a few days. But some testifying that the leather tore, and others that the seams ripped, the Court referred the matter to a committee of shoemakers and tanners, who reported as follows:—

"We apprehend this: that the leather is very bad, not tanned, nor fit to be sold for serviceable leather; but it wrongs the country, nor can a man make good work of a great deal of it. And we find the workmanship bad also: First, there is not sufficient stuff put in the thread, and instead of hemp it is flax, and the stitches are too long, and the threads not drawn home, and there wants wax on the thread, and the awl is too big for the thread. We ordinarily put in seven threads, and here is but five; so that, according to our best light, we lay the cause both upon the workmanship and the badness of the leather.

"Goodman Gregory, upon this testimony, seemed to be convinced that he had not done his part, but then laid the fault on Goodman Meigs, that he was the more slight in it through his encouragement, who said to him, 'Flap them up: they are to go far enough.' In this statement he was confirmed by two witnesses, who had heard Meigs say to him, 'Flap them up together: they are to go far enough.'"

Goodman Meigs being called to propound his damage, instanced five particulars: 1st, damage to his name; 2d, damage to Mr. Evance, to whom he had engaged himself to supply him with these goods for exportation to the value of thirty pounds sterling; 3d, damage in having his wares turned back upon his hands, Mr. Evance having refused to accept them; 4th, hinderance in his trade, people having on account of these shoes shunned to buy any wares of him; 5th, money paid several men for satisfaction.

"The plaintiff and defendant professing, upon the Court's demand, that they had no more to say, and the court considering the case as it had been presented, debated, and proved, found them both faulty. Goodman Gregory had transgressed rules of righteousness, both in reference to the country and to Goodman Meigs, though his fault to Goodman Meigs is the more excusable because of that encouragement Goodman Meigs gave him to be slight in his workmanship; though he should not have taken any encouragement to do evil, and should have complained to some magistrate, and not have wrought such leather in such a manner into shoes, by which the country, or whomsoever wears them, must be deceived. But the greater fault and guilt lies upon John Meigs for putting such untanned, horny, unserviceable leather into shoes, and for encouraging Goodman Gregory to slight workmanship upon a motive that the shoes were to go far enough, as if rules of righteousness reached not other places and countries.

"The Court proceeded to sentence, and ordered Goodman Meigs to pay ten pounds as a fine to the jurisdiction, with satisfaction to every particular person, as damage shall be required and proved. And further, the Court ordered that none of the faulty shoes be carried out of the jurisdiction to deceive men, the shoes deserving rather to be burnt than sold, if there had been a law to that purpose; yet in the jurisdiction they may be sold, but then only as deceitful ware, and the buyer may know them to be such. They ordered also Goodman Gregory, for his slight, faulty workmanship and fellowship in the deceit, to pay five pounds as a fine to the jurisdiction, and to pay the charges of the court, and that he require nothing of Goodman Meigs for his loss of time in this work, whether it was more or less; and the court thought themselves called speedily and seriously to consider how these deceits may be for time to come prevented or duly punished."

If the contemporary records of the jurisdiction were extant, we should probably find some legislation prompted by this case. Allusion to such legislation is made on the town-records a little later, when sealers of leather were appointed, and sworn "to discharge the trust committed to them in sealing leather according to the Jurisdiction General Court's order." It was at the same time ordered that calf-skins, deer-skins, and goat-skins which are fully tanned should be sealed, and shoemakers were allowed to use them for upper leather; but, as such shoes were inferior to those made of neat's leather, "the court ordered that every shoemaker in this town, mark all those shoes he makes of neat's leather, before he sell them, with a N, — upon the lap withinside, below the place where they be tied." "It was propounded to the shoemakers, that, seeing hides are now near as cheap as ordinarily they are in England, shoes might be sold more reasonable than they have been; and the shoemakers promised they would consider of it."

We have already seen that biscuit was shipped to Virginia and the West Indies. But, according to English usage, bread was made in the shop of the baker for families in the town. It was of three grades: the white loaf, the wheaten loaf, and the household loaf. " Every person within this jurisdiction, who shall bake bread for sale, shall have a distinct mark for his bread, and keep the true assizes hereafter expressed and appointed." Then follows the assize fixing the weight of a penny white loaf, a penny wheaten loaf, and a penny household loaf respectively, when the bushel of wheat is at three shillings and diminishing the weight of the loaf as the price of wheat increases. When a bushel of wheat cost three shillings, which seems to have been regarded as a minimum price, the weight of the penny white loaf was to be eleven and a quarter ounces; the weight of the penny wheaten loaf, seventeen and a quarter ounces; and the weight of the penny household loaf, twenty-three ounces. When wheat was at six shillings and sixpence per bushel, which is the highest price named in the tariff, the penny white loaf must weigh six ounces, the penny wheat loaf nine and a half ounces, and the penny household loaf twelve and a quarter ounces.

The inspector, having been sworn to the faithful discharge of his office, "is hereby authorized to enter into any house, either with the constable or marshal, or without, where he understands that any bread is baked for sale, and to weigh such bread as often as he seeth cause; and, after one notice or warning, to seize all such bread as he findeth defective in weight, or not marked according to this order. And all such forfeitures shall be divided, one third to the officer for his care and pains, and the rest to the poor of the place."

Iron-works were projected as early as 1665. John Winthrop, jun., interested in mining, and Stephen Goodyear, interested in every enterprise which promised to be advantageous to New Haven, united in setting up a bloomery and forge, at the outlet of Saltonstall Lake. The people of New Haven favored the undertaking by contributing labor in building a dam, and by conceding the privilege of cutting on the common land all the wood needed for making charcoal. They hoped that the works would bring trade, and that Winthrop would fix his residence in New Haven. The ore was transported from North Haven, partly by boats down the Quinnipiac and up Farm River, and partly by carts. After two or three years, Goodyear having died, and Winthrop having ceased to think of New Haven as a place of residence, the works were leased to Capt. Clark and Mr. Payne of Boston. Iron continued to be made for some years, but the institution did not fulfil the hopes of its projectors, or of the public.

CHAPTER XII.

RELIGION AND MORALS.

TWO classes of writers differing widely in their feelings towards the Puritan emigrants who came to New England resemble each other in manifesting a singular ignorance. The planters of New England never were advocates of religious liberty; and there is equal sciolism in eulogising them as such, and in criticising them for inconsistency with their professions when they expelled from their territory those who publicly dissented from their religious opinions and from their forms of worship. If the Puritans had been in power in England, they would have suppressed the ritualism of Laud as heartily as Laud punished non-conformity. Overpowered in England, they came to America to find freedom to worship according to their own consciences, and not to establish religious liberty for all men of every creed. The restrictions which had been placed upon them, and the sufferings to which they had been subjected in their native land, instead of leading them to be tolerant of other forms of Christianity, served rather to render them more earnest to secure to themselves, and to those who should be like-minded, the territory to which they had emigrated, and upon which they were to expend their labors and their estates.

They saw no other way of securing the end for which they had exiled themselves, than that of exclusiveness and intolerance.

In accordance with such convictions and feelings, the planters of the New Haven Colony not only established in the several plantations, churches such as they approved, but took care that no other than "approved churches" should be gathered, and that, if they should find it impossible to prevent the formation of other churches, the members of them should have no political power. It was ordered:—

"That all the people of God within this jurisdiction, who are not in a church way, being orthodox in judgment, and not scandalous in life, shall have full liberty to gather themselves into a church estate, provided they do it in a Christian way, with due observation of the rules of Christ, revealed in his Word; provided also, that this Court doth not, nor hereafter will, approve of any such company of persons, as shall join in any pretended way of church-fellowship, unless they shall first, in due season, acquaint both the magistrates and the elders of the churches within this colony where and when they intend to join, and have their approbation therein. Nor shall any person, being a member of any church which shall be gathered without such notice given and approbation had, or who is not a member of some church in New England approved by the magistrates and churches of this colony, be admitted to the freedom of this jurisdiction."

It is not sufficient to say, that, according to the theory and practice of the New Haven Colony, the approved churches were established by law; but since the seven men who were chosen to be the foundation work covenanted together as a church before they organized themselves as a civil court, it would be more accurate to say that the civil authority was instituted by the church, than that the church was established by the state. This method of organization was undoubtedly designed to secure "the purity and peace of the ordinances to themselves and their posterity;" that is, to exclude, as far as they could, all other forms of Christianity. Such was their design, whatever may be the verdict of the present age respecting the breadth of their scope, or the equilibrium of their justice. It is easy to see that such a foundation could not, and ought not to, endure through all the changes of opinion introduced by their posterity and by later emigrants. It is not easy to show that it was either unrighteous or impolitic as a temporary arrangement designed to secure to exiles from their native land the peaceable enjoyment of that "purity of the ordinances" for which they had left their homes, and in regard to which they were all of one mind.

The "approved churches" were of the Congregational order, in distinction from Independency on the one hand and from diocesan or presbyterial combination on the other. Some of the planters were High Church Separatists, regarding it as wrong to be in fellowship with the Church of England. Those who were more liberal had lost all desire for Episcopacy, if for no other reason because it was for them impracticable. To organize congregations, and place them under the government of the English hierarchy, would have been a surrender of themselves to the yoke they had slipped from. However they differed one from another in their theories of the church, the people of New England had, before the settlement of New Haven, with one accord, practically renounced Episcopacy. The planters of

Salem seem to have had no plan for their ecclesiastical organization till the time for action was close at hand. The adoption of Congregationalism was a surprise, at least to some of them. A few expressed their dissent by worshipping apart from the majority, and according to the forms prescribed by act of Parliament. After the violent suppression of this schism, there was no attempt among the Puritans of New England to organize congregations in connection with the Church of England. Some of them, when they returned to the mother country, showed by their adhesion to the national church that they had not been Congregationalists through conviction that Episcopacy was unlawful. Others, on their return home, conscientiously dissented from the established religion, and cast in their lot with the Separatists, however feeble and despised.

Presbyterianism was but little known to most of the planters of New Haven; and what Davenport had learned of it by his experience in Holland had led him to dislike a classis almost as much as a bishop.

Adopting Congregationalism, the people of the New Haven Colony, like their brethren throughout New England, intended by it something as different from Independency as from Presbyterianism or Episcopacy. Their views and feelings may perhaps be illustrated by a quotation from one of themselves better than in any other way. John Wakeman, who resided at New Haven, on a lot at the corner of Chapel and York Streets vacated by the removal to Milford of the widow Baldwin to whom it was originally allotted, was for some years the treasurer of the jurisdiction, the representative of the plantation in the Colonial Court, and a deacon of the church. Drawing near to the end of life he felt himself called to profess his belief, not only in the facts which underlie Christianity, but in that theory of the Christian Church which prevailed in New England. In his last will and testament he writes:—

"I, John Wakeman of New Haven, being weak in body, but of sound understanding and memory, in expectation of my great change, do make this my last will and testament. First, I commend my soul into the hands of my Lord Jesus Christ, my Redeemer, trusting to be saved by his merits and intercession, and my body to be buried at the discretion of my executors and friends, in hope of a joyful resurrection; testifying my thankfulness to God for the free manifestation of his grace to me in Christ, and for the liberty and fellowship vouchsafed me with his people in his ordinances in a Congregational way, which I take to be the way of Christ, orderly walked in according to his rules; but I do testify against absolute independency of churches, and perfection of any in light or actings, and against compulsion of conscience to concur with the church without inward satisfaction to conscience, and persecuting such as dissent upon this ground, which I take to be an abuse of the power given for edification by Christ, who is (the) only lord of the conscience."

This profession of Mr. Wakeman agrees, for substance, with the doctrine concerning Congregationalism taught by the elders of the churches, and received by the people. Even that part of it which relates to freedom of conscience, and the abuse of power in persecuting, fairly represents the public sentiment of the colony, so far as erroneous thinking, apart from the promulgation of error, is concerned; for, while banishing or otherwise maltreating those who dissented from the majority, the law-makers were careful to declare that the offenders were not punished for wrong thinking, but for "broaching, publishing, and maintaining" their erroneous sentiments. The law against heresy reads,—

"Although no creature be lord or have power over the faith and consciences of men, nor may constrain them to believe or profess against their consciences, yet to restrain or provide against such as may bring in dangerous errors or heresies, tending to corrupt and destroy the souls of men, it is ordered, That if any Christian within this jurisdiction shall go about to subvert or destroy the Christian faith or religion by broaching, publishing or maintaining any dangerous error or heresy, or shall endeavor to draw or seduce others thereunto, every such person so offending, and continuing obstinate therein, after due means of conviction, shall be fined, banished, or otherwise severely punished, as the court of magistrates duly considering the offence, with the aggravating circumstances and danger like to ensue, shall judge meet."

Winthrop's journal affords a telling illustration of the maintenance of this distinction in the neighboring colony of Massachusetts. Recording the punishment of a Baptist, who was too poor to be fined, he says, "He was ordered to be whipped, not for his opinion. but for reproaching the Lord's ordinance, and for his bold and evil behavior, both at home and in the court." That the distinction was not merely theoretical, is evident from the fact that many Baptists were unmolested, among them the first two presidents of Harvard College. Dunster, the first president, was an avowed anti-pedobaptist; yet he held the office for fourteen years, and might have held it longer had he not, in a moment of excitement, burst the bonds of his usual discretion, and inveighed openly, in the church at Cambridge, against infant baptism. For this offence he was obliged to resign, but suffered no further molestation. His successor, while approving of infant baptism, held that immersion was the only mode; and his peculiarity in this respect was known before his election. "Mr. Mather and Mr. Norton were desired by the overseers of the college to tender unto Rev. Mr. Charles Chauncey the place of president, with the stipend of one hundred pounds per annum, to be paid out of the country treasury; and withal to signify to him that it is expected and desired that he forbear to disseminate or publish any tenets concerning immersion in baptism, and celebration of the Lord's Supper at evening, or to expose the received doctrine therein.[1]" Mr. Chauncey agreed to this stipulation, and was never disturbed.

There were Baptists at New Haven, but no action was taken against them by the civil authority. Perhaps their immunity is sufficiently accounted for when we learn that the wife of Gov. Eaton was one of them. "The first discovery of her peremptory engagement was by her departing from the assembly after the morning sermon when the Lord's Supper was administered, and the same afternoon, after sermon, when baptism was administered, judging herself not capable of the former, because she conceited herself to be not baptized, nor durst she be present at the latter, imagining that pedobaptism is unlawful." Mr. Davenport, finding that others of his flock were also astray, undertook to prove in a sermon on the next Lord's Day, that "baptism is come in place of circumcision, and is to be administered unto infants;" which he himself says was done

[1] Mass. Hist. Coll., X., p. 175. Pierce's History of Harvard College.

"with a blessing from God for the recovery of some from this error, and for the establishment of others in truth. Only Mrs. Eaton [received] no benefit by all, but continued as before." It is, however, more probable that the immunity was due to the discretion of the dissenters, who did not attempt, so far as appears, to make proselytes. That there was some jocose talk about banishment, as if such a penalty might follow the dissemination of their opinions, appears in the trial of Mrs. Brewster for sundry vituperative speeches concerning the church, its pastor and the magistrates. A maid testified that "she heard Mrs. Brewster, speaking aloud to Mrs. Eaton concerning banishment, say, they could not banish her but by a general court, and, if it come to that, she wished Mrs. Eaton to come to her and acquaint her with her judgment and grounds about baptizing, and she would by them seduce some other women, and then she, the said Mrs. Brewster, would complain to the court of Mrs. Eaton, and the other women should complain of her, as being thus seduced. and so they would be banished together, and she spoke of going to Rhode Island. Mrs. Brewster confesseth the charge, but saith she spoke in jest and laughing.[1]"

---

[1] The action of the church in reference to Mrs. Eaton may be seen in the Appendix to Bacon's Historical Discourses.

The pastor, finding that she had received no benefit from his sermon, put himself " to a further task for her good," writing a treatise which was read to her in private. This effort, however, was as fruitless as the former. What course the church might have taken with her for what they regarded as the error of her judgment, or for turning her back on its ordinances, does not appear; for, at this stage of the proceedings, "divers rumors were spread up and down the town of her scandalous walking in her family." " Upon inquiry, it appeared the reports were true, and more evils were discovered than we had heard of. We now began to see that

While the few Baptists in the colony were quiet in their dissent, the Quakers were more troublesome. The first to appear was Humphrey Norton, who, having been banished from Plymouth, came to Southold, whence, within six months after his banishment from Plymouth, he was sent as a prisoner to New Haven. This was in 1658. It is an illustration of the prevalent neglect to distinguish between the jurisdiction court and the court of the principal plantation, that he was indicted before the plantation court of New Haven. Mr. Leete of Guilford and Mr. Fenn of Milford were, indeed, called in to assist; and the proceedings were afterward read to, and approved by, the court of the jurisdiction. The charges against Norton were:—

"1. That he hath grievously and in manifold wise traduced, slandered, and reproached Mr. Youngs, pastor of the church at Southold, in his good name, and the honor due to him for his work's sake, together with his ministry, and all our ministers and ordinances.

"2. That he hath endeavored to seduce the people from their

God took us off from treating with her any further about the error of her judgment till we might help forward by the will of God her repentance for those evils in life, believing that else these evils would by the just judgment of God hinder from receiving light." Seventeen specifications of "scandalous walking" were presented to the church; the first charging her with striking her mother-in-law, the second with an assault upon her step-daughter, and all showing a violent, ungoverned temper. After waiting nine months for satisfaction, "with much grief of heart and many tears the church proceeded to censure," cutting her off from its communion.

The conduct of Mrs. Eaton was so strange as to suggest the conjecture that she was either insane, or in that state of nervous excitement which borders on insanity, and that medical treatment would have been more appropriate than church discipline.

due attendance upon the ministry and the sound doctrines of our religion settled in this colony.

"3. That he hath endeavored to spread sundry heretical opinions, and that undei expressions which hold forth some degree of blasphemy, and to corrupt the minds of people therein.

"4. That he hath endeavored to vilify or nullify the just authority of the magistracy and government here settled.

"5. That in all these miscarriages he hath endeavored to disturb the peace of this jurisdiction.

The sentence was, in the excess of punishment which it ordered, worthy of the High Commission, or of the Star Chamber. It discovers in the court a hatred of the prisoner's opinions, which is but thinly covered by the specification of overt crimes. Norton was fined, whipped, branded, and banished.

At the session of the colonial court next following, the proceedings against Norton having been approved, laws were enacted against "a cursed sect lately risen up in the world, which are commonly called Quakers," imposing fines on any who should bring them into the colony, or harbor them; requiring Quakers coming in about "their civil, lawful occasions," upon their first arrival, to appear before the authority of the place, and from them have license to pass about and issue their lawful occasions; and providing penalties if they attempt to seduce others, if they revile or reproach, or any other way make disturbance or offend. If a Quaker having fallen under these penalties, and having been sent out of the jurisdiction, should presume to return, penalties increasing in severity are provided for the second, the third, and the fourth offence. Penalties are also provided for bringing into the jurisdiction Quaker books, and for circulating or concealing them.

The cruelty of laws whose penalties culminated in "tongues bored through with a hot iron" must be revolting, even to those who justify the fathers of the New Haven Colony in intrusting with political power only such as were of the "religion settled in this colony." But such penalties were not peculiar to New Haven or to New England. In England, two years earlier, a Quaker by the name of James Naylor had been bored through the tongue, and otherwise tormented. So that, however true it may be that "emigration tends to barbarism," the severest punishment with which Quakers were threatened by the people of New Haven was not invented on this side of the Atlantic.

Either these laws were very effective in deterring persons of the troublesome and hated sect from remaining within the jurisdiction, or there was little occasion for the terror which led to their enactment. Only three instances are found, subsequent to the enactment of the laws against Quakers, in which action is taken against persons thus denominated. The first occurred a few days after the laws were enacted, and resulted in a fine imposed upon an inhabitant of Greenwich for the miscarriages of himself and his wife in the use of the tongue against elders and magistrates. In the second, a seaman was sent on board his vessel lying in the harbor of New Haven; and the master was required to keep him on board till he should carry him out of the jurisdiction. The third concerned a Quaker brought over from Southold: it was ordered that the offender "be whipped, and that he be bound in a bond of fifty pounds for his good behavior for the time to come, to carry it in a comely and inoffensive manner."

Besides Baptists and Quakers, there were no sectaries in the colony of New Haven till after its absorption into Connecticut. Thirteen years after the union, the Lords of the Privy Council, through their commissioners for trade and foreign plantations, sent out a schedule of questions concerning the condition of Connecticut. The twenty-sixth inquiry was as follows: viz., "What persuasion in religious matters is most prevalent? and among the varieties which you are to express, what proportion in number and quality of people [does] one hold to the other?" To this question Gov. Leete replied one year later, "Our people in this colony are, some of them, strict Congregational men, others more large Congregational men, and some moderate Presbyterians. The Congregational men of both sorts are the greatest part of the people in the colony. There are four or five Seventh-day men, and about so many more Quakers." The "moderate Presbyterians" to whom the governor alludes were a party in the church at Hartford, including Mr. Stone, the pastor, who maintained that Congregationalism was "a speaking aristocracy in the face of a silent democracy." He, and those who agreed with him in thus magnifying the authority of the elders, were naturally called Presbyterians by those who magnified the rights of the brotherhood;[1] but there was no outward separation of them from "Congregational men," either "strict" or "large," and they did not call themselves

[1] Gov. Leete was a member of the church in Guilford, which from its beginning would never have a ruling elder.

Presbyterians, but claimed that theirs was genuine Congregationalism. The condition of the united colony fourteen years after the union being such as Gov. Leete represents, we may conclude that in the colony of New Haven, previous to the union, there was to all intents and purposes entire ecclesiastical uniformity.

As another inquiry of the commissioners related to religion, we may as well record the reply of Gov. Leete. Though covering the whole territory of Connecticut, it throws light on the religious condition of that portion of it which a few years before had been the jurisdiction of New Haven. The twenty-seventh inquiry was: "What course is taken for the instructing of the people in the Christian religion? How many churches and ministers are there within your government, and how many are yet wanting for the accommodation of your corporation?" The reply was, "(1) Great care is taken for the instruction of the people in the Christian religion, by ministers catechising of them, and preaching to them twice every Sabbath day, and sometimes lecture days; and so by masters of families instructing or catechising their children and servants, being so required to do by law. (2) In our corporation are twenty-six towns, and there are one and twenty churches in them. (3) There is, in every town in our colony, a settled minister, except it be in two towns new begun; and they are seeking out for ministers to settle amongst them."

It was held in those days, that there should be in every church, if possible, a pastor, a teacher, a ruling elder, and one or more deacons. In the church at New Haven Mr. Davenport was chosen pastor, and Robert

Newman and Matthew Gilbert deacons, soon after the organization. In 1644 Rev. William Hooke was ordained teacher; and about the same time Robert Newman, one of the deacons, was ordained ruling elder.[1] "Thus," says Dr. Bacon, "the church became completely supplied with the officers which every church in that day was supposed to need. It had within itself a complete presbytery,—a full body of ordained elders, competent to maintain a regular succession, without any dependence on the supposed ordaining power of ministers out of the church, and without any necessity of resorting to the extraordinary measure of ordination by persons specially delegated for that purpose. The three elders—one of whom was to give attention chiefly to the administration of the order and government of the church, while the others were to labor in word and doctrine—were all equally and in the same sense 'elders,' or 'overseers,' of the flock of God. The one was a mere elder; but the others were elders called to the work of preaching. The distinction between pastor and teacher was theoretical, rather than of any practical importance. Both were in the highest sense ministers of the gospel; as colleagues they preached by turns on the Lord's Day, and on all other public occasions; they had an equal share in the administration

---

[1] Robert Newman returned to England, and no one was appointed to succeed him as ruling elder. Mr. Hooke also returned to the mother country, and was succeeded by Rev. Nicholas Street. Mr. Street was born in Taunton, England, was educated at Oxford University, and had been teacher of the church in Taunton in the colony of Plymouth. He was installed at New Haven, according to the church record, Nov. 26, or, as Davenport writes in a letter to John Winthrop, jun. (Mass. Hist. Coll. XXXVII., 507), Nov. 23, 1659.

of discipline; and if Mr. Davenport was more venerated than Mr. Hooke, and had more influence in the church and in the community generally, it was more because of the acknowledged personal superiority of the former in respect to age and gifts and learning, than because of any official disparity. The Cambridge platform, which was framed in 1648, and with which Mr. Davenport, in his writings on church government, fully agrees, says, in defining the difference between pastors and teachers, 'The pastor's special work is to attend to exhortation, and therein to administer a word of wisdom; the teacher is to attend to doctrine, and therein to administer a word of knowledge; and either of them to administer the seals of that covenant, unto the dispensation of which they are alike called; as also to execute the censures: being but a kind of application of the Word: the preaching of which, together with the application thereof, they are alike charged withal.' The pastor and teacher gave themselves wholly to their ministry and their studies, and accordingly received a support from the people: they might properly be called clergymen. The ruling elder was not necessarily educated for the ministry: he might without impropriety pursue some secular calling; and, though he fed the flock occasionally with 'a word of admonition,' the ministry was not his profession. Inasmuch as he did not live by the ministry, he was a layman."

But there was perhaps no other church in the colony provided with a presbytery complete according to the Cambridge platform, than that of New Haven. The church at Guilford had for its pastor Rev. Henry Whitfield, under whose guidance most of the people had crossed the ocean; and for its teacher, Rev. John Higginson, a son-in-law of its pastor. But, to borrow the language of one of its later pastors, "they never had, and upon principle never would admit, a ruling elder. Although in all other things Mr. Whitfield and Mr. Davenport and their churches exactly agreed, yet in this they were quite different. I have made diligent inquiry into the subject, many years ago, with old people who were personally acquainted with the first members of the church. They all invariably agree, that as Mr. Whitfield was never ordained in any sense at Guilford, but officiated as their pastor by virtue of his ordination in England, so neither he nor the church would allow of a ruling elder; and the ancient tradition in the church here was, that New Haven, and afterward other churches in the colony, conformed their judgment and practice to Mr. Whitfield's and his church's judgment.[1]" After the return of Mr. Whitfield to England, Mr. Higginson was both pastor and teacher, until 1659, when he removed to Salem. At Milford Mr. Prudden was the only preaching elder, Rev. John Sherman, a resident of the town, having declined the office of teacher to which the church had elected him; but Zachariah Whitman, as ruling elder, was associated with Mr. Prudden in the care of the church. Mr. Prudden, dying in 1656, was succeeded, after an interim of four years, by Rev. Roger Newton, who, like his predecessor, was the only preaching elder. No records of the church at Southold of an earlier date than 1745 being extant, we cannot ascertain whether it had a ruling elder; but there is no

---

[1] Letter of Rev. Thomas Ruggles, author of a History of Guilford, to Rev. Dr. Stiles; printed in Mass. Hist. Coll., X. 91.

reason to doubt that Mr. Youngs was its only preaching officer. At Stamford Rev. John Bishop was both pastor and teacher; as was Rev. Abraham Pierson at Branford, when, with the approbation of the Jurisdiction Court, a settlement had been made, and a church had been gathered, in that place.

The preaching elders were maintained from the treasury of *the church*, and not of the town, the treasury being supplied by contributions made every Lord's Day; but these contributions were, if not from the beginning, certainly very soon after the beginning, made in accordance with a pledge which every inhabitant was required to give, that he would contribute a certain amount yearly for the maintenance of the ministry. The law respecting such pledges reads as follows:—

"It is ordered, that when and so oft as there shall be cause, either through the perverseness or negligence of men, the particular court in each plantation, or, where no court is held, the deputies last chosen for the General Court, with the constable, or other officer for preserving peace, and so forth, shall call all the inhabitants, whether planters or sojourners, before them, and desire every one particularly to set down what proportion he is willing and able to allow yearly, while God continues his estate, toward the maintenance of the ministry there. But if any one or more, to the discouragement or hindrance of this work, refuse or delay, or set down an unmeet proportion; in any and every such case, the particular court, or deputies and constable as aforesaid, shall rate and assess every such person, according to his visible estate there, with due moderation and in equal proportion with his neighbors. But if after that he deny or delay, or tender unsuitable payment, it shall be recovered as other just debts. And it is further ordered, That if any man remove from the plantation where he lived, and leave or suffer his land there, or any part of it, to lie unimproved, neither selling it, nor freely surrendering it to the plantation, he shall pay one-third part what he paid before for his movable estate and lands also. And in each plantation where ministers' maintenance is allowed in a free way without rating, he shall pay one-third part of what other men of the lowest rank enjoying such accommodations, do pay; but if any removing, settle near the said plantation, and continue still to improve his land, or such part of it as seems good to himself, he shall pay two-thirds of what he paid before when he lived in the plantation, both for movable estate and land, or two-thirds part of what others of like accommodation pay."

There, is perhaps, an intimation in the law, that the amount which each inhabitant should pay for the maintenance of the elders was determined, in some of the plantations, by assessors and not by himself. Practically there could not be much difference in the two methods, since, if the "free way without rating" was practised, the order of the court obliged non-resident proprietors and unwilling residents to pay according to their taxable estates.

The general synod at Cambridge, which in 1648 prepared, agreed to, and published the system of ecclesiastical polity known as the Cambridge platform, included representatives of the churches in the colony of New Haven; and this platform fairly represents the Congregationalism of these churches from their organization to the formation of the Saybrook platform in the early part of the eighteenth century. The same synod took action on the confession of faith published by the Westminister Assembly of divines, as follows:—

"This synod, having perused and considered, with much gladness of heart and thankfulness to God, the confession of faith published of late by the reverend assembly in England do judge it to be very holy, orthodox, and judicious in all matters of faith;

and do therefore freely and fully consent thereunto, for the substance thereof. Only in those things which have respect to church government and discipline, we refer ourselves to the platform of church discipline agreed upon by this present assembly."

The Presbyterian party being at that time in the ascendant in England, the synod adopted the Westminster Confession, instead of framing one for themselves, for the sake of vindicating in the mother country the orthodoxy of New England Congregationalists. They say in their preface:—

"We, who are by nature Englishmen, do desire to hold forth the same doctrine of religion, especially in fundamentals, which we see and know to be held by the churches of England." "By this, our professed consent and free concurrence with them in all the doctrinals of religion, we hope it may appear to the world, that, as we are a remnant of the people of the same nation with them, so we are professors of the same common faith, and fellow-heirs of the same common salvation."

If the Church of England had been at that time Episcopal, the Cambridge Synod would with equal willingness have adopted the doctrinal part of the Thirty-Nine Articles. These articles they heartily received, according to the interpretation generally given to them in the reign of Elizabeth, in the first part of the reign of James I., and by the Calvinistic party in the Church of England subsequently. The pastors and teachers of the churches in the New Haven colony retained the Calvinistic theology in which they had been indoctrinated in the universities, and believed, as did their teachers, that it was consistent with and embodied in the Thirty-Nine Articles. After the restoration of the Thirty-Nine Articles in the national church of England, the churches of Connecticut publicly agreed with the dissenters in the mother country, in adopting them as a standard of orthodoxy. The Heads of Agreement which accompany the Saybrook platform say, "As to what appertains to soundness of judgment in matters of faith, we esteem it sufficient that a church acknowledge the Scriptures to be the word of God, the perfect and only rule of faith and practice, and own either the doctrinal part of those commonly called the articles of the Church of England, or the confession, or catechisms, shorter or longer, compiled by the assembly at Westminster, or the confession agreed on at the Savoy, to be agreeable to the said rule." This declaration, though made after the first generation had passed away, would have been uttered by the fathers as willingly as by their children, if justified by an appropriate occasion.

In each plantation there was a building in which the church assembled for worship. It was built and owned by the proprietors of the plantation, and was used for meetings of the General Court as well as of the church. Having this double design, it was not called a church or a church-house, as an edifice used only for church services would naturally be denominated, but a meeting-house. This two-fold use of the edifice did not offend the religious sentiment of the people; for the court was composed of church-members who came together in a religious spirit to serve God in the business of the court as truly as they served him in the ordinances of the church. It was not a temporary expedient such as a people believing in a more thorough separation of

Church and State might adopt in a new plantation till they were able to provide more appropriately for each; but it was in its design a permanent arrangement befitting a theocratic constitution of society.

The meeting-houses in the several plantations differed

A MEETING-HOUSE OF THE SEVENTEENTH CENTURY.

in size, but were similar in external appearance and internal arrangement. The meeting-house at Guilford was, however, of stone, as were a few of the principal dwellings in that plantation. That at Milford was of wood, was forty feet square, and had a roof in shape like a truncated pyramid surmounted by a "tower." That at New Haven was of wood, was fifty feet square, and had a roof like that of the Milford house, and a "tower and turret." There were also "banisters and rails on the meeting-house top," which probably enclosed that higher and flatter portion of the roof from which the tower ascended. It was built in accordance with an order of the General Court, passed Nov. 25, 1639. The estimated cost was £500; and, as the last instalment of the tax levied to raise that sum was made payable in the following May, one may infer that the expectation was that it would be finished within a year. It stood in the market-place, certainly near its center, and presumably exactly upon it.[1] The frame being insufficient to support the weight of the tower and turret, it became necessary to shore up the posts. In time it was found that the shores were impaired by decay, and fears were expressed that the house would fall. In January, 1660, there was a discussion at a general court concerning the meeting-house. Some were in favor of taking down both the tower and the turret. Some were for removing the turret, and allowing the tower to remain. Some thought that both tower and turret might be retained, if the shores

[1] See in Mass. Hist. Coll. XL., p. 474, a curious essay on the laying out of towns. The author is unknown, and it is without address or date. It seems to have been written before the settlement of New Haven, but lays down the same principles as ruled in laying out New Haven. The meeting-house is to be "the centre of the whole circumference." The houses are to be orderly placed about it. Then there is to be a first division of lands extending from the center one-half the distance to the outside boundary, to be improved in the earlier years of the settlement, before the second division comes into use.

were renewed, and the frame were strengthened with braces within the house. In conclusion it was "determined, that, besides the renewing of the shores, both turret and tower shall be taken down." Probably the order to take down the tower and turret was not executed, for a committee on the meeting-house reported, Aug. 11, 1662, that "they thought it good that the upper turret be taken down. The thing being debated, it was put to vote, and concluded to be done, and left to the townsmen to see to get it done."

The internal arrangement of a meeting-house is shown in the accompanying plan. Behind the pulpit was the seat of the teaching elders; immediately in front of it was the seat of the ruling elder; and before the seat of the ruling elder was the seat of the deacons, having a shelf in front of it, which ordinarily hung suspended from hinges, so as to present its broad surface to the congregation, but, when needed for a communion-table, was elevated to a horizontal position. The report of the committee for seating people in the meeting-house at New Haven, in 1656, shows that the deacons were expected to sit one at each end of their official seat, and that each of them had his own place,—four men being appointed to sit before Deacon Gilbert's seat, and three women before Deacon Miles's seat. In every such meeting-house the sexes were seated apart, the men on one side, and the women on the other side, of the middle "alley." The soldiers' seats were, however, an exception to the rule, one-half of them being on the women's side of the house. In the meeting-house at New Haven the "forms" between the "alleys" were long enough to accommodate seven persons, but only two or three were assigned to those near the pulpit, the space allowed to each person having some proportion to his dignity. At "the upper end" were five cross-seats and "one little seat." The seat-

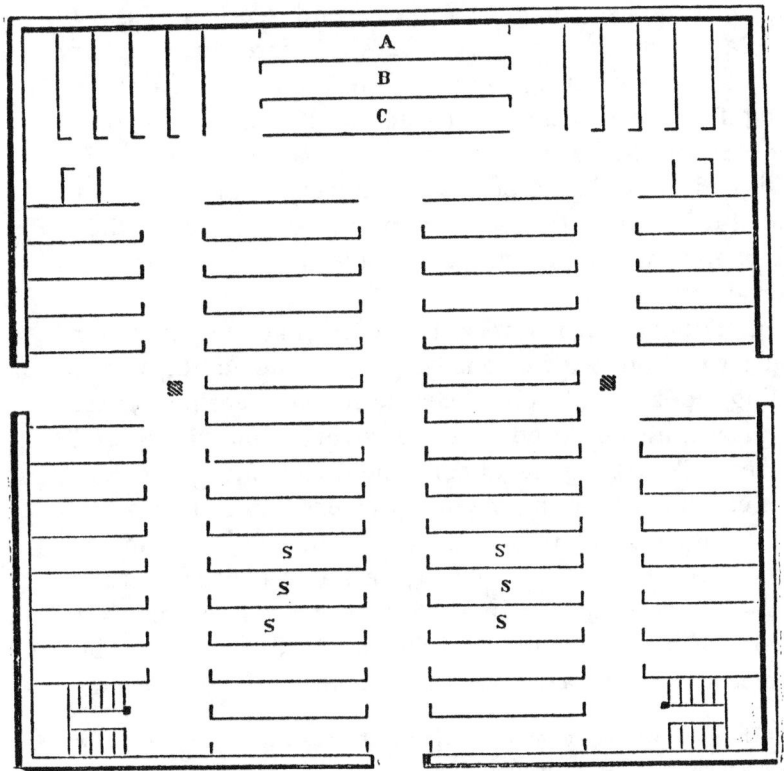

GROUND-PLAN OF A MEETING-HOUSE.
A. Teaching Elders. B. Ruling Elders. C. Deacons. S. Soldiers.

ing of 1656 assigns two men to "the bench before the little seat," and, on the opposite side of the house, two women to "the seat before the little seat." In like manner persons were assigned to sit in front of every front seat in the house. The first seating which is recorded placed only proprietors and their wives. The second was more liberal, including apparently all heads of families, but, with the exception of "Mr. Goodyear's daughters," no unmarried women. This more liberal policy in the assignment of seats rendered it necessary to place benches in the "alleys," before every front seat. In the meeting-house at New Haven there were two pillars, one on that part where the men were seated, and one on the women's side. Apparently they were designed to aid in supporting the weight of the tower and turret. On the accompanying ground-plan they are represented as placed in the side "alleys," half way from front to rear.

In January, 1647, "it was ordered that the particular court with the two deacons, taking in the advice of the ruling elder, should place people in the meeting-house, and it was also ordered that the governor may be spared therein.[1]" At a general court held the tenth of March, this committee having meanwhile performed their duty, "the names of people, as they were seated in the meeting-house, were read in court, and it was ordered they should be recorded." In 1656, nine years later, another record was made, and in 1662 a third record of the names of people as they were seated in the meeting-

[1] The governor may have been spared, because, his wife being now excommunicate, no seat could be assigned to her by name. It will be seen, however, that there was plenty of room for her in the seat with "old Mrs. Eaton." Nine years later, the governor's mother being now dead, the seat was assigned to his wife under the adroit circumlocution, "The first as it was," but the committee's faculty of circumlocution failed when they came to the bench in front of that seat, and they wrote, "Before Mrs. Eaton's seat."

house. As a comparison of these records may assist the reader to note the increase of the congregation and the change in its personnel, we have transcribed them to be printed in Appendix IV. At the town meeting at which the second list of names was read, "it was agreed that (because there want seats for some, and that the alleys are so filled with blocks, stools, and chairs, that it hinders a free passage) low benches shall be made at the end of the seats on both sides of the alleys, for young persons to sit on." But these additional seats did not suffice, for about twelve months later the townsmen, or, as we now term them, the selectmen, were "desired to speak with some workmen to see if another little gallery may not for a small charge be made adjoining that [which] is already." This mention of the gallery prompts us to suggest, that, as with few exceptions the persons who had seats assigned to them by name were heads of families, young men and young women sat in the gallery, as was the general custom in New England in later generations. That the interior of the building was cared for and kept free from dust, is evident from the minute, "It is ordered that sister Preston shall sweep and dress the meeting-house every week, and have one shilling a week for her pains."

The people of each plantation gathered together on the morning of every Lord's day to a sanctuary not unlike that which has been described. The first drum was beaten about eight o'clock in the tower of the meeting house and through the streets of the town. When the second drum beat, families came forth from their dwellings, and walked in orderly procession to the house of God, children following their parents to the door, though not allowed to sit with them in the assembly. The ministers in the pulpit wore gowns and bands as they had done in England, their Puritan scruples reaching not to all the badges of official distinction which they had been accustomed to see and to use, but only to the surplice.

There is, perhaps, no way in which one can more accurately conceive of the ritual of worship in these churches than by reading what has been written by a contemporary, concerning worship in New England and especially in Boston. Lechford [1] says:—

"The public worship is in as fair a meeting-house as they can provide, wherein, in most places they have been at great charges. Every Sabbath or Lord's day they come together at Boston by ringing of a bell, about nine of the clock or before. The pastor begins with solemn prayer, continuing about a quarter of an hour. The teacher then readeth and expoundeth a chapter. Then a psalm is sung; whichever, one of the ruling elders dictates. After that, the pastor preacheth a sermon, and sometimes *ex tempore* exhorts. Then the teacher concludes with prayer and a blessing.

"Once a month is a sacrament of the Lord's Supper, whereof notice is given usually a fortnight before, and then all others departing save the church, which is a great deal less in number than those that go away, they receive the sacrament, the ministers and ruling elders sitting at the table, the rest in their seats or upon forms. All cannot see the minister consecrating unless they stand up and make a narrow shift. The one of the teaching elders prays before, and blesseth and consecrates the bread and wine, according to the words of institution; the other prays after the receiving of all the members; and next communion they change turns; he that

---

[1] Lechford was a lawyer, who, being disbarred for talking with a juryman out of court, returned to England.

began at that ends at this; and the ministers deliver the bread in a charger to some of the chief, and peradventure give to a few the bread into their hands, and they deliver the charger from one to another, till all have eaten; in like manner the cup, till all have drunk, goes from one to another. Then a psalm is sung, and with a short blessing the congregation is dismissed. Any one, though not of the church, may, in Boston, come in and see the sacrament administered if he will; but none of any church in the country may receive the sacrament there without leave of the congregation, for which purpose he comes to one of the ruling elders, who propounds his name to the congregation before they go to the sacrament.

"About two in the afternoon they repair to the meeting-house again; and then the pastor begins as before noon, and, a psalm being sung, the teacher makes a sermon. He was wont, when I came first, to read and expound a chapter also before his sermon in the afternoon. After and before his sermon he prayeth.

"After that ensues baptism, if there be any; which is done by either pastor or teacher, in the deacon's seat, the most eminent place in the church, next under the elder's seat. The pastor most commonly makes a speech or exhortation to the church and parents concerning baptism, and then prayeth before and after. It is done by washing or sprinkling. One of the parents being of the church, the child may be baptized, and the baptism is in the name of the Father and of the Son and of the Holy Ghost. No sureties are required.

"Which ended, follows the contribution, one of the deacons saying, 'Brethren of the congregation, now there is time left for contribution, wherefore, as God hath prospered you, so freely offer.' Upon some extraordinary occasions, as building or repairing of churches or meeting-houses, or other necessities, the ministers press a liberal contribution, with effectual exhortations out of Scripture. The magistrates and chief gentlemen first, and then the elders and all the congregation of men, and most of them that are not of the church, all single persons, widows and women in absence of their husbands,[1] come up one after another one way

---

[1] Mrs. Brewster, in the absence of her husband, who had sailed for England in Lamberton's ship, went forward with her gift "because her

and bring their offerings to the deacon at his seat, and put it into a box of wood for the purpose, if it be money or papers; if it be any other chattel, they set it or lay it down before the deacons, and so pass another way to their seats again."

The sermons were much longer than would be endured at the present day; but were not regarded by the hearers as too long, such was the interest which the people felt in the exposition of the Scriptures, and so little else was there to occupy their intellectual and spiritual faculties. Long sermons, however, were not a peculiarity of New England. The churches in the mother-country were commonly supplied with hour-glasses, one hour being the ordinary measure of a sermon; but when an able preacher turned the glass to signify that he wished to speak longer, the congregation would give visible, if not audible, expression of their approval.

After the contribution, candidates were "propounded" for admission to the church, or, having been previously announced as candidates, were, on their assenting to the covenant of the church, formally received into its communion. If there were any matters of offence requiring censure, they were then attended to, "sometimes till it be very late." "If they have time after this, is sung a psalm, and then the pastor concludeth with a prayer and a blessing."

In the church at New Haven it was the custom for

husband had commanded her." but was charged with saying, "It was as going to mass or going up to the high altar." She denied "that ever she spake of mass or high altar in reference to the contributions," but adroitly quoted the text, "when thou bringest thy gift to the altar," alleging that she first heard it applied to the contributions by her irreproachable seat-mate, Mrs. Lamberton.

the assembly to rise and stand while the preacher read the passage of Scripture which he had selected as a text for his sermon. But Hutchinson says that this was a peculiarity of that church, and quotes a letter from Hooker to Shepard, referring to the Sunday when the practice commenced in the afternoon, Mr. Davenport having preached a sermon in the morning advocating such an expression of reverence for the word of God.

Stated religious services in addition to those of the Lord's Day were held on other days of the week, the arrangement of them differing probably in the several plantations. In New Haven the church had a meeting by themselves on Tuesday, or "third day," as their scruples required them, at least for a time, to term the third day of the week. On Thursday, or "fifth day," there was a public lecture open to all.[1] Allusion is also made in the records to neighborhood-meetings, not only during the year preceding the formation of a church and a government, but so late as May, 1661.

"A plantation whose design is religion" ought to be distinguished for morality. Such being the design of all the plantations combined in the colony of New Haven, we naturally expect to find it standing higher than midway in a list of Christian communities arranged according to their respective degrees of ethical purity. All the proprietors were, or desired to become, church-

---

[1] I am not sure that either the church-meeting or the lecture-service was held every week. The lecture probably occurred regularly, whatever the interval; the church-meeting may have been appointed by the elders whenever there was occasion. I think, however, that church-meetings were always on third day, and lectures always on fifth day.

members, and all had evinced the sincerity of their religious professions by coming into the wilderness for the sake of their religion. Such men were personally moral, and, so far as they could control their children, their servants, and the strangers who sojourned among them, they preserved their community free from vice. It is true that the records supply evidence that the moral law was sometimes transgressed. Indeed, if one should judge solely from the number of cases brought to trial, he might come to the conclusion that there was a low state of morals in the colony. But a community governed by Puritans differed from other communities, both in the comprehensiveness of the moral code enforced by the civil law, and in the strictness with which laws enacted in the interest of morality were enforced. Probably more cases were brought before the court, in proportion to the number of crimes committed, than in any community of the present day. In our time the civil law aims to protect society from the destructive power of immorality, and this is the limit of its endeavor in behalf of morality. If there be any laws on the statute-book designed to protect an individual from himself, or to enforce the duties which man owes to God, such laws are ancient, and, for want of enforcement, are practically obsolete.

The whole duty of a man comprises his duties to himself, his duties to his fellow-beings, and his duties to God. Puritan law enforced the obligations of the first and third, as well as of the second division. Drunkenness and unchastity were trespasses which the offender committed against himself,—trespasses from which the innocent were to be deterred by penalties threatened, and, whenever there was transgression, by penalties inflicted. Blasphemy was an outrage upon the being spoken against, and willful absence from public worship was to rob God of the outward honor rightfully belonging to him: there were therefore laws to protect the rights of God by punishing such impiety.

The field in which ethical purity was enforced by law, being considerably wider than in modern times, the moral sentiment of society being high-toned, and magistrates being conscientiously diligent in maintaining law, there were more criminal prosecutions than would occur under modern laws and modern administration in a community equally virtuous and of equal population. Allowing for the breadth of the Puritan code of morals, and the conscientiousness with which law was enforced, one must conclude that the people of the New Haven colony were more moral than the people inhabiting the same territory have been during any equal period in modern times. Antecedent to the union with Connecticut, there was no trial of an English person for murder. There is incidental evidence that there was one trial for adultery, though the record of it is lost. There were executions for crimes of unnatural lust, but the imperfection of the records renders it impossible to determine how many. Trials for fornication, drunkenness, and theft were not as numerous in proportion to the population as on the same territory in our own time.

Generally, offenders were either servants or artisans temporarily resident. But in a comparatively few cases the children of proprietors so far deviated from the strictly moral life required by Puritan law, as to be summoned before the magistrates. When this happened, it usually appeared that they had been misled by servants, bond or hired. One such case illustrates the firmness and impartiality with which law was administered. The daughter of a magistrate was, by order of the court of magistrates, whipped for "consenting to go in the night to the farms with Will. Harding to a venison feast; for stealing things from her parents; and yielding to filthy dalliance with the said Harding." Neither her father who was a member of the court, nor her father's "cousin" who presided, however they may have shrunk and faltered, refused to administer the same measure as they would have administered to the humblest apprentice.

Passing out of the zone in which morality was protected by civil law, into the region where conscience and public sentiment ruled, we find the colonists superior rather than inferior to their descendants and successors. In the sobriety which governs animal appetites; in the observance of the rules of righteousness between man and man; in the carefulness with which honor was given to those to whom honor was due, and especially to the Supreme Ruler, they excelled.

Having said so much in commendation, we must in truthfulness testify, that, like the saints whose sins are recorded on the pages of Holy Writ, they were human and therefore imperfect. Even among church-members there were cases of gross immorality. In a single church there was one case of lying, one of fraud, one of drunkenness, and one of unnatural lust. These exceptional outbreaks of wickedness are conspicuous by reason of the general sobriety, righteousness, and godliness of the community in which they occurred.

If there was any sin to which Puritans were especially liable, it was avarice. Watchful against carnality and ungodliness, they were less suspicious of that lust of acquiring, which under the guise of such virtues as industry, frugality, and domestic affection, sometimes held them in a bondage of which they were little aware. Hence there were frequent appeals to the court for justice between man and man in regard to contracts, and in one instance a complaint from the deacons of the church in the principal plantation that "the wampum that is put into the church-treasury is generally so bad that the elders to whom they pay it cannot pay it away." The court, appointing a committee to inquire further concerning the matter, found that "the contributions for the church-treasury are by degrees so much abated that they afford not any considerable maintenance to the teaching officers, and that much of the wampum brought in is such, and so faulty, that the officers can hardly, or not at all, pass it away in any of their occasions." Those who abated their contributions too much, or cast into the treasury of the church worthless money, were certainly wrong; but perhaps those who in our day are accustomed to receive and count the contributions of churches, could testify that such manifestations of avarice are not peculiar to ancient times.

The outward honor shown to those who were worthy of honor was in the seventeenth century rendered as being of moral obligation. Good morals included good manners, and good manners were so far forth good morals. The Puritan gave to the fifth commandment so broad a scope that it required outward expressions of reverence for all superiors in age or station. It would be impossible now to re-establish the manners of the seventeenth century, or to convince any considerable part of society that the young owe to their superiors in age any such degree of deference as was then acknowledged to be due. But even to one who believes that outward signs of reverence were then excessive, there may perhaps be more of fitness and beauty in the manners of the olden time, notwithstanding such excess, than in the opposite extreme sometimes exhibited in modern society. Certainly, as reverence for superiors was then universally held to be of moral obligation, the people of New Haven colony are to be credited for the general rendition of honor to whom honor is due.

CHAPTER XIII.

LEARNING.

PROTESTANT Christianity places so much emphasis on individual accountability to God that consistency requires a Protestant community to provide that every person shall be able to read, in order that he may read the Scriptures. The Puritan fathers of New England established schools as early as, or earlier than, they organized churches, and with direct reference to religious instruction as the ultimate end. Under the caption "Children's Education," the New Haven law reads as follows :—

"Whereas, too many parents and masters, either through an over tender respect to their own occasions and business, or not duly considering the good of their children and apprentices, have too much neglected duty in their education while they are young and capable of learning, It is Ordered, That the deputies for the particular court in each plantation within this jurisdiction for the time being, or where there are no such deputies, the constable or other officer or officers in public trust, shall, from time to time, have . a vigilant eye over their brethren and neighbors within the limits of the said plantation; that all parents and masters do duly endeavor, either by their own ability and labor, or by improving such school-master or other help and means as the plantation doth afford or the family may conveniently provide, that all their children and apprentices, as they grow capable, may, through God's blessing, attain at least so much as to be able duly to read the Scriptures and other good and profitable printed books in the English tongue, being their native language; and, in some competent measure, to understand the main grounds and principles of Christian religion necessary to salvation."

The statute then proceeds to provide for its enforcement, imposing fine after fine, and finally authorizing the court of magistrates if "such children or servants may be in danger to grow barbarous, rude, and stubborn," to "take such children or apprentices from such parents or masters, and place them for years, boys till they come to the age of one and twenty, and girls till they come to the age of eighteen years, with such others who shall better educate and govern them, both for public conveniency and for the particular good of the said children or apprentices."

We learn from the statute that the end for which schools were instituted was that children might not grow "barbarous, rude and stubborn." From the history of the schools we shall further find that the planters had in view not only to secure the colony from the existence of a dangerous class, but to qualify some of their youth to be leaders of the people in the following generation.

The first planters of the earliest plantation in the colony brought with them a school-master. A few months after the arrival of the company at Quinnipiac, and apparently as soon as a room for the school could be provided, he commenced to teach. Michael Wigglesworth, who was his pupil in the summer of 1639, says, "I was sent to school to Mr. Ezekiel Cheever, who at that time taught school in his own house; and under him, in a year or two I profited so much, through the blessing of God, that I began to make Latin and to get on apace." The revision of the town records sanctioned by the General Court, after the unfaithfulness of Secretary Fugill had been discovered, gives the following minute concerning Mr. Cheever's school:—

"For the better training up of youth in this town, that through God's blessing they may be fitted for public service hereafter, either in church or commonweal, it is ordered that a free school be set up, and the magistrates with the teaching elders are entreated to consider what rules and orders are meet to be observed, and what allowance may be convenient for the school-master's care and pains, which shall be paid out of the town's stock. According to which order £20 a year was paid to Mr. Ezekiel Cheever, the present school-master, for two or three years at first; but that not proving a competent maintenance, in August, 1644, it was enlarged to £30 a year, and so continueth."

After Mr. Cheever's difficulty with the church it was uncomfortable for him to reside in New Haven, and he soon removed to Ipswich. In October, 1650, "it was propounded that a school-master be provided for the town," and the matter was referred to a committee; but some time elapsed before a school-master was found whom the town was willing to reward with so large a salary as they had paid to Mr. Cheever. Mr. Jeanes, one of the proprietors of the town, was willing to teach, and, in March, 1651, "it was propounded to know whether the town would allow any salary to Mr. Jeanes for teaching school.[1] Much debate was about it, but

[1] William Jeanes, whose house was at the corner of Chapel and Church Streets. I have seen it stated that Rev. Thomas James, who lived at the corner of Chapel and York Streets, taught school in New Haven; but after diligent search I conclude that this is a mistake occasioned by the similarity of his name to that of Jeanes.

nothing was ordered in it at present; only it was propounded to him, that if the town would allow him £10 a year, whether he would not go on to teach and take the rest of the parents of the children by the quarter; but he returned no answer." On further reflection Mr. Jeanes concluded to accept the town's offer, so that in May the town "ordered that he should have £10 for this year." In October " Mr. Jeanes informed the town that he is offered a considerable maintenance to go to Wethersfield to teach school, yet if the town will settle that £10 a year upon him formerly ordered, he is willing to stay here in the work he is. Whereupon it was voted that for three years he have £10 a year as formerly ordered, and upon the same terms as before." For some reason Mr. Jeanes did not continue to teach for so long a period as the town had engaged itself to him; for, in October, 1651:—

"The secretary was desired to speak with Mr. Goodyear to use some means to bring the school-master hither, who, they hear, is coming, but wants transportation;" and, about a fortnight later, "the governor acquainted the court that now the school-master is come, and some course must be taken to provide for his lodging and diet; and to repair the school-house; and consider what the town will allow him a year; and what his work shall be; therefore it is necessary a committee should be chosen to treat with him. The court considered of the motion, and chose the ruling elder, the four deputies, and the treasurer, as a committee to treat with him and provide for him; and declared that they are willing to allow him £30 a year out of the treasury, or any greater sum as they can agree, not exceeding £40, and that his work should be to perfect male children in the English after they can read in their Testament or Bible, and to learn them to write, and to bring them on to Latin as they are capable, and desire to proceed therein."

Three days later —

"The committee appointed at the last court to treat and agree with the school-master, acquainted the court with what they had done; viz., that he propounded to have £20 a year and the town to pay for his chamber and diet (which they have agreed with Mr. Atwater for, for five shillings per week); that the town pay toward his charges for coming hither thirty shillings; that he have liberty once a year to go to see his friends, which we propounded to be in harvest time; that his pay be good, and some of it such as wherewith he may buy books and defray charges in his travel; that if he be called away (not to the same work, but to some other employment which may be for the honor of Christ) he may have liberty. And for this he will teach the children of this town (having the benefit of strangers to himself) after they are entered and can read in the Testament; to perfect them in English; and teach them their Latin tongue as they are capable; and to write. After consideration the town voted to accept the terms propounded."

The school-master thus provided was John Hanford, afterward settled in the ministry at Norwalk. When he had taught about four months :—

"The governor acquainted the court that he hears the school-master is somewhat discouraged, because he hath so many English scholars which he must learn to spell, which was never the town's mind, as appeared in the order which was now read. And it was now ordered that the school-master shall send back such scholars as he sees does not answer the first agreement with him, and the parents of such children were desired not to send them."

Seven months after Mr. Hanford had commenced his school :—

"The governor informed the court that one of Norwalk had been with him to desire liberty for Mr. Hanford's remove to be helpful to that plantation in the work of the ministry: also Mr. Hanford himself, who saith he finds his body unable, and that it will not stand with his health to go on in his work of teaching school, and therefore desires liberty to take his opportunity; which liberty he did reserve when he agreed with the town; the record of which agreement being read, it so appeared. Therefore, if his mind was so set, they could not hinder him; but a convenient time of warning was desired, which he granted, if it was a month or two."

On the same day when the aforesaid action was taken, releasing Mr. Hanford, "brother Davis's son was propounded to supply the school-master's place, and the magistrates, elders, and deacons, with the deputies for the court, were chosen as a committee to treat with him about it." It is probable, however, that Mr. Davis was not employed; for the governor informed the court, Nov. 8, 1652:—

"That the cause of calling this meeting is about a school-master, to let them know what he hath done in it. He hath written a letter to one Mr. Bowers, who is school-master at Plymouth, and desires to come into these parts to live, and another letter about one Mr. Rowlandson, a scholar, who, he hears, will take that employment upon him. How they will succeed, he knows not; but now Mr. Jeanes is come to the town, and is willing to come hither again if he may have encouragement. What course had been taken to get one he was acquainted with, and that. if either of them come, he must be entertained; but he said, if another come, he should be willing to teach boys and girls to read and write, if the town thought fit; and Mr. Jeanes being now present, confirmed it. The town generally was willing to encourage Mr. Jeanes's coming, and would allow him at least ten pounds a year out of the treasury, and the rest he might take of the parents of the children he teacheth, by the quarter, as he did before, to make it up a comfortable maintenance. And many of the town thought there would be need of two school-masters, for if a Latin school-master come, it is feared he will be discouraged if many English scholars come to him. Mr. Jeanes, seeing the town's willingness for his coming again, acknowledged their love, and desired them to proceed no further at this time; for he was not sure he shall get free where he is, and if he do, he doubts it will not be before winter. Therefore no more was done in it at present."

About seven months later (June 21, 1653):—

"The governor acquainted the town that Mr. Bowers, whom they sent for to keep school, is now come, and that it hath been difficult to find a place for his abode; but now Thomas Kimberly's house is agreed upon, and he intends to begin his work next fifth day if the town please; with which the town was satisfied, and declared that they would allow him as they did Mr. Hanford,— that is, twenty pounds a year, and pay for his diet and chamber; and they expected from him that work which Mr. Hanford was to do: and some that had spoken with him, declared that upon these conditions he was content."

Mr. Bowers continued to teach the town school for about seven years. He was at first troubled, as Mr. Hanford had been, with so many "children sent to him to learn their letters and to spell, that others, for whom the school was chiefly intended, as Latin scholars," were neglected. The town, hearing of this, charged two of the selectmen (as such officers are now called, or townsmen, as they were then denominated) to send all such children home, and desired the school-master not to receive any more such. He does not appear to have been hindered in his usefulness after his first year by this or any other difficulty, till the last year of his service. He then informed the court, April 23, 1660, "that the number of scholars at present was but eighteen, and they are so unconstant that many times there are but six or eight. He desired to know the town's mind whether they would have a school or no school, for he could not satisfy himself to go on thus. The reason of it was inquired after, but not fully discovered. But that the school might be settled in some better way for the furtherance of learning, it was referred to the consideration of the court, elders, and townsmen, who are desired to prepare it for the next meeting of the town." At the next meeting "the governor declared that the business of the school had also been considered by the committee, but was left to be further considered when it appears what will be done by the jurisdiction general court concerning a colony school."

The institution of a colony school at New Haven, a few months later, put an end to the town school, absorbing into itself all the boys in the plantation whose parents wished them to learn Latin.

The question naturally rises in the mind of one who studies in the early town records of New Haven, the history of its schools, What provision was there for children who had not yet learned to read? So far as appears, no provision was made at the public expense for children not sufficiently advanced to enter the town school; but parents were obliged either personally to teach their children, or to pay for their instruction in private schools. So early as February, 1645, "Mr. Pearce desired the plantation to take notice that if any will send their children to him, he will instruct them in writing or arithmetic." Probably other inhabitants from time to time taught the rudiments of learning as they could obtain pupils. Mr. Jeanes seems to have occupied a middle position between such teachers of private schools and the master of the public school, being regarded as less competent than those who received their maintenance wholly from the town, and yet worthy to be encouraged by a grant from the public treasury when a more learned man than he was not to be obtained.

At Guilford, Rev. John Higginson added to his work as teaching elder of the church, that of school-master for the town. At a general court, Oct. 7, 1646, a committee was appointed to collect *the contributions* for the maintenance of the elders, and "it was ordered that the additional sum toward Mr. Higginson's maintenance with respect to the school shall be paid by the treasurer out of the best of *the rates* in due season according to our agreements." As it was at the same time further ordered " that whoever shall put any child to school to Mr. Higginson, shall not put for less than a quarter's time at once, and so all shall be reckoned with quarterly, though they have neglected to send them all the time, after the rate of four shillings per quarter, by the treasurer," we may infer that the school was not free to those who sent their children, though a fixed salary was assured to the master by the town. When Mr. Higginson, after Mr. Whitfield's departure, became the only elder of the church, other persons were successively employed as school-masters. Jeremiah Peck, afterward an ordained minister, was school-master from 1656,— in which year he was married to a young lady of Guilford,—to 1660, when he removed to New Haven to take charge of the grammar school established in that year by the colony.

According to Lambert, "the first school in Milford was kept by Jasper Gunn, the physician;" and the colonial records in 1657 preface an order, that "endeavors shall be used that a school-master shall be procured in every plantation where a school is not already set up," with the statement that "New Haven hath provided that a school-master be maintained at the town's charge, and Milford hath made provision in a comfortable way.[1]"

These town schools were chiefly intended for such as could remain long enough "to make Latin." The teachers were men of liberal education, and were procured to teach, because they were capable of teaching something more and higher than the rudiments of learning. In every plantation there were inhabitants who could teach children as much as the law required that they should learn, which, as we have seen, was at first only reading.

To show, that, as the colony grew in years it required a greater minimum of scholarship, we cite the addition made by the General Court in 1660 to the law requiring that all children should be taught to read. "To the printed law concerning the education of children, it is now added that the sons of all the inhabitants within this jurisdiction shall (under the same penalty) be learned to write a legible hand so soon as they are capable of it." The reader should take notice, however, that the earlier order refers to all children and apprentices, and the later to boys only. The standard to which Mr. Davenport would have brought the people by moral suasion, if not by authority of law, was even higher than that enforced by the court; for, when he delivered

---

[1] The omission of Guilford in this mention of towns which in May, 1657, were maintaining schools, leads me to think that Mr. Peck commenced his school in 1657; but I have allowed the date of his commencement to remain as it is in Sibley's Harvard Graduates. Perhaps he commenced as the master of a private school.

up all his power and interest as a trustee of Mr. Hopkins's bequest in aid of a college, he embraced the opportunity to express his desire "that parents will keep such of their sons constantly to learning in the schools whom they intend to train up for public serviceableness; and that all their sons may learn, at the least, to write and cast up accounts competently, and may make some entrance into the Latin tongue." As this communication was made at the meeting when the order was passed requiring that boys should be taught to write, it would seem that the freemen were moved by Mr. Davenport's communication to pass the order, but did not think it expedient to require arithmetic and Latin.

It was designed from the beginning, that "a small college should be settled in New Haven.[1]" In laying

[1] While they looked forward to the establishment of a college at home, the people of New Haven in 1644 appointed collectors to "receive of every one of this plantation whose heart is willing thereunto, a peck of wheat or the value of it," for "the relief of poor scholars at the college at Cambridge." The amount of this contribution may be learned from the following record in 1645. "Mr. Atwater, the present treasurer, informed the court that he had sent from Connecticut forty bushels of wheat for the college, by Goodman Codman, for the last year's gift of New Haven, although he had not received so much." This contribution of *college corn* became an annual institution, though sometimes there was less enthusiasm than at first. In 1647 "the governor propounded that the college corn might be forthwith paid, considering that the work is a service to Christ to bring up young plants for his service, and besides it will be a reproach that it shall be said New Haven is fallen off from this service." A few weeks later "it was desired that as men had formerly engaged themselves to contribute a portion of corn to the college, that they would not now be slack in carrying it to the collectors, but that within seven or eight days at farthest those that are behind would pay, for it is a service to Christ, and may yield precious fruit to the colonies hereafter, being that

out their town the freemen reserved the tract called "Oyster-shell Field" "for the use and benefit of a college," and in March, 1648, directed a committee, empowered to dispose of vacant lots "to consider and reserve what lot they shall see meet and most commodious for a college, which they desire may be set up as soon as their ability will reach thereunto." The subject has been brought before the General Court for the jurisdiction, at least as early as 1652; for the town of Guilford voted in June of that year:—"That the matter about a college at New Haven is thought to be too great a charge for us of this jurisdiction to undergo alone, especially considering the unsettled state of New Haven town, being publicly declared from the deliberate judgment of the most understanding men to be a place of no comfortable subsistence for the present inhabitants there; but if Connecticut do join, the planters are generally willing to bear their just proportions for erecting and maintaining a college there. However, they desire thanks to Mr. Goodyear for his proffer to the setting forward of such a work." The records of the jurisdiction for that year having been lost, we are indebted to an allusion to this offer twelve years afterward by Mr. Davenport in some remarks in a town meeting, for the knowledge that the offer of Mr. Goodyear alluded to by the Guilford people was an offer to give his house and home-lot for the use of the college.

Notwithstanding the damper which Guilford put upon

the commissioners have taken order that none should have the benefit of it but those that shall remain in the country for the service of the same."

the attempt to set up a college, the people of New Haven continued to hope, and about two years afterward again agitated the subject. At a general court May 22, 1654, "the town was informed that there is some motion again on foot concerning the setting up of a college here at New Haven, which, if attained, will in all likelihood prove very beneficial to this place; but now it is only propounded to know the town's mind, and whether they are willing to further the work by bearing a meet proportion of charge, if the jurisdiction, upon the proposal thereof, shall see cause to carry it on. No man objected, but all seemed willing, provided that the pay which we can raise here, will do it." The next year, at a general court May 21, 1655, the subject was "revived; and in some respects this seems to be a season, some disturbance being at present at the college in the Bay,[1] and it is now in-

---

[1] The disturbance at Harvard College alluded to was occasioned by the outburst of President Dunster's long pent-up conviction that infant baptism was unscriptural. Probably some of the leading men at New Haven were aware, when in the preceding year they made a motion for setting up a college, that a storm was brewing at Cambridge; for about three weeks previously the General Court of Massachusetts had commended to the "pious consideration and special care of the officers of the college and the selectmen of the several towns not to permit or suffer any such to be continued in the office or place of teaching, educating, or instructing of youth or child in the college or schools, that have manifested themselves unsound in the faith or scandalous in their lives, and not giving due satisfaction according to the rules of Christ; forasmuch as it greatly concerns the welfare of the country that the youth thereof be educated not only in good literature, but sound doctrine." Mr. Davenport and Mr. Hooke knew what this meant as well as President Dunster himself, who resigned in the following month. When it was publicly mentioned in town meeting at New Haven that there had been some disturbance in the college at the Bay, the college had been eleven months without a president.

tended to be propound to the General Court: therefore, this town may declare what they will do by way of encouragement for the same; and it would be well if they herein give a good example to the other towns in the jurisdiction, being free in so good a work." Mr. Davenport and Mr. Hooke were both present upon this occasion, and " spake much to encourage the work;" and a committee was appointed " to go to the several planters in this town, and take from them what they will freely give to this work." On the 30th of the same month, at a general court for the jurisdiction:—

"The governor remembered the court of some purposes which have formerly been to set up a college at New Haven; and informed them that now again the motion is renewed, and, that the deputies might be prepared to speak to it, letters were sent to the plantations to inform them that it would now be propounded. He acquainted them also that New Haven has in a free way of contribution raised above three hundred pounds to encourage the work, and now desired to know what the other towns will do. The magistrate and deputies from Milford declared, that, if the work might comfortably be carried on, their town would give one hundred pounds; but those from the other towns seemed not prepared, as not having taken a right course, and therefore desired further time to speak with their towns again, and take the same course New Haven hath done, and they will then return answer: and for a committee to receive these accounts, and upon receipt of them to consider whether it be meet to carry on the work, and how; and whatever considerations and conclusions may be meet for the furtherance of it; they agree that each town choose some whom they will entrust therein, and send them to New Haven upon Tuesday come fortnight, which will be the 19th of June, to meet in the afternoon, by whom also they promise to send the account, what their several towns will raise for the work; the major part of which committee meeting, and the major part of them agreeing, shall conclude what shall be done in this business."

The time was not ripe, however, for setting up a college; and these endeavors produced no substantial fruit except a bequest in aid of the intended college, which Mr. Hopkins made at the solicitation of Mr. Davenport. In May, 1659, however, Mr. Hopkins being now deceased, the General Court of the jurisdiction took action for establishing a grammar school for the colony, being probably stimulated thereto by the desire to secure Mr. Hopkins's bequest for such an institution of learning as it was possible for them to establish, since they could not compass a college. The order of the Court reads as follows; viz:—

"The Court looking upon it as their great duty to establish some course (that, through the blessing of God), learning may be promoted in the jurisdiction as a means for the fitting of instruments for public service in church and commonwealth, did order that £40 a year shall be paid by the treasurer for the furtherance of a grammar school for the use of the inhabitants of the jurisdiction, and that £8 more shall be disbursed by him for the procuring of books of Mr. Blinman,[1] such as shall be approved by Mr. Davenport and Mr. Pierson [2] as suitable for this work. The appointing of the place where this school shall be settled, the person or persons to be employed, the time of beginning, &c., is referred to the governor, deputy-governor, the magistrates, and ministers settled in the jurisdiction, or so many of them as upon due notice shall meet to consider of this matter. The deputy-governor, with the deputies of Guilford, did propound Mr. Whit-

[1] Rev. Richard Blinman, "after he had labored about ten years in the ministry at New London, removed to New Haven in 1658. After a short stay in that town, he took shipping, and returned to England."—*Trumbull*, vol. i., chap. 13. The New Haven town records show that he assisted Mr. Davenport in the work of the ministry after Mr. Hooke left and before Mr. Street came.

[2] Rev. Abraham Pierson of Branford.

field's house [1] freely for the furtherance of this work, who did also declare that they judged it reasonable that if the said school should be settled in any other place by those who are appointed to determine this question, that the like allowance should be made by that plantation where it falls, answerable to what by Guilford is now propounded."

More than a year, however, elapsed after this order was passed before the colony school went into operation. Meantime Mr. Davenport, having agreed with the other surviving trustees of Mr. Hopkins what part of his bequest should inure to the benefit of New Haven, transferred to the court of magistrates his rights as a trustee to receive and manage this part of the bequest:—

"At a court of magistrates held at New Haven, May 28, 1660, Mr. John Davenport, pastor to the church of Christ at New Haven, delivered into the hands of the court, to be kept for the use of the magistrates and elders of this colony, as is specified in his writing to them, certain writings concerning a trust committed to himself with some others, for the disposal of an estate given by the worshipful Edward Hopkins, Esquire, deceased, for the furtherance of learning in these parts, with resignation of his power and interest therein, so far as he might with preserving in himself the power committed to him for the discharge of his trust (which is more fully and particularly expressed in the records of the General Court), which was thankfully accepted."

A few days afterward, a general court for the juris-

---

[1] The house thus offered by Gov. Leete and the Guilford deputies is still standing near the railway-station in Guilford. Its appearance and its internal arrangements have been somewhat changed, however, by alterations made in 1868. Mr. Ralph D. Smith's description of it, as it was in 1859, may be found in this volume, in the chapter on domestic and social life, and in Palfrey's History of New England.

diction was held at New Haven, the record of which contains the following document:—

"QUOD FELIX, FAUSTUMQUE SIT!

"On the fourth day of the fourth month, 1660, John Davenport, pastor to the church of Christ at New Haven, presented to the Honored General Court at New Haven as followeth,—

"MEMORANDUM.

"1. That sundry years past it was concluded by the said General Court that a small college, such as the day of small things will permit, should be settled in New Haven, for the education of youth in good literature, to fit them for public services in church and commonwealth, as it will appear in the public records.

"2. Hereupon the said John Davenport wrote unto our honored friend, Edward Hopkins, Esq., then living in London, the result of those consultations; in answer whereunto the said Edward Hopkins wrote unto the said John Davenport a letter, dated the thirtieth of the second month, called April, 1656, beginning with these words: 'Most dear sir, the long-continued respects I have received from you, but especially the speakings of the Lord to my heart by you, have put me under deep obligation to love and a return of thanks beyond what I ever have or can express,' &c. Then after other passages (which, being secrets, hinder me from showing his letter), he added a declaration of his purpose in reference to the college about which I wrote unto him: 'That which the Lord hath given me in those parts, I ever designed the greatest part of it for the furtherance of the work of Christ in those ends of the earth; and, if I understand that a college is begun and like to be carried on at New Haven for the good of posterity, I shall give some encouragement thereunto.' These are the very words of his letter, but

"3. Before Mr. Hopkins could return an answer to my next letter, it pleased God to finish his days in this world. Therefore, by his last will and testament (as the copy thereof transcribed and attested by Mr. Thomas Yale doth show), he committed the whole trust of disposing of his estate in these countries,—after some personal legacies were paid out,—unto the public uses mentioned, and bequeathed it to our late honored governor, Theophilus Eaton, Esq., his father-in-law, and to the aforesaid John Davenport, and joined with them in the same trust Capt. John Cullick and Mr. William Goodwin.

"4. It having pleased the Most High to afflict this colony greatly by taking from it to himself our former ever-honored governor, Mr. Eaton, the surviving trustees and legatees met together to consider what course they should take for the discharge of their trust, and agreed that each of them should have an inventory of the aforesaid testator's estate in New England, in houses and goods and lands (which were prized by some in Hartford intrusted by Capt. Cullick and Mr. Goodwin), and in debts, for the gathering-in whereof some attorneys were constituted, empowered, and employed, by the three surviving trustees, as the writing in the magistrates' hands will show.

"5. Afterward at another meeting of the said trustees, they considering that by the will of the dead they are joined together in one common trust, agreed to act with mutual consent in performance thereof, and considering that by the will of the testator two of New Haven were joined with two of Hartford, and that Mr. Hopkins had declared his purpose to further the college intended at New Haven, they agreed that one-half of that estate which should be gathered in, should be paid unto Mr. Davenport for New Haven; the other half to Capt. Cullick and Mr. Goodwin to be improved for the uses and ends forenoted, where they should have power to perform their trust; which, because they could not expect to have at Hartford, they concluded would be best done by them in that new plantation unto which sundry of Hartford were to remove and were now gone; yet they agreed that out of the whole, an £100 should be given to the college at Cambridge in the Bay, the estate being £1,000, as Capt. Cullick believed it would be, which we now see cause to doubt, by reason of the sequestrations laid upon that estate and still continued by the General Court at Hartford, whereupon some refuse to pay their debts, and others forsake the purchases they had made, to their great hinderance of performing the will of the deceased according to the trust committed to them, and to the endamagement of the estate.

"6. The said John Davenport acquainted the other two trustees with his purpose to interest the honored magistrates and elders of this colony in the disposal of that part of the estate that was, by their agreement, to be paid thereunto, for promoting the college-work in a gradual way, for the education of youth in good literature, so far as he might with preserving in himself the power committed to him for the discharge of his trust. They consented thereunto. Accordingly on the election day, it being the thirtieth day of the third month, he delivered up into the hands of the honored governor and magistrates, the writings that concern this business (viz., the copy of Mr. Hopkins's last will and testament, and the inventory of his estate in New England, and the appraisement of his goods, and the writings signed by the surviving trustees for their attorneys, and some letters between the other trustees and himself), adding also his desire of some particulars for the well performing of the trust, as followeth:—

"I. He desireth of New Haven Town, *First*, That the rent of the oyster-shell field, formerly separated and reserved for the use and benefit of a college, be paid from this time forward toward the making of some stock for disbursement of necessary charges towards the college till it be set up, and afterward to continue for a yearly rent as belonging to it, under the name and title of college land.

"*Secondly*, That if no place can be found more convenient, Mrs. Eldred's lot be given for the use of the college and of the colony grammar school, if it be in this town, else only for the college.

"*Thirdly*, That parents will keep such of their sons constantly to learning in the schools whom they intend to train up for public serviceableness, and that all their sons may learn, at the least, to write and cast up accounts competently, and may make some entrance into the Latin tongue.

"*Fourthly*, That if the colony settle £40 per annum for a common school, and shall add an £100 to be paid toward the building or buying of a school-house and library in this town, seeing thereby this town will be freed from the charges which they have been at hitherto to maintain a town school, they would consider what part of their former salary may be still continued for future supplies toward a stock for necessary expenses about the college or school.

"II. He humbly desireth the honored General Court of the

colony of New Haven, *First*, That the £40 per annum formerly agreed upon to be paid by the several plantations for a common grammar school be now settled in one of the plantations, which they shall judge fittest, and that a school-master may forthwith be provided to teach the three languages, Latin, Greek and Hebrew, so far as shall be necessary to prepare them for the college, and that, if it can be accomplished, that such a school-master be settled by the end of this summer or the beginning of winter, the payments from the several plantations may begin from this time.

"*Secondly*, That, if the common school be settled in this town, the honored governor, magistrates, elders, and deputies would solemnly and together visit the grammar school, once every year at the court for elections, to examine the scholars' proficiency in learning.

"*Thirdly*, That for the payments to be made by the plantations for the school, or out of Mr. Hopkins's estate toward the college, one be chosen by themselves, under the name and title of steward or receiver for the school and college, to whom such payments may be made, with full power given him by the court to demand what is due and to prosecute in case of neglect, and to give acquittances in case of due payments received, and to give his account yearly to the court, and to dispose of what he receiveth in such provisions as cannot be well kept, in the best way for the aforesaid uses, according to advice.

"*Fourthly*, That unto that end a committee of church-members be chosen, to meet together and consult and advise in emergent, difficult cases, that may concern the school or college, and which cannot be well delayed till the meeting of the General Court, the governor being always the chief of that committee.

"*Fifthly*, The said John Davenport desireth that while it may please God to continue his life and abode in this place (to the end that he may the better perform his trust in reference to the college), he be always consulted in difficult cases, and have the power of a negative vote, to hinder anything from being acted which he shall prove by good reason to be prejudicial to the true intendment of the testator, and to the true end of this work.

"*Sixthly*, That certain orders be speedily made for the school, and, when the college shall proceed, for it also, that the education of youth may be carried on suitably to Christ's ends, by the counsel of the teaching elders in this colony: and that what they shall conclude with consent, being approved by the honored magistrates, be ratified by the General Court.

"*Seventhly*, Because it is requisite that the writings which concern Mr. Hopkins's estate be safely kept, in order thereunto the said John Davenport desireth that a convenient chest be made, with two locks and two keys, and be placed in the house of the governor or of the steward, in some safe room, till a more public place (as a library or the like) may be prepared, and that one key be in the hand of the governor, the other in the steward's hand; that in this chest all the writings now delivered by him to the magistrates may be kept, and all other bills, bonds, acquittances, orders, or whatsoever writings that may concern this business, be put and kept there; and that some place may be agreed on where the steward or receiver may lay up such provisions as may be paid in, till they may be disposed of for the good of the school or college.

"*Eighthly*, Because our sight is narrow and weak in viewing and discerning the compass of things that are before us, much more in foreseeing future contingencies, he further craveth liberty for himself and other elders of this colony to propound to the honored governor and magistrates what hereafter may be found to be conducible to the well carrying on of this trust according to the ends proposed, and that such proposals may be added unto these, under the name and title of USEFUL ADDITIONALS, and confirmed by the General Court.

"*Lastly*, He hopeth he shall not need to add what he expressed by word of mouth, that the honored General Court will not suffer this gift to be lost from the colony, but, as it becometh Fathers of the Commonwealth, will use all good endeavors to get it into their hands, and to assert their right in it for the common good, that posterity may reap the good fruit of their labors and wisdom and faithfulness, and that Jesus Christ may have the service and honor of such provision made for his people, in whom I rest.

"To these motions I desire that the answer of the Court, together with this writing, may be kept among the records for the school and college.

JOHN DAVENPORT."

To this communication the General Court responded as follows:—

"The Court being deeply sensible of the small progress or proficiency in learning that hath yet been accomplished in the way of more particular town schools of later years in this colony, and of the great difficulty and charge to make pay, &c., for the maintaining children at the schools or college in the Bay, and that notwithstanding what this Court did order last year or formerly, nothing hath yet been done to attain the ends desired, upon which considerations and other like, this Court for further encouragement of this work doth now order that, over and above the £40 per annum, granted the last year for the end then declared, £100 stock shall be duly paid in from the jurisdiction treasury, according to the manner and times agreed and expressed in the court records, giving and granting that special respect to our brethren at New Haven, to be first in embracing or refusing the court's encouragement or provision for a school, whether to be settled at New Haven town or not; but if they shall refuse, Milford is to have the next choice, then Guilford, and so in order every other town on the main within the jurisdiction have their liberty to accept or refuse the court's tender; yet it is most desired of all that New Haven would accept the business, as being a place most probable to advantage the well carrying on of the school for the ends sought after and endeavored after thereby; but the college after spoken of is affixed to New Haven, if the Lord shall succeed that undertaking. It is further agreed that all and every plantation who have any mind to accept the propositions about the school, shall prepare and send in their answer unto the committee chosen of all the magistrates and settled elders of this jurisdiction, to order, regulate, and dispose all matters concerning the school (as the providing instruments and well carrying on of the business) from time to time as they shall judge best, before the 24th of the June instant, that so if any plantation do accept, the committee may put forth their endeavors to settle the business; but if all refuse, then it must be suspended until another meeting of this General Court.

"And for further encouragement of learning and the good of posterity in that way, Mr. John Davenport, pastor of the Church of Christ, at New Haven, presented a writing, as before appears, whereby and wherewith he delivered up all his power and interest as a trustee by Mr. Hopkins, for recovering and bestowing of all that legacy given by him for the end of furtherance to the settlement of a college at New Haven; he also propounded therewith, what he apprehends hath been granted and set apart by the town of New Haven for the same end, with a request that matters thereabouts might be ordered and carried on according to such propositions as are therein set down. All which the General Court took thankfully, both from the donors and Mr. Davenport, and accepted the trust, and shall endeavor by God's help to get in the said estate and improve it to the end it was given for.

"By way of further answer to what was propounded by Mr. Davenport in his writing presented, the Court declared that it was their desire that the colony school may begin at the time propounded, and to that end desire that endeavors may be put forth by the committee of magistrates and settled elders formerly appointed, for the providing a school-master, &c., to whom also they leave it to appoint a steward or receiver, which steward or receiver they empower as is propounded, and to settle a committee from among themselves to issue emergent cases, and to take order that a chest be provided wherein the writings may be laid up that concern this business. The Court further declared that they do invest Mr. Davenport with the power of a negative vote, for the reason and in the cases according to the terms in his writing specified, and that they shall be ready to confirm such orders as shall be presented, which in the judgment of the Court shall be conducible to the main end intended.

"It is ordered for encouragement of such as shall diligently and constantly, to the satisfaction of the civil authority in each plantation, apply themselves to due use of means for the attainment of learning, which may fit them for public service, that they shall be freed from payment of rates with respect to their persons: provided that if any such shall leave off, or not constantly attend those studies, they shall then be liable to pay rates in all respects as other men are.

"It is ordered that if the colony school shall begin any time within the first half year from this court of election, that £40 shall be paid by the treasurer for this year, and if it shall begin at any time before the election next, that £20 shall be paid by the treasurer upon that account.

": To the printed law concerning the education of children, it is now added, that the sons of all the inhabitants within this jurisdiction shall, under the same penalty, be learned to write a legible hand, so soon as they are capable of it."

The next record concerning the colony school which we find, was made by the town of New Haven, and is as follows:—

"1660, June 21st.
"The orders made by the General Court in May last, also a writing of Mr. Davenport by him then delivered in to the General Court concerning a school and college, were both read; after which the governor declared that formerly the Court had taken care that schools of learning might be settled in the several plantations, but finding that means did not attain the end propounded, they have now, as by their order read appears, provided for the settling of a colony school (for teaching of Latin, Greek and Hebrew), in some one of the plantations, which they first tender to New Haven to accept if they shall see cause so to do upon the encouragement they have agreed upon; viz., £100 stock for the providing a house for the master to live in and a school-house, and £40 per annum. Sergeant Jeffrey desired that the town [   ] the compass of the business. To which it was answered that it appears by the order read, that the jurisdiction allows £100 stock and £40 per annum for the salary; but what it comes to more, that town which accepts their tender must make up. After the business had been debated and considered, it was, by the vote of the town, generally declared, that upon the jurisdiction's encouragement, the school shall be settled at New Haven. To which end, Mr. Gilbert, Lieutenant Nash, Sergeant Munson, and John Cooper were appointed a committee to provide a house for the school-master and a school-house, and therein to use their best discretion whether to buy or build, so as may answer the end, yet with as good husbandry for the town as may be."

At the same court "it was also by the governor propounded concerning Oyster-shell Field, that as it hath been from the first intended (as hath been often said) for the use of a college, that it might now be actually set apart for that use, as Mr. Davenport in his writing hath desired, which was also debated; and the town generally showed their willingness, that if it shall please God in his providence so to order it that a college be settled and set up at New Haven, that then the Oyster-shell Field shall be set apart for that use. But to do it before that was not granted."

From the colony records we extract the following:—

"At a meeting of the committee for the school, June 28th, 1660, there were present the governor,[1] the deputy-governor,[2] Mr. Treat, Mr. Davenport, Mr. Street. It was agreed that Mr. Peck, now at Guilford, should be school-master, and that it should begin in October next, when his half-year expires there; he is to keep the school, to teach the scholars Latin, Greek, and Hebrew, and fit them for the college; and for the salary, he knows the allowance from the colony is £40 a year; and for further treaties, they must leave it to New Haven, where the school is; and for further orders concerning the school and well carrying it on, the elders will consider of some against the court of magistrates in October next, when things, as there is cause, may be further considered. Mr. Crane and Mr. Pierson came after the business was concluded, and what is above written was read to them, and they fully approved of it; and after that, being read to Mr. Gilbert, he approved of it also."

At a town meeting in New Haven, July 25 of the same year, the governor communicated the action of the committee as above, and "further informed that upon the eleventh of July, Mr. Peck coming over him-

[1] Newman.   [2] Leete.

self, with such of the court and townsmen as could be got together, had a treaty with him, who propounded that unto the £40 per annum allowed by the jurisdiction, £10 per year, with a comfortable house for his dwelling, and a school-house, and the benefit of such scholars as are not of the jurisdiction, and such part of the accommodations belonging to the house lately purchased of Mr. Kitchel (at a moderate price), as he shall desire, with some liberty of commonage, all which the town now consented to, and by vote determined to allow to Mr. Peck; which the governor now promised to give him information of."

According to the arrangement thus made, the colony school went into operation in the autumn of 1660. At the General Court held in May of the following year, "there were sundry propositions presented by Mr. Peck, school-master, to this court, as followeth:—

"*First*, That the master shall be assisted with the power and counsel of any of the honored magistrates or reverend elders, as he finds need, or the case may require. 2. That *rectores scholæ* be now appointed and established. 3. What is that the jurisdiction expects from the master? Whether any thing besides instruction in the languages and oratory? 4. That two indifferent men be appointed to prove and send to the master such scholars as be fitted for his tuition. 5. That two men be appointed to take care of the school, to repair and supply necessaries, as the case may require. 6. Whether the master shall have liberty to be at neighbors' meetings once every week? 7. Whether it may not be permitted that the school may begin but at eight of the clock all the winter half-year? 8. That the master shall have liberty to use any books that do or shall belong to the school. 9. That the master shall have liberty to receive into and instruct in the school, scholars sent from other places out of this jurisdiction, and that he shall receive the benefit of them, over and above what the jurisdiction doth pay him. 10. That the master may have a settled habitation, not at his own charge. 11. That he shall have a week's vacation in the year to improve, as the case may require. 12. That his person and estate shall be rate-free in every plantation of this jurisdiction. 13. That half the year's payment shall be made to, and accounts cleared with, the master, within the compass of every half-year. 14. That £40 per annum be paid to the school-master by the jurisdiction treasurer, and that £10 per annum be paid to him by New Haven treasurer. 15. That the major part of the aforesaid payments shall be made to the school-master in these particulars as followeth; viz., 30 bushels of wheat, 2 barrels of pork, and 2 barrels of beef, 40 bushels of Indian corn, 30 bushels of pease, 2 firkins of butter, 100 pounds of flax, 30 bushels of oats. *Lastly*, That the honored Court would be pleased to consider of and settle these things this court time, and to confirm the consequent of them, the want of which things, especially some of them, doth hold the master under discouragement and unsettlement; yet these things being suitably considered and confirmed, if it please the honored Court further to improve him who at present is school-master, although unworthy of any such respect, and weak for such a work, yet his real intention is to give up himself to the work of a grammar school, as it shall please God to give opportunity and assistance.

"The Court, considering of these things, did grant as followeth; viz., to the second, they did desire and appoint Mr. John Davenport, sen., Mr. Street and Mr. Pierson, to take that care and trust upon them; to the third, they declared that besides that which he expressed, they expected he would teach them to write so far as was necessary to his work; to the fourth, they declared that they left it to those before mentioned; to the eighth, they declared that he should have the use of those books, provided a list of them be taken; the ninth they left to the committee for the school; and the rest they granted in general, except the pork and butter, and for that they did order that he should have one barrel of pork and one firkin of butter, provided by the jurisdiction treasurer, though it be with some loss to the jurisdiction, and that he should have wheat for the other barrel of pork. This being done, Mr. Peck seemed to be very well satisfied."

The school thus established continued only about two years, being discontinued partly on account of the paucity of scholars, and partly on account of the expense of litigation with Connecticut concerning her assumption of title to the territory of New Haven, which threatened to exhaust the treasury. The vote to discontinue is thus recorded:—

"At a General Court held at New Haven, for the jurisdiction, Nov. 5, 1662, it was propounded as a thing left to be issued at the next General Court after May last, by the committee for the school, whether they would continue the colony school or lay it down. The business being debated, it came to this conclusion, that, considering the distraction of the time, that the end is not attained for which it was settled no way proportionable to the charges expended, and that the colony is in expectation of unavoidable necessary charges to be expended, did conclude to lay it down, and the charges to cease when this half-year is up at the end of this month."

How far the school came short of attaining the end for which it was established, may be seen in the light of some remarks made by Mr. Davenport in a town meeting held the preceding August. "Mr. Davenport further propounded to the town something about the colony school, and informed them that the committee for the school made it a great objection against the keeping of it up, that this town did not send scholars to it, only five or six; now, therefore, if you would not have that benefit taken away, you should send your children to it constantly, and not take them off so often; and further said that he was in the school, and it grieved him to see how few scholars were there."

The colony school being discontinued, the town of

New Haven negotiated with George Pardee, one of their own people, to teach the children "English and to carry them on in Latin so far as he could. The business was debated, and some expressed themselves to this purpose, that it is scarce known in any place to have a free school for teaching English and writing, but yet showed themselves willing to have something allowed by the public, and the rest by the parents and masters of such that went to school; and in the issue twenty pounds was propounded and put to vote, and by vote concluded to be allowed to George Pardee for this year out of the town treasury, and the rest to be paid by those that sent scholars to the school, as he and they could agree. This, George Pardee agreed to, to make trial of for one year. He was also advised to be careful to instruct the youth in point of manners, there being a great fault in that respect, as some expressed."

Our history of schools in the colony of New Haven might here come to a conclusion, for, when the year expired for which Mr. Pardee was engaged, the colony of New Haven had become absorbed into the colony of Connecticut, and thus lost not only its name but its existence as a jurisdiction.

But it will not be deemed improper to add that within two years after the union, the town of New Haven, stimulated by its desire to secure to itself that part of Gov. Hopkins's bequest which was in the power of Mr. Davenport, established a "grammar or collegiate school," and invited Mr. Samuel Street to be the schoolmaster. The town appropriated £30 per annum, and the Hopkins estate in the hands of Mr. Davenport yielded by this time £10 more. A few months afterward, Mr. Davenport came into the town meeting, and "desired to speak something concerning the school; and first propounded to the town whether they would send their children to the school, to be taught for the fitting them for the service of God in church and commonwealth. If they would, then he said that the grant of that part of Mr. Hopkins's estate formerly made to this town stands good; but if not, then it is void, because it attains not the end of the donor. Therefore he desired they would express themselves. Upon which Roger Alling declared his purpose of bringing up one of his sons to learning; also Henry Glover, one of William Russel's; John Winston; Mr. Hodson; Thomas Trowbridge; David Atwater; Thomas Mix; and Mr. Augur said that he intended to send for a kinsman from England. Mr. Samuel Street declared that there were eight at present in Latin, and three more would come in in summer, and two more before next winter. Upon which Mr. Davenport seemed to be satisfied, but yet declared that he must always reserve a negative voice, that nothing be done contrary to the true intent of the donor, and that it be improved only for that use; and therefore, while it can be so improved here, it shall be settled here; but if New Haven will neglect their own good herein, he must improve it otherwhere unto that end that may answer the will of the dead."

As this declaration of Mr. Davenport was made in February, 1668, and he removed to Boston some two or three months afterward, having in the previous September received a call to the pastorate of the first church there, it may be inferred that the people of New Haven had some reason at that time to apprehend that they might lose the benefit of the Hopkins bequest. On the 18th of April, however, Mr. Davenport executed a deed of trust, in which he conveyed unto " William Jones, assistant of the colony of Connecticut, the Rev. Mr. Nicholas Street, teacher of the church of Christ at New Haven, Mr. Matthew Gilbert, Mr. John Davenport, jun., and James Bishop, commissioned magistrates, Deacons William Peck and Roger Alling, and to their successors," his interest in the Hopkins bequest; reserving "full power of a negative voice, while it shall please God to continue my living and abiding in this country or any part of it;" appending the condition that the rent of Oyster-shell Field and of Mrs. Eldred's lot should be to the use of the school; and declaring null and void his former conveyance for the encouragement of a "colony school," on the ground that the colony school had been dissolved by the act of the General Court of the colony of New Haven.[1]

The Hopkins Grammar School thus established, has, with some intermissions which occurred early in its history, afforded to the boys of New Haven from that time to the present day, opportunity " to be taught for the fitting them for the service of God in church and commonwealth." It opens its doors so indiscriminately to the children of all classes of people, Christian, Jewish, and pagan, that the following action of the town may perhaps awaken the risibles of the reader:—

"At a town meeting in New Haven, Dec. 9, 1728, Voted, That the land lying in the governor's quarter in New Haven called the Oyster-shell Field be put into the hand of the school committee in New Haven commonly known by the name of Hopkins Committee, as they now be or hereafter shall be, according to their

[1] See Appendix V.

constitution or custom, by them to be improved for the upholding and maintaining a grammar school in the first parish in this town, for the education of children of Congregational or Presbyterian parents only, and no other use whatsoever forever hereafter; and if it shall hereafter be thought most advantageous to make sale of the lands commonly called the Oyster-shell Field as aforesaid, and the major part of proprietors in this town shall agree thereto, the money thereby produced shall be past into the hands of said committee to be improved as aforesaid, and to no other use whatsoever."

CHAPTER XIV.

MILITARY AFFAIRS.

EACH of the colonies of New England had its military chieftain. A captain was as necessary as a magistrate. Miles Standish came with the pilgrims from Leyden to Plymouth; but, so far as appears, he came as a soldier rather than as a Separatist. He was a man of pure morals, but never identified himself with the church at Plymouth. It was not required in that colony, as it was in Massachusetts and in New Haven, that military officers should be church-members. Of the expedition sent by Massachusetts against the Pequots in 1636, John Endicott was chief captain; John Underhill, Nathanael Turner, and William Jenningson, were subordinate captains; and there were other inferior officers. As the number of privates did not exceed one hundred in number, Underhill, in his narrative of the expedition, apologizes for the unusual proportion of officers. "I would not have the world wonder at the great number of commanders to so few men, but know that the Indians' fight far differs from the Christian practice, for they most commonly divide themselves into small bodies; so that we are forced to neglect our usual way, and to subdivide our divisions to answer theirs, and not thinking it any disparagement to any captain to go forth against an enemy with a squadron of men, taking the ground from the old and ancient practice when they chose captains of hundreds and captains of thousands, captains of fifties and captains of tens. We conceive the captain signifieth the chief in way of command of any body committed to his charge for the time being; whether of more or less, it makes no matter in power, though in honor it does."

Eaton and Davenport not knowing, when they left England, that they should settle afar from their friends in Massachusetts, had not been careful to bring with them a military chief. During the winter they spent at the Bay they found a valuable accession to their company in Nathanael Turner, one of the three captains of the first Pequot expedition who were subordinate only to Endicott. Having lost his house at Lynn (then called Sagus) by fire, in January, 1637, "with all that was in it save the persons," he was free to listen to proposals from a company, which, with large resources, proposed to settle at Quinnipiac. He listened, and was persuaded to take part in the responsibilities and rewards of the undertaking. Capt. Turner was invested with military command at Quinnipiac during the time of the provisional authority which preceded the permanent settlement of civil affairs in the plantation; for, on the 25th of November, 1639, only thirty days after the organization of the court, and, so far as appears on the record, before any appointment of military officers had been made, it was "ordered that every one that bears arms shall be completely furnished with arms; viz., a musket, a sword, bandoleers, a rest, a pound of powder, twenty bullets fitted to their musket, or four pounds of pistol-shot or swan-shot at least, and be ready to show them in the market-place upon Monday, the 16th of this (sic) month, before Capt. Turner and Lieut. Seeley, under the penalty of twenty shillings fine for every default or absence."

On the first day of September following, "Mr. Turner was chosen captain to have the command and ordering of all martial affairs of this plantation, as setting and ordering of watches, exercising and training of soldiers, and whatsoever of like nature appertaining to his office; all which he is to do with all faithfulness and diligence, and be ready at all times to do whatsoever service the occasions of the town may require." This seems to have been a permanent appointment; for he continued in office, till, having determined to visit the mother country, he had embarked in Lamberton's vessel. Then "the governor propounded whether the military affairs of the town may be comfortably carried on without a captain, or whether it were not convenient to choose a captain instead of Capt. Turner, not knowing when he will return. After some debate, Mr. Malbon was chosen captain, with liberty to resign his place to Capt. Turner at his return."

Robert Seeley, above mentioned as lieutenant before the adoption of the fundamental agreement, was formally elected to that office Aug. 6, 1642. In 1649 he asked the town to excuse him from further service, but the Court was unwilling to do so; and, "it was propounded that the men in the town would underwrite what they would give toward the maintenance of Lieut. Seeley in his place." Before the settlement of New Haven, Seeley had been the lieutenant of Capt. Mason in the expedition from Connecticut against the Pequots in 1637. He had passed Quinnipiac in the chase of the Pequots westward, and, unless Turner was with him in that pursuit, had been the first of those who soon afterward settled there as planters to set his eyes on its hills and meadows, its creeks, rivers, and fair haven.

Soon after the inspection of arms appointed in November, 1639, it was ordered that a similar inspection should take place quarterly; and it was defined that "every one that beareth arms" meant "every male from sixteen to sixty years of age, who shall dwell or sojourn within this plantation or any part of the bounds and limits of it for a month together." The number of persons thus made subject to military duty was in 1642 not less than two hundred and seventeen, as there were then thirty-one watches, each consisting of seven men. The whole company was divided into four squadrons each commanded by a sergeant; and the squadrons being trained in succession, one on Saturday of each week for four weeks, there was every fifth week a general training of the whole company, which occurred always on Monday. The squadron-training was omitted that week. At a later date the number of general trainings was reduced to six in a year; and after the organization, in 1645, of a volunteer artillery company, whose members were exempt from squadron-training, the four squadrons were exercised two at once, and only required to train each six times a year.

Besides the officers already mentioned, "the trained band" had an ensign, four sergeants, and four corporals. In 1642 the ensign, or antient as he was usually styled, was Francis Newman, afterward governor of the jurisdiction. The sergeants contemporary with him were William Andrews, Thomas Munson, John Clark, and Thomas Jeffrey; and the corporals were Thomas Kimberley, John Moss, John Nash, and Samuel Whitehead.

Fines for absence and late-coming, whether on days of general training or on squadron days, were given up to the military officers and company for their encouragement, "to be disposed in powder and shot, that they may set up marks to shoot at, or may furnish themselves for their military exercises." A portion of Oyster-shell Field was set apart for a "shooting-place;" and here, on training-days, the soldiers were exercised in target practice.

The arms which the militia were required to show were, in the revision of the orders, specified as "a good serviceable gun, a good sword, bandoleers, a rest, all to be allowed by the military officers; one pound of good gunpowder, four pounds of bullets, either fitted for his gun, or pistol bullets, with four fathom of match fit for service with every matchlock, and four or five good flints fitted for every firelock piece, all in good order, and ready for any sudden occasion, service, or view." The order makes it indifferent whether the gun be a matchlock or a firelock; only if the soldier have a firelock, he must be furnished with a sufficiency of flints, and if his gun is a matchlock, he must have a sufficiency of match. Any musket of the seventeenth century would seem to us ludicrously inferior to those with which modern soldiers are provided; but even the matchlock gave its possessor, so long as he had a rest and a match, immense superiority over an enemy destitute of fire-arms.

The muskets of that day had no bayonet; but soldiers were sometimes exercised in the use of the pike, a weapon consisting of a long wooden shaft pointed with steel. New Haven, while requiring each soldier to be equipped with a musket at his own cost, provided pikes at the public expense.

"It is ordered that a convenient company and number of pikes be provided at the town's charge, that the military and artillery companies may be trained and exercised in the use of them, but no man hereby to be freed from providing, and at all times continuing furnished, with all other arms, powder, and shot, as before expressed; and that a chest be made in some convenient place in the meeting-house, to keep the said pikes from warping or other hurt or decay. And Thomas Munson and the rest of the sergeants undertook to have it done without delay; and Mr. Pearce was appointed to give out and lay up the pikes from time to time, that they receive no damage betwixt times of service; and in consideration hereof and of some bodily weakness, he is at present freed from training, and allowed to provide a man to watch for him."

In respect to defensive armor, the following order gives information: "It is ordered that when canvas and cotton-wool may conveniently be had, due notice and warning shall be given; and then every family within the plantation shall accordingly provide and after continue furnished with a coat well made, and so quilted with cotton-wool as may be fit for service, and a comfortable defense against Indian arrows; and the tailors about the town shall consider and advise how to make them, and take care that they be done without unnecessary delay."

Capt. Turner was by virtue of his office chief captain of the watch, appointing the watch-masters and designating the watchmen to be subject to each, though not without the approval of the magistrates. "It is ordered that a constant and strict watch shall be kept every night in this plantation from the first of March to the last of October every year ordinarily, leaving extraordinary cases, either of mildness or of sharpness of weather or times of danger, to the governor and magistrates, who may remit or continue the watch longer, or increase and order them as seasons and occasions may require. But in the ordinary course the watch is every night to consist of one intrusted as master of the watch (who is diligently to attend and observe all the orders made by this court for the watch while they remain in force), and of six other watchmen. This watch-master is to be appointed yearly, and the six watchmen to be sorted, as may be most convenient in respect of their dwellings, by the captain, with approbation of the magistrates. But if by death, remove, or any other occasion, after the watches are settled in their course for the year, a breach be made, and so cause of an alteration, the captain shall with all convenient speed order and settle them again, so as may be most convenient for the town, and shall give seasonable warning to all the watch-masters whom it concerneth, that the service may go on without interuption or disorder."

What the orders for the watch were, may be learned from the following record: "At a court holden the 3d of June, 1640, all the masters of the watches received their charge and orders as followeth:—

"1. The drummer is to beat the drum at the going down of the sun.

"2. The master of the watch is to be at the court of guard

within half an hour after the setting of the sun, with his arms complete.

"3. All the watchmen are to be there within an hour after the setting of the sun, with their arms complete and their guns ready charged; and if any of them come after the time appointed, or be defective in their arms, they are to pay one shilling fine; for total absence five shillings fine. And if the master of the watch transgress, either in late coming, defectiveness in arms, or total absence, his fine is to be double to the watchmen's fine in like case.

"4. The master of the watch is to set the watch an hour after sunset, dividing the night into three watches, sending forth two and two together to walk their turns, as well without the town as within the town and the suburbs also, and to bring to the court of guard any person or persons whom they shall find disorderly or in a suspicious manner within doors or without, whether English or Indians, or any other strangers whatsoever, and keep them there safe until the morning, and then bring them before one of the magistrates. If the watchmen in any part of their watch see any apparent common danger which they cannot otherwise prevent or stop, then they are to make an alarm by discharging their two guns, which are to be answered by him that stands at the door to keep sentinel, and that also seconded by beating of the drum. And if the danger be by fire, then with the alarm the watchmen are to cry *fire, fire*. And if it be by the discovery of an enemy, then they are to cry *arm, arm*, all the town over, yet so as to leave a guard at the court of guard.

"5. The master is to take care that one man always stand sentinel in a sentinel posture without the watch-house, to hearken diligently after the watchmen, and see that no man come near the watch-house or court of guard; no, not those of the present watch who have been walking the round, but that he require them to stand, and call forth the master of the watch to question, proceed, or receive them, as he shall see cause. The master of the watch is also to see that none of the watchmen sleep at all, and that none of their guns remain uncharged till the watch break up (and then they may discharge), and also that no man lay aside his arms while the watch continues.

"6. Every master of the watch in his course is to warn both his own watch and the master of the succeeding watch, four and twenty hours before they are to watch, and not to do it slightly, but either to do it themselves or to leave the warning with some sufficient for such a trust.

"*Lastly*, If any master of the watch shall fail either in the warning or ordering of the watch in any of the forenamed particulars, or shall break up the watch in the morning before it have been full half an hour daylight, or neglect to complain to one of the magistrates of the neglects or defects of any of the watchmen, he is to be fined by the court according to the quality of his offence."

In 1645 "it is ordered that the market-place be forthwith cleared, and the wood carried to the watch-house, and there piled for the use and succor of the watch in cold weather, and the care of this business is committed to the four sergeants." From a record four years later it appears that this work of clearing the market-place was to be performed by the inhabitants, each working in his turn either personally or by proxy; that some trees were then still standing; and that some of the inhabitants had not yet done their share of the labor. Probably a wood-pile had been provided sufficient for "the use and succor" of the watch for four years; after the lapse of which time "it was propounded that some wood might be provided for the watch. The sergeants were desired to inquire who hath not wrought in the market-place, that they might cut some wood out, and in the meantime the treasurer was to provide a load."

"In 1647 it was propounded that men would clear wood and stones from their pale sides, that the watchmen in dark nights might the more safely walk the rounds without hurt thereby."

On Sabbath and lecture days and other days ordinary and extraordinary, of solemn worship, the watch was kept as at night.

"The sentinels and they that walk the round in their course, shall diligently attend their trust and duty, and shall have their matches lighted during the time of meeting, if they serve with matchlock pieces."

At first all who belonged to the watch, that is to say all persons subject to military service, were required to come every Lord's day to the meeting completely armed; and all other adult males were required to bring their swords, "no man exempted save Mr. Eaton, our pastor, Mr. James, Mr. Samuel Eaton, and the two deacons." Afterward, when the military company had been divided into four squadrons, it was ordered that one squadron in its course should come to public worship with arms complete, and "be at the meeting-house before the second drum hath left beating, their guns ready charged with a fit proportion of match for matchlocks, and flints ready fitted in their firelock pieces, and shot and powder for five or six charges at least." Such an order must have secured for each service of public worship a guard of fifty full-armed men, and one hundred and fifty more equipped with swords. However, one of the rules of the artillery company requiring that "every one of this company purposely coming to any general or particular court, or to the ordinances at any public meeting, whether on the Lord's days, lecture days, days of solemn fasting or thanksgiving, shall carry and wear his sword by his side," affords ground for an inference that the order requiring the whole adult male population to wear their swords, had in 1645 been repealed or become inoperative.

The other plantations conducted their military affairs in a manner similar to that of New Haven. Indeed, the colony laws concerning military affairs so closely resemble those of the principal plantation as to suggest a common origin. They specify the arms with which every male within the jurisdiction shall be equipped; require that "every captain or chief officer chosen in any of the plantations, for the military affairs, shall from time to time be propounded to the next general court after he is chosen, for approbation and confirmation;" enjoin inspection of arms "once in each quarter of a year at least, but oftener if there be cause;" provide that "there shall be every year at least six training days;" order that "a fourth part of the trained band in every plantation shall in their course come constantly to the worship of God every Lord's day, and (such as can come) on lecture days; to be at the meeting-house at latest before the second drum hath left beating, with their arms complete, their guns ready charged, their match for their matchlocks and flints ready fitted to their firelock guns, with shot and powder for at least five shots besides the charge in their guns;" and "that a strict watch be kept in the night in all the plantations within this jurisdiction." Exemption from military duty is defined as follows; viz.: "Upon consideration of public service and other due respects, it is ordered that all magistrates within this jurisdiction, and teaching elders, shall at all times hereafter be freed, not only in their persons, but each of them shall have one son or servant, by virtue of his place or office, freed from all watching, warding, and training. And it is further ordered that all elders, deputies for courts intrusted for judicature, all the chief military officers (as captains, lieutenants, and ensigns), the jurisdiction treasurer, deacons, and all physicians, school-masters, and surgeons, allowed by authority in any of these plantations, all masters of ships and other vessels above fifteen tons, all public millers constantly employed, with others for the present discharged for personal weakness and infirmity, shall, in their own persons, in time of peace and safety, be freed from the said services. And that all other seamen and ship-carpenters, and such as hold farms above two miles from any of the plantations, train only twice a year at such times as shall be ordered either by the authority or by the military officers of the plantation. But all persons freed and exempted from the respective services as before, shall yet in all respects provide, keep, and maintain in a constant readiness, complete arms, and all other military provisions as other men; magistrates, and teaching elders excepted, who yet shall be constantly furnished for all such sons and servants as are hereby freed from the forementioned services."

The artillery company at New Haven seems in later years to have become so far a colonial company that "Mr. Chittenden of Guilford" was one of its sergeants. A company of troopers was organized in 1656. "It is ordered that sixteen horses shall be provided and kept in the five towns upon the main, in this jurisdiction, with suitable saddles, bridles, pistols, and other furniture that is necessary toward the raising of a small troop for the service of the country, in an equal proportion as they can be divided, according to the estate of each plantation, which is as followeth: Six from New Haven, four from Milford, two from Stamford, and four from Guilford and Branford, and that the persons who shall freely undertake or be appointed thereunto, shall be free from rates, both for their persons and the said horses, also from training with the foot company, and from any press for themselves and horses to other public service, and shall have what other privileges are granted to troopers in the Massachusetts or Connecticut colonies, provided that such men who shall be appointed to this service shall be diligent in the use of all due means to fit themselves and horses for the same at home in their several plantations, after which this Court will consider how they may be improved in a public way of training."

At the same court it was "ordered, that, for the encouragement of soldiers in their military exercise, every plantation shall provide a partisan for their lieutenant, colors for their ensign, halberds for their sergeants, with drums fit for service, with a certain number of pikes, as hereafter expressed. New Haven being furnished, Milford is to have sixteen pikes, Stamford sixteen, Guilford twelve, Southold and Branford eight apiece; and, further, that half a pound of powder for every soldier be allowed by every town out of their town rate, once in a year, to the chief officer, to be by him bestowed upon them, according to their due deserts, to be spent as he shall order, by shooting at a mark three times a year, for some small prize which each town shall provide, in value not above five shillings a time, and not less than two shillings sixpence, which shall be ordered either to one or more, as the officer shall appoint; and that each town provide a good pair of hilts for soldiers to play at cudgels with; and that they exercise themselves in playing at backsword, &c.; that they learn how to handle their weapons for the defence of themselves and offence of their enemies; and that the deputies of each plantation speak to the teaching elders there to take some fit opportunity to speak to the soldiers something by way of exhortation to quicken them to a conscientious attendance to this duty; and that soldiers in time of their vacancy do exercise themselves in running, wrestling, leaping, and the like manly exercises, the better to fit their bodies for service and hardship; and that all other exercises, as stool-ball, nine-pins, quoits, and such like games, be forbidden, and not to be used till the military exercise of the day be finished, and the company dismissed from that service."

The colony of New Haven, though always prepared for war, had no opportunity for great or brilliant achievements. The Indians in their immediate neighborhood were peaceable and friendly; and though tribes more remote sometimes threatened hostilities against the whole European population of New England, and though war with the Dutch was at one time imminent, yet the period of which our history treats, exhibits no battles like those of the Pequot war immediately preceding it, or of the wars subsequent to the union with Connecticut.

There was no disturbance at all during the first five years. The union of the towns into a colony, and of the four colonies into a confederation, was hastened by portents of a general war with the Indians. The same year in which the union was consummated, the commissioners of the United Colonies, feeling that they were under obligation to defend Uncas, the sachem of the Mohegans, and the ally of the English, from the vengeance of the Narragansetts, requested Connecticut and New Haven to undertake this service. Accordingly six soldiers were sent from New Haven to Norwich in a shallop, "to join with eight from Hartford for Uncas's defence against the assaults which may be made upon him by the Narragansett Indians." This squad of soldiers remained with Uncas till messengers from the commissioners of the United Colonies had for the moment dissuaded the Narragansetts from their hostile purposes against the Mohegans. Two years later, the Narragansetts, having in violation of their promise resumed hostilities, assistance was again sent to Uncas from New Haven and from Connecticut. These auxiliaries remained with him several months. A special meeting of the commissioners of the United Colonies being meanwhile called, they determined that an immediate war with the Narragansetts was both justifiable and necessary. New Haven was required to send thirty of the three hundred soldiers composing the army of invasion. In three days after the declaration of war, a company of forty men ready to march was raised in Massachusetts, as the first fruits of her quota of one hundred and ninety men. The arrival at Mohegan of this advanced company, relieved the Connecticut and New Haven men so long absent from their homes on garrison duty; and the spirited preparations made by the English induced the Narragansetts to sign articles of peace, which made it unnecessary for New Haven to send her quota to the war. From time to time the Narragansetts broke and renewed their promises, till, in King Philip's war, which occurred after the union of New Haven with Connecticut, they were driven from their territory, never to repossess it.

Simultaneously with the first of the expeditions to Mohegan, there was danger in the west as well as in the east; the Dutch being involved in an Indian war, and the Indians being not careful to distinguish between Dutch and English. The same month in which the shallop was sent to Norwich, the Dutch governor proposed that one hundred soldiers should be raised out of the English plantations, and led by Capt. Underhill[1] of Stamford, to assist the Dutch against the Indians, promising to pay the whole expense "by bills of exchange

[1] Capt. John Underhill, formerly of Boston. After, if not in consequence of, the preaching of antinomianism at Boston, he fell into the vilest immorality, and found it expedient to change his residence. Removing first to Piscataqua, he came afterward to Stamford. There he was well received on account of his professional ability, the town agreeing to pay him a salary as their captain; and the jurisdiction, upon his application for a loan of £20 to supply his present occasions, ordering that if the lending of this £20 may be a means to settle the captain, and if they conceive his settlement may tend to their comfort and security, and if the town of Stamford will see the said sum duly repaid, the jurisdiction is willing to lend the said sum to prevent the snares of larger offers for his remove." Very soon, however, after this endeavor to retain him in the colony of New Haven, Underhill was secured by the Dutch, and intrusted with the chief command in the war they were waging with the Indians. After some good service rendered on Long Island, he led a force of one hundred and thirty men to Greenwich, surprised an Indian village in the night, and, by a terrific slaughter, almost equalling in the number of the slain that in which he had been a principal actor at Mystic fort, persuaded the natives to terminate a conflict in which they were so inferior to their foes.

into Holland." Stamford, being nearest to the scene of danger, was disposed to join with the Dutch in chastising the merciless savages. But the General Court, "not clearly understanding the rise and cause of the war, and remembering that they could not make war without the consent of the other confederate colonies, did not see how they might afford the aid propounded without a meeting and consent of the commissioners for the rest of the jurisdictions. But if peace be not settled this winter, so soon as the commissioners may meet in the spring, both the ground of the war and the aid or assistance desired may be taken into due consideration; and if in the meantime there be want of corn for men and food for cattle, in supply of what the Indians have destroyed, these plantations will afford what help they may."

We hear nothing more of the proposal that the English should join with the Dutch to chastise the Indians. On the contrary, we find the Dutch, a few years afterward, when their own troubles had come to an end, charged with selling firearms to the Indians, and inciting them to hostilities against Connecticut and New Haven, between which colonies and the Dutch there were some matters in dispute. This quarrel was still further inflamed when news came of war between Holland and England, so that in the spring of 1653 the commissioners of the United Colonies, by a vote of seven to one, declared war against the colony of New Netherlands, having, as the majority believed, sufficient evidence that the Dutch governor had plotted with the Indians for the destruction of the English. In the autumn, by a similar vote of seven to one, they declared war against Ninigret, sachem of the Niantics. But the General Court of Massachusetts, nullifying the action of the commissioners, on the ground that the evidence of a plot was insufficient, refused to contribute her quota of troops. The General Court of New Haven jurisdiction, declaring that the Massachusetts General Court and Council "have broken their covenant with us in acting directly contrary to the articles of confederation," saw themselves "called to seek for help elsewhere," and could "conclude of no better way than to make their address to the State of England." Connecticut joined with them, and the appeal was successful. Cromwell, listening to their declaration, that, "unless the Dutch be either removed or subjected, so far at least that these colonies may be freed from injurious affronts, and secured against the dangers and mischievous effects which daily grow upon them by their plotting with the Indians, and furnishing them with arms against the English, and that the league and confederation betwixt the four united English colonies be confirmed and settled according to the true sense (and, till this year, the continued interpretation) of the articles, the peace and comfort of these smaller western colonies will be much hazarded," sent a fleet to subjugate New Netherlands.

The plan, as formed after the arrival of the fleet at Boston, was, to raise an army to co-operate with the ships, to consist of two hundred from Massachusetts, two hundred from the ships, two hundred from Connecticut, "and one hundred and thirty-three from this colony, which the court must now agree to raise in equal proportion, which was done as follows; viz.,

From New Haven, fifty; from Milford, twenty-one; from Guilford, seventeen; from Stamford, twenty; from Southold, fourteen; from Branford, eleven; New Haven and Milford having one or two less in proportion than the rest, because of seamen that are to go from thence, which, if not provided for, will put them above their proportion. Of which one hundred and thirty-three, these officers were chosen: Lieut. Seeley, captain; Lieut. Nash, lieutenant; Richard Baldwin, of Milford, ensign; Sergt. Munson, Sergt. Whitehead, Sergt. Tibballs, of Milford, and Sergt. Bartlett, of Guilford, sergeants; Robert Basset, chief drummer, and Anthony Elcott to be under him; Mr. Augur, and John Brockett, surgeons; and Mr. Pierson is chosen and appointed to go along with this company as their minister, for their encouragement, spiritual instruction, and comfort; and the corporals are, Corp. Boykin, John Cooper, Henry Botsford of Milford, and Thomas Stevens of Guilford; but this last is only for this present service, and that he proceed no higher in any other office, because he is not a freeman and that the chief military officer be acquainted with it."

The caveat of the court, in respect to Corp. Stevens, illustrates the care taken by the New Haven Colony to commit military authority to none but church-members. For some reason,—perhaps for the reason that no church-member could be found who would willingly go,—an exception to the rule was allowed in this instance; but Corp. Stevens was made to understand that he could rise to no higher office, and that his rank would cease when the expedition returned.

"The Court, considering the great weight of this business, and that all good success depends upon God's blessing, did therefore order that the fourth day of the next week shall be set apart by all the plantations of this jurisdiction, to seek God in an extraordinary way, in fasting and prayer, for a blessing upon the enterprise abroad, and for the safety of the plantations at home.

"The Court considered of what provisions were necessary to send forth with these men for a month, and agreed upon six tuns of beer, six thousand biscuits, nine barrels of pork, six barrels of beef, four hogsheads of pease, three hogsheads of flour, six firkins of butter, five hundred (pounds) of cheese, three anchors of liquor, trays, dishes or cans, pails, kettles; and that every man have a good firelock musket, with other arms suitable; a knapsack, with one pound of powder, and twenty-four musket bullets, or four pounds of pistol shot; and, for a stock beside, in the whole, two barrels of powder, three hundred weight of musket bullets, and one hundred weight of pistol shot, with twenty spades and shovels, ten axes, and ten mattocks."

"It is ordered that the charges of soldiers, horse or foot, wherever provided for, shall be at the jurisdiction's charge in equal proportion."

"It is ordered that the magistrates and deputies at New Haven shall be a committee to order matters which concern this design, but cannot now be foreseen, as occasions present, and what they do is to stand good as if the court did it."

"It is ordered that Johnson's lighter shall be pressed to attend the service, for transporting of men and provisions as there is occasion."

"It is ordered that all vessels which come into any harbor in this jurisdiction, which may be fit to attend this service, shall be made stay of for the same, on behalf of the commonwealth of England, till further order."

"It is ordered that as soon as the army is past, watching and warding shall begin in an extraordinary way, as may suit with every town's conveniency and safety, and then all Indians are to be restrained from coming into any of our plantations without leave."

These preparations for war were ordered on the 23d of June, the governor having on that day "acquainted the Court with some letters he had received from Mr. Leete from Boston, informing that the design against the Dutch is like to go on." But the design did not go on, for in a few days came news of peace concluded between England and Holland. At the next session held July 5, "the governor informed the Court that there were with him this day since dinner two men, sent as messengers from the Dutch governor, to inquire of the truth of the peace which they hear by report is concluded betwixt England and Holland, who desired that two or three lines might be sent to certify the same; which the Court desired the governor to do, and ordered that a copy of the proclamation should be sent also; both which were presently done, and the messengers dismissed."

New Haven being thus restrained from executing her design against the Dutch, turned her attention to Ninigret, who, emboldened by the nullifying attitude of Massachusetts, was preparing to destroy the Indian tribes friendly to the English. In August she despatched Lieut. Seeley, Connecticut sending also Capt. Mason, to carry a present of powder and lead to the Montauk Indians, on Long Island, and explain that with it they were "not to offend or hurt Ninigret or any other Indians, but to defend themselves if they are invaded." At the meeting of the commissioners in September, Massachusetts consented, though, as the result showed, not very heartily, to active hostilities against Ninigret. It was determined to raise an army of forty horsemen and two hundred and sixty footmen, the quota of New Haven being thirty-one. Sixteen of these were immediately sent, with two seamen to carry them and their provisions by water, eight from New Haven, three from Milford, three from Stamford, two from Guilford, and two from Branford.

The Court also "agreed of provisions to be sent for a month as followeth: Six barrels of beer, five hundred pounds of bread, one barrel of beef, one barrel of pork, one hundred pounds of cheese, one barrel of pease, and three gallons of strong water; with every man two pounds of powder and shot answerable, for a stock; besides one pound of powder and shot answerable, which every man is to carry with him; with some coats, every man his knapsack and musket, and other fit arms for the service; six trays, six dishes, and one kettle; and for the chief officer for this colony in this service, the Court chose Lieut. Seeley, and Sergt. Jeffrey for sergeant; and the other fifteen men are to be forthwith pressed, that they may be in readiness to attend further service if they be called to it."

The 13th of October being the time agreed upon for the meeting of the troops from the different colonies at the place of rendezvous, it was "ordered that upon the twelfth day of this month, being the fifth day of the week, shall be a day of humiliation to seek God for a blessing upon this enterprise in hand."

Contrary to the wishes of New Haven and of Connecticut, no fighting was done by the troops thus sent against the sachem of the Niantics. Willard, the commander-in-chief, receiving his appointment from Massachusetts, seems to have been as reluctant to engage in hostilities as the power which appointed him. The commissioners, at their next meeting, nearly a year afterward, censured him for his inactivity, and referred the matter to the General Courts of the several colonies. New Haven, in response, expressed the opinion that he had not obeyed his instructions, but declined to propose any penalty till the other colonies had acted. They were powerless to punish a citizen of Massachusetts whose conduct Massachusetts approved, even if she had not, as Trumbull charges, predetermined it.

The failure of the expedition against the Niantics made it necessary to employ an armed vessel to cruise in the Sound, "to hinder Ninigret from going against the Long Island Indians." The vessel was commanded by John Youngs, son of the pastor at Southold (a plantation belonging to New Haven), and four men were sent with him by vote of the jurisdiction. This service continued about a year, and seems to have effectually prevented the hostile incursions of Ninigret into Long Island.

With this exception, there seems to have been no military service required by the New Haven colony from the time of the Niantic expedition to the union with Connecticut, other than the regular trainings in each plantation; though for several years immediately subsequent to that expedition, wars between Indian tribes excited frequent alarms among the English, and stimulated them to unusual diligence in military exercise.

CHAPTER XV.

THE ABORIGINES.

THE small tribes of Indians which originally possessed the territory of the New Haven colony had lived in fear of the Pequots and the Mohawks. Delivered from fear of their eastern enemies by the extinction of the Pequot tribe, they gladly received the English planters, hoping that the people, by whose wonderful prowess this deliverance had been effected, would protect them from their enemies in the west.

"The Mohawks," says Trumbull, "had not only carried their conquests as far southward as Virginia, but eastward as far as Connecticut River. The Indians, therefore, in the western parts of Connecticut, were their tributaries. Two old Mohawks, every year or two, might be seen issuing their orders and collecting their tribute, with as much authority and haughtiness as a Roman dictator.

"It is indeed difficult to describe the fear of this terrible nation, which had fallen on all the Indians in the western parts of Connecticut. If they neglected to pay their tribute, the Mohawks would come down against them, plunder, destroy, and carry them captive at pleasure. When they made their appearance in the country, the Connecticut Indians would instantly raise a cry from hill to hill, 'A Mohawk! A Mohawk!' and fly like sheep before wolves, without attempting the least resistance. The Mohawks would cry out in the most terrible manner in their language, importing, 'We are come, we are come, to suck your blood!' When the Connecticut Indians could not escape to their forts, they would immediately flee to the English houses for shelter; and sometimes the Mohawks would pursue them so closely as to enter with them, and kill them in the presence of the family. If there was time to shut the door, they never entered by force; nor did they upon any occasion do the least injury to the English."

In the articles of agreement in which Momaugin, sachem of Quinnipiac, and his council, conveyed land to Theophilus Eaton, John Davenport, and others, English planters at Quinnipiac, they refer to "heavy taxes and eminent dangers which they lately felt and feared from the Pequots, Mohawks, and other Indians, in regard of which they durst not stay in their country, but were forced to fly and to seek shelter under the English at Connecticut;" mention "the safety and ease that other Indians enjoy near the English, of which benefit they have had a comfortable taste already since the English began to build and plant at Quinnipiac;" and stipulate "that if at any time hereafter they be affrighted in their dwellings assigned by the English unto them as before, they may repair to the English plantation for shelter, and that the English will there in a just cause endeavor to defend them from wrong."

The Quinnipiacs at New Haven numbered "forty-seven men or youth fit for service," and covenanted "not to receive or admit any other Indians amongst them without leave first had and obtained from the English." Montowese, whose land adjoined that of Momaugin on the north, reported his company as being "but ten men besides women and children." The Indians of Guilford were of the same tribe as the Quinnipiacs of New Haven, for Shaumpishuh, the squaw sachem at Guilford, was sister of Momaugin, and signed with him the deed of sale to Eaton and Davenport. After she sold her land at Guilford to Whitfield and his partners in the purchase, she came to reside with her brother at East Haven,[1] bringing with her thirty-four of her people; of the rest a few removed to Branford, and about thirty-three persons remained at Guilford. Of the latter company, one was blind, and another was "a dumb old man."

These statistics favor the opinion that the territory of the New Haven colony, when the English began to build and plant upon it, was but sparsely inhabited. Momaugin had about one square mile for every one of his people, and Montowese had thirteen square miles for each of his ten men. The Wepowaugs were apparently more numerous than the Indians at New Haven. Perhaps it was because this tribe was so powerful, that the English settlement at Milford was fortified with palisades. Trumbull speaks in terms indefinite indeed, but fitted to convey the impression that Ansantaway, their sachem, had some hundreds of warriors; specifying five different settlements in the town of Milford, and making mention of oyster-shells "so deep that they never have been ploughed or dug through to this day." De Forest thinks that Trumbull's estimate was too

[1] De Forest, History of the Indians of Connecticut, p. 167.

high. He says, "The territories of this clan stretched fifteen or eighteen miles along the coast, and comprehended nearly the present townships of Monroe, Huntington, Trumbull, Bridgeport, Stratford, Milford, Orange and Derby. In numbers it seems to have been considerable; and large heaps of shells have been found along the coast, showing what must have been the natives' favorite and principal food. These heaps, however, do not necessarily prove the large population which people often suppose; for they were probably the accumulations of centuries, and their foundations may have been laid by some race which came and disappeared before the foot of a Paugussett or Wepowaug ever left its print on these shores. In fact, eating oysters is not such a marvellous feat that large piles of oyster-shells must of necessity indicate a great number of consumers. We must consider also that, as the natives depended little upon agriculture for a subsistence. and as hunting was a less certain and more laborious mode of supply than fishing, a very large proportion of their food consisted of the produce of the sea, and especially of shell-fish." Slender as is our knowledge of the Wepowaugs, we know even less of the tribes on the coast west of them. Fairfield and Norwalk were purchased for Connecticut, and Stamford for New Haven. The records of Stamford inform us that Capt. Nathanael Turner, the agent of New Haven, purchased of Ponus, sagamore of Toquams, and his brother Wascussue, sagamore of Shippan, the territory now occupied by Stamford, Ponus reserving a piece of ground for himself and the other Indians to plant upon. The tribe to which Ponus and his family belonged were called Siwanoys. Greenwich was also acquired for New Haven, though for a time the inhabitants repudiated her authority, and placed themselves under the protection of the Dutch. It is said that the sachems of whom Patrick and Feaks purchased Greenwich, were sons of Ponus. The red men resident in the vicinity have been estimated at from three hundred to five hundred, but even the latter number was largely increased during the war which the Dutch waged with the Indians, many of whom fled to Greenwich from their customary abodes nearer to New Amsterdam. This temporary accession to the aborigines inhabiting the territory claimed by New Haven was more than balanced by the terrible slaughter executed by Underhill in the service of the Dutch, who, surprising a village in Greenwich, put to death in a single night, by lead, steel, and fire, according to the estimate of the natives, five hundred of its inhabitants.

With the exception of Southold, which was purchased of the Montauks, a tribe always friendly to the English, the territory of New Haven colony was acquired from the Indians mentioned or alluded to in the preceding paragraph. It will be seen that the colony had less reason to apprehend collision with the aborigines on its own territories than if these had been united in a single tribe, under one chieftain. A sagamore who had only a score or two of warriors, even if smarting under the infliction of wrong, would not be so quick to resort to hostilities as one who counted his tribe by hundreds. It was, however, the policy of the New Haven people, to avoid conflict with the red men as much as possible, and to cultivate their friendship. They were, indeed, earnest for war with Ninigret in 1653 and 1654, seeing no other way to secure peace than by fighting for it; but their history, as a whole, evinces a ruling desire to live in amity with their Indian neighbors. They were careful to deal justly with them in all public dealings, and to avenge any injuries inflicted upon them by the greed or passion of individuals. This is true of the fathers of New England in general; but Hubbard, a Massachusetts historian, testifies of New Haven, in particular, "They have been mercifully preserved from harm and violence all along from the Indians, setting aside a particular assault or two, the means whereof hath been a due carefulness in doing justice to them upon all occasions against the English, yet far avoiding any thing looking like servility or flattery for base ends." It was a memorable testimony which, as Winthrop relates, a Pequot gave in favor of the foe who had extinguished the tribal existence of his people. "Those at New Haven, intending a plantation at Delaware, sent some men to purchase a large tract of land of the Indians there, but they refused to deal with them. It so fell out that a Pequot sachem (being fled his country in our war with them, and having seated himself, with his company, upon that river ever since) was accidentally there at that time. He, taking notice of the English and their desire, persuaded the other sachem to deal with them; and told him that howsoever they had killed his countrymen, and driven them out, yet they were honest men, and had just cause to do as they did, for the Pequots had done them wrong, and refused to give such reasonable satisfaction as was demanded of them. Whereupon the sachem entertained them, and let them have what land they desired."

As respects New Haven in particular, her records show a disposition to do justice to the Indian. Take the following cases for evidence:—

"June 25, 1650. A seaman that went in Michael Taynter's vessel was brought before the governor, and accused by Wash, an Indian, that he, having hired him to show him the way to Totoket and agreed for twelvepence, when he was upon the way Wash asked him for his money: the man gave him tenpence, lack two wampum. Wash said he must have twelvepence, else he would not go; whereupon the seaman took him by the arm, pulled him, and threw him down, and stamped upon him, and, in striving broke his arm. The seaman said he agreed with him for tenpence, and gave him so much; but Wash would not go, and struck him first, and he cannot tell that he broke his arm, for it was sore before. Whereupon Mr. Besthup and Mr. Augur, two surgeons being desired to give their advice, said, to their best apprehension the arm was broken now, though by reason of an old sore, whereby the bone might be infected, might cause it the more easily to break. The Court was called, but none came to the governor but Mr. Crane, Mr. Gibbard, and Francis Newman. They would have persuaded Wash to have taken some wampum for satisfaction, but he would not hear of it, but said he desired it might be healed at the man's charge. Whereupon the Court desired Mr. Besthup to do the best he could to heal it, and promised him satisfaction, and, for the present, sent the man to prison. But, quickly after, Philip Leeke, John Jones, and Edward Camp, became his bail, and bound themselves in a bond of £10, that, upon a month's warning left with Philip Leeke, the man should make his appearance here before authority. And David Sellevant and Robert Lord become sureties, and engaged to bear them harmless."

"March, 1664. Nathanael Thorpe being called before the Court for stealing venison from an Indian called Ourance, Ourance was called, and asked what he had to say against Nathanael Thorpe. Nasup, on his behalf, declared that Ourance had killed a deer, and hanged some of it upon a tree, and brought some of it away, and coming by (on the sabbath day, in the afternoon) Nathanael Thorpe's house, his dog barked, and Nathanael Thorpe came out and asked Ourance what he carry, and Ourance said venison, and further said that he had more a little walk in the wood. Then Nathanael Thorpe said to him that the wolf would eat it. Ourance said, No, he had hanged it upon a tree. Then he said that Nathanael Thorpe said to him, Where, where? and he told him a little walk, and to-morrow he would truck it. Then to-morrow Ourance went for the venison, and two quarters of it was gone, and he see this man's track in the snow, and see blood. Then he came to Nathanael Thorpe, and tell him that he steal his venison; but Nathanael Thorpe speak, Ourance lie, and that he would *tantack* him. And Ourance further said that he whispered to Nathanael Thorpe, and told him if he would give him his venison he would not discover him; but still he peremptorily denied it, and told many lies concerning it, and, after it was found in an outhouse of his, he said he had trucked the week before."

Thorpe, having confessed his guilt:—

"He was told seriously of his sin, and of his falseness, and that after he seemed to hold forth sorrow before the magistrates; yet then he spake falsely, and said that it was a little before morning he rose out of his bed and did it, and that now he saith it was in the evening, before he went to bed; and he was told the several aggravations of his sin, as that it seemed to be contrived on the Lord's day, staying at home by reason of some bodily weakness, and that he had done it to an Indian, and to a poor Indian, and when himself had no need of it, and so often denying it, &c., whereby he makes the English and their religion odious to the heathen, and thereby hardens them. So the Court proceeded to sentence, and for his theft declared, according to the law in the case, that he pay double to the Indian, viz., the venison, with two bushels of Indian corn; and for his notorious lying, and the several aggravations of his sin, that he pay as a fine to the plantation twenty shillings, and sit in the stocks the Court's pleasure. And he was told, that, were it not that they considered him as sometimes distempered in his head, they should have been more sharp with him. Then Nathanael Thorpe declared that he desired to judge himself for his sin, and that the Lord would bless their good counsel to him, that so he might take warning for the future, lest it be worse with him."

Not contenting themselves with mere justice, the New Haven colony were also kind and helpful to their Indian neighbors. Take, for evidence and illustration, the following action of the town of New Haven concerning a field which the Indians desired to have fenced:—

"The governor acquainted the town that the Indians complain that the swine that belong to the town, or farms, do them much wrong in eating their corn; and now they intend to take in a new piece of ground, and they desired the English would help them to fence it, and that those who have meadows at the end of their ground would fence it, and save them fencing about. Sergeant Jeffrey and John Brockett were desired to go speak with them, to know what ground it is which they intend to take in, and to view it, and see what fencing it may be, and give them the best direction they can. The sagamore also desires the town to give him a coat. He saith he is old and poor, and cannot work. The town declared themselves free that he should have a coat given him at the town's charge."

At the next meeting it was

"Ordered, concerning the Indians' land spoken of the last court, that Thomas Jeffrey, John Brockett, William Tuttle, and Robert Talmadge shall be a committee to view the ground which they say is theirs, and to advise them for the best about fencing; the meadow lying against their ground bearing its due proportion; and that some men be appointed at the town's charge to show them how, and help them in their fencing; that so we may not have such complaints from them of cattle and hogs spoiling their corn, which they say makes their squaws and children cry."

At a later date it was

"Ordered that the townsmen shall treat with the Indians, getting Mr. Pierson and his Indian for interpreters, and make a full agreement in writing what we shall do, and what they shall be bound to; and let them know that what their agreement is, we expect they shall perform it."

In this agreement threescore days' work was promised to the Indians toward their fence, and the town voted that the work "should be done by men fit and able for the work, and be paid for out of the town treasury."

Just and kind treatment of the aborigines was required of the English by politic prudence as well as by Christian benevolence. The action concerning the sagamore's coat and the fence around his land was taken in 1653, when, throughout all the colonies, there was some fear of a general combination of Indians against the English. New Haven does not seem to have felt any present distrust of the tribes within her borders, but the intermingling of neighborly kindness with orders for special military preparation and precautions suggests that the manifestations of kindness may have proceeded, not from pure benevolence, but from a complex motive in which prudence was a considerable element.

An illustrative instance of this politic prudence occurred in the second year of the plantation at Quinnipiac, and before civil government had been formally instituted. The planters at Wethersfield, having some quarrel with Sowheag, the sachem of the place, had driven him from his reservation near their village, and he had removed to Middletown. Sowheag, in prosecution of the quarrel, had incited, or at least encouraged, the Pequots to make an attack on Wethersfield, in which six men and three women were killed, and had ever since entertained and protected the Pequot warriors by whom these murders were committed. The Pequot war being now ended, so that the Connecticut people were at liberty to attend to Sowheag, they required him to give up these murderers; and, upon his refusal, the General Court, in August, 1639, ordered a levy of one hundred men to be sent to Mattabeseck, as Middletown was then called, to take them by force. But the Court also determined to obtain the advice and consent of their friends at Quinnipiac before carrying their design into execution.

"Gov. Eaton and his council," says Trumbull, "fully approved of the design of bringing the delinquents to condign punishment, but they disapproved of the manner proposed by Connecticut. They feared that it would be introductive to a new Indian war. This, they represented, would greatly endanger the new settlements, and be many ways injurious and distressing. They wanted peace, all their men and money, to prosecute the design of planting the country. They represented that a new war would not only injure the plantations in these respects, but would prevent the coming over of new planters whom they expected from England. They were therefore determinately against seeking redress by an armed force. Connecticut, through their influence, receded from the resolution which they had formed with respect to Sowheag and Mattabeseck."

Eaton, though not at that time, as Trumbull carelessly assumes, governor of New Haven jurisdiction, may have had some provisional power or trust, such as was abrogated by the first action of the Court when civil government was settled two months afterward. Certainly his voice gave expression to the public opinion of his plantation. His determined opposition to the p oposed war upon Sowheag is easily accounted for by the nearness of Middletown to New Haven, and by the still closer contiguity of Montowese, a son of Sowheag, whose wigwam was but one hour distant from the English houses at Quinnipiac.

That this pacific policy of New Haven was not carried to a hazardous extreme, is evident from the punishment inflicted on one of these Pequot murderers, who, of his own accord, came to Quinnipiac, presuming, perhaps, on the manifested leniency of that plantation. The trial of Nepaupuck, which commenced the day after civil government was instituted at Quinnipiac, has already been mentioned. A more particular account of it is here appropriate, and may perhaps be best given *verbatim* from the record.

"October 26th, 1639. The civil affairs of the plantation being settled as before, by the providence of God an Indian called Messutunck, *alias* Nepaupuck, who had been formerly accused to have murderously shed the blood of some of the English, of his own accord, with a deer's head upon his back, came to Mr. Eaton's, where by warrant the marshal apprehended and pinioned him; yet notwithstanding, by the subtlety and treachery of another Indian his companion, he had almost made an escape; but by the same providence he was again taken and delivered into the magistrates power and by his order safely kept in the stocks till he might be brought to a due trial. And the Indian who had attempted his escape was whipped by the marshal's deputy.

"October 28th, 1639. The Quinnipiac Indian sagamore with

divers of his Indians with him were examined before the magistrate and the deputies for this plantation concerning Nepaupuck. They generally accused him to have murdered one or more of the English, and that he had cut off some of their hands and had presented them to Sassacus the Pequot sachem, boasting that he had killed them with his own hands.

"Mewhebato, a Quinnipiac Indian, kinsman to the aforesaid Nepaupuck, coming at the same time to intercede for him, was examined what he knew concerning the murders charged upon the said Nepaupuck. At first he pretended ignorance, but with a distracted countenance, and in a trembling manner. Being admonished to speak the truth he did acknowledge him guilty according to the charge the other Indians had before made.

"All the other Indians withdrawing, Nepaupuck was brought in and examined. He confessed that Nepaupuck was guilty according to the tenure of the former charge, but denied that he was Nepaupuck. Mewhebato being brought in, after some signs of sorrow, charged him to his face that he had assisted the Pequots in murdering the English. This somewhat abated his spirit and boldness; but Wattoone, the son of Carroughood a councilor to the Quinnipiac Indian sagamore, coming in charged him more particularly that he had killed Abraham Finch, an Englishmen, at Wethersfield, and that he himself, the said Wattoone, stood upon the island at Wethersfield and beheld him, the said Nepaupuck, now present, acting the said murder.

"Lastly, the Quinnipiac sagamore and the rest of the Indians being called in, to his face affirmed that he was Nepaupuck, and that he had murdered one or more of the English as before.

"Nepaupuck being by the concurrence of testimony convinced, confessed he was the man, namely Nepaupuck, and boasted he was a great captain, had murdered Abraham Finch, and had his hands in other English blood. He said he knew he must die, and was not afraid of it, but laid his neck to the mantel-tree of the chimney, desiring that his head might be cut off, or that he might die in any other manner the English should appoint; only, he said, fire was God and God was angry with him; therefore he would not fall into his hands. After this he was returned to the stocks, and, as before, a watch appointed for his safe custody.

"A general court 29th of October, 1939. A general court being assembled to proceed against the said Indian Nepaupuck, who was then brought to the bar and being examined as before, at the first he denied that he was that Nepaupuck which had committed those murders wherewith he was charged; but when he saw that the Quinnipiac sagamore and his Indians did again accuse him to his face, he confessed that he had his hand in the murder of Abraham Finch, but yet he said there was a Mohawk of that name that had killed more than he.

"Wattoone affirmed to his face that he, the said Nepaupuck, did not only kill Abraham Finch, but was one of them that killed the three men in the boat or shallop on Connecticut River, and that there was but one Nepaupuck and this was he and the same that took a child of Mrs. Swain at Wethersfield. Then the said Nepaupuck being asked if he would not confess that he deserved to die, he answered, 'It is *weregin*.[1]'

"The Court having had such pregnant proof, proceeded to pass sentence upon him according to the nature of the fact and the rule in that case, 'He that sheds man's blood, by man shall his blood be shed.' Accordingly his head was cut off the next day and pitched upon a pole in the market-place."

If Nepaupuck had been a lawyer, he might have demurred not only to the indictment for murder of one who had killed in war the enemies of his tribe, but also to the jurisdiction of a power which had been in existence but a single day, and did not even then claim as its own, the territory where a crime was alleged to have been committed two years before. But his untutored mind approved of that principle of natural justice, according to which, in every instance in which English blood was shed by an Indian, the English required life for life without regard to territorial limitation. His own people acted upon the same principle, and he justified it when it recoiled upon himself.

[1] Well, or good. Some dialects used *n* in place of *r*. Eliot's Bible has *wunnegin* in Gen. i. 10, "God saw that it was *wunnegin*."

In making common cause throughout all the colonies against Indian murderers, certainly the English did no injustice. They had a right thus to combine for the protection of life. In deciding whether they were justifiable in treating as murderers those who had shed English blood in war, it should be taken into consideration, that, as Capt. Underhill expresses it, "the Indians' fight far differs from the Christian practice." Civilized nations have agreed that soldiers shall not be held individually responsible for homicide in battle; but this agreement would not cover such homicides as those of which Nepaupuck was convicted, and of which Indian warriors were customarily guilty whenever they could surprise an unarmed foe. Fighting with a people wholly uncivilized, the English planters in New England were obliged to deviate from the usages established among civilized nations, and adapt their practice to the exigencies of their situation.

Another execution of an Indian occurred in 1644, near the close of the war between the Indians and the Dutch. A savage named Busheage, not discriminating between the two Europeon nations whose settlements were so little space apart, came into a house at Stamford, none being at home but a woman and her infant, and, with a lathing hammer, which he picked up and examined as if with intent to purchase, struck the woman as she stooped down to take her child out of the cradle. The wound was not fatal, but the woman became hopelessly insane. Busheage, being delivered to the English, was tried, convicted, and sentenced to death. Winthrop says, "The executioner would strike off his head with a falchion, but he had eight blows at it before he could effect it, and the Indian sat upright and stirred not all the time."

Four years later Stamford was the scene of another tragedy. Taphanse, a son of Ponus, the sachem of the place, brought news into the town that an Indian named Toquatoes, living up near the Mohawks, had said at their wigwams that he would kill an Englishmen; that they had offered him wampum not to do it; that he had gone again and reported that he had done it, and that he had gone away in haste, and left some of the Englishman's clothing. From that time, Mr. John Whitmore, one of the principal inhabitants, was missing. Two months afterward, Uncas, sachem of the Mohegans, coming to Stamford to assist his English friends to investigate the matter, was at once conducted by Taphanse to the place where lay the remains of the murdered man. Uncas and his Mohegan companions were satisfied that Taphanse was himself guilty of the murder, but he escaped before they could apprehend him. Fifteen years afterward being arrested and examined, he was pronounced "guilty of suspicion," but "not guilty in point of death."

As the people of New Haven had to do not only with the aborigines within their borders, but with some who were without, we have occasion to describe some of their Indian neighbors who dwelt beyond the limits of the jurisdiction. Prominent among these was Uncas, sachem of the Mohegans. De Forest, in "The Indians of Connecticut," thus describes him: "In person, Uncas is said to have been a man of large frame and great physical strength. His courage could never be doubted, for he displayed it too often and too clearly in war. No sachem, however, was ever more fond of overcoming his enemies by stratagem and trickery. He seemed to set little value upon the glory of vanquishing in war, compared wtih the advantages it brought him in the shape of booty, and new subjects, and wider hunting-grounds. He favored his own men, and was, therefore, popular with them; but all others who fell under his power he tormented with continual exactions and annoyances. His nature was selfish, jealous, and tyrannical; his ambition was grasping, and unrelieved by a single trait of magnanimity."

Originally, a Pequot, and by blood a kinsman of Sassacus, chief sachem of the Pequots at the time when the Pequot tribe was extinguished by the English, Uncas had allied himself still more closely with the royal family of his tribe by marrying a daughter of Sassacus. But, previous to the Pequot war, he had broken friendship with Sassacus, and become an exile from his tribe. The outbreak of hostilities between the English and the Pequots was to him, therefore, a welcome opportunity for revenge. With a score or two of followers he joined the expedition of Capt. Mason against his native tribe ln 1637, which, without the guidance of Uncas and Wepuash, would probably have been fruitless. Uncas had profited by the success of that expedition as much, perhaps, as the English. The number of his followers was increased by such captured Pequots as were allowed to join his people, and by other Indians who appreciated the advantage he might derive from being the ally of the wonderful white men.

Uncas married, and probably before the Pequot war, a daughter of Sebequanash, sachem of the Hammonassets, and by this marriage acquired a large tract of land on the shore of Long Island Sound, extending westward from Connecticut River till it touched the land of the Guilford branch of the Quinnipiacs. This he sold to Mr. Fenwick and the planters of Guilford, and withdrew to the east side of the Connecticut River, to a region, which, as it had formerly belonged to his ancestors, the Pequot sachems, was now assigned to him as his portion of the spoils of war. When at the height of his power, and during that portion of his career when history mentions him most frequently, his residence was commonly at Norwich. But in 1644 he seems to have been residing, at least temporarilly, on his Hammonasset land; for in December of that year, in town meeting at New Haven, "upon complaint made by some of the planters of Totoket that the Mohegan Indians have done much damage to them by setting their traps in the walk of their cattle, it was ordered that the marshal shall go with Thomas Whitway to warn Uncas, or his brother, or else Foxon, to come and speak with the governor and the magistrates." At this time Uncas, having sold a strip of land on the shore, still claimed for his son by his Hammonasset wife the northern part of the land which she had inherited. He and his son united in a deed conveying it to the planters of Guilford in January, 1663. The mark of Uncas affixed to the deed is a rude image of a turtle; and that of his son Ahaddon, *alias* Joshua, is a still more unsuccessful attempt to represent a deer.

The rising power of Uncas and his alliance with the English drew upon him the hatred of other Indian chiefs, especially of Miantinomoh, head sachem of the

Narragansetts. Miantinomoh, while professing friendship for the English, was suspected of complicity in a plot for the destruction of all white men throughout New England, and of those Indians who could not be detached from their cause. After prompting several vain attempts to assassinate Uncas, Miantinomoh attacked him without warning, and without regard to an engagement that he would not make war upon Uncas without permission of the English. Miantinomoh being defeated and taken prisoner, Uncas desired for his own security to put him to death; but not venturing to do so without the consent of his white allies, brought him to Hartford, and asked the advice of the governor and magistrates of Connecticut. As these occurrences had taken place in the summer of 1643 and the commissioners of the confederate colonies were to hold their first meeting in September, it was resolved to refer the whole matter to their decision, Miantinomoh being meanwhile left in the custody of the English. The commissioners determined "that as it was evident that Uncas could not be safe while Miantinomoh lived, but that either by secret treachery or open force his life would be continually in danger, he might justly put such a false and blood-thirsty enemy to death." It was further determined that if Uncas should be assailed on account of the execution of Miantinomoh, the English would, upon his desire, assist him against such violence.

The meeting of the commissioners was at Boston; and their determination in regard to Miantinomoh was kept secret till Hopkins and Fenwick, commissioners from Connecticut, and Eaton and Gregson, commissioners from New Haven, had arrived home, some intimation having been received that if it was determined to give Miantinomoh back to Uncas, these gentlemen would be seized while on their journey home, and held as hostages for the safety of the sachem.

The commissioners had stipulated that Miantinomoh should not be tortured, and that his execution should not take place within the jurisdiction of the English. Accordingly, when the decision of the commissioners was made known, Uncas, coming to Hartford, received his prisoner, and led him not only beyond the jurisdiction of Connecticut, but to the place of his capture near Norwich. When they came upon the plain where the battle had been fought, Wawequa, a brother of Uncas, was walking behind Miantinomoh. Upon a signal from his brother, Wawequa silently raised his tomahawk, and sunk it into the head of the captive, killing him with a single blow.

We have given this story of Miantinomoh and his execution, not because it is a part of the history of New Haven, but because it explains some parts of that history. It was this execution which occasioned the sending of the six soldiers from New Haven a few weeks after the event, the similar expedition about two years afterward, and perhaps the temporary residence of Uncas west of the Connecticut River in the intervening time. The uneasiness observable for some years among the Indians is also sometimes ascribed to the execution of Miantinomoh; but possibly, if he had continued to live, there might have been not only rumors of war, but an actual coalition of many tribes against the English. More than any other chieftain of his time he possessed the qualities necessary for combining whatever elements of hostility were lying separated and scattered among the aborigines; and the people of New Haven and of the other colonies seem to have felt that the danger of a general and destructive war was diminished by this victory of Uncas over Miantinomoh.

Uncas, though a faithful ally of the colonists, was utterly unteachable in regard to English civilization, morals, and religion. Standing over the fallen Miantinomoh, he cut a piece of flesh from the shoulder of his foe, and ate it, exclaiming, "It is the sweetest meat I ever ate! It makes my heart strong!" De Forest says, "He oppressed the Pequots who were subject to him; he abused and plundered those who were not properly his subjects; he robbed one man of his wife; he robbed another man of his corn and beans; he embezzled wampum which he had been commissioned to deliver to the English; and he and his brother Wawequa took every opportunity of subjecting, or at least plundering, their neighbors. The colonists, however, did not encourage him in these acts of violence; and sometimes, as the records of those times show, administered to him sharp rebukes, and even punishment."

Happening to be in New Haven on other business when the commissioners were in session there in 1646, he was called to answer several charges, one of which was that he had beaten and plundered some Indians employed by Englishmen to hunt near New London. Uncas acknowledged that he had done wrong in using violence so near an English settlement, but did not appear very penitent for his ill treatment of the Indians. The next year the commissioners met at Boston, and Uncas was again summoned to answer many complaints brought against him. That from New London being renewed, he was fined one hundred fathom of wampum, to be divided among those who had suffered wrong at his hands. On this occasion Uncas did not appear in person, but was represented by Foxon, a sagamore who had been associated with him, apparently from the beginning of his upward career, and by diplomatic ability had contributed much to the success of his chief. Foxon was held in reputation, as the apostle Eliot informs us, even among the Massachusetts tribes, "as the wisest Indian in the country." He made a dexterous defence on this occasion, declaring that he had never heard of some of the misdeeds charged; positively denying others; justifying, as in accord with the laws and customs of the Indians, the appropriation of Obechiquod's wife when her husband had fled from the territories of his sachem, leaving her behind; and admitting the charge that Wawequa, at the head of one hundred and thirty Mohegans, had attacked and plundered the Nipmucks, carrying away thirty-five fathoms of wampum, ten copper kettles, ten large hempen baskets, and many bear-skins, deer-skins, and other articles of value; but claiming that Uncas, with his chief men, was at New Haven when it was done, and knew nothing of the affair; that he never shared in the spoils, and that some of his own Indians were robbed at the same time.

So far was Uncas from receiving with favor the religion of his allies, that a contemporary mentions him as an opposer of Mr. Fitch, the first minister of Norwich, in his endeavors to instruct the Mohegans in Christianity. "I am apt to fear," says Gookin in his "Historical Collections of the Indians in New England," "that a great obstruction to his labors is in the sachem of those Indians, whose name is Uncas, an old and wicked, wilful man, a drunkard, and otherwise very vicious, who hath always been an opposer and underminer of praying to God." Fitch himself, in a letter to Gookin, gives similar testimony, saying that Uncas and the other sachems "at first carried it teachably and tractably, until at length the sachems did discern that religion would not consist with the mere receiving of the Word, and that practical religion will throw down their heathenish idols and the sachem's tyrannical monarchy; and then the sachems, discerning this, did not only go away, but drew off their people, some by flatteries and others by threatenings, and would not suffer them to give so much as an outward attendance to the ministry of the word of God."

When Uncas went with Capt. Mason to fight against his native tribe, he was accompanied by another sagamore called by the English, Wequash, or Wequash Cook. Perhaps his name in the Indian language was a word of three syllables, as Wequashcuk. He was of the Niantic tribe, the eldest son of its chief sachem, but for some reason had not succeeded to his father's place. As he is sometimes called a Pequot, it is surmised that his mother was a Pequot, and of so low rank that her children, according to Indian law and custom, were obliged to give place to an uncle, who, upon the death of their father, became chief sachem of the Niantics. This uncle of Wequash was none other than Ninigret, whom we have already had occasion to mention as, in later times, an enemy of the English. Wequash, in 1637, when Uncas and he went with Mason, was acknowledged as a sagamore by a few followers; but as the whole number of Indians in that expedition was only seventy, and Uncas was so much more prominent than Wequash that the latter is barely mentioned by the historians, it is evident that his clan was not numerous. Probably as a sagamore, he was more nearly on a par with Montowese than with Momaugin.

When Mason, after a march of about two miles before dawn of day, drew near to Mystic Fort, he sent for his Indian allies to come to the front. Only Uncas and Wequash came. Mason inquired of them where the fort was. They replied that it was on the top of the hill at whose foot they were now standing. "He demanded of them where were the other Indians. They answered that they were much afraid. The captain sent to them not to fly, but to surround the fort at any distance they pleased, and see whether Englishmen would fight." These timid allies did but very little fighting, but they were interested and astonished observers. The destruction of the fort and of its occupants made, doubtless, upon all of them a profound impression of respect for English power; but in the mind of Wequash it awakened a spirit of inquiry in regard to the Englishmen's God, which led him finally to a hearty and influential reception of Christianity. An account of his religious experience may perhaps be best given in the language of an anonymous contemporary:—

"This man, a few years since, seeing and beholding the mighty power of God in our English forces, how they fell upon the Pequots, when divers hundreds of them were slain in an hour, the

Lord as a God of glory in great terror did appear to the soul and conscience of this poor wretch in that very act; and though before that time he had low apprehensions of our God, having conceived him to be (as he said) but a mosquito God or a God like unto a fly; and as mean thoughts of the English that served this God, that they were silly, weak men; yet from that time he was convinced and persuaded that our God was a most dreadful God; and that one Englishman by the help of his God was able to slay and put to flight an hundred Indians.

"This conviction did pursue and follow him night and day, so that he could have no rest or quiet because he was ignorant of the Englishman's God: he went up and down bemoaning his condition, and filling every place where he came with sighs and groans. Afterward it pleased the Lord that some English well acquainted with his language did meet with him; thereupon, as a hart panting after the water brooks, he enquired after God with such incessant diligence that they were constrained constantly for his satisfaction to spend more than half the night in conversing with him.

"Afterward he came to dwell amongst the English at Connecticut; and travailing with all his might and lamenting after the Lord, his manner was to smite his hand on his breast and to complain sadly of his heart, saying it was much *matchet* (that is, very evil), and when any spake with him, he would say, 'Wequash no God, Wequash no know Christ.' It pleased the Lord, that, in the use of the means, he grew greatly in the knowledge of Christ and in the principles of religion, and became thoroughly reformed according to his light, hating and loathing himself for his dearest sins, which were especially these two, lust and revenge. This repentance for the former was testified by his temperance and abstinence from all occasions or matter of provocation thereunto; secondly, by putting away all his wives, saving the first, to whom he had most right. His repentance for the latter was testified by an eminent degree of meekness and patience, that now, if any did abuse him, he could lie down at their feet; and if any did smite him on the one cheek, he would rather turn the other than offend them (many trials he had from the Indians in this case); secondly, by going up and down to those he had offered violence or wrong unto, confessing it, and making restitution.

"Afterward he went amongst the Indians, like that poor woman of Samaria, proclaiming Christ, and telling them what a treasure he had found, instructing them in the knowledge of the true God; and this he did with a grave and serious spirit, warning them with all faithfulness to flee from the wrath to come, by breaking off their sins and wickedness. This course of his did so disturb the devil that ere long some of the Indians, whose hearts Satan had filled, did secretly give him poison, which he took without suspicion; and, when he lay upon his death bed, some Indians who were by him wishing him, according to the Indian manner, to send for a powwow, that is, a wizard; he told them, 'If Jesus Christ say that Wequash shall live, than Wequash must live; if Jesus Christ say that Wequash shall die, then Wequash is willing to die, and will not lengthen out his life by any such means.' Before he died, he did bequeath his child to the godly care of the English for education and instruction, and so yielded up his soul into Christ's hands.[1]"

This anonymous witness, who was apparently a New England minister visiting the mother country, amplifies more than any other the story of Wequash's conversion and subsequent Christian life; but his story is in the main corroborated by contemporaries writing over their own names. Winthrop thus records the case:—

"One Wequash Cook, an Indian, living about Connecticut River's mouth, and keeping much at Saybrook with Mr. Fenwick, attained to good knowledge of the things of God and salvation by Christ, so as he became a preacher to other Indians, and labored much to convert them, but without any effect, for within a short time he fell sick, not without suspicion of poison from them, and died very comfortably."

[1] New England's First Fruits, London, Printed by R. O. and G. D. for Henry Overton, and are to be sold at his shop in Popes-head-alley 1643.

The fervent Thomas Shepard writes in a letter to a friend:—

"Wequash, the famous Indian at the river's mouth, is dead, and certainly in heaven; gloriously did the grace of Christ shine forth in his conversion; a year and a half before his death he knew Christ; he loved Christ; he preached Christ up and down, and then suffered martyrdom for Christ; and when he died, he gave his soul to Christ, and his only child to the English, rejoicing in this hope that the child should know more of Christ than its poor father ever did."

Roger Williams, mentioning Wequash in his "Key into the Indian Languages," says:—

"Two days before his death, as I passed up to Connecticut River, it pleased my worthy friend Mr. Fenwick, whom I visited at his house in Saybrook Fort at the mouth of that river, to tell me that my old friend Wequash lay very sick. I desired to see him, and himself was pleased to be my guide two miles where Wequash lay. Amongst other discourse concerning his sickness and death, in which he freely bequeathed his son to Mr. Fenwick, I closed with him concerning his soul. He told me that some two or three years before, he had lodged at my house, when I acquainted him with the condition of all mankind and his own in particular; how God created man and all things; how man fell from God and his present enmity against God, and the wrath of God against him until repentance. Said he, 'Your words were never out of my heart to this present, and me much pray to Jesus Christ.' I told him, so did many English, French, and Dutch, who had never turned to God, nor loved him. He replied in broken English, 'Me so big-naughty heart; me heart all one stone!' Savory expressions, using to breathe from compunct and broken hearts and a sense of inward hardness and unbrokenness. I had many discourses with him in his life, but this was the sum of our last parting until our general meeting."

Though Wequash did but little active fighting at Mystic, he drew upon himself by his alliance with the

English the deep hostility of some of his own race, This hatred may have been afterward intensified by his espousal of the religion of the white men. But if he died by poison, it was doubtless his friendship for the English which inflamed his murderers.

Indeed, from the first, his friends feared that his life was in danger. Capt. Stoughton, sending home to the governor and council of Massachusetts a report of his expedition westward in pursuit of the remnant of the Pequots, says, " For Wequash, we fear he is killed; and if he be, 'tis a mere wicked plot; and seeing he showed faithfulness to us, and for it is so rewarded, it is hard measure to us-ward; and what is meet to be done therein is difficult for me to conclude. I shall, therefore, desire your speedy advice."

If Wequash was in Stoughton's expedition, as this mention of him suggests, he must have been a valuable source of information in regard to Quinnipiac, for he was in some way connected with the Indians of that place. A deed, in which Uncas conveyed land to the planters of Guilford, denies the ownership of other Indians, who "have seemed to lay claim to these lands aforesaid, as the sachem squaw of Quinnipiac, and Wequash through her right, the one-eyed squaw of Totoket and others." Wequash himself, a few weeks previous to this sale by Uncas, had signed a deed conveying a tract of land to Mr. Whitfield, alleging that he derived his title from the sachem squaw of Quinnipiac. For some reason which does not appear on the record, the proprietors of New Haven accounted themselves under obligation to Wequash; for, under date of Nov. 29, 1641, "it is ordered that Wequash shall have a suit of clothes made at the town's charge." As this was but a few months before his death, and during that year and a half which he spent in going up and down preaching to the Indians, it may be conjectured that it was in reward for such evangelistic labor expended on the red men of Quinnipiac. But if such were the occasion of the gift, why should it not appear on the record? More probably it was for information in regard to Indian conspiracies; for, nine months after this gift to Wequash, and only one month after his decease, a friendly sagamore came to Mr. Ludlow at Fairfield, as he worked in his hayfield, and discovered a plot, desiring "a promise that his name might be concealed, for, if it were known, it would cost him his life, and he should be served as Wequash was for being so faithful to the English." Promise of concealment was made, and he related what he knew concerning the plot in which Miantinomoh was concerned. It designed, first, the assassination of Uncas, and then a general and simultaneous massacre of the English. "As soon as the Sabbath was past, Mr. Ludlow rode to New Haven, and there intended to take advice with them, and so to proceed to Connecticut. But when he came to New Haven, and procured Mr. Eaton, Mr. Goodyear, and Mr. Davenport, to give him meeting, and opened things unto them, they presently declared there was an Indian from Long Island that had declared the same to them *verbatim*.[1]" If this testimony be trustworthy, it would seem that the death of Wequash was the first fruits of a plot which intended the destruction of all the English, and of their Indian allies.

[1] Relation of the Indian plot. Mass. Hist. Coll., XXIII. p. 161.

The reader may form some idea of Wequash's wardrobe, when he learns, that two months previous to the gift of the English clothes by New Haven, he received from Mr. Whitfield, in payment for his land in Guilford, "a frieze coat, a blanket, an Indian coat, one fathom of Dutchman's coat, a shirt, a pair of stockings, a pair of shoes, a fathom of wampum."

The story of Wequash naturally leads to an account of efforts within the colony of New Haven for the civilization and evangelization of the aborigines. Wequash was described on his tombstone at Lyme as the first convert among the New England tribes; but this statement seems to have been made by one imperfectly informed in regard to Plymouth and Massachusetts. Palfrey mentions by name several Indians of whom English Christians in those colonies entertained, at an earlier date, "good hopes in their hearts." The success of the evangelistic work of Eliot and the Mayhews in Massachusetts, a few years after the death of Wequash, enkindled such interest in the mother country that a corporation was created by act of Parliament, "for the promoting and propagating of the gospel of Jesus Christ in New England." Its charter directed that the commissioners of the United Colonies of New England, or such as they should appoint, should have power to receive and dispose of the moneys brought in "in such manner as should best and principally conduce to the preaching and propagating of the gospel amongst the natives, and the maintenance of schools and nurseries of learning for the education of the children of the natives." The funds thus provided were chiefly expended in the older colonies; but, in Connecticut, Mr. Blinman, the minister of New London, and in the colony of New Haven, Mr. Pierson, the minister of Branford, were employed by this corporation. The efforts of Mr. Fitch of Norwich to instruct his heathen neighbors have been already mentioned. "The minsters of the several towns where Indians lived," says Trumbull, "instructed them as they had opportunity; but all attempts for Christianizing the Indians in Connecticut were attended with little success. They were engaged a great part of their time in such implacable wars among themselves, were so ignorant of letters and the English language, and the English ministers in general were so entirely ignorant of their dialect, that it was extremely difficult to teach them. Not one Indian church was ever gathered by the English ministers in Connecticut. Several Indians, however, in one town and another, became Christians, and were baptized and admitted to full communion in the English churches." This testimony of Trumbull was intended to cover the territory which had belonged to the colony of New Haven as truly as the other part of Connecticut. Of the ministers of the New Haven colony, Mr. Pierson seems to have been most proficient in the Indian tongue; he "and his Indian" being employed as interpreters in the negotiation of important business. He preached to the red men in their own language, and commenced to prepare a catechism, a part of which being submitted to the commissioners of the United Colonies, at their meeting, in 1656, they advised that it be completed, and "turned into the Narragansett or Pequot, and for that purpose they spake with and desired Thomas Stanton to advise with Mr. Pierson about a fit season to meet and translate the same." Mr. Pierson, displeased at the absorption of New Haven by Connecticut, removed out of the colony. Perhaps a few years more of perseverance might have produced a much greater result, and brought to view some fruits of the labor expended, which, by reason of its untimely cessation, have remained unknown.

But, though comparatively little was accomplished by preaching to the Indians in their own tongue, many youth, being received into English families, were instructed as if they had been born in the house; so that after a few years from the beginning, there were civilized and Christian Indians living among the English, speaking English, wearing English cloth, owning land, following trades, and frequenting public assemblies on the Lord's day.

CHAPTER XVI.

DOMESTIC AND SOCIAL LIFE.

IN a former chapter the mansion of Gov. Eaton has been described with nearly as much of detail as it is now possible to give. The fame of three other houses, as handed down by tradition, has also been mentioned. President Stiles relates, on the authority of one of the mechanics who demolished the Allerton house, that the wood was all of oak, and of the best joiner-work. Ranking next to these four were other houses of framed timber, smaller and less stately, but equal and similar to the ordinary dwelling-house of the seventeenth and the first half of the eighteenth century, a few specimens of which still remain in almost every ancient town. In shape they differed one from another as old houses differ in the same neighborhood in England; but they probably were copies, in most cases, of some style of house prevalent in the country or parish where the emigrant had been born. Commonly they had two stories, though some, being in the lean-to shape, showed a second story only in front. Often the second story projected over the first; and this style, though not devised for such an end, but copied from numerous examples in the mother country, was regarded as especially convenient for defensive warfare

DOMESTIC AND SOCIAL LIFE. 349

against savage foes. Lower in rank than these framed buildings were log houses, which, when small and built with little expenditure of joiner-work, were called huts rather than houses; as on a western prairie a log cabin is even now distinguished from a log house.

In Guilford several dwellings, as well as the meeting-house, were built of stone. In the summer of 1651 the record was made, "The meeting-house appointed to be thatched and clayed before winter." This order indicates that the stone was  not laid in mortar, but, as many stone chimneys which have lasted to our time, in clay. In the course of years the clay had fallen out, and the walls, that they might exclude the cold winds of winter, needed to be again pointed with this substitute for mortar. The order to thatch, shows that in Guilford, if not in the other plantations, a thatched roof was thought worthy to cover their most honored edifices.

WHITFIELD HOUSE, AS SEEN FROM THE SOUTH.

WHITFIELD HOUSE, AS SEEN FROM THE WEST.

Among the dwellings in Guilford which were built of stone, was that of Mr. Whitfield, the minister. It is mentioned by Palfrey, in his "History of New England" as "the oldest house in the United States now standing as originally built, unless there be older at St. Augustine in Florida." Since the publication of Mr.

Palfrey's History, great changes have been wrought in the appearance and internal arrangement of the house, but it still preserves an aspect of antiquity. The following description, with the accompanying plans, was furnished to Mr. Palfrey by Mr. Ralph D. Smith of Guilford:—

"The walls are of stone, from a ledge eighty rods distant to the east. It was probably brought on hand-barrows, across a swamp, over a rude causey which is still to be traced. A small addition, not here represented, has in modern times been made to the back of the house; but there is no question that the main building remains in its original state, even to the oak of the beams, floors, doors, and window-sashes. The following representations of the interior exhibit accurately the dimensions of the rooms, windows, and doors, the thickness of the walls, &c., on a scale of ten feet to the inch.[1] The single dotted lines represent fireplaces and doors. The double dotted lines represent windows. In the recesses of the windows are broad seats. Within the memory of some of the residents of the town, the panes of glass were of diamond shape.

"The height of the first story is seven feet and two-thirds. The height of the second is six feet and three-quarters. At the southerly corner in the second story there was originally an embrasure, about a foot wide, with a stone flooring, which still remains. The exterior walls are now closed up, but not the walls within.

"The walls of the front and back of the house terminate at the floor of the attic, and the rafters lie upon

---

[1] In this volume the horizontal sections of the house are reduced in size, so tha 'he scale is twenty feet to the inch.

them. The angle of the roof is 60°, making the base and sides equal. At the end of the wing, by the chimney, is a recess, which must have been intended as a

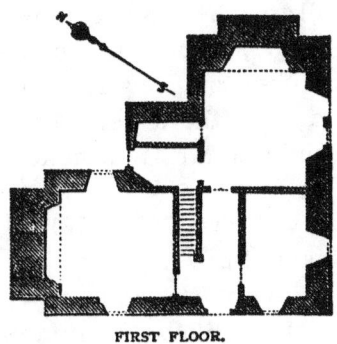

FIRST FLOOR.

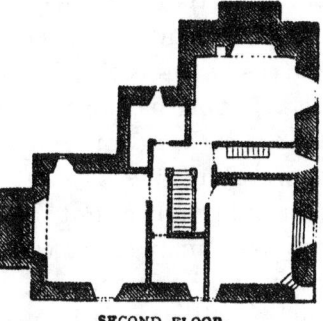

SECOND FLOOR.

place of concealment. The interior wall has the appearance of touching the chimney, like the wall at the northwest end; but the removal of a board discovers two closets, which project beyond the lower part of the building."

The Whitfield house differed from the typical New England dwelling, both in the material of which it was built, and in its interior arrangement. Houses were usually supported, not by walls of stone, but by frames of heavy timber. White oak was a favorite wood for this purpose, and some of the larger pieces were considerably more than a foot square. Mr. Whitfield, though he was a man of wealth, had no more apartments in his dwelling than the average New Eng-

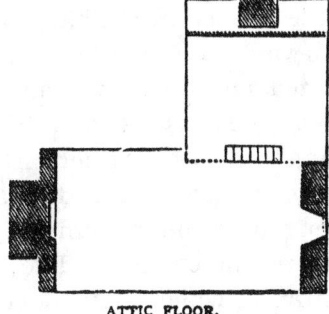

ATTIC FLOOR.

land planter. It is not easy to conjecture where he had his study, nor where he lodged his ten children, some of whom were nearly or quite adult when he came to Guilford. His house seems small for the requirements of his family and of his calling, and surprisingly small in contrast with that of the minister of New Haven. Mr. Davenport had but one child; but there were thirteen fireplaces in his house, while in Mr. Whitfield's there were but five.

A framed house not exceeding that of Mr. Whitfield in its dimensions, would have but one chimney, which would be in the middle of the house, and not in the outer wall, as in a house of stone. Such a chimney measured about ten feet in diameter where it passed through the first floor, being even larger in the cellar and tapering as it ascended; the fireplace in one of the apartments of the first floor being six or eight feet long. A door in the middle of the front side of the house opened into a hall, which contained the principal stairway on the side opposite to the entrance, and opened on the right hand and on the left into front rooms used as parlors, but furnished, one or both of them, with beds, which, if not commonly in use, stood ready to answer such drafts upon hospitality as are frequent in a new country, where all traveling is by private conveyance. The apartment most used by the family, in which they cooked and ate their food, and in winter, gathered about the spacious fireplace, was in the rear of the chimney. At one end of it was a small bed-room, and at the other, a buttery.

The frame of such a house was covered with clapboards or with shingles, and, after a little experience, the planters learned to prefer cedar shingles to perishable and inflammable thatch as a covering for the roof. The floors were of thick oak boards, fastened with wooden pins. The rooms were plastered only on the sides, the joists and floor above being exposed to view. In the parlors, the side contiguous to the chimney was usually wainscoted, and thus displayed wide panels from the largest trees of the primeval forest. The window-sashes, bearing glass cut into small diamond-shaped panes, and set with lead, were hung with hinges to the window-frames, and opened outward. The doors were of upright boards, fastened together with battens, and had wooden latches. The outside doors were made of two layers of board, one upright and one transverse, fastened together with clinched nails so arranged as to cover the door with diamond-shaped figures of equal dimension. The front door was made in two valves, which, when closed, met in the middle, and were fastened in that position by a wooden bar, placed across from one lintel to the other, and secured by iron staples.

Farm houses were commonly built near a spring, which supplied water for domestic use, as well as for the cattle. If a well was dug, either in town or in country, the water was drawn from it by means of a sweep moving vertically on a fulcrum at the top of a post. From the lighter end of the well-sweep a smaller pole or rod, with a bucket attached, was suspended. When the bucket had been lowered and dipped, the sweep was so nearly poised that the water could be drawn up with little effort. The following record shows that pumps were not unknown: "Robert Johnson desired that he might have liberty to make a well in the street near his house. The Court, fearing some danger might come by it, propounded that he, and his neighbors joining with him, would put a pump in it; whereupon he took time to speak with them, and consider of it." This was in 1649. Six years afterward, when the younger Winthrop was expected to spend the winter in New Haven, Mr. Davenport writes to him that Mrs. Davenport had taken care of his apples, had provided twenty loads of wood, thirty bushels of wheat, fifty pounds of candles, tables, and some chairs, and a cleanly, thrifty maid-servant for Mrs. Winthrop, and had caused the well to be cleaned, and a new pump to be set up.

In the seventeenth century, as compared with the present day, household furniture was rude and scanty, even in England; and doubtless emigration to a new country deprived the planters of New England of some domestic conveniences which they might have possessed if they had remained at home. A few of the most distinguished men in New Haven had tapestry hangings in their principal apartments; and Gov. Eaton had, in addition to such luxuries, two Turkey carpets, a tapestry carpet, a green carpet fringed, and a small green carpet, besides rugs; but the mansion of a planter who had been a London merchant is no more fit to be taken as a fair specimen of contemporary dwellings than the hut in which the pit-man in a saw-pit sheltered his family. The floors in the house of a planter whom his neighbors called "Goodman," and generally in the houses of men to whose names the title of Mr. was prefixed, were bare of carpets. Excepting the beds, which stood in so many of the apartments, the most conspicuous and costly piece of furniture in the house was, perhaps, a tall case of drawers in the parlor. It was called a case of drawers, and not a bureau, for at that time a writing-board was a principal feature of a bureau. If, as was sometimes the case, there were drawers in the lower part, and a chest at the top, it was called a chest of drawers. This form, being in itself less expensive, received less of ornament, and was to be found even in the cottages of the poor. Still another form had drawers below and doors above, which, being opened, revealed small drawers for the preservation of important papers or other articles of value. This form was sometimes called a cabinet. After the death of Gov. Eaton "there was found in his *cabinet* a paper fairly written with his own hand, and subscribed also with his own hand, having his seal also thereunto affixed," which was accepted as his last will and testament, "though not testified by any witnesses, nor subscribed by any hands as witnesses." The inventory of Gov. Eaton does not mention a cabinet, but specifies among the items "in the green chamber," which was evidently the most elegant of his apartments, a cupboard with drawers. This was doubtless, under a more homely name, the same piece of furniture, which, in the probate record, is called a cabinet.

The inventory of Gov. Eaton makes no mention of a clock, and probably there was none in the colony of New Haven while he lived, unless his friend Davenport had so early become the possessor of the "clock with appurtenances," which, after the death of its owner, was appraised at £5.

At a later date a clock outranked the case of drawers

however elegant, by its greater rarity and greater cost. For a long time after their first appearance, clocks were to be found only in the dwellings of the opulent, the generality of the people measuring time by noon-marks and sun-dials.

Table furniture, as compared with that of the present day, was especially scanty. Forks were not in common use in England till after the union of New Haven with Connecticut, though, as Palfrey suggests, there was a very liberal supply of napkins as if fingers were sometimes used for forks. Spoons used by families of the middle class were commonly of a base metal called alchymy, though some such families had a few spoons of silver. But if silver ware was not in general use, families of opulence seem to have been well supplied with it. Gov. Eaton had, including the basin and ewer presented to Mrs. Eaton by the Eastland Fellowship, £140 worth of plate. Mr. Davenport's plate was appraised at £50. One of the items was a silver tankard, still preserved in the family [1]

Table-dishes were generally of wood or of pewter, though China and earthen ware are specified in the inventory of Mr. Davenport's estate. Vessels of glass are also sometimes mentioned in inventories. Drinking-vessels, called cans, were cups of glass, silver or pewter, with handles attached to them. Porringers were small, bowl-shaped vessels, for holding the porridge commonly served for breakfast or supper. Usually they were of pewter and supplied with handles. Meat was brought to the table on platters of pewter or of

[1] An engraving of it may be seen in "The Davenport Family," by A. B. Davenport, Supplementary Edition, p. 404,

wood, and from these was transferred to wooden trenchers; which, in their cheapest form, were square pieces of board, but often were cut by the lathe into the circular shape of their porcelain successors.[1]

In all but the most wealthy families, food was cooked in the apartment where it was eaten, and at the large fireplace, which by its size distinguished the most frequented apartment of the house. A trammel in the chimney, by means of its hook, which could be moved up or down according to the amount of fuel in use at the time, held the pot or kettle at the proper distance above the fire. At one end of the fireplace was an oven in the chimney. Supplementary to these instruments for boiling and baking were a gridiron, a long-handled frying-pan, and a spit for roasting before the fire. At the end of the room, pewter platters, porringers, and basins, when not in use, were displayed on open shelves; and hanging against the wide panels of the wainscot were utensils of tin and brass, the brightness of the metals showing forth the comparative merit of the housekeeping. The brass-ware included such articles as the ladle, the skimmer, the colander, and the warming-pan.

The diet of the planters necessarily consisted chiefly

[1] Persons are still living, who can remember when wooden trenchers were in general use in England, instead of the porcelain plates which even the poorest householder now provides. A middle-aged farmer in Sussex told me that in his childhood trenchers were more common than plates, and pointed out a mill where the trenchers were turned; and I have recently seen in a newspaper an account, by a living graduate of the Wykeham School at Winchester, of the table fare in that school when he was a boy, in which he says that they ate on square trenchers.

of domestic products, though commerce, as we have seen, supplied the tables of the wealthy with sugar, foreign fruits and wines. Kine and sheep were few during the early years of the colony, but there was such an abundance and variety of game that the scarcity of beef and mutton was but a small inconvenience.[1] In towns, venison brought in by English or Indian hunters was usually to be obtained of the truck-master; and at the farms, wild geese, wild turkeys, moose, and deer, were the prizes of the sharp-shooter. The air in spring and autumn was sometimes perceptibly darkened with pigeons; the rivers were full of fish; on the sea-shore there were plenty of clams, oysters and mussels. Poultry and swine soon multiplied to such an extent that they could be used for the table; and within ten years from the foundation of New Haven, beef had become an article of export. The abundance of game, of pork, and of poultry, doubtless hastened the exportation of this commodity. Tillage produced besides the maize, the beans, and the squashes, indigenous to the country, almost every variety of food to which they had been accustomed in England.

The diet for breakfast and supper was frequently porridge made of meat, sometimes salt meat, and of pease, beans, or other vegetables. Frequently it was mush and milk. A boiled pudding of Indian meal, cooked in the same pot with the meat and vegetables which followed it, was often the first and principal course at

---

[1] Winthrop, before his wife came out, writes to her, "We are here in a paradise. Though we have not beef and mutton, yet (God be praised) we want them not: our Indian corn answers for all. Yet here is fowl and fish in great plenty."

dinner. It seems to have been assigned to the first course in the interest of frugality, to spare the more expensive pork and beef. Of esculent roots the turnip was far more highly prized and plentifully used than the potato. Tea and coffee had not yet come into general use so as to be articles of commerce even in England, but beer was the common drink of Englishmen at home and in America. A brew-house was regarded as an essential part of a homestead in the New Haven colony, and beer was on the table as regularly as bread.[1]

While the breakfast, dinner, and supper, described above, may be taken as a specimen of the diet frequently appearing on the table of a New England family in the seventeenth century, they are by no means to be regarded as a rule from which there was no variation. There were flesh-days and there were fish-days in every week; and on Saturday, the oven being heated for baking bread, a pot of beans was put in, which, being allowed to remain for twenty-four hours, furnished a warm supper for the family when they returned from public worship. There was variation from and addition to the ordinary fare on those numerous occasions when friends, traveling on horse-back, stopped to spend the night, or to rest in the middle of the day. Then the table was burdened with variety and abundance according to the means of the family and the provi-

[1] New Haven Town Records, Dec. 1, 1662. "Deacon Peck informed the town that they were much troubled to supply the elders with wheat and malt, and he feared there was want: therefore desired the town to consider of it. The deputy-governor urged it that men would endeavor to make a present supply for them."

dence of the mistress. Feasting reached its acme on the day of the annual thanksgiving, when there was such plenty of roast meats, and so extraordinary an outcome from the oven, that ordinary diet was for some days afterward displaced by the remains of the feast.

No picture of domestic life in New England could be complete which did not exhibit the family observing the annual thanksgiving. Rejecting Christmas because of the superstitions which had attached themselves to it, the Puritans established in its place another festival, which became equally domestic in the manner of its observance. Children who had left their parents to prepare for the duties of adult life, or to occupy homes which they themselves had established, were gathered again in the home of their nativity, or under the roof of those whom they had learned since they were married to call father and mother. Here they recounted the blessings of the year; and united in giving thanks to God. If there were children's children, they came with their parents, and spent the hours which remained after worship in feasting and frolic.

Family worship was an important feature of domestic life in a Puritan household. It was important because of its frequency, regularity, and seriousness. Whenever the family came to the table for breakfast, dinner, or supper, there was a grace before meat, and when they left it, a grace after meat, every person standing by his chair while the blessing was asked, and the thanks were given. The day was begun with worship, which included the reading of Scripture and prayer, and ended with a similar service, all standing during the prayer. A member of Gov. Eaton's family reports:—

"It was his custom, when he first rose in the morning, to repair unto his study; a study well perfumed with the meditations and supplications of a holy soul. After this, calling his family together, he would then read a portion of the Scripture among them, and after some devout and useful reflections upon it, he would make a prayer not long, but extraordinarily pertinent and reverent; and in the evening some of the same exercises were again attended. On the Saturday morning he would still take notice of the approaching Sabbath in his prayer, and ask the grace to be remembering of it and preparing for it; and when the evening arrived, he, besides this, not only repeated a sermon, but also instructed his people with putting of questions referring to the points of religion, which would oblige them to study for an answer; and if their answer were at any time insufficient, he would wisely and gently enlighten their understanding; all which he concluded by singing a psalm."

In the New Haven colony, the Lord's day began, according to the Hebrew manner of reckoning, at sunset. Saturday was the preparation day. The diet for the morrow was made ready so far as was possible, and the house was put in order. The kitchen floor received its weekly scrubbing, and the floor of the parlor was sprinkled anew with the white sand from the sea-shore. Before the sun had disappeared beneath the western horizon, the ploughmen had returned from the fields; the mistress and her maids had brought the house-work to a stop. Because "the evening and the morning were the first day" they began their Sabbath observance at evening. It was because Saturday evening was a part of the Lord's day that the master of a house added to the usual family worship some endeavor to impart religious instruction to his children and servants

New Haven retained its custom of beginning the Lord's day at evening, through the seventeenth and eighteenth centuries. Whatever may have been the disadvantages of the custom, they were of a worldly, and not of a spiritual, nature. Perhaps less labor was accomplished; though it admits of question whether the subtraction of an hour or two from the work-time of Saturday did not by a more thorough restoration of strength to the laborer increase rather than diminish the labor accomplished. There can be no question that the New Haven custom was more favorable to the religious improvement of the Lord's day than that, which, by exacting extra hours of labor on Saturday, occasions unusual fatigue at the end of the week. It is also indisputable that the New Haven custom exerted a refining influence by means of the social intercourse on Sunday evening, for which it afforded opportunity. Every house was then dressed; and every person, even if obliged on other days to delve and drudge, was in his best apparel. Sunday in the New Haven colony was at once a holy day and a holiday, the Puritan restraint with which it was kept till sunset giving place in the evening to recreation and social converse.

Though young men were by law forbidden " to inveigle or draw the affections of any maid without the consent of father, master, guardian, governor, or such other who hath the present interest or charge, or, in the absence of such, of the nearest magistrate, whether it be by speech, writing, message, company-meeting, unnecessary familiarity, disorderly night-meetings, sinful dalliance, gifts," or any other way, yet every respectable young man knew of some house where he might meet on Sunday evening one of the maidens whom he had seen in the opposite gallery of the meeting-house, without fear that her father, master, guardian, or governor would be displeased.

The marriages which resulted from these Sunday evening visits of the young men, were not solemnized by a minister of religion, but, according to the Puritan view of propriety, by a magistrate.[1] The requirement that marriage should be contracted before an officer of the civil authority, was a protest against the position that marriage is a sacrament of the church. It is said that the first marriage in Guilford was celebrated in the famous mansion of the minister, "the wedding table being garnished with the substantial luxuries of pork and pease." Probably this was the marriage of the pastor's daughter to Rev. John Higginson. But though the bride was his own daughter, Mr. Whitfield had no legal authority to pronounce the couple husband and wife. Clandestine marriage was carefully prevented by the requirement that the intention of the parties should be three times published at some time of public lecture or town meeting, or "be set up in writing upon some post of their meeting-house door, in public view, there to stand so as it may be easily read, by the space of fourteen days." Although the same statute required that the marriage should be in "a public place," this requirement was sufficiently answered when spectators were present; and usually marriages were solemnized at the home of the bride, and accompanied, as in the Whitfield mansion, with feasting.

[1] I have seen a parish register in England where for a century all marriages are recorded as solemnized by the clergymen, then, without a word of explanation, all marriages for several years are recorded as contracted before a justice of the peace; then, without explanation, the record returns to its old formula. Marriage by a magistrate marks the time of the commonwealth.

A marriage implied a new home,—perhaps a farm to be cut out of the primeval forest, and a house to be built with lumber yet in the log. A portion of the work had preceded the marriage, but a life-long task remained. The people were generally frugal and industrious, and the women in their sphere were as truly so as the men. The mistress and her maids, if she had them, were as busy in the house as the master and his servants in the fields. Besides the housework, the dairy-work, the sewing, and the knitting, there was everywhere spinning, and in some houses weaving. They spun cotton, linen and wool. New Haven probably had in its Yorkshire families special skill in the manufacture of cloth. Johnson, speaking in his "Wonder Working Providence" of that part of Mr. Rogers's company which began a settlement in Massachusetts and called it Rowley after the name of their former home in Yorkshire, says, "They were the first people that set upon making of cloth in the western world, for which end they built a fulling mill, and caused their little ones to be very diligent in spinning cotton, many of them having been clothiers in England." This industry, so far at least as spinning is concerned, spread through the whole community. Every farmer raised flax, which his wife caused to be wrought into linen; and wherever sheep were kept, wool was spun into yarn for the knitting-needles and the loom. A young woman who could spin, between sunrise and sunset, more than thirty knots of warp or forty of filling, was in high estimation among sagacious neighbors having marriageable sons. This industry occupied a chamber in the dwelling-house, or a separate building in the yard. The music of the wheel was frequently accompanied with song. Tradition relates that when Whalley and Goffe were concealed at Milford in a cellar under a spinning-shop, the maids, being accustomed to sing at their work, and unaware that any but themselves were within hearing, sang a satirical ballad concerning the regicides, and that the concealed auditors were so much amused that they entreated their friend, the master of the family, to procure a repetition of the song.

The simple, regular life of a planter's family was favorable to health. As compared with the present time there was but little excitement and but little worry for man or woman. As compared with Old England in the seventeenth century, New Haven, during the twenty-seven years in which it was a separate jurisdiction, might be called a healthy region. England was then often ravaged by the plague. In Sandwich in Kent there were, on the 12th of March, 1637, that is, about six weeks before the first company of New Haven planters sailed from London, "seventy-eight houses and one hundred and eighty-eight persons infected." On the 30th of June, that is, four days after the Hector arrived in Boston, "twenty-four houses and tents were shut up, in which were one hundred and three persons. From the 6th of July to the 5th of October there were buried in St. Clement's parish about ten every week who died of the plague." While Mr. Davenport was vicar of St. Stephen's, the city of London was visited with a pestilence which swept away thirty-five thousand of its inhabitants. The parish register records the vote of the parishioners "that Mr. Davenport shall have of the parish funds in respect of his care and pains taken in time of the visitation of sickness, as a gratuity, the sum of £20."

In coming to New Haven, the planters found a more salubrious or certainly a less deadly atmosphere than they had breathed in England; nevertheless they were grievously afflicted with sickness, malaria having been more prevalent than in the other New England colonies.

"It is not annual," says Hubbard, "as in Virginia, there being sundry years when there is nothing considerable of it, nor ordinarily so violent and universal; yet at some times it falls very hard upon the inhabitants, not without strange varieties of the dispensations of Providence; for some years it hath been almost universal upon the plantations, yet little mortality; at other times, it hath been very mortal in a plantation or two, when others that have had as many sick, have scarcely made one grave; it hath been known also in some years that some one plantation hath been singled out and visited after a sore manner when others have been healthy round about." Much has been written of the depression which settled upon the town of New Haven in consequence of the failure of its expectations in regard to commerce; but perhaps the prevalence of malaria may have had much to do with the discouragement of the people, for, as this disease in modern times takes away the energy and hopefulness of the patient, so it was then, as Hubbard testifies, "attended with great prostration of spirits."

The following record shows not only that the years 1658 and 1659 were very sickly in the principal plantation, but that there was a general remissness in paying the physician. At a town meeting, Jan. 29, 1660:—

"Mr. Augur declared that (it having pleased God to visit the town sorely by sickness the two last years) his stock of physic is gone, and how to procure more out of his returns he saw not, being disabled by the non-payment of some and the unsuitable payment of others.· To get supplies, those that were Mr. Augur's debtors were called upon to attend their duty. It was also declared that if Mr. Augur see cause to bring any of them to the court, it will be witnessed against as a wrong to the public, that a physician should be discouraged."

As Mr. Augur had signified about a year before, his intention to lay down the practice of physic because his pay was not brought in with satisfactory promptness, and the neglect to pay him had been "witnessed against as an act of unrighteousness," probably there was some temporary virtue in the witnessing of the General Court in his behalf.

Mr. Augur was at this time the only physician in the town of New Haven, Mr. Pell and Mr. Westerhouse having removed some years before. That he was not in high repute appears from attempts which were made to procure another physician. In November, 1651, soon after Mr. Pell's removal:—

"The governor acquainted the Court that there is a physician come to the town, who, he thinks, is willing to stay here, if he may have encouragement. He is a Frenchman; but hath lived in England and in Holland a great while, and hath good testimonials from both places, and from the University of Franeker where he hath approved himself in his disputations able in understanding in that art; and Mr. Davenport saith, he finds in discourse with him, that his abilities answer the testimony given. Now the town may consider what they will do in the case, for it is not good to neglect such providences of God when they are offered. The Court, after consideration, desired the former committee to speak with him, and desire his settling amongst us; and that he may have a house provided, and encouraged in provisions and what also is necessary, to the value of ten pounds."

The committee reported soon after "that they had spoken with the French doctor, and find his wants so many that ten pounds will go but a little way in providing for him." But so strong was the desire to have Dr. Chais remain, that a house was procured, and furniture was loaned by divers persons. In less than three months "the magistrates and elders were desired to speak with the doctor, and see if they cannot settle a more moderate price for his visiting of sick folk than he hath yet taken;" and in a little more than a year after the town had invited him to settle, they consented "that he shall have liberty to go, as he sees he hath opportunity."

Unable to retain Dr. Chais, some obtained medical advice and medicines from John Winthrop, jun., who resided at Pequot, afterward named New London. Mr. Davenport sends an Indian, as a special messenger, with a letter dated Aug. 20, 1653, inquiring how he can best consult with him about the state of his body, whether by coming to Pequot to sojourn for a time, or by accompanying Winthrop on a journey,—which he has heard that the latter intends to make to Boston,—or by waiting for Winthrop to visit New Haven after his return from the Bay. In the spring of 1655, he says, "The winter hath been extraordinarily long and sharp and sickly among us " " My family hath been kept from the common sickness in this town, by the goodness and mercy of

God, this winter; only Edmund, my man-servant, hath been exercised with it near unto death." Soon after this, Winthrop took Mr. Malbon's house, and for the space of two or three years resided part of the time in New Haven, very much to the content of those who did not think highly of Mr. Augur's skill. The town were so desirous of securing Winthrop, that they would have freely given the use of the house; but he was a man unwilling to be put under obligation, and therefore the house was sold to him for £100 to be paid in goats at his farm on Fisher's Island. He ceased to reside in New Haven before the great sickness of 1658 and 1659, and sold the house back to the town in the last named year. Mr. Davenport, writing to him during the sickness, mentions such symptoms as gripings, vomitings, fluxes, agues and fevers, giddiness, much sleepiness, and burning. He says, "It comes by fits every other day." He informs him that the supply of medicine he had left with Mrs. Davenport is spent. "The extremities of the people have caused her to part with what she reserved for our own family, if need should require." He adds in a postscript, "Sir, my wife desires a word or two of advice from you, what is best to be done for those gripings and agues and fevers; but she is loth to be too troublesome; yet as the cases are weighty, she desires to go upon the surest ground, and to take the safest courses, and knoweth none whose judgment she can so rest in as in yours."

With all the despondency resting upon the town, there was mingled the same comfort which comforts all communities afflicted with malaria; namely, the conviction that the evil is not so great as in some other places. Mr. Davenport, when writing that "many are afflictively exercised," adds, "though more moderately in this town, by the mercy of God, than at Norwalk and Fairfield. Young Mr. Allerton, who lately came from the Dutch, saith they are much more sorely visited there, than these parts are. It is said that at Maspeag the inhabitants are generally so ill that they are likely to lose their harvest through want of ability to reap it."

It is evident that the care of the sick must have been an important part of domestic life in New Haven while these malarial diseases prevailed. With more or less of skill, and more or less of success, every family nursed its sick. There was sickness alike in the hut of the mean man, and in the mansion of the governor. Death with impartial step entered where he pleased. With what degree of skill the disease was combated at first, the reader may guess from the declaration of Hubbard that the "gentle conductitious aiding of nature hath been found better than sudden and violent means by purgation or otherwise; and blood-letting, though much used in Europe for fevers, especially in the hotter countries, is found deadly in this fever, even almost without escaping."

The restraint which the Puritans put upon their feelings appears, perhaps, more wonderful when death entered the house, than at any other time. We have a detailed report of the manner in which Gov. Eaton carried himself when his eldest son was called to die:—

"His eldest son he maintained at the college until he proceeded master of arts; and he was indeed the son of his vows, and the son of great hopes. But a severe catarrh diverted this younng gentlemen from the work of the ministry, whereunto his father had once devoted him: and a malignant fever, then raging in those parts of the country, carried off him with his wife within two or three days of one another. This was counted the sorest of all the trials that ever befell his father in the days of the years of his pilgrimage, but he bore it with a patience and composure of spirit truly admirable. His dying son looked earnestly on him, and said, 'Sir, what shall we do?' Whereto, with a well ordered countenance, he replied, 'Look up to God!' And when he passed by his daughter, drowned in tears on this occasion, to her he said, 'Remember the sixth commandment; hurt not yourself with immoderate grief; remember Job, who said, "The Lord hath given, and the Lord hath taken away; blessed be the name of the Lord." You may mark what a note the spirit of God put upon it,—" In all this Job sinned not, nor charged God foolishly." God accounts it a charging him foolishly when we don't submit unto him patiently.' Accordingly he now governed himself as one that had attained unto the rule of weeping as if he wept not; for, it being the Lord's day, he repaired unto the church in the afternoon, as he had been there in the forenoon, though he was never like to see his dearest son alive any more in this world. And though, before the first prayer began, a messenger came to prevent Mr. Davenport's praying for the sick person who was now dead, yet his affectionate father altered not his course, but wrote after the preacher as formerly; and when he came home, he held on his former methods of divine worship in his family, not, for the excuse of Aaron, omitting anything in the service of God. In like sort, when the people had been at the solemn interment of this his worthy son, he did with a very unpassionate aspect and carriage then say, 'Friends, I thank you all for your love and help, and for this testimony of respect unto me and mine: the Lord hath given, and the Lord hath taken; blessed be the name of the Lord.' Nevertheless, retiring hereupon into the chamber where his daugter then lay sick, some tears were observed falling from him while he uttered these words, 'There is a difference between a sullen silence or a stupid senselessness under the hand of God, and a child-like submission thereunto.'"

Not all Puritans attained so near to the Puritan ideal as Theophilus Eaton, but all had something of his self-control. They governed themselves as seeing Him who is invisible.

Social life among the planters of tho New Haven colony had for its basis contemporary social life in England, but was modified by Puritanism, and by emigration to a wilderness. Some features of it which seem strange to one who is acquainted only with the present age, were brought with them across the water, and disappeared earlier than in the old country. They brought with them English ideas of social rank, of the relative duties of parents and children, of the reserve and seclusion proper for young women, and of the supervision under which young people of the different sexes might associate. They did not originate the public sentiment or the legislation on these subjects which provokes the merriment of the present age.

Their religious convictions of course influenced their social life. It would be impossible that any community as homogenous and earnest in religion as they were, should not have some peculiarity springing from this source. A peculiarity of the Puritans was seriousness. Such convictions as they cherished will necessarily produce more than an average seriousness of manner; and if this be true in a prosperous community whose tranquility has not been disturbed for a generation, we should expect to find even more seriousness among a people who have expatriated themselves for their religious convictions. If we again take Theophilus Eaton as an illustration, he was a man of gravity when residing in

London and in the East countries. He would have been such if the Puritan party had been in power, and he consequently in security. He was probably more so by reason of the annoyances and dangers to which he and his friends were exposed. Having undertaken to establish a new plantation in the wilderness, his greater responsibility would naturally produce a deeper seriousness. A member of his family testifies that "he seldom used any recreations, but, being a great reader, all the time he could spare from company and business, he commonly spent in his beloved study." It would be an error, however, to suppose that this seriousness had with it no admixture of gayety, for Hubbard, who was partly his contemporary, describes him as "of such pleasantness and fecundity of harmless wit as can hardly be paralleled."

Residence in a new country also influenced social life, but not as much as in many other cases of removal to a wilderness. It has been said in modern time that emigration tends to barbarism; but this could not have been true in their case, in any considerable degree. From the first Sabbath, they maintained the public worship of God. Before the first year had passed, their children were gathered into a school. Laws were as diligently executed as anywhere in the world. Every plantation had in it, from the first some persons of polite manners, to whom those of less culture looked up with respect. The principal plantation was a compact and populous town, and some of its inhabitants were not only refined, but wealthy. The peculiarity of their social state was not that they were more barbarous than other Englishmen, but it consisted rather in that mutual dependence and helpfulness usually to be found in a new country. News from home was communicated to the neighbors. Letters of intelligence, an institution which during the existence of the colony began to give place to printed newspapers, were passed from hand to hand.[1] Corn was husked and houses were "raised" by neighborly kindness. The whole plantation sympathized with a family afflicted with sickness, and the neighbors assisted them in nursing and watching. Families entertained travelers after the manner of Christians of the first centuries, and highly prized their visits and seasons of fellowship, and opportunities for learning the news of the day. The train-band and the night watch were also peculiar features of the social system incident to a plantation in the wilderness. Comparing the social state in the New Haven colony with that which now obtains on the same teritory, we find more manifestations of social inequality. This appears in the titles prefixed to names. The name of a young man had no prefix till he became a master workman. Then, if he were an artisan or a husbandman, he might be addressed by the honorary title of Goodman, and his wife might be called Goodwife or Goody. A person who employed laborers but did not labor with them was distinguished from one whose prefix was Goodman, by the prefix Mr. This term of respect was accorded to elders, magistrates, teachers, merchants, and men of wealth, whether engaged in merchandise, or living in retirement from

[1] Notice on page 419 what Mr. Davenport says of "the two Weekly Intelligences." These were, I think, two numbers of a printed periodical.

trade.¹ Social inequality was also strikingly manifest in the "seating of the meeting-house," the governor and deputy-governor being seated on the front form, and allowed its whole length for the accommodation of themselves and their guests, while others were disposed behind them and in the end seats, according to social position; but a back seat of the same length as those in front was considered sufficiently long for seven men. The women on the other side of the house were arranged with the same consideration of rank. No seats were assigned to persons inferior to a goodman and a goodwife.

Although many of the people were much confined at home during the week by domestic industry, all assembled every Sunday for worship. In but few cases was the attendance perfunctory. They went to the house of God from a sense of duty, but they went with a willing mind. They were interested, not only in the worship and instruction of the church, but in the assembly. Their social longings were gratified with the announcement of intended marriages, with "bills" asking the prayers of the church for the sick, for the recently bereaved, for those about to make a voyage to Boston; or with "bills" returning thanks for recovery from a dangerous illness or for a safe return from a journey or voyage. Besides such personal items as reached their ears by way of the pulpit, others came to them in a more private way as they spoke with ac-

¹ In Massachusetts it was "ordered that Josias Plastowe shall, for stealing four baskets of corn from the Indians, return them eight baskets again, be fined five pounds, and hereafter to be called by the name of Josias and not Mr. as formerly he used to be."

quaintances, dwelling in a different quarter or at the farms. It was a satisfaction to persons, who during the week, had seen only the inmates of their own houses and a few neighbors, even to look on such an assembly.

Let the reader fancy himself entering the market-place in New Haven town, while Stephen Metcalf and Robert Bassett, "the common drummers for the town," are sounding the second drum on a Sunday morning. The chimney-smoke rises not only from the habitations of the town, but from as many Sabbath-day houses as there are families dwelling at the farms.[1] From every direction families are approaching the square. The limping Wigglesworth, whose lameness was afterwards so severe "that he is not able to come to the meeting, and so is many times deprived of the ordinances," starting early from his house (which was in Chapel street, near the intersection since made by High street), is the first to enter the south door of the sanctuary. Seeley, straight and stalwart in contrast with this poor cripple, stands near, conversing with the mas-

---

[1] A Sabbath-day house was a hut, in one end of which horses might be sheltered, and in the other end was a room having a fireplace and furnished, perhaps, with a bench, a few chairs, and a table. Here the owners arrived soon after the first drum, and, if cold, kindled a fire. Here they deposited their lunch, and any wraps which might be superfluous in the meeting-house. Hither they came to spend the intermission of worship. The writer remembers such houses in a country parish near New Haven. where he visited when a child. In one of them he spent an intermission, dividing his attention, when in the room devoted to the human inmates, between doughnuts and the open fireplace with its rusty fire-dogs and large bed of live coals; but preferring the company of the pony behind the chimney to that of the solemn people before the fire. He was born a little too late to remember Sabbath-day houses in New Haven, but his father has told him where this and that family had such accommodations.

ter of the watch, as the watchmen move away to patrol the town. Following Wigglesworth comes "the right worshipful Stephen Goodyear, Esquire," deputy-governor, and his neighbor, the reverend teacher of the church, William Hooke,[1] afterward chaplain to Oliver Cromwell, wearing gown and bands. On the east side of the market-place, the pastor, also in gown and bands, comes in solitary meditation through the passage which the town had given him between Mr. Crane's lot and Mr. Rowe's lot, "that he may go out of his own garden to the meeting-house." His family, that they may not intrude upon him in this holy hour, come through the public street. Gov. Eaton, with his aged mother leaning on his arm, walks up on the opposite side of the same street, and crosses over from Mr. Perry's corner, followed by his honored guests and the rest of his numerous household. When all but a few tardy families have reached the meeting-house, the drums cease to beat. The squadron on duty for the day march in, and seat themselves on the soldiers' seats near the east door, which is "kept clear from women and children sitting there, that if there be occasion for the soldiers to go suddenly forth, they may have free passage."

Days of extraordinary humiliation were appointed by the General Court from time to time in view of public calamities or apprehended danger. On such days there were two assemblies; and abstinence from labor and amusements was required as on the Lord's Day, though with less rigidness of interpretation, the prohibition crystallizing in later times into the formula, "All servile

[1] Mr. Hooke had the lot which had been Zachariah Whitman's, at the corner of Chapel and College streets.

labor and vain recreations on said day are by law forbidden." On Thanksgiving Day, as we learn from Davenport's letter to Winthrop, in which he mentions Gov. Newman's sickness and death, there were also two services in the meeting-house. Adding these occasional assemblies to those of the Lord's Day, we find that the whole population were often called together. But there were, besides, convocations on lecture-days, occasional church-meetings, and in the several neighborhoods " private meetings wherein they that dwelt nearest together gave their accounts one to another of God's gracious work upon them, and prayed together, and conferred, to their mutual edification " These private meetings were held weekly, and in the day-time, as appears from a question which Mr. Peck, the school-master, propounded to the court, " whether the master shall have liberty to be at neighbors' meetings once every week." Assemblies for worship were certainly a very important feature in social life.

Almost equally prominent were military trainings. Soldiers were on duty every night. One-fourth of the men subject to bear arms were paraded before the meeting-house every Sunday, and were at frequent intervals trained on a week-day. Six times in a year the whole military force of the plantation was called out. A general training brought together, not only those obliged to train, but old men, women, and children, as spectators of the military exercises, and of the athletic games with which they were accompanied. Almost as many people were in the market-place on training-day as on Sunday, and those who came had greater opportunity for social converse than on the day of worship. The enjoyment which each experienced in watching the manœuvres of the soldiers, and the games of cudgel, backsword, fencing, running, leaping, wrestling, stool-ball, nine-pins, and quoits, was enhanced by sharing the spectacle with the multitude, meeting old friends, and making acquaintance with persons of congenial spirit.

Election-days were also occasions when the people left their homes, and came together. The meeting of a plantation court did not indeed bring out the wives and daughters of the planters as a general training did; but when the annual election for the jurisdiction took place, the pillion was fastened behind the saddle, and the goodwife rode with her goodman to the seat of government to truck some of the yarn she had been spinning, for ribbons and other foreign goods, as well as to gather up the gossip of the year. On such occacasions a store of cake was provided beforehand, and "election cake" is consequently one of the institutions received from our forefathers.

For several years there were two fairs held annually at the town of New Haven, one in May, and one in September, for the sale of cattle and other merchandise. These of course attracted people from all parts of the jurisdiction.

In addition to these public assemblies of one kind and another, there was daily intercourse between neighbors. Women sometimes carried their wheels from one house to another, that they might spin in company. There were gatherings at weddings and at funerals. There was neighborly assistance in nursing and watching the sick. There was, as has already been related, social visiting in the evening after the Lord's Day.

There were house-raisings, when the neighbors assembled to lift and put together the timbers of a new dwelling; and house-warmings, when, being again invited, some months later, they came to rejoice with those who had taken possession of a new dwelling. There were huskings in the autumn when the maize had been gathered and brought in; but in the plantation of New Haven single persons were not allowed to "meet together upon pretence of husking Indian corn, out of the family to which they belong, after nine of the clock at night, unless the master or parent of such person or persons be with them to prevent disorders at such times, or some fit person entrusted to that end by the said parent or master."

In view of the frequency with which the planters were convened in greater or less companies, it is evident, that, however affected by their Puritanism and by emigration to a wilderness, they were a social people. They did not retire within themselves to live recluse from human converse, but endeavored to purify their social life. In this respect New Haven resembled the other New England colonies, but, contrary to a somewhat prevalent opinion, did not go as far as the other colonies in attempts to control social life by legislation.[1] "Mixt dancing" was discountenanced, and, by construction, forbidden, but there was no legal prohibition of dancing. The General court, referring in 1660 to some former

[1] Professor Kingsley, in a note to his historical discourse, delivered on the two hundredth anniversary of the settlement of New Haven, traces the impression that there had been "blue laws" at New Haven as far back as the year 1767, when Judge Smith of New York, having heard of such a code, embraced the opportunity afforded by a visit to New Haven to examine the early records of the colony. "A lie will travel round the world while Truth is putting on her boots."

laws of a very general nature, designed to restrain idle or evil living or miscarryings, declared in explanation :—

"Now that it may more clearly be understood what we judge to be such miscarriages or misdemeanors amongst such persons, as do thus tend to discourage God's work under our hands, and may prove hurtful and hindersome to the profiting of our posterity rising, we do express that not only such night meetings unseasonably, but corrupt songs and foolish jesting or such like discourses, wanton and lascivious carriages, mixt dancings, immoderate playing of any sort of sports and games, or mere idle living out of an honest calling industriously, or extravagant expenses by drinking, apparel, and so forth, have all and every of them such a tendency."

Gaming by shuffle-board was prohibited, as was shuffle-board at taverns, and by minors, but there was no enactment against shuffle-board as such. Card-playing was not forbidden, but the explanatory declaration of the General Court cited above, was on one occasion publicly read as a warning to Samuel Andrews, Goodwife Spinage, and James Eaton, when, being summoned before the Court, they were charged with allowing young persons to play cards in their houses. Goodwife Spinage said "that the scholars had played at cards there [at her house] on the last days of the week and on play-days in the afternoon, but in the evening, never." Andrews "confessed he had done wrong, and professed his hearty sorrow." Eaton "acknowledged that he might have spent his time better, and if it were to do again, he would not do it, being it is judged unlawful and gives offence; but for the thing itself, unless all recreation be unlawful, he cannot see that what he hath done is evil." The Court suspended judgment. "hoping that this will be a warning to them to take heed of such evil practices, and to improve their houses to better purposes for time to come than herein they have done." But as if Eaton had given less satisfaction than the others, he was called again some three months afterward, when he declared unto the Court that he understood that there were "reports abroad of his miscarriage in suffering some young persons to be at his house at an unseasonable time, which report he acknowledged to be true, and professed his hearty sorrow for it, and his desire to see the evil of it more and more, and that God would help him for time to come to keep a conscience void of offence toward God and toward man.[1]"

There were in New Haven no sumptuary laws, and, so far as appears, there was, with the exception of the explanatory declaration of 1660, no attempt to restrain extravagance in apparel, either by legal enactment or by the concentration of public opinion. In Massachusetts, Winthrop writes, about six months after the settlement at New Haven was begun, that "the Court, taking into consideration the great disorder general throughout the country in costliness of apparel and

---

[1] Some of the descendants of this James Eaton, or as his name is more commonly written, James Heaton, claim that he was a son of Theophilus Eaton, jun., the younger son of Gov. Eaton, alleging that he gave the name Theophilus to one of his sons, that the name has been repeated in every generation since, and that their famlly still possess land in North Haven, east of the Quinnipiac, which belonged to the governor. I cannot find that the governor had any land east of the Quinnipiac, except at Stony River. Any presumptive evidence afforded by the name Theopilus disappears when we learn from the parish register of St. Stephen's that Theophilus, son of Theophilus and Anne Eaton, was baptized March 11, 1631, and from the New Haven records that James Eaton took the oath of fidelity April 4, 1654. Theophilus Eaton, jun., could not have been eight years old when James Eaton was born.

following new fashions, sent for the elders of the churches, and conferred with them about it, and laid it upon them, as belonging to them to redress it by urging it upon the consciences of their people, which they promised to do. But little was done about it; for divers of the elders' wives were in some measure partners in this general disorder." Some years previously there had been an order of the Court prompted by similar feelings, and having a similar design. Afterward there were in different years several orders designed to restrain extravagance in apparel, especially "amongst people of mean condition," one of them especially providing that "this law shall not extend to the restraint of any magistrate or other public officer of this jurisdiction, or any settled military officer, or soldier in time of military service, or any other whose education and employments have been above the ordinary degree, or whose estates have been considerable, though now decayed."

But nothing similar to this is found on the records of New Haven. Some writer, noticing that both Plymouth and New Haven differed from Massachusetts in that they did not attempt to regulate dress, says that Plymouth was too poor, and New Haven too rich, for such legislation. Perhaps, however, New Haven was restrained from enacting sumptuary laws more by its mercantile character than by its wealth. Its leading men had been accustomed not only to wear rich clothing themselves, and to see it worn by others, but to iucrease their estates by selling cloth to all comers who were able to pay for it. Their feelings were, consequently, different from those of a man like Winthrop, who had never been a merchant, and had, like other

English country gentlemen, regarded rich apparel as a prerogative of the gentry.

As Gov. Eaton's wearing apparel was appraised after his death at £50, it would seem that he could not have favored sumptuary legislation consistently with his own habits, unless he did it in the aristocratic spirit of the Massachusetts law. Considering how much greater purchasing power there was then in fifty pounds sterling then there is now, we must conclude that in his dress, as well as in the furniture of his house, he "maintained a port in some measure answerable to his place."

CHAPTER XVII.

HISTORY OF THE COLONIAL GOVERNMENT TO THE RESTORATION OF THE STUARTS.

WE have seen that the colony of New Haven, when it entered into combination with Connecticut, Plymouth, and Massachusetts, consisted of the plantations at New Haven, Southold, and Stamford, and that Guilford and Milford were shortly afterward received as component parts of the jurisdiction. In the spring of 1644, Totoket, or Branford, "a place fit for a small plantation, betwixt New Haven and Guilford," was sold to Mr. Swain and others of Wethersfield upon condition that they should join in one jurisdiction with New Haven and the other plantations, upon "the fundamental agreement settled in October, 1643, which they, duly considering, readily accepted." Southampton, on Long Island, having placed itself under the jurisdiction of Connecticut, a minority of the people, with their minister, Mr. Abraham Pierson, preferring the theocratic constitution of New Haven, removed to Branford, and united themselves with the company from Wethersfield. From this time to its dissolution the jurisdiction consisted of the six plantations of New Haven, Southold, Stamford,[1] Guilford, Milford, and Branford.

[1] Greenwich was regarded as a part of Stamford.

In two important particulars New Haven differed from the other colonies. It was part of its "fundamental law," as we have already seen, that only church-members should be free burgesses or voters. By "fundamental" was meant unchangeable. In our day it is generally allowed that a people have the right to change the constitution of their government; and most written constitutions recognize their own mutability by indicating the method in which a change may be wrought. But the fundamental law established by the planters of Quinnipiac on "the fourth day of the fourth month, called June, 1639," and afterward assented to by the other plantations constituting the jurisdiction of New Haven, was designed to be unalterable. It was understood to be a compact, or agreement, from which those who had assented to it could not recede. In the words of the colonial constitution, "it was agreed and concluded as a fundamental order not to be disputed or questioned hereafter, that none shall be admitted to be free burgesses in any of the plantations within this jurisdiction for the future, but such planters as are members of some or other of the approved churches in New England.[1]"

The second particular in which New Haven differed from the other colonies was in the disuse of juries. In the plantation courts, and in the courts of the jurisdiction, the judges determined all questions of fact, as well as of law, and of discretionary punishment. It has been thought by some that Gov. Eaton's residence

---

[1] In Massachusetts only church-members could be made freemen, till the law was changed by command of King Charles the Second. But the requirement of church-membership was not " a fundamental law."

in the Baltic countries suggested this departure from English law. But if suggested by anything he had seen in other lands, it was doubtless commended to him and to others who acted with him in establishing a new government, by its conformity to the institutions of Moses.

The records give no evidence that the disuse of juries occasioned any trouble; but Hubbard thus criticises this peculiarity of New Haven; "Those who were employed in laying the foundation of New Haven colony, though famed for much wisdom, experience and judgment, yet did they not foresee all the inconveniency that might arise from such a frame of government, so differing from the other colonies in the constitution thereof, manifest in their declining that prudent and equal temperament of all interests in their administration of justice, with them managed by the sole authority of the rulers without the concurrence of a jury, the benefit of which had been so long confirmed by the experience of some ages in our own nation; for where the whole determining, as well both matter of fact as matter of law, with the sentence and execution thereof, depends on the sole authority of the judges, what can be more done for the establishing of an arbitrary power?"

Hubbard also testifies as follows concerning the limitation of the right of suffrage: "There had been an appearance of unquietness in the minds of sundry, upon the account of enfranchisement and sundry civil privileges thence flowing, which they thought too shortly tethered up in the foundation of the government." His testimony on this subject is confirmed by that of the records, as will hereafter appear.

The colonial government, for ten years after its establishment, experienced no greater trials than the petty injuries and insults from the Dutch already mentioned in the chapters on industrial pursuits and military affairs. But in 1653, England and Holland being at war, the Dutch at Manhattan evinced greater hostility than usual against their English neighbors. It was believed throughout the colonies of Connecticut and New Haven that they had plotted to form a general conspiracy of Indians to massacre the English. Trumbull, who lived a century later, seems to have had entire confidence in the testimony. He says, " Nine sachems, who lived in the vicinity of the Dutch, sent their united testimony to Stamford 'that the Dutch governor had solicited them, by promising them guns, powder, swords, wampum, coats, and waistcoats, to cut off the English.' The messengers who were sent declared 'that they were as the mouth of the nine sagamores, who all spake they would not lie.' One of the nine sachems afterward came to Stamford with other Indians, and testified the same. The plot was confessed by a Wampeag and a Narragansett Indian, and was confirmed by Indian testimonies from all quarters. It was expected that a Dutch fleet would arrive, and that the Dutch and Indians would unite in the destruction of the English plantations. It was rumored that the time for the massacre was fixed upon the day of the public election, when the freemen would be generally from home."

Connecticut and New Haven were naturally much alarmed, and became clamorous for war. The commissioners, after investigation, declared war by a vote of seven to one. Mr. Bradstreet of Massachusetts voted against the declaration, and the general court of that jurisdiction, being then in session, certified the commissioners that "they did not understand they were called to make a present war against the Dutch." This action of the General Court expressed the general sentiment of its constituency. Less irritated against the Dutch on account of previous injuries, and less exposed to present danger, the people of Massachusetts were less ready to believe that war was imperatively necessary and unquestionably just.

Not content with the communication they had made, the General Court of Massachusetts proceeded to put on record a declaration that the commissioners had no power by the Articles of Agreement to determine the justice of an offensive or vindictive war and to engage the colonies therein. This declaration gave great offence to the other colonies, particularly to Connecticut and New Haven, where the spirit of war was most rife: —

"At a general court held at New Haven for the jurisdiction the 29th of June, 1653, the governor acquainted the Court with what was done at the commission last at Boston, concerning the war propounded against the Dutch, and particularly with an interpretation of the General Court of the Massachusetts of the Articles of Confederation, wherein they declare that the commissioners have not power to act so far in matters of that nature as to make an offensive war. These writings were read; and the interpretation was much disliked by the Court, knowing that if it stood, the combination of the colonies must be broken, or made useless.

"The governor also acquainted the Court with a late conference which himself, Capt. Astwood, and Mr. Leete have had with the magistrates and General Court of Connecticut jurisdiction, and that they have agreed to send the mind of both the General Courts to the Massachusetts concerning the interpretation (that from this colony the Court desired the governor to draw up, which is hereafter entered), and also again to desire aid and assistance from them in this undertaking against the Dutch, according as the commissioners had agreed, that is, five hundred men, from all the colonies, with suitable provisions for such a design; but if that be not yielded, that then they would give leave that we use some means whereby volunteers may be procured out of their colony, with shipping, victuals, and ammunition, fit for that service. And the better to further and accomplish it, it is agreed that four persons shall be sent as agents or commissioners from the two general courts; that is, two from Connecticut and two from hence. Wherefore the Court did now choose and appoint Mr. William Leete, one of the magistrates of this jurisdiction, and Mr. Thomas Jordan, one of the deputies for the General Court for Guilford, for this service, who are to have commission and instructions from this Court to authorize and direct them to act and negotiate in this business, and to give the commissioners a call to sit here at New Haven the first or second Thursday in August next, which answer to the Massachusetts declaration, and the commissions and instructions are as followeth:—

"*The Answer of this General Court to the Massachusetts Declaration.*

"Upon information of a question propounded by the honored General Court of the Massachusetts concerning the power of the commissioners to determine the justice of an offensive war and the answer of the committee thereto, this Court hath considered and compared the Articles of Confederation and the interpretation together, and desire they, may, without offence, express their thoughts and apprehensions in the case.

"The confederation betwixt the colonies was no rash and sudden engagement; it had been several years under consideration. In *anno* 1638 there was a meeting at Cambridge about it, but some things being then propounded inconvenient for the lesser colonies, that conference ended without fruit, and the four jurisdictions, though knit together in affections, stood, in reference one to another, loose and free from any express covenant or combination, till, upon a new invitation and propositions from the Massachusetts, another meeting was appointed at Boston, in May, 1643; so that magistrates, deputies, and freemen, especially those of the Massachusetts, had about five years' time to consider what they were about, the compass and consequences of such a consociation, and probably did improve it, and saw cause to renew the treaty so long suspended.

"2. After a large and serious debate of the committee chosen and empowered by the several jurisdictions (the General Court for the Massachusetts, then sitting at Boston, and being acquainted, and from time to time advised with, concerning all and every article treated of), the 19th of May, 1643, a firm agreement was made and concluded, wherein the other jurisdictions, by their deputies, the Massachusetts, both by their deputies, and by the General Court, considering that we were all of one nation and religion, and all of us came into these parts of America with one and the same end and aim, and could it have been done with conveniency, had communicated in one government and jurisdiction, thought it their bounden duty, without further delay, to enter into such a present consociation as whereby the four jurisdictions might be, and continue, one, according to the tenor and true meaning of the Articles of Agreement; and that thenceforth they all be, and be called by the name of, the United Colonies of New England.

"3. Though all the plantations which already are, or hereafter may be, duly settled within the limits of each of these four colonies, are to be, and forever to remain, under the government of the same, and each colony to have peculiar jurisdiction within itself as an entire body, as expressed in the third and sixth articles, yet till now that was never understood to cross or abate the power of the commissioners in things proper to the confederation. The colonies uniting did, for themselves and their posterities, enter into a perpetual league of friendship and amity, for offence and defence, mutual advice and succor, upon all just occasions for the joint safety and welfare, as in the second article. The charge of all just wars, whether offensive or defensive, to be borne by the four colonies in their several proportions, and the advantage of all such wars (if God give a blessing) to be accordingly divided, as in the fourth article; and for the managing and concluding all such affairs, by express agreement, eight commissioners are to be chosen (all in church fellowship, and all to bring full power from their several general courts), namely, two by and out of each colony, to hear and examine, weigh and determine, all affairs of war and peace, leagues, aids, charges, and numbers of men for war, division of spoils, or whatever is gotten by conquest, receiving of more confederates or plantations into combination with any of these confederates, and all things of like nature which are the proper concomitants or consequents of such a confederation for amity, offence, or defence; and if these eight commissioners, when they meet, agree not, any six of them agreeing have power to settle and determine the business in question; but if six do not agree, then such propositions, with their reasons to be sent and referred to the four general courts, as in the sixth article. They were also to endeavor to frame and establish agreements and orders in general cases of a civil nature, wherein the plantations are interested, for preserving peace among themselves, and preventing (as much as may be) all occasions of war or differences with others, as about the speedy passage of justice in each jurisdiction to all the confederates equally as to their own, as more largely appears in the eighth article, so that certainly, and without question, these four colonies have, by a perpetual covenant, invested the commissioners with power suiting such a confederation, and without it the combination must either break or prove useless.

"4 As questions and scruples may arise and grow about the justice of an offensive war, so conscience may be exercised in a defensive war, and concerning leagues and aids. Jehoshaphat, the king of Judah, sinned and was rebuked by two prophets, Jehu and Eliezer, for joining with and helping Ahab and Ahaziah, kings of Israel. If, therefore, the General Court for the Massachusetts do now conceive and interpret that the power given to the commissioners (men of the same nation, of the same religion, members of approved churches, who came into these parts for the same ends and spiritual aims, and who had communicated in one and the same government and jurisdiction, had not distance of place hindered) in an offensive war is a contradiction and absurdity in policy, a scandal to religion, a violation of fundamental law, a bondage, and prostituting itself to strangers, and so forth, they may, at their next meeting, upon the same or like grounds conclude against leagues, aids, a defensive war, and other parts of trust and power wherewith the commissioners by the articles are invested, and the three other colonies or the general court for any one of them may do the like; but we fear in so doing we shall draw guilt upon ourselves in violating a perpetual league, so deliberately and firmly made, be covenant-breakers, and provoke God against us.

"5. It may be considered when a just war in ordinary cases may be called offensive or vindictive. When God gave the land of Canaan, their cities, vineyards, and so forth, to the children of Israel, Israel was the staff or sword in God's hand, by his appointment to punish a rebellious people, the measure of whose sins was then full; but ordinarily and in reference to men, lawful wars are to defend, recover, secure, or to get satisfaction, in case of just possessions or rights injuriously invaded, seized, or endangered by others, with respect to persons, estates, or honors, when other means will not serve: such a war was David's against the children of Ammon (2 Sam. x.); and such, we conceive, was the late war of England against Scotland, and their present war against the Dutch.

"6. Such leagues and confederations have been made and continued among other people and provinces, some in a subordination, some in a consociation, upon some several articles and covenants, wherein power hath been granted, and yet customs, privileges, and parts of government reserved for the safety of the whole and conveniency of the parts, as may appear in the different agreements and settlements of the Netherland Provinces, and the confederations of the cantons of the Switzers.

"7. We know of no fundamental law of these colonies violated or impaired by the Articles of Confederation, as (till now, we conceive) they have been clearly and fully understood by the whole committee and by the General Court of the Massachusetts, whose heads and hands were in the contriving and framing of them; nor is there any such delegating of others, especially of strangers, as is intimated. The freemen of the colonies generally choose their own respective commissioners, such as in whom they may confide, and accordingly they are invested with power according to the combination covenant, and for these ten years we have found the blessing of God upon our uniting, and his presence and assistance upon the meetings and conclusions of the commissioners.

"8. According to the intent of the colonies and contrivers of the confederation, hath been the practice in all former times. The commissioners have met and treated with power only limited to the articles. The Indians, French, and Dutch, have had recourse to them in all matters of war, leagues, aids, and so forth, from time to time; but this most clearly appears in *anno* 1645, when the meeting was at Boston, and the General Court for the Massachusetts had some agitations with the commissioners about an offensive war with the Narragansett Indians, if the war now propounded against the Dutch may be called offensive. The General Court would have sent a commission after the soldiers gone from Boston, but not yet out of the jurisdiction, conceiving that if otherwise any blood should be shed, the actors might be called to account for it. It was answered that though it did belong to the authority of the several jurisdictions (after the war and number of men was agreed by the commissioners) to raise the men and provide means to carry it on, yet the proceeding of the commissioners and the commission given was as sufficient as if it had been done by the General Court, for,

First, It was a case of such urgent necessity as could not stay the calling of a court or council.

Secondly, In the Articles of Confederation power is given to the commissioners to consult, order, and determine, all affairs of war, and the word *determine* comprehends all acts of authority belonging thereto.

Thirdly, The commissioners are the sole judges of the necessity of the expedition.

Fourthly, The General Court have made their commissioners their sole counsel for these affairs.

Fifthly, Their counsels could not have had their due effect, except they had power to proceed in this case as they have done, which were to make the commissioners' power and the main end of their confederation to be frustrate, and that merely for observing a ceremony.

Sixthly, The commissioners having had the sole power to manage the war for number of men, time, place, and so forth, they only know their own counsels and deferminations, and therefore none can grant commissioners to act according to these but themselves.

Seventhly, To send a new commission after them or any confirmation of that which they have, would cast blame upon the commissioners, and weaken their power, as if they had proceeded unwarrantably.

After much time spent in such agitations, the General Court of the Massachusetts allowed the proceedings of the commissioners for the matter, and further agreed that it did belong to the commissioners only, to appoint one to have command in chief over all the forces sent from the several colonies.

"9. In the uniting of these colonies, it was agreed and covenanted that if any of the confederates shall hereafter break any of these present articles, or be any other way injurious to any one of the other jurisdictions, such breach of agreement or injury shall be duly considered and ordered* by the commissioners for the other jurisdictions, that both peace and this present confederation may be entirely preserved without violation, as in the eleventh article. And it is a rule in law concerning legal acts, that all expressions and sentences, though of a doubtful construction, be understood for the confirming of them as far as rationally may be. Then certainly in confederations and covenants, blood may not be drawn out by forced interpretations contrary to clear words, sentences, the scope and purpose of all the articles, and to the practice of all time since, to nullify and infringe them.

"10. The premises considered, we conceive the interpretation made by the committee and approved both by the magistrates and deputies of the General Court for the Massachusetts apparently tends to the breaking of the league of confederation betwixt the colonies; and though, by an order of June 3d, 1653, they declare they have no such intention, that satisfies no more than if a man maimed and made forever useless should be told his life for a time should be spared. This colony conceiveth (and is accordingly affected) that it had been much better for them never to have combined. They are more exposed to enemies and dangers now than before, while that interpretation stands in force at the Massachusetts. The commissioners from thence are like to be sent with a limited commission, and no fruit can be expected from such a meeting; all they can do is to look up to Him to whom all the shields of the earth belong, and, in the second place, to seek advice and help elsewhere."

"*The commission and instructions of Mr. William Leete, one of the magistrates for New Haven jurisdiction, and Mr. Thomas Jordan, one of the deputies for the General Court of the same jurisdiction, joined to two agent or commissioners of Connecticut, sent as a committee to treat with the honorable colony of the Massachusetts. as hereunder is more particularly expressed.*

"Whereas all the confederated colonies, but especially these two smaller and more westerly jurisdictions, are in imminent danger of an invasion of war, both from the Dutch (if once they be strengthened with forces, either from the Netherlands or elsewhere) and from the Indians hired and engaged by the Dutch (as by much Indian testimony is proved) to cut off the English, not only of Hempstead, Middleborough, &c., within the Dutch limits, who are threatened and exposed to ruin for their faithfulness to the English nation and their countrymen in these parts, but the plantations within the United Colonies; you are to treat with the governor, council, commissioners, and General Court of the Massachusetts, or any of them, as you find or may procure opportunity, that, for the honor of the English nation, the peace and safety of the English in all this part of America,—by war, if no other means will serve,—the Dutch, at and about Manhatoes, who have been and still are likely to prove, injurious and dangerous neighbors, may be removed, and that (according to the commissioners' late agreement at Boston) five hundred men may be speedily raised out of the four colonies in proportion then settled, and, without delay, employed in this public service.

"But if the governor, council, commissioners, General Court, &c., as above, think fit to increase that number (the Dutch being now more strongly fortified), or upon other considerations much importing the welfare of the whole confederation in these times of exercise, these two colonies of Connecticut and New Haven do jointly desire that without offence three magistrates of this jurisdiction may give a call, according to the fifth article in the Confederation, to the commissioners, to meet at New Haven, the fourth or eleventh day of August next, all invested with full power from their several jurisdictions, according to the Articles of Confederation, without any other limits than have hitherto been used.

"The General Court have also, as you know, perused and considered the interpretation of the Articles of Confederation, made by a committee at Boston, and approved both by magistrates and deputies of the Massachusetts General Court, and by way of answer, do now return their apprehensions enclosed in a letter to the governor, deputy governor, and commissioners of that colony, which we herewith deliver to you, and you are to present it to the governor, &c., that if God bless our and your endeavors, the late interpretation may be recalled, and the confederation settled according to the first intendment, and the progress it hath had in the hands of the commissioners hitherto with a blessing. We commend you to Him who can prosper both your travel and occasions, and rest.

"BY THE GENERAL COURT FOR NEW HAVEN COLONY,
"The 29th of June, 1653.
"FRANCIS NEWMAN, *Secretary*."

"*Further instructions for Mr. Leete and Mr. Jordan, if they cannot prevail in the former propositions.*

"You are to propound and desire from the governor, &c., liberty to strike up a drum, or in some other way to treat for the raising of volunteers to assist these two colonies in an expedition for their safety; and if leave be granted (for we would give no offence), you may speak with such military officers in whom you may confide, for the better furtherance of the work.

"BY THE GENERAL COURT FOR NEW HAVEN COLONY,
"The 29th June, 1653.
"FRANCIS NEWMAN, *Secretary*."

"*Further instructions for Mr. William Leete and Mr. Thomas Jordan, if they cannot prevail in the former propositions.*

"1. For the number, there may be two, three, or four hundred men, provided that such agreements and conclusions may be firmly settled in writing, that these two colonies may with conveniency send such a proportion of men as they may spare, that they may have at least an equal share, both in power to order and command in all affairs, and in the success and advantage of the business in all respects, if God give a blessing; but herein they that by agreement stay with the stuff, or be ordered as reserve or an auxiliary army to guard the plantations, or to watch against any invasions or assaults of the Indians upon the plantations, to be reckoned as part of our number, and to share equally with the rest; and herein due consideration be had of shipping for the service, what great guns will be necessary, with suitable provision, with victuals, &c., and you will warily consider the quality and disposition of the men with whom you treat, and their company they are like to bring, that they be such as with whom we may join the same way, both of church administration and civil government; we would be loath to bring Rhode Island or any of that stamp or frame near us.

"2. If ships should come from England, bringing such commissions as may suit the service propounded, while you are in those parts, it is hereby left to your discretion to treat and conclude with them for the public good, according to the tenor of your instructions, though we cannot prescribe all particulars.

"3. In case the governor, &c., should send an answer to all propounded, in a letter sealed, neither treating nor acquainting you with the contents, you may, in time and place convenient, avoiding offence, open the letter, and consider what is written, that you may the better proceed in any thing to be done by you according to directions now given; and if any letters come from England, which you may rationally conceive concern public affairs, you are to send them with all speed, though you hire a messenger. The wise and good God assist you according to the weight of your work. We rest.

"BY THE GENERAL COURT FOR NEW HAVEN COLONY,
"June 29, 1653.
"FRANCIS NEWMAN, *Secretary*."

These documents from the pen of Gov. Eaton will perhaps acquaint the reader as well and as briefly as it were possible to do it, with the nature of the controversy which arose between New Haven and Massachusetts. The errand of Leete and Jordan and their associates from Connecticut produced no immediate fruit, the governor and council of Massachusetts claiming that they could do nothing in the vacation of the General Court, but offering to assemble the court on the thirtieth day of August, a few days before the next meeting of the commissioners.

When the commissioners met in September, a communication was received from the General Court of Massachusetts to the intent that, having considered the letters and papers from the General Courts of Connecticut and New Haven, they thought it unjust to be placed "under a dilemma either to act without satisfaction against their light or to be accounted covenant-breakers." After further correspondence, both parties retaining as firmly as ever their antagonistic position, the commissioners determined to adjourn *sine die*, and return without loss of time to their other occasions. This would have been practically a dissolution of the confederation. The General Court, learning that the commissioners were about to disperse, manifested a more conciliatory spirit, voting, "That by the Articles of Confederation, so far as the determinations of the commissioners are just, and according to God, the several colonies are bound before God and man to act accordingly, and that they sin and break covenant if they do not; but otherwise we judge we are not bound, neither before God nor men."

In view of this communication, the commissioners were so far pacified that they proceeded to business;

"referring all further questions to the addresses the Massachusetts shall please to make to the other General Courts." But the very first matter presented for their consideration renewed the old dispute. It was a complaint that Ninigret had made a hostile raid upon the Indians of Long Island, tributaries and friends of the English, in which two sachems and about thirty other Indians were slain, and divers women taken captive. The commissioners immediately dispatched messengers to bring Ninigret's answer to this complaint. Upon return of the messengers, bringing an insolent reply from Ninigret, and reporting that he had allowed his men to insult and threaten them, the commissioners declared war against him, and determined to raise for its prosecution an army of 250 men.

In reply to the requisition on Massachusetts for her contingent of 166 soldiers, the commissioners received the following paper:—

" In answer to a letter of the honored commissioners for raising forces to make a present war against Ninigret; the council for the Massachusetts assembled at Boston, the 24th of September, 1653, taking into their consideration the votes of the commissioners for raising 250 men to make war upon Ninigret, and having perused the grounds and reasons thereunto presented in their papers, do not see sufficient grounds either from any obligation of the English towards the Long Islanders, or from the usage the messengers received from the Indians, or from any other motive presented unto our consideration, or from all of them; and therefore dare not to exercise our authority to levy force within our jurisdiction to undertake a present war against the said Ninigret."

Upon receipt of this communication, the commissioners protested that by this overt act "the Massachusetts have actually broken their covenant." Resenting this imputation, the General Court of Massachusetts addressed letters to the General Courts of the other colonies, proposing that "a committee be chosen by each jurisdiction to treat and agree upon such explanation or reconciliation of the Articles of Confederation as shall be consistent with our true meaning, the nature of the confederacy, and the power and authority of every government."

The General Court of New Haven, upon receipt of this communication and the report which their commissioners made of "the debate they had for ten days with the Massachusetts General Court before they could sit as commissioners, and after with what they did when the commissioners sat," declared that they saw no cause to choose any committee for the purpose mentioned.

"The Articles of Confederation in their judgment want neither alteration nor explanation, and they are fully satisfied in them as they are." "What the commissioners of this colony did the Court approved; but considering what the Massachusetts General Court and council have done, this Court all agreed, and cannot but declare that they have broken their covenant with us in acting directly contrary to the Articles of Confederation; upon which consideration this Court see themselves called to seek for help elsewhere, and can conclude of no better way than to make their addresses to the State of England."

The letter in which the Court communicated to the General Court of Massachusetts the declarations thus recorded, was, in the first place, sent to Hartford, and, being approved by the General Court of Connecticut, was, by their direction, signed by the secretary of that colony, as well as by the secretary of New Haven. The General Court of Plymouth, some months afterward, replied to Massachusetts in a communication of similar import, but doubtless more pungent by reason of the indisputable disinterestedness of that colony. They say:—

"The unexpected and less welcome intelligence that we received upon the return of our commissioners from their last and most uncomfortable meeting hath administered just ground to us to let you understand how sadly we resent, and how deeply we are affected with that sad breach of the confederation, on your part acted, especially at such a time as this, wherein our enemies may be occasioned not only to insult over us, but also to reproach the name of God and his ways which we profess; which, upon whose account it will be charged, we leave to consideration and pass on to express our thoughts in answer to yours dated the 13th of September, 1653, which, after due consideration, we conceive (reserving due respects to yourselves dissenting) that the Articles of Confederation are so full and plain that they occasion not any such queries for their full explanation, or meeting of a committee for such a purpose, it seeming unto us to be obvious to any impartial eye, that, by the said articles, the commissioners are the representatives of the several colonies, and therefore what they act and determine, according to that power given them in such matters as are expressly included in the said articles, may justly be interpreted as the sense, reason, and determination of the several jurisdictions which have substituted them thereunto, and the several colonies may and ought to acquiesce in as if themselves had done it."

When the time for the next meeting of the commissioners was near, the question was raised in the General Court at New Haven, whether commissioners should be chosen. The result of the debate is thus recorded:—

"The Court, having found such ill fruit from the Massachusetts, of the two former meetings, are discouraged to send; yet that they might show themselves followers of peace, and that they earnestly desire to continue their confederation upon the terms it first began, and for sundry years hath been carried on, did agree and choose the governor and Francis Newman commissioners for the year ensuing, and particularly for the next meeting at Hartford, if it hold; and Mr. Leete and Mr. Goodyear are chosen to supply, if the providence of God order it so that one or both of the others should be hindered; but with this direction from the Court, that if the mind of the Massachusetts remain as they have formerly declared, which hath made the other three colonies look upon the confederation as broken by the Massachusetts, they conceive there can be no fruit of their meeting, but only to consider the eleventh article, and require such satisfaction from the delinquent colony as they shall judge meet."

No sooner had the commissioners assembled than they "fell upon a debate of the late differences betwixt the Massachusetts and the other colonies, in reference to the government of the Massachusetts' declaration or interpretation of the articles, bearing date June the 2d, 1653, and their not acting by raising of forces against Ninigret in September last, according to the determination of the commissioners; and, after some agitations and writing about the same, the commissioners for the Massachusetts presented the ensuing writing:—"

"To the intent all former differences and offences may be issued, determined, and forgotten, betwixt the Massachusetts and the rest of the confederate colonies, we do hereby profess it to be our judgment, and do believe it to be the judgment of our General Court that the commissioners, or six of them, have power, according to the articles, to determine the justice of all wars, &c.; that our General Court hath and doth recall that interpretation of the articles which they sent to the commissioners at Boston, dated the 2d of June, 1653, as it appears by that interpretation and concession of our Court presented to the commissioners in September last, and do acknowledge themselves bound to execute the determinations of the commissioners, according to the literal sense and true meaning of the Articles of Confederation, so far as the said determinations are in themselves just, and according to God."

Thus ended the open quarrel between Massachusetts and the other colonies. But when the commissioners, proceeding to make war upon Ninigret, gave the appointment of the commander-in-chief to Massachusetts, Major Willard, their appointee, carried out the policy of his colony almost as closely as if no army had been sent. The commissioners censured him, but he doubtless felt assured that in his own colony his conduct was approved. News of peace between England and Holland having arrived before Massachusetts retracted her offensive interpretation of the articles, the subject of hostilities against the Dutch was no more agitated, and gradually the United Colonies settled into tranquility.

During this quarrel with Massachusetts, Connecticut and New Haven had been vexed with internal dissension. As these colonies had been more clamorous for war than those more remote from the Dutch, so the zeal of those plantations in these colonies which were most exposed to danger exceeded that of others. The people of Stamford and Fairfield were not only ready to engage in the fight with such forces as Connecticut and New Haven might be able to raise, but were enraged because the authorities of their respective colonies were not as rash as themselves. Trumbull says, "The town of Fairfield held a meeting on the subject, and determined to prosecute the war. They appointed Mr. Ludlow commander-in-chief. He was the center of the evidence against the Dutch; had been one of the commissioners at the several meetings relative to the affair; had been zealous and active for the war; and conceiving himself and the town in imminent danger unless the Dutch could be removed from the neighborhood, too hastily accepted the appointment." But, as Fairfield belonged to Connecticut, it is not our task to relate what took place at Fairfield, nor what happened in consequence to Mr. Ludlow. Stamford, in the new Haven colony, wrote to the colonial authorities, "stirring up to raise volunteers to go against the Dutch, and that themselves will send forth ten men well furnished for the war." The governor communicated this letter to the General Court, Nov. 22, 1653, and, at the same time a letter from Mr. Ludlow, giving information of the action taken by Fairfield; and an anonymous letter to Robert Basset of Stamford, "which is to stir up to stand for the State of England, as they pretend, and to stand for their liberties, that they may all have their votes, and shake off the yoke of government they have been under in this jurisdiction." These writings having been read:—

"The Court considered whether they are called at this time to send forth men against the Dutch, and after much debate and consultation had with most of the elders in the jurisdiction, the issue was, which the Court by vote declared, that, considering the hazards and dangers attending such a design, especially now, it being so near winter, and the want of suitable vessels, and the like, they see not themselves called to vote for a present war, but to suspend a full issue till Connecticut jurisdiction be acquainted with it, and give notice what they will do; but if they agree to carry it on now, then this Court agrees to join with them, and to meet again to consider and order, as the case may require."

At the same court two magistrates who had been sent to Stamford "to settle a right understanding of things for the better quieting of their spirits who are in a mutinous way," reported that they found the people "for the most part full of discontent with the present government they are under, pleading that they might have their free votes in the choice of civil officers, making objection against their rates, and propounded to have their charges of watching and warding in the summer past, with some works about their meeting-house for their defence, borne by the jurisdiction, and that they might have twelve men sent them at the jurisdiction charge to lie there all winter for their defence, with some other things; and after much debate with them to quiet them, which did little prevail with them, an order from the committee of Parliament in England sent to this colony was read to them, requiring them to submit to the government they are under, which did somewhat allay their spirits for the present, and they desired further time to consider of things, and they would in some short time send their mind to the governor in writing."

A similar spirit of discontent prevailed at Southold, which was liable to be attacked by Ninigret, transporting his men across the Sound in canoes. John Youngs, a son of the pastor, was the leader of the disaffected at Southold, and was in communication with Robert Basset, the boldest and most active of the disaffected at Stamford. Young, Basset, and three other inhabitants of Stamford, were put nnder bonds "to attend their oath of fidelity to the jurisdiction, maintain the laws here established, and not disturb the peace of the colony, or of any plantation therein." Each made a separate confession.

"Concerning John Youngs, he did now acknowledge that he hath miscarried many ways, speaking rash and foolish words, and such as have tended to sedition, was unsatisfied that he had not his vote in choosing military officers, and that such he would not follow as he did not choose. He is sorry he hath given such just offence, and hopes he shall take warning, and walk to better satisfaction hereafter." "Robert Basset said, concerning that letter he received without a name subscribed, he did not do as he ought in so weighty a business, not considering of it, nor seeing that in it which he since sees; but something being in it which suited his present affection against the Dutch, and his corrupt opinion concerning the votes, whereby his eyes were then blinded, he is heartily sorry for it, and if God had not stopped him, for aught he knows, it might have wrought great disturbance; and for his disturbing the peace of the colony, and opposing the ways of government, he sees his evil in it in some measure, and hopes he shall see it more, for he is convinced that the way of government here settled is according to God, which he hath not honored as he ought, and had he honored God, he would have helped him to honor the government, which he did not, and is heartily sorry for it. Concerning the uncomfortable words in the town meetings at Stamford which have tended much to disturb the peace of that place, and much grieve the hearts of God's people, which doth now cause sorrow of heart in him, he hopes, that, as he hath been an instrument of dishonor to God in that place, so he desires to be an instrument of his honor there. Concerning the letter which he carried from Stamford, wherein he was employed by the town, at that time he apprehended it for the peace of the place, but he now sees that he did not then see the bottom of it, for it did tend to dishonor the government here, and prefer another government before it; these and other his miscarriages he said he was sorry for, and desires the Court to be merciful to him, hoping he shall be watchful hereafter; and added that he looks upon this as an aggravation of his sin, that all this was against his oath of fidelity, and from the great pride of his spirit."

Mr. Youngs soon recovered the confidence of the magistrates and other loyal people. The next year after his submission he appeared in company with Capt. Tappan of Southampton before the commissioners, in behalf of the English on the east end of Long Island, and their Indian allies in the neighborhood, petitioning for aid against Ninigret's hostile invasions. At the suggestion of these gentlemen, seconded by letters from some of the chief men of that neighborhood, the commissioners ordered "a vessel sufficiently manned and armed, as the case may require, to attend Ninigret's motions and, as much as may be, hinder his intrusions upon the Island." Of this vessel Youngs was appointed commander, with instructions to "take in from Saybrook or New London, six, ten, or twelve men, well armed and fitted for the service, as any of the magistrates of Connecticut shall direct; with which force you shall improve your best endeavors to disturb his passage to, and prevent his landing upon, Long Island, by taking, sinking, and destroying so many of his canoes employed in that service as shall come within your power." In later years Youngs became a freeman, and appears on the records as Capt. John Youngs. It is doubtful, however, whether he was ever in his true inwardness reconciled to the fundamental law of New Haven; for, after the arrival of the Connecticut charter, he took the earliest opportunity of transferring to Connecticut the allegiance of himself and of Southold. After the absorption of New Haven into Connecticut, he "became the most prominent man of the town" of Southold, and was honored with important trusts under the colonial government.

The vexed question of war with the Dutch brought to open expression a dissatisfaction in the New Haven colony, which, though latent at other times, was real and wide-spread. Those who were not voters felt that suffrage was too much restricted by the fundamental law. The dissatisfaction was deepest in regard to the choice of military officers. It often happened that there was in the train-band a man plainly more fit to be its commander than any of those who were church-members. But however great a man's military genius might be, he could neither be an officer, nor have any voice in determining who should give the word of command, unless he was a member of some approved church. This was the grievance of John Youngs, in whose plantation there seems to have been a remarkable scarcity of military capacity among the church-members. The records disclose, however, similar cases of dissatisfaction in other plantations. In 1655 the General Court so far yielded to the influence of public opinion as to record:—

"It is agreed, that if in any plantation in this jurisdiction there be none among the freemen fit for a chief military officer, it shall be in the power of the General Court to choose some other man, as they shall judge fit, in whom they may confide."

One instance of manifested dissatisfaction should be specially mentioned in order to exhibit also the protest of the General Court against it. In 1661, at the first court held under the administration of Gov. Leete, John Benham acknowledged that he had circulated an offensive writing, and desired forgiveness.

"The Court was willing to accept his acknowledgment, provided that they heard not further against him. Upon this the Court saw cause to declare as followeth; viz., That whereas we have been occasioned (upon some reports of grievance from sundry non-freemen, that just privileges and liberties are denied them, which they apprehend are allowed them by our first fundamental law) to take the matter into consideration. and upon a serious review of things of this nature, and of our law, we do see cause to declare unto all godly and peaceable inhabitants of this colony that we are grieved to hear of some uncomfortable manner of acting by such unsatisfied persons in a seeming factious, if not seditious manner, which we wish all (who would not be looked upon as disturbers of our peace and troublers of our Israel) to be warned from after appearings in such wise; and we hope they shall have no cause to complain of any injury by our withholding of just rights, privileges, or liberties, from any to whom they belong, so as to hurt the promotion of our chief ends and interests, professed and pretended by all at our coming, combining, and settling in New England, as by the Articles of Confederation and otherwise may be made to appear, which must engage us to seek, secure, and advance the same by law, and from which we cannot be persuaded to divert, so as to commit our more weighty civil or military trusts into the hands of either a crafty Ahithophel or a bloody Joab (as some abusive meddlers do seem to hint unto us, in a paper we met withal), though such should seem to be better accomplished with either natural or acquired abilities above those that are as well lawful as entitled freemen; whose earnest desire is that all planters would make it their serious endeavor to come in by the door to enjoy all privileges and bear all burdens equal with themselves, according to our foundation settlements and universally professed ends, and that there may be no disorderly or uncomely attempts to climb up another way, or to discourage the hearts or weaken the hands of such as yet bear the burden of the day in public trusts, which will be afflicting and hurtful to the ends aforesaid."

Although this last manifestation of discontent occurred twelve months later than the end of the period to be covered by this chapter, it seems appropriate to connect it with earlier manifestations, so as to complete what should be said of that "unquietness in the minds of sundry upon the account of enfranchisement, and sundry civil privileges thence flowing, which they thought too shortly tethered up in the foundation of the government."

The restoration of peace with the Dutch brought internal quiet to New Haven; the discontent with restricted suffrage subsiding into its usual latent condition. The reconciliation with Massachusetts, begun in the autumn of 1654, after her commissioners in her name had retracted her offensive interpretation of the Articles, was completed in the spring of 1655, when Gov. Eaton informed the General Court of New Haven "that he hath received from the General Court of the Massachusetts an order, whereby they confirm what their commissioners did last year at Hartford, in recalling their interpretation of the Articles of Confederation, so offensive to the other colonies, which order is by this Court accepted and appointed to be entered next after the conclusions of the commissioners at that meeting."

In 1655 Gov. Eaton presented to the General Court a digest of the laws of the colony, which he had been requested to prepare. The Court approved of what he had done, but desired him "to send for one of the new books of laws in the Massachusetts colony, and to view over a small book of laws newly come from England, which is said to be Mr. Cotton's, and to add to what is already done as he shall think fit, and then the Court will meet again to confirm them, but in the meantime (when they are finished) they desire the elders of the jurisdiction may have the sight of them for their approbation also." A few months later, "the laws which at the Court's desire have been drawn up by the governor, viewed and considered by the elders of the jurisdiction, were now read and seriously weighed by this Court, and by vote concluded and ordered to be sent to England to be printed, with such oaths, forms, and precedents as the governor may think meet to put in; and the governor is desired to write to Mr. Hopkins, and Mr. Newman to his brother, to do the best they can to get five hundred of them printed." Ten months after this order for printing was made:—

"The governor informed the court that there is sent over now in Mr. Garret's ship five hundred law-books, which Mr. Hopkins hath gotten printed, and six paper books for records for the jurisdiction; with a seal for the colony, which he desires them to accept as a token of his love. The law-books cost, printing and paper, £10.10; the six paper books £2.8. The law-books are now ordered to be divided as followeth: New Haven, 200; Milford, 80: Guilford, 60; Stamford, 70, a part of which for Greenwich; Southold, 50; Branford, 40. For every of which books, each plantation is to pay twelve pence in good country pay (wheat and pease were propounded) to the governor, Mr. Hopkins having ordered him to receive it here upon his own account, and therefore it must be made up in quantity, else he would be a great loser by it."

Greenwich, though nominally purchased and established as a plantation by authority of the colony of New Haven, had always been a wayward daughter. The inhabitants soon revolted, and placed themselves under the government of the New Netherlands; but the Dutch, being remonstrated with, relinquished their claim. In 1665,—

"The deputies of Stamford propounded that they have and do still suffer great inconvenience and damage by Greenwich, who pound their cattle off the common, besides their disorderly walking among themselves, admitting of drunkenness among the English and Indians, whereby they are apt to do mischief, both to themselves and others; they receive disorderly children or servants, who fly from their parents' or masters' lawful correction; they marry persons in a disorderly way, besides other miscarriages; and therefore, if the Court see meet, they desire some course may be taken to reduce them to join with Stamford in this jurisdiction, and the rather because they pretend to shelter themselves under the commonwealth of England, who, we are confident, will not approve of such carriages. The Court considered of the several particulars, and remembered how Greenwich at first was by Mr. Robert Feak, the first purchaser of the said lands, freely put under this jurisdiction; though after Capt. Patrick did injuriously put himself and it under the Dutch, yet after, it was by agreement at Hartford with the Dutch governor, 1650, to be resigned to New Haven jurisdiction again, and since we hear that the Dutch do exercise no authority over them; all which, being considered, the Court did agree and order that a letter should be written to them from this court, and sent by the deputies of Stamford, requiring them, according to the justice of the case, to submit themselves to this jurisdiction, which, if they refuse, then the Court must consider of some other way."

After more than a year of resistance, the people of Greenwich signed the following engagement:—

"At Greenwich, the 6th of October, 1656. We, the inhabitants of Greenwich, whose names are underwritten, do from this day forward freely yield ourselves, place, and estate, to the government of New Haven, subjecting ourselves to the order and dispose of that general court, both in respect of relation and government, promising to yield due subjection unto the lawful authority and wholesome laws of the jusisdiction aforesaid, to wit, of New Haven." The Court, receiving this written engagement, ordered that "they are to fall in with Stamford, and be accepted a part thereof, and, from the time of their submission, they are freed from rates for one whole year."

The submission of Greenwich, signed in the next preceding October, was presented to the court May 27, 1657. This was the last general court in which Eaton presided, and only twice afterward did he hold a court of magistrates. He died suddenly in the following January. "Having worshipped God with his family after his usual manner, and upon some occasion with much solemnity charged all the family to carry it well unto their mistress who was now confined by sickness, he supped, and then took a turn or two abroad for his meditations. After that, he came in to bid his wife good night, before he left her with her watchers; which, when he did, she said, 'Methinks you look sad.' Whereto he replied, 'The differences risen in the church of Hartford make me so.' She then added, 'Let us even go back to our native country again.' To which he answered, 'You may, but I shall die here.' This was the last word that ever she heard him speak; for, now retiring unto his lodging in another chamber, he was overheard about midnight fetching a groan; and unto one sent in presently to inquire how he did, he answered the inquiry with only saying, 'Very ill,' and without saying any more, he fell asleep in Jesus." "This man," says Hubbard, "had in him great gifts and as many excellencies as are usually found in any one man. He had an excellent princely face and port, commanding respect from all others; he was a good scholar, a traveler, a great reader, of an exceeding steady and even spirit, not easily moved to passion, and standing unshaken in his principles when once fixed upon, of a profound judgment, full of majesty and authority in his judicatures so that it was a vain thing to offer to brave him out."

As Eaton had been elected to the chief magistracy annually from the institution of the colonial government, so Stephen Goodyear had been with equal regularity chosen deputy-governor. Naturally he would have succeeded to the place vacated by the death of Eaton; but his absence on a visit to England obliged the freemen to look elsewhere for a chief magistrate. At the court of election in the following May, Francis Newman, who had for some years been secretary of the jurisdiction, was chosen governor, and William Leete, deputy-governor. Mr. Davenport writes to his friend the younger Winthrop:—

"The last election day was the saddest to me that ever I saw in New Haven, by our want of him whose presence was wont to make it a day of no less contentment than solemnity. Being weary after my sermon, I was absent from the Court. The first news that I heard from thence added to my sorrow, for I heard that Mr. Goodyear was wholly left out in the choice of magistrates; whereas I had been secure, thinking they purposed to choose him governor. But the day following, upon inquiry into the cause of it, I received such answer as cleared unto me that it came to pass, not by any plot of men, but by the overruling providence of God. For the proxies generally voted for Mr. Goodyear to be governor and Mr. Leete deputy, and none of them gave their votes for Mr. Goodyear to be deputy-governor if the former failed, nor to be magistrate, but put in blanks to both, taking it for granted that he would be chosen governor. But before they proceeded to election, some of the deputies of the court propounded and urged the necessity of great expediency, in respect of our condition at present, of having the governor present among us. Hereunto the freemen generally consented; and hereby the election fell upon Mr. Newman to be governor, and Mr. Leete deputy-governor, for this year. To this latter the proxies for the most part concurred; and most of the present freemen. The votes of the present freemen and some few proxies carried the election for governor to Mr. Newman by plurality of votes, which he strongly refused; but importunity of many in the court at last overcame him to accept it; and some of Mr. Goodyear's friends spake earnestly, when these two were chosen, to hinder his being chosen to magistracy, alleging such reasons as they had."

Mr. Goodyear was so generally regarded as second only to Gov. Eaton in all qualifications requisite for the chief magistracy, that, if he had lived to return, he would probably have been called, as soon as an election occurred, to the high position for which his only disqualification in May, 1653, was absence from the colony. His death occurred in London, not long afterward; the melancholy tidings of it having been received before the 20th of October, at which date proceedings were commenced for the settlement of his estate.

Mr. Newman and Mr. Leete were re-elected in 1659 and 1660. On the 17th of October of the latter year a court of magistrates was held, at which the following record was made, the governor being absent:—

"By reason of the afflicting hand of God on New Haven by much sickness, the Court could not pitch upon a day for public thanksgiving through the colony for the mercies of the year past, and did therefore leave it to the elders of the church at New Haven, as God may be pleased to remove his hand from the governor and others, to give notice to the rest of the plantations what day they judge fit for that duty, that we may give thanks and rejoice before the Lord together."

Gov. Newman died Nov. 18, 1660. Mr. Davenport, in a letter to his friend Winthrop, thus communicates the particulars of his decease:—

"We hoped he was in a good way of recovery from his former sickness, and were comforted with his presence in the assembly two Lord's days, and at one meeting of the church on a week day, without sensible inconvenience. And on the morning of the day of public thanksgiving, he found himself encouraged to come to the public assembly. But after the morning sermon he told me that he found himself exceedingly cold from head to toe; yet having dined, he was refreshed, and came to the meeting again in the afternoon, the day continuing very cold. That night he was very ill; yet he did not complain of any relapse into his former disease, but of inward cold, which he and we hoped might be removed by his keeping warm and using other suitable means. I believe he did not think that the time of his departure was so near, or that he should die of this distemper, though he was always prepared for his great change. The last day of the week he desired my son to come to him the next morning to write a bill for him to be prayed for, according to his direction. My son went to him after the beating of the first drum; but finding himself not fit to speak much, he prayed him to write for him what he thought fit. When the second drum beat, I was sent for to him. But before I came, though I made haste, his precious immortal soul was departed from its house of clay unto the souls of just men made perfect. We were not worthy of him, a true Nathanael, an Israelite indeed, who served God in Christ in sincerity and truth. He honored God in his personal conversation, and in his administration of chief magistracy in this colony; and God hath given him honor in the hearts of his people."

On the 27th of July, 1660, about four months previous to the death of Gov. Newman, the ship Prudent Mary, commanded by Capt. Pierce, a noted shipmaster in the trade between New England and the mother country, arrived at Boston, bringing intelligence that the Stuarts had been restored to the throne in the person of Charles II. In the vessel which brought these tidings came Edward Whalley and William Goffe, both members of the High Court which had condemned to death the father of the reigning monarch.

CHAPTER XVIII.

THE STUARTS AND THE REGICIDES.

THE tidings which came to Boston on the 27th of July, 1660, were not entirely unexpected. A new parliament had been summoned to meet in April; and the result of the elections had shown that it was to consist chiefly of persons friendly to a government by king, lords, and commons. So much as this must have been already known in New England by earlier ships than that of Mr. Pierce. His arrival was anxiously expected. Mr. Davenport writes to Winthrop just one week before Pierce cast anchor at Boston, "Sir, I humbly thank you for the intelligences I received in your letters, and for the two weekly intelligences which Brother Miles brought me, I think from yourself, and which I return enclosed, by this bearer, with many thanks. I did hope that we might have received our letters by Capt. Pierce before this time. But we have no news lately from the Bay. Brother Rutherford and Brother Alsop are both there, so also is our teacher Mr. Street. The two former, I hope, will return next week. Then, probably, we shall have some further news. The Lord fit us to receive it as we ought, whatever it may be."

The restoration of the Stuarts was not received in

New England joyfully. The change from a kingdom to a commonwealth twenty years before had injured New England in its material interests by checking the emigration which was pouring into it population and wealth. But this disadvantage had been outweighed, in the judgment of the Puritan colonists, by the elevation of men in sympathy with themselves to supreme power and authority in what they called the State of England. They were more earnest to secure "the ends for which they had come hither" than to obtain a larger price for their corn and cattle, and they were confident that these ends would not be frustrated by any action of the home government so long as Puritans were in power in England. But what effect upon the colonies the restoration of the Stuarts might produce, it was impossible to foresee.

When the time arrived for the next election in New Haven jurisdiction, it was difficult to find suitable persons willing to accept office. John Wakeman and William Gibbard were nominated for the magistracy in the plantation court of New Haven, notwithstanding their protest; Mr. Wakeman, who had had some thought of removing to Hartford, saying, when questioned if he intended to stay at New Haven, that "he was not resolved whether to go or stay, but rather than he would accept of the place, he would remove." In the court of elections for the jurisdiction they were both elected magistrates, "but neither of them took the oath." Mr. Benjamin Fenn of Milford being elected magistrate, took the oath "with this explanation before the oath was administered, that he would take the oath to act in his place, according to the laws of this jurisdiction; but in case any business from without should present, he conceived he should give no offence if he did not attend to it, who desired that it might be so understood." Mr. William Leete was chosen governor, Mr. Matthew Gilbert deputy-governor, and Mr. Robert Treat and Mr. Jasper Crane, magistrates. It does not appear that any of these four hesitated to take the oath proper to their place.

By the terms of his restoration, Charles II. had left to Parliament to determine who should be excepted from an act of general amnesty. The act, when passed, excepted all who had been directly concerned in the death of the former king. But because Whalley and Goffe had left England before they had been marked for punishment, the people of Massachusetts felt no embarrassment in receiving and entertaining them. Major Daniel Gookin, one of their fellow-passengers in the Prudent Mary, offered them the hospitality of his house in Cambridge; and in Cambridge they remained till the following February, often visiting Boston and other towns in the neighborhood. They came, it is said, under the assumed names of Edward Richardson and William Stephenson: but their secret, notwithstanding this disguise, was known to many; so that when intelligence came that they had been excepted in the act of amnesty, some of the magistrates were alarmed, and the more because it was known that they had been seen and recognized by Capt. Thomas Breedon, a royalist who had since sailed for England. The governor therefore convened his council to consider and determine whether the proscribed regicides should be apprehended. The council considered, but came to no determination. Four days afterward Whalley and Goffe relieved their friends in Massachusetts by departing for New Haven.

Only a fortnight after their arrival at Boston, Mr. Davenport had mentioned them in a letter to the younger Winthrop, and declared his purpose of inviting them to his house after the meeting of the commissioners in September, alleging, as a reason for delay, his desire to keep the guest-chamber ready for an expected visit from Mr. and Mrs. Winthrop during the meeting of the commissioners. His interest in them at that time seems to have been that of a person in sympathy with them in politics and religion, who had heard a good report of their quality and godliness, but was unacquainted with their personal history and connections. On a little piece of paper wafered to the side of the letter, he adds this postscript: "Sir, I mistook, in my letter, when I said Col. Whalley was one of the gentlemen, &c. It is Commissary-Gen. Whalley, sister Hooke's brother, and his son-in-law who is with him is Col. Goffe; both godly men, and escaped pursuit in England narrowly." He had doubtless received this information from Mr. William Jones and his wife,[1]

[1] William Jones, having married as his second wife Hannah, youngest daughter of Theophilus Eaton, July 4, 1659, came in the following year from London to New Haven, where, on the 23d of May, 1662, he took the oath of fidelity with the following qualification: "That whereas the king hath been proclaimed in this colony to be our sovereign, and we his loyal subjects, I do take the said oath with subordination to his majesty, hoping his majesty will confirm the said government for the advancement of Christ's gospel, kingdom. and ends, in this colony, upon the foundations already laid; but in case of the alteration of the government in the fundamentals thereof, then to be free from the said oath." The same day he was admitted a freeman; and five days afterward, at a court of election for the jurisdiction, he was chosen a magistrate.

who, having crossed the Atlantic in the ship with these distinguished strangers, had come to New Haven to occupy the mansion which Mrs. Jones, the daughter of Gov. Eaton, had inherited from her father. The identification of Whalley as Mrs. Hooke's brother must in time have recalled to memory many things he had learned from his colleague in reference to Goffe, who was the husband of Mrs. Hooke's niece. If he had not already heard that the latter, when a major-general in the army, with his headquarters at Winchester, had resided in the family of Mr. Whitfield, formerly pastor of the church in Guilford, he may have learned it from the same persons who had assisted him to identify the brother-in-law of his former colleague.

The greater ease of escaping from New Haven into New Netherlands, may have influenced Whalley and Goffe to go thither rather than remain in Hartford, where they tarried awhile, and were hospitably entertained by Gov. Winthrop. But the presence at New Haven of persons intimately acquainted with the friends in England on whom they were dependent for remittances of money, may also have had some weight in their minds in determining where to hide themselves.

A journey of nine days from Cambridge brought them by way of Hartford and Guilford to New Haven, March 7, 1661, where they appeared openly as Mr. Davenport's guests. But intelligence having reached Boston, while they were on their journey, that a royal proclamation for their arrest had been issued in January, on information supplied by Capt. Breedon, it soon followed them to New Haven, and rendered it unsafe for them to be seen in public. Accordingly, on the

27th of March, they went to Milford, as if on a journey to New Netherlands; but in the night they returned to Mr. Davenport's, where they remained in concealment till the 30th of April.

Further reports of their residence at Cambridge having reached England, another royal order for their arrest was issued in March, and reached Boston on the 28th of April. It was blunderingly addressed, "*To our trusty aud well-beloved, the present governor or other magistrate or magistrates of our plantation of New England.*" The governor of Massachusetts, having delayed till sufficient time had elapsed for the news to be forwarded to New Haven, gave two young men, recently come from England, Thomas Kellond, merchant, and Thomas Kirk, shipmaster, a commission to prosecute the search in Massachusetts, with letters of commendation from himself to the governors of Plymouth, Connecticut, New Haven, and New Netherlands. On Tuesday, May 7, about six P. M., Kellond and Kirk, with John Chapin as guide, left Boston. On Friday they had an interview with Gov. Winthrop at Hartford. They say in the report, "The honorable governor carried himself very nobly to us, and was very diligent to supply us with all manner of conveniences for the prosecution of them, and promised all diligent search should be made after them in that jurisdiction, which was afterward performed." Learning from Winthrop that the "colonels," as Whalley and Goffe were called, had gone from Hartford toward New Haven, the pursuivants rode on Saturday to Guilford, where resided Deputy-Gov. Leete, chief magistrate of New Haven colony since the death of Gov. Newman.

Leete received them in the presence of several other persons. Looking over their papers, "he began to read them audibly; whereupon we told him (says their report) it was convenient to be more private in such concernments as that was." Retiring with them to another room, and thus giving opportunity for the rest of the company to disperse, Leete assured them that he had not seen the colonels for nine weeks; that is, since the time when they passed through Guilford on the way from Hartford to New Haven. The pursuivants replied that they had information that the persons they were in pursuit of had been in New Haven since then, and desired him to furnish them with horses for their further journey. The horses were "prepared with some delays." Coming out from the governor's house, they were told on their way to the inn by one Dennis Scranton (Crampton?) that the colonels were secreted at Mr. Davenport's, "and that, without all question, Deputy Leete knew as much." Other persons reported that they had very lately been seen between the houses of Mr. Davenport and Mr. Jones.

Confirmed by these tidings in the belief that they were upon the track of the fugitives, the pursuivants returned to Leete, and demanded military aid and "a power to search and apprehend." But he "said he could do nothing until he had spoken with one Mr. Gilbert and the rest of his magistrates." He offered, however, to give them a letter to Mr. Gilbert. By the time the governor had made ready his letter, the sun was too far on its way toward the western horizon to justify any expectation that they could conclude a conference with magistrate Gilbert before the going down of the sun should put an end to all secular transactions. They seem to have come to the conclusion, that, in the circumstances, it was better to stay in Guilford than to go on to New Haven, and, by their presence there on the Sabbath, notify the friends of the regicides that search would be made for them on the morrow. But their presence in Guilford was already known in New Haven, for some one who heard the governor read their commission had occasion soon after to send an Indian runner on an errand to New Haven.

At daybreak on Monday they left Guilford for New Haven, bearing the letter of Gov. Leete, advising Mr. Gilbert to call the town court together, and, by their advice and concurrence, to cause a search to be made. But, early as they started, a messenger had been sent before them to warn Gilbert that they were coming. "To our certain knowledge (they say) one John Meigs was sent a horseback before us, and by his speedy and unexpected going so early before day, was to give them an information; and the rather because by the delays which were used it was break of day before we got to horse; so he got there before us." Leete arrived, the pursuivants say in their report, "within two hours or thereabouts after us, and came to us to the court-chamber, where we again acquainted him with the information we had received, and that we had cause to believe they were concealed in New Haven, and thereupon we required his assistance and aid for their apprehension; to which he answered, that he did not believe they were. Whereupon we desired him to empower us, or order others for it; to which he gave us this answer, that he could not, nor would not, make us magistrates."

Magistrate Crane, of Branford, had arrived in company with Leete. Gilbert, who was not at home when the pursuivants inquired for him, having at last made his appearance, and Mr. Fenn having been summoned from Milford,—perhaps by Mr. Gilbert in person,— the magistrates and the deputies for New Haven held a consultation which lasted five or six hours. The issue of it, as communicated to Kellond and Kirk, was that "they would not nor could not do anything until they had called a general court of the freemen." The pursuivants protested against the delay, and threatened the magistrates and the colony with the resentment of his Majesty. The reply was "we honor his Majesty, but we have tender consciences." The magistrates then held a second consultation of two or three hours; after which, being further pressed "to their duty and loyalty to his Majesty, and whether they would own his Majesty or no, it was answered, they would first know whether his Majesty would own them."

New Haven was a government formed by the people without any charter or commission of any kind from England; and its magistrates feared that by acting under a mandate directed to the Governor of New England they might be acknowledging a governor-general, and thus betray the trust committed to them under oath by the freemen of the colony. They would do nothing, therefore, without a general court.

Evening coming on before the magistrates made their last reply to the pursuivants, it was too late to send forth on that day a warrant for convening the court. On Tuesday it was sent to the several plantations, and the court was held on Friday. The pursuivants, however, could not wait so long for a meeting which promised so little. Offering "great rewards to English and Indians who should give information that they might be taken," they departed on Tuesday for New Amsterdam, not without hope of finding, and, with the help of the Dutch governor, apprehending the fugitives. From New Amsterdam they returned by sea to Boston, where, on the 30th of May, they made oath to the truth of the written report which they delivered to Gov. Endicott.

On the Saturday when Kellond and Kirk were in Guilford, Whalley and Goffe, leaving the house of Mr. Jones, in which they had been secreted since the 30th of April, went to the mill[1] two miles north of the town, where they remained till Monday. We can easily conjecture that they did not make themselves visible at the mill till the last customer had departed, and that they went away on Monday morning before the earliest grist was brought. Beyond the mill all was an un-

---

[1] Dr. Bacon places the mill to which the regicides went for concealment till the Sabbath was past, at Westville; but I do not find on the records evidence that there was at that time any other mill than that on Mill River. This mill having become rotten, and new mill-stones being required for it, an unsuccessful attempt had been made not long before to bring the water from the Beaver Pond in a trench, so that an overshot mill might be set up in the town. On the first day of December, 1662, there was a general court, at which nothing was said about the mill, and on the third day of the same month a special meeting was held and "the occasion of coming together" was "the sad providence of God that was fallen out in the burning of the mill." Doubtless it was burned after the meeting, two days before. It was regarded as a calamity, not only because of the loss of the property, but because of the inconvenience of going to Milford for meal. The mill was soon after rebuilt in the same place. The mill-house, which was consumed by fire in 1662, was doubtless the same which in 1661 sheltered the regicides.

broken wilderness; so that if the pursuivants had come to New Haven on Saturday, furnished with a search-warrant, the fugitives might, at any moment, by retiring a few miles into the forest, have become secure. Probably this was their design after Mr. Jones had learned from the Indian runner what was going on in Guilford; but as their enemies did not leave Guilford till Monday, they deemed it safe to sleep under a roof.

No more appropriate time could be suggested for the allusion which Mr. Davenport is believed to have made to the regicides in the pulpit, than the Sabbath intervening between the two nights they spent at the mill. In a series of sermons substantially reproduced afterward in a book entitled "The Saint's Anchor-Hold," he inculcated among other duties that of sympathizing with and helping those who, for Christ's sake, are in trouble.

"Brethren, it is a weighty matter to read letters and receive intelligence in them concerning the state of the churches. You need to lift up your hearts to God, when you are about to read your letters from our native country, to give you wisdom and hearts duly affected, that you may receive such intelligences as you ought; for God looks upon every man, in such cases, with a jealous eye, observing with what workings of bowels they read or speak of the concernments of his church." . . . . "The Christian Hebrews are exhorted to call to remembrance the former days in which, after they were illuminated, they endured a great fight of afflictions partly whilst they were made a gazing stock both by reproaches and afflictions, and partly whilst they became companions of them that were so used. Let us do likewise. and own the reproached and persecuted people and cause of Christ in suffering times.

"Withhold not countenance, entertainment, and protection, from such, if they come to us from other countries, as from France, or England, or any other place. Be not forgetful to entertain strangers, for thereby some have entertained angels unawares Remember them that are in bonds, as bound with them, and them who suffer adversity, as being yourselves also in the body. The Lord required this of Moab, saying, 'Make thy shadow as the night in the midst of the noonday;'—that is, provide safe and comfortable shelter and refreshment for my people in the heat of persecution and opposition raised against them:—'hide the outcasts, betray not him that wandereth: let mine outcasts dwell with thee, Moab; be thou a covert to them from the face of the spoiler.' Is it objected, But so I may expose myself to be spoiled or troubled? He therefore, to remove this objection, addeth, 'For the danger is at an end, the spoiler ceaseth; the treaders down are consumed out of the land.' While we are attending to our duty in owning and harboring Christ's witnesses, God will be providing for their and our safety, by destroying those that would destroy his people.[1]"

On Monday, May 13, Whalley and Goffe were conducted by Mr. Jones and two other friends some three miles into the wilderness beyond the mill, where, a booth having been constructed, the colonels spent two nights. Having found a hatchet at the moment when one was needed for constructing the booth, they called the place Hatchet Harbor. On Wednesday, Kellond and Kirk being now far on their way to New Amsterdam, it was safe for Whalley and Goffe to come nearer to the habitations of men, and they were on that day conducted to West Rock, or Providence Hill, as they named it, by Richard Sperry, one of the three friends

[1] But as a copy of the book was presented by Davenport to Sir Thomas Temple in August, 1661, it would seem that the discourse from which the above is extracted must have been preached at an earlier date. The time intervening between May and August would hardly suffice for sending the manuscript to England, and receiving in return the printed copies.

who had guided them to Hatchet Harbor. Here were several huge fragments of trap rock, placed so as, with the aid of hemlock boughs, to shield the space amidst them from the wind, and some of them projecting overhead so as to afford shelter from rain. This cluster of rocks, which has ever since been called the Judges' Cave, was the refuge of these hunted regicides from May 15 to June 11. They were supplied with food from day to day by the faithful Sperry, whose house at the foot of the hill, though much nearer than any other, was nearly a mile distant. It is not unreasonable to conjecture that they went down in the evening to Sperry's house to sleep, and returned early in the morning to the cave, though tradition allows only that they sometimes came to the house in stormy weather. Probably not more than three or four persons knew that they were in Sperry's neighborhood; perhaps of the few who knew that he supplied their wants and guarded the approach to their privacy, none but himself had ever seen the Judges' Cave.

On Friday, two days after Whalley and Goffe had removed from Hatchet Harbor to West Rock,—

"At a meeting of the General Court for the jurisdiction, May 17, 1661, the deputy-governor declared to the Court the cause of the meeting; viz., that he had received a copy of a letter from his Majesty, with another letter from the governor of the Massachusetts, for the apprehending of Col. Whalley and Col. Goffe; which letters he showed to the Court, and acquainted them that forthwith upon the receipt of them he granted his letter to the magistrate of New Haven, by advice and concurrence of the deputies there to make present and diligent search throughout their town for the said persons accordingly; which letter the messengers carried, but found not the magistrate at home; and that he himself followed after the messengers, and came into New Haven soon after them, the 13th of May, 1661, bringing with him Mr. Crane, magistrate at Branford; who, when they were come, sent presently for the magistrates of New Haven and Milford, and the deputies of New Haven Court. The magistrates thus sent for not being yet come, they advised with the deputies about the matter, and after a short debate with the deputies, were writing a warrant for search for the aforesaid colonels; but the magistrates before spoken of being come, upon further consideration (the matter being weighty) it was resolved to call the General Court for the effectual carrying on of the work. The deputy-governor further informed the Court that himself and the magistrates told the messengers that they were far from hindering the search, and they were sorry that it so fell out, and were resolved to pursue the matter as that an answer should be prepared against their return from the Dutch.

"The Court being met, when they heard the matter declared, and had heard his Majesty's letter and the letter from the governor of the Massachusetts, they all declared they did not know that they were in the colony, or had been for divers weeks past, and both magistrates and deputies wished a search had been sooner made; and did now order that the magistrates take care and send forth warrant that a speedy, diligent search be made throughout the jurisdiction, in pursuance of his Majesty's command, according to the letters received, and that from the several plantations a return be made, that it may be recorded.[1]

[1] The following is a copy of one of the warrants, and of the return made by the searchers :—

May 17, 1661.

For the Marshal or Deputies at Milford.

You are to make diligent search, by the first, throughout the whole town of Milford and the precincts thereof, taking with you two or three sufficient persons, and calling in any other help you shall see need of, who are hereby required to attend for your assistance upon call; and this to be in all dwelling houses, barns or other buildings whatsoever and vessels in the harbor, for the finding and apprehending of Colonel Whalley and Colonel Goffe, who stand charged with crimes as by his Majesty's letter appears; and being found, you are to bring them to the Deputy-Governor,

"And whereas there have been rumors of their late being here at New Haven, it hath been inquired into and several persons examined, but could find no truth in those reports, and for any thing yet doth appear, they are but unjust suspicions and groundless reports against the place, to raise ill surmises and reproaches."

Learning that Mr. Davenport was suspected of concealing them, Whalley and Goffe left West Rock on the 11th of June, and showed themselves publicly, that he might be relieved from suspicion. It is not known at the present day where they spent the time between the 11th and the 22d of the month. Mr. Davenport, in a letter to Sir Thomas Temple, says that they came on the 22d of June "from another colony where they were, and had been some time, to New Haven.[1]"

or some other magistrate, to be sent over for England, according to his Majesty's order. Hereof fail not at peril.

By order of the General Court,
As attest, WILLIAM LEETE, *Deputy Governor.*

JASPER CRANE,
MATTHEW GILBERT,
ROBERT TREAT.

In the marshal's absence, I do appoint and empower you, Thomas Sanford, Nicholas Camp, and James Tapping to the above named powers, according to the tenor of the warrant; and to make a return thereof under your hands to me by the first.

ROBERT TREAT.

We, the said persons, appointed to serve and search by virtue of this our warrant, do hereby declare and testify that to our best light we have the 20th of May, 1661, made diligent search according to the tenor of this warrant, as witness our hands.

THOMAS SANFORD,
NICHOLAS CAMP,
JAMES TAPPING,
LAWRENCE WARD. his **I** mark.
} *Searchers.*"

[1] It has been said that "Mr. Davenport's statement looks like a prevarication." Doubtless it was, as every thing which the New Haven

Perhaps they made a visit to Connecticut, and allowed themselves to be seen there in order to divert attention from New Haven. On Saturday, June 22, they came to New Haven, and remained till Monday, causing Mr. Gilbert, who, since the election on the 19th of May, had been deputy-governor, to be informed that they were ready to surrender, if necessary, and choosing to do so rather than bring ruin upon their friends. But on Sunday some persons came to them advising not to surrender; and so on Monday they disappeared while the magistrates were consulting together, and taking measures for their arrest. "Thereupon a diligent search was renewed, and many were sent forth on foot and horseback to recover them into their hands." From a letter of Edward Rawson, secretary of the colony of Massachusetts to Gov. Leete, it may be inferred that these pursuers went to Branford. But if the regicides were seen going in that direction, as if they would return to Connecticut, it was only to mislead, for the same night they were lodged in their former retreat at West Rock.[1] "They continued there

people said about the two regicides was, a prevarication, but there is no reason to doubt that the statement was literally true. Mr. Davenport was a subtile casuist, but was not reckless of the truth.

[1] I conjecture that going eastward as far as Neck Bridge, they hid themselves under it till the pursuers had ridden over, and then, passing up by the side of the stream to the mill, went by Mill Rock to the house of Sperry. The conjecture accounts for the tradition that they were under the bridge when Kellond and Kirk passed over it; in which form the tradition has no inherent probability.

The tradition that they were concealed in the Allerton house, I cannot account for quite so satisfactorily. Stiles relates that their friend, Mrs. Eyers, hearing that the pursuers were coming, sent the colonels out of the house with directions to return immediately. They returning, she (says Hutchinson, who had access to a diary of Goffe, not now extant), sometimes venturing to a house near the cave, until the 19th of August, when the search for them being pretty well over, they ventured to the house of one Tomkins, near Milford, where they remained two years without so much as going into the orchard. After that they took a little more liberty, and made themselves known to several persons in whom they could confide; and each of them frequently prayed, and also exercised, as they term it, or preached at private meetings in their chamber."

The regicides, lying concealed at West Rock, Gov. Leete received on the 30th of July a letter written by order of the council of Massachusetts informing that they had heard from the agent of their colony in London that many complaints were made against New England in general, and that though the address to his

concealed them in a closet, and promptly replied, when the pursuers asked for the colonels, that they had been there, but had recently gone away. Mrs. Eyers, granddaughter of the Isaac Allerton who came in the Mayflower, was born Sept. 27, 1653, and therefore was in June, 1661, less than eight years of age. If, therefore, Whalley and Goffe were concealed in the house where she lived, they were concealed by the contrivance of her step-grandmother, the widow Allerton, rather than of the person who afterward became the owner of the Allerton mansion, and the wife of Simon Eyers. The tradition may have been handed down by her, but she could not have been the principal actor. Perhaps the colonels were entertained in this house from Saturday, June 22, to Monday, June 24, and went from Mrs. Allerton's toward Neck Bridge after they learned that the magistrates had issued a warrant for their arrest. This would account for another tradition; viz., that Marshal Kimberley attempted to arrest them between the town and Neck Bridge, but found them so skilled in the art of self-defence that he was obliged to go back for assistance. For further information in regard to Mrs. Eyers and the Allertons, see Dr. Bacon's letter to Hon. John Davis, in Mass. Hist. Coll. XXVII. 243.

Majesty which Massachussets had made, came seasonably and had a gracious answer, yet the commissioners for the Plantations had taken notice that the other colonies had neglected thus to recognize the king. The secretary adds,—

"Further I am required to signify to you as from them that the non-attendance with diligence to execute the king's majesty's warrant for the apprehending of Colonels Whalley and Goffe will much hazard the present state of these colonies, and your own particularly, if not some of your persons, which is not a little afflictive to them; and that in their understanding there remains no way to expiate the offence and preserve yourselves from the danger and hazard but by apprehending the said persons, who, as we are informed, are yet remaining in the colony, and not above a fortnight since were seen there, all which will be against you. Sir, your own welfare, the welfare of your neighbors, bespeak your unwearied pains to free yourself and neighbors. I shall not add, having so lately, by a few lines from our governor and myself looking much this way, communicated our sense and thoughts of your and our troubles, and have as yet received no return, but commend you to God and his rich grace for your guidance and direction in a matter of such moment, as his Majesty may receive full and just satisfaction, the mouths of all opposers stopped, and the profession of the truth that is in you and us may not in the least suffer by your actings is the prayer of
 Sir, your loving friend,
  EDWARD RAWSON, *Secretary*.
 In the name and by order of the Council."

The above was written on the 4th July, 1661, but remained in the hand of the writer till the 15th of the same month, when he added,—

"Sir, since what I wrote, news and certain intelligence is come hither of the two colonels being at New Haven from Saturday to Monday, and publicly known; and, however, it is given out that they came to surrender themselves, and pretended by Mr. Gilbert that he looked when they would have come in and delivered up themselves, never setting a guard about the house nor endeavoring to secure them, but, when it was too late, to send to Totoket, &c. Sir, how this will be taken is not difficult to imagine. To be sure, not well; nay, will not all men condemn you as wanting to yourselves, and that you have something to rely on, that you hope, at least, will answer your ends? I am not willing to meddle with your hopes, but if it be a duty to obey such lawful warrants, as I believe it is, the neglect thereof will prove uncomfortable. Pardon me, sir; it is my desire you may regain your peace (and if you please to give me notice when you will send the two colonels); though Mr. Woodgreen is bound hence within a month, yet if you shall give me assurance of their coming, I shall not only endeavor, but do hereby engage, to cause his stay a fortnight, nay, three weeks, rather than they should not be sent."

At a general court held at New Haven for the jurisdiction, Aug. 1, 1661:— "the governor informed the Court of the occasion of calling them together at this time, and among the rest the main thing insisted on was to consider what application to make to the king in the case we now stood, being like to be rendered worse to the king than the other colonies, they seeing it an incumbent duty so to do. The governor informed also the Court that he had received a letter from the Council in the Bay, which was read, wherein was intimated of sundry complaints in England made against New England. and that the committee in England took notice of the neglect of the other colonies in their non-application to the king.

"Now the Court, taking the matter into serious consideration, after much debate and advice concluded that this writing should be sent to the Council in the Bay, the copy whereof is as followeth:"—

"HONORED GENTLEMEN,—Yours dated the 4th of July (61), with a postscript of the 15th, we received July 30, which was communicated to our general court Aug. 1, who considered what you please to relate of those complaints made against New England, and of what spirit they are represented to be of, upon occasion of that false report against Capt. Leveret, whom we believe to have more wisdom and honesty than so to report, and we are assured that New England is not of that spirit. And as for the other colonies' neglect in non-application with yourselves to his Majesty last year, it hath not been forborne upon any such account; as we for our parts profess, and believe for our neighbors, but only in such new and unaccustomed matters we were in the dark to hit it in way of agreement as to a form satisfactory that might be acceptable; but since that of your colony hath come to our view, it is much to our content, and we solemnly profess from our hearts to own and say the same to his Majesty, and do engage to him full subjection and allegiance with yourselves accordingly, with profession of the same ends in coming with like permission and combining with yourselves and the other neighbor colonies, as by the preface of our articles may appear; upon which grounds we both supplicate and hope to find a like protection, privilege, immunities, and favors, from his royal Majesty. And as for that you note of our not so diligent attendance to his Majesty's warrant, we have given you an account of before, that it was not done out of any mind to slight or disown his Majesty's authority in the least, nor out of favor to the colonels; nor did it hinder the effect of their apprehending, they being gone before the warrant came into our colony, as is since fully proved; but only there was a gainsaying of the gentlemen's earnestness, who retarded their own business to wait upon ours without commission; and also out of scruple of conscience and fear of unfaithfulness to our people (who committed all our authority to us under oath) by owning a general governor, unto whom the warrant was directed, as such implicitly, and that upon misinformation to his Majesty given, though other magistrates were mentioned, yet (as some thought) it was in or under him, which oversight (if so it shall be apprehended) we hope, upon our humble acknowledgment, his Majesty will pardon, as also that other and greater bewailed remissness in one, in not securing them till we came and

knew their place, out of over-much belief of their pretended reality
to resign up themselves, according to their promise, to save the
country harmless, which failing is so much the more lamented, by
how much more we had used all diligence to press for such a
delivery upon some of those who had shown them former kindness, as had been done other where, when as none of the magistrates could otherwise do anything in it, they being altogether
ignorant where they were or how to come at them, nor truly do
they now, nor can we believe that they are hid anywhere in this
colony, since that departure or defeatment. But however the consequence prove, we must wholly rely on the mercy of God and the
king, with promise to do our endeavor to regain them if opportunity serve. Wherefore in this our great distress we earnestly
desire your aid to present us to his Majesty in our cordial owning
and complying with your address, as if it had been done and said
by our very selves, who had begun to draw up something that way,
but were disheartened through sense of feebleness, and incapacity
to procure a meet agent to present it in our disadvantaged state,
by these providences occurring; hoping you will favor us in this
latter and better pleasing manner of doing, which we shall take
thankfully from you, and be willing to join in the proportionate
share of charge for a common agent to solicit New England affairs
in England, which we think necessary to procure the benefit of all
acts of indemnity, grace, or favor, on all our behalfs, as well as in
other respects to prevent the mischiefs of such as malign and seek
to misinform against us, of which sort there be many to complot
nowadays with great sedulity. If you shall desert us in this
affliction, to present us as before, by the transcript of this our letter or otherwise, together with the petition and acknowledgment
herewithal sent, we shall yet look up to our God, that deliverance
may arise another way."

This letter manifests a fear of evil results to the
colony and to the magistrates from their neglect to
apprehend the regicides. It was doubtless drawn up
by Gov. Leete, who by this time was so much in fear
for himself and for the colony that the fugitives would

not have been safe if he had known where to put his hand on them. The freemen allowed this letter to be sent as the sense of the colony; and perhaps a majority sympathized with Leete in the feeling that the safety of the colony required their extradition if found, and agreed with him in the belief that they were not at that time within its territory; but a few were more courageous, and quietly allowing the letter to be sent as the official declaration of the colony, kept to themselves their knowledge that Whalley and Goffe were still within the jurisdiction. Of this number were Gilbert and Davenport, though even they were probably not aware that the fugitives were so near that they could see the turret of the building in which the court was held, and hear the rattle of the drum which convened it.

The difference of opinion on this subject which now obtained among the leading men seems to have occasioned some sharpness of feeling. Mr. Hooke, Whalley's brother-in-law, and formerly teacher of the church at New Haven, writes from England about ten weeks after this general court, to Mr. Davenport, "I understand by your letter what you have lately met with from Mr. Leete, &c.," and proceeds to explain that a certain letter from a friend in England to Mr. Street, was not designed to caution New Haven people against befriending the regicides, but only against doing it openly. "The man was in the country when he wrote it, who sent it up to the city to be sent by what hand he knew not, nor yet knoweth who carried it; and such were the times that he durst not express matters as he would, but he foresaw what fell out among you, and was willing yon should be secured as well as his other friends, and therefore he wrote that they might not be found among you, but provided for by you in some secret places. . . . I hope yet all will be well; though now I hear (as I am writing) of another order to be sent over, yet still I believe God will suffer no man to touch you. I am almost amazed sometimes to see what cross capers some of you do make. I should break my shins should I do the like." Gov. Leete had apparently understood the cautionary letter to Mr. Street as advising an entire withholding of entertainment from the regicides, and had changed his position by cross caper, such as Mr. Hooke thought himself incapable of executing.

Another intimation that Mr. Leete had become more penitent than others approved, is contained in a letter to Mr. Gilbert from Robert Newman, formerly ruling elder in the church at New Haven, but now resident in England. He writes, "I am sorry to see that you should be so much surprised with fears of what men can or may do unto you. The fear of an evil is ofttimes more than the evil feared. I hear of no danger, nor do I think any will attend you for that matter. Had not W. L. written such a pitiful letter over, the business, I think, would have died. What it may do to him I know not: they have greater matters than that to exercise their thoughts." On the same day another friend in England wrote to Gilbert, "We are very apt to be more afraid than we ought to be, or need to be."

The letter drawn up by Gov. Leete, and sanctioned by the General Court on the 1st of August, was sent to Boston by special messengers, who were to " see what could be done in the case." Twenty days later another court was held, occasioned by information that Massachusetts had, on the 7th of August, formally proclaimed the king. Anxious not to come short in demonstrations of loyalty, "it was voted and concluded as an act of the General Court," that the king should be proclaimed.

"And for the time of doing it, it was concluded to be done the next morning at nine of the clock, and the military company was desired to come to the solemnizing of it. And the form of the proclamation is as followeth:—

"Although we have not received any form of proclamation by order from his Majesty or Council of State, for the proclaiming his Majesty in this colony, yet the Court taking encouragement from what hath been in the rest of the United Colonies, hath thought fit to declare publicly and proclaim that we do acknowledge his Royal Highness, Charles the Second, King of England, Scotland, France, and Ireland, to be our Sovereign Lord and King, and that we do acknowledge ourselves the inhabitants of this colony to be his Majesty's loyal and faithful subjects." GOD SAVE THE KING.

These public demonstrations of loyalty were prompted in large measure by fear of evil consequences to the colony, on account of its neglect to apprehend the regicides. They were supplemented with every possible attempt to secure the aid of those whose position enabled them to make intercession with the king. Before the official communication of Secretary Rawson had been received at New Haven, a letter from Davenport to Deputy-Gov. Bellingham was on its way to Boston, enclosing what he calls an apology. In August, fearing that his apology had miscarried, he wrote to Sir Thomas Temple, enclosing a copy of the apology, and very humbly beseeching his good offices in averting from the colony of New Haven the displeasure of the king. In September Gov. Leete went to Boston, probably on his way to or from the meeting of the commissioners of the United Colonies of Plymouth, to consult with friends there how he might escape the punishment of his neglect. The result of the conference was a letter from John Norton, teacher of the church at Boston, to Richard Baxter, one of the king's chaplains. It is to be inferred from Norton's letter that there had been a change in Leete's spirit since he received Kellond and Kirk in his house at Guilford and read their instructions aloud in the presence of his neighbors. Norton says:—

"He, being conscious of indiscretion and some neglect (not to say how it came about) in relation to the expediting the executing of the warrant, according to his duty, sent from his Majesty for the apprehending of the two colonels, is not without fear of some displeasure that may follow thereupon, and indeed hath almost ever since been a man depressed in his spirit for the neglect wherewith he chargeth himself therein. His endeavors also since have been accordingly, and that in full degree; as, besides his own testimony, his neighbors attest they see not what he could have done more."

At their meeting in September, the commissioners of the United Colonies issued an order forbidding the entertainment of Whalley and Goffe, and requiring all persons who knew where they were to make known their hiding-place. This order, with the other proceedings, was signed by William Leete and Benjamin Fenn, commissioners for New Haven, the last named an inhabitant of Milford, where Whalley and Goffe where then concealed. There is no evidence that Fenn was in the secret, and no good reason can be alleged why he should have been embarrassed with useless information.

Whalley and Goffe remained in Milford from Aug. 19, 1661, till July, 1664, when, hearing that four royal commissioners had arrived in Boston, charged to inquire after persons attainted of high treason, they thought it necessary to leave the place where they had so long resided. At first they retired to their cave on West Rock. But after they had remained there eight or ten days, some Indians, in their hunting, discovered the cave with the bed in it. This being reported, they were obliged to find another temporary retreat, the location of which is unknown. Probably they were unwillingly tarrying in New Haven till arrangements could be made for their removal to a less suspected and less frequented place. Starting on the 13th of October, and traveling only by night, they directed their steps toward Hadley, Mass., a plantation in the remotest north-western frontier of the New England settlements, recently established by emigrants from Hartford and Wethersfield. Here they were, by pre-arrangement, received and concealed by Mr. John Russell, the minister of the town. With him they both continued to reside till the death of Whalley, about ten years afterward. But with their removal to Hadley their connection with the History of the New Haven colony ceases.

CHAPTER XIX.

CONNECTICUT PROCURES A CHARTER WHICH COVERS THE TERRITORY OF NEW HAVEN.

KING JAMES THE FIRST incorporated by letters-patent the "Council established at Plymouth in the county of Devon for the planting, ruling, and governing of New England in America," and granted unto them and their successors and assigns all that part of America lying between the fortieth and forty-eighth degree of north latitude, and extending from sea to sea. This "Council for New England," having sold patents to New Plymouth and Massachusetts, granted to its president, Robert, Earl of Warwick, a territory supposed to be bounded on the east and north by New Plymouth and Massachusetts, and the grant was confirmed by King Charles the First. On the 19th of March the said Robert, Earl of Warwick, conveyed his title to the right honorable William, viscount Say and Seal, the right honorable Robert, Lord Brook, the right honorable Lord Rich, and the honorable Charles Fiennes, Esq., Sir Nathaneal Rich, Knt., Sir Richard Saltonstall, Knt., Richard Knightly, Esq., John Pym, Esq., John Hampden, John Humphrey, Esq., and Herbert Pelham, Esq., their heirs and assigns, and their associates, forever. He describes the territory as "all that part of New England in America which lies and extends itself from a river there called Narragansett River, the space of forty leagues upon a straight line near the sea-shore toward the south-west, west and by south, or west, as the coast lieth towards Virginia, accounting three English miles to the league; and also all and singular the lands and hereditaments whatsoever, lying and being within the lands aforesaid, north and south in latitude and breadth, and in length and longitude, of and within all the breadth aforesaid, throughout the main lands there, from the Western Ocean to the South Sea."

The first planters of Hartford, Windsor, and Wethersfield settled themselves in the territory thus conveyed by the Earl of Warwick, without asking leave of the patentees. Some years afterward, a fort having been meanwhile built at Saybrook by the patentees, the colonial government purchased of Mr. Fenwick, the representative of the patentees, the fort and the lands upon the river. In the articles of agreement Mr. Fenwick also promises that "all the lands from Narragansett River to the fort of Saybrook, mentioned in a patent granted by the Earl of Warwick to certain nobles and gentlemen, shall fall under the jurisdiction of Connecticut if it come into his power," but makes no mention of, or allusion to, the territory occupied by the New Haven colony.

So far as appears, no claim was made by Connecticut to the territory of New Haven till 1660. In that year the town of New Haven, wishing to "set out the bounds with lasting marks," between them and Connecticut, appointed Mr. Yale, William Andrews, John Cooper,

CONNECTICUT PROCURES A CHARTER. 447

John Brocket, and Nathaniel Merriman, a committee to do it with the help of Montowese, the late proprietor. Connecticut took offence at the proceedings of this committee, and sent to New Haven the following letter:—

"Honored Gentlemen,—This Court having received informaton, not only by what appears in one of your laws respecting the purchase of land from the Indians, wherein there is a seeming challenge of very large interests of lands, and likewise by what intelligence we have had of your stretching your bounds up toward us, by marking trees on this side Pilgrims' Harbor,[1] which things, as ye intrench upon our interest, so they are not satisfying or contentful, nor do we apprehend it a course furthering or strengthening that friendly correspondency that we desire and ought to be perpetuated betwixt neighbors and confederates; especially in that we conceive you cannot be ignorant of our real and true right to those parts of the country where you are seated, both by conquest, purchase, and possession; and though hitherto we have been silent and altogether forborne to make any absolute challenge to our own, as before, yet now we see a necessity at least to revive the memorial of our right and interest, and therefore do desire that there may be a cessation of further proceedings in this nature, until upon mature consideration there may be a determinate settlement and mutual concurrence twixt yourselves and this colony in reference to the dividing bounds twixt the two colonies. It is further desired and requested by us that if there be anything extant on record with you that may further the deciding this matter, it may be produced, and that there may be a time and place appointed, when some deputed for that end, furnished with full power, may meet, that so a loving issue may be effected to prevent further troubles. And in case there be no record of grant or allowance from this

---

[1] Pilgrims' Harbor, it appears, was so called before this letter was written. It was probably a hut where travelers between Hartford and New Haven found shelter. If the regicides ever made use of it, it was after this letter was written. It was not, as President Stiles suggests, called Pilgrims' Harbor because the regicides lodged in it.

colony, respecting the surrender not only of lands possessed by you and improved, but also such lands as it seems to us that you, under some pretended or assumed right, have induced by your bounds within your liberties, that you would be pleased to consider on some speedy course, whereby a compliance and condescendency to what is necessary and convenient for your future comfort may be obtained from us, the true proprietors of these parts of country. We desire your return to our General Court in reference to our propositions, with what convenient speed may be, that so what is desired by us in point of mutual and neighborly correspondence, according to the rules of justice and righteousness, may be still maintained and continued."

Action was taken on this letter at a general court held at New Haven for the jurisdiction, May 20, 1661. It was "ordered that a committee be chosen by this Court for the treating with and issuing of any seeming difference betwixt Connecticut Colony and this, in reference to the dividing bounds betwixt them, and of some seeming right to this jurisdiction, which they pretend in a letter sent to this General Court."

This order was passed thirteen days after the General Court of Connecticut had desired and authorized Gov. Winthrop to act as the agent of the colony in presenting their address to the king, and in procuring a patent. Though the extant copy of the letter in which Connecticut for the first time lays claim to the territory of New Haven bears no date, it was written about the time when they were considering the expediency of applying for the charter which they soon after obtained. They had no copy of the conveyance from the Earl of Warwick; and if they had possessed a copy, or even the original, Mr. Fenwick had conveyed to them only what his agreement specified. It is evident that about this time they conceived the design of procuring a royal charter which should secure to them the whole territory conveyed to Lord Say and Seal and others, by the Earl of Warwick, even if it should include the territory of New Haven. They justified themselves in doing so on the ground, that, having paid a large sum to Mr. Fenwick, they ought to have received for it all the territory covered by the patent which he and his associates possessed. They felt and represented to the aged Lord Say and Seal that Mr. Fenwick had dealt hardly with them, and that they ought to receive whatever was reserved by him as the representative of the patentees. While they were all agreed that it was right for Connecticut to acquire, if possible, a legal title as extensive as the patent from the Earl of Warwick, the New Haven people having paid nothing to the patentees, they were not of one mind as to the disposition to be made of New Haven; some holding that New Haven should be at liberty to join with them or not, while others maintained that the welfare of all parties justified the compulsion of New Haven into union with Connecticut. Gov. Winthrop was himself of the first-mentioned party; for when Davenport, hearing what was going on at Hartford, wrote to his friend, warning him "not to have his hand in so unrighteous an act as so far to extend the line of their patent, that the colony of New Haven should be involved within it," Winthrop replied,[1] "that the magistrates had agreed and

---

[1] The extract is from Davenport's report of Winthrop's letters in "New Haven's Case Stated." Winthrop wrote twice "from two several places:" first from Middletown, and again from New Amsterdam "at his going away." This looks as if he did not pass through New Haven in

expressed in the presence of some ministers, that, if their line should reach us (which they knew not, the copy being in England), yet New Haven Colony should be at full liberty to join with them or not."

Embarking at New Amsterdam some time in August, Winthrop went to England, both to transact business of his own and to execute the commission with which he was intrusted by Connecticut. He was most favorably received by Lord Say and Seal to whom he carried a letter from the General Court of Connecticut. His lordship writes to him, Dec. 14, 1661:—

"For my very loving friend, Mr. John Winthrop, living in Coleman Street, at one Mrs. Whiting's house, near the church.

"MR. WINTHROP,—I received your letter by Mr. Richards, and I would have been glad to have had an opportunity of being at London myself to have done you and my good friends in New England the best service I could; but my weakness hath been such, and my old disease of the gout falling upon me, I did desire leave not to come up this winter, but I have writ to the Earl of Manchester, lord chamberlain of His Majesty's household to give you the best assistance he may; and indeed, he is a noble and worthy lord, and one that loves those that are godly. And he and I did join together, that our godly friends of New England might enjoy their just rights and liberties; and this, Col. Crowne, who, I hear, is still in London, can fully inform you. Concerning that of Connecticut, I am not able to remember all the particulars; but I have written to my lord chamberlain, that when you shall attend him (which I think will be best for you to do, and therefore I have enclosed a letter to him in yours), that you may deliver it, and I

---

going from Hartford to his place of embarkation. A passage in a shallop down the river was more convenient for one who was on the way to Europe than a horseback-ride through the country. From a letter of Willet to Winthrop printed in Mass. Hist. Coll., xli., p. 396, it appears that Winthrop went to England by way of Holland.

have desired him to acquaint you where you may speak with Mr. Jesup, who, when we had the patent, was our clerk, and he, I believe, is able to inform you best about it, and I have desired my lord to wish him so to do. I do think he is now in London. My love remembered unto you, I shall remain,

"Your very loving friend,
"W. SAY AND SEAL."

Lord Say and Seal, and the other Puritan lords and gentlemen to whom the Earl of Warwick conveyed his title to Connecticut, had secured the territory for the purpose of establishing a Puritan colony, and with the expectation that some of themselves would personally engage in the enterprise. Twenty-five years before, Winthrop himself had been constituted their agent, with instructions "to provide able men to the number of fifty at the least, for making of fortifications and building of houses at the river Connecticut and the harbor adjoining, first for their own present accommodations, and then such houses as may receive men of quality, which latter houses we would have to be builded within the fort." Not one, however, of the lords and gentlemen named by Warwick in his conveyance, came to Connecticut. Of the "men of quality" who in 1635 signed the agreement with Winthrop, the only one that came over was George Fenwick; and he was not one of the original patentees, but had become partner in the company subsequent to the conveyance from the Earl of Warwick in 1631. He seems from the day of his arrival to have full power to dispose of everything belonging to the company; and in his conveyance of the fort and the lands on the river to the colony of Connecticut he makes no mention of any other conveyor than himself. His whole conduct is that of a principal rather than of an agent. He had doubtless acquired from the other partners all their rights. At what date he had become sole proprietor, we cannot determine. Perhaps it was before he came over in 1639; for most of the patentees were then and had been for some time so earnestly and deeply engaged in saving their native land from the encroachments of tyranny, that they must have relinquished the idea of emigration. Notably, two of them, Viscount Say and Seal and John Hampden, had committed themselves to resist the requirement of ship-money; and Hampden was prosecuted rather than Say and Seal, only because his case had a prior standing on the docket. At all events, Fenwick talks and acts, in 1644 and 1645, as if he were sole proprietor. In 1644 he makes the conveyance before mentioned, to the colony of Connecticut in his own name; and in 1645 he makes a free gift to the plantation of Guilford of land, which in his sale to the colony of Connecticut, he had reserved for his plantation of Saybrook. His letter of gift is so illustrative of his character and of the condition of Guilford as to deserve transcription in full. It is as follows:—

"MR. LEETE,—I have been moved by Mr. Whitfield to enlarge the bounds of your plantation, which otherwise, he told me, could not comfortaby subsist, unto Hammonassett River; to gratify so good a friend, and to supply your wants, I have yielded to his request, which, according to his request, by this bearer I signify to you for your own and the plantation's better satisfaction, hoping it will be a means fully to settle such who, for want of fit accommodation, begun to be wavering amongst you; and I would commend to your consideration one particular, which, I conceive, might tend to common advantage, and that is, when you are all suited to your present content, you will bind yourselves more strictly for continuing together; for however in former times (while chapmen and money were plentiful) some have gained by removes, yet in these latter times it doth not only weaken and discourage the plantation deserted, but also wastes and consumes the estates of those that remove. Rolling stones gather no moss in these times, and our conditions now are not to expect great things. Small things, nay, moderate things, should content us. A warm fireside, and a peaceable habitation, with the chief of God's mercies, the gospel of peace, is no ordinary mercy, though other things were mean. I intended only one word, but the desire of the common good and settlement hath drawn me a little further.

"For the consideration Mr. Whitfield told me you were willing to give me for my purchase, I leave it wholly to yourselves. I look not to my own profit, but to your comfort. Only one thing I must entreat you to take notice of, that when I understood that that land might be useful for your plantation, I did desire to express my love to Mr. Whitfield and his children, and therefore offered him to suit his own occasions, which he, more intending your common advantage than his own particular, hath hitherto neglected; yet my desire now is that you would suit him to his content; and that he would accept of what shall be allotted him as a testimony of my love intended to him, before I give up my interest to your plantation, and that therefore he may hold it free from charge as I have signified to himself. I will not now trouble you further, but with my love to yourself and plantation, rest

"Your loving friend and neighbor,
"SAYBROOK, Oct. 22, 1645." "GEORGE FENWICK."

Lord Say and Seal, though he had long since relinquished the expectation of removing to America, retained the friendly feeling he had ever cherished toward the planters of New England, and was in a position, when Connecticut sought a royal charter, where his influence was very powerful. Although he had opposed the tyranny of Charles the First, he was a royalist in principle, and disapproved of the extreme measures to which the popular party were carried by the current of events. During the commonwealth he lived in retirement, and was among the first to move, when opportunity offered for the restoration of the ancient constitution. As a reward for his services, Charles the Second had made him lord privy seal.

The Earl of Manchester, whom Say and Seal mentions in his letter to Winthrop, was also a Puritan. He likewise, and for similar reasons, was high in office, and high in favor with the king. Forced to resign his commission as commander-in-chief of one of the grand divisions of the parliamentary army, by the intrigues of men who wished to eliminate both royalty and aristocracy from the constitution, he, too, had lived for years in retirement, waiting for an opportunity to assist in restoring the ancient form of government. He was now lord chamberlain, and more active in public affairs than his aged friend Say and Seal.

Winthrop himself was singularly well qualified for the negotiation in which he had engaged. A university scholar, he had made the tour of the Continent as far as to Constantinople before he emigrated to New England. Gifted by nature, and polished with the best European culture, he was qualified to converse on those subjects which were everywhere discussed in society, and by his experience in America was able to discourse of a country full of marvels to Englishmen, whether they had traveled on the Continent or journeyed only within their native land.

Every thing seemed to favor his undertaking. Though the colony had no copy of the old patent, one was found among the papers of Gov. Hopkins, and was by his executor delivered to Winthrop. The lord chamberlain, moved by the lord privy seal, as well as by his own love to "those that are godly," lent to the Puritan colony his influence with the king. Mather relates that Winthrop had a ring which his grandfather received from King Charles the First, and that the acceptance of his Majesty of this souvenir of his father effectually pledged him to favor the suppliant who offered it.

The new charter was in every respect as Winthrop would desire it to be. The boundaries of the territory it confirmed to Connecticut were the same as in the patent of 1631. "With regard to powers of government, the charter was" (says Bancroft) "still more extraordinary. It conferred on the colonists unqualified power to govern themselves. They were allowed to elect all their own officers, to enact their own laws, to administer justice without appeals to England, to inflict punishments, to confer pardons, and, in a word, to exercise every power, deliberative and active. The king, far from reserving a negative on the acts of the colony, did not even require that the laws should be transmitted for his inspection; and no provision was made for the interference of the English government, in any event whatever. Connecticut was independent except in name."

Clearly the terms of the charter were dictated by Winthrop. Both the boundaries and the powers of government were such as he asked for. He was resolved, when he left Hartford, to ask for all the territory included by the old patent, even if the line should reach so as to include a sister colony.

What, then, was his expectation in regard to the Jurisdiction of New Haven? Plainly it was, if we may trust his own testimony, that New Haven should be at liberty to join with them or not. Though he had no intention of absorbing New Haven by compulsion, he believed that it would be to the advantage of all to be united in one jurisdiction by mutual agreement. There were in the colony of New Haven some who were of the same opinion. Gov. Leete, "both by speech and letter," urged Winthrop to include New Haven within the territory he should ask for Connecticut. Leete may have been more solicitous for comprehension at that time than two or three years later; for Winthrop embarked when New Haven was more apprehensive of the royal displeasure than at any other time. Connecticut, in reply to New Haven's Case Stated, says, "By your then chief in government, our governor was solicited to include New Haven within our patent, both by speech and letter; and friends in England were improved by some of you to persuade to and promote the same, and, according to your desires, attended the best expedient to express sincerity of love, *your case and condition at that time duly considered.*" The obvious interpretation of this language is that Leete desired, in the danger which threatened New Haven, that she might be allowed to take shelter under the royal charter which Connecticut hoped to obtain. Two letters from Leete to Winthrop, found among the Winthrop papers enclosed in a slip of paper which was indorsed "Mr. Leete's letter about procuring patent," still more clearly prove that Leete desired the comprehension of New Haven, and that he

CONNECTICUT PROCURES A CHARTER. 457

desired it in order to secure her safety from danger impending on account of the regicides. The first of the letters is doubtless that which Connecticut refers to in her answer to New Haven's Case Stated.[1] A few words in this letter are italicised for the convenience of the reader. Under date of Aug. 6, 1661, he writes:—

" *To the Right Worshipful John Winthrop, Esq.*

" HONORED SIR,—I waited with expectation to have seen you at Guilford, or met you at New Haven, to have presented you with something I had prepared, petition-wise, for the king; that, if you had pleased, we might have had your furtherance about it; but not meeting you, I went toward New London, thinking to find you there; but when I came at Saybrook I heard of your being gone near a week before, and so I was wholly disappointed: since which time I have sent it to the Council at Boston, as also a letter of our General Court, signifying our accord to own their address, and to acknowledge ourselves in like relation and with like affection to his Majesty.[2] All which I suppose we should have done by you, could we have seen you and yours,[3] and had your consent; for we are desirous ever to maintain the stamp of the United Colonies; but seeing we were disappointed, we were necessitated to apply ourselves to the Bay, and are now thither sending this enclosed letter and petition; yet, lest any miscarrying or interruption there should fall out as from them, and for fuller testimony of us and our loyalty to his Majesty, I have sent . . . (*nonnulla desunt*) . . . and hope it shall not meet with a check from his

[1] Since writing the above I have noticed that Leete in a letter to Winthrop, which may be found on p. 484, alludes to a letter of similar import with that here given, which he wrote when Winthrop was in England. According to Leete, the purport of the letter to England was "to make your patent a covert, but no control to our jurisdiction, until we accorded with mutual satisfaction to become one."

[2] This letter may be found on p. 438.

[3] Fitz John and Waitstill, sons of Winthrop, accompanied their father to Europe.

Majesty. If it should, it would grieve me, but if it find favor, and herein his Majesty's clemency shall further shine as toward such despised ones, it will bring forth (I believe) great cheering and cordialness, with growth of loyalty; which I shall seek to further as I shall be in capacity. Good sir, mind us, and with first opportunities please to deal upon our account. I have written to the Bay, that some apt personage may be procured to be the common agent for New England, to wait upon all turns when any thing *pro* or *con* should be on hand about New England affairs, which I am informed they think needful also. *I wish that you and we could procure one patent to reach beyond Delaware*, where we have expended a thousand pounds to procure Indian title, view, and begin to possess. If war should arise between Holland and England, it might suit the king's interest; a little assistance might so reduce all to England. *But our chief aim is to purchase our own peace*, which I desire we all pursue, as I hope you will, and for which we pray, as for your health, success, and welfare. With chiefest respects to yourself, Mr. Fitz and Mr. Wait, wishing your safe and speedy return to your good family, and us that long for it, resting

"Yours cordially to love and honor you,
"WILLIAM LEETE.
"GUILFORD, Aug. 6, (61).

"Pray, Sir, give us a word of intelligence how matters go, timely, *as may concern us*.

"If any thing be needful as to form or emendation in writing, good Sir, let it be done, and we shall recompense it."

The other letter, enclosed with this by Winthrop for preservation, was written after Winthrop's return from Europe. It bears date June 25, 1663, and is as follows:—

"*For the honored John Winthrop, Esquire, Governor of Connecticut Colony, these dd.*

"MUCH HONORED AND DEAR SIR,—By this first opportunity, with or indeed somewhat before my meet capacity to write, by reason of extraordinary pain in the one side of my face and teeth, I have adventured to perform that duty to congratulate your so safe return, which hath so long been sought, waited, and hoped for, as the medium to bring a comfortable issue to our perturbing exercises, always giving out my confident apprehensions of your acting in the Patent business so as to promote peace and love to mutual satisfaction, without any intendment to infringe our liberty or privileges in the least thereby, when you came to manifest your ingenuous sense of things; and therefore all my laboring with our neighbors of Connecticut hath been for a respite of all things till your return, and that no preparations might be given in that interim, to hinder *a loving accord and compliance between us which truly I am and ever have been a friend to encourage, according as I have said, or at any time written to yourself or Mr. Stone.* But I fear some physicians of our time may be too highly conceited of curing diseases by violent fomentations, which I ever judged not to be your method, but rather by gradual ripening and softening supplements, which I am yet more confirmed to believe since I see your letter unto Major Mason, a copy whereof Major Thompson and Mr. Scott sent enclosed (as they say) in one from them, all which letters have been opened and tossed up and down about the country in reports, before they came to my view, which is even now done, and so if any inconvenience be thereby occasioned, I hope you will not impute it unto me. But truly I hear of great irritations of spirits amongst our people, by reports of opposite speeches or writings, that are said to come from yourself; but I hope all will come to a fair reconcilement in due time, and which I still wait and long for. Thus hoping you will pardon the want of more ample expressions or other attendance upon you in time of my long continuing illness, with all humble and best respects presented to yourself, good Mrs. Winthrop, Mr. Fitz John, Mr. Wait, and all yours, I take leave, resting

"Your assured loving friend to serve,

"WILLIAM LEETE.

"GUILFORD, June 25, (63)."

These overtures by Mr. Leete toward a union with Connecticut were very obnoxious to those who, regarding the limitation of suffrage to church-members as of paramount importance, were less alarmed than Mr. Leete for the safety of themselves and of the colony. Mr. Davenport writes to Winthrop, June 22, 1663: "As for what Mr. Leete wrote to yourself, it was his private doing, without the consent or knowledge of any of us in this colony; it was not done by him according to his public trust as governor, but contrary to it." Probably this movement of Leete for union with Connecticut was what the letters of Hooke to Davenport and of Newman to Gilbert, cited in the preceding chapter, refer to. It does not appear that any public attack was made upon him; but the little apologetic speech with which he opened the court of election in the spring of 1662 indicates that those who thought that his proposal to Winthrop to include New Haven was not done by him according to his public trust as governor, but contrary to it, had in a private way made it warm for him. "The governor declared that through the goodness of God they had been carried through another year, though with much infirmity and weakness, and himself more than ordinary, yet not so but through reflection God had brought him to the sight of it, but yet was free to be responsible for any public transaction, and should be ready to give answer to any brother or brethren coming to him in an orderly way, desiring to find pardon and acceptance with God, and acknowledging their patience and love in passing by any thing that hath been done amiss. None objecting, they proceeded to vote."

The charter bore the date, April 23, 1662. It was first made public in this country at the meeting of the commissioners for the United Colonies at Boston in September. A letter from the General Court of Connecticut to the commissioners, dated August 30, makes no reference to the charter, but proposes a special meeting of the commissioners "in case any matters needful to be considered should, at the return of our worthy governor and the agents for the Massachusetts, be presented." A letter sent by the commissioners during their session, to the governor of Rhode Island says, "We have read and perused a charter of incorporation under the broad seal of England, *sent over the last ship*, granted to some gentlemen of Connecticut." For some time after the charter had come into his possession, Winthrop expected to return home that summer, and be himself the bearer of the document; but, changing his plans, and deciding to spend a second winter abroad, he had sent it by another hand. The arrival of the charter, therefore, preceded the return of the envoy by whom it was procured. It was read at the meeting of the commissioners, who "took notice of his majesty's favor as being very acceptable to them, and advised that wherein others may be concerned, the said gentlemen with such others do attend such ways as may conduce to righteousness, peace, and amity, and that the favor showed to the said colony, or any other, may be jointly improved for the benefit of all concerned in the said charter." In the margin of that copy of the records of the commissioners printed in Hazard's State Papers is the following note: "We cannot as yet say that the procurement of this patent will be acceptable to us or our colony.— William Leete, Benjamin Fenn."

At the General Assembly or Court of Election held at Hartford, Oct. 9, 1662,—

"THE PATENT or CHARTER was this day publicly read in audience of the freemen, and declared to belong to them and their successors; and the freemen made choice of Mr. Wyllys, Capt. John Talcott, and Lieut. John Allyn, to take the charter into their custody in behalf of the freemen, who are to have an oath administered to them by the General Assembly for the due discharge of the trust committed to them."

CHAPTER XX.

CONTROVERSY WITH CONNECTICUT.

AT the session of the General Court of Connecticut at which the charter was received, Capt. John Youngs of Southold appeared, and presented the following certificate, signed by thirty-two persons:—

"SOUTHOLD, Oct. 4, 1662.

"Having notice of Mr. Wyllys of Connecticut jurisdiction, Long Island comes within the patent, and also that the Court is to be held at Hartford, and thither we are desired by Mr. Wyllys to send our deputies from these towns of Long Island; we therefore of Southold, whose names are underwritten, do desire and have appointed Capt. John Youngs to be our deputy, and do hereby give him full power to speak and act in our behalf as occasion shall serve."

Upon this certificate Capt. Youngs was admitted to sit as the deputy of Southold, and the following minute was entered on the record:—

"This Court being informed by Capt. John Youngs and some other gentlemen of quality, that the inhabitants of Southold, the major part of them, have sent up and empowered him to act as their deputy, and he as their agent tending to submit their persons and estates unto this government according to our Charter; this Court doth own and accept them, and shall be ready to afford them protection as occasion shall require, and do advise the said inhabitants to repair to South and East Hampton, to the authority there settled by this Court, in case of any necessary occasion, to require the assistance of authority. And this Court doth hereby accept and declare Capt. John Youngs to be a freeman of this corporation, and do grant him commission to act in the plantation of Southold as need requires, according to his commission. And this Court doth order the inhabitants of Southold to meet together, to choose a constable for that town; and Capt. John Youngs is authorized to administer oath to the said constable for the due execution of his office. And we do advise and order Capt. Youngs to see that the minister be duly paid his meet and competent maintenance."

When the magistrates of Connecticut agreed, before the departure of Winthrop for Europe, that if it should be found that their boundary included New Haven, their brethren of that colony should be at liberty to unite with them or not at their option, they had no thought of such a temptation as beset them when Southold applied to be received under their jurisdiction. They were tempted to divide and conquer when they ought in fairness and good faith, by postponing action on the proposal of the Southold people, to have shown courtesy to a sister colony with which they were confederate. The signers of the application were probably, as Capt. Youngs alleged, a major part of the freemen of Southold; but they were under oath of allegiance to New Haven, and in revolting to Connecticut were acting as individuals and not in a court of the plantation. Connecticut, after acknowledging New Haven as a sister colony and becoming confederate with it, could not justly receive one of its plantations, even if a general court of the plantation had voted to change its allegiance. If possible, it was a still greater outrage to do it in the absence of municipal action.

Having thus robbed New Haven of Southold, the same General Court proceeded to take under the government and protection of Connecticut a few disaffected persons in Guilford, without even pretending that they were a majority of the inhabitants or of the freemen. The record reads,—

" Several inhabitants of Guilford tendering themselves, their persons and estates, under the government and protection of this colony, this Court doth declare that they do accept and own them as members of this colony, and shall be ready to afford what protection is necessary. And this Court doth advise the said persons to carry peaceably and religiously in their places toward the rest of the inhabitants that yet have not submitted in like manner. And also to pay their just dues unto the minister of their town; and also all public charges due to this day."

In like manner Stamford and Greenwich were received. "This Court doth hereby declare their acceptance of the plantations of Stamford and Greenwich under this government upon the same terms and provisions as are directed and declared to the inhabitants of Guilford; and that each of those plantations have a constable chosen and sworn."

As no disaffected inhabitants of New Haven, Milford, or Branford appeared, no action was attempted for comprehending those plantations further than to appoint Mr. Matthew Allyn, Mr. Wyllys, Mr. Stone, and Mr. Hooker a committee " to go down to New Haven to treat with the gentlemen and others of our loving friends there, according to such instructions as shall be directed to the said committee by this Court."

About a week later a court of magistrates was held at New Haven, at which the governor, the deputy-governor, Mr. Jones, Mr. Fenn, Mr. Treat, and Mr. Crane were present. The committee from Connecticut, arriving in New Haven while the magistrates were in session, presented a copy of the charter, and with it the written declaration which may be found below, to the intent that Connecticut desired "a happy and comfortable union."

In the record of their proceedings the magistrates make no express mention of the committee or of their documents; but "it was agreed and ordered that the twenty-ninth day of this month be kept a day of extraordinary seeking of God by fasting and prayer for his guidance of the colony in this weighty business about joining with Connecticut colony, and for the afflicted state of the church and people of God in our native country, and in other parts of the world." But though no mention is made in the record of the court of magistrates, of the documents received from Connecticut, it subsequently appears that the magistrates and elders returned a written reply.

At a meeting of the freemen of New Haven colony, held at New Haven, Nov. 4, 1662, the governor informed them they were not ignorant of the occasion of this meeting, they knowing that some gentlemen of Connecticut had been here, and had left a copy of their patent, and another writing under their hands, both of which were now read, and also the answer of our committee to their writing, which writing and answer are as followeth:—

"*To our Much Honored and Reverend Friends of New Haven, Milford, &c., to be communicated to all whom it may concern:—*

"We declare that through the good providence of the Most High, a large and ample patent and therein desirable privileges and immunities from his Majesty, being come to our hands (a copy whereof we have left with you to be considered), and yourselves upon the sea-coast being included and interested therein, the king having united us in one body politic, we according to the commission wherewith we are intrusted by the General Assembly of Connecticut do declare in their name that it is both their and our earnest desire that there may be a happy and comfortable union between yourselves and us, according to the tenor of the charter, that inconveniences and dangers may be prevented, and peace and truth strengthened and established, through our suitable subjection to the terms of the patent, and the good blessing of God upon us therein. We do desire a seasonable return hereunto.

"MATTHEW ALLYN,
SAMUEL WYLLYS,
SAMUEL STONE,
SAMUEL HOOKER,
JOSEPH FITCH."

"*To our Much Honored and Reverend Friends, the Commissioners from the General Court of Connecticut, to be communicated, &c.*

"MUCH HONORED AND REVEREND,—We have received and perused your writing, and heard the copy read of his Majesty's letters patent to Connecticut colony, wherein though we do not find the colony of New Haven expressly included, yet to show our desire that matters may be issued in the conserving of peace and amity with righteousness between them and us, we shall communicate your writing and the copy of the patent to our freemen, and afterwards with convenient speed return their answer. Only we desire that the issuing of matters may be respited until we may receive fuller information from the Honored Mr. Winthrop or satisfaction otherwise, and that in the meantime this colony may remain distinct, entire, and uninterrupted, as heretofore, which we hope you will see cause lovingly to consent unto, and signify the same to us with convenient speed.

"WILLIAM LEETE,
MATTHEW GILBERT,
BENJAMIN FENN,
JASPER CRANE,
ROBERT TREAT,
WM. JONES,
JOHN DAVENPORT,
NICHOLAS STREET,
ABRAH. PIERSON,
ROGER NEWTON.

"NEW HAVEN, 17th of October, 1662."

"Then the governor told them that they had heard the writings and patent, and there were two things in their writing to be answered to: first, that they declare us to be, by the king, made one body politic with them, and interested in their patent; second, they desire a happy and comfortable union for peace and truth's sake, &c. : now to these two you must give answer; and then dismissed the assembly to consider of it for the space of one hour and a half, and then to meet again at the beat of the drum.

"Then, the company being come together in the afternoon, the governor told them that they knew what was left with them, for they had heard the patent and the writings read; therefore he desired to know their minds, for he hoped they might have some help from among ourselves, mentioning Mr. Davenport.

"Then Mr. Davenport, pastor of the church of Christ at New Haven, said that according to this occasion he should discharge the duty of his place, and should read to them his own thoughts (which he had set down in writing), which he desired might remain his own till they were fully satisfied in them, and further said he should leave others to walk according to the light that God should give them in this business; and so read some reasons why we were not included in the patent, and also why we might not voluntarily join with them, and so, upon desire of some, left his writing with them to consider of.

"Then the governor told them that they had heard the thoughts of Mr. Davenport concerning both the parts of the writing, and [he] had left them with them that they might do that which may be to God's acceptance; therefore he desired them to speak their minds freely, for he desired that the freemen themselves would give the substance of the answer voluntarily. The governor further said that for his part he should not be forward to lead them in this case, lest any should think him ambitious of the place, but desired that that might be done which is according to the will of God. Then, the matter being largely debated, at last came to this conclusion, to have an answer drawn up out of these three heads: first, that there be due witness-bearing against their sin; secondly, that there may be a deferring of things till Mr. Winthrop's coming or we [have] satisfaction otherwise, and that we remain in the same state as we are till then; thirdly, that we can do nothing till we consult with the other confederates.

"Then the advice of the commissioners about this patent was read, and considered how contrary to that righteousness, amity, and peace, our neighbors of Connecticut had carried toward us. Then they considered of a committee to draw up an answer into form, and to annex some weighty arguments thereunto, to send to the general assembly of Connecticut, and considered also about making address to his Majesty if our answer prevail not. The committee appointed was the magistrates and elders of this colony in general, with Brother Law of Stamford, and these to conclude according to the major part of them in session. It was left with this committee to send this answer, &c., to what person they see most convenient, to be communicated to their general assembly.

"The freemen expressed themselves desirous that the magistrates would go on in their work, and they looked upon themselves bound to stand by them according to our laws here established."

"The answer of the freemen drawn up into form by the committee, and sent to Connecticut General Assembly, is as followeth: viz.,—

"HONORED GENTLEMEN,—We have heard both the patent and the writing read, which those gentlemen (who said they were sent from your General Assembly) left with our committee, and have considered the contents according to our capacities. By the one we take notice of their declared sense of the patent and also of your desire of our uniting with yourselves upon that account. By the other we understand that his Majesty hath been graciously pleased (at your earnest petition) to grant liberty to the colony of Connecticut to acquire, have, possess, and purchase, &c., whatever lands, &c., you have gained or shall gain by lawful means within the precincts or lines therein mentioned, and also of his abundant grace to allow and establish you to be one body politic, for managing all your public affairs and government in a religious and peaceable manner, to the intents and purposes by his Majesty and the adventurers therein professed, over all persons, matters, and things, so gained by purchase or conquest, at your own proper costs and charges, according as yourselves informed you had already done. Now, whatever is so yours, we have neither purpose nor desire to oppose, hurt, or hinder in the least; but what ourselves (by like lawful means) have attained, as to inheritances or jurisdiction as a distinct colony, upon our most solemn and religious covenants, so well known to his Majesty and to all, we must say that we do not find in the patent any command given to you nor prohibition [permission?] to us to dissolve covenants or alter the orderly settlements of New England, nor any sufficient reason why we may not so remain to be as formerly. Also, your beginning to procure and proceeding to improve the patent without us doth confirm this belief; but rather it seems that a way is left open to us to petition for the like favor, and to enter our appeal from your declared sense of the patent and signify our grievances. Yet if it shall appear (after a due and full information of our state) to have been his Majesty's pleasure so to unite us as you understand the patent, we must submit according to God; but for the present we cannot answer otherwise than our committee hath done, and likewise to make the same request unto you, that we may remain distinct as formerly, and may be succored by you as confederates, at least that none occasion be given by yourselves for any to disturb us in our ancient settlements until that either by the Honored Mr. Winthrop, by our other confederates, or from his Majesty, we may be resolved herein. All which means are in our thoughts to use, except you prevent, for the gaining of a right understanding, and to bring a peaceable issue or reconcilement of this matter; and we wish you had better considered than to act so suddenly to seclude us from patent privilege at first if we are included as you say, and to have so proceeded since, as may seem to give advantage unto disaffected persons to slight or disregard oaths and covenants, and thereby to rend and make division, manage contention and troubles in the townships and societies of this colony, and that about religious worship, as the enclosed complaint may declare, which seems to us a great scandal to religion before the natives, and prejudicial to his Majesty's pious intention, as also to hold forth a series of means very opposite to the end pretended, and very much obscured from the beauty of such a religious and peaceable walking amongst English brethren, as may either invite the natives to the Christian faith, or unite our spirits in this juncture, and this occasion given before any conviction tendered or publication of the patent amongst us, or so much as a treaty with us in a Christian, neighborly way; no pretence for our dissolution of government till then could rationally be imagined. Such carriage may seem to be against the advice and mind of his Majesty in the patent, as also of your honored governor, and to cast reflection upon him, when we compare these things with his letters to some here; for the avoiding whereof we earnestly request that the whole of what he hath written to yourselves, so far as it may respect us in this business, may be fully communicated to our view in a true copy or transcript of the same. We must profess ourselves grieved hereat, and must desire and expect your effectual endeavors to repair these breaches and restore us to our former condition as confederates, until that by all or some of these ways intimated we may attain a clear resolution in this matter. Unto what we have herein propounded we shall add that we do not in the least intend any dislike to his Majesty's act, but to show our sense of your actings first and last, so much to our detriment, and to manifest the consequent effects to God's dishonor, as also to give you to know how we understand the patent, hoping that you will both candidly construe and friendly comply with our desires herein, and so remove the cause of our distraction and sad affliction that you have brought upon this poor colony: then shall we forbear to give you further trouble, and shall pray to the God of spirits to grant us all humility, and to guide us with his heavenly wisdom to a happy issue of this affair in love and peace; resting, gentlemen, your very loving friends and neighbors, the freemen of the Colony of New Haven.

"℔ JAMES BISHOP, *Secretary*,
" *In the name and by order and consent of the Committee and freemen of New Haven Colony.*

" *Postscript.*—We have also thought fit to send our reasons enclosed, which are the ground of this answer we return, and desire the whole may be read and communicated to the General Assembly, entreating an answer with all convenient speed, or from the committee if so empowered."

Four days previous to this Court of the Jurisdiction, there had been a general plantation court at New Haven, when, after Deputy-Gov. Gilbert had read the charter, the written declaration of the committee from Connecticut, and the reply of the magistrates and elders, "Mr. John Davenport, pastor of the church of Christ at New Haven, declared unto the town that he wrote to Mr. Winthrop, before he went to England, not to have any hand in such an unrighteous act as to involve us in their patent. To which he wrote to him in two letters, one from Mattabesick, and another from the Manhatoes at his going away, part of which was read, wherein he expressed his contrary purpose and the expressions of some other of their magistrates to the same purpose. And also Mr. Davenport presented a letter, which he received the last night from Mr. Richard Law of Stamford, and read it to the town, wherein was intimated their sad state by reason of the turbulent carriages of some of their inhabitants which Connecticut colony had admitted and so dismembered us, and some would say they were rebels against the king and the jurisdiction of Connecticut. Also he further informed the town of the treaty they had with those gentlemen of Connecticut aforesaid, and how they had showed them the wrong they had done us, in dismembering of us at Stamford, Guilford, and Southold, and all this before they had consulted with us, and showed them their evil therein, but received no satisfaction from them about it.

"Mr. Davenport also propounded sundry reasons to be considered, both why we were not included in Connecticut patent, and also why we may not voluntarily join with them, with some directions what answer to return, that so they may see their evil in what they have done, and restore us to our former state, that so we and they may live together in unity and amity for the future.

"The Deputy-Governor declared that the things spoken by Mr. Davenport were of great weight, and he desired all present would seriously consider of them.

"Mr. Street, teacher of the church of Christ at New Haven, declared that he looked upon the reasons propounded by Mr. Davenport to be unanswerable, and that both church and town had cause to bless God for the wisdom held forth in them, and wished them to keep the ends and rules of Christ in their eye, and then God would stand by them; and did second the directions given, with one Scripture out of Isa. xiv. 32, and from thence did advise that our answers should be of faith and influenced with faith, and not of fear.

"The matter was largely debated, and sundry expressed themselves as disliking the proceeding of Connecticut in this business, as Lieut. Nash, Mr. Tuttle, Mr. Powell, &c., and desired some answer might be given that way, with a desire of restoring us to our former state again, and then by general vote declared their disapproving of the manner of Connecticut colony's proceeding in this business."

There being no meeting of the General Court of Connecticut till the following spring, and their committee returning no written reply to the communication from New Haven, though, in a personal interview as is intimated in New Haven's Case Stated, they signified their persistence in their "own will and way," New Haven through its committee forwarded an appeal to his Majesty, but advised their friends in London who served them in the business, to communicate their papers first to Winthrop, that if possible the difference between the colonies might be settled without further recourse. Accordingly the papers were shown to Winthrop, and he stopped the proceeding of the appeal to the king by engaging that Connecticut should cease its injurious treatment of New Haven. In fulfilment of that engagement he wrote a letter dated March 3d, 166$\frac{2}{3}$, to Major Mason, Deputy-Governor of Connecticut and, in the absence of Winthrop, its acting governor, to be communicated to the other magistrates, which is as follows:—

"GENTLEMEN,—I am informed by some gentlemen who are authorized to seek remedy here, that since you had the late patent, there hath been injury done to the government of New Haven, and in particular at Guilford and Stamford in admitting several of the inhabitants there unto freedom with you, and appointing officers, which hath caused division in said towns, which may prove of dangerous consequence if not timely prevented, though I do hope the rise of it is from misunderstanding, and not in design of prejudice to that colony, for whom I gave assurance to their friends that their rights and interests should not be disquieted or prejudiced by the patent. But·if both governments would with unanimous agreement unite in one, their friends judged it would be for advantage to both; and further I must let you know that testimony here doth affirm that I gave assurance before authority here, that it was not intended to meddle with any town or plantation that was settled under any other government. Had it been any otherwise intended or declared, it had been injurious in taking out the patent, not to have inserted a proportionable number of their names in it. Now upon the whole, having had serious conference with their friends authorized by them, and with others who are friends to both, to prevent a tedious and chargeable trial and uncertain event here, I promised them to give you speedily this

representation, how far you are engaged, if any injury hath been
done by admitting of freemen, or appointing officers, or any other
unjust intermeddling with New Haven Colony in one kind or other
without the approbation of the government, that it be forthwith
recalled, and that for future there will be no imposing in any
kind upon them, nor admitting of any members without mutual
consent; but that all things be acted as loving, neighboring
colonies, as before such patent granted. And unto this I judge
you are obliged, I having engaged to their agents here that this
will be by you performed, and they have thereupon forborne to give
you or me any trouble. But they do not doubt but upon future
consideration there may be such a right understanding between
both governments that an union and friendly joining may be established to the satisfaction of all, which at my arrival I shall also
endeavor (God willing) to promote. Not having more at present
in this case, I rest

"Your humble servant,

"JOHN WINTHROP.

"*For Major John Mason, Deputy-Governor of Connecticut Colony, and the rest of the Court there at Hartford, dd.*"

This letter, or a copy of it in Winthrop's handwriting, was by him delivered to the agents of the New
Haven Colony, and by them sent to Gov. Leete. A
year after the date thereof, the Connecticut committee
allege that it had never been seen by Major Mason or
themselves, and intimate that it was sent to Guilford to
be forwarded to Hartford. Gov. Leete evidently had
regarded it as a copy sent to him to inform him how
the negotiation stood between the agents who acted
for the two colonies in London. Winthrop's letter was
so satisfactory to the agents of New Haven (as is evident from the letter itself) that they did not proceed
with the intended appeal to the king. When received
by Leete, it was equally satisfactory to the magistrates

and elders who were in charge of New Haven's case. The letter, being dated March 3, reached New Haven not many weeks before Winthrop's arrival in June.

At a general assembly, held at Hartford in March, 166⅔, the Court "voted and desired the deputy-governor, Mr. Matthew Allyn, Capt. John Talcott, and Lieut. John Allyn, and for a reserve to the major, Mr. Wyllys, as a committee to go down to New Haven to treat with our honored and loving friends about their union and incorporation with this colony of Connecticut. And in case the committee cannot effect a union according to instructions given them by the Court, that then they endeavor to settle a peace in the plantations until such time as they and we may be in a further capacity of issuing this difference, and to act in reference hereunto as they judge most meet." Another order was "that in case the committee do not issue an agreement with New Haven gentlemen according to their instructions, before their return, that then all propositions and instructions from the Court, respecting union with that people, are void and of none effect."

Three of this committee were in New Haven a few days afterward, where they made the following communication:—

"*Some Proposals to the Gentlemen of New Haven, &c., in reference to their Firm Settlement and Incorporation with us of Connecticut:*—

"1. We shall in no wise infringe or disturb them in their order of church government, provided we remain free from any impositions from the supreme powers of England.

"2. That those who have been of the magistracy in New

Haven Colony shall be invested with full power to govern the people within those limits until our General Assembly in May next.

"3. That there shall yearly be nominated to election a proportionable number of assistants in the plantations of New Haven, Milford, Branford, and Guilford, as shall be for the rest of the plantations in our colony.

"4. That those who have been freemen of New Haven colony shall be forthwith admitted freemen of our corporation, unless any person be justly excepted against unto us.

"5. That New Haven, Milford, Branford, Guilford, shall be a distinct county wherein there shall be chosen yearly such civil officers as may carry on all causes of judicature amongst themselves which extend not to life, limb, or banishment.

"6. That there shall be, once a year at the least, a court of assistants at New Haven to prevent unnecessary trouble and expense to those that do appeal from the sentence of the former court, and to hear and determine all matters that respect life, limb, and banishment.

"7. That each of the forementioned towns shall have liberty to send two of their freemen as deputies to our next General Assembly.

"8. Whatever privileges else you shall propound consonant to the tenor of our charter, we shall be ready to attend you therein.

"9. That, in case these our proposals be not accepted before our departure, then they are to be void and of no effect.

"MATH. ALLYN,
SAM. WYLLYS,
JOHN ALLYN.

'NEW HAVEN, March 20, '6⅔."

The answer of New Haven to these proposals, in the handwriting of William Jones, is as follows:—

"Whereas we discern by the order of the General Court of Connecticut, dated March the 11th, 166⅔. that the gentlemen their committee were limited to conclude at this present meeting with us, otherwise their power ceases; our answer in general is that we are not in a capacity so to do:—

"1. First, because we are under an appeal to the king whereunto we do adhere, and therefore cannot act contrarily without dishonor to his Majesty, and prejudice to our own right until his royal determination be known in the question depending between us.

"2. Because we cannot in conscience conclude to dissolve our distinct colony by uniting with Connecticut without the express consent of the other colonies declared from their general courts respectively.

"3. Because we are limited by our freemen not to conclude anything for altering our distinct colony state and government without their consent.

"Yet shall we, in order to an issue betwixt us with love and peace, which we desire them by all loving carriages to promove in the interim of our deliberation, consider of their propositions and communicate them to our freemen, as we may have a convenient opportunity.

"But whereas we observe in their propositions that Stamford is left out, as if it were no member of us, we must and do profess ourselves unsatisfied with that omission, because we apprehend ourselves bound to seek and provide for their liberties and comforts as our own.

"WILLIAM LEETE,
"*In the name of our Committee.*
"NEW HAVEN, 20th of 1st mo. ($\frac{6\,2}{6\,3}$)."

On the 6th of May a general court for the jurisdiction was held at New Haven, when "the governor informed the Court of the state of things in reference to Connecticut, and how the committee had acted; and the proposals of the gentlemen of Connecticut were read with the answer of our committee.

"It was propounded whether we should make any alteration of the usual time of our election, we standing in the state we do and waiting for an answer to our appeal. After debate, it was concluded as best to go on with our election as formerly, and make no alteration, but stand in the same state we were when we made an appeal, and, if anything should come from Connecticut by way of prohibition, then to have a protest ready to witness against them, we being under an appeal to his Majesty.

"It was also propounded, whether we should not send up a remonstrance of our grievances by their unsuitable carriages towards us in the state wherein we are, it being a question whether the general assembly of Connecticut is rightly informed of our state; a draft whereof (being prepared) was read and well approved for the substance of it and, after debate upon it, was by vote concluded to be sent, only with alteration of some passages therein, which was done and sent to Major John Mason, that by him it might be communicated to their general assembly.[1]"

In accordance with the resolution recited above, the annual election was held on the 29th of May, when the officers chosen, "all took oath for the year ensuing, or until our foundation settlements be made null." On the same day a general court for the jurisdiction was held, at which the "governor told the court that they knew how we stood in reference to Connecticut Colony, and that there was a committee appointed for the last year: therefore propounded, whether they would empower the same again; which being voted, it was concluded both for the same persons and the same power as the last year."

[1] The remonstrance may be found in Appendix No. VI.

Gov. Winthrop arrived not long afterward from Europe. The New Haven people were earnestly desiring his arrival, hoping that he would, in accordance with the spirit of the letter he had written to Major Mason and the other magistrates of Connecticut, "come with an olive-branch." The earliest intimation of his being in Hartford is in a letter to him from Davenport, who writes:—

"*To the Right Worshipful John Winthrop, Esquire, Governor of Connecticut, these present at Hartford.*

"HONORED SIR,—These are to congratulate your safe arrival and return to your family, where you have been ardently desired and long expected. Blessed be our good God, in Jesus Christ, who hath, at last, mercifully brought you off from court-snares and London-tumults and European troubles, and from all perils at sea, and hath preserved your precious life and health, and hath carried yourself, with your two sons, as upon eagles' wings, above the reach of all hurtful dangers, unto your habitation, and hath kept your dear wife and all your children alive, and made them joyful by your safe and comfortable return unto them. Together with them, I also, and my wife and son and daughter, rejoice herein, as in a gracious answer of many prayers and in persuasion that you are come with an olive-branch in your mouth; according to the encouragement and assurance which I have received in some letters to myself from Capt. Scott and from Mr. Halstead; and from one sent to Mr. Leete, which is either the protograph or a copy of your letter to Major Mason, which seems to be written by yourself, but the seal was broken open before it came hither. Whether he hath that letter from Major Thompson, which you mention, or not, I know not. But I hear he hath one from Mr. Whitfield, the contents whereof I have not heard. Sir, give me leave to take notice of one passage in yours [that there is nothing but misunderstanding that could occasion such apprehensions of any injury done to New Haven or their concernments; and those friends above mentioned were fully satisfied thereof, and wondered much that it was not better understood *by yours*]. It was written in the line, *them;* that being blotted out, it is interlined, *yours;* which makes the sense of the whole very dark to me. For if, by *yours*, be meant our committee of magistrates, elders, and deputies, intrusted by the freemen of this colony to treat with our friends of Connecticut, I shall wonder at their wondering. For : 1. That manifest injury is done to this colony, is proved by instances in the writings sent to Connecticut and to England. 2. Nor did we misunderstand the patent, but saw and pleaded that New Haven Colony is not mentioned therein, and that it was not the King's purpose, nor yours, to destroy the distinction of colonies, nor our colony-state; and, in that confidence, desired that all things might stand, *in statu quo prius*, till your return; which, when we could not obtain, we were compelled to appeal to the King; yet, out of tender respect to your peace and honor, advised, as you know, our friends to consult with you before they prosecuted our appeal or delivered my letter to my lord chamberlain. Our friends at Connecticut regarded not our arguments, which yet, I know, are pleadable and would bear due weight in the Chancery and at the Council Table, and one of them yourself is pleased to establish in your letter to Major Mason. 3. Nor is it to be wondered at, if we had misunderstood the things which we wanted means to understand from yourself; who neither in your letter to me from London, dated May 13, 1662, which I received by Mr Ling, nor in your next, dated March the 7th this year, signified to me any other thing than that New Haven is still a distinct colony, notwithstanding the Connecticut patent. I do the more insist on this, because I am told that Mr. Stone, in a letter which he sent unto one in Fairfield (*ni fallor*), saith that he had received a letter from Mr. Winthrop, who wondereth that New Haven do question their being under Connecticut, or to that purpose; which is understood as concluding the dissolution of this colony, which, I perceive by what yourself and others have written, is a misunderstanding of your meaning, so that the misunderstanding is to be wondered at in them, not in us. As for what Mr. Leete wrote to yourself, it was his private doing, without the consent or knowledge of any of us in this colony; it was not done by him according to his public trust as governor, but contrary to it. If they had treated with us, or should yet, as with a distinct colony, we should readily agree with them in any rational and equal terms, for the settling of neighborly peace and brotherly amity between them and us, mutually, who have already, as you see, patiently suffered wrong, for peace's sake, in hope of a just redress, at your return into these parts. I would not have mentioned these matters in this letter (which I intended only for a supply of my want of bodily fitness for a journey to Hartford, to give you a personal visit, in testimony of my joy for your safe arrival and return), but that the expression 'forenoted compelled me to speak something to it. I long to see your face, and am in hope that shortly, after your first hurries are over, we shall enjoy your much-desired presence with us in your chamber at my house, which shall be as your own while it is mine. Then we may have opportunity, by the will of God, to confer placidly together, and to give and receive mutual satisfaction, through a right understanding of what is done in our concernments. Myself, my wife, my son and daughter, do jointly and severally present our humble service to your honored self and Mrs. Winthrop, with our respectful and affectionate salutations to your two sons and to all your daughters, praying that blessings from heaven may be multiplied upon you and them, through Jesus Christ, in whom I rest, Honored Sir,

"Yours, obliged to honor and serve you in the Lord,
"JOHN DAVENPORT.
"N. H., the 22nd day of the 4th month, called June, 1663."

Gov. Leete's letter to Winthrop congratulating him on his safe return and expressing confidence that he would be a medium to bring the strife between the colonies to a comfortable issue, has been given in the preceding chapter. That the New Haven people were disappointed in their hope that through Winthrop's influence Connecticut would reverse its action, will appear in the sequel; but Winthrop's reasons for disappointing them are not on record. A cloud of mystery envelops the matter, and we can only exhibit the facts.

That Leete and some others of the New Haven committee began very soon to doubt whether things would come to a comfortable issue by means of Winthrop, appears in a letter which Leete wrote to Winthrop on the 20th of July:—

"*For the Right Worshipful John Winthrop, Esquire, Governor of Connecticut Colony, at Hartford, These:—*

"Much Honored Sir,—In my last I informed you of your very acceptable letter sent us by Major Thompson and Mr. Scott jointly attesting it; the purport whereof suited well with mine to you in England, to make your patent a covert, but no control to our jurisdiction, until we accorded with mutual satisfaction to become one, which I have been and still am a friend to promove in a righteous and amicable way. But truly, I think, a just expedient hath not hitherto been seasonably attended to accomplish the same; but rather that which hath irritated, and so conduced to the contrary; which to behold hath been a grief to some. [It hath been a grief] to see the strings of the instrument so stretched as to make it untunable to play in consort, the chief music which I delight to hear, especially in jarring times; and therefore hoped and longed to see it taken into the hand of a more knowing artist, and one apt and inclined to make uniting and composing melody, as (in my understanding) was sweetly begun to be sounded in the language of your letter. But as yet we find not such harmonious effects to ensue in a practical way as were to be wished for. Wherefore I am desired by our committee, or some of them, to write unto yourself, earnestly entreating that you would please to send us a plain, positive, and particular answer in writing to this question, viz., whether the contents of that your letter aforesaid shall be performed to us or no, according to the genuine sense thereof. Good sir, be pleased that either your own or your committee's answer may be sent us by Mr. Pierson, who intends to visit and wait upon you for the same, as I also should have done, had not something more than ordinary interrupted, together with some hopes we might enjoy your presence here, before your going into the Bay, as was intimated to us. So with many thanks

and chiefest respects presented from myself and wife unto you all, acknowledging our great engagements for your love and sympathy in your last expressed, I take leave, and remain
"Your cordial friend and servant,
"WILLIAM LEETE."
"GUILFORD, July 20, 1663."

"SIR,—Hearing that you sought for your own copy but could not find it when Mr. Jones and Mr. John Davenport were with you, I have here enclosed sent a true copy of your letter as it came to my hands."

From the letter and its postscript we may infer that two of the committee had conferred with Winthrop in a personal interview, and that upon their report Leete doubted whether Winthrop would abide by the agreement he had made in London with Major Thompson and Mr. Scott acting in behalf of New Haven.

On the 19th of August, there was a session of the General Assembly of Connecticut at Hartford, but there is nothing in the record to show that the governor was present. Action was taken concerning New Haven as follows: viz., "This court doth nominate and appoint the deputy-governor, Mr. Wyllys, Mr. Daniel Clark, and John Allyn, or any three or two of them, to be a committee to treat with our honored friends of New Haven, Milford, Branford, and Guilford, about settling their union and incorporation with this colony of Connecticut; and they are empowered to act according to the instructions given to the committee sent to New Haven in March last; and, in case they cannot effect a union, they are hereby authorized publicly to declare unto them that this Assembly cannot well resent[1] their proceeding in civil government as a dis-

---

[1] *Resent*, to feel back in return; to think over.

tinct jurisdiction, being included within the charter granted to Connecticut corporation; and likewise they are publicly to declare that this Assembly doth desire and cannot but expect that the inhabitants of New Haven, Milford, Branford, Guilford, and Stamford, do yield subjection to the government here established according to the tenor of our charter, which is publicly to be read in New Haven." On the 26th of the same month, three of this committee, Messrs. Wyllys, Clark, and Allyn, were in New Haven, where they renewed the proposals made by Connecticut in March. The New Haven committee responded by sending the following communication in the handwriting of William Jones:—

"NEW HAVEN COMMITTEE'S PROPOSALS, AUG. 26, 1663.

"*To the Honored Committee from the General Assembly of Connecticut, Mr. Wyllys, Mr. Clark, and Mr. Allyn.*

"GENTLEMEN,—In order to a friendly treaty and amicable composure of matters in difference between us, we earnestly desire you would restore us to our entire colony state by disclaiming that party at Guilford and Stamford; and so doing, we offer the following queries to your consideration, as matter for such treaty: viz.,—

"1. Whether the fundamental laws for government, especially that touching the qualifications of freemen, shall be the same with Boston or ours (i. e.), members of some one or other of our churches.

"2. Whether our church order and privileges shall not be infringed nor disturbed, and that both the choice and calling in of ministers in each plantation be established a church right forever.

"3. Whether all our present freemen shall be forthwith admitted and empowered to act as your own freemen to all intents and purposes.

"4. Whether any of our former adjudications in our distinct colony state shall be liable to appeals or be called in question.

"5. Whether we shall be immediately established a distinct county, and to have so many magistrates as necessary, four at least, with a president chosen yearly by our own county court, together with other inferior officers to be nominated by ourselves.

"6. Whether any appeals shall be at any time allowed from our county court in ordinary cases, unless to our own court of assistants, and that upon weighty grounds and with good caution, to prevent trouble and charge to the county.

"7. Whether there shall not be a court of assistants at New Haven yearly, or oftener if need require, to try capital causes and hear such appeals, consisting of our own and such other magistrates as we shall desire by order from our president.

"8. Whether all our present magistrates and officers shall remain in full power to govern the people as formerly, until new be orderly chosen at the next election court after this agreement.

"9. Whether all rates and public charges granted or levied or due in each colony before this agreement, be paid and discharged by the inhabitants proportionably in a distinct way, and not otherwise.

"10. Whether at the next election there shall be a committee chosen and appointed of your and our ablest ministers and other freemen, to consult and prepare a body of laws out of your and our laws most consonant to Scripture.

"11. Whether until such a body of laws be framed and agreed upon anew mutually, all matters in our towns and courts shall be issued and done according to our own laws as formerly.

"11. Whether all our plantations according to their anciently reputed and received bounds shall not so remain unalterably, but receive confirmation by authority of the patent.

"That such treaty shall not be binding to us without consent of our confederates and general court of freemen.

"Whether the freemen in each of our towns may not make orders for the town affairs.

"These imperfect queries we at present offer to your consideration, reserving liberty to propound what further we shall see needful, allowed by the patent.

"WILLIAM LEETE,
"*In the name and with consent of the committee.*"

The next day the Connecticut committee, in reply to these queries, sent the following communication:—

"OUR PROPOSALS IN ANSWER TO THE QUERIES PRESENTED FROM NEW HAVEN COMMITTEE, AUG. 27, '63.

"In answer to the queries propounded to our consideration by the honored committee of New Haven, we present:—

"In reference to the proceedings of the Assembly at Connecticut, October last, in entertaining several that presented themselves from Guilford and Stamford, desiring to submit to our government, which (though according to our charter we apprehend we had power to admit them or any other within our precincts, yet) *consideratis considerandis pro modo et ordine*, we shall grant that prudent considerations might have directed us in the first place to have had some treaty with our honored friends of these plantations for an orderly settling of themselves with us into a body politic according to our charter, and therefore we are ready to retract those commissions that have been given to any persons that have been settled in public employ either at Guilford or Stamford. And it is our earnest desire that no former conceived injuries on your part or on ours may obstruct our proceeding with you to an amicable settlement of union as one corporation, and with clemency and candidness each part may accept such proposals as are presented to prudent and serious consideration. And we do hereby declare the propensity and readiness of our spirits fully and finally to obliterate the memorial of all former occasions administered to us, as matter of grievance or offence respecting any of you.

"1. For the first query, we answer that the pattern of foundation from which we cannot vary is our charter, nor dare we admit of any fundamental varying from the tenor thereof, but what laws may be concurring therewith and conducible to the public weal of church and state we are ready to grant the establishment thereof; and particularly for qualification of freemen we are ready to grant that they shall be men of a religious carriage, visibly so, having and possessing some competency of estate, and shall bring a certificate affirmative that they are thus qualified from the deacons of the church and two of the selectmen of the town where they live, and, if there be no deacons, then some other known and approved persons with the selectmen as before.

"2. That the church order and privileges within these plantations, New Haven, Milford, Branford, Guilford, and Stamford, shall not be infringed or disturbed by us, or any from us, and that the choice and call of the church-officers in each plantation shall remain a church-right forever.

"3. That upon our and your union all the present freemen within these plantations shall be forthwith invested with full power to be and act as freemen of Connecticut corporation in all concerns.

"4. That all former transactions in courts and administrations as a distinct jurisdiction shall be totally freed from future callings into question in the Court at Connecticut or elsewhere within our precincts, unless anything controversial be at present dependent in the Court here.

"5. That the plantations forementioned be immediately upon our union established a distinct county, and to have so many officers as may be sufficient to carry on matters of civil judicature as a county, and shall have power to try and issue all cases according to the tenor of our charter, provided that such cases as respect life, limb, banishment, or total confiscation, shall be issued by a court of assistants, which shall be once a year, or oftener if any thing extraordinary fall out within any of these plantations necessitating the same, which court of assistants shall consist of such as are chosen and ordained yearly for these plantations, whereof one shall be the president of the county or moderator of the courts kept in this county, and chosen to that place by the civil officers that attend the county courts; unto which officers for the constituting of the court of assistants shall be added three assistants out of the corporation such as shall be yearly appointed thereunto by the General Assembly held in May, and such as are grieved at the sentence of the county court shall have liberty upon good caution to appeal to the court of assistants; and that all cases tried by this court or the county court dependent twixt party and party respecting damage to the sum of forty shillings or upwards, and likewise capital crimes and offenses, shall be tried by a jury either of six or twelve freemen, according as the nature of the case require, but in capital cases by a jury of twelve at all times. And further that all civil officers except assistants or commissioners shall be yearly chosen by themselves for and within the precincts of the plantations aforesaid.

"6. That the Worshipful Mr. Leete, Mr. Gilbert, Mr. Jones, Mr. Fenn, Mr. Treat, and Mr. Crane, be and remain in magistratical power within this county, and any three or more of them, as they see cause, to have power to keep a county court, they choosing out from amongst themselves a moderator *pro tempore*, in the president's absence, whom we hereby nominate to be Worshipful Mr. Leete for the county, and this to stand in force until an orderly election of officers at general election in May next, at which time the freemen of these plantations shall nominate their proportion of assistants with other plantations in this corporation to be put to election; and such as shall be yearly chosen by the freemen to that place, together with such as the General Assembly shall commissionate within these plantations, shall for future carry on civil judicature within the county, and they being chosen and sworn to choose out of themselves a president for that year.

"7. That until the election in May next, all matters of civil judicature within this county shall be issued and determined according to the laws that have been formerly established by New Haven Assembly or such as are in force in the corporation as the officers of this county see cause to attend, being no way repugnant to the tenor of our charter.

"8. That the neighboring plantations either on the Island or main shall have liberty to appeal from the sentence of their courts unto the court of assistants held at New Haven as before declared.

"9. We mutually approve of a committee of the ablest persons that may be had amongst yourselves aud us, to compact a body of laws out of ours and yours, that may be most suitable to further the establishment of peace and righteousness and the upholding of a well-ordered government in Church and State.

"10. That the ancient real and established bounds between plantation and plantation shall forever be and remain unalterable.

"11. That the freemen of these plantations shall have power to choose all public county officers except assistants, to wit, commissioners, deputies, and constables. As for selectmen who are to order the civil, prudential affairs of the respective towns, they to be yearly chosen by a major vote of the approved inhabitants, with other necessary town officers in your respective places in this county.

"12. That all public charges and levies, due for time past and until this instant, shall be defrayed by the respective towns in this county as formerly, and for those several persons within this county that have subjected to Connecticut government, that they shall also be rated after the sum of a penny per pound for their ratable estates, with the rest of the inhabitants in their respective towns as before expressed.

"Unto these proposals we whose names are subscribed desire a return from the honored committee, whether you are willing to accept of them, to the settlement of your union with our corporation.

"SAMUEL WYLLYS,
DANIEL CLARK,
JOHN ALLYN.

"NEW HAVEN, 27 August, 1663."

The negotiation between the colonies was at this time in a dead-lock; New Haven refusing to submit, or even negotiate, unless Connecticut would "first restore us to our right state again," and Connecticut offering nothing more than "to retract those commissions that have been given to any persons that have been settled in public employ either at Guilford or Stamford." New Haven insisted that Connecticut should not only retract these commissions, but, by two other retractions, disclaim those who had revolted from New Haven to Connecticut, and admit that New Haven was a distinct colony. In September, the controversy was brought before the commissioners of the United Colonies on the following complaint:—

"*The Complaint of the Commissioners of New Haven, in behalf of that Colony, humbly presented to the rest of the Honored Commissioners, for their Advice, Aid, and Succor, as followeth:—*

"Viz., that sundry of the inhabitants of several of our towns have been taken under the government of Connecticut, and by them encouraged to disown our authority. They refuse to observe their oaths of fidelity, to attend our courts or meetings called by our authority, or to perform other duties with the rest of our people, and so our settled order and peace is much prejudiced.

2. "That constables or officers are, by Connecticut's authority, appointed and set up amongst us, who are very troublesome to us. These things and the sad consequences thereof are so aggrieving to the generality of our people, and like to bring forth such uncomfortable effects, that we cannot but present the matter to your serious consideration, to take some effectual course that such actings may be recalled or forborne, and the articles of confederation duly observed towards us, a distinct colony, your observant confederates.

"In the name of the Colony of New Haven.

"WILLIAM LEETE,
BENJAMIN FENN.

"BOSTON, 17th September, 1663."

"*An Answer to New Haven Gentlemen.*

"The commissioners for Connecticut do conceive that there is no such cause of complaint at present from New Haven as hath been mentioned in their paper, there having been divers friendly treaties about the matters in difference, and very amicable propositions and tenders formerly, and now again very lately, propounded by a committee from the court of Connecticut, who had of late a friendly conference upon it with the committee of New Haven, and a copy of those propositions was presented now by Mr. Wyllys, one of the magistrates and one of the said committee of Connecticut, and the said amicable propositions were now read to all the commissioners, and not disliked by them; and we hope they are yet in a fair way of further treaty toward a friendly compliance, and are assured that the court at Connecticut did never intend to do, nor will do, any injury or wrong to them, but will be ready to attend all just and friendly ways of love and correspondence; and, whatever hath been now suggested by way of complaint, we doubt not but they will return a fair and satisfactory answer to them when they have notice thereof.

"JOHN WINTHROP,
JOHN TALCOTT.

"SEPTEMBER 17, 1663."

"New Haven's Reply.

" The commissioners of New Haven Colony cannot approve of the answer or apology of Connecticut commissioners, in saying that they conceive there is no ground for our complaint, the case being as related, and can prove nothing being done to reverse or satisfy upon that account, or promised but conditionally and in treaty only, wherein we have and do desire to carry as amicably towards them as they towards us; but how it should be said that the court of Connecticut neither intended nor would do us any wrong, while such injuries as are complained of are not righted, nor yet absolutely promised so to be, we see not, and therefore cannot but desire the sense of the commissioners upon the acting complained of, while it is not known how far those propositions mentioned will be satisfactory to our people, nor what issue will be attained for settlement of affairs according to confederation (in case), which we still cleave unto.

"WILLIAM LEETE,
BENJAMIN FENN."

" *The Answer of the Massachusetts and Plymouth to the Complaint of New Haven is as followeth:—*

" The commissioners of the Massachusetts and Plymouth, having considered the complaint exhibited by New Haven against Connecticut for infringing their power of jurisdiction, as in the said complaint is more particularly expressed, together with the answer returned thereto by Connecticut commissioners, with some other debates and conferences that have passed between them, do judge meet to declare, that the said colony of New Haven being owned in the Articles of Confederation as distinct from Connecticut, and having been so owned by the colonies jointly in this present meeting in all their actings, may not by any act of violence have their liberty of jurisdiction infringed by any other of the United Colonies, without breach of the Articles of Confederation, and that where any act of power hath been exerted against their authorfty, that the same ought to be recalled, and their power reserved to them entire, until such time as in an orderly way it shall be otherwise disposed; and for particular grievances mentioned in their complaint, that they be referred to the next meeting of the commissioners at Hartford, where Connecticut, having timely notice, may give their answer thereto, unless in the meantime there be an amicable uniting for the establishment of their peace, the which we are persuaded will be very acceptable to the neighboring colonies.

"SIMON BRADSTREET, *President*.
THOMAS DANFORTH.
THOMAS PRINCE.
JOSIAH WINSLOW."

By this time Winthrop, as appears from his signature to one of the above documents, had shown that he accorded with the other leading men of Connecticut in their policy toward New Haven. He doubtless feared that if Connecticut, following the advice which he sent from London, should fully and unconditionally retract what she had done, and acknowledge New Haven as a distinct colony, the party of which Davenport and Gilbert were leaders would be able to prevent the success of any negotiations for union under one government. For the sake of the common good he repudiated the engagement he had made, and joined in the effort to force New Haven into submission. He shows, however, the reluctance of a noble mind to do so mean an act, keeping himself in the background, avoiding appointment on the committees successively sent to

New Haven, and absenting himself from the court when on the 8th of October the following action was taken in regard to New Haven:—

" This court doth declare that they can do no less for their own indemnity than to manifest our dissatisfaction with the proceedings of the plantations of New Haven, Milford, Branford, &c., in their distinct standing from us in point of government; it being directly opposite to the tenor of the charter lately granted to our colony of Connecticut, in which charter these plantations are included. We also do expect their submission to our government, according to our charter and his majesty's pleasure therein expressed; it being a stated conclusion of the Commissioners that jurisdiction right always goeth with patent. And whereas, the aforesaid people of New Haven, &c., pretend they have power of government distinct from us, and have made several complaints of wrongs received from us, we do hereby declare that our Council will be ready to attend them, or a committee of theirs, and if they can rationally make it appear that they have such power, and that we have wronged them according to their complaints, we shall be ready to attend them with due satisfaction. (The Governor absent when this vote passed.) The Court appoints Mr. Wyllys and the Secretary to draw up a letter to th New Haven gentlemen, and inclose this act of the court in it."

This action of the General Assembly was probably taken after the receipt of, and with reference to, the contents of the following communication from the New Haven committee:—

"HONORED GENTLEMEN,—Seeing that it hath pleased the Almighty who is our defence, at this session of the Commissioners, not to suffer any mine to spring for subverting that ancient wall of New England's safety, which Himself hath erected upon the foundation of our so solemn and religious confederation, but further unanimously to establish the same, we thought it might not be unacceptable on our part to present you with our request at this season of your General Assembly's meeting, that you would observe to do according to their conclusions, reminding to recall all and every of your former acts of a contrary tendency and please to signify the same to us before our General Court held the 22d inst., who will then expect it before they return answer to your committee's proposals. Your cordial and ready attendance unto this our request, we conceive will be no obstruction to an amicable treaty for compliance, but rather the contrary if the Lord shall please to own and succeed such endeavors as means for the better flourishing of religion, and righteousness with peace, in this wilderness. And we cannot apprehend that you need to fear any damage to your patent hereby from his majesty's taking offence at so honest a carriage, there being no express interdiction of New Haven colony inserted therein, nor any intendment of your agent to have it so injuriously carried against us. And now also have you the encouragement of all your confederates to apologize upon that account, in case any turbulent spirits should suggest a complaint, whom the righteous God can countermand and disappoint, to whose wisdom and grace we recommend you and all your weighty concernments; resting, gentlemen, your very loving and expectant confederates.

"THE COMMITTEE FOR NEW HAVEN COLONY.
"BY JAMES BISHOP, *Secretary*.
"NEW HAVEN, Oct. 6, 1663."

At the General Court for the jurisdiction of New Haven, held Oct. 22, there were read to the freemen the above communication from the New Haven committee to the General Assembly at Hartford, the late decision of the Commissioners maintaining the colony State of New Haven, and the letter of Winthrop to Major Mason and "the rest of the Court there at Hartford." "The deputies also signified the mind of the freemen, as not at all satisfied with Connecticut committee's proposals, but thought there should be no more treaty with them unless they first restore us to our right state again."

"The matter was largely debated, and the Court considering how they of Connecticut do cast off our motion in the forementioned letter and give us no answer, but that contrary thereunto is reported, as that they have further encouraged those at Guilford and Stamford; therefore this court did now order that no treaty be made by this colony with Connecticut before such acts of power exerted by them upon any of our towns be revoked and recalled, according to Honored Mr. Winthrop's letter engaging the same, the Commissioners' advice, and our frequent desires."

At the same court, "after large debate thereupon, it was concluded as best for us, and most feasible as the case now stands with us, that we seek a letter of exemption from his Majesty, and leave the matter concerning a patent in our instructions to our agents in England as they shall judge best." For the management of this affair, a committee was appointed, and for its expenses a rate of three hundred pounds was levied. And as there were many falling off to Connecticut, it was "ordered that the magistrates do give forth their warrants according to law, to attach and make seizure of such personal estate in proportion, for the payment of their rates, who, upon legal demand made, have or shall refuse the same, and that the orders provided in case of distresses be carefully attended; provided that for the preservation of the public peace, in case of resistance and forcible rescue, violence be not used to occasion the shedding of blood saving in their own defence, but that such officer or officers, so by force of arms resisted in discharge of their duty, make report of such resistance and rescue with sufficient proof to the magistrate or magistrates or other officer of the plantation where it happens, in due season to be presented to the General Court."

New Haven, having taken much encouragement from the decision of the Commissioners in her favor, was further strengthened by the reception of two communications from his Majesty's government, acknowledging her as a distinct colony. One was only indirectly addressed by the home government to New Haven, but the other was especially precious as being under his Majesty's "own princely hand, and sign manual in red wax annexed," and addressed expressly to the governor and assistants of New Haven colony as well as to its confederates. A court of magistrates held in December improved the opportunity to issue the following most loyal proclamation, viz :—

"Whereas the King's Majesty, by his letter under his own princely hand, and sign manual in red wax annexed, bearing date the 21st of June, 1663, from his royal court at Whitehall, directed to his trusty and well-beloved subjects, the governors and assistants of the Massachusetts, Plymouth, New Haven, and Connecticut colonies in New England; and the Lords of his Majesty's most honorable Privy Council, in their letter from his Majesty's court aforesaid, bearing date the 24th of June in the year aforesaid, superscribed, 'For his Majesty's special service, To our very loving friend, John Endicott, Esquire, Governor of his Majesty's plantations in New England, and to the Governor and Council of the colony of the Massachusetts with the rest of the governors of the English plantations in New England respectively,' and by order of the General Court of Boston entered upon record in that court, particularly directed to the governor of the said colony of New Haven, in which letters his Majesty hath commanded this colony many matters of weight, very much respecting his Majesty's service and the good of this country in general, expecting upon his displeasure the strict observance thereof, which this court (most of the towns of this colony being situate by the seaside and so fitly accommodated to fulfil his Majesty's commands) are resolved to their utmost to obey and fulfil; but in their consultation thereabout they find, through the disloyal and seditious principles and practices of some men of inconsiderable interests, some of his Majesty's good subjects in this colony have been seduced to rend themselves from this colony, by which division his Majesty's affairs in these parts (in case some speedy course be not taken for the prevention thereof) is like to suffer, the peace of this country to be endangered, and the heathen amongst us scandalized; the which if we should connive at, especially at this time, his Majesty having so particularly directed his royal commands to this colony as aforesaid, we might justly incur his displeasure against us: this Court doth therefore in his Majesty's name require all the members and inhabitants of this colony heartily to close with the endeavors of the Governor and assistants thereof, for the fulfilling his Majesty's commands in the said letters expressed, and in order thereunto to return to their due obedience and paying their arrears of rates for defraying the necessary charges of the colony, and other dues, within six days after the publication hereof, unto such person or persons as are or shall be appointed to collect the same in attendance to the laws and orders of this colony. All which being done, this court shall forever pass by all former disobedience to the government; but if any shall presume to stand out against his Majesty's pleasure so declared as aforesaid concerning this colony, at your peril be it: this court shall not fail to call the said persons to a strict account, and proceed against them (as disloyal to his Majesty and disturbers of the peace of this colony) according to law."

This Declaration, as it is called in the records, was published in the several plantations. At Stamford it "was violently plucked down" by the Connecticut constable, and "with reproachful speeches rejected, though sent in his Majesty's name, and by the authority of our court of magistrates." When published at Guilford,

Bray Rossiter and others who had submitted to Connecticut went to Hartford, claiming protection. "At a meeting of the Council the 28th of December, Mr. Bray Rossiter, John Bishop, Isaac Crittenden, and John Rossiter presented a declaration dated at New Haven, Dec. 18, 1663, signed by James Bishop, Secretary, which declaration was ordered by the court of magistrates at New Haven aforesaid to be published, &c., as the said declaration declareth; the said Mr. Rossiter also complaining of some threatening expressions that have been by some vented against divers that have submitted to the government of Connecticut.

"This Council having considered the premises, and fearing the peace of the colony will be interrupted by these motions unless some speedy course be taken to prevent it, do nominate and appoint Mr. Wyllys, John Allyn, and Mr. Wait Winthrop, to go to Guilford to treat with Mr. Leete and any other whom Mr. Leete shall desire to join with himself about the indemnity of the persons and estates of those that have actually joined to our government, according to these following instructions:—

"1. If the said Mr. Leete will give security by his word for the indemnity of the aforesaid persons and estates, then you are to propound some propositions for our uniting, according to private instructions.

"2. If they will attend any such propositions, if you cannot come to a conclusion and issue, you are to appoint a meeting at Middletown for a further treaty, where this Council will send a committee fully empowered to conclude all matters between us and New Haven and the rest.

"3. If none of these propositions will be attended by them, then you are in his Majesty's name, and by order from the Council of this colony, to require them to forbear putting in execution their aforesaid declaration against any of those that have joined to our government, and also to administer the oath of a constable to John Meigs, and to require him to use his utmost endeavor to maintain the peace of this colony amongst those at Guilford that have joined to the government of this colony."

To his certificate of the appointment of this committee, the Secretary adds, " Mr. James Richards is desired to attend the service also."

The visit of this committee to Guilford is thus related in " New Haven's Case Stated:—"

"On the 30th of December, 1663, two of your magistrates, with sundry young men and your marshal, came speedily to Guilford, accompanying Rossiter and his son, and countenancing them and their party against the authority of this General Court, though you know how obnoxious they were formerly to this jurisdiction, for contempt of authority and seditious practices, and that they have been the ringleaders of this rent; and that Bray Rossiter, the father, hath been long and still is a man of a turbulent, restless, fractious spirit, and whose designs you have cause to suspect to be to cause a war between these two colonies, or to ruin New Haven Colony: yet him you accompanied in opposition to this colony, without sending or writing before to our governor to be informed concerning the truth in this matter. Sundry horses, as we are informed, accompanied them to Guilford, whither they came at unseasonable hour, about ten o'clock in the night, these short days, when you might rationally think that all the people were gone to bed, and by shooting of sundry guns, some of yours, or of their party in Guilford, alarmed the town; which, when the governor took notice of, and of the unsatisfying answer given to such as inquired the reason of that disturbance, he suspected, and that not without cause, that hostile attempts were intended by their company; whereupon he sent a letter to New Haven to inform the magistrates there concerning matters at Guilford, that many were affrighted, and he desired that the magistrates of New Haven would presently come to their succor, and as many of the troopers as could be got,[1] alleging for a reason, his apprehension of their desperate resolutions. The governor's messenger also excited to haste, as apprehending danger and reporting to them that Branford went up in arms hastening to their relief at Guilford, which the governor required with speed. Hereupon New Haven was also alarmed that night by beating the drum to warn the town militia to be ready. This fear was not causeless, for what else could be gathered from the preparations of pistols, bullets, swords, &c., which they brought with them, and the threatening speeches given out by some of them, as is attested by the depositions of some and subscriptions of others, which we have by us to show when need requires; and your two magistrates themselves, who ought to have kept the king's peace among their own party, and in their own speeches, threatened our governor that if any thing was done against those men, viz., Rossiter and his party, Connecticut would take it as done against themselves, for they were bound to protect them."

Although it was so late in the evening when the "honored gentlemen" from Hartford arrived in Guilford, the following correspondence passed between them and Gov. Leete:—

"GUILFORD, Dec. 30, 1663.

"WORTHY SIR,—After the presentation of our service to yourself, you may please to understand that we underwritten, being a committee authorized by the Council of the Colony of Connecticut, do desire that yourself would be pleased to give us a meeting to-morrow about nine of the clock, to treat of such things as present concernments do require.

"Sir, we desire your answer by the bearer.

"Yours, SAMUEL WYLLYS.
JOHN ALLYN.
JAMES RICHARDS.
WAIT WINTHROP.

"*These for Wm. Leete, Esquire, at his house in Guilford.*"

[1] At a general court for New Haven, Dec. 31, 1663, "Mr. Jones acquainted the town with the business of Guilford the last night, and how

"GUILFORD, Dec. 30, 1663.

"HONORED GENTLEMEN,—My answer sent before by Jonathan Gilbert was in earnest, to let you know my true capacity and resolution, from which I cannot recede, and rest,
"Yours in what I may,
"WILLIAM LEETE.
"*For Mr. Wyllys, Mr. John Allyn, Mr. Richards, Mr. Wait Winthrop.*"

The record of a general court, occasioned by the visit of the Connecticut gentlemen to Guilford, which was held at New Haven, Jan. 7, $166\frac{3}{4}$, indicates that though Leete refused to give them audience, they had at least some informal conference with him in regard to the Declaration lately published in New Haven. The record is as follows: viz.,—

"The publishing of the former Declaration at Guilford occasioned Mr. Rossiter and his son to go up to Connecticut, and there obtain two of their magistrates, marshal, and sundry others to come down to Guilford on the 30th of December last; who coming into the town at an unseasonable time of night, their party, by shooting off sundry guns, caused the town to be alarmed unto great disturbance, and some of them giving out threatening speeches, which caused the governor to send away speedily to Branford and New Haven for help, which caused both those towns to be alarmed also to great disturbance, the same night, which caused sending of men both from New Haven and Branford. Now, for the gaining of a right understanding of the business, and to consider what to do upon this and the like accounts, occasioned the calling of this court, though the weather proved very unseasonable.

"But the Court being met together (so many of them as could possibly stay), the governor related the whole business to the best of his remembrance; and among other things he informed the they had sent away six troopers to see what the matter is, but ordered them not to provoke, neither by word nor action, but to keep the peace."

Court that those gentlemen of Connecticut, that came down with Mr. Rossiter and his son, did earnestly desire that there might be at least a suspension of the execution of that Declaration till there might be another conference betwixt them and us, wherein they hoped matters might come to a more comfortable issue; and they very earnestly pressed for such a thing, urging how dangerous the contrary might be, for they said that what we did to those men whom they had admitted, they must take it as done to Connecticut colony. Therefore he now desired to know the mind of the Court, whether they would yield to them so far or no; but the Court, considering how fruitless all former treaties had been, and that they had formerly ordered that there should be no more treaty with them unless they first restore us those members which they had so unrighteously taken from us, therefore did now again confirm the same, and in the issue came to this conclusion: to desire Mr. Davenport and Mr. Street to draw up in writing all our grievances, and then, with the approbation of as many of the committee as could come together, to send it to Connecticut unto their General Assembly, which accordingly was done in March next, which writing you have recorded after the conclusions of this Court with arguments annexed and sundry testimonies both from Guilford and Stamford.

"Then it was also propounded, whether this Court would confirm the former Declaration sent forth by the magistrates, which was by vote concluded."

The writing which Mr. Davenport and Mr. Street were requested to draw up, was entitled "New Haven's Case Stated." Under this title it may be found in Appendix No. VII., and with it a draught of an answer in the handwriting of the secretary of Connecticut. There is no evidence that any answer was ever forwarded to New Haven. In the opinion of Hollister, "good judgment was shown in abstaining from an attempt to answer it." Hollister says, "In all our New England colonial papers, I have not found a more touching and eloquent narrative, nor have I ever seen a more convincing argument." Before this plea of New Haven reached Hartford, the Council of Connecticut had appointed another committee to go to Guilford and New Haven. From a note inserted in their instructions it appears that Gov. Winthrop was to precede them, and make in person such preparation as he could, for their success. These are their instructions: viz.,—

"It is agreed by the Council, that if our honored friends of New Haven, Guilford, Branford, Milford, and Stamford, will treat with us for an accommodation, then we will grant and confirm to them all such privileges as they shall desire, which are not repugnant to the tenor of our charter.

"(This following particular is not to be put in execution before we hear what our honored governor and the rest effect there.)

"But if they will not treat with us and agree for their settlement, then they are hereby ordered to read the charter at a public meeting (if they can attain it), and to declare that we expect their submission to his Majesty's order therein contained; and also, to commission those now in place to govern the people there according to law until further order be taken, and to draw up a declaration which shall be publicly made known to the people, whereby they may be informed what rational and Christianlike propositions have been made to the gentlemen there, in several treaties for the settlement of their and our union."

The correspondence between the committees of the two colonies which has been preserved is as follows: viz.,—

"24th 12 m., 1663 [24th February, 1663¼]

"GENTLEMEN,—In order to treaty we propound as a necessary expedient that you redintegrate our colony by restoring our members at Stamford and Guilford, that the confederation may be repaired and preserved; then we have power from our general court to treat with you and to settle agreement, according to God, between your colony and ours, for future peace between us, for ourselves and our posterity mutually, which we shall readily attend upon our receipt of your positive consent to the premises testified by your joint subscription thereunto, being made an authentical act.

"WILLIAM LEETE,
MATTHEW GILBERT,
WILLIAM JONES,
BENJAMIN FENN,
JASPER CRANE,
ROBERT TREAT,"

"GENTLEMEN,—In answer to your proposals, and as an expedient for the promoting of peace, we propound as followeth:—

"1. In reference to your dissatisfactions respecting divers persons of Guilford and Stamford, and to prevent divisions in those plantations, it is agreed that they be ordered to submit to the same authority with their neighbors in those places.

"2. It is agreed that all the elected officers in New Haven, Guilford, Milford, Branford, be hereby authorized to administer justice to the people in those plantations according to law, and the people to choose new officers at New Haven at their usual time for that purpose for the management of their affairs within those plantations, with due caution that our patent be no way violated thereby.

"3. That all motions or occasions tending to obstruct further union be carefully shunned, and that all past grievances be buried, upon a penalty on any that shall revive them.

"4. And that it be referred to the prudent consideration of those in place of authority, both in Church and Commonwealth, to think of accommodations most conducible to the settlement of religion and righteousness upon the firmest basis of peace, truth, and unity, for the benefit of posterity; and that some suitable persons do meet to that purpose, when either the much-honored Mr. Winthrop or Mr. Leete shall judge it a fit season, that so brotherly amity may be propagated to future ages.

"SAMUEL WYLLYS,
HENRY WOLCOTT,
JOHN ALLYN,
JAMES RICHARDS.

"Feb. 25, 1663."

"Gentlemen,—As to your first article in your paper sent us, we query whether it be an authentic act as done by you, or not, till it be confirmed by your General Assembly; which, if it be, we desire that you do signify so much under your hands, as also that they are positively restored to this jurisdiction by virtue thereof.

"WILLIAM LEETE,
"*In the name of the rest of the magistrates.*
"FEB. 25, 1663."

"Gentlemen,—In answer to yours we return that we are ready to make authentic what we have proposed to you, if you please to treat with us as they are propounded.

"JOHN ALLYN,
"*In the name of the Committee.*

"We expect your answer, whether you please thus to treat with us or not,"

A little yielding on either side in this crisis might have led on to negotiation. If Connecticut had ordered those who revolted to her from New Haven, "to submit to the same authority with their neighbors," the New Haven committee were bound by promise to negotiate, but not bound thereby to give up her existence as a distinct colony. Some of her people, would, perhaps, have been willing to do so; but there were others who would never have consented to any arrangement which would annul the fundamental law of New Haven concerning suffrage. Davenport, the champion of this party, writes a few days after the above written correspondence: "The premises being duly weighed, it will be your wisdom and way to desist wholly and forever from endeavoring to draw us into a union under your patent." But New Haven, however divided on the question of uniting with Connecticut, was unanimous in refusing to treat till she was redintegrated and acknowledged as a distinct colony. If Connecticut had fully believed that by retracting she could set in motion measures which would result in the absorption of New Haven, she might have sacrificed to the pride of her sister colony the required punctilio. But fearing that the party whose desire was, "that we may for the future live in love and peace together as distinct neighbor colonies, as we did above twenty years together before you received and misunderstood and so abused your patent," might become masters of the situation, she would not otherwise than conditionally retract what she had done.

CHAPTER XXI.

NEW HAVEN SUBMITS.

THE negotiation between the two colonies was thus in dead-lock, when, "at the close of a long summer day, as the Sabbath stillness in Boston was beginning, two ships of war—the Guinea, carrying thirty-six guns, and the Elias, carrying thirty — came to anchor off Long Wharf. They were the first vessels of the royal navy that had ever been seen in that harbor. Officers went on board and brought back intelligence to the town, that the ships had sailed ten weeks before from England, in company with two others, — the Martin, of sixteen guns, and the William and Nicholas, of ten,—from which they had parted a week or two before in bad weather; and that the fleet conveyed three or four hundred troops, and four persons charged with public business. These were Col. Richard Nicolls, Sir Robert Carr, Col. George Cartwright, and Mr. Samuel Maverick.[1] " The other vessels had anchored at Portsmouth three days earlier.

The arrival of these royal commissioners brought to a speedy issue the controversy between Connecticut and New Haven. They were instructed to require the colonies to assist in reducing under English authority

[1] Palfrey.

all the territory occupied by the Dutch, the king claiming it as of right belonging to the English and bestowing it on his brother the Duke of York. As the territory thus granted was to be bounded on the east by the Connecticut River, New Haven experienced a sudden change of heart toward Connecticut, preferring to submit to her jurisdiction rather than be subjected to the rule of a man who was a royalist, a Romanist, and a Stuart.

Connecticut was also alarmed, or else feigned to be, at the arrival of the commissioners. As soon as possible she sent a delegation to New Haven to persuade her loving friends there to come under the Winthrop charter in order to avoid a common danger. These delegates, one of whom had recently been in Boston, alleged, moreover, that the leading men of Massachusetts earnestly desired that Connecticut and New Haven should come to an agreement, as it had been ascertained that the commissioners had instructions to take advantage of disputes between colonies as well as of every other expedient for reducing all New England under the immediate government of the king.

In less than three weeks after the arrival of the commissioners, Gov. Leete assembled his Court at New Haven.

"The governor acquainted them with the occasion of this Court, that there had Mr. Whiting and Lieut. Bull of Hartford been lately with most of the magistrates, and brought a letter from Mr. Wyllys to Mr. Jones; and they signified that Mr. Whiting being lately in the Bay, and having speech with many friends there, he was hastened away by them to communicate matters above at Connecticut, and also to us, showing themselves very sensible of danger of detriment to the country by reason of any differences between the colonies, now the king's commissioners were come over; and they looked upon this difference of ours with Connecticut to be the greatest, and therefore they declared that they were sent to this purpose, and declared this to be the advice of the best part in the Bay, though they had no letter, that this difference be made up betwixt us, being very sensible of danger to all by this means, and therefore they judge this the best way for all our safety, to stand for the liberties of our patents, and so Connecticut and they would have us join with them upon that account, for they conceive a great advantage given to the commissioners by our standing off. Now we told them, for our parts, we could do nothing in it ourselves, but after much debate and urging we signified to them thus much: that if Connecticut would come and assert their claim to us in the king's authority, and would secure what at any time they had propounded to us, and would engage to stand to uphold the liberties of their patent, we would call the General Court together that they may consider of it, and be ready to give them an answer, and said for our parts, we did not know but we might bow before it, if they assert it and make it good. They urged to have something from us as grounds of certainty that we would so do, but we told them that we would not do so. Now the Court was desired to consider of it, what answer should be given if they should so come. Much debate there was upon it, and something pleaded upon the danger of standing as we now are, if the king's commissioners come amongst us; much was also said by some against, and declared that they see no reason of such a motion, making that a question to be answered before we knew it would be put to us; also that there had not been a full summons to all the plantations for this General Court; also it was questioned whether the General Court, if it were full, had any power to deliver up the colony state without the consent of the whole body of freemen at least. But notwithstanding all that was said, it came to a vote as followeth: that if Connecticut do come down and assert their right to us by virtue of their charter, and require us in his Majesty's name to submit to their government, that then it be declared to them that we do submit, referring all arguments between us to the final issue of the commissioners of our confederates.

"The vote passed in the affirmative; but after the vote was passed there appeared some dissatisfaction, and there was further advice and consideration taken in the case, and much was said that it was necessary the freemen should be acquainted with it, and in the issue came to another vote, which was this: That if they of Connecticut come and make a claim upon us in his Majesty's name and by virtue of their charter, then we shall submit to them until the commissioners of the colonies do meet; and so the governor, the deputy-governor, and magistrates, or so many of them as can be got together, were appointed to give the answer to Connecticut men if they come."

At the annual meeting of the Commissioners of the United Colonies in September, Connecticut protested against the admission of Messrs. Leete and Jones as Commissioners for New Haven colony, "because it doth not appear that they are a colony, or have any power of government distinct from us, confirmed by regal authority." The dispute being thus brought before them, the representatives of Massachusetts and Plymouth declared "that as the occasion thereof was acted without their cognizance, and the grounds not being fully known to them, they could, as to the right of the cause, add nothing to what was passed by the commissioners at their meeting in 1663: yet considering how much the honor of God as well as the weal of all the colonies, as themselves therein interested, are concerned in the issue, they heartily and affectionately commended such a compliance between them, that the sad consequences which would inevitably follow upon their further contentions might be prevented."

"At a general court of the freemen of the jurisdiction held at New Haven, Sept. 14, 1664, the governor acquainted them with the occasion of calling them together at this time, and that was something they had met withal lately at the meeting of the commissioners at Hartford, as in the writings may appear, which writings that concerned us were all now read, with a letter also subscribed by Mr. Samuel Wyllys and Mr. John Allyn, directed to James Bishop, to be communicated to this Assembly. The governor further said that it was a season to advise and consider together in what state it is best for us to appear when the commissioners from England come to visit us, whether in the state we now are, or under a regal stamp (as they call it), in joining with Connecticut. There was much debate, and divers spake that to stand as God hath kept us hitherto is our best way; but some desired to understand the vote of the last General Court, so the secretary went home to fetch it, and in the mean space, while he was gone, the assembly was broken up, and no more done at this time."

The General Assembly of Connecticut met in October, and passed the following order:—

"This Court desires and appoints Mr. Shearman and the secretary to go to New Haven, &c., and by order from this Court, in his Majesty's name, to require all the inhabitants of New Haven, Milford, Branford, Guilford, and Stamford to submit to the government here established by his Majesty's gracious grant to this colony, and to take their answer And they are here authorized to declare all the present freemen of New Haven, Milford, Branford, Guilford, and Stamford, that are qualified according to law, to be freemen of this corporation, so many of them as shall accept of the same and take the freemen's oath. And they are hereby authorized to make as many freemen as they shall by sufficient testimony find qualified according to order of court, in that respect, and to administer the oath of freedom to them.

"They are also to declare that this Court doth invest William Leete, Esquire, William Jones, Esquire, Mr. Gilbert, Mr. Fenn, Mr. Crane, Mr. Treat, and Mr. Law, with magistratical power, to assist in the government of those plantations and the people thereof, according to the laws of this corporation, or so many of their own laws and orders as are not contradictory to the tenor of our charter, until May next; and if any of these above-named refuse to accept to govern the people as aforesaid, then Mr. Shearman and the secretary are hereby authorized to appoint some other fit persons in their room, and to administer an oath to them for the faithful execution of the trust committed to them."

For some reason Mr. Richards was desired to go in place of Mr. Shearman to Stamford, where, Mr. Law having been won over, they found no great difficulty in persuading the town to submit. The committee originally appointed visited Milford on the 17th of November, where they issued a call for a meeting of all householders, as follows:—

"These are in his Majesty's name to will and require you forthwith to warn all the inhabitants at your town of Milford, being householders, to meet at the meeting-house this day about one of the clock, to attend such occasions with Mr. Shearman and myself, as are given us in charge by the General Court of Connecticut; whereof fail not. JOHN ALLYN, *Secretary*,"
"*To Joseph Waters, to execute.*"

The people of Milford, assembling in response to this call, voted to submit to Connecticut. "No one person voted against it."

On the 19th of the same month, Mr. Shearman and Secretary Allyn were present at a town-meeting in New Haven, where Mr. Jones, who at the election in May had been chosen deputy-governor, and was therefore moderator of the plantation court, "acquainted the town that the occasion of the meeting was that there were some gentlemen from Connecticut that had something to acquaint the town withal, and he thought the business in general was to require our submission to Connecticut, with some other propositions. He further minded the town of the peace and unity that God had hitherto continued amongst us, and the many blessings both on the right hand and left that we enjoyed under this government; and also told the town that we are a people in combination with others, and therefore could not give a full answer without first acquainting the other plantations, and then that we ourselves were not a full meeting of the town, divers of the farms having not warning. But, the gentlemen being come in, Mr. Jones desired to see their commission. They declared that they should show it to persons deputed, but after, read it, and then declared what they had to say to the town. The persons were Mr. John Allyn and Mr. Samuel Shearman. These gentlemen urged to have the matter put to vote, but they were told that the town-meeting was not full. But Mr. Allyn said that if Mr. Shearman did consent, which he thought he would, he should take the boldness to put it to vote himself; but his speech was disliked, and after, witnessed against, and they were desired to withdraw awhile, and the town would consider to give them an answer; and so they did, and the town considering of it came to this conclusion as their present answer by a general vote, only one dissenting, which answer follows their declaration. The gentlemen aforesaid being called in again, the answer was read to them. They desired a copy of it; which was granted, they leaving a copy of what they had declared, which they promised, and is here inserted as followeth."

The declaration of the Connecticut committee was

in accordance with their instructions. The answer of the New Haven town-meeting, though not preserved, was doubtless substantially what the moderator had already stated: viz., that submission to such a demand must come from the colony of New Haven, and not from its several plantations.

The committee visited also Branford and Guilford, where the answers they received to their requirement of submission were in accordance with that of New Haven.

Submission to Connecticut was now the manifest destiny of New Haven, and the only remaining question respected the mode. The royal commissioners had obliterated the Dutch power in America, and New Haven was included in the territory given to the Duke of York. A "distinct colony state" being out of the question, the best practicable condition was to become a part of Connecticut. The course of events had at last brought all but a very few to this conclusion. However strongly they were attached to the peculiarities of their colony, including, as most important of all, its limitation of suffrage, and however deeply offended with the insult their colony had received from Connecticut, they saw that submission was a necessity. If there were a few who still desired "to stand as God hath kept us hitherto," they were, since the reduction of New Netherlands, so few that nothing could be accomplished. All that the leading men now hoped for was that the colony might die decently. Not consenting that the plantations should separately transfer allegiance, they required that the General Court of the jurisdiction should assemble and vote its submission.

If any thing was wanting to bring the last man to despair of maintaining a distinct colony state, it was a formal determination by the royal commissioners of the boundary between Connecticut and New York. If New Haven was in Connecticut, the distinct colony of New Haven was at an end; but the other alternative was worse.

Winthrop with several associates had been appointed by the General Assembly of Connecticut, at their session in October, to go to New York, "to congratulate his Majesty's Honorable Commissioners." They were empowered, "if an opportunity offer itself that they can issue the bounds between the Duke's patent and ours, so as in their judgment may be to the satisfaction of the Court, to attend the same." Winthrop had been present with the Commissioners, and rendered them important aid, in negotiating the surrender of New Amsterdam in the preceding August; but still further to prepare the way for an issue that would be to the satisfaction of the Court, an order had been passed "that Col. Nicolls and the rest of the Commissioners be presented with four hundred bushels of corn as a present from this colony."

The decision of the Commissioners was rendered on the thirtieth day of November. After assigning Long Island, which Connecticut claimed as one of the "adjacent islands," mentioned in her charter, to his Royal Highness the Duke of York, they proceeded to declare "that the creek or river called Momoronock, which is reputed to be about twelve miles to the east of West Chester, and a line drawn from the east point or side, where the fresh water falls into the salt at high-water mark, north-north-west, to the line of the Massachusetts, be the western bounds of the said colony of Connecticut; and all plantations lying westward of that creek and line so drawn to be under his Royal Highness's government, and all plantations lying eastward of that creek and line to be under the government of Connecticut."

Thirteen days after this authoritative determination of this western boundary of Connecticut, the Jurisdiction of New Haven held its last general court. "The freemen of New Haven, Guilford, Branford, and part of Milford, and as many of the inhabitants as were pleased to come," assembled to put an end to their distinct colony state, by submission to Connecticut.

"The governor acquainted them with the occasion of calling them together; and that is, some of Connecticut gentlemen having made demand of our submission to their government, in his Majesty's name, the answers of these three towns were with promise of further answer when they should consider of the matter together; and therefore to set their thoughts a-work about it, something was propounded to them and left with them to consider of till the morning.

"In the morning, the assembly being come together, the governor propounded to know what was the issue of their thoughts in the business left with them. After some debate, the answer was drawn up in writing, and read, and after serious consideration put to vote, and so was concluded with universal consent, not any one opposing.

"*The vote of the freemen and other inhabitants of the colony met together at New Haven, the 13th of December,'64, in answer to what Mr. John Allyn and Mr. Samuel Shearman declared in our several towns in November last as followeth:—*

"1. First that by this act or vote we be not understood to justify Connecticut's former actings, nor anything disorderly done by our own people upon such accounts.

"2. That by it we be not apprehended to have any hand in breaking or dissolving the confederation.

" Yet in testimony of our loyalty to the king's Majesty, when an authentic copy of the determination of his Commissioners is published to be recorded with us, if thereby it shall appear to our committee that we are by his Majesty's authority now put under Connecticut patent, we shall submit, as from a necessity brought upon us by their means of Connecticut aforesaid, but with a *salvo jure* of our former right and claim, as a people who have not yet been heard in point of plea."

A committee having been appointed for consummating matters with Connecticut, and the following letter having been read and approved, it was sent to the authorities of Connecticut with the aforesaid vote.

" HONORED GENTLEMEN,—We having been silent hitherto as to the making of any grievance known unto the king's commissioners, notwithstanding what may be with us of such nature from the several transactions that have been amongst us, are desirous so to continue the managing of these affairs in ways consistent with the ancient confederation of the United Colonies, choosing rather to suffer than to begin any motion hazardful to New England settlements. In pursuance whereof (according to our promise to your gentlemen sent lately to demand our submission, though in a divided if not dividing way, within our towns severally seeking to bring us under the government by yourselves already settled, wherein we have had no hand to settle the same, and before you had cleared to our conviction the certain limits of your charter, which may justly increase the scruple of too much haste in that and former actings upon us), the generality of our undivided people have orderly met this 13th of December, 1664, and by the vote enclosed have prepared for this answer to be given, of our submission, which being done by us, then for the accommodating of matters betwixt us in amicable wise, by a committee empowered to issue with you on their behalf and in the behalf of all concerned, according to instructions given to the said committee. We never did nor ever do intend to damnify your moral rights or just privilege, consistent with our like honest enjoyment, and we would hope that you have no further scope towards us, not to violate our covenant interest, but to accommodate us with that we shall desire and the patent bear, as hath been often said you would do. And surely you have the more reason to be full with us herein, seeing that your success for patent bounds with those gentlemen now obtained, seems to be debtor to our silence before them, whenas you thus by single application and audience issued that matter. You thus performing to satisfaction, we may still rest silent, and according to profession by a studious and cordial endeavor with us to advance the interest of Christ in this wilderness and by the Lord's blessing thereupon, love and union between us may be greatly confirmed and all our comforts enlarged; which is the earnest prayer of, gentlemen, your loving friends and neighbors,

"*The Committee appointed by the freemen and inhabitants of New Haven colony now assembled.*

"℔ JAMES BISHOP, *Secretary*.

"NEW HAVEN, Dec. 14, 1664."

The submission of New Haven was an unqualified triumph for Connecticut. There had been a time when she would have modified the qualifications for suffrage, and made them as nearly comfortable to those in New Haven as the home government would allow. The qualifications she had proposed to New Haven in the preceding year are almost exactly what Massachusetts adopted when the royal commissioners demanded, in the king's name, that church-membership should not be insisted on. At that time, she seemed willing to permit New Haven to have a court in which magistrates might, without a jury, try and determine causes. She even seemed willing to exempt the churches of New Haven County from that Erastian control, which, in the session of the General Assembly when Mr.

Shearman and Secretary Allyn were appointed to demand the submission of New Haven, commended "to the ministers and churches in this colony to consider whether it be not their duty to entertain all such persons who are of an honest and godly conversation, having a competency of knowledge in the principles of religion, and shall desire to join with them in church fellowship by an explicit covenant; and that they have their children baptized; and that all the children of the church be accepted and accounted real members of the church, and that the church exercise a due Christian care and watch over them; and that when they are grown up, being examined by the officers in the presence of the church, it appears in the judgment of charity they are duly qualified to participate in the great ordinance of the Lord's Supper, by their being able to examine themselves and discern the Lord's body, such persons be admitted to full communion. The Court desires that the several officers of the respective churches would be pleased to consider whether it be not the duty of the Court to order the churches to practise according to the premises, if they do not practise without such an order."

But New Haven, instead of securing these concessions by capitulating when they were offered, had obstinately refused, and had now submitted without any definite assurance of peculiar privileges. Plainly, they were expecting that their loving friends would accommodate them with everything they might "desire and the patent bear." Their letter of submission mentions with other matters, a committee they had appointed to communicate their desires, and alleges that the silence of New Haven when Connecticut prosecuted her claim before the royal commissioners was a reason why Connecticut should be magnanimous in her concessions. How bitter must have been the disappointment at New Haven, when Connecticut, in response to the letter of submission, alluded to every topic it contained except the appointment of the committee "for the accommodating of matters betwixt us in amicable wise." New Haven had unconditionally surrendered.

The response of Connecticut to the letter of submission was as follows:—

"HARTFORD, Dec. 21, 1664.

"HONORED GENTLEMEN,—We have received yours, dated the 14th of this instant, signed by James Bishop, &c., wherein you are pleased to mention your silence hitherto, as to the making any grievance known to his Majesty's commissioners, notwithstanding what may be with you, &c. We can say the same, though we had fair opportunities to present any thing of that nature. As for your desire to manage affairs consistent with the Confederation, the present motion will (we hope) upon a candid review not appear any way dissonant therefrom, for besides the provision made in one of the Articles of Confederation for two colonies uniting in one, there was special provision, as you well know, made at the last session of the commissioners, to that purpose, conjoined with pathetical advice and counsel to an amicable union. Our too much forwardness with New Haven, &c., is not so clear, seeing those plantations you inhabit are much about the center of our patent, which our charter limits, as also the enclosed determination of his Majesty's honorable commissioners, will to your conviction be apparent. That our success for patent bounds with the king's commissioners is debtor to your silence, seems to us strange, when your non-compliance was so abundantly known to those gentlemen; yea, the news of your motions when Mr. John Allyn was last with you, was at New York before our governor's departure thence, notwithstanding your silence, and yet so good an issue obtained. We desire such reflections may be buried in perpetual silence, which only yourselves necessitating thereunto shall revive them, being willing to pursue truth and peace as much as may be with all men, especially with our dear brethren in the fellowship of the gospel, and fellow-members of the same civil corporation, accommodated with so many choice privileges, which we are willing, after all is prepared to your hands, to confer upon you equal with ourselves; which we wish may at last produce the long-desired effect of your free and cordial closure with us, not attributing any necessity imposed by us further than the situation of those plantations in the heart of our colony, and therein the peace of posterity in those parts of the country is necessarily included, and that after so long liberty to present your plea where you have seen meet. Gentlemen, we desire a full answer as speedily as may be, whether those lately empowered, accept to govern according to their commission; if not, other meet persons to govern, may by us be empowered in their room. Thus desiring the Lord to unite our hearts and spirits in ways well pleasing in his sight.

"Which is the prayer of your very loving friends,

"THE COUNCIL OF THE COLONY OF CONNECTICUT.

"Signed by their order by me, JOHN ALLYN, *Secretary*."

New Haven made but one more effort to obtain concessions. The effect was neither vigorous nor effectual. The following letter ended its resistance to the will of Connecticut.

"NEW HAVEN, Jan. 5, 1665.

"HONORED GENTLEMEN,—Whereas, by yours, dated Dec. 21, 1664, you please to say that you did the same as we in not making any grievance known to the commissioners, &c.; unto that may be returned that you had not the same cause so to do, from any pretence of injury by our intermeddling with your colony or covenant interest: unto which we refer that passage. For our expressing desires to manage all our matters in consistency with the Confederation, we hope you will not blame us; how dissonant or consonant your actings with us have been, we leave to the confederates to judge, as tbeir records may show. That article which allows two colonies to join, doth also with others assert the justness of each colony's distinct right until joined to mutual satisfaction, and the provision made in such case the last session we gainsay not, when the union is so completed, and a new settlement of the confederation by the respective general courts accomplished. Their pathetical advice and counsel for an amicable union we wish may be so attended; in order whereunto we gave you notice of a committee prepared to treat with you for such an accommodation, unto which you give us no answer, but instead thereof, send forth your edict from authority upon us before our conviction for submission was declared to you. The argument from our intermixt situation is the same now as it was before our confederating and ever since, and affords no more ground now to disannul the covenant than before. We might marvel at your strange why we should think your success should be debtor to our silence, and that because the news of our non-compliance was with the commissioners; as if the mere news of such a thing contained the strength of all we had to say or plead. Gentlemen, we entreat you to consider that there is more in it than so, yea, that still we have to allege things of weight, and know where and how, if we chose not rather to abate and suffer, than by striving, to hazard the hurting yourselves or the common cause. We scope not at reflections, but conviction and conscience-satisfaction, that so brethren in the fellowship of the gospel might come to a cordial and regular closure, and so walk together in love and peace to advance Christ's interest among them, which is all our design; but how those high and holy ends are like so to be promoved between us without a treaty for accommodation, we have cause to doubt, yet that we may not fail in the least to perform whatever we have said, we now signify, that having seen the copy of his Majesty's commissioners' determination (deciding the bounds betwixt his highness the Duke of York, and Connecticut's charter), we do declare submission thereunto according to the true intent of our vote, unto which we refer you. As to that part of yours concerning our magistrates' and officers' acceptance, their answer is, that they having been chosen by the people here to such trust, and sworn thereunto for the year ensuing, and until new be orderly chosen, and being again desired to continue that trust, they shall go on in due observance thereof, according to the declaration left with us by Mr. John Allyn and Mr. Samuel

Shearman, bearing date Nov. 19, 1664, in hope to find that in a loving treaty for accommodating matters to the ends professed by you, unto which our committee stands ready to attend, upon notice from you, truth and peace may be maintained. So shall we not give you further trouble, but remain, gentlemen, your very loving friends and neighbors.
"*The committee appointed by the freemen and inhabitants of New Haven Colony, signed ℈ their order, ℈ me,*
"JAMES BISHOP, *Secretary*."

This reiterated appeal for a "loving treaty" brought forth no response, and the people of the late colony of New Haven found that they were not to be allowed to retain any of the peculiarities they had so highly prized under the old jurisdiction. Deputies from the plantation of New Haven appeared and sat in the General Assembly of Connecticut in the following April. An act of indemnity was at that time passed as follows: "This Court doth hereby declare that all former actings that have passed by the former power at New Haven, so far as they have concerned this colony (whilst they stood as a distinct colony), though they in their own nature have seemed uncomfortable to us, yet they are hereby buried in perpetual oblivion, never to be called to account." At the election in May four gentlemen who had been magistrates under the New Haven jurisdiction were appointed magistrates of Connecticut.

A very large majority of the people formerly under the jurisdiction of New Haven soon became satisfied with their new relation. Branford, however, was an exception. In the words of Trumbull, "Mr. Pierson and almost his whole church and congregation were so displeased that they soon removed into Newark in

New Jersey. They carried off the records of the church and town, and, after the latter had been settled about five and twenty years, left it almost without inhabitants. For more than twenty years from that time there was not a church formed in the town. People from various parts of the colony gradually moved into it, and purchased the lands of the first planters, so that in about twenty years it became resettled. In 1685 it was re-invested with town privileges."

Most of all, Davenport, who, on the other side of the sea, had devised the peculiar constitution of New Haven, who had seen the establishment of successive plantations according to the pattern he had set, and the combination of them under a colonial government, was distressed at the ruin of his plans and his hopes. In April, 1666, Winthrop wrote requesting him to preach the election sermon in May, and suggesting that he would have been asked to preach the preceding year, but that the union was not then complete. Davenport, who had just entered his seventieth year, and was suffering with malaria, writes of his "unfitness for such a journey," mentions the intention of his colleague to visit Boston as a reason why he himself must remain at home, and adds, " I have sundry other weighty reasons whereby I am strongly and necessarily hindered from that service, which may more conveniently be given by word of mouth to your honored self, than expressed by writing." Retaining the letter in his hand two days, he writes in a postscript: "The reason which it pleased you to give why I was not formerly desired to preach at the election, holdeth as strong against my being invited thereunto now. For we are not yet fully joined, by the Court's refusal of our freemen to vote in the last election, when they came thither to that end, in obedience to their absolute summons, and about twenty of ours were sent home as repudiated after they had suffered the difficulties and hazards of an uncomfortable and unsafe journey, in that wet season.[1]" Writing his reply the same day he received Winthrop's invitation, he ruled his spirit; but, after two days of musing, he gives vent to his disappointment in the complaint that the freemen of New Haven were not, as such, received and treated under the expected treaty of accommodation as freemen of Connecticut. A year later he writes to Winthrop with something of his former cordiality and abandon, as if time had softened his resentment. But he never recovered from the disappointment which fell upon him like a blow at the extinction of the little sovereignty whose foundations he had laid. New Haven, as Palfrey rightly says, "ceased to be attractive to him. It was rather the monument of a great defeat and sorrow." He speaks in a letter to a friend in Massachusetts of "Christ's interest in New Haven Colony as miserably lost." In this state of mind he received an invitation to the pastorate of the First Church in Boston, there to champion the cause of orthodoxy against the half-way covenant. Contrary to the wishes of his church and congregation, he determined to accept the invitation. Mr. John Hull of Boston writes in his

[1] These freemen of New Haven Colony doubtless presented themselves as voters in response to a public summons directed to freemen of Connecticut. As they had not taken the oath of allegiance to that colony, they were repudiated.

diary, under date of May 2, 1668: "At three or four in the afternoon came Mr. John Davenport to town, with his wife, son, and son's family, and were met by many of the town. A great shower of extraordinary drops of rain fell as they entered the town; but Mr. Davenport and his wife were sheltered in a coach of Mr. Searl, who went to meet them."

Mr. Davenport's ministry in Boston was of short duration. He died in less than two years after the date given above. His removal from New Haven doubtless helped to obliterate the bitter feelings produced by the controversy between Connecticut and New Haven. The union of the two colonies was in itself so desirable, that resentment against what was wrong in the means of accomplishing it yielded to the stronger feeling of satisfaction with the result. After two centuries, New Haven scarcely remembers that she was once a distinct colony.

APPENDIX.

APPENDIX I.

AUTOBIOGRAPHY OF MICHAEL WIGGLESWORTH.

[From the N. E. Hist. and Gen. Reg., vol. xvii.]

I WAS born of Godly Parents, that feared ye Lord greatly, even from their youth, but in an ungodly Place, where ye generality of ye people rather derided then imitated their piety, in a place where, to my knowledge, their children had Learnt wickedness betimes, In a place that was consumed wth fire in a great part of it, after God had brought them out of it.[1] These godly parents of mine meeting with opposition & persecution for Religion, because they went from their own Parish Church to hear ye word & Receiv ye Ls supper &c took up resolutions to pluck up their stakes & remove themselves to New England, and accordingly they did so, Leaving dear Relations friends & acquaintace, their native Land, a new built house, a flourishing Trade, to expose themselves to ye hazzard of ye seas, and to ye Distressing difficulties of a howling wilderness, that they might enjoy Liberty of Conscience & Christ in his ordinances. And the Lord brought them hither & Landed them at Charlestown, after many difficulties and hazzards, and me along with them being then a child not full seven yeers old. After about 7 weeks stay at Charls Town, my parents removed

---

[1] In the copy of the N. E. Hist. and Gen. Register which belongs to the N. H. Col. Hist. Society is this manuscript note:—

" Hedon, a village in the East Riding of Yorkshire, on the river Humber, three miles from Hull, was almost entirely consumed by fire in the year 1656. H. D."

The initials are those of Mr. Horace Day, a former secretary of the Society.

again by sea to New Haven in yᵉ month of October. In or passage thither we were in great Danger by a storm which drove us upon a Beach of sand where we lay beating til another Tide fetcht us off; but God carried us to or port in safety. Winter approaching we dwelt in a cellar partly under ground covered with earth the first winter. But I remember that one great rain brake in upon us & drencht me so in my bed being asleep that I fell sick upon it; but yᵉ Lord in mercy spar'd my life & restored my health. When yᵉ next summer was come I was sent to school to Mr. Ezekiel Cheever who at that time taught school in his own house, and under him in a year or two I profited so much through yᵉ blessing of God, that I began to make Latin & to get forward apace. But God who is infinitely wise and absolutely soverain, and gives no account concerning any of his proceedings, was pleased about this time to visit my father with Lameness which grew upon him more & more to his dying Day, though he liv'd under it 13 yeers. He wanting help was fain to take me off from school to follow other employments for yᵉ space of 3 or 4 yeers until I had lost all that I had gained in the Latine Tongue. But when I was now in my fourteenth yeer, my Father, who I suppose was not wel satisfied in keeping me from Learning whereto I had been designed from my infancy, & not judging me fit for husbandry, sent me to school again, though at that time I had little or no disposi .on to it, but I was willing to submit to his authority therein and accordingly I went to school under no small disadvantage & discouragement seeing those that were far inferior to me, by my discontinuance now gotten far before me. But in a little time it appeared to be of God, who was pleased to facilitate my work & bless my studies that I soon recovered what I had lost & gained a great deal more, so that in 2 yeers and 3 quarters I was judged fit for yᵉ Colledge and thither I was sent, far from my parents and acquaintace among strangers. But when father and mother both forsook me, then the Lord took care of me. It was an act of great self Denial in my father that notwithstanding his own Lameness and great weakness of Body wᶜʰ required the service & helpfulness of a son, and having but one son to be yᵉ staff of his age & supporter of his weakness he would yet for my good be content to deny himself of that comfort and Assistace I might have Lent him. It was also an evident proof of a strong Faith in him, in that he durst adventure to send me to ye Colledge, though his Estate was but small & little enough to maintain himself & small family left at home. And God Let him Live to see how acceptable to himself this service was in giving up his only son to ye Lord and bringing him up to Learning; especially ye Lively actings of his faith & self denial herein. For first, notwithstanding his great weakness of body, yet he Lived til I was so far brought up as that I was called to be a fellow of ye Colledge and improved in Publick service there, and until I had preached several Times; yea and more than so, he Lived to see & hear what God had done for my soul in turning me from Darkness to light & fro the power of Sathan unto God, wch filled his heart ful of joy and thankfulness beyond what can be expressed. And for his outward estate, that was so far from being sunk by what he spent from yeer to yeer upon my education, that in 6 yeers time it was plainly doubled, wch himself took great notice of, and spake of it to my self and others to ye praise of God, wth Admiration and thankfulness. And after he had lived under great & sore affliction for ye space of 13 yeers a pattern of faith, patience, humility & heavenly mindedness, having done his work in my education and receivd an answer to his prayers God took him to his Heavenly Rest where he is now reaping ye fruit of his Labors. When I came first to ye Colledge, I had indeed enjoyed ye benefit of religious & strict education, and God in his mercy and pitty kept me from scandalous sins before I came thither & after I came there, but alas I had a naughty vile heart and was acted by corrupt nature & therefore could propound no Right and noble ends to my self, but acted from self and for self. I was indeed studious and strove to outdoe my compeers, but it was for honor & applause & prefermt & such poor Beggarly ends. Thus I had my Ends and God had his Ends far differing from mine, yet it pleased him to Bless my studies, & to make me grow in knowledge both in ye tongues & Inferior Arts & also in Divinity. But when I had been there about three yeers and a half; God in his Love

& Pitty to my soul wrought a great change in me both in heart & Life, and from that time forward I learnt to study with God and for God. And whereas before that, I had thoughts of applying my self to ye study & Practice of Physick, I wholly laid aside those thoughts, and did chuse to serve Christ in ye work of ye ministry if he would please to fit me for it & to accept of my service in that great work.

APPENDIX II.

LETTER OF NATHANAEL ROWE TO JOHN WINTHROP.

To the worshipful & much respected Friende Mr. Winthrop, Magistrate liveing att Boston in New Ing:

MOST LOVING & KINDE SIR,—My humblest service remembered to you, I now wth much consideratione (and thinkinge of all things & bussinesses) doe now write to you. First of all my father sent mee to this countrie verie hastelie (& overmuch inconsideraely), indeed it is a sore griefe to mee yt I should charge my prudent & most deare father wth the evill of rash doeinge of thinges; but yet being compelled in this time of straightness, I must say itt. My father sent with mee pvtiones enough for to serve mee a yeare or twoe; as meale, flower, buttar, beefe. I, haveinge lost my meale and flower, was compelled to sell the rest of my pvicon, & indeed, being counselled soe to doe, I immediately did itt. Then Mr. Eaton and Mr. Davenport haveinge noe direct order w^t to doe, wished me & sent me unto Mr. Eaton, the marchant's brother, to be instructed in the rudiments of the Lattine tongue (in wch wth practise, I shalbe prettie skilfull). I lived with him about a month, & verily in y^t space he spake not one word to mee, *scilicet*, about my learninge, & after he went awaie, I lived an idle life, because I had noe instructor. After all this, I was sent (by Mr. Bellinghas order) unto Mr. Willis of Linne, the school-maister: and theire I liveing privately gott the best part of my Lattine-tongue, but yet not by his instructiones, butt indeed onelie by seeinge his manner of teachinge, & gathering thinges of my selfe, & also by bribeinge (or giveing gifts to) his sonnes for patternes; of which Mr. Willis never knew as yett. This last half yeare hath binne spent in receiveing instructiones frome

Mr. Dunster, whoe (blessed be God for it) hath binne a guide to leade mee onne in the waie of hummane litterature, & alsoe in divine. Thus much for my cors in this lande: seeing, sir, you out of your fountaine of wisdome, doe adjudge that it is my father's will & pleasure that I should betake myselfe to one thinge or other, whereby I mighte gett my livinge (O TEMPORA, O MORES!) why for my part I shall be willinge to doe anie thinge for my father (God assistinge mee) att Quille-piacke, as to help to cleare growr de, or hough upp grownde, *quia enim, qui humiliatur, is vero tempestivô exaltabitur.* But, I pray you, sir, to make the waie cleare for mee to goe to England, so that I may speake more fullie to my father & wth my friends, soe that if my father hath caste his affections off frome mee (which, if I had but one serious thought that waie, it would be the distractinge of my spirite all the daies I have to live. The curse of the parent is the greatest heviness & burden to [the] soule of a child yt is; my father never made anie such thing knowne to mee) that I might not loose those opportunities that are offerred to mee by one of my uncles, whome I am certain will doe mee anie good, & if my father be offended wth mee, then, if I be att London, I feare not but tha[t] my uncle will pacifie my father's wrathe. Thus I end.

       Yor observant servant,

           NATH. ROWE.

APPENDIX III.

LAMBERTON'S SHIP.

SO much interest is felt in Lamberton's ship that I have felt inclined to bring together what the early writers have recorded concerning the vessel herself and concerning the atmospheric phenomenon which the superstition of the times connected with her loss.

Winthrop mentions her thrice. When the news of her departure had reached Boston, he records that "this was the earliest and sharpest winter we had since we arrived in the country, and it was as vehement cold to the southward as here," adding, as one illustration, "At New Haven, a ship bound for England was forced to be cut out of the ice three miles." In the following June, when solicitude had nearly or quite given place to despair, he writes, "There fell a sad affliction upon the country this year, though it more particularly concerned New Haven and those parts. A small ship of about one hundred tons set out from New Haven in the middle of the eleventh month last (the harbor being then so frozen as they were forced to hew her through the ice near three miles). She was laden with pease and some wheat, all in bulk, with about two hundred West India hides, and store of beaver and plate, so as it was estimated in all at five thousand pounds. There were in her about seventy persons, whereof divers were of very precious account, as Mr. Gregson, one of their magistrates, the wife of Mr. Goodyear, another of their magistrates (a right godly woman), Captain Turner, Mr. Lamberton, master of the ship, and some seven or eight others, members of the church there. The ship never went voyage before, and was very crank-sided, so as it was conceived she was overset in a great tempest which happened soon after she put to sea, for she was never heard of after." Two years afterward, that is, in June, 1648, he writes, as if the news had just reached him, "There appeared over the harbor at New Haven, in the evening, the form of the keel of a ship with three masts, to which were suddenly added the tackling and sails, and presently after, upon the top of the poop, a man standing with one hand akimbo under his left side, and in his right hand a sword stretched out toward the sea. Then from the side of the ship which was from the town arose a great smoke which covered all the ship and in that smoke she vanished away; but some saw her keel sink into the water. This was seen by many, men and women, and it continued about a quarter of an hour."

Hubbard, who was born in 1649, says, "The main founders of New Haven were men of great estates, notably well versed in trading and merchandising, strongly bent for trade and to gain their subsistence that way, choosing their seat on purpose in order thereunto, so that if the providence of God had gone along with an answerable blessing, they had stood fair for the first born of that employment. But that mercy, as hath since appeared, was provided for another place, and a meaner condition for them; for they quickly began to meet with insuperable difficulties, and though they built some shipping and sent abroad their provisions into foreign parts; and purchased lands at Delaware and other places to set up trading-houses for beaver, yet all would not help; they sank apace, and their stock wasted, so that in five or six years they were very near the bottom: yet, being not willing to give over, they did, as it were, gather together all their remaining strength, to the building and loading out one ship for England, to try if any better success might befall them for their retrievement. Into this ship they put, in a manner, all their tradable estates, much corn, large quantities of plate, and sundry considerable persons also went, amongst whom was Mr. Gregson forementioned, who, besides his own private occasions, carried with him some estate in order to the procuring of a patent; but all this, though done by very wise men, yet hath since been thought to be carried by a kind of infatuation; for the ship was ill-built, very walt-sided, and, to increase the inconveniency thereof, ill-laden, the lighter goods at the bottom: so that understanding men did even beforehand conclude in their deliberate thoughts a calamitous issue, especially being a winter voyage, and so in the dead of winter that they were necessitated with saws to cut open the ice, for the passage of the ship frozen in for a large way together; yet were all these things overlooked, and men went on in a hurry till it was too late, when such circumstances as these were called to mind. The issue was, the ship was never heard of, foundered in the sea, as is most probable, and with the loss of it their hope of trade gave up the ghost, which was gasping for life before in New Haven. But this was not all the loss; besides the goods, there were sundry precious Christians lost, not less than ten belonging to the chnrch there, who, as Mr. Cotton's expression upon it was, went to heaven in a chariot of water, as Elijah long before in a chariot of fire. There were also some writings of Mr. Hooker's and Mr. Davenport's lost, that never were at all or not fully repaired."

In another place discoursing of memorable accidents he says, "Another deplorable loss befell New England the same year. wherein New Haven was principally concerned and the southern parts of the country: for the inhabitants of that town, being Londoners, were very desirous to fall into a way of traffic, in which they were better skilled than in matters of husbandry; and to that end had built a ship of one hundred tons, which they freighted for London. intending thereby to lay some foundation of a future trade: but either by the ill form of her building or by the shifting of her lading (which was wheat, which is apt to shift its place in storms), the vessel miscarried, and in her seventy persons, some of whom were of the principal part of the inhabitants, with all the wealth they could gather together."

Hubbard makes no mention of the apparition in the air which followed the loss of the ship, and Winthrop, who was no sceptic in regard to supernatural interventions, records it without intimating that he regarded it as a miracle; but Mather, who wrote about as long after the occurrence as did Hubbard, has given us the story with the superstitious interpretation attached to it by some, at least, of his contemporaries. Desir-

540   APPENDIX III.

ing to give it accurately, he wrote to Rev. James Pierpont, the successor of Davenport in the pastorate of the church at New Haven, and received from him the following letter in reply:—

"REVEREND AND DEAR SIR.—In compliance with your desires I now give you the relation of that apparition of a ship in the air, which I have received from the most credible, judicious, and curious surviving observers of it.

"In the year 1647,[1] besides much other lading, a far more rich treasure of passengers (five or six of which were persons of chief note and worth in New Haven) put themselves on board a new ship, built at Rhode Island, of about one hundred and fifty tons, but so walty that the master (Lamberton) often said she would prove their grave. In the month of January, cutting their way through much ice, on which they were accompanied with the Rev. Mr. Davenport, besides many other friends, with many fears, as well as prayers and tears, they set sail. Mr. Davenport in prayer with an observable emphasis used these words: 'Lord, if it be thy pleasure to bury these our friends in the bottom of the sea, they are thine, save them.' The spring following, no tidings of these friends arrived with the ships from England; New Haven's heart began to fail her: this put the godly people on much prayer, both public and private, that the Lord would (if it was his pleasure) let them hear what he had done with their dear friends, and prepare them with a suitable submission to his holy will. In June next ensuing, a great thunder-storm arose out of the north-west; after which (the hemisphere being serene) about an hour before sunset, a ship of like dimensions with the aforesaid, with her canvas and colors abroad (though the wind northerly), appeared in the air coming up from our harbor's mouth, which lies southward from the town, seemingly with her sails filled under a fresh gale, holding her course north, and continuing under observation, sailing against the wind for the space of half an hour.

"Many were drawn to behold this great work of God; yea, the very children cried out, 'There's a brave ship.' At length, crowding up as far as there is usually water sufficient for such a vessel, and so near some of the spectators, as that they imagined a man might hurl a stone on board

[1] Pierpont was in error in regard to the year. The ship sailed in January, 1646, New Style.

her, her main-top seemed to be blown off, but left hanging in the shrouds; then her mizzen-top; then all her masting seemed blown away by the board, quickly after the hulk brought to a careen, she overset and so vanished into a smoky cloud, which in some time dissipated, leaving, as everywhere else, a clear air. The admiring spectators could distinguish the several colors of each part, the principal rigging, and such proportions, as caused not only the generality of people to say, 'This was the mould of their ship, and this was her tragic end;' but Mr. Davenport also in public declared to this effect, that God had condescended, for the quieting of their afflicted spirits. this extraordinary account of his sovereign disposal of those for whom so many fervent prayers were made continually. Thus I am, sir, Your humble servant,

"JAMES PIERPONT."

APPENDIX IV.

SEATING THE MEETING-HOUSE.

AT a general court held the 10th of March, 164$\frac{8}{7}$, the names of people as they were seated in the meeting-house were read in court, and it was ordered they should be recorded, which was as followeth:—

"FIRST FOR THE MEN'S SEATS, VIZ.:

"*The middle seats have to sit in them:*

"1st seat, the governor and deputy-governor.
"2d seat, Mr. Malbon, magistrate.
"3rd seat, Mr. Evance, Mr. Bracey, Mr. Francis Newman, Mr. Gibbard.
"4th seat, Goodman Wigglesworth, Bro. Atwater, Bro. Seeley, Bro. Miles.
"5th seat, Bro. Crane, Bro. Gibbs, Mr. Caffinch, Mr. Ling, Bro. Andrews.
"6th seat, Bro. Davis, Goodman Osborne, Anthony Thompson, Mr. Browning, Mr. Rutherford, Mr. Higginson.
"7th seat, Bro. Camfield, Mr. James, Bro. Benham, Wm. Thompson, Bro. Lindon, Bro. Martin,
"8th seat, Jno. Meigs, Jno. Cooper, Peter Brown, Wm. Peck, Jno. Gregory, Nicholas Elsey.
"9th seat, Edw. Bannister, Jno. Harriman, Benj. Wilmot, Jarvis Boykin, Arthur Halbidge.

1	Mr. Pell, Mr. Tuttle, Bro. Fowler.
2	Thom. Nash, Mr. Allerton, Bro. Perry.
3	Jno. Nash, David Atwater, Thom. Yale.
4	Robert Johnson, Thom. Jeffrey, John Punderson.
5	Thom. Munson, Jno. Livermore, Roger Alling, Joseph Nash, Sam. Whitehead, Thomas James.

SHORT SEAT. Jno. Clarke, Mark Pearce.

1. Jeremy Whitnell, Wm. Preston, Thom. Kimberley, Thom. Powell.
2. Daniel Paul, Richard Beckley, Richard Mansfield, James Russell.
3. Wm. Potter, Thom. Lamson, Christopher Todd, William Ives.
4. Hen. Glover, Wm. Thorp, Matthias Hitchcock, Andrew Low.

1. John Moss, Luke Atkinson, Jno. Thomas, Abraham Bell.
2. George Smith, John Wakefield, Edw. Patteson, Richard Beach.
3. John Bassett, Timothy Ford, Thom. Knowles, Robert Preston.
4. Richd. Osborne, Robert Hill, Jno. Wilford, Henry Gibbons.
5. Francis Brown, Adam Nicolls, Goodman Leeke, Goodman Dayton.
6. Wm. Gibbons, John Vincent, Thomas Wheeler, John Brockett.

REV. JOHN DA

1 Gov. Eaton, Dep. Gov. Goodyear.
2 Mr. Malbon.
3 Mr. Evance, Mr. Bracey, Mr. Francis Newman, Mr. Gibbard.
4 Goodman Wigglesworth, Bro. Atwater, Bro. Seeley, Bro. Miles.
5 Bro. Crane, Bro. Gibbs, Mr. Caffinch, Mr. Ling, Bro. Andrews.
6 Bro. Davis, Goodman Osborne, Anthony Thompson, Mr. Browning, Mr. Rutherford, Mr. Higginson.
7 Bro. Camfield, Mr. James, Bro. Benham, Wm. Thompson, Bro. Lindon, Bro. Martin.
8 Jno. Meigs, Jno. Cooper, Peter Brown, Wm. Peck, Jno. Gregory, Nicholas Elsey.
9 Edw. Bannister, Jno. Harriman, Benja. Wilmot, Jarvis Boykin, Arthur Halbidge.

1   SOLDIERS' SEATS.
1   "   "
3   "   "

1 First middle seat, vacant or occupied by children and servants.
2
3

MARCH 10,

———

VENPORT.

Old Mrs. Eaton, Mrs. Gov. Eaton (?)	1
Mrs. Malbon, Mrs. Gregson, Mrs. Davenport, Mrs. Hooke.	2
Elder Newman's wife, Mrs. Lamberton, Mrs. Turner, Mrs. Brewster.	3
Sister Wakeman, Sister Gibbard, Sister Gilbert, Sister Miles.	4
Mr. Francis Newman's wife, Sister Gibbs, Sister Crane, Sister Tuttle, Sister (Ann) Atwater.	5
Sister Seeley, Mrs. Caffinch, Mrs. Perry, Sister Davis, Sister Cheever, Jno. Nash's wife.	6
David Atwater's wife, Sister Clarke, Mrs. Yale, Sister Osborne, Sister Thompson.	7
Sister Wigglesworth, Goody Johnson, Goody Camfield, Sister Punderson, Goody Meigs, Sister Gregory.	8
Sister Todd, Sister Boykin, Wm. Potter's wife, Matthias Hitchcock's wife, Sister Cooper.	9

SOLDIERS' SEATS.	1
" "	2
" "	3
Probably occupied by children or servants.	1
	2
	3

1646-7.

---

1. Mrs Bracey, Mrs. Evance.
2. Sister Fowler, Sister Ling, Sister Allerton.
3. Sister Jeffrey, Sister Rutherford, Sister Livermore.
4. Sister Preston, Sister Benham, Sister Mansfield.
5. Sister Alling, Goody Bannister, Sister Kimberly, Goody Wilmot, Sister Whitnell, Mrs. Higginson.

SHORT SEAT.
Sister Potter, the midwife.
Old Sister Nash.

1. Sister Powell, Goody Lindon, Mrs. James.
2. Sister Whitehead, Sister Munson, Sister Beckley, Sister Martin.
3. Sister Peck, Joseph Nash's wife, Peter Brown's wife, Sister Russell.
4. Sister Ives, Sister Bassett, Sister Patteson, Sister Elsey.

1. Jno. Thomas's wife, Goody Knowles, Goody Beach, Goody Hull.
2. Sister Wakefield, Sister Smith, Goody Moss, James Clarke's wife.
3. Sister Brockett, Sister Hill, Sister Clarke, Goody Ford.
4. Goody Osborne, Goody Wheeler, Sister Nicolls, Sister Brown.

APPENDIX IV. 543

"*In the cross seats at the end.*

" 1st seat, Mr. Pell, Mr. Tuttle, Bro. Fowler.
" 2d seat, Thom. Nash, Mr. Allerton, Bro. Perry.
" 3d seat, Jno. Nash, David Atwater, Thom. Yale.
" 4th seat, Robert Johnson, Thom. Jeffrey, John Punderson.
" 5th seat, Thom. Munson, Jno. Livermore, Roger Alling, Joseph Nash, Sam. Whitehead, Thomas James.
" In the other little seat, John Clarke, Mark Pearce.

"*In the seats on the side, for men.*

" 1st, Jeremy Whitnell, Wm. Preston, Thom. Kimberly, Thom. Powell.
" 2d, Daniel Paul, Richard Beckley, Richard Mansfield, James Russell.
" 3d, Wm. Potter, Thom. Lamson, Christopher Todd, William Ives.
" 4th, Hen. Glover, Wm. Thorp, Matthias Hitchcock, Andrew Low.

"*On the other side of the door.*

" 1st, John Moss, Luke Atkinson, Jno. Thomas, Abraham Bell.
" 2d, George Smith, John Wakefield, Edw. Patteson, Richard Beach.
" 3d, John Bassett, Timothy Ford, Thom. Knowles, Robert Preston.
" 4th, Richd. Osborne, Robert Hill, Jno. Wilford, Henry Gibbons.
" 5th, Francis Brown, Adam Nicolls, Goodman Leeke, Goodman Dayton.
" 6th, Wm. Gibbons, John Vincent, Thomas Wheeler, John Brockett.

"SECONDLY FOR THE WOMEN'S SEATS.

"*In the middle.*

" 1st seat, old Mrs. Eaton.

"2d seat, Mrs. Malbon, Mrs. Gregson, Mrs. Davenport, Mrs. Hooke.

" 3d seat, Elder Newman's wife, Mrs. Lamberton, Mrs. Turner, Mrs. Brewster.

"4th seat, Sister Wakeman, Sister Gibbard, Sister Gilbert, Sister Miles.

"5th seat, Mr. Francis Newman's wife, Sister Gibbs, Sister Crane, Sister Tuttle, Sister Atwater.

" 6th seat, Sister Seeley, Mrs. Caffinch, Mrs. Perry, Sister Davis, Sister Cheever, Jno. Nash's wife.

" 7th seat, David Atwater's wife, Sister Clarke, Mrs. Yale, Sister Osborne, Sister Thompson.

" 8th seat, Sister Wigglesworth, Goody Johnson, Goody Camfield, Sister Punderson. Goody Meigs, Sister Gregory.

"9th seat, Sister Todd, Sister Boykin, Wm. Potter's wife, Matthias Hitchcock's wife, Sister Cooper.

"*In the cross seats at the end.*

" 1st, Mrs. Bracey, Mrs. Evance.

" 2d, Sister Fowler, Sister Ling, Sister Allerton.

" 3d, Sister Jeffrey, Sister Rutherford, Sister Livermore.

" 4th, Sister Preston, Sister Benham, Sister Mansfield.

"5th, Sister Alling, Goody Bannister, Sister Kimberly, Goody Wilmot, Sister Whitnell, Mrs. Higginson.

"*In the little cross seat.*

" Sister Potter the midwife, and old Sister Nash.

APPENDIX IV.   545

"*In the seats on the side.*

"1st seat, Sister Powell, Goody Lindon, Mrs. James.
"2d seat, Sister Whitehead, Sister Munson, Sister Beckley, Sister Martin.
"3d seat, Sister Peck, Joseph Nash's wife, Peter Brown's wife, Sister Russell.
"4th seat, Sister Ives, Sister Bassett, Sister Patteson, Sister Elsey.

"*In the seats on the other side of the door.*

"1st seat, Jno. Thomas's wife, Goody Knowles, Goody Beach, Goody Hull.
"2d seat, Sister Wakefield, Sister Smith, Goody Moss, James Clarke's wife.
"3d seat, Sister Brockett, Sister Hill, Sister Clarke, Goody Ford.
"4th seat, Goody Osborne, Goody Wheeler, Sister Nicolls, Sister Brown."

Nine years later (Feb. 11, 165⅝) the names of people as they were seated in the meeting-house were again recorded as follows:—

"*The long seats in the middle, for men.*

" 1. The governor and the deputy-governor.
" 2. Mr. Newman, magistrate.
" 3. Mr. Wakeman, Mr. Gibbard, John Gibbs, William Davis.
" 4. William Judson, Mr. Goodenhouse, Mr. Mullener, John Nash.
" 5. Henry Lindon, William Andrews, John Cooper, Roger Alling, William Thompson.
" 6. Thom. Munson, Sam. Whitehead, William Potter, Math. Moulthrop, Jno. Peakin, John Harriman, Christopher Todd.
" 7. Jno. Benham, Jarvis Boykin, Nich. Elsey, Ro. Talmadge, Jer. How, Jno. Thompson, James Bishop.

35

"8. Jno. Moss, Jno. Brockett, Thos. Morris, Andrew Low, Thos. Wheeler, Rich. Miles, jun., Jno. Thompson, jun.

"9. William Gibbons, William Paine, Jno. Winston, Edw. Parker, Edward Preston.

" The cross seats at upper end."

"1. Mr. Tuttle, Mr. Jno. Davenport, William Fowler, Mr. Allerton, sen.

"2. Mr. Caffinch, David Atwater, Mr. Rutherford, Mr. Yale.

"3. Thomas Jeffrey, Jno. Punderson, Mr. Augur, Mr. Daniel.

"4. William Peck, William Bradley, Thomas Mullener.

"5. Jos. Nash, William Russell, Jer. Osborne, Geo. Constable, Rich. Gregson, Francis Brown, Allen Ball, Thomas Johnson.

"In the little seat.

"Mr. Bowers, Thom. Kimberly.

"In the seats on the side, on both sides of the door.

"1. Thomas Powell, James Russell, John Hodson, Joseph Alsop.

"2. Richard Beckley, Henry Glover, John Chidsey, Thom. Mix.

"3. Abraham Doolittle, Matthias Hitchcock, John Jones, Thom. Lamson.

"4. Geo. Smith, John Thomas, James Clark, Geo. Pardee.

"5. Benj. Wilmot, Edwa. Hitchcock, Edwa. Patteson, Robert Hill.

"6. John Hall, Jno. Wakefield, Timothy Ford, Matthew Rowe.

"7. Nathaniel Merriman, John Tuttle, Thom. Barnes, Peter Mallory.

"8. William Bassett, John Benham, Martin Tichener, Philip Leeke.

"9. Edward Camp, John Johnson, William Holt, Isaac Whitehead.

REV. JOHN DA

REV. MR. H

Mr. Gilbert's Seat.

Jer. Whitnell, Rich. Johnson, Ephraim Pennington, Rich. Hull.

Rob. Seeley, Rob. Johnson, Tho. Mitchell, Thomas Wheeler, Senior.

1 Governor Eaton, Dep. Gov. Goodyear.

2 Mr. Newman, magistrate.

3 Mr. Wakeman, Mr. Gibbard, John Gibbs, William Davis.

4 William Judson, Mr. Goodenhouse, Mr. Mullener, John Nash.

5 Henry Lindon, William Andrews, John Cooper, Roger Alling, William Thompson.

6 Thom. Munson, Sam. Whitehead, Wm. Potter, Math. Moulthrop, Jno. Peakin, John Harriman, Christopher Todd.

7 Jno. Benham, Jarvis Boykin, Nich. Elsey, Ro. Talmadge, Jer. How, Jno. Thompson, James Bishop.

8 Jno. Moss, Jno. Brockett, Thos. Morris, Andrew Low, Thos. Wheeler, Rich. Miles, jun., Jno. Thompson, jun.

9 William Gibbons, William Paine, Jno. Winston, Edw. Parker, Edward Preston.

1 SOLDIERS' SEATS.

2   "   "

3   "   "

(Against the soldiers' seats.)

1 Jno. Sackett, James Eaton (Heaton) Ralph Lines, Isaac Beecher, Abra. Kimberley.

2 John Alling, Edward Perkins, Sam. Marsh, Joseph Benham.

3 Henry Morell, Sam. Hodskins, William Blayden.

Rob. Pigg, William Thorp, Henry Bristow, Thom. Beamont.

Mr. Tuttle, Mr. Jno. Davenport, William Fowler, Mr. Allerton, sen. — 1

Mr. Caffinch, David Atwater, Mr. Rutherford, Mr. Yale. — 2

Thomas Jeffrey, Jno. Punderson, Mr. Augur, Mr. Daniel. — 3

William Peck, William Bradley, Thomas Mullener. — 4

Jos. Nash, William Russell, Jer. Osborne, Geo. Constable, Rich. Gregson, Francis Brown, Allen Ball, Thos. Johnson. — 5

BENCH BEFORE LITTLE SEAT.
Henry Gibbons,
Jno. Vincent.
LITTLE SEAT.
Mr. Bowers.
Thom. Kimberly

Goodw. Beecher, the elder, Goodw. Munson, Goodw. Boykin, Goodw. Beamont, old Goodw. Johnson.

---

1 Thomas Powell, James Russell, John Hodson, Joseph Alsop.

2 Richard Beckley, Henry Glover, John Chidsey, Thom. Mix.

3 Abraham Doolittle, Matthias Hitchcock, John Jones, Thom. Lamson.

4 Geo. Smith, John Thomas, James Clarke, Geo. Pardee.

Edward Watson.

5 Benj. Wilmot, Edwa. Hitchcock, Edwa. Patteson, Robert Hill.

6 John Hall, Jno. Wakefield, Timothy Ford, Matthew Rowe.

7 Nathaniel Merriman, John Tuttle, Thom. Barnes, Peter Mallory.

8 William Bassett, John Benham, Martin Tichener, Philip Leeke.

9 Edward Camp, John Johnson, William Holt, Isaac Whitehead.

VENPORT.
OOKE(?)

Deacon Miles' Seat.
Goodw. Whitnell, Goodw. Watson, Goodw. Halbidge.

Goodw. Harriman. Goodw. Glover, Goodw. Andrews, James Russell's wife.

Mrs. Theop. Eaton.

Mrs. Newman.   2

Mrs. Goodenhouse, Mrs. Gilbert, Mrs. Miles, Mrs. Wakeman.   3

Mrs. Gibbard, Mrs. Tuttle, Goodwife Gibbs, Goodwife Davis.   4

Jno. Nash's wife, Mrs. Caffinch, Mrs. Rutherford, Goodwife Lindon, Da. Atwater's wife.   5

Goodwife Punderson, Mrs. Yale, Rob. Johnson's wife, Goodwife Seeley, Goodwife Todd, Goody Bradley.   6

Goodwife Camp, Goo. Osborne, Goo. Thompson, Goo. Moulthrop, Goo. Potter, Will Russell's wife.   7

Goodw. Talmadge, Goodw. Parker, Goodw. Bishop, Goodw. Wheeler, Goodw. Hitchcock, Goodw. Clarke.   8

Goodw. Wilmot, sen., Goodw. Wilmot, jun., Goodw. Brockett, Goodw. Hall, Goodw. Paine.   9

SOLDIERS' SEATS.   1
"   "   2
"   "   3

First middle seat, vacant or occupied by children.   1
2
3

1 Goodw. Judson, Goodw. Mansfield, Goodw. Cooper.
2 Mrs. Allerton, the elder, Mr. Goodyear's daughters.
3 Mrs. Bowers, Goodw. Fowler, Goodw. Jeffrey.
4 Goodwife Preston, senior, William Peck's wife, Goodw. Kimberly, the elder.
  Sam. Whitehead's wife, Goodw. Benham, the elder, Jer. Howe's wife.
5 Widow Peck, Tho. Johnson's wife, Goodw. Ball, Goodw. Mitchell, Goody Hull, Goodw. Thorp, Goodw. Wakefield.

Goodw. Low, Goodw. Elsey.

1 Mrs. Daniell, Mrs. Mullener, Mrs. Powell, Goodw. Chidsey.
2 Goodw. Mix, Mrs. Hodson, Goodw. Patteson, Goodw. Beckley.
3 Goodw. Moss, Goodw. Thomas, Goodw. Doolittle, Goodw. Alsop.
4 Goodw. Bassett, Goodw. Smith, Goodw. Gibbons, Goodw. Morris.

5 Goodw. Ford, Goodw. Rowe, Goodw. Winston, Goodw. Hill.
6 Goodw. Tichener, Goodw. Leeke, Goodw. Pennington, Goodw. Pardee.
7 Goodw. Barnes, Goodw. Merriman, Jno. Benham's wife, Edwa. Camp's wife.
8 Goodw. Mallory, Goodw. Atkinson, Goodw. Marsh, Goodw. Hodskins.

Goodw. Pigg.
Goodw. Browne.

THE SHORT SEAT.
Goodw. Nash, the elder.
Roger Alling's wife.

FEBRUARY 11, 1655-6.

"*Against the soldiers' seats.*

"1. Jno. Sacket, James Eaton, Ralph Lines, Isaac Beecher, Abra. Kimberley.

"2. John Alling, Edward Perkins, Sam. Marsh, Joseph Benham.

"3. Henry Morrell, Sam. Hodskins. William Blayden.

"*On the bench before the little seat.*

"Henry Gibbons, Jno. Vincent.

"*Before the governor's seat.*

"Rob. Seeley, Rob. Johnson, Tho. Mitchell, Thomas Wheeler, senior.

"*Before Mr. Gilbert's seat.*

"Jer. Whitnell, Rich. Johnson, Eph. aim Pennington, Rich. Hull.

"*Before Mr. Tuttle's seat.*

"Rob. Pigg, William Thorpe, Henry Bristow, Thom. Beamont.

"*Before the Pillar.*

" Edward Watson.

"THE WOMEN'S SEATS.

"*The long seats.*

"The first as it was.

" In the second, Mrs. Newman added.

"3. Mrs. Goodenhouse, Mrs. Gilbert, Mrs. Miles, Mrs. Wakeman.

"4. Mrs. Gibbard, Mrs. Tuttle, Goodwife Gibbs, Goodwife Davis.

"5. Jno. Nash's wife, Mrs. Caffinch, Mrs. Rutherford, Goodwife Lindon, Da. Atwater's wife.

" 6. Goodwife Punderson, Mrs. Yale, Rob. Johnson's wife, Goodwife Seeley, Goodwife Todd, Goody Bradley.

" 7. Goodwife Camp, Goo. Osborne, Goo. Thompson, Goo. Moulthrop, Goo. Potter, Will. Russell's wife.

" 8. Goodw. Talmadge, Goodw. Parker, Goodw. Bishop, Goodw. Wheeler, Goodw. Hitchcock, Goodw. Clark.

" 9. Goodw. Wilmot, sen., Goodw. Wilmot, jun., Goodw. Brockett, Goodw. Hall, Goodw. Paine.

"Cross seats.

" 1. Mrs. Allerton the elder, Mr. Goodyear's daughters.

" 2. Mrs. Bowers, Goodw. Fowler, Goodw. Jeffrey.

" 3. Goodwife Preston, senior, William Peck's wife, Goodw. Kimberley the elder.

" 4. Sam. Whitehead's wife, Goodw. Benham the elder, Jer. Howe's wife.

" 5. Widow Peck, Tho. Johnson's wife, Goodw. Ball, Goodw. Mitchell, Goody Hull, Goodw. Thorpe, Goodw. Wakefield.

"In the short seat.

" Goodw. Nash the elder, Roger Alling's wife.

"In the seat before them.

" Goodw. Pigg, Goodw. Browne,

"In the side seats all along.

" 1. Mrs. Daniell, Mrs. Mullener, Mrs. Powell, Goodw. Chidsey.

" 2. Goodw. Mix, Mrs. Hodson, Goodw. Patteson, Goodw. Beckley.

" 3. Goodw. Moss, Goodw. Thomas, Goodw. Doolittle, Goodw. Alsop.

" 4. Goodw. Bassett, Goodw. Smith, Goodw. Gibbons, Goodw. Morris.

"5. Goodw. Ford, Goodw. Rowe, Goodw. Winston, Goodw. Hill.

"5. Goodw. Tichener, Goodw. Leeke, Goodw. Pennington, Goodw. Pardee.

"6. Goodw. Barnes, Goodw. Merriman, Jno. Benham's wife, Edwa. Camp's wife.

"8. Goodw. Mallory, Goodw. Atkinson, Goodw. Marsh, Goodw. Hodskins.

"*Before Mrs. Eaton's seat.*

"Goodw. Harriman, Goodw. Glover, Goodw. Andrews, James Russell's wife.

"*Before the pillar.*

"Goodw. Low, Goodw. Elsey.

"*Before Dea. Miles' seat.*

"Goodw. Whitnell, Goodw. Watson, Goodw. Halbidge.

"*Before Mrs. Allerton's seat.*

"Goodw. Judson, Goodw. Mansfield, Goodw. Cooper.

"*Permitted to sit in the alley (upon their desire) for convenience of hearing.*

"Goodw. Beecher the elder, Goodw. Munson, Goodw. Boykin, Goodw. Beamont, old Goodw. Johnson."

Another seating of the meeting-house is recorded Feb. 20, 166½.

"*In the long seats for men.*

"1. Mr. Gilbert, with such other as may be called to magistracy.

"2. Mr. Jones, Mr. John Davenport, Jr., Mr. Yale, Mr. William Gibbard.

APPENDIX IV.

"3. Mr. Goodenhouse, Mr. Tuttle, William Judson, John Gibbs, Lieut. Nash.

"4. Mr. Hodson, William Andrews, John Cooper, Roger Alling, James Bishop.

"5. William Thompson, William Potter, Matthew Moulthrop, Christopher Todd, William Bradley, John Harriman.

"6. Henry Glover, Nicholas Elsey, John Moss, John Thompson, John Brockett, John Winston, Thomas Mix.

"7. Jeremy Howe, Nathaniel Merriman, Thomas Barnes. George Smith, Timothy Ford, Ralph Lines, William Gibbons.

"8. Robert Hill, William Meeker, Ephraim Howe, Thomas Harrison.

"9. Edward Parker, Thomas Lamson, William Trowbridge, John Alling, Edward Preston.

"In the short seats at the upper end.

"1. Mr. Rutherford, Mr. Mullener, John Punderson, David Atwater.

"2. Mr. Field, Mr. Augur, Mr. Nathaniel Street, Ensign Munson.

"3. Sergt. Whitehead, Sergt. Russell, Joseph Alsop, John Chidsey.

"4. Thomas Trowbridge, Thomas Johnson, Jeremiah Osborne, Allen Ball.

"In the long seat next the wall.

"John Gilbert, Geo. Pardee, Wm. Holt.

"In the little seat.

"Thomas Kimberley, James Russell.

"Before this seat.

"Hen. Gibbons, Wm. Basse .,

MINIST

Deacon Miles.

Jeremiah Whitnell, Thos. Morris, Richard Johnson.

Thos. Wheeler, Wm. Thorp, Richard Hull, Francis Brown.

1 Mr. Gilbert.

2 Mr. Jones, Mr. John Davenport, jr., Mr. Yale, Mr. William Gibbard.

3 **Mr. Goodenhouse, Mr. Tuttle,** William Judson, John Gibbs, Lieut. Nash.

4 Mr. Hodson, William Andrews, John Cooper, Roger Alling, James Bishop.

5 William Thompson, William Potter, Matthew Moulthrop, Christopher Todd. William Bradley. John Harriman.

6 Henry Glover, Nicholas Elsey, John Moss, John Thompson, John Brockett, John Winston, Thomas Mix.

7 Jeremy Howe, Nathaniel Merriman, Thos. Barnes, Geo. Smith, Timothy Ford, Ralph Lines, William Gibbons.

8 Robert Hill, William Meeker, Ephraim Howe, Thomas Harrison, Matthew Rowe, John Johnson, Jos. Mansfield.

9 Edward Parker, Thomas Lamson, William Trowbridge, John Alling, Edward Preston.

1 SOLDIERS' SEATS.

2 "   "

3 "   "

1 Sam. Blackley, Will. Wooden, Hen. Humiston, Wm. Wilmot.

2 Ellis Mew, James Brooks, John Osbill, James Dennison.

3 Wm. Chatterton, John Ware.

FEBRUARY 2(

Sister Andrews, Sister Boykin.

Jeremiah Hull, Edward Perkins.

John Jackson. STEPS OF STAIRS.

Hen. Bristow, John Hall, Thos. Beamont, Hen. Lines.

Mr. Rutherford. Mr. Mullener, John Punderson, David Atwater. 1

Mr. Field, Mr. Augur, Mr. Nathanael Street, Ensign Munson. 2

Sergt. Whitehead, Sergt. Russell, Joseph Alsop, John Chidsey. 3

Thomas Trowbridge, Thomas Johnson, Jeremiah Osborne, Allen Ball. 4

LITTLE SEAT.
Thomas Kimberly, James Russell.

Hen. Gibbons, Wm. Bassett.

John Gilbert, Geo. Pardee, Wm. Holt.

Thos. Powell, William Paine, James Clarke, Abraham Doolittle. 1

Matthias Hitchcock, Andrew Low, Benj. Wilmot, John Thomas, Humph. Spinage. 2

Edward Patteson, John Tuttle, Richard Sperry. 3

John Sacket, Sam. Marsh, Peter Mallery, Robert Foot. 4

John Potter, Abraham Dickerman, Isaac Beecher, Thos. Kimberly, jr. 1

Jonathan Tuttle, James Eaton, John Clark, Isaac Turner. 2

John Benham, Geo. Ross, Martin Tichener, Philip Leeke. 3

Anthony Elcot, Joseph Benham, Richard Newman, Joseph Potter. 4

Henry Morrell, Samuel Hodskins, John Brown, Wm. Pringle. 5

E R.

Deacon Peck.

Sister Parker, Sister Beamont, Goodwife Ball.

Sister Harriman, Sister Glover, Sister Munson, James Russell's wife.

Mrs. Goodyear, Mrs. Gilbert. 1

Mrs. Gregson, Mrs. Davenport, Mrs. Street, Mrs. Jones. 2

Sister Miles, Sister Peck, Sister Lindon, Sister Tuttle, Sister Gibbard. 3

Sister Davis, Sister Gibbs, Sister Rutherford, Sister Hodson, Sister Nash. 4

Sister Atwater, Sister Johnson, sen., Sister Judson, Sister Bishop, Sister Mix. 5

Sister Bradley, Sister Todd, Sister Moss, Sister Moulthrop, Goodwife Potter, Wm. Russell's wife. 6

Sister Osborne, Sister Thompson, Sister Talmadge, Sister Brockett, Sister Smith, Sister Doolittle. 7

Goodwife Mansfield, Goodwife Hitchcock, Goodw. Harrison, Sister Merriman, Sis. Barnes, John Johnson's wife 8

Ephraim Howe's wife, Ralph Lines's wife, John Potter's wife, Goodwife Spinage, Benj. Wilmot's wife, John Alling's wife. 9

SOLDIERS' SEATS. 1

"   " 2

"   " 3

First middle seat, vacant or occupied by children and servants. 1

2

3

), 1661-2.

1 Sister Field, Sister Clark, Goodwife Sperry.

2 Mrs. Allerton, Mrs. Mullener, Mrs. Yale, Mrs. Yale, Hannah Lamberton.

3 Sister Punderson, Sister Kimberly, Sister Elsey.

4 Thomas Trowbridge's wife, Wm. Trowbridge's wife, Sister Thorp, Sister Daniel.

5 Sister Howe, Thos. Johnson's wife, Sister Brown, Goodwife Paine.

Sister Cooper.

1 Sister Powell, Sister Jones, Sister Chidsey, Goodwife Alsop.

2 Sister Whitehead, Sister Humiston, Sister Bassett.

3 Goodwife Pardee, Sister Thomas, Goodwife Gibbons, Goodwife Rowe.

4 Goodwife Meeker, Sister Marsh, John Tuttle's wife, Thos. Tuttle's wife.

1 Sister Tichener, Sister Leeke, Goodwife Dickerman, Goodwife Foot.

2 John Benham's wife, Joseph Benham's wife, Edward Preston's wife, Goodwife Hodskins.

3 Goodwife Mallery, Hen. Lines's wife, John Brown's wife, Goodwife Beecher.

4 Goodwife Newman, Goodwife Humiston, Joseph Potter's wife, Goodwife Wooden.

Sister Pennington, Sister Bristow.

LITTLE SHORT SEAT.

Sister Alling, Sister Parmelee.

Sister Mitchell, Sister Low, Sister Holt, Sister Hall, Sister Morris, Goodwife Ford, Sister Jackson.

STEPS OF STAIRS.

APPENDIX IV.

"In the side seats above the door.

"Thos. Powell, William Paine, James Clarke, Abraham Doolittle.

"2. Matthias Hitchcock, Andrew Low, Benj. Wilmot, John Thomas, Humph. Spinage.

"3. Edward Patteson, John Tuttle, Richard Sperry.

"4. John Sacket, Sam. Marsh, Peter Mallery, Robert Foot.

"Below the door.

"1. John Potter, Abraham Dickerman, Isaac Beecher, Thos Kimberley, Jr.

"2. Jonathan Tuttle, James Eaton, John Clark, Issac Turner.

"3. John Benham, Geo. Ross, Martin Tichener, Philip Leeke.

"4. Anthony Elcot, Joseph Benham, Richard Newman, Joseph Potter.

"5. Henry Morrell, Samuel Hodskins, John Brown, Wm. Pringle.

"Against the soldiers' seat.

"1. Sam. Blackley, Will. Wooden, Hen. Humiston, Wm. Wilmot.

"2. Ellis Mew, James Brooks, John Osbill, James Dennison.

"3. Wm. Chatterton, John Ware.

"Before the governor's seat.

"Thos. Wheeler, Wm. Thorp, Richard Hull, Francis Brown.

"Before Deacon Miles his seat.

"Jeremiah Whitnell, Thos. Morris, Richard Johnson.

"On the steps.

"John Jackson.

APPENDIX IV.

"Before Mr. Rutherford's seat.

"Hen. Bristow, John Hall, Thos. Beamont, Hen. Lines.

"Before the pillar.

"Jeremiah Hull, Edward Perkins.

"In the long seats for women.

"1. Mrs. Goodyear, Mrs. Gilbert.
"2. Mrs. Gregson, Mrs. Davenport, Mrs. Street, Mrs. Jones.
"3. Sister Miles, Sister Peck, Sister Lindon, Sister Tuttle, Sister Gibbard.
"4. Sister Davis, Sister Gibbs, Sister Rutherford, Sister Hodson, Sister Nash.
"5. Sister Atwater, Sister Johnson, sen., Sister Judson, Sister Bishop, Sister Mix.
"6. Sister Bradley, Sister Todd. Sister Moss, Sister Moulthrop, Goodwife Potter, Wm. Russell's wife.
"7. Sister Osborne, Sister Thompson, Sister Talmadge, Sister Brockett, Sister Smith, Sister Doolittle.
"8. Goodwife Mansfield, Goodwife Hitchcock, Goodwife Harrison, Sister Merriman, Sister Barnes, John Johnson's wife.
"9. Ephraim Howe's wife, Ralph Lines's wife, John Potter's wife, Goodwife Spinage, Benj. Wilmot's wife, John Alling's wife.

"In the short seats at the upper end.

"1. Mrs. Allerton, Mrs. Mullener, Mrs. Yale, Hannah Lamberton.
"2. Sister Punderson, Sister Kimberley, Sister Elsey.
"3. Thomas Trowbridge's wife, Wm. Trowbridge's wife, Sister Thorp, Sister Daniel.
"4. Sister Howe, Thos. Johnson's wife, Sister Brown, Goodwife Paine.

"*In the long seat next the wall.*

"Sister Mitchell, Sister Low, Sister Holt, Sister Hall, Sister Morris, Goodwife Ford, Sister Jackson.

"*In the little short seat.*

"Sister Alling, Sister Parmelee.

"*Before this seat.*

"Sister Pennington, Sister Bristow.

"*In the side seats above the door.*

"1. Sister Powell, Sister Jones, Sister Chidsey, Goodwife Alsop.

"2. Sister Whitehead, Sister Humiston, Sister Bassett.

"3. Goodwife Pardee, Sister Thomas, Goodwife Gibbons, Goodwife Rowe.

"4. Goodwife Meeker, Sister Marsh, John Tuttle's wife, Thos. Tuttle's wife.

"*Below the door.*

"Sister Tichener, Sister Leeke, Goodwife Dickerman, Goodwife Foot.

"2. John Benham's wife, Joseph Benham's wife, Edward Preston's wife, Goodwife Hodskins.

"3. Goodwife Mallery, Hen. Lines's wife, John Brown's wife, Goodwife Beecher.

"4. Goodwife Newman, Goodwife Humiston, Joseph Potter's wife, Goodwife Wooden.

"*Before Deacon Peck's seat,*

"Sister Parker, Sister Beamont, Goodwife Ball.

"*Before Mrs. Goodyear's seat.*

"Sister Harriman, Sister Glover, Sister Munson, James Russell's wife.

"*Before Mrs. Allerton's seat.*

"Sister Field, Sister Clark, Goodwife Sperry.

"*Before the pillar.*

" Sister Cooper.

"Sister Andrews and Sister Boykin had liberty, for convenience of hearing, to sit in the alley."

APPENDIX V.

HOPKINS GRAMMAR SCHOOL.

[The full text of Mr. Davenport's Deed of Trust mentioned on p. 291.]

To all Christian people to whom these presents shall come, I John Davenport, sen., pastor of the Church of Christ at New Haven in New England, send greeting:

Whereas Edward Hopkins, Esquire, sometime of Hartford in the colony of Connecticut in New England aforesaid, governor, and since in Old England deceased, by his last will and testament in writing, bearing date the 7th of March, 1657, did give and bequeath to his father-in-law Theophilus Eaton, Esquire, then governor of New Haven colony, the said John Davenport, Mr. John Cullick and Mr. William Goodwin sometime of Hartford aforesaid, all the residue and remainder of his estate in New England (his due debts being first paid and legacies discharged), and also the sum of £500 out of his estate in Old England within six months after the decease of his wife, Mrs. Anne Hopkins, by the advice of Mr. Robert Thompson and Mr. Francis Willoughby to be made over and conveyed into the hands of the said trustees in New England, in full assurance of their trust and faithfulness in dispose of the said remainder of his estate in New England and of the said £500 in Old England, according to the true intent and purpose of him, the said Edward Hopkins, declared in his said will, viz., for the encouragement and breeding up of hopeful youths, both at the grammar school and college, for the public service of the country in these foreign plantations, as in and by the will doth and may more fully and at large appear.

And whereas the said Mr. William Goodwin and the said John Davenport, the only surviving trustees of the above-named

Edward Hopkins, by an instrument or writing under our hands and seals bearing date the 27th of April, 1664, having agreed upon an equitable division, settlement, and dispose of the said remainder of estate above mentioned, received or secured by us severally, or our attornies, and of the said £500, to the use or us s aforesaid; whereby the sum of £412, part of the said remainder besides the full moiety or half part of the said £500, when it shall become due and received as aforesaid, is by me, the said John Davenport, to be disposed of according to the true intent and meaning of the said testator, as in the said instrument or writing agreed upon: KNOW YE THEREFORE that I, the said John Davenport, in pursuance of the said trust in me reposed, and that the grammar school or college at New Haven already founded and begun may be provided for, maintained, and continued for the encouragement and bringing up of hopeful youths in the languages and other good literature, for the public use and service of the country, according to the sincere and true intent of the donor as above mentioned, and to no other use, intent, or purpose whatsoever, do give, grant, infeoff, and confirm, and have by these presents given, granted, infeoffed, and confirmed unto Mr. William Jones, assistant of the colony of Connecticut, the Reverend Mr. Nicholas Street, teacher of the Church of Christ at New Haven, Mr. Matthew Gilbert, Mr. John Davenport, jun., and James Bishop, commissioned magistrates, Deacon William Peck, and Roger Alling, and to their successors to be nominated, appointed, and chosen as hereafter in these presents is ordered and directed, the said sum of £412, and the said moiety or half-part of the said £500, and all and every other sum or sums of money, or other estate which is or may be due by virtue of the aforesaid grant or agreement forever, under the name or title of the Committee of Trustees for the said trust, invested hereby with full power and authority to improve and dispose of the said sums or estate as before expressed, and to oversee, regulate, order, and direct the said grammar or collegiate school according to their best skill, understanding, and ability, in pursuance of the said trust and ends, in full assurance that they, the said committee and their successors regularly chosen and appointed, shall so manage and dispose of the said sums or other estate herein mentioned, to the true ends, purposes, and intents of the said donor, in his last will and testament declared and expressed, and to the true meaning and intent of me, the said John Davenport, in these presents before declared and directed, or to be hereby further declared and directed, and not otherwise: that is to say, for the purchasing a farm or farms for a yearly revenue for the schoolmaster, or building such dwelling-house for the schoolmaster as the said committee, their successors, or the major part of them, shall judge necessary and convenient; and the said house and present school-house (being granted and confirmed by the said town of New Haven for the use of the said school) to uphold, maintain, and keep in good and sufficient repair from time to time, out of the rents, issues, and profits of the said money or estate so given and granted as aforesaid. And the said committee, or the major part of them, or of their successors, meeting together from time to time, in some convenient place and agreeing, are hereby fully empowered and authorized to consult, determine, and conclude, act, and do in the premises as is above ordained, appointed and directed, and to conclude, act, and do, all other thing or things thereabouts in pursuance of the said trust and the true meaning and intent of the foresaid donor, as fully and amply as I, the said John Davenport, by virtue of the trust to me committed in and by the said will, or by any other way or means whatsoever might lawfully do in the dispose of the said estate, all, or any part of it, to the ends aforesaid; and do further invest them, the said committee and their successors, and the major part of them, with full power, authority, and trust, to order, regulate, and direct the said collegiate school, by such laws and rules as are by me provided, or shall be further as additionals by them, or the major part of them, judged necessary and expedient for the better ordering, regulating, and directing of the said school for the advancement of learning and good government therein; and to make choice of such school-master (and usher, if need be) as they shall approve of to be sufficiently qualified to undertake such a charge, and able to instruct and teach the three learned languages, Latin, Greek, and Hebrew, so far as shall be necessary to prepare and fit youth for the college; and to state and allow out of the said rents and profits such yearly stipend and salary toward his or their encouragement and maintenance as they, the said committee, or the major part of them, or of their successors, shall judge meet and convenient; and also upon just grounds, either insufficiency, wilful neglect of trust, scandal, or the like causes, to exclude or remove him or them upon due proof and conviction of such offences, and to provide, to nominate, and choose some other fit person or persons in his or their room and place. And that there may be a certain and orderly succession of able and fit persons to manage the several trusts herein before mentioned in the room and place of any of the said committee or trustees before named, that shall die or remove his or their dwelling from New Haven aforesaid, the said committee, or the major part of them surviving, shall immediately, or at furthest within three months after, choose such other person or persons of known integrity and faithfulness, to succeed in the room and place of any such person or persons so dying or removing as aforesaid, that the work may be carried on (in the said grammar or collegiate school) hereby committed to them, that so learning may be duly encouraged and furthered therein, in the training up of such hopeful youth as, in time, by the blessing of God upon good endeavors, may be fitted for public service in church and commonwealth, for the upholding and promoting of the kingdom of our Lord Jesus Christ in these parts of the earth, according to the true and sincere desire and ends of the aforesaid Worthy Donor in his said last will and testament mentioned and expressed. And because I stand under an engagement to attend the will of the said donor deceased, that his ends may be attained in the dispose of his said legacy, if the said committee or their successors shall find the said ends by this grant not attained at New Haven, and that the said grammar or collegiate school hereby endowed and provided for, should be dissolved and wholly cease, I do obtest them by the will of the dead, which no man may alter, and by the trust committed to me and them, whereof we must give our account to the great Judge of all, that this gift of the said Edward Hopkins, Esquire, deceased, be by them the said committee wholly transferred and disposed of elsewhere, where the said ends may be attained. But if the true ends of the testator and of this settlement be attained at New Haven, I stand firm to the place in this my grant, reserving nevertheless to myself in all cases, matters, and things respecting the laying out or improvement of the said estate, as aforesaid, for the said school, full power of a negative voice whilst it shall please God to continue my living and abiding in this country, or any part of it, to hinder and prevent any act or acts, thing or things, to be acted or done in or about the premises, to the detriment of the said estate, or contrary to the said trust to be committed and hereby transferred to the said committee and their successors aforesaid, upon this further condition, that the rent, profit, and improvement of the Oyster-shell Field, containing by estimation forty acres, more or less, formerly separated and reserved for the use and benefit of a college at New Haven, and also one other field commonly called Mrs. Eldred's lot, containing by estimation three acres more or less, be to the use of the said school at New Haven forever settled, ratified, and confirmed by the said town accordingly. And to prevent any further re-interruption which this settlement by me made may meet with by reason of a former grant of the abovesaid sum or sums of money and estate for encouragement of a colony school at New Haven, made by a memorandum in writing under my hand, containing sundry particulars to that purpose, and bearing date the fourth day of the fourth month, 1660, the same being registered in the records of the then General Court, and by the said Court at the time approved and accepted, as by the said records, page 260, doth appear, I therefore, the said John Davenport, in regard that the said Court by their act bearing date the 5th of November, 1662, for sundry reasons therein alleged, did lay down and discharge the said school, and withdraw the yearly exhibition by them formerly allowed, whereby (the said school being so dissolved) the said grant by me made became null and void: I do therefore hereby declare the same to be null and void accordingly, any thing in the said writing or memorandum to the contrary notwithstanding. And the grant herein made of the premises to be good against the same, and against all or any other pretences whatsoever, according to my true intent and meaning herein before declared and expressed. In witness whereof I have hereunto set my hand and seal the eighteenth day of the second month, commonly called April; one thousand six hundred, sixty and eight.

JOHN DAVENPORT, Senior. { L. S. }

Signed, sealed, and delivered by the Reverend Mr. John Davenport, senior, as his act and deed, in the presence of

BENJAMIN LING,
JOHN HODSON.

This is a true record of the original examined by me.

JAMES BISHOP, *Recorder*.

APPENDIX VI.

NEW HAVEN'S REMONSTRANCE.

THE Remonstrance or Declaration sent to the General Assembly of Connecticut Colony from this Court is as follows:—

GENTLEMEN,—The professed grounds and ends of your and our coming into these parts are not unknown, being plainly expressed in the prologue to that solemn confederation entered into by the four colonies of New England, printed and published to the world, namely: to advance the kingdom of our Lord Jesus Christ, and to enjoy the liberties of the gospel in purity with peace, for which we left our dear native country and were willing to undergo the difficulties we have since met with in this wilderness, yet fresh in our remembrance; being the only ends we still pursue, having hitherto found by experience so much of the presence of God with us, and of his goodness and compassion towards us in so doing these many years. Yet, considering how unanswerable our returns have been to God, how unfruitful, unthankful, and unholy under so much means of grace and such liberties, we cannot but lament the same, judge ourselves and justify God, should he now at last (after so long patience towards us) bring desolating judgments upon us, and make us drink of the dregs of that cup of indignation he hath put into the hands of his people in other parts of the world, or suffer such contentions (in just displeasure) to arise among us as may hasten our calamity and increase our woe, which we pray the Lord in mercy to prevent. And, whereas, in the pursuance of such ends, and upon other religious and civil considerations, as the security of the interest of each colony within its self in ways of righteousness and peace, and all and every of the said colonies from the Indians and other enemies, they did judge it to be their bounden duty for mutual strength and helpfulness for the future in all their said concernments, to enter into a consociation among themselves, thereupon fully agreed and concluded by and between the parties or jurisdictions in divers and sundry articles, and at last ratified as a perpetual confederation by their several subscriptions, whereunto we conceive ourselves bound to adhere, until with satisfaction to our judgments and consciences we see our duty, with like unanimous consent of the confederates, orderly to recede, leaving the issue unto the most wise and righteous God.

As for the Patent upon your petition granted to you by his Majesty, as Connecticut Colony, so far, and in that sense, we object not against it, much less against his Majesty's act in so doing, the same being a real encouragement to other of his subjects to obtain the like favour upon their humble petition to his Royal Highness in the protection of their persons and purchased rights and interests, is also a ground of hope to us. But, if the line of your Patent doth circumscribe this Colony by your contrivement, without our cognizance or consent, or regard to the said confederation on your parts, we have and must still testify against it, as not consistent (in our judgment) with brotherly love, righteousness and peace. And that this Colony (for so long a time a confederate jurisdiction, distinct from yours and the other colonies) is taken in under the administration of the said Patent in your hands, and so its form being dissolved, and distinction ceasing, there being no one line or letter in the Patent expressing his Majesty's pleasure that way, although it is your sense of it, yet we cannot so apprehend, of which we have already given our grounds at large in writing, we shall not need to say much more, nor have we met with any argumentative or rational convictions from you, nor do we yet see cause to be of another mind. As for your proceedings upon pretence of the Patent towards us, or rather against us, in taking sundry inhabitants of this Colony under your protection and government, who (as you say) offered themselves, from which a good conscience and the obligation under which most of them stood to this Colony should have restrained them, without the consent of the body of this Colony first had, and in concurrence with them, upon mature deliberation and conviction of duty yet wanting, we cannot but again testify against as disorderly in them, and which admission on your parts we conceive your Christian prudence might have easily suspended, for prevention of that great offence to the consciences of your confederate brethren and those sad consequences which have followed, disturbing the peace of our towns, destroying our comforts, and hazard of our lives and liberties by their frequent threats and unsufferable provocations, hath been and is with us a matter of complaint both to God and man; especially when we consider that thus you admitted them, and put power into their hands, before you had made any overture to us or had any treaty with us about so weighty a business, as if you were in haste to make us miserable, as indeed in these things we are at this day.

And seeing upon the answer returned to your propositions made by you afterwards of joining with you in your governments, finding ourselves so already dismembered, and the weighty gronnds and reasons we then presented to you, we could not prevail so far with you as to procure a respite of your further proceedings until Mr. Winthrop's return from England, or the grant of any time that way, which was thought but reasonable by some of yourselves, and the like seldom denied in war to very enemies, we saw it then high time and necessary (fearing these beginnings) to appeal unto his Majesty, and so we did, concluding according to the law of appeals in all cases and among all nations, that the same (upon your allegiance to his Majesty) would have obliged you to forbear all further process in this business, for our own parts resolving (notwithstanding all that he had formerly suffered) to sit down patient under the same, waiting upon God for the issue of our said appeal.

But seeing that notwithstanding all that we had presented to you by word and writing, notwithstanding our appeal to his Majesty, notwithstanding all that we have suffered (by means of that power you had set up, viz., a constable at Stamford), of which informations have been given you, yet you have gone further to place a constable at Guilford, in like manner, over a party there, to the further disturbance of our peace and quiet, a narrative whereof, and of the provocations and wrongs we have met with at Stamford, we have received, attested to us by divers witnesses, honest men, we cannot but on behalf of our appeal to his Majesty, whose honor is highly concerned therein, and of our just rights, but (as men exceedingly afflicted and grieved) testify in the sight of God, angels, and men, against these things; our end therein being not to provoke or further any offence, but rather, as a discharge of duty on our parts as brethren and Christian confederates, to call upon you to take some effectual course to ease and right us in a due redress of the grievances you have caused by these proceedings, such, and that after you had complimented us with large offers of patent privileges, with desire of a treaty with us for union of our colonies. And you know as your good words were kindly accepted, so your motion was fairly answered by our committee, that in regard we were under an appeal to his Majesty, that being limited by our freemen not to conclude any thing for altering our distinct colony state and government without their consent and wihout the approbation of the other confederate colonies, they were not in present capacity so to treat; but did little suspect such a design on foot against us, the effect whereof quickly appeared at Guilford before mentioned. But we shall say no more at this time, only to tell you, whatever we suffer by your means, we pray the Lord would help us to choose it rather than to sin against our consciences, hoping the righteous God will in due time look upon our affliction, and incline his Majesty's heart to favor our righteous cause.

Subscribed in the name and by order of the General Court of New Haven Colony.

℔ JAMES BISHOP,
Secretary.

NEW HAVEN, May 6, 1663.

APPENDIX VII.

NEW HAVEN'S CASE STATED.

[*To the honored John Winthrop, Esq., Governor, or to the honored Major Mason, Deputy Governor of Connecticut Colony, to be communicated to the honored the General Assembly for the said Colony.*]

HONORED 'AND BELOVED IN THE LORD,—We, the General Court of New Haven Colony, being sensible of the wrongs which this Colony hath lately suffered by your unjust pretences and encroachments upon our just and proper rights, have unanimously consented, though with grief of heart, being compelled thereunto, to declare unto you and unto all whom the knowledge thereof may concern, what yourselves do or may know to be true, as followeth,

1. That the first beginners of these plantations by the seaside in these western parts of New England, being engaged to sundry friends in London and in other places about London (who purposed to plant, some with them in the same town, and others as near to them as they might), to provide for themselves some convenient places by the sea-side, arrived at Boston in the Massachusetts (having a special right in their Patent, two of them being joint purchasers of it with others, and one of them a patentee and one of the assistants chosen for the New England Company in London), where they abode all the winter following, but not finding there a place suitable for their purpose, were persuaded to view these parts, which those that viewed approved, and before their removal, finding that no English were planted in any place from the fort (called Saybrook) to the Dutch, purposed to purchase of the Indians, the

natural proprietors of those lands, that whole tract of land by the sea-coast for themselves and those that should come to them, which they also signified to their friends at Hartford, in Connecticut Colony, and desired that some fit men from thence might be employed in that business, at their proper cost and charges who wrote to them. Unto which letter having received a satisfying answer, they acquainted the court of magistrates of Massachusetts Colony with their purpose to remove and the grounds of it, and with their consent began a plantation in a place situated by the sea, called by the Indians Quillipiac, which they did purchase of the Indians the true proprietors thereof, for themselves and their posterity, and have quietly possessed the same about six and twenty years, and have buried great estates in buildings, fencings, clearing the ground, and in all sorts of husbandry, without any help from Connecticut or dependence upon them. And by voluntary consent among themselves they settled a civil court and government among themselves, upon such fundamentals as were established in Massachusetts by allowance of their patent, whereof the then governor of the Bay, the Right Worshipful Mr. Winthrop sent us a copy to improve for our best advantage. These fundamentals all the inhabitants of the said Quillipiac approved, and bound themselves to submit unto and maintain, and chose Theophilus Eaton, Esq., to be their governor, with as good right as Connecticut settled their government among themselves and continued it above twenty years without any patent.

2. That when the help of Mr. Eaton our governor and some others from Quillipiac was desired for ending of a controversy at Wethersfield, a town in Connecticut Colony; it being judged necessary for peace that one party should remove their [371] dwellings, upon equal satisfying terms proposed, the governor, magistrates, etc., of Connecticut offered for their part that if the party that would remove should find a fit place to plant in upon the river, Connecticut would grant it to them; and the governor of Quillipiac (now called New Haven), and the rest there joined with him and promised that if they should find a fit place for themselves by the sea-side, New Haven would grant it to them, which accordingly New Haven per-

formed and so the town of Stamford began and became a member of New Haven Colony, and so continueth unto this day. Thus in a public assembly in Connecticut was the distinct right of Connecticut upon the river and of New Haven by the sea-side declared with consent of the governor, magistrates, ministers and better sort of the people of Connecticut at that time.

3. That sundry other townships by the sea-side, and Southold on Long Island (being settled in their inheritances by right of purchase of their Indian proprietors), did voluntarily join themselves to New Haven to be all under one jurisdiction, by a firm engagement to the fundamentals formerly settled in New Haven, whereupon it was called New Haven Colony. The general court being thus constituted, chose the said Theophilus Eaton, Esq.; a man of singular wisdom, godliness and experience to be the governor of New Haven Colony, and they chose a competent number of magistrates and other officers for the several towns. Mr. Eaton so well managed that great trust that he was chosen governor every year while he lived. All this time Connecticut never questioned what was done at New Haven, nor pretended any right to it, or to any of the towns belonging to this colony, nor objected against our being a distinct colony.

4. That when the Dutch claimed a right to New Haven and all along the coast by the sea-side, it being reported they would set up the prince of Orange's arms, the governor of New Haven to prevent that, caused the king of England's arms to be fairly cut in wood and set upon a post in the highway by the sea-side, to vindicate the right of the English, without consulting Connecticut, or seeking their concurrence therein.

5. That in the year 1643, upon weighty considerations, an union of four distinct colonies was agreed upon by all New England (except Rhode Island) in their several general courts, and was established by a most solemn confederation, whereby they bound themselves mutually to preserve unto each colony its entire jurisdiction within itself respectively, and to avoid the putting of two into one by any act of their own without consent of the commissioners from the four united colonies, which were

from that time and still are called and known by the title of *the four United Colonies of New England;* of these colonies New Haven was and is one. And in this solemn confederation Connecticut joined with the rest and with us.

6. That in the year 1644, the General Court for New Haven Colony, then sitting in the town of New Haven, agreed unanimously to send to England for a Patent, and in the year 1645, committed the procuring of it to Mr. Gregson, one of our magistrates, who entered upon his voyage in January that year from New Haven, furnished with some beaver in order thereunto as we suppose, but by the providence of God, the ship and all the passengers and goods were lost at sea in their passage toward England, to our great [loss] and the frustration of that design for that time; after which the troubles in England put a stop to our proceedings therein. This was done with the consent and desire of Connecticut to concur with New Haven therein; whereby the difference of times and of men's spirits in them may be discovered, for then the magistrates of Connecticut with consent of their General Court knowing our purposes, desired to join with New Haven in procuring that patent for common privileges to both in their distinct jurisdictions, and left it to Mr. Eaton's wisdom to have the patent framed accordingly. But now they seek to procure a patent without the concurrence of New Haven, and contrary to our minds expressed before this patent was sent for, and to their own promise, and to the terms of the confederation; and without sufficient warrant from their patent they have invaded our right, and seek to involve New Haven under Connecticut jurisdiction.

7. That in the year 1646, when the commissioners first met at New Haven, Kieft, the then Dutch governor, by letters expostulated with the commissioners, by what warrant they met at New Haven without his consent, seeing it and all by the sea-coast belonged to his principals in Holland, and to the Lords the States General. The answer to that letter was framed by Mr. Eaton, governor of New Haven and then president of the commission, approved by all the commissioners, and sent in their names, with their consent, to the then Dutch governor, who never replied thereunto.

8. That this colony in the reign of the late King Charles the first, received a letter from the committee of Lords and Commons for foreign plantations, then sitting at Westminster, which letter was delivered to our governor, Mr. Eaton, for freeing the several distinct colonies of New England from molestations by the appealing of troublesome spirits unto England, whereby they declared that they had dismissed all causes depending before them from New England, and that they advised all inhabitants to submit to their respective governments there established, and to acquiesce when their causes shall be there heard and determined; as it is to be seen more largely expressed in the original, which we have subscribed,

Your assured friends,

PEMBROOK, MANCHESTER, WARWICK,
W. SAY & SEAL, FR. DACRE, etc., DENBIGH.

In this order they subscribed their names with their own hands, which we have to show, and they inscribed or directed this letter,

To our worthy friends, the governor and assistants of the plantations of New Haven, in New England.

Whereby you may clearly see that the right honorable the earl of Warwick and the lord viscount Say and Seal (lately one of his majesty's that now is, King Charles the Second his most honorable privy council, as also the right honorable earl of Manchester still is), had no purpose, after New Haven Colony situated by the sea-side was settled to be a distinct government, that it should be put under the patent for Connecticut, whereof they had only framed a copy, before any house was erected by the sea-side from the fort to the Dutch, which yet was not signed and sealed by the last king for a patent, nor had you any patent till your agent Mr. Winthrop procured it about two years since.

9. That in the year 1650, when the commissioners for *the four United Colonies of New England* met at Hartford, the now Dutch governor being then and there present, Mr. Eaton, the then governor of New Haven Colony, complained of the

Dutch governor's encroaching upon our colony of New Haven, by taking under his jurisdiction a township beyond Stamford, called Greenwich. All the commissioners (as well for Connecticut as for the other colonies) concluded that Greenwich and four miles beyond it belongs to New Haven jurisdiction, whereunto the Dutch governor then yielded, and restored it to New Haven Colony. Thus were our bounds westward settled by consent of all.

10. That when the honored governor of Connecticut, John Winthrop, Esq., had consented to undertake a voyage for England to procure a patent for Connecticut in the [year] 1661, a friend warned him by letter not to have his hand in so unrighteous an act, as so far to extend the line of their patent that the colony of New Haven should be involved within it. For answer thereunto, he was pleased to certify that friend in two letters which he wrote from two several places before his departure, that no such thing was intended, but rather the contrary, and that the magistrates had agreed and expressed in the presence of some ministers, that if their line should reach us (which they knew not, the copy being in England), yet New Haven Colony should be at full liberty to join with them or not. This agreement, so attested, made us secure, who else could have procured a patent for ourselves, within our own known bounds, according to purchase, without doing any wrong to Connecticut in their just bounds and limits.

11. That notwithstanding all the premises, in the year 1662, when you had received your patent under his majesty's hand and seal, contrary to your promise and solemn confederation and to common equity, at your first general assembly (which yet could not be called general without us, if we were under your patent, seeing none of us were by you called thereunto), you agreed among yourselves to treat with New Haven Colony about union, by your commissioners chosen for that end, within two or three days after that assembly was dissolved, but before the ending of that session you made an unrighteous breach in our colony, by taking under your patent some of ours from Stamford, and from Guilford, and from Southhold, contrary to your engagements to New Haven Colony, and without our con-

sent or knowledge. This being thus done, some sent from you to treat with us showed some of ours your patent, which being read, they declared to yours that New Haven Colony is not at all mentioned in your patent, and gave you some reasons why they believed that the king did not intend to put this colony under Connecticut without our desire or knowledge; and they added that you took a preposterous course in first dismembering this colony, and after that treating with it about union, which is as if one man purposing to treat with another about union first cut off from him an an arm and a leg and an ear, then to treat with him about union. Reverend Mr. Stone also, the teacher of the church at Hartford, was one of the committee, who being asked what he thought of this action, answered that he would not justify it.

12. After that conference, our committee sent, by order of the General Court, by two of our magistrates and two of our elders a writing containing sundry other reasons for our not joining with you, who also finding that you persisted in your own will and way, declared to you our own resolution to appeal to his majesty to explain his true intendment and meaning in your patent, whether it was to subject this colony under it or not; being persuaded, as we still are, that it neither was or is his royal will and pleasure to confound this colony with yours, which would destroy the so long continued, and so strongly settled distinction of *the four United Colonies of New England*, without our desire or knowledge.

13. That accordingly we forthwith sent our appeals to be humbly presented to his majesty by some friends in London, yet out of our dear and tender respect to Mr. Winthrop's peace and honor, some of us advised those friends to communicate our papers first to honored Mr. Winthrop himself, to the end that we might find out some effectual expedient to put a good end to this uncomfortable difference between you and us; else to present our humble address to his majesty. Accordingly it was done, and Mr. Winthrop stopped the proceedings of our appeal by undertaking to our friends that matters should be issued to our satisfaction, and in order thereunto he was pleased to write a letter to Major Mason your deputy governor, and the

rest of the court of Connecticut Colony, from London, dated March 3d, 1662, in these words:—

GENTLEMEN,—I am informed by some gentlemen who are authorized to seek remedy here, that since you had a late patent there hath been injury done to the government of Newhaven, and in particular at Guilford and Stamford in admitting several of the inhabitants there unto freedom with you, and appointing officers, which hath caused division in the said towns, which may prove of dangerous consequence if not timely prevented, though I do hope the rise of it is from misunderstanding and not in design of prejudice to that colony, for whom I gave assurance to their friends that their rights and interests should not be disquieted or prejudiced by the patent. But if both governments would with unanimous agreement unite in one, their friends judged it would be for advantage to both; and farther, I must let you know that testimony here doth affirm that I gave assurance before authority here, that it was not intended to meddle with any town, or plantation that was settled under any other government. Had it been any otherwise intended or declared, it had been injurions in taking out the patent not to have inserted a proportionable number of their names in it. Now upon the whole, having had serious conference with their friends authorized by them, and with others who are friends to both, to prevent a tedious and chargeable trial and uncertain event here, I promised them to give you speedily this representation, how far you are engaged, if any injury hath been done by admitting of freemen, or appointing officers, or any other intermeddling with New Haven Colony in one kind or other without approbation of the governments, that it be forthwith recalled, and that for the future there will be no imposing upon them nor admitting of any members without mutual consent, but that all things be acted as loving, neighbouring colonies, as before such patent granted. And unto this I judge you are obliged, I haveing engaged to their agents here that this will be by you performed, and they have thereupon forborne to give you or me any further trouble. But they do not doubt but upon future consideration there may be such a right understanding between both governments that a union and friendly jotning may be established to the satisfaction of all, which at my arrival I shall endeavor (God willing) to promote. Not having more at present in this case, I rest,

Your humble servant

JOHN WINTHROP.

APPENDIX VII. 573

The copy of this letter was sent to Mr. Leete unsealed, with Mr. Winthrop's consent, and was written by his own hand, and the substance of this agreement between some of our friends in London is fully attested by them in their letters to some of us. Say not that Mr. Winthrop's acting in this agreement is nothing to you, for he acted therein as your public and common agent and plenipotentiary, and therefore his acting in that capacity and relation are yours in him.

14. That after Mr. Winthrop's return, when some from you treated again with our committee about union, it was answered by our committee that we could not admit any treaty with you about this matter till we might treat as an entire colony, our members being restored to us whom you have unrighteously withheld from us, whereby also those parties have been many ways injurious to this government, and disturbers of our peace, which is and will be a bar to any such treaty till it be removed, for till then we cannot join with you in one government without our fellowship in your sin.

15. That after this, nothing being done by you for our just satisfaction, at the last meeting of the commissioners from the four United Colonies of New England, at Boston on the —— day of September, 1663, the commissioners from New Haven Colony exhibited to the other commissioners their confederates, a complaint of the great injuries done to this colony by Connecticut, in the presence of your commissioners, who for answer thereunto showed what treaties they had made with New Haven, but that plea was inconsiderable through your persisting in unrighteously withholding our members from us, whereby our wounds remain unhealed, being kept open and continually bleeding. The result of the commissioner's debates about that complaint was in these words, "The commissioners of Massachusetts and Plymouth having considered the complaints exhibited by New Haven against Connecticut, for infringing their power of jurisdiction, as in the complaint is more particularly expressed, together with the answer returned thereto by Connecticut commissioners, with some other debates and conferences that have passed between them, do judge meet to

declare, that the said Colony of New Haven being owned in the Articles of Confederation as distinct from Connecticut, and having been so owned by the colonies in this present meeting, in all their actings, may not by any act of violence have their liberty of jurisdiction infringed by any other of the United Colonies without breach of the Articles of Confederation, and that where any act of power hath been exerted against their authority that the same ought to be recalled, and their power reserved to them entire, until such time as in an orderly way it shall be otherwise disposed. And for particular grievances mentioned in their complaint, that they be referred to the next meeting at Hartford," etc.

We suppose that when they speak of disposing it otherwise in an orderly way, they mean with our free consent, there being no other orderly way by any act or power of the United Colonies for disposing the colony of New Haven otherwise than as it is a distinct colony, having entire jurisdiction within itself, which our confederates are bound by their solemn confederation to pursue inviolate.

16. That before your general assembly in October last, 1663, our committee sent a letter unto the said assembly, whereby they did request that our members by you unjustly rent from us should be by you restored unto us, according to our former frequent desires, and according to Mr. Winrhrop's letter and promise to authority in England, and according to justice and according to the conclusion of the commissioners in their last session at Boston, whereunto you returned a real negative answer contrary to all the promises, by making one Brown your constable at Stamford; who hath been sundry ways injurious to us and hath scandalously acted in the highest degree of contempt, not only against the authority of this jurisdiction but also of the king himself, pulling down with contumelies the declaration which was sent thither, by the Court of magistrates for this colony, in the king's name, and commanded to be set up in a public place that it might be read and obeyed by all his majesty's subjects inhabiting our town of Stamford.

17. That thereupon at a general court held at New Haven for the jurisdiction, the 22d of Octoher, 1663, the deputies for this

general court signified the mind of our freemen as not at all satisfied with the proposal of the committee from Connecticut, but thought there should be no more treaty with them unless they first restore us to our right state again. The matter was largely debated, and this general court considering how they of Connecticut do cast off our motion in the forementioned letter and give us no answer. but that contrary thereunto, as is reported, they have further encouraged those at Guilford and Stamford, therefore this court did then order that no treaty be made by this colony with Connecticut before such acts of power exerted upon any of our towns be revoked and recalled, according to honored Mr. Winthrop's letter engaging the same, the commissioners' advice, and our frequent desires.

18. That in this juncture of time we received two letters from England, mentioned in the following declaration published by the court of magistrates upon that occasion, in these words; Whereas this colony hath received one letter under his majesty's royal hand and seal (manual in red wax) annexed, bearing date the 21st of June, 1663, from his royal court at Whitehall, directed To his trusty and well beloved subjects the governors and assistants of the Massachusetts, Plymouth, New Haven and Connecticut colonies in New England; and one other letter from the lords of his majesty's most honorable privy council, from his majesty's court aforesaid, bearing date the 24th of June in the year aforesaid, superscribed, For his majesty's special service, and directed To our very loving friend John Endicott, Esquire, governor of his majesty's plantations in New England, and to the governor and council of the colony of the Massachusetts, with the rest of the governors of the English plantations in New England respectively, and by order of the general court at Boston recorded in the court it is particularly directed to the governor of the colony of New Haven; in which letters his majesty hath commanded this colony many matters of weight, very much respecting his majesty's service and the good of his country in general, expecting upon displeasure the strict observance thereof, which this Court (this colony being situated by the sea-side, and so fitly accommodated to fulfil his majesty's commands) are resolved to

their utmost to obey and fulfil. But in their consultation thereabout, they find through the disloyal and seditious principles and practices of some men of inconsiderable interests, some of his majesty's good subjects in this colony have been seduced to rend themselves from this colony, by which division his majesty's affairs in these parts are like to suffer, the peace of this country to be endangered, and the heathen among us scandalized, in case some speedy course be not taken for the prevention thereof, the which if we should connive at, especially at this time his majesty having so particularly directed his royal commands to this colony aforesaid, we might justly incur his displeasure against us. This court therefore doth in his majesty's name require all the members and inhabitants of this colony heartily to close with the endeavors of the governor and assistants thereof for fulfilling his majesty's commands in the said letter expressed, and in order thereunto to return to their due obedience and paying their arrears of rates for defraying the necessary charges of the colony, and other dues, within six days after the publication hereof, unto such person or persons as are or shall be appointed to collect the same, in attendance to the laws and orders of this colony. All which being done this court shall forever pass by all former disobedience to this government; but if any shall presume to stand out against his majesty's pleasure so declared as aforesaid concerning this colony, at their peril be it. This Court shall not fail to call the said persons to a strict account and proceed against them as disloyal to his majesty and disturbers of the peace of this colony, according to law.

19. This declaration being grounded in general upon his majesty's commands expressed in these letters, and in special in orders to the preservation of his majesty's customs in that case provided for by act of this present parliament, which act was sent inclosed with the letter to our governor, requiring his strict observance of the same under the penalty of displacing and a thousand pounds fine, and therefore in case any difference should arise to his majesty upon these accounts, we must be inforced to lay the cause of it at your door, because when it was sent to the several towns of this colony, and set up in

public places to be seen and read of all, that all might obey it, it was at Stamford violently plucked down by Brown your constable, and with reproachful speeches rejected, though sent in his majesty's name, and by the authority of our court of magistrates. And after it was published at Guilford, Bray Rosseter and his son hastened to Connecticut to require your aid against this government, which accordingly you too hastily performed, for on the 30th of December, 1663, two of your magistrates with sundry young men and your marshal came speedily to Guilford accompanying Rosseter and his son, and countenancing them and their party against the authority of this general Court, though you know how obnoxious they were formerly to this jurisdiction, for contempt of authority and seditious practices, and that they have been the ringleaders of this rent, and that Bray Rosseter the father hath been long and still is a man of a turbulent, restless, factious spirit, and whose design you have cause to suspect to be to cause a war between these two colonies, or to ruin New Haven colony; yet him you accompanied in opposition to this colony, without sending or writing before to our governor to be informed concerning the truth in this matter. Sundry horses, as we are informed, accompanied them to Guilford, whither they came at unseasonable hour, about ten o'clock in the night these short days, when you might rationally think that all the people were gone to bed, and by shooting of sundry guns, some of yours or of their party in Guilford alarmed the town, which when the governor took notice of, and of the unsatisfying answer given to such as inquired the reason of that disturbance, he suspected, and that not without cause, that hostile attempts were intended by their company, whereupon he sent a letter to New Haven to inform the magistrates there concerning matters at Guilford, that many were affrighted, and he desired that the magistrates of New Haven would presently come to their succor and as many troopers as could be got, alleging for a reason his apprehension of their desperate resolutions. The governor's messengers also excited to haste, as apprehending danger and reporting to them that Branford went up in arms hastening to their relief at Guilford, which the governor required with speed. Hereupon New Haven was also alarmed that night by beating the drum, etc., to warn the town militia to be ready, etc. The fear was not causeless, for what else could be gathered from the preparations of pistols, bullets, swords, etc., which they brought with them, and by the threatening speeches given out by some of them, as is attested by the depositions of some and subscriptions of others, which we have by us to show when need require; and your two magistrates themselves, who ought to have kept the king's peace among their own party and in their own speeches, threatened our governor that if any thing was done against those men, i. e., Rosseter and his party, Connecticut would take it as done against themselves, for they were bound to protect them; and they rose high in threatenings, yet they joined therewith their desire of another conference with New Haven, pretending their purpose of granting to us what we would desire, so far as they could, if we would unite with them; but still they held our members from us and upheld them in their animosities against us. Is this the way to union? and what can you grant us which we have not in our own right within ourselves without you? Yea, it is the birthright of our posterity which we may not barter away from them by treaties with you. It is our purchased inheritance, which no wise man would part with upon a treaty to receive in lieu thereof a lease of the same, upon your terms who have no right thereunto. And why is our union with you by our coming under your patent urged now as necessary for peace? seeing we have enjoyed peace mutually while we have been distinct colonies for about twenty years past. And why do you separate the things which God hath joined together, viz., righteousness and peace, seeing you persist in your unrighteous dealing with us, and persuade us to peace. It is true we all came to New England with the same ends, and that we all agree in some main things, but it doth not follow from thence we ought therefore to unite with you in the same jurisdiction, for the same may be said of all the united colonies, which nevertheless are distinct colonies.

20. That upon a more diligent search of your patent, we find that New Haven colony is not included within the line of your patent, for we suppose that your bounds, according to the expression of your patent may be in a just grammatical construction so cleared, as that this colony, in every part of it may be mathematically demonstrated to be exempted from it.

21. That the premises being duly weighed, it will be your wisdom and way to desist wholly and forever from endeavoring to draw us into a union under your patent by any treaty for the future, and to apply yourselves to your duty towards God, the king, and us. 1st, Towards God, that you fear him, and therefore repent of your unrighteous dealing with us, and reform what you have done amiss, by restoring our members without delay unto us again, that you may escape the wrath of God which is revealed from heaven against all unrighteousness and against all that dishonor his holy name, especially among the heathen, which you have done thereby. 2. Toward the king, that you honor him by looking at us as a distinct colony within ourselves, as you see by the premises his majesty doth, and by restorin[g] us to our former entire state, and our members to us in obedience to his majesty who hath commanded us, as a distinct colony, to serve him in weighty affairs, and wherein if you hinder us (as you will if you still withhold our members from us, as much as in you lyeth), you will incur his majesty's just and high displeasure, who hath not given you in your patent the least appearance of a just ground for your laying any claim to us. 3. Towards us, your neighbors, your brethren, your confederates, by virtue whereof it is your duty to preserve unto us our colony state, power, and privileges, against all others that would oppose us therein or encroach upon us. Is Rosseter of such value with you that what this jurisdiction doth against them your colony will take it as done to themselves? But if it be said, as one of your committee is reported to express it, that you must perform your promise to them, as Joshua and elders of Israel did to the Gibeonites, do you not see the sundry disparities between that vow and yours? or do you indeed make conscience of your vow to Gibeonites, if you term them so, and without regard to your consciences break your promise and most solemn confederation to Israelites? Doubtless it will not be safe for this colony to join in one government with persons of such principles and practices; no treaty will be able to bring us to it. We believe that our righteous God, to whom we have solemnly and publicly commended and committed our righteous cause, will protect us against all that shall any way wrong and oppress us;

neither will we at all doubt the justice of his majesty, our king as well as yours, and of his most honorable council, but that upon hearing the business opened before them they will effectually relieve us against your unjust encroachments, as the matter shall require. We desire peace and love between us, and that we may for the future live in love and peace together as distinct neighbor colonies, as we did above twenty years together before you received and misunderstood and so abused your patent, and in hope that our uncomfortable and afflictive exercises, by your encroachments upon our rights would issue therein, we have so long borne what we have suffered for peace' sake; now it is high time that we bring these unbrotherly contests, wherewith you have troubled us, to a peaceable issue. In order thereunto, we do offer you this choice, either to return our members unto us voluntarily, which will be your honor and a confirmation of our mutual love, or to remove them to some other plantation within your own bounds, and free us wholly from them; for we may not bear it that such fœdifragous, disorderly persons shall continue within the towns belonging to this colony, to disturb our peace, despise our government, and disquiet our members, and disable us to obey the king's commands. But if they stay where they now are, we shall take our time to proceed according to justice; especially with Brown, for his contempt of the declaration, and therein of the king's commands and of the authority of this jurisdiction, and with Bray Rosseter and his son for all their seditious practices.

Lastly for prevention of any misapprehension, we crave leave to explain our meaning in any passages in this writing, which may seem to reflect censure of unrighteous dealing with us, upon your colony or general assembly, that we mean only such as have been active instruments therein.

From the committee, by order of the General Court of New Haven Colony,

JAMES BISHOP, *Secretary.*]

NEW HAVEN, March 9, $168\frac{3}{4}$.

APPENDIX VII.

[*In these papers is a copy of the answer of the New Haven Case Stated, and New Haven Plea, March, 166¾.*

HONORED GENTLEMEN AND NEIGHBORS, — We have, according to our promise in our last to you (sent by your messengers), considered what you sent to us, and, by way of answer, we return as followeth.

You are pleased to term our claims and our claiming our interest, an unjust pretence and encroachment upon your just and proper rights. To untie this knot and pretence of yours, in all the particulars of it, states the whole case you have presented in your large schedule and multiloquous pennings; therefore as methodically as we can, and curt, as the little time we have allowed and our other weighty concernments will permit, in few words we have addressed ourselves for resolution and your conviction.

It is not a pretence, but a reality that we do and have acted upon; we are a delegated power and act under a superior head, yours and ours, if we both know our standing, upon whose interest we do and must act; and our acting so shows our loyalty to our sovereign and is no way dissonant to a religious rule, and therefore our consciences not to be charged with delinquency therein (we forbear to gird, though we have your copy for it before us); and if with a single, not self-willed eye, you be pleased to peruse and weigh what we have already promised, the next particular in order is resolved; we will set to it a seal, a broad seal, which we doubt not will confirm the justice of all our actings toward yourselves, if our great forbearance prove not prejudicial to us, we being trustees in charge; and then if what we claim be just and really just, what you assume to yourselves belongs to us; what you have aspersed us withal, apply it to yourselves; if you can disprove what we have rightly affirmed, then you must countermand our allegation with as eminent a delegation and sealed with as broad a seal also, yet then it would not be so eminently evident, but doubtful and admit a trial, because the plea of priority would be ours and not yours, and you well know that is a good plea in the law.

As for your consultations with friends in England, intentions and ends propounded to yourselves, we see no more argument of force in such precedaneous discourses than in a dream of rich

APPENDIX VII.

revenues to an awaking poor man; of the same nature it is to be one joining in the purchase of the Massachusetts patent and a patentee, because the privileges thereof extend not beyond the limits of the same, for our purchasing of one piece of land gives us no right to our neighbor's field; and it is a difficult undertaking to maintain your Indian purchase from the right owner thereof, or to plead a better right than Connecticut who had the right of conquest, and as added to conquest a deed of gift from the great sachem Sowheag, and under both those rights possessing; and by the court of Connecticut allowing you a plantation right in that place, and then calling whom their agent that possessed the same, we may well question the foundation of your government, unless you can find and show a Connecticut court record allowing the same.

And as for Stamford's being joined to New Haven government by consent of Connecticut, there is no record extant that we can find; but provided it be true as you say, they are but words of course, as the case now stands, because the conclusion follows not upon the premises, but rather all your many instances are but so many flourishes as blinding mists, to darken the truth as now it is.

Your high prizing of Mr. Eaton, that worthy man deceased, who we own was wise, grave and godly, and we could also say that we have had governors not much inferior, who now with him lie in the dust, but such applauses little promote our state concernments in this present contest; wherefore we shall pass them over as not so pertinent.

But you say from the first you maintained your Quilipiage against the claim of the Dutch, by hewing out the King's Arms in wood, and advancing them (marble and brass are the more lasting); but we of Connecticut maintain our rights and claim now, by the king's arms in wax, which is a confirming seal to his royal pleasure in express words and directions for our settlement for ever hereafter.

You say all New England consented that New Haven should be and were a distinct government, except Rhode Island. It is likely that is a mistake, for Piscataway was then a government, and Agamenticus, and several other planted places more eastward, whose consent and approbation was never sought for as we suppose, but if it were as is said, there is no danger to yield to it or argument in it to advantage.

The main argument as follows is the combination and solemn confederation, unto which we answer.

1. The combination did not constitute a government with power and privileges, only amicable compliance and mutual helpfulness in common concernments, as bordering friends and neighbors in a distracted wilderness.

2. The casual inducement of the combination was a former exigence felt (as in the Pequot War) and for future feared, as *vis unita fortior*, to deter a common enemy from future attempts in like kind, and to promote mutual welfare.

3. As a vow is disannulled by the contradiction of a superior, so where the word of a king is there is power; and we having the word of a king, with a religious loyalty we are to observe it when we may do so, without sin in doing so.

4. It is our duty (when without sin we may so do it) to obey our king in his lawful commands, when every year we take our solemn oaths exactly to attend all his and our lawful appointments.

These particular arguments also answer the common title of the four united colonies, for by the combination came in that union.

And for a title of a Colony, it is not a title of honour properly, neither doth it imply government; the basis of our government is not that empty title, but as subjects of his royal majesty by his abundant grace we are created and made a body politic and corporate with power and privileges, and the extent of our corporation ordered to be all that part of his majesty's dominions in New England, bounded as our charter expresseth, and entrusting us with the care of all the plantations therein and the government of all the people thereof; and because it is a duty incumbent on us to be faithful to our trust, we do declare and claim (not with a flourish of empty words) as under our government, all those plantations which you possess and have formerly governed as peculiarly belonging to our corporation, requiring your subjection to our order and laws in observance to the order and appointment of our royal sovereign and yours.

Then you improve as another argument that Mr. Gregson intended to procure a patent, and was employed therein by yourselves, with the consent of Connecticut, for the procuring of power and privileges, for both are implied by your mention of a patent, though there be no enforcing argument for what you intend it in these presents, yet we must take notice of what may appear as contradiction and our advantage, for this endeavor succeeded the combination, and therefore it was then the conclusion both of yourselves and us (as you say) that our combination was not sufficient, patent right was requisite, yet perusing the preface to the combination, we question the truth of it, it being neither upon record and that preface in plain and full words expressing that by reason of sad distractions in England by which we were hindered both from seeking and reaping the comfortable fruits of protection, &c., which is the great privilege conferred by letters patents, and if then patent right was requisite, now we have obtained it and you are included within it, wherefore ready submission would better become you than bold insultings and charges. We pass particulars briefly, knowing that a word to the wise is sufficient.

You say Connecticut sought a patent without your consent, when you had formerly taken in their consent to Mr. Gregson's intention as before: we say as before we have said, we can find no record witnessing the same; but to take off your causeless offence herein, we doubt not but you well know that we paid hundreds of pounds to Mr. Fenwick and his agents for patent rights several years together, and we will now inform you we had a full promise and engagement for the sending and delivering into our possession that patent which we had paid so dear for, the date of the grant of which patent did precede the combination, or your knowledge of a place called Quilipiage in New England, and this patent which we now have is but that which formerly we should have had, with some small addition and inconsiderable alteration, and neither that addition or alteration reflecting upon yourselves in any measure. Our owning of you in a tacit way we doubt not but will be judged a favour in the true sense, of such as have eyes to see and hearts to understand.

As for your letter from the Lords of the Council, persons whom we highly honour as yourselves do, yet we suppose it was sent in the time of the great distractions in England, when the king was separate from his parliament, but now we have received letters patent confirmed by broad seal and writ of privy seal, king, council, and parliament all consenting, and not only owning of, but establishing us with corporation power and privileges, upon which we may act more boldly than on a presumption only, and are bound to act so, and that under oath and by royal appointment.

Your affirming Connecticut had no patent but within these two years last past we have fully answered it before; a patent formally confirmed and possessed we had not till of late, though we had payed a considerable sum, and had the same firmly engaged. Had we had it before, we should have acted upon it as now we do, and probably more vigorously.

Greenwich settled by the commissioners was in the time of ignorance which doth not alienate a true proper right forever.

As for that friend's warning letters to our honored governor, &c., we know not what they were, but it is attested that your then governor desired our honored governor to include New Haven within our charter, and by a letter and improving his interest in some friends he further endeavored the same.

You affirm, if New Haven were within the patent they should have been warned to the first general assembly, for we could not constitute a general assembly without them; this is hardly worth an answer, but to prevent a cavil, the power and privilege was not conferred on New Haven but on Connecticut, and this evidently appears, because the favour extended is unto those that formerly had purchased, conquered, and now petitioned; and we should have acted imprudently, disorderly and justly offensive to our associates so to have done, before we had discovered his majesty's favour towards them in his gracious grant, and preferring others less obliged.

The next particular presented is the rent and disturbance thereby to your government and orderly constitution (as you say) by our admission of some of your members under our protection. Those of your members (as you term them) clearly perceiving themselves included, and advisedly considering their duty for willing and ready observance of his majesty's pleasure and appointment, and for obedience unto our corporation power as ready subjects to both, owning us as we are truly delegated, we could not without some danger but accept of them, confirming security and protection, and do conclude the like ready obedience from yourselves would have been more regular and comfortable to yourselves at last; the event will discover.

Now to give you a short answer to our honored governor's letter to Major Mason, which as yet never came to our honored major or our hands; if it be with you, you had done well if you had sent it us.

2. As for his engagement, it was after we had received your members (as you term them), it evidently appears, the complaint being upon that account.

3. We had then received our letters patent, and acted according to our instructions and directions in them from his majesty; our true loyalty to his gracious appointments and our proceedings therein his majesty hath determined and warranted pleadable in law against himself and his successors, and so we stand free.

But in respect of the honor of our worshipful governor, as we are able we shall answer.

1. Our governor knew the extent of the patent, the desire of your then governor, as by letter and persuasion of friends appears, and therefore in the order of the patent acted innocently and blamelessly, expressing his great courtesy and tender respect towards you, and this bluster of yours is a very ungrateful return for all his love, favour and tenderness.

2. Yourselves could not but be well acquainted with what we expressed, before you sent into England unto our honored governor by way of complaint, for you had received a copy of the patent by our first committee sent from Connecticut unto you.

3. You know that the absolute power was now in the hands of the corporation of Connecticut to do according to the tenor thereof, and not in our governor's power to alter the same.

4. Our honored governor receiving your complaint (and from a tender affection and favour towards yourselves) endeavored to do his utmost to promote your desires; and what a reward he hath for his labour of love from you, the world may judge.

5. Lastly, this cannot advantage your cause nor be an evidence in your plea, for he passeth no engaging promise to you

therein, but as a friend persuading those whom it altogether concerns to do what possibly and fairly may be done, with the highest engaging expressions adventuring as far as may be to do you a kindness, which you should have accepted if you had known yourselves.

For the commissioners' last act in relation to those our concernments, their caution introduced in relation to the Dutch, is a wary answer, saving our allegiance to his majesty and interest by patent, which you may accept of as our present answer to your allegation, for there is a stronger argument in it than yours alleged.

And for your mathematical measures and discovery, it might do us some service in the line betwixt us and the Massachusetts, if you have an able artist, when he is desired by them and us to attend that service; but our charter is the true astrolobe for our south bounds.

Gentlemen, these shadows being flush and fled, in the next place we shall make some short return to your sharp reproofs, and answer your arguments briefly.

Our return to the narrative gives you a full answer to all your arguments, yet to silence cavils full of empty adored conceits, to each argument we shall take the pains to give a short answer, only premising to prevent tautology.

1. Yourselves have proclaimed our king, owned him your sovereign and yourselves his subjects, and the places you possess part of his majesty's dominions abroad, and in your present writing declaring that you intend (if not already attempted) to improve means for obtaining a patent.

3. You well know a king in his own dominions is by all men termed *pater patriæ*, and in Scripture record he is said to be a nursing father, and then all his subjects or his children bound to obey. (Eccles. viii. 2; 1 Pet. ii, 13, 14.)

1. Argument: That Connecticut in entertaining some inhabitants of Stamford, Guilford, and Southold, they did it by a pretended power against the just right of New Haven Colony and without their knowledge or consent.

This assumption is false, both in the pretended power mentioned, and the just right as you apply it. For, 1. Our power is real, not pretended; it is formally legal, as by our letters patent doth undeniably appear, being ratified by broad seal. 2. For your just right, that appears to be your pretence and presumption only, and it cannot be maintained unless you can show a deed of gift sealed as ours and precedent also. And 3dly, Whereas you say what we did was without your knowledge and consent, we answer: 1. Your consent was not absolutely requisite, the places possessed by them being within our charter limits and the government of the people committed to our care, and they claiming it as their privilege, and ourselves clearly perceiving it to be so, could not deny them without unfaithfulness in our trust.

Hence your prolix discourses (by way of explication of this argument) respecting the 5th and 8th commandment, reflect upon yourselves as the transgressors, withstanding your ready obedience to the order and appointment of your nursing father, and attempting to intrude, and actually disturbing of us in our just rights. As for your purchase of the Indians, it is very questionable whether you purchased of the right owners; but if you did, as yourselves say, yet you purchased but land of them and not jurisdiction power, about which is our only contest.

2. Argument: Connecticut have assumed to themselves power of jurisdiction over part of our members without just right thereunto.

This assumption is altogether false, for, 1, We assumed not this power to ourselves; our letters patent are our witness, which declare that his royal majesty, of his abundant grace, certain knowledge and mere motion, hath created and made us a body politic and corporate, to exercise our government over all, yourselves not excepted, which is sufficient to discover our just right beyond exception, and to cavil against it is only to bid battle to a shadow.

As for your mathematical demonstration, we judge it not worthy to be weighed in the balance of reason, it is so unreasonable. 1. If we exceed our line and limits it is a trespass against the king: when his attorney general appears, then we will plead our patent, for his royal majesty of his abundant grace hath made it pleadable against himself and for the best behoof of the governor and company. 2. If you had a patent and there were to be a line settled for peace between us, we

APPENDIX VII.

should readily attend you therein, but we cannot understand that his majesty hath yet given you distinct from us a mathematical line.

3. Argument: Connecticut have acted contrary to promise and confederation.

ANS.— In nonage the contradiction of a superior makes void: a father disannuls the child's act, that is powerless; for the dispose or gift of government is only the gift of the nursing father within his own territories and dominions; if otherwise, it was blamable folly to be at such large expense to procure a patent, when the commissioners might have granted it for an inconsiderable sum, and it will be the like folly in yourselves, especially being minded and forewarned of it; the true question here is whether his majesty's appointment or the commissioners' is of most force and valid.

4. Argument: Connecticut have done contrary to the general rule of love and righteousness.

ANS.— 1. In every argument we find the question begged. 2. Hence the assumption is false. But 3dly, to apologize for our love and righteousness: 1. For love by your then chief in government our governor was solicited to include New Haven within our patent, both by speech and letter, and friends in England were improved by some of you to persuade to and promote the same, and according to your desires attended the best expedient to express sincerity of love, your case and condition at that time duly considered; and since by our many loving insinuations, solicitings, and loving treaties, both for your own good and ours, and large offers of immunities and liberties as great as our own, and as far as we could possibly extend our charter; what could we have done more. 2. For righteousness: the extremity of justice we have not used, but the moderation of justice; we might have immediately declared you under our government, required your subjection, upon refusal severely censured, and have justified what we had done; yet we have used much patience, forbearance, waiting, and expense of much time and charges, if possibly we might have gained you without much extremity, and we doubt not but understanding judges will interpret it an extreme condescendency and chargeable labor of love; besides for righteousness,

you were included in our former patent grant, which was before
your being or your plantation, and at chargeable purchase to
ourselves, and this our patent expresses it a valuable consideration of our present confirmation. And now having so fully expressed ourselves and informed yourselves, we can appeal to all
the Christian world for judges.

5. Argument: If the general assembly upon the receipt of
your patent agreed to treat with New Haven about union, and in
the interim accept of some of your members without your consent, they dealt unrighteously, but so Connecticut did.

Ans.— This argument looks like a chaos, there is so much
jumble in it; it is hypothetical with a sequel in the first proposition, which is to be denied as a *non sequitur*, for both may
be without any unrighteousness, for it is the king that hath
united you and us; to have refused the ready submission of
any, had become unrighteousness towards the persons tendering that obedience, and a negligent retarding of the king's
appointment; the vote for a treaty for union only respected the
modus, for a more placid entertainment of what in duty and
loyalty was to be attended. If authority entertains one that
voluntarily offers himself, persuades another, commands a third,
he sins in neither, nor though he had determined to treat with
them together before that; and truly the greatest danger of dismembering, and loosing an ear, is in refusing submission to his
majesty's lawful appointment.

Argument 6th: Connecticut pleads a power over New Haven
by virtue of a patent, and it gives them no such power, whereby
they abuse that patent and deal unrighteously.

Ans.— This answered before, and it is too favorable to say it is
like two sentences in one sense, rather six sentences and no
sense; like men spoken of in the prophet, that have eyes and see
not, hearts and understand not.

To the remaining arguments we say, and sufficient is said to
maintain it: 1. That our entertainment of those members was
righteous, our promise of protection lawful; therefore that we
may avoid unrighteousness, and it perform we must. 2. Their
submission was righteous and commendable: we dare not call
good evil. 3. Then if Joshua took himself bound to keep
promise with the Gibeonites who acted wilily, and were of that

people which were appointed to destruction, much more must we, when people of our own language, nation, profession, and friends, are appointed and ordered under our care and protection, keep our promise with them, allowing them an interest in our privileges which are common to them as well as to ourselves.]

SUPPLEMENTARY

History and Personnel

OF TOWNS BELONGING TO THE

COLONY OF NEW HAVEN

INCLUDING

BRANFORD, GUILFORD, MILFORD,

STRATFORD, NORWALK,

SOUTHHOLD,

ETC.

ALSO OTHER INTERESTING INFORMATION

COMPILED BY
ROBERT ATWATER SMITH
OF WASHINGTON, D. C.

ASSISTED BY
BESSIE B. BEACH
OF BRANFORD, CONN.
AND
LUCY M. HEWITT
OF NEW HAVEN, CONN.

BRANFORD.

NO historian has failed to recognize the indomitable courage and dauntless energy of the early settlers of New England, who, abandoning the struggle for freedom of thought and action in their native land, sought a fitting home in an unknown and unexplored country. Whether the writer has reveled in fact or fiction, the characters of John Davenport and Theophilus Eaton and their faithful band of supporters ever endure with an unsullied reputation and a perennial fame. However rigid their line of duty, it has radiated in myriad lines of "light and truth" in the institutions which they have founded, the arts and trades which they have encouraged, and the government which they have sustained. When resigning comparative wealth and position in England for the tenets of their belief, they could not conscientiously yield an allegiance to another colony whose views might differ from theirs.

They consistently refused the amicable and flattering proffers of the people of Massachusetts and braved a sterner fate. Thus it transpired that they continued their passage to Quinnipiac. As soon as they possessed their "fair haven" of rest, and even before establishing their civil and ecclesiastical affairs, these early-day saints evolved the theory of expansion and looked about for continued accessions. The region destined to become an integral part of the new colony, designated as "a place fit for a small plantation betwixt New Haven and Guilford," at once claimed their attention and after due deliberation was deemed a desirable acquisition.

December 11, 1638, this tract was purchased from the Indians for the compensation of "eleven coats of trucking cloth and one coat of English cloth made after the English manner," and the reservation of sufficient land for a home for the tribe, which consisted of ten men with their families.

This might appear to be a very meager remuneration for the territory, but the sagacity of the Indian had already discerned the trading advantages to be secured from the proximity of the English. The deed of sale was signed by Montowese and Sausounck with John Clarke as interpreter. The signature of Montowese was a bow and arrow; that of Sausounck, a rude hatchet.

Samuel Eaton, brother of Theophilus Eaton, obtained from the Court, September 1, 1640, a grant of this purchase, known as Totokett, "for such friends as he shall bring over from old England and upon such terms as shall be agreed betwixt himself and the committee chosen for that purpose." He sailed for England intending to return with a band of colonists and settle this plantation, but conditions had changed, and he found no one willing to emigrate; so he accepted a parish near London and did not return to fulfill his agreement.

Thus some years passed and the territory was not occupied, and only used for hunting and fishing,—its further disposition being left to the discretion of the Court.

During this interval the Dutch explorers had crowded in and established a trading post, since known as Dutch House wharf, but its existence was of short duration.

The colony at Wethersfield had retained its connection with the parent church at Watertown, Mass., and for seven years there had been no settled pastor. Without such controlling influence its church relations "fell into unhappy contentions and animosities" to such an extent that no adjustment of the difficulties appeared probable or possible. Therefore a separation was advised and arranged. There had also been many new arrivals in the colony who could not obtain suitable or agreeable lands upon which to locate, and they gladly joined the dissenting partisans in their project of removal.

The unoccupied possessions of the New Haven colony presented desirable advantages for a new settlement, and the claim of Samuel Eaton was purchased by "Mr. Swaine and others" for £12 or £13, an advance upon the previous sale. "They joyning in one jurisdiction with New Haven and the forenamed plantations upon the same fundamental agreement, settled October, 1643, which they duly considering readylye accepted."

This purchase included a territory extending seven and one-half miles on the Sound — four and one-half miles in width on the north, ten miles back; bounded on the west by Stony or Farm river, Furnace pond, now Lake Saltonstall, and by a line extending directly north from the head of the lake; on the east by the Guilford line. These boundaries have varied but little in over two centuries, although it is a prevailing tradition supported by collateral records that Branford actually held in possession more land than was mentioned in the original purchase. As early as 1649 a difficulty arose on this subject and there were frequent litigations settled by arbitration. In 1674 there was a final settlement by the commissioners.

It would appear that the Indians were content as they quietly receded upon the arrival of the English and were ever friendly in their intercourse with them and upon occasion submitted to their legal decisions. While on the other hand, the settlers made stringent laws for the protection of the rights of the Indians.

In the grants and for some time later, the place retains the original name of Totokett, which means "the tidal river," with some reference to the meadows along its banks.

In nearly every colony the settlers, clinging to the associations and traditions of the mother country, had adopted an English nomenclature for their new homes; so with the coming of the white man, the name of Totokett gradually disappears. There is no record extant of a vote to change the name of the plantations, but as if by universal assent, in a few years the name Brainford or Branford appears in their records and transactions.

Brenford or Brainford, in England, was a town on the river Brent, seven miles from London, a place of great historic as well as histrionic interest, and it is supposed that some of the settlers emigrated from that place and bestowed the name of their native town upon their new abiding place.

Early in the spring of 1644 the new proprietors took possession of their purchase. It is probable that they came from Wethersfield in vessels, down the Connecticut river and through Long Island sound. They were joined by others from New Haven and all numbered forty men, many of whom were accompanied by wives and children. Prominent among them were: William Swaine and his sons Samuel and Daniel, John Plum, Richard

Harrison, Thomas Blatchly, Robert Rose, John and Francis Linsley, William Palmer, Thomas Sargent, Robert Abbott, Edward Treadwell, Samuel Nettleton, John Norton, John Hill, John Ward, Daniel Dod, Thomas Richards, Jonathan England, Edward Frisbie, Richard Lawrence, Richard Mather, Sagismond Richalls, William Merchant, Luther Bradfield, Thomas Fenner, John Edwards, Robert Meeker, Thomas Whitehead, Richard Lawrence, with Rev. John Sherman, who accompanied them as their pastor. Jasper Crane, George and Lawrence Ward, Thomas Morris, and Thomas Luptor came from New Haven.

Their first homes were along the north and west banks of the river, leaving the Indian reservation, which still retains the name of Indian Neck, on the opposite side. These houses were probably of a rude construction as the first meeting house, built in 1644, was a block house with a thatched roof, surrounded by a palisade of cedar logs twelve feet high.

In 1645 the first division of lands was made, each proprietor having previously received a home lot of three acres. "This dai it is ordered that the meadow in this plantation shall be divided into four parts and then divided by lott· viz., all the meadow that lyeth on the right hand side of the towne that is earliest settled shall be in the first dividend; and all the meadow that lyeth by the river on the left side and all upwards from that place where it is considered a bridge must be built is for the 2nd dividend.— Also 3dly, all the meadow that lyeth downe the river from the place where formerly it was considered a bridge must be and all that lyeth within the compass of that piece of ground called the plaine shall be in the 3rd dividend.—4thly all the meadow left beside in the towne that is knowne shall be in the 4th dividend. This meadow is to be bounded and prized by Robert Rose, William Palmer, Samuel Swaine and Thomas Blatchly, with all convenient speede and then the lott to be cast."

It is difficult to locate these original allotments as they were in detached pieces in order that there might be an equal distribution of meadow, upland and forest; and they made frequent exchanges of their portions as their various occupations and pursuits demanded.

As early as October, 1644, the church was so well organized that the congregation gathered for regular services under the ministration of Rev. John Sherman. They conformed to the rules and customs of the parent colony of New Haven.

Each man carried firearms when he went to meeting, and those appointed kept guard during the service; all persons were fined for neglecting to carry their arms, for being late at meeting, or for leaving before the close of the service.

Their pastor was also a teacher, and thus the cause of education received early attention, and with instructors possessing such mental attainments as John Sherman, Mr. Pierson, and Mr. Bowers, the influence then and later cannot be overestimated.

In 1655 laws were enacted by Governor Eaton for the establishment of schools, with a penalty for neglecting the education of children. It was not, however, until 1678 that there was a regular teacher, John Arnold, employed.

The records show that they soon became a busy people, and while subservient to the jurisdiction of New Haven, they arranged their affairs of local government with prudence and wisdom. A clerk was appointed to keep the town's book; an agent to arrange civil affairs; a general cowherd who was of importance in caring for their property; the salary of the minister, Mr. Sherman, was agreed upon and a house built for him. The provision for his successor, Mr. Pierson, is recorded as follows: " It is ordered that the minister's pay shall be brought each half year. For every milch cow he shall have two pounds of butter in part pay every year; for the rest, for the first half year in beef or pork or Indian corn or wampum; for the second half year, in wheat and peas good and marketable."

For their better protection a fence five miles in extent was built, beginning at the "head of the Ba" and extending "to the sea where the Indians dwell," which must have enclosed the entire settlement. This fence, which was of logs, was built by division of labor among the settlers, each man to build a section at the time when his name should be drawn by lot. Their herds were kept outside this fence during the day, in charge of the keeper.

Their first season was spent in arranging and developing their plan of settlement. There were doubtless men of various trades among the planters who could provide for the exigencies of the first years, but very soon a smith was called from a neighboring plantation, and John Nash came from New Haven to attend a mill.

As their needs increased small industries were established and their agricultural and trading pursuits formed a community of interest based upon the system of barter and exchange.

Their maritime and commercial enterprise was closely allied with that of New Haven, which afforded them much encouragement and opportunity for progress.

They built their houses upon their allotments of land, which were in most instances approached by lanes, with a total disregard for their appropriation for a highway, which did not become an established feature except in a modified sense. The first road extended from Furnace pond, along the summit of the hills, probably following the trail of the wily Indian, who always selected the most elevated country for his expeditions. This became the connecting thoroughfare with New Haven and in the course of time was continued toward Guilford.

In the division of lands and levying the proportion of expenses they held absolute authority. They were allowed deputies at the General Court of New Haven, and very soon a magistrate was elected, and with the union of the colonies the General Assembly, May 11, 1665, decreed "that Lt. Samuel Swaine, Lawrence Ward, and John Wilford are chosen Comrs. for ye Town of Branford to assist in keeping a Town Court; to administer the freeman's oath to all those that were formerly freemen there or to so many as will accept of it and to as many others as by sufficient evidence they judge qualified according to law."

There was little demand upon their military prowess for the horrors and atrocities of the Indian wars were wholly abated and they were on amicable terms with all adjacent tribes. Upon the occasion of the war provoked by the encroachments of the Dutch at Manhadoes in 1654, Branford responded with alacrity, and furnished its quota of eleven men. Mr. Pierson was appointed to accompany the force as their minister, "for their incouragement, spirituall instruction, and comfort." With the abrupt termination of the contest between England and Holland and the submission of New Netherland, there was a cessation of hostilities between these colonies. They were again called upon to aid in suppressing the depredations of the treacherous Ninigret, but this expedition was also concluded without bloodshed.

In 1664, Charles II. granted New Netherlands to his brother, the Duke of York, and with the usual recklessness of the royal prerogative he extended this territory to the Connecticut river. This conflicted with the formal charter which he had granted two years before to John Winthrop as governor of the Connecticut settlements.

To the chagrin of the New Haven people this latter charter included their town. As an affair of state this might have been favorably regarded, but when their church discipline was in danger of shipwreck or total annihilation, they arose in wrath and indignation and would not be appeased, for Winthrop's charter rejected their "fundamental law." They debated the case with much obstinacy and tenacity of purpose, and only yielded an assent when a more "imminent deadly peril" menaced them —that of submission to the royal governors.

Mr. Davenport and Mr. Pierson maintained a strict allegiance to their principles and could not endure to have their high ideal of government so cruelly frustrated.

And, as on previous occasions, Mr. Pierson with his usual tact and diplomacy gathered the "faithful few" about him and they withdrew from the scene of years of labor and success.

Dr. Trumbull in his "History of Connecticut," "the most careful and conscientious chronicle of the colonial history of these states," affirms that "Mr. Pierson and almost his whole church were so displeased that they removed to Newark, New Jersey. They carried off the records of the church and town,[1] and after it had been settled about five and twenty years left it without inhabitants."

Against such authority it may be in vain to hazard a doubt or admit a demurrer. However the case, Branford arose as the Phœnix from the ashes of its defeat and desolation to higher and better things.

Mr. Pierson secured a successor to continue his work—Mr. John Bowers, a graduate of Harvard College who had been called to

---

[1] While Dr. Trumbull is usually very accurate in his work, this statement is incorrect, as Mr. Henry Rogers, of New Haven, informs the writer that the Branford town records, dating back to 1645, are still in the possession of the town, and in an excellent state of preservation.

New Haven as a teacher, by Governor Eaton. He was a man of broad culture and of high social standing in the colony, having married a daughter of Thomas Gregson. June 20, 1667, the Plantation covenant was signed by forty-seven free-holders endorsing their adherence to the Congregational order.

Worthy purchasers arrived to secure houses and lands.

At a town meeting, October 4, 1667, "It was agreed that John Wilford, Thomas Blatchly, John Collins and Michael Taintor should be chosen and employed and empowered to buy Richard Harrison's house and lands in behalf of the towne, for a minister, and all that were present did engage the value of their estates for the same."

"The people who remained acted nobly in manifesting their attachment to the Gospel and its institutions; and their firm purpose to adhere to the principles which had inspired and guided them in their first efforts to establish a settlement."—*Rev. T. P. Gillet, "Branford; Past and Present, a semi-centennial sermon, 1850."*

PERSONAL SKETCHES.

REV. ABRAHAM PIERSON was born in Yorkshire, England; graduated at Trinity College, Cambridge; ordained to Episcopal orders and preached for some time in Yorkshire. He married Abigail, daughter of Rev. Jonathan Wheelwright of Lincolnshire. Adopting non-conformist views, he came to America in 1639, in the pursuit of religious freedom. He became a member of the Congregational church at Boston, and preached at Lynn until 1640, when various circumstances decided him with a part of his congregation to remove to Long Island. Here they laid the foundations of Southampton, but after a few years of arduous labor they found themselves under the jurisdiction of Connecticut, which was very liberal in church government and not in accordance with their views. Mr. Pierson with a few followers recrossed the Sound to join the new colony at Totokett. Here Mr. Pierson received a cordial welcome and was accepted as their settled pastor. He was eminently successful as a pastor and teacher for over twenty years. He was intimately associated with Mr. Davenport of New Haven in ecclesiastical affairs, and they were co-laborers in the cause of education. In 1659 they were appointed to formulate plans for the establishment of a grammar school in New Haven and to approve the books. In the following year they were elected trustees of the school. He was selected to assist in compiling "a history of the gracious providences of God to New Haven." Mr. Pierson was conversant with the Indian language, often acting as interpreter, especially before the Court. For his labors among the Indians he received a regular salary paid by a missionary society in England, known as "The Commissioners for the United Colonies of New England." He prepared a catechism for their instruction entitled "Some Helps for the Indians: a catechism," printed at Cambridge, 1658, of which there are only two copies extant, one in the Lenox Library, New York, the other in the British Museum. He himself possessed a library containing 440 volumes.

Mr. Pierson opposed the union of the colonies with "great inflexibility," taking a prominent part in the controversy. Many of his congregation were agreeable to his views and they determined to seek a new field of usefulness. They signed a covenant of remonstrance, organized a society, and embarked for New Jersey in 1666. Here they established their church in conformity to their views and founded the present city of Newark. For twelve years Mr. Pierson ministered to this church, " his life full of piety to God and service to his fellowmen." He died in 1678, aged 72.

Children of Rev. Abraham Pierson–Abigail Wheelwright.

Abraham, b. Lynn, 1640; d, 1708; m. Abigail Clark of Milford.
Thomas, b. Southampton, 1641-2; d. 1684; m. Marie Taintor.
John, b. Southampton, 1643; d. 1671.
Abigail, b. Southampton, 1644; m, John Davenport, Jr.
Grace, b. Branford, July 23, 1650; m. Samuel Kitchell.
Susanna, b. Branford, Dec. 10, 1652; m. John Ball.
Rebecca, b. Branford; m. Joseph Johnson.
Theophilus, b. Branford, Mar. 15, 1657.
Isaac.
Mary.

REV. ABRAHAM PIERSON, JR., was born at Lynn, Mass., 1640; graduated at Harvard College, 1668; accompanied his father to Southampton and Branford. While at the latter place he married Abigail Clark of Milford. He was settled as colleague with his father at Newark, ordained at Killingworth, Conn. In 1700 he was one of the ten ministers selected as trustees of Yale College, and in 1701 he was chosen president of the college with the title of "Rector of Yale College." He was distinguished for his talents and profound learning. He died at Killingworth, 1708.

THOMAS PIERSON, brother of Rev. Abraham Pierson, "was a weaver, and while quietly pursuing his calling was ready to bear his full share of the burdens devolving upon the settlers of a new colony." He married Maria, daughter of Richard Harrison, November 27, 1662. He removed to Newark, where he held many offices.

REV. JOHN SHERMAN was born at Dedham, Essex county, England, December 26, 1613. He was the son of Edmund Sherman, known as "old Father Sherman," who died in New Haven, 1641. He was educated at Emanuel College, Cambridge, but as he would not sign the articles upon which graduation depended, he left college before taking his degree under the character of a college Puritan. He came to New England, 1634–5, and preached at Watertown, Mass., as assistant to Rev. George Philips. The records show that he was assigned a house lot at Wethersfield, 1636, and from there he migrated to Milford, 1639. While there he was employed as a teacher. He was invited to join the colony at Totokett as their pastor, and also acted as judge and magistrate.

After the death of Mr. Philips, 1646, he returned to Watertown, preaching there until he died, 1685. "He was a man of superior intellectual endowments; the best mathematician in the country, and left voluminous manuscripts on the Science of Astronomy."

His first wife, Mary, died in New Haven, September 8, 1646, leaving six children. His second wife was Mary Launce, whom he met in the family of Governor Eaton. She was the granddaughter of Thomas Darcy, Earl of Rivers, and under the guardianship of Edward Hopkins. She survived her husband, dying in 1710. She was the mother of twenty children. Mr. Sherman was at Totokett between the death of his first wife and his second marriage.

Inscription on his tombstone at Watertown, Mass.: "To the memory of John Sherman, a man of the greater piety, dignity and candor, well versed in theology, in the pulpit a Chrysostom, and in the liberal arts especially mathematics exceedingly skillful. He was the faithful pastor of the church at Watertown, in New England, and an overseer and fellow of Harvard College. After he had been an undaunted servant of Christ for forty-five years he was removed when ripe for his departure and received the palm from his Redeemer on the 8 of August, 1685, in the 72 year of his age."

The will of Rev. John Sherman was dated August 6, 1685. In it are named thirteen children who survived him. Sons: Bezaleel, Daniel, Samuel, John, James. Daughters: Abigail, m. Samuel Willard; Mercy, m. Samuel Barnard; Mary, Grace, Elizabeth, Abiah, Hester, Barren. He died August 8, 1685.

THOMAS MULLINER was the first settler in Totokett, coming before the country was bought by the New Haven colony in 1638, and gaining ownership from the Indians. He was the son of Thomas and Elizabeth Mulliner of Ipswich, England, each of whom left him a legacy in their respective wills, dated 1625 and 1627. "A restless and independent spirit," who preferred an isolated life. He had located near the sea, which section retains the name of Mulliner's Neck. He objected to being ignored by the grant to New Haven, claiming land included in their purchase. He evidently had been trained to the occupation of his father, that of joiner, as in 1647 the governor informed the Court that the King's arms had been carved for the town by Mr. Mulliner and was to be set upon a post on the highway.

The Mulliners, father and son, were troublesome for many years, and were frequently arraigned before the Court for trespassing upon the territory of the settlers and violating their laws. "Samuel Swayne complayned of Mr. Mulliner for neglecting of traynings, watchings & bringing of his armes when it was his turne one the Lord's days." "February 5, 1644, Thomas Mulliner sen. and Thomas Mulliner his son were under bonds of £100 to keep the publique peace and be of good behaviour towards all people especially towards the Inhabitants of Totokett." Thomas, sen., died in 1690. November 10, 1691, Thomas, jr., with his wife, Martha Browne, yielded their claim to the land and were granted 200 acres in the northwest corner of the town. Later they sold to Nathaniel Johnson and removed to Westchester, N. Y.

THOMAS WHITWAY was quietly settled in the region afterward known as Foxon. He had a house lot in Wethersfield, and local history records that he joined the emigration to Totokett, yet he is never identified with the early settlers although on friendly terms with them. He understood the Indian language, and was of service as an interpreter. As early as 1644 he went as messenger to Uncas to summon him to settle with the governor and magistrates for "damage to their cattell." April 21, 1651, he was chosen "pound herd." He died December 12, 1651, leaving no heir and his lands were reclaimed by the town.

JOHN PLUM came from Dorchester to Wethersfield, where he appears to have taken an active part in all public affairs, ecclesiastical as well as state. He was associated with Mr. Swaine as deputy, 1642. With Robert Rose he was fined, "failing in proof,' for preferring grievances against the minister, Mr. Smith. He was one of a committee appointed to consider ways and means of improving the ground of the plantation. Upon his arrival at Branford he was also regarded as a man of affairs, for he was appointed in 1645 to keep the town's book — the first town clerk. His death, which occurred in 1648, is the first on the records of the town. "Mistrs Plume and her sonn Samuell Plume brought into ye court an inventorie of the estate of Mr. John Plume deceased, amounting to 3661: 9s: 1d, prised by Robert Rose, Robert Abut, & Lawrence Ward, upon oath the 4th of September, 1648."

His son Samuel removed to Newark. Dorcas Plum married John Liman of Hartford, January 12, 1664.

DANIEL DOD was one of the emigrants who came to Boston before 1640. He came to Branford from Wethersfield with his wife, Mary, "and after a few years several sons and daughters sat around his table." "They did not long endure the hardships and trials of pioneer life," for his wife died in 1657, leaving six small children. He himself died in 1666, leaving an estate of £146 to be divided among his children, with Richard Lawrence and Lawrence Ward their guardians. His eldest daughter, Mary, had married Aaron Blatchly, and when they removed to Newark, in 1666, took three young brothers with her. The remaining brother, Stephen, found a home with a sister who had removed to Guilford. Daniel, the son of Stephen, joined his kinsmen in Newark, and thus all the descendants bearing the name of Dod are of Newark extraction. There have been many distinguished men in the Dod family, especially in the ministry.

Children of Daniel Dod and Mary ———.

Mary, bap. June 1, 1651; m. Aaron Blatchly.
Hannah, bap. June 1, 1651; m. —— Fowler.
Daniel, bap. June 1, 1651.
Ebenezer, b. Dec. 11, 1651.
Daughter, b. March 29, 1653.
Stephen, b. Feb. 16, 1656; d. Oct. 6, 1691; m. Sarah Stevens.
Samuel, b. May 2, 1657.

ROBERT ROSE was a native of Ipswich, Suffolk county, England. He and his wife, Margery, each aged forty years, with eight children, came in the ship Francis to Boston in 1634 He first located in Watertown, Mass., but better opportunities induced him to join the pioneer settlement in Connecticut, where he occupied "adventure lands" in Wethersfield. He had also an allotment of 312 acres. These circumstances gave him preëminence among the colonists, yet he appeared to have little ambition to be a ruler in temporal affairs as he filled but one public office, that of constable in 1639. His name often appears in connection with Mr. Swaine and Mr. Plum, especially in affairs spiritual. His was a leading mind in the dissensions which led to the early disruption of that colony. His attitude in Branford was that of a worthy citizen aiding and adjusting the affairs of the community. He was liberal in his views, broad in his charities, highly respected and venerated in his life and by succeeding generations. He was regarded as a very wealthy man, owning ten horses when there were not as many more in the town He dispensed material aid to his less fortunate neighbors, giving the Sunday's milking to the poor, which was one instance of his beneficence. He died April 4, 1665. His estate was valued at £616: 17s.

Last Will and Testament of Robert Rose of Branford, made August 25, 1664.

"1. I give to my son Jonathan a hundred pounds. 2. When all my debts are payd then I give to my wife one-third part of my whole estate 3. I give to my son Jonathan five pounds more. 4. I give to my daughter Hannah ten pounds more. 5. It is my will that all the rest of my estate shall be equally divided into eight parts amongst my other eight children as followeth: That is to each of them alike part but my son John & daughter Mary & my daughter Elizabeth both shall have but twenty pounds of that part that falls to them but the rest of that part which falls to them shall be given to their children. I give unto the church of Branford six pounds, thirteen shillings, four pence."

The
ROBERT ROSE
mark

Lawrence Ward
Samuel Swaine

His Bible, printed in England, 1599, was for many generations in the possession of descendants, several of whom were deacons of the Congregational church.

His legacy to the church of Branford was its first donation.

In the geographical nomenclature of the town are found Rose's hill and Rose's brook, both adjacent to his estate.

Children of Robert Rose and Margery ———.

John, b. 1619.
Robert, b. 1619.
Elizabeth, b. 1621; m. Michael Taintor (?).
Mary, b. 1623.
Samuel, b. 1625.
Sarah, b. 1627.
Daniel, b. 1631.
Dorcas, b. 1632; m. Daniel Swaine, July 26, 1653; m. 2d, John Collins.
Jonathan.
Hannah.

His sons Samuel and Daniel settled in Wethersfield, and Robert in Stratford.

ELIZABETH, widow of John Potter of New Haven, who died in 1643, and of Edward Parker, who also died in New Haven, July, 1662, married Robert Rose of Branford, who died in 1665. Elizabeth Rose made her will July 23, 1677, but died July 28, before signing it. She appointed her two sons, John Potter and John Parker, joint executors of this will. The will was admitted to probate. "The fact that her heirs agreed to stand by a void will is conclusive proof that she was a woman of merit and had the respect of her children."

WILLIAM SWAINE, "gentleman," aged fifty years, came from London, 1635, in the "Elizabeth and Ann." Received a grant of sixty acres at Watertown, Mass. He was made a freeman, and served as representative in Massachusetts in May, 1636, and in September of the same year he held court in the new colony of Wethersfield, where he had acquired "adventure lands." He was appointed with Roger Ludlow and Andrew Ward as commissioners to govern the people until the adoption of the constitution in 1639. He was a member of the Court which tried the first offender; enacted the first law, and declared war against the Pequots in 1637. Becoming involved in "divers grievances" pertaining to the adjustment of church differences, he was one of the foremost projectors of the scheme of removal from Wethersfield. His name appears prominently in the purchase of the plantation of Totokett, where he settled in 1644. He was successively deputy, juror, and magistrate.

During the Pequot war, two daughters of William Swaine were captured by the Indians and taken to Pequot, now New London. Here they were rescued by a Dutch trading vessel and transferred to the care of Lion Gardiner, then in command at Saybrook, at a cost of £10 to the latter, who writes in 1660: "I am yet to have thanks for my care and charge about them."

His daughter Mary married in New Haven, name not known. Mr. Swaine held an estate of 435 acres in Branford, which he did not occupy long, as his death must have occurred in the first years of the settlement of the colony, when his name disappears from the records.

SAMUEL SWAINE, son of William, born in England, was in Watertown in 1635; also at a later date in Wethersfield; "one of the founders of the church and town of Branford." In 1653, "propounded to the Court and approved as the chief military officer of Branford." He was deputy to New Haven, 1651-63. As a friend and coadjutor of Mr. Pierson, he accompanied him

BRANFORD.   611

to Newark. The tradition is that Elizabeth Swaine, daughter of Samuel, was the first to land on the shore of Newark, having been handed up by her lover, Josiah Ward, who hastened to secure this distinction for her.

In his will Samuel Swaine gives all his estate to his "beloved wife Joanna."

Children of Samuel Swaine and Joanna ———.

Elizabeth, b. 1647; m. Josiah Ward; m. 2d, David Ogden.
Mary, b. March 1, 1649; d. Nov. 10, 1655.
Phebe, b. May 24, 1654.
Mary, b. June 12, 1656.
Christiana, b. April 25, 1659; m. Nathaniel Ward.
Sarah, b. Oct. 7, 1661; m. Thomas Johnson.
Abigail, m. Eleazar Lampson.
Joanna, m. Jasper Crane, Jr.

DANIEL SWAINE, son of William, was born in England. Probably with his father in Watertown and Wethersfield. His name is in the list of freemen in Branford, 1669; deputy at Hartford, 1673–77. His home lot was centrally located. He married Dorcas, daughter of Robert Rose, July 26, 1653. He died in 1691.

Children of Daniel Swaine and Dorcas Rose.

Debora, b. April 24, 1654; m. Peter Tyler, Nov. 20, 1671.
Daniel, b. Dec. 23, 1655: d. 1684.
Dorcas, b. Dec. 2, 1657; m. John Taintor.
John, b. May 22, 1660; d. 1694.
Jonathan, b. Jan. 12, 1662.

JASPER CRANE, a merchant from London, who took a prominent part in the settlement of New Haven; signed the first agreement of the free planters in Mr. Newman's barn, July 1, 1639. His house lot was on the public square adjoining that of Mr. Davenport, and his estate was estimated at £480. He was interested in every enterprise pertaining to the advancement and growth of the colony of New Haven, and he at once joined the company who settled at Totokett, although he may have retained his home in New Haven for some years. He represented Branford as deputy at the General Court, 1653-57; from 1658-66 he served as magistrate, and was intimately associated with Governor Leete; in 1664 he was appointed commissioner to administer the oath of allegiance; one of the signers of the resolution to form a new colony at Newark, and at that time he was so highly esteemed that his name precedes that of the pastor, Mr. Pierson. He did not at once remove to Newark, as he was residing in Branford in 1668, but on his arrival there he was equally respected and was elected their first magistrate. He died at Newark, October 19, 1681, and was probably the last survivor of the subscribers to the "Fundamental agreement."

Children of Jasper Crane and ———.

John, b. in England.
Hannah, b. in England; m. Thomas Huntington.
Delivered, bap. in New Haven, June 12, 1642.
Mercy, bap. in New Haven, March 1, 1645.
Micah, bap. in New Haven, Nov. 3, 1647.
Azariah, b. 1651; m. Mary, dau. of Robert Treat.
Jasper, b. 1651; m. Joanna Swaine.

EDWARD FRISBIE, "the Immigrant," with his wife Hannah, was one of the first settlers who entered his name for land in 1645. He must have been an extensive land owner and acquired much additional property, as the conditions of his will, dated 1689, dispose of many valuable tracts in different parts of the town. His large family of eleven children displayed marked traits of character and ability. Their descendants in succeeding generations include many distinguished members. His son John was a member of the State Legislature, 1690-92.

Children of Edward Frisbie and Hannah ———.

John, b. July 27, 1650; m. Ruth, dau. of Rev. John Bowers; d. 1694.
Edward, b. July 11, 1652.
Benoni, b. 1654; d. 1700.
Samuel, b. Oct. 7, 1655; d. 1681.
Abigail, b. Oct. 7, 1657; m. William Hoadley, Jr.
Jonathan, b. Oct. 28, 1659; d, April 7, 1695.

Josiah, b. Jan. 19, 1661; d. March 13, 1712.
Caleb, b. 1667.
Ebenezer, b. Sept. 5, 1672; d. 1714.
Silence, b. Sept. 5, 1672; m. Joshua Austin of New Haven.
Hannah, b. 1669 (?); m. Nathaniel Harrison.

ROBERT ABBOTT was admitted a freeman at Watertown, Mass., 1634; was granted thirty-five acres of land besides a home lot of ten acres. His name remained on the list of proprietors at that place, although he was residing in Wethersfield in 1641. August 6, 1642, he was admitted a freeman in New Haven. He had land allotted to him in East Haven and Branford, but continued to reside in New Haven until May 6, 1645. He died intestate in 1658, and in 1660 his estate was distributed, reserving £10 for the two younger children. In 1659 his widow, Marie, married John Robins.

Children of Robert Abbott and Marie ———.

Peter, b. before 1649.
Sarah, b. before 1649; m. Matthew Rowe.
Deborah, b. before 1649.
Abigail, b. Oct. 2, 1650.
John, b. April 20, 1652.
Benjamin, b. Jan. 10, 1653.
Daniel, b. Feb. 12, 1654.
Mary, b. May 13, 1656.

THOMAS BLATCHLY, aged 20, came to Boston, 1635, in the Hopewell. He was a merchant residing in Hartford in 1640; in New Haven, 1643; and for many years after 1644 in Branford, where he received an allotment of land. He was representative at the General Assembly, 1667, after the union of the colonies—also elected, 1668-69, but was absent. He signed the Newark covenant and later the plantation and church covenant of Branford. He was assigned a house lot in Newark, but evidently did not become a permanent resident there, for in 1668 he was admitted an inhabitant of Guilford, where his son Moses had settled. After a time he removed to Boston, where he died in 1674.

The value of his estate in Connecticut was £79, and that in Boston £128. His widow Susanna married Richard Bristow. Miriam Blatchly, his daughter, married Samuel Pond, the ancestor of Lieutenant-Governor Pond of Milford.

Aaron Blatchly, his son, who settled in Newark, had married Mary Dod and brought suit against the estate of Daniel Dod on account of a marriage settlement. The claim was not allowed because of the small estate.

Children of Thomas Blatchly and Susanna ———.

Aaron, b. 1647; m. Mary Dod.
Moses, b. March 29, 1650; m. Susannah Bishop of Guilford.
Miriam, b. March 1, 1653; m. Samuel Pond, Jan. 5, 1669.
Abigail, m. Ed. Ball.

ROGER BETTS, one of the Watertown settlers, came from Wethersfield to Totokett, having taken the oath of fidelity in New Haven in 1644. His three children, Samuel, Peter, and Mercy, were baptized in New Haven, July 1, 1651, his daughter Hannah being older. He with his family joined Thomas Betts of Guilford, who settled in Milford, 1658. In the Betts genealogy he is mentioned as a possible relation. He died in Milford and his widow married John Cabell of Fairfield. She died in 1683, leaving her property to her son, Samuel Betts, with instructions to pay legacies to the other children.

Children of Roger Betts and Ann ———.

Hannah.
Samuel, bap. in New Haven, July 1, 1651.
Peter, bap. in New Haven, July 1, 1651; d. Oct. 3, 1653.
Mercy, bap. in New Haven, July 1, 1651.
Roger, b. in Branford, Feb. 20, 1652.
Mary, b. in Branford, Feb. 29, 1653.

WILLIAM PALMER in 1636 received a grant of twenty acres of land at Watertown, Mass. Probably he soon followed the fortunes of the new colony at Wethersfield, as he is known to have participated in the war against the Pequots, for which service he was rewarded with bounty lands. His claims as a leading man at Totokett are indisputably established by the records. " Moreover it is ordered that Mr. Palmer in consideration of some former expense and also for the good services he has done the town, and also for the public business that he is to do the town for one year following as they call him thereunto, he is to have that piece of meadow which lyeth at the end or side of his lot to the neck and also upland apportionable to it." Which shows that Mr. Palmer was the first town agent.

He died 1656.

MICAH PALMER, who was a planter, was his son. He married Elizabeth Butler. In 1676 his estate was valued at £45.

His will, dated November 12, 1681, gave one-third of his estate to his wife Elizabeth, and he mentions his sons John, Daniel, Micah and three other children.

Children of Micah Palmer and Elizabeth Butler, m. January 3, 1662-3.

Elizabeth, b. Oct. 3, 1662-3.
Michael, b. Feb. 8, 1664.
John, b. Dec. 24, 1666.
Mary, b. Oct. 24, 1669.
Micah, b. Aug. 19, 1671.
Mary, b. May 25, 1673.
Daniel, b. Sept. 13, 1675.
Joshua, b. Dec. 25, 1677.

JOHN and FRANCIS LINSLEY came from the northwest of London. John became a permanent resident of Branford, building his house on Mulliner's Neck Path. John Linsley, jr., came from Guilford, 1654, after the death of his wife Ellen, and died 1684; a possible relation. John Linsley, sen., married July 9, 1655, Sarah Pond, a widow from Windsor. She was the mother of Samuel Pond, then a youth of seven years, who accompanied her to Branford, and 1669 married Miriam Blatchly. John Linsley, sen., lived until 1698.

Children of John Linsley and Sarah Pond.

Benjamin, b. July 10, 1656; d. March 29, 1660.
Elizabeth, b. June 18, 1658; d. July 11, 1659.
Jonathan, d. May 3, 1725; m. Dorcas Phipper of Milford, Sept. 24, 1705.

In the inventory of July 13, 1698, children Mary and Hannah are mentioned.

FRANCIS LINSLEY is presumed to be the brother of John Linsley, sen., as their relations were very intimate. Francis Linsley was speedily inducted into office. "The second month, the tenth day, 1646. This day it was agreed by the town and Francis Linsley that the said Francis shall keep the heard of cows and heifers from the 16 of this month to the 16 of the 9th & he is to call for them by the sun half an hour high in the morning and to bring them home in the evening and he must blow a horn or make some other noise before he come in the morning and also in the evening that we may be ready to turn them out of our yards and to return them in the evening." They further arrange that he is to have one Sabbath out of four. Also if any of the cattle are astray, he is to look for them four days at his own expense. This was probably his occupation for the following five years. In 1666 he removed with his wife and three daughters to Newark.

Children of Francis Linsley and Susannah Culpepper, m. July 24, 1655.

Debora, b. April 22, 1656.
Ruth, b. Feb. 4, 1657.
Bethia, b. March 4, 1659.

GEORGE and LAWRENCE WARD were brothers, mentioned in the allotment of lands in New Haven in 1641. They received two lots on East Water street fronting the harbor. Their estates were estimated at £30 and £10. They were ship carpenters and may have found further opportunies for plying their trade in the necessities of a new settlement.

GEORGE WARD, who signed the agreement of 1639, was represented at New Haven as having a family of six persons, and when he died in Branford in 1653, he left a widow and four children. Samuel and Josiah Ward who settled in Newark were probably his sons.

LAWRENCE WARD was active in discharging official duties. He was one of the "searchers" sent to Milford by the Governor to assist in the capture of the regicides, Goffe and Whalley, which expedition proved a failure. He was deputy at the General Court of New Haven, 1654–64; and was a member of the General Assembly at Hartford, 1665–66; he was collector of customs and excise on wines and strong liquors, for which he received 3s. for each £1 collected. He with his family of seven children removed to Newark.

JOHN WARD was the son of Joyce Ward, a widow of Wethersfield, who mentions him in her will dated 1640. He lived in Branford many years; was representative in 1666; and signed the Plantation and Church covenant in 1667. In 1661, he testifies that he is about thirty-six years of age. His will bears date of 1694.

Children of John Ward and Sarah ———.

John, b. 1649; m. dau. of Henry Lyon; 2, Abigail Kitchell
Mary, b. 1654; m, Samuel Harrison.
Nathaniel, b. 1656; m. Christiana Swaine.
Hannah, b. 1658; m. Jonathan Baldwin.
Elizabeth, b. 1660.
Dorcas, m. Joseph Harrison.
Deborah, m. Eliphalet Johnson.
Phebe, m. John Cooper.
Sarah, m. John Rogers.

JOHN ENGLAND died in Branford, 1655, leaving a widow but no children. His estate was valued at £121 6s. 11d., of which he gave £10 to Jonathan Sargent.

BRANFORD.

JOHN NORTON is supposed to have been the third son of Richard Norton and Ellen Rowley of London. His name appears upon the Branford records as one of the first settlers, where he lived with his wife Dorothy, who died 1652, leaving three young daughters who were born in Branford, and a son John, who died 1657. He married a second wife Elizabeth, who died leaving a son John. He assisted in the legal transactions of the place. In 1659 he removed to Farmington, and was one of the first proprietors in the division of lands in that place. He died there November 5, 1709.

Children of John Norton and Dorothy ———, who d. Jan. 24, 1652.

Elizabeth, b. 1645; m. John Plumb of Milford.
Hannah, b. 1646; m. Samuel North of Farmington.
Dorothy, b. March 1, 1649.
John, b. March 24, 1651; d. Jan. 15, 1657.

Children of John Norton and Elizabeth ———, who d. Nov. 6, 1657.

John, b. Oct. 14, 1657; m. Ruth More; d. April 25, 1725.

Children of John Norton and Elizabeth Clark.

Samuel, b. May 13, 1659; died August 20, 1659.
Thomas, b. 1660; m. Hannah Rose.

THOMAS FENNER was a trader carrying on a business by boat or vessel between Hartford and Branford or New Haven. His inventory taken two days after his death, May 15, 1647, would indicate that he had a stock of merchandise in both Hartford and Branford. It is evident that he died while away on a trip to Hartford.

EDWARD TREDWELL was from Ipswich, England. He was one of the early settlers of Branford, coming in 1644, where he was living in 1648 and perhaps later, as he does not appear at Southold, L. I., until 1659. He lived at that place many years, dying, 1718, very aged. It was probably his son Samuel Tredwell who was made a freeman in Fairfield, 1670, and in 1673 he received from that town a pasture and a building lot of fourteen acres.

RICHARD HARRISON came from West Kirby, Cheshire, England, to Virginia. He may have become interested in the maritime trade between the colonies, for in a very short time he came to New Haven accompanied by two sons, Richard, Jr., and Thomas. He was evidently aged, as he is called "old Harrison" in the Branford records. He signed the division of lands July 1, 1646, and remained in Branford until his death, which occurred October 25, 1653. His daughter, Maria, married Thomas Pierson, brother of Rev. Abraham Pierson.

Children of Richard, Sen., and Sarah ———.
Benjamin, who remained in Virginia.
Nathaniel, who remained in Virginia.
Richard, Jr., of Branford and Newark.
Thomas, of Branford.
Maria, who married Thomas Pierson.

RICHARD HARRISON, Jr., may have resided for some time in New Haven, but he was in Branford as early as 1645, where he had a house lot. He joined the Newark colony and removed there with his family. His house and lands in Branford were purchased in 1667 for £60 by a committee as a permanent home for the minister. As a signature to this deed he affixed his mark with a wax seal bearing a design of three roses.

THOMAS HARRISON, who remained in Branford, in 1688 gives his age as fifty-eight years. In 1667 he purchased the estate of Jasper Crane, which is described on the records: "a dwelling house with all outhouses, barns, stables, orchards, gardens, yard or yards about my now dwelling house." This is regarded as the first frame house which was built, He is the ancestor of a long line of descendants, many of whom have achieved marked success in professional life, and others have been called to positions of great trust and honor in public life.[1] When he died in 1696, his

---

[1] Notably among these, and worthy of the highest esteem, was the late Governor Henry Baldwin Harrison, of New Haven.

estate was estimated as the largest in the town, £192. He was twice married; his first wife was Mary, widow of John Thompson, of New Haven; March 29, 1666, he married Elizabeth Stent. He died 1704.

Children of Richard Harrison, Jr.

Benjamin, b. Jan. 30, 1655.
Ann, b. Nov. 2, 1657.
George, b. Dec. 31, 1658.

Children of Thomas Harrison and Mary Thompson, widow, m. 1652.

Thomas, b. March 1, 1657; m. Margaret Stent.
Nathaniel, b. Dec. 13, 1658; m. Abigail Frisbie.

Children of Thomas Harrison and Elizabeth Stent, m. March 26, 1666.

Elizabeth, b. Jan., 1667; m. William Barker.
Mary, b. Feb. 10, 1668; m. John Linsley.
John, b. March 1, 1670.
Samuel, b. August 11, 1673.

JONATHAN SEARGENT and his family were among the earliest settlers. August 10, 1651, his children went to New Haven and were baptized,—Jonathan, Hannah, Thomas and John. They were at this time all adults, "and able to walk to New Haven." He died Dec. 12, 1651, and his wife seven days later.

Thomas Seargent was a teacher from 1684 until 1691. He died in Branford, 1700.

John Seargent became a planter at Guilford Dec. 11, 1672, where he died, 1675.

Jonathan Seargent, with his sister Hannah, who had married Benjamin Baldwin, removed to Newark, and the family became extinct in Connecticut.

LUTHER or LESLY BRADFIELD is mentioned in the Wethersfield records, and in 1644 settled at Branford, locating near the shore. He died July 26, 1655, leaving a family. His daughter died July 29 of the same year. His widow, Mary, married George Adams, 1657. This is the first marriage on the records.

There was a son, Samuel Bradfield, and a daughter, Maria, who married John Whitehead.

GEORGE ADAMS, who was interested in the iron works, died 1675. His will dated 1670 mentions his widow and son John.

John Adams, his son, died 1677, and having no near relations gave " to Noah Rogers and Eleazar Stent all his estate equall."

CHARLES TAINTOR, the father of Michael Taintor, being deprived by confiscation of a large estate in Wales, migrated to America with his family, which consisted of a wife and four children. He was in New England in 1643, and with Capt. Jagger in the exodus from Wethersfield, settled in Fairfield. He was interested in foreign voyages and was lost at sea 1654. His son Michael, however, for obvious reasons, settled in Branford before 1650, where he had a house lot. He was master of a vessel trading with Virginia.

He, with his son John, then seventeen years of age, signed the new plantation and church covenant. In 1669 he was Judge of the Court of Branford and commissioner to arrange the bounds between Branford and New Haven; also between Branford and Guilford; and for several sessions a member of the Connecticut General Assembly.

" In him we find the ship-master and man of enterprise, the legislator and consistent Christian professor, the commissioner and judge, the puritan and patriarch; evidently bringing up his family in the fear of God. From all that can be known of him it appears evident that he was a man of influence and discretion, and posterity held his name in great respect and veneration, probably not so much from the splendor of his career as from the disinterested nobleness and integrity of his character." He died 1673, his wife Elizabeth, daughter of Robert Rose (?), having died in 1659. His estate was inventoried at £166.

His son John, "who possessed many of the virtues and qualities of his father," died in 1699, leaving no children His will contained the following bequest, "I do give to the town of Branford that part of my homelot lying between Stephen Foot's homelot and what was my Father Swaine's, to the street on the north of said land, that I do give to said town of Branford to build a public meetinghouse, and to continue for that use so long as they shall maintain a meetinghouse there unless the town see fit to build elsewhere, and then that land to be in common or what other use the town see meet . . .;" as well as a legacy of £4 for the church. This tract of land was accepted and became the public common or "Green," and the church building was erected thereon the following year.

All the Taintors in this country are supposed to be descendants of Michael Taintor, as his brothers are not known to have had children, and no names of any other family are to be found.

Children of Michael Taintor and Elizabeth Rose (?).

John, b. March 26, 1650; m. Dorcas Swaine.
Michael, b. Oct. 12, 1652; m. Mary Loomis, of Windsor; (2) Mabel Butler.
Elizabeth, b. June 22, 1655; m. Noah Rogers, April 8, 1673.
Johanna, b. April 29, 1657; m. Josiah Gillet, of Windsor, June 30, 1676.
Sarie, b. Oct. 12, 1658.

Children of Charles Taintor.

Michael.
Charles, Jr.
Joseph.
Marie, m. Thomas Pierson, son of Rev. Abraham Pierson.

JOHN WILFORD, a merchant, came from London. He was in New Haven, 1641, when lands were allotted to him in "ye Great Plaine"; he took the oath of fidelity, 1644, and was named in the seating of the church, 1646. He evidently went to Branford in that year, as he was elected town clerk at that place, 1648, succeeding John Plum. He was a member of the General Assembly for twenty sessions, from 1665 to 1676. While prominent in affairs of state he was enterprising in business. He was connected with the iron works at Furnace Pond, and their supplies were stored at his house. He died 1678, without children, leaving his entire estate to his nephew, John Wilford, of London, after the death of his wife. His widow married Thomas Topping, who was for a number of years a member of the Governor's Council of State. She contested the will, declaring that the property belonged to herself before marriage. Her claim was disputed by Richard Wilford, agent of John, of London, who settled permanently in Branford as early as 1698. He was a school teacher and land surveyor and the ancestor of the Wilford family.

Lydia Wilford Topping, d. Nov. 3, 1694.

RICHARD LAWRENCE was a deacon of the church of Branford. His name frequently occurs upon the records as a party to legal transactions. He was highly esteemed. His home was near Mulliner's Neck. He signed the Newark covenant and removed from Branford, 1667, and was settled at Passaic, New Jersey, 1668.

Children of Richard Lawrence and ——— ———, b. in Branford.

Ebenezer, b. Jan. 17, 1651.
Edward, b. July 15, 1654; d. Nov. 12, 1655.
Sarah, b. March 25, 1657.
Bothia and Esther were baptized in New Haven, June 1, 1651.

RICHARD WILLIAMS removed to Fairfield, 1658.

Children of Richard Williams and ——— ———.

Samuel, b. Sept. 13, 1655.
Daniel, b. April 15, 1657.

JOHN EDWARDS with his son Thomas came from Wethersfield, 1647. At this date he signed an agreement to share all expenses with the other proprietors of Branford. He died in 1664.

JOHN HILL was living in Branford, 1644-48. He had a wife Frances and four children. He may have lived some time in Guilford. He died, 1673 or '78. His inventory is entered on the records as that of John Hill of Branford, but without date, and appraised by Moses Croft and John Frisbie.

SIGISMOND RICHALLS was a landowner, and in 1676 he was estimated as worth £30, 10s. He died Dec. 27, 1692.

THOMAS and JOHN WHITEHEAD were probably the youth brought over from England by Francis Halle at the request of their uncle, Thomas Allcote of Roxbury, Mass., who promised to pay the expense of their passage upon their arrival; but Mr. Allcote was then dead. There was no provision for the youth, and Thomas was employed by Mathias Hitchcocke and later by David Atwater. John became a member of the household of Jasper Crane, and accompanied him to Branford. He married March 9, 1661, Martha, daughter of Lesly Bradfield. He signed the new Plantation and Church covenant and resided in Branford until his death. His widow and seven children were present at the signing of his inventory, January 8, 1695. He owned a house and upland at Indian Neck.

Children of John Whitehead and Martha Bradfield.

Hannah, m. Peter Tyler, Dec. 25, 1688.
John, b. Feb. 20, 1665.
Martha, b. Jan. 10, 1667.
Damaris, b. Jan. 20, 1669.
Samuel, b. Nov. 24, 1672.
Eliphalet, b. Sept. 27, 1674.
Elizabeth, b. Oct., 1677.
Thomas, b. Feb. 27, 1680.

ROBERT MEEKER took the oath of fidelity in New Haven July 1, 1644, and then removed to Branford, where he appeared to be a person of some standing. He married Susan Tuberfield, 1651. He removed to Fairfield before 1670.

SAMUEL NETTLETON was a landowner and in Branford until 1668. November 4, 1647, he appeared before the Governor and upon oath testified "that he had bought a pare of shooes of Goodman Megs of New Haven, russed, clossed in the inside at the side seames, for his wife. She put tnem on on the Lord's day, and the next third day they were ripped, the soales being good, neither shranke nor hornie, that I could perceive. And he also testifyed that for and in consideration of satisfaction from Goodman Megs he expecteth a new pare."

Maria, wife of Samuel Nettleton, died October 29, 1658.

Hannah Nettleton, a daughter, married Thomas Linsley, July 10, 1656.

THOMAS MORRIS and his son-in-law, Thomas Lupton, although associated with the purchasers of Totokett, did not own lands in that plantation.

WILLIAM MERCHANT and **RICHARD MATHER** do not appear to have continued any permanent connection with the colony.

ED. BALL, a surveyor, who had married a daughter of Thomas Blatchly, removed to Newark, where he was appointed high sheriff.

PERSONNEL OF GUILFORD.

IN addition to the information given on pages 160-171 of this volume something further in relation to the first settlers of Guilford will be of interest to the reader.

It is stated in the John Stone Family Genealogy (189), page 150, that the first ship, the St. John, commanded by Captain Russell, sailed from England on May 20, 1639, and arrived at New Haven between July 10th and 15th, 1639. The list of persons (in alphabetical order) who are believed to have come in this first ship and to have settled, with a few exceptions, in Guilford is as follows:

John Bishop,	John Jordan,
Francis Bushnell,	Thomas Jones,
Francis Chatfield,	Henry Kingsnorth,
William Chittenden,	Robert Kitchell,
Thomas Cook,	William Leete,
Abraham Cruttenden,	John Mepham,
Henry Dowd,	William Plane,
William Dudley,	John Parmelin,
Richard Gutridge,	Thomas Nash,
John Hoadley,	Thomas Norton,
William Hall,	John Stone,
John Hughes,	William Stone,
Rev. Henry Whitfield.	25 names.

The names of the Guilford settlers that came to New Haven in the second ship in July, 1639, are believed to be as follows:

Francis Austin,	Thomas Dunk,
George Bartlett,	Thomas French,
Edward Benton,	George Highland,
Samuel Blachley,	John Johnson,

GUILFORD. 627

William Boreman,
Richard Bristow,
Alexander Chalker,
John Caffinch, rem. to N. H.,
Samuel Desborough,
John Scranton,
John Sheader, or Sheather,
Jacob Sheafe,

John Linsley,
Thomas Mills,
Thomas Reif,
William Somers,
John Stevens,
Edward Seward,
Jasper Stillwell,
Benjamin Wright.

24 persons.

Of the forty-eight planters in the lists of 1650 and 1652, noted on pages 166 and 167, those not mentioned in the alphabetical lists above are as follows: Stephen Bishop, Thomas Betts, Thomas Chatfield, George Chatfield, Abraham Cruttenden, Jr., John Evarts, John Fowler, Rev. John Higginson, Richard Hughes, George Hubbard, Thomas Jordan, John Parmelin, Jr., Thomas Stevens.

LIEUT. GEORGE BARTLETT (16 –1669) came in the second ship to New Haven in 1649. He removed from Guilford to Branford and died there August 3, 1669, and his widow died there the next month. He married September 14, 1650, Mary Cruttenden (b. 163 ; d. Sept. 11, 1669), daughter of Deacon Abraham Cruttenden (16 –1683) and Mary —— (16 –1664). They had seven or more children. See "The Bartlett Family," 1876, page 114, by Levi Bartlett, and also another Bartlett Family Book of 1892, page 112, by Bartlett. Also see New Eng. Hist. & Gen. Register, vol. 52, pages 466–469.

JOHN BISHOP came in the first ship (St. John) that came direct from England to New Haven. He died in Guilford before January 7, 1661, when his inventory was taken. His widow Ann survived him, and her will was probated in Hartford, June, 1676. He had three or more children. The sons, John (16 –1683) and Stephen (16 –1690), lived and died in Guilford, and both had large sized families.

EDWARD BENTON came in the second ship (   )

which came to New Haven direct from England. He lived in Hartford in 1659, but was again in Guilford in 1669. He died, October 28, 1680. His wife Ann (16 –1671) had ten or more children. (See the N. Eng. Gen. Reg., vol. 54, page 175.)

THOMAS BETTS (1616–1688) removed from Milford to Guilford before 1650. After 1658 he was in Milford, and in 1664 in Norwalk, where he died. He had nine or more children. Five sons are recorded as proprietors in Norwalk in 1694. (See Selleck's History of Norwalk.)

SAMUEL BLACHLEY (or Blakesley) came in the second ship to New Haven. He married, December 5, 1650, Hannah Potter.

WILLIAM BOREMAN probably came in the second ship to New Haven. No information concerning him is found in Savage's Genealogical Dictionary.

FRANCIS BUSHNELL (16 –1646) and wife Rebecca had some six children, four of them being born in England. His daughter Sarah (1625-1688) married Rev. John Hoadley (16 – 1693), returned to England with her husband, and died at Rolvenden, Kent, July 28, 1668. He was ancestor of David Bushnell, who in the time of the war of the American Revolution invented the first submarine boat and submarine torpedo, the "American Turtle"; also of Cornelius S. Bushnell (1829–1896) of New Haven, Conn., who after a great deal of work succeeded in inducing President Lincoln to order the contract to be made for Ericsson's "Monitor," and was very prominent in preparing the ways and means for its construction. (For further particulars of this family see N. Eng. Gen. Reg., vol. 53, page 208.)

ALEXANDER CHALKER (16 –167) married, September 29, 1649, Catherine Post (16 –168), daughter of Stephen Post (15 –1659) of Saybrook. He removed to Saybrook where he had some seven or more children. He died before 1673, as his widow was married September 25, 1673, to John Hill.

GUILFORD. 629

FRANCIS CHATFIELD (16 -164) is believed to have died without wife or children. George Chatfield, his brother, lived in Guilford with his wife, Sarah Bishop, daughter of John Bishop (16 -166). She died September 20, 1657. No children survived her. He married March 29, 1658, Isabel Nettleton, daughter of Samuel Nettleton. She had three or more children. He removed to Killingworth in 1663, and died there June 7, 1671.

THOMAS CHATFIELD removed to New Haven. There he married Ann Higginson, daughter of Rev. Francis Higginson. He removed to East Hampton, Long Island, which was then under the jurisdiction of New Haven Colony, and died there without leaving any descendants.

MAJOR WILLIAM CHITTENDEN (1593–1661) and wife, Joan Sheaffe (16 -1668), came to New Haven from East Guilford, County Sussex, England. He had nine children, and was lieutenant and magistrate in Guilford. (See " Chittenden's Family," 1882, page 225, by Dr. Alvan Talcott.)

THOMAS COOKE (16 -1692) signed the agreement on board the St. John on June 1, 1639. He had two children, Thomas and Sarah. Sarah married Thomas Hall of Guilford. He married March 30, 1668, for second wife, Hannah Lindon, who died July 7, 1676, and he died December 1, 1692.

DEACON ABRAHAM CRUTTENDEN (1610–1683), one of the signers of the "Covenant" of June 1, 1639, with wife Mary (16 -1664) and some four children, arrived in New Haven and Guilford in 1639. He had three more children in Guilford. On May 31, 1665 he married Mrs. Johanna (   ) Chittenden (16 -1668), the widow of William Chittenden. A large number of his descendants are to be found at the present time, as all of his seven children were married, and with perhaps one exception, all had children. (See N. Eng. Reg., vol. 52, pages 466–469.)

SAMUEL DESBOROUGH (16 -1690), who probably came to New Haven in the second ship, returned to England with his family in the autumn of 1650, with his minister, Rev. Henry Whitfield, and died in England December 10, 1690, at his family estate of Elsworth, Cambridge. (For further account of his life in England see Savage's Genealogical Dictionary, vol. 2, pages 41-42.)

WILLIAM DUDLEY married in 1636 at Oakeley in Surrey, England, Jane Lutman (b.   , 16   ; d. May 1, 1674). He had five or more children, and died in Guilford March 5, 1684. Among other descendants is the Hon. Wm. W. Dudley of Indiana, Commissioner of Pensions 1881-1884. The Dudley Family Genealogies of 1848, 144 pages; 1862, 160 pages; and 1886-94, by Dean Dudley, 1,400 pages, give extensive information concerning the Dudley family.

HENRY DOWD, one of the signers of the compact of June 1, 1639, died or was buried August 31, 1668. Probably with his wife Elizabeth (16 -1683) there were also brought over from England some of his eight children, for the last birth recorded by Savage is in 1653. In 1680 all but two of the children were living.

JOHN EVARTS (16 -1669) was a freeman in Concord in March 1638. Probably some of his children were born in England. He removed to Guilford about 1650. There his wife, the mother of his children, died, and he married Mrs. Elizabeth Parmelee, the widow of John Parmelee. His sons John, Judah, Daniel and heirs of James were proprietors in Guilford in 1685. A daughter Elizabeth married Peter Abbott of Fairfield and was killed by her husband, who also attempted to kill his only child Hannah. Although undoubtedly insane, he was executed October 16, 1667.

DEACON JOHN FOWLER (16 -1677) with his father-in-law, George Hubbard (16 -1683), removed from Milford to Guilford about 1649. He died in May, 1677. His wife, Mary Hubbard, died April 13, 1713. Of his six or more children, three daughters died young, and the fourth, Mehitable, died in 1751, unmarried, aged 95 years. The name has been transmitted through the two sons, Abraham and John. (See the Fowler Genealogies, Boston, 1857; No. 2, 8vo., pp. 12; No. 3, 12mo., pp. 42, Milwaukee, 1870.)

THOMAS FRENCH was in Charlestown in 1638. He removed to Guilford in 1650 or before. Of several children only Ebenezer and John lived to middle age. A daughter Mary married September 14, 1665, John Evarts, and died in a few years. (See the N. Eng. Hist. and Gen. Reg. of 1893.)

RICHARD GUTRIDGE (Savage changes the name to Goodrich) was one of the signers of the compact of June 1, 1639. Nothing more concerning him is found in the Genealogical Dictionary. In the History of Guilford it is stated that he died May 7, 1676.

Rev. JOHN HIGGINSON (1616–1708), son of Rev. Francis Higginson (1587–1629) of Salem, Mass., came from Saybrook in 1641 to Guilford, where he married   , 165 , Sarah Whitfield, daughter of Rev. Henry Whitfield (1597–165), by whom he had several children. He was a colleague of Rev. Henry Whitfield. In 1659 he was in Salem and about to take a ship for England when he was induced to remain at Salem and become their pastor, and at which place he died December 9, 1708. He married   , 1676, Mrs. Mary (Blackman) Atwater (1635–1709,) widow of Joshua Atwater (1612–1676), a merchant of Boston.

GEORGE HIGHLAND (or Hyland) perhaps came in the second ship to New Haven in July, 1639. He died January 21, 1692. He had four daughters. Two of them married Halls, one of whom had a son Highland. Mary Highland married February 1, 1692–3, Capt. Thomas Hall (1662–1753) and removed to Middletown. They must have returned to Guilford, for he died in Guilford. (See Tuttle Family Book, 1883, page 43)

WILLIAM HALL, who came over in the first ship in 1639, perhaps married his wife Esther after he arrived in New Haven Colony, as his first child, John, was born in 1648. He died March

8, 1669, and his widow died in 1683. The sons, John and Samuel, married and had children. (See Halls of New England, 1883, 789 pages, Albany.)

Rev. JOHN HOADLEY, born January, 1617, probably at Rolvenden, County Kent, England, came with relatives to New Haven in 1639. He was a signer of the compact of June 1, 1639. He married June 14, 1642, Sarah Bushnell, daughter of Francis Bushnell. (See Bushnell note on page   .) In 1653 he returned to England and was made Court Chaplain by Cromwell. In 1655 his wife and family followed him to Edinburgh. There he had three children. In 1662 he removed to Rolvenden, where he had two more children, making a total of twelve children. There he died July 28, 1668. His wife died November 1, 1693, at Halstead in Kent, where her son John was the rector.

GEORGE HUBBARD was in Wethersfield in 1636, probably came there from Watertown, and was a representative from Wethersfield in the first General Assembly in 1643. He removed to Milford and is recorded on the Milford map of 1646. (See map opposite page 155.) In 1650 he was in Guilford, where his wife Mary died September 16, 1676. He died January , 1683. From his seven or more children a large number of people have descended. (See the Hubbard Genealogy, 1895, 512 pages, N. Y.)

RICHARD HUGHES perhaps came over in the second ship. He died before 1659, for in that year his widow Mary married William Stone. Samuel Hughes of Guilford, a proprietor in 1665, was probably his son.

JOHN HUGHES was a signer of the compact of June 1, 1639. He did not remain long in Guilford, but removed elsewhere.

JOHN JORDAN (16 –1650) came over in the first ship (St. John). He died about January 1, 1649–50. He married about 1640 Anna Bishop (16 –16), daughter of John Bishop (16 –1660) and Ann   (16 –1676) of Guilford.

JOHN JOHNSON probably came over to New Haven in the second ship. He married in Guilford, October 1, 1651, Mrs. Elizabeth (Disbrow) Relfe, who had been divorced from her husband Thomas Relfe, he having deserted her and gone to Long Island. She died December 23, 1661, and he died in 1681. In his will four children are mentioned, viz: John, Ruth, Isaac and Abigail.

THOMAS JORDAN, a younger brother of John, perhaps came in the first ship with his brother, but being under age did not sign the conpact, so was not mentioned in the list. He was from Kent County, England, and went home in 1655. His daughter Elizabeth (16 –March 4, 1701) married June 1, 1669, Andrew Leete (16 –1702) of Guilford. She had six children. All of them were living at the death of their parents.

THOMAS JONES, one of the signers of the compact of June 1, 1639, possibly married his wife Mary after coming to New Haven Colony. She had three children before 1650 and died December 5, 1650. He soon after married a widow Carter, went to England and died there of small-pox in 1654. A son Nathaniel and daughter Sarah, who married June 8, 1665, John Pratt of Saybrook, remained in New England.

HENRY KINGSNORTH, one of the signers of the compact, died in 1668. He married Mary Stevens, daughter of John Stevens. She married June 2, 1669, John Collins (16 –1704), and died before 1700, for in that year he married again.

ROBERT KITCHELL (1604-167) with wife, Margaret Sheaffe, and three or more children came in the first ship to New Haven, or rather to Quinnipiac. He removed to Newark, N. J., and died there. His widow came back to Connecticut and died in Greenwich in 1679. Through his daughter, Mrs. Hannah (Kitchell) Peck, and his son Samuel he had numerous descendants, the author of this History being one of them. (See Kitchell Genealogy, 1879, New York, 8vo., pp. 80.)

Gov. WILLIAM LEETE (1611-1683), a signer of the compact,

was a very prominent person in Guilford. Assistant in 1643, Deputy-Governor in 1658, Governor 1661-65, Deputy-Governor of Connecticut Colony 1670-76, and Governor 1676-83. His first child, John, born in 1639, is said to have been the first white child born in Guilford. Of his three wives, the first, Ann, who was buried September 1, 1668, was probably the mother of all of his children. His second wife, Mrs. Sarah Rutherford, widow of Henry Rutherford (16   -16   ), married to him in 1671, died February 10, 1674; and his third wife, Mrs. Mary (   ) Street, widow of Rev. Nicholas Street (16 -16   ), and before her marriage to Mr. Street the widow of Francis Newman (16 -16   ), died a few months after her husband, who died April 16, 1683. Gov. William Leete will long be remembered for the aid given to the regicides by delaying their pursuers, and by sending them word warning them of their danger. (See Leete Genealogy, 1874, pp. 168, New Haven.)

JOHN LINSLEY probably came in the second ship to New Haven Colony. He removed before 1667 to Branford; and further information concerning him will be given under the chapters on the Planters of Branford.

JOHN MEPHAM, a signer of the compact, was one of the seven pillars at the foundation of the church in 1643. He died in 1647 leaving an only son John. His widow married in 1649 Timothy Baldwin (16   -166) of Milford; she married in 1666 as her third husband Thomas Tapping of Milford.

THOMAS NASH (15   -165), a signer of the compact of June 1, 1639, remained in New Haven. (See ante., page 134; also the Nash Family Gen., 304 pages, 1853, Hartford, Conn.)

THOMAS NORTON, a signer of the compact, died in 1648. As he married his wife, Grace Wells, in 1625 he was very probably less than fifty years of age at the time of his death. Before coming to New Haven he was a warden in the church in Ocgley, Surrey County, England, where the Rev. Henry Whitfield was rector. His children, two sons, Thomas and John, and four daughters, Ann, Grace, Mary and Abigail all married, so that his descendants are very numerous. (See History of Goshen, Conn., 1897; also Norton Family Gen., at present in MSS.)

JOHN PARMELEE (Parmily, Permely, Parmal.e or Parmelin) was one of the signers of the Plantation Covenant of June 1, 1639 (old style). He died in New Haven November 8, 1659. The will was probated January 3, 1659–60; amount £78, 13s. He gave to his son John, probably the only son that outlived him, a large share of his property, the remainder to his daughter Hannah, the wife of John Johnson, and to his widow Elizabeth, who, as stated above, married John Evarts. He married first Hannah   , and second Elizabeth Bradley, who died in New Haven January   , 1683. His house lot was on the site of the present First Congregational Church. Spencer T. Parmalee of New Haven, the founder of the Mathushek Piano Co. was a descendant.

WILLIAM PLANE, a signer of the compact, was executed at New Haven in 1646. No record of children is found.

JOHN SCRANTON, possibly one of the company that came in the second ship to New Haven with his wife Joanna, who died in 1651. He married in 1663 Mrs. Adeline (   ) Hill, widow of Robert Hill. He died August 27, 1671; his widow died in 1685. The children, Thomas, John and Sarah, all by the first wife, married and left descendants. Probably most all persons of this name in Connecticut are descendants of this John Scranton (16 – 1671). (See Scranton Genealogy, 1855, 104 pages, Hartford, Conn.)

EDWARD SEWARD, possibly a passenger in the second ship, or he may be the Edward Seward who was in Ipswich in 1637, and perhaps the person who went back to England and then returned to New England He was in Guilford in 1650, and died there a few years after. No record found of wife or family. The Sewards of Connecticut of the present century are descended from Lieut. William Seward (1627–1689), who settled in Guilford after 1652.

JOHN SHEADER (or Sheather) was probably a passenger in the second ship. Some of his five children, if not all, married and had children. Two of the sons, John and Samuel, removed to Killingworth.

JACOB SHEAFFE (1616–1659) came with his mother, Mrs. Joanna Sheaffe (15 –1659), to Guilford with Rev. Henry Whitfield, who had married his sister. In 1642 he removed to Boston where he married in 1643 Margaret Webb, only child of Henry Webb (16 –1660) of Boston. He had six or more children. The inscription on his tombstone states that he died March 22, 1659. A son, Jacob, was born July 23, 1659, four months after his death. His estate was the largest of any one who had died at that time in Boston.

WILLIAM SOMERS died before 1650. Nothing more is found in Savage or elsewhere concerning him.

JOHN STONE (16 –1687), a signer of the compact, by wife Mary   had five or more children; four of the sons married and had families. (See The Family of John Stone of Guilford, 1888, 184 pages, Albany.)

WILLIAM STONE, also a passenger on the first ship (St. John), by wife Hannah had four or more children. He married in 1659 Mrs. Mary (   ) Hughes, widow of Richard Hughes of Guilford, and died November   , 1683.

The Stone family (descendants of these two men, John and William Stone), for several years have had family reunions at New Haven, Milford, Guilford, West Haven and elsewhere on the Connecticut shore of Long Island Sound, where they gathered together and renewed their family intercourse, read historical papers concerning the family, &c. A large and exhaustive genealogy of descendants of William Stone (16 –1683) is being compiled by Charles Stone Smith of Terryville, Conn. A list of descendants in the male line for a few generations is printed as an appendix in the John Stone Family Genealogy noted above.

Rev. HENRY WHITFIELD (1597-165), the pastor of the people who formed the Guilford Plantation, arrived in New Haven on the St. John (according to the John Stone Family Book) between July 10 and 15, 1639, with a portion of his parishioners. He built in Guilford the celebrated stone house which is still in existence and one of the oldest houses in the United States north of St. Augustine, Florida. He went back to England in 1650, leaving a portion of his family in the New Haven Colony and never returned to the Colony, dying not many years after at Winchester. Of his large family only the daughters Abigail, who married Rev. James Fitch (162 -16), and Sarah, who married Rev. John Higginson (1616-1708), are recorded.

BENJAMIN WRIGHT, probably one of the second company that came to New Haven, after living in Guilford some years removed to Killingworth (now Clinton), where he died March 29, 1677. His widow, Jane, died October 26, 1684, leaving three sons and three daughters. The daughters were married at the time of her death and probably her sons also.

ADDENDA.

Three brothers, Francis, Thomas and George Chatfield, were in Guilford in 1639 or soon after. Francis signed the compact of June 1, 1639; his brothers Thomas and George may have come with him, but being younger did not sign the conpact, or what is more probable came in the second ship which brought the remainder of the Guilford company. Francis died unmarried in Guilford in 1647. Thomas removed to New Haven, there married Ann Higginson (16 -16), daughter of Rev. Francis Higginson (1587-1629) of Salem, who had come to New Haven with her mother and brothers, and from there removed to Easthampton, Long Island, where he was long a magistrate of the Connecticut Colony jurisdiction. George Chatfield married first Sarah Bishop (b.   , 16   ; d. Sept. 30, 1657), who left no children; he married second Isabel Nettleton (16 -16), daughter of Samuel Nettleton. In 1663 he removed to Killingworth, Conn., where he died June 9, 1671, leaving three children, viz: John, b. April 8, 1661; George, b. Aug. 18, 1668; Mercy, b. April 26, 1671.

THOMAS DUNK was in Guilford in 1645, but is not mentioned in the list of 1650. He was in Saybrook in 1662 and on the east side of Connecticut River in 1673. His first wife, Mary Price, daughter of William Price of Newington, Butts, County Surrey, England, and widow of Philip Petersfield of Turnstile Alley, in the parish of Holborn, at the age of sixteen or seventeen years, came to New Haven about 1644. She lived with Mrs. George Lamberton some two years, married about 1647 or 1648 Thomas North, and had three children by him. After his death she married Thomas Dunk. No children are recorded. In 1670 she went to England to obtain her father's estate and probably died there. (See affidavits in New Eng. Reg., vol. 11, pages 159–160, which give the age and home in England of some of the persons making the affidavits, one of them being Mrs. Margaret (Lamberton) Goodyear.) On July 10, 1677, Thomas Dunk married Elizabeth Stedman and had Thomas, b. August 6, 1678. She died October 8, 1678, and he died August 9, 1683.

PERSONNEL OF MILFORD (WEPOWAUG)

1639–1646.

FOLLOWING is a list of residents of Milford recorded on the Map of 1646, and whether they came from New Haven or Wethersfield. Those marked 1 came from New Haven; those marked 2 from Wethersfield:

2	John Astwood (Atwood),	1	John Fowler,
2	Thomas Baker,	2	Dr. Jasper Gunn,
1	John Baldwin,	2	Edmund Harvey,
1	Joseph Baldwin.	2	Philip Hatley,
1	Nathaniel Baldwin,	2	George Hubbard,
1	Timothy Baldwin,	2	John Lane,
1	Richard Baldwin,	2	Thomas Lawrence,
1	Mrs. Martha Beard,	2	Henry Lyon,
2	Andrew Benton,	1	Richard Platt,
2	John Birdseye,	2	Robert Plum,
2	Francis Bolt,	1	John Pocock,
2	Henry Botsford,	1	James Prudden,
2	Nathaniel Briscoe,	1	Rev. Roger Prudden,
2	William Brooks,	2	Edward Riggs,
2	Alexander Bryan,	2	John Rogers,
1	Dea. Thomas Buckingham,	2	Thomas Sanford,
2	John Burwell,	2	Rev. John Sherman,
2	Nicholas Camp,	2	William Slough,
2	Thomas Canfield,	1	John Smith, Sr.,
2	Dea. George Clark,	1	Henry Stonhill,
2	George Clark, Jr.,	1	John Stream,
2	Samuel Cooley.	1	Edmund Tapp,
1	Robert Dennison,	2	Thomas Tapping,

MILFORD.

2 William East,
1 Benjamin Fenn,
2 John Fletcher,
1 Thomas Ford,
1 William Fowler,
1 William Fowler, Jr.,

2 Roger Terrill,
1 Thomas Tibballs,
2 Micah Tomkins,
1 Thomas Welch,
2 Thomas Wheeler,
1 Zechariah Whitman.

JOHN ASTWOOD (or Atwood) (1609–1654) was first in Roxbury. He came over on the ship *Hopewell*, Captain Bundocke, in the spring of 1636, aged 26 years; was a husbandman from Stanstead Abbey, County Herts. While living in Roxbury he had a wife, Martha, who may have come over on the same ship. He was made a freeman March 3, 1635-6, removed to Milford and there in 1640 married Mrs. Sarah (   ) Baldwin (16 –1669), widow of Sylvester Baldwin (15 –1638). He was chosen representative in 1643 and '44, an Assistant of the Colony at a later date, and a Commissioner of the United Colonies in 1653. As an agent for the Colonies to "petition for aid to reduce the Dutch" he went to England in 1654 and died at Aberthy, Eng., in July (?) 1654. Will made June 27; probated August 31, 1654.

THOMAS BAKER (16 –16) in 1650 removed to East Hampton, L. I., and is probably the same person who was recorded as an Assistant of Connecticut Colony from 1658 to 1663.

JOHN BALDWIN (16 –1681), a son of Sylvester Baldwin (15 –1638), who died on the ship *Martin* in 1638 on the way to Boston, by his first wife, Mary   (16 –1652), had seven or more children. He married   , 1653, Mary Bruen (16 – 16), and by her had seven children, all of these latter through their mother trace back to royal lines and to William the Conqueror. Mary Bruen was a daughter of Obadiah Bruen (1606–168) of Bruen, Stapleford, Cheshire, England. About 1667 or 1668 he removed to Newark, N. J., but returned to Milford where he died June   , 1681. He was buried June 21, 1681. In his will, made May 24, 1681, he mentions all of his children except Samuel, Mary and Sarah, who had probably died before 1681. (For

MILFORD. 641

further information see Baldwin Family Book, 1889, pages 1373, by Judge C. C. Baldwin, Cleveland, Ohio.)

JOSEPH BALDWIN (16 -1690) by wife, Hannah   (16 - 16   ), had four sons and five daughters. About 1663 he removed to Hadley; was a freeman there in 1666. He married for a second wife Mrs. Isabel (   ) Northam, widow of James Northam (16 -16) of Hartford, and before that a widow of   Catlin (16 -16); her son, John Catlin (16 -17), married Mary Baldwin, one of Joseph's daughters. For a third wife he married Mrs. Elizabeth (   ) Warriner (b.   , 16 ; d. April 25, 1696), widow of William Warriner (16 -1676) of Springfield; he died   , 1690 at Hadley.

NATHANIEL (16 -1650), JOSEPH AND TIMOTHY were brothers, sons of Richard Baldwin (15 -16) of Clholesbury, Buckinghamshire, Eng. He with his wife, Abigail Camp (b.   , 162 ; d. March 22, 1647-8), daughter of Nicholas Camp (159 - 165), was in Milford in 1639. He died   , 1650, leaving three sons and a daughter Abigail.

TIMOTHY BALDWIN (16 -1665) had a town lot in New Haven in 1640, but is not recorded there as a resident. By his wife, Mary (16 ; d. July 21, 1647), he had three daughters. He married   , 1647, Mrs. Mary (   ) Mepham (b.   , 16 ; d. before 1670), widow of John Mepham (16 -164) of Guilford. By this second wife he had three or more children. There were no descendants of this settler in the Baldwin line. His son Timothy had no sons that grew up and were married. (See Baldwin Family Book. Milford "Memorial Bridge" pamphlet.)

MRS. MARTHA (   ) BEARD (15 -1647), with her husband James (?) Beard (15 -1638), came to New England in 1638 on the ship *Martin*. He died on board the ship before reaching Massachusetts Colony. She had three sons, James (16 -1642), who d. unmarried, Jeremy, who also d. unmarried in 16 , and Capt. John Beard (16 -16) and three daughters, Martha (16 -16),
41

who married John Stream (16 –1685), Sarah, who married Nicholas Camp, Jr. (1629-1706), and ――――

RICHARD BALDWIN (16 –1665), eldest son of Sylvester Baldwin (15 –1638), who died on the ship *Martin* soon after June 21, 1638, when " his *nuncup*. will was made" and which was probated in Boston , 163 . He with his mother, Sarah ( ) Baldwin (15 ; d. Nov., 1689), brother John and sisters Sarah, Mary, Martha and Ruth lived in Milford and died there July 29, 1665. He married , 1642, Elizabeth Alsop (16 –16), sister of Joseph Alsop (1621-1698), and had five sons and six daughters.

ANDREW BENTON (16 –16) in Milford in 1639 removed to Hartford after 1660 and died in 1683. By his first wife he had three sons and two daughters; by his second wife, Ann (16 –1686), he had one son and two daughters.

JOHN BIRDSEYE (16 –168) removed in 1649 to the adjoining town of Stratford. In his will, which was drawn August 22, 1689, he mentions his second wife, Mrs. Alice ( ) Tomlinson (16 –169), widow of Henry Tomlinson (16 –1681), and his son John and daughter Joanna, wife of Timothy Wilcockson, whom she married December 28, 1664.

FRANCIS BOLT (16 –1649) came to Boston in the ship *Martin* in 1638 with the Baldwins. He joined the church in 1640, and it is believed had wife Susanna, a son Philip and daughter Susanna, who are mentioned in the records of Milford.

HENRY BOTSFORD (16 –1686) by wife, Elizabeth (16 –16), who joined the church in 1640, had one son and five daughters, all of whom grew up, were married and had children. He died between February 1, 1685-6, the date of his will, and April 15, 1686, the date of the inventory.

NATHANIEL BRISCOE (16 –1683), born about 1620, baptized , 1629, at Little Missenden, England, was son of Nathaniel Briscoe (15 –16) and Elizabeth   (b.   , 15 ; bur. Nov. 20, 1642, at Watertown, Mass.) of Watertown, Mass., the "rich tanner." He was an usher in Harvard College, Cambridge, in 1639. According to Lambert's History he came to Milford from Wethersfield. He married   , 164 , Mehitable   (16 –16) and had sons Nathaniel (1646–1691), James (1649–1710) and Abigail. (For further information concerning this family see Bond's Hist. of Watertown; also a pamphlet on the Biscoe family published in London in 1888.)

WILLIAM BROOKS (16 –1684) at Milford 1640 or after; married Mrs. Sarah (   ) Wheeler (16 –1666), widow of William Wheeler (16 –16). She was probably a second wife. Nothing further found in Savage concerning this settler.

JOHN BROWN (16 –16) had a wife, Mary, and a family of three sons and five daughters. He removed about 166 to Newark, N. J., where probably further record of him and his family may be found.

ALEXANDER BRYAN (or Bryant) (1602–1679), son of Thomas Bryan of Alesbury, Eng., was baptized there September 29, 1602. He had a wife, Anna Baldwin (b.   , 16 ; d. Feb. 20, 1661), daughter of Robert and Joanna Baldwin of   , Eng. From 1668 to 1678 he was Assistant Governor of Connecticut Colony. He was a prominent merchant, owned land in Norwalk, but probably never resided there. He married after 1661 Mrs.   (   ) Fitch (16 –16), widow of Samuel Fitch of Milford and Hartford. (See pamphlet of 12 pages reprinted from the Baldwin Family Book.)

DEACON THOMAS BUCKINGHAM (16 –1657) was one of the New Haven Company who arrived at Quinnipiac in 1638 and removed to Milford in 1659; he probably came with that company to Massachusetts Colony in 1637; it is possible that he was from the neighborhood of the home of the Rev. Peter Prudden (16 – 1656); was a minister before coming to New England. It is very probable that those of the New Haven Company who left New Haven by 1640 and went to Milford had been under the ministration of this minister in England, and for that reason followed him to whatever place he should settle. Deacon B. by his wife, Hannah Hawkins (?) (16 –1647), had sons and daughters. He went to Boston "to seek for them a Pastor" (says the Church Record) and died there in 1657. His grandson, Rev. Stephen Buckingham (16 –17), was a member of Yale College Corporation 1718–1732; his sons were, and his descendants have been, prominent men in their day and generation. From him was descended Governor and U. S. Senator William H. Buckingham (16 –167) of Connecticut. (See the Buckingham Family Book, 1872, pp. 594, Hartford, Ct., by Rev. F. W. Chapman.)

JOHN BURWELL (16 –1649) was from Herts Co., but dying so early (Aug. 17, 1649), Milford records do not contain much information concerning him. He had five sons and a daughter Elizabeth, born   , 1647. His wife, Alice   (b.   16 ; d. Dec. 19, 1649). A line of ancestry to English Lords and members of the Royal family is said to be found in this family.

NICHOLAS CAMP (1597–1652-8), perhaps son of John Campe (15 –1630) of Nasing, England, had three wives, possibly more; by his wife Sarah (15 –1645) he had Abigail (162 –1648), wife of Nathaniel Baldwin (16 –1650), Nicholas (1629–1707), William (163 –17), and perhaps others. Her name is engraved on the Memorial Bridge; she died Sept. 1, 1645, and was the first adult person buried in Milford; her infant twin sons born in August died in November, 1645. Married his second wife 1646, Mrs. Edith (   ) Tilley (16 –164), widow of John Tilley (16 – 1645) of Windsor, had one daughter, Abigail Camp (b. Aug. 29, 1647; d.   , 16). For his third wife he married July 14, 1652, Mrs. Kattern (   ) Thompson (16 –16), widow of Anthony Thompson (16 –1648) of New Haven. Evidently he died before 1658, for in that year she is called in New Haven records "Widow Camp." He probably had no children by the third wife.

SERGT. THOMAS CANFIELD (16 –1689) with his wife, Phebe

Crance (16 -16), who probably was in some way related to the Henry and Benj. Crane of Wethersfield, Conn., was a prominent man in Milford, a sergeant of militia, and a representative to the Connecticut Colony 1673-74; he left two sons and seven or more daughters. (For further information see Orcutt's History of New Milford, "History of Thomas Canfield and Matthew Canfield," 1897, Dover, New Jersey, pp. 228, by Fred. Canfield.)

DEACON GEORGE CLARK (16 -1690) with his wife, Mary (16 -16), came from Wethersfield to Milford in 1639. Three of his sons were prominent in Milford affairs: George (16 -17) was an ensign; one of his daughters, Sarah (16 -17), became the mother of Jonathan Law (16 -16), Gov. of Connecticut Colony in 17 . Savage states he " was called carpenter for distinction and this is all I know about him." (See also " Clark Genealogy," by Albert Clark Patterson, Washington, D. C., 1875, pp. 16.)

GEORGE CLARK (16 -1690), the "Farmer," was a brother of Hon. Daniel Clark (16 -16) of Windsor, Conn., one of the patentees under the charter from Charles II. They with their brother John Clark (16 -16) of Guilford, came from   , England, where they had property which is mentioned in the wills of these three brothers; possibly Samuel Clark of New Haven was another brother. His only son, John, died without leaving any children; a daughter, Ruth (16 -17), married Thomas Fitch (164 -168) of Norwalk; her grandson, Thomas Fitch (16 -1774), was Governor of Connecticut Colony (17 -17); Abigail (16 -16) married Rev. Abraham Pierson (16 -17), the first Rector of Yale College; Sara (16 -17) married   , 16 , Capt. Reynold Marvin (16 -1676), the celebrated Indian fighter; she married   , 1677, Capt. Joseph Sill, (1636-1696).

SAMUEL COOLEY (16 -1684).

ROBERT DENNISON (16 -16) was in Milford in 1645; he married in 165 Esther   (16 -16); had John, 1654; Samuel, 1656; Esther, 1658; Hannah, 1662. He removed to Newark, N. J., in 1667, with the Branford people that went there at that time. (See Dennison Family Genealogy, 1881, pp. 423, Worcester, Mass.) Of children of first wife, James settled in East Haven; Mary (16 –1692) married in Milford Robert Dalglish or Douglass (16 –1691) and went to Newark.

WILLIAM EAST (16 –1681), according to Savage, was in Milford in 1639; he had Solomon, baptized 1643, who probably died young. In 1676 he had a second wife, Mrs. Mary (Baldwin) Plumb (b. April 21, 1621; d.   , 1708), widow of Robert Plumb (16 –1655). He died in 1681 without leaving any children.

BENJAMIN FENN (16 –1672) was a proprietor in Dorchester in 1637. It is suggested by Savage that he "may have come over in the *Mary and James* in 1630, but his name is not mentioned until 1638." It is more probable that he came over with the New Haven Company, or perhaps with the friends and parishioners of the Rev. Peter Prudden (15 –1656), who came in the *Bristol* at a later period in 1637, according to the History of New Haven (1887), page   . He was a man of prominence in Milford, was a Representative, Assistant Governor, 1665–72; his estate at his death was large, both here and in England; he left lands in Aylesbury, but he was only credited with £80 in New Haven records in 1638; probably he in later years received additional funds from property in England, for his estate was inventoried at £   in 1672. He left sons and daughters. An unbroken line of Benjamin Fenns for ten generations can be recorded in this country.

DEACON JOHN FLETCHER (1602–1661) before coming to Milford was in Wethersfield; he joined the church in 1641; according to Savage he had then been living in Milford for two years. His only son, Samuel, born in 1649, died young. Of his six daughters, five were married when his wife, Mary Ward (1607–168), made her will in 1679, she then being the widow of John Clark (16 –1674). (See Fletcher Family History, 1881, pp. 563, by Ed. H. Fletcher.)

MILFORD. 647

THOMAS FORD (16 -1661), in Milford among the first settlers, married Elizabeth Knowles (16 -1673), daughter of Alex. Knowles (16 -1663) of Fairfield; he had two sons and three daughters; one of them Lydia (1662-1747), married John Newton (1656-1699), a son of Rev. Roger Newton (16 -1683), the second minister of Milford. In March, 1663, Mrs. Elizabeth (Knowles) Ford married Eliezer Rogers (16 -16).

LT. WILLIAM FOWLER (b , 15 ; d. Jan. 25, 1660-1) was one of the seven pillars of the foundation of the church. He was a builder of the first mill of the colony, which has now been in the possession of the Fowler family for ten generations. " It is now acknowledged to be the oldest business (or manufacturing) establishment in the country." No record of his wife is known. In the New Haven list of 1638, he had a family of three, and an estate of £800, as he brought his sons William and John with him, and who were undoubtedly minors in 1638, judging from the dates of their marriages, which took place in 1643 and 1647. (See Fowler Genealogy, 1870, pp. 42, Milwaukee.)

DEACON JOHN FOWLER (16 -1677) removed from Milford to Guilford about 1649, where he died May , 1677; his widow, Mary Hubbard, daughter of George Hubbard (16 -1683) of Milford and Guilford, died April 13, 1703. He had two sons and four daughters; none of the daughters were married; one of these daughters, Mehitable Fowler, born in 1656, died March 18, 1751, being 95 years old at her death.

WILLIAM FOWLER, JR. (16 -1682), whose name is also engraved on the Memorial Bridge, as well as that of his father, Lt. William Fowler, married , 164 , Mary Tapp (162 -16), daughter of Edmund Tapp (15 -1653); for many years he lived in New Haven. In 1645 he built the mill at what is now called Whitneyville, where Eli Whitney, the inventor of the cotton gin, established in 1798, a factory for manufacturing fire-arms. He married in 1670 Mrs. Elizabeth (Alsop) Baldwin (16 -16), widow of Richard Baldwin (1622–1665), and left sons and daughters who married and left descendants.

STEPHEN FREEMAN (16 –1675) in Milford in 1646; had a house-lot, but did not become a resident until 1658. In a few years he removed to Newark, N. J.; there Thomas Judd of Waterbury married his daughter Sarah, and perhaps he came back to Connecticut; his widow, Hannah (16 –16), may have married Robert Porter (16 -1689) of Farmington, Conn. (See Freeman Genealogy (1875), pp. 456, Boston). He married , 165 , Hannah Atwood (16 –16), daughter of Captain Atwood (1604–1654), and had Hannah, b. 1655; Mary, 1658; Samuel, 1662; Martha and Sarah. (See Freeman.)

DR. JASPER GUNN (1606-1670) with his wife(?) Ann (1610–16), or what is more probable, his sister Ann, came in the ship *Defense* in July, 1635, settled at Roxbury, and was a proprietor there May 25, 1636; he was at Milford at an early date; according to Lambert he came there from Wethersfield. Savage states that he was in Hartford from 1646 to 1657, and then removed to Milford. He left four sons, Jobama (16 –16), Abel (16 –169), Daniel (16 –1690), Samuel (16 –16), and daughter Mehitable Fenn. Judging from the dates of marriage of his children, most of them, if not all, were born in this country. On the Memorial Bridge his wife's name is engraved as *Sarah.* In his will he calls John Smith (16 –1684) and Joseph Peck (16 –1701) his brothers. N. G. Pond suggests that they were probably brothers-in-law. In that case Sarah might have been a sister of Joseph Hawley (16 –16) of Stratford, as it is believed that Mrs. John Smith was Grace Hawley, a sister of that Joseph Hawley.

EDMUND or EDWARD HARVEY (16 ; d. May 22, 1648) was in Milford in 1639; came from Wethersfield. Savage states that he was a merchant, and brought two daughters with him, one aged nine years, the other four; perhaps also brought a wife, but more probably was a widower, for he married about 1640, Martha (16 -16), and had Josiah, baptized December

MILFORD. 649

29, 1640, and Hannah, b.   , 1646; he removed to Fairfield and died there May 22, 1648, leaving a daughter in England aged 22 years, two more as above stated aged 18 and 14 years (in 1648), all by a former wife. His widow married Nathan Gold (16 - 1684) of Fairfield.

PHILIP HATLEY was in Milford in 1639; he went back to London in 1649; nothing more concerning him found in Savage.

THOMAS HINE (16 -1698) was at Milford in 1646 or before. His will was made May 9, 1694; he died about 1698; had twelve or more children. For a tradition of his rescuing an Indian from certain death, see Lambert's History of New Haven Colony, also History of Derby, pages 711-717. See Hine Family Genealogy (1898), St. Paul, Minn., pages 239, by Judge Robert Clark Hine.

GEORGE HUBBARD (16 -1683) was in Milford in 1643; he removed to Guilford in 1650 with his son-in-law, John Fowler (16 -1677). For further particulars see Personnel of Guilford Colony; also Hubbard Genealogy (1895), pp. 312, N. Y.

JOHN LANE (16 -Sept. 10, 1669) came from Wethersfield to Milford in or before 1640 with his wife Kattareen (?) who died before 1662, for in that year he married Mrs. Mary (   ) Camp (16 -Jan., 1680), widow of Edward Camp (16 -1669), of New Haven, by whom he probably had no children. His daughter Kattareen (163 -167) married Nov. 8, 1653, John Tuttle (1631-1683) of New Haven; their descendants are recorded in the Tuttle Family Book. His son Isaac removed to Middletown. His will mentions Samuel, Edward and Mary Camp, the children of his wife by her first husband, Edward Camp. See the Lane Genealogies, Vol. 2 (189), pp. 296. His will was made Sept. 10, 1669; inventory taken Sept. 16, 1669; amount £441 15s. 1d.

THOMAS LAWRENCE, one of the Wethersfield people, died in 1648. Nothing further learned of him in Savage or in Lambert.

MILFORD.

HENRY LYON (16 –1712) removed from Milford to Fairfield before 1652, when he married the only daughter of William Bateman (16 –1658), who in his will, made March 24, 1656, gave one-half of his estate to his son-in-law, Henry Lyon.

DEACON RICHARD PLATT (1603-1684) was the son of John Platt (15 –16), of Bovington, England. With his wife, Mary (b. 16 ; d. Jan. 24, 1675-6), he probably brought four children: Mary, John, Isaac and Sarah; although in the New Haven list of 1639 his family is only numbered as four instead of six. His estate at that time was £200. The inventory of his estate in 1683 amounted to £ . U. S. Senator Thomas C. Platt, of New York, is a descendant. The town of Plattsville, N. Y., was named after a member of this family. See Platt Lineage (1891), pp. 398, New York, by Lewis Platt.

ROBERT PLUMB (1617-1655) in Milford in 1639; came from Wethersfield. He married Jan. 9, 1642, Mary Baldwin (1621-1708), daughter of Sylvester Baldwin (15 –1638). He had a daughter, Mary, and five sons. His widow married in 1676 William East (16 –1), and died in 1708. U. S. Senator P. B. Plumb, of Kansas, was a descendant of this emigrant. See Plumb Genealogy (1893), pp. 102, Luzerne, Peary Co., Pa., by H. B. Plumb. Only one son, John, left descendants to bear the family name.

JOHN POCOCK (or Peacocke).

JAMES PRIME (16 –1685) at his death in 1685 left a widow, a son James, a daughter Sarah, wife of Thomas Frior, and a daughter Rebecca, who married April 1, 1677, Walter Smith (16 –1709) of Milford. See Prime Family (1888), pp. 118, New York, by E. D. G. Prime, D.D.

JAMES PRUDDEN (16 –1648), probably older brother of Rev. Peter Prudden (1601-1656), had according to New Haven Records in 1638 a family of three persons and an estate of £10.

MILFORD. 651

As his daughter Ann married in 1640, and his daughter Elizabeth married in 1648 or before, they must have been with him in New Haven, and consequently he must have been at that time a widower; no record has been found of his wife in New England.

REV. PETER PRUDDEN (1601-1656) had at New Haven in 1638 or '39, an estate of £500, a family of four, and at his death in July, 1656, he also still possessed lands in Edgton, York County, England, where he may have been born, and where he married his wife, Joanna Boyse. He had three sons, Samuel (163 -1685), who lived in Milford; Rev. John (1646-1725), who died at Newark (?), N. J.; and Peter, baptized in 1652 and who died young. Of his six daughters several married and left descendants. The widow married Sept. 19, 1671, Capt. Thomas Willett (16 -1674) and after 1674 Rev. John Bishop (16 -1693) of Stamford. Her will was made Nov. 8, 1681, in which she mentions all her children that were living, and she probably died soon after.

THOMAS REED (16 -16) may be the same person who was living in Newtown, L. I. Reed Family (1860), pp. 596, Boston.

SERGEANT EDWARD RIGGS (1605-166), son of Edward Riggs (1585-1672) and Elizabeth (15 -1635) of Roxbury. He came from Wethersfield in 1640, or before. In 1654 he removed to Paugussett (afterwards called Derby). He married at Roxbury in 1635 Elizabeth Roosa, and had Edward, Samuel, Joseph and Mary. Gen. Joseph Wheeler, U. S. A., retired, of Alabama, is a descendant. Consult the Riggs Family Genealogy, by Wallace. In 1666 Edward Riggs removed to Newark with his family, except Samuel, who remained in Derby.

WILLIAM ROBERTS (16 -16) came from Wethersfield before 1645.

MILFORD.

JAMES ROGERS (1615-1688), although his name is not recorded on the map of Milford, is engraved on the "Memorial Bridge" as one of the first settlers. He was a brother of John Rogers (16 -1684), and came over to New England in the ship *Increase*. He was early in Stratford, where he married before 1640 Elizabeth Rowland (16 -169), daughter of Henry Rowland (16 -1691) of Stratford. He had six children in Stratford and Milford and removed to New London after 1658. He was considered, next to Gov. Winthrop, the richest man in Connecticut Colony. His widow married before 1691   Wheeler, for she is mentioned in her father's will as Elizabeth Wheeler "who had been wife of James Rogers."

JOHN ROGERS (16 -1684).

EDWARD SANFORD (16 -1681) was in Dorchester in 1634, and in Milford in 1639. By his wife Sarah   (b.   , 16 ; d. May 14, 1681), whom he married in Massachusetts, he had Ezekiel and Sarah, and in Milford, Mary, Samuel, Thomas, Ephraim and Elizabeth. He died in October, 1681. Many of his descendants are to be found in Connecticut and the states further west.

REV. JOHN SHERMAN (b. Dec. 26, 1613; d. Aug. 8, 1685), born at Dedham, Essex County, England; a graduate of Trinity College, Cambridge, in 1633; embarked in April, 1634, in the Elizabeth at Ipswich, England. He reached Boston in June, was at Watertown and later at Wethersfield, Conn., and soon after 1640 he was in Middletown. He was a representative from Milford in 1643; preached a short time in 1645 in Branford. His wife Mary   died at Milford September 8, 1644, and he married in 1645 Mary Launce (b.   , 162 ; d. March 9, 1710), a maiden in the family of Governor Eaton, of New Haven. He removed to Watertown, Mass., in 1647, became their pastor, and remained there the rest of his life. He was stricken with fever and delirium in the pulpit of his son at Sudbury, where he

MILFORD.

preached his last sermon July 5, 1685, and died Aug. 8, 1685. By both wives he had some fourteen or more children.

WILLIAM SLOUGH (16 –165) was in New Haven in 1644, and in 1645 he removed to Milford, where he joined the church in 1648. He married in 1647, or earlier, Elizabeth Prudden (16 – 16), daughter of James. Had a daughter Hadidiah, bap. 1648, and James, b. Jan. , 1650; d. February of same year. He was executed in New Haven for some offence against the law. The widow married Feb. 18, 1653, Roger Prichard (16 –1671) of Milford, who removed soon after to New Haven, where he died.

JOHN SMITH (16 –1684), "The Farmer," was in Milford in 1640 (?), and may have come in one of the three ships that sailed from England direct to New Haven in 1639. He might have been one of the parishioners of Rev. Peter Prudden in his English home, but could not arrange matters so as to be able to come with his pastor in 1637 and followed on at a later date. He married Grace Hawley (16 –1690), probably a sister or near relative of Joseph Hawley (16 –16) of Stratford, who joined the church in 1642. Their first child, Ephraim, was baptized Oct. 13, 1644. From the amount of property left by him at his death (£513 3s. 9d.), the inventory was taken in December, 1684, it is probable that he belonged to a family of wealth in England. Of his descendants many have been prominent in professional and business life, of the former class was U. S. Senator Orrin Smith Ferry (1823–1875), of the latter, Winthrop Brinsmade Smith (1808–1887), a millionaire publisher of Cincinnati, and in later years a banker in Philadelphia. See the N. E. Register of July, 1891, also the Henry Whitney Family Book (1886), Vol. 1, page 127 and onwards, where over 500 descendants are recorded in that volume and in Vols, 2 and 3.

JOHN SMITH (16 –1704),—"Ye Smith," The Blacksmith,— was in Milford, according to Lambert, in 1643. He may have been married at that time, but the first marriage recorded is his marriage on July 19, 1665, to Sarah Fowler (16 –169) daughter of Lt. William Fowler (16 –1683), by whom he had four or more children. In 1694 he married Mrs. Clement (Hosmer) Hunt (b. , 163 ; d. Sept. 29, 1695), widow of Jonathan Hunt (16 – 16) and daughter of Thomas Hosmer (1604–1687) of Hartford. Her tombstone (see Milford Tombstone Records, No. 398) is to be found in the Milford cemetery.

HENRY STONHILL (or Stonell) was in New Haven in 1638, and is rated on the list of that year as having no family and possessed an estate of £300. His lot was on the northwest corner of Church and George streets, and reached from George street north to Crown street. He went to Milford in 1639 and joined the church in 1641. Soon after 1646 he returned to England. He was dismissed by the Milford church to Thomas Goodwin's church in London.

ENSIGN JOHN STREAM (1621–1685) is probably the person who came with his Uncle Zachariah Whitman (15 –1666) in the *Truelove* from London to Boston in 1635, aged 14 years. He married Dec. 20, 1649, Martha Beard (16 –16), daughter of James (?) Beard (15 –1638), who died on the ship *Martin* while coming to New England. His son John (164 –1687) died without children, so that the name of Stream ceased, but through the daughters, Mrs. Abigail Tibballs, Mrs. Mary Baldwin and Mrs. Martha Cooley, there are descendants at the present time.

SERGT. THOMAS TIBBALLS (1615–1703) embarked at London in the *Truelove* in 1835. He was engaged in the Pequot War of 1637, and by that means gained his knowledge of Quinnipiac and the country west, so that he was able to pilot the Milford settlers from New Haven (Quinnipiac) to the region that they had purchased from the Indian owners. In 1691 he received a grant of land (50) for his services rendered in the Pequot War. By his first wife, Mary, who died June , 1644, he had Mary or Mercy, baptized Feb. ,1643–4, and Samuel, b. April 14, 1644.

Mary married July 12, 1664, Nicholas Smith (16 -17)—Sevearsmith, a Dutchman. He had a second wife, whom he married probably in 1644. By her he had a son John, baptized   , 1645, and five or more other children. He died probably in May, 1703, as his estate was probated June 1, 1703. Gen. Joseph Wheeler, U. S. A., retired, is a descendant through his eldest daughter Mary.

EDMUND TAPP (15 -1653) one of the seven pillars at the foundation of the Milford church Aug. 22, 1638, in New Haven, had on the New Haven list of 1638 an estate of £800 and a family of seven. There is no record of any son growing to maturity. Four daughters are mentioned, leaving a fifth child unrecorded. Possibly he had no wife living at the time but had six children. His name is engraved on the Memorial Bridge, also that of his wife Ann, but no date of her death is given on the stone. His daughter Ann (162 -16) married William Gibbard (16 -16), Mary (16 -166) married   , 1645, Lt. William Fowler (16 - 1682), Elizabeth (16 -16) married Lt. John Nash (16 -16), and Jane (1628-1703) married Governor Robert Treat (1622-1710). For records of descendants of these daughters see The Fowler Family pamphlet (18   ), pp.   , by   ; The Nash Family book (185), Hartford, pp.   , by Rev.   Nash; The Treat Family Genealogy (1893), by John H. Treat, Salem, Mass., pp. 637.

CAPTAIN THOMAS TAPPING (16 -168) was an Assistant and Representative. He was in Wethersfield previous to 1639, joined the church with wife Emma in 1640. By this wife he had four or more children. He may have lived for a time in Southampton, L. I. On October 20, 1666, he made a contract at Milford for marriage with Mrs. Mary   Baldwin (16 -1671), widow of Timothy Baldwin (16   -1665). Before June , 1678, he had married Mrs. Lydia   Wilford (16 -Nov. 1694), widow of John Wilford (16 -16) of Branford. He removed to Branford, where on Oct. 5, 1688, he deeded to sons Elnathan and James his lands in Southampton, Long Island; also other property to daughters,

Mrs. Mary (Tapping) Quinny (16 –17) and Mrs. Martha (Tapping) Herrick (16 –17). His widow on October , 1688, had transactions with the sons, and she died Nov. , 1694.

MICAH TOMPKINS (16 –16) came to Milford from Wethersfield in 1639 or soon after. He and his wife Mary joined the church in 1643. They had some eight or more children. In 1666 he removed to Newark, N. J., and in 1667 he bought a large tract of land from the Indians on the Passaic River where the city of Newark is now laid out.

ROGER TYRRELL.

THOMAS WELCH (16 –1681), one of the founders of the Milford church in 1639, married , 164 , Hannah Buckingham (16 –1684), daughter of Deacon Thomas Buckingham (15 –1657). He died Aug. 12, 1681. For account of descendants of his only son Thomas, see Orcutt's History of New Milford.

THOMAS WHEELER (16 –16).

ZECHARIAH WHITMAN (1595–1666), brother of John Whitman (1614-1692) of Weymouth, Mass., came to Massachusetts in the *Truelove*, aged 40 years, with wife Sarah Biscoe, aged 25 years, and son Zechariah, aged two and a half years. He was at Milford in 1639. He was one of the trustees in the first deed, one of the judges chosen by the settlers to act in civil affairs, and one of the seven pillars of the church. His name is engraved on the Memorial Bridge. His wife was a cousin of Nathaniel Biscoe (162 –1683). See Whitman Genealogy (1889) by Chas. H. Farnam of New Haven, Conn., pp. 1261. He d. April 23, 1666; his wife Sarah, b. 1619; d. Jan. 2, 1670–71; no children mentioned in his will.

PERSONNEL OF STRATFORD.

WILLIAM BEARDSLEY (1604-1660), a mason, came in the *Planter* in 1635, aged 30, with wife Mary, aged 26; children, Mary, aged 4 years; John, aged 2 years; Joseph, aged 6 months. He was a freeman of Massachusetts December 7, 1636; was a representative from Stratford in 1645; will dated September 28, 1660; inventory taken February 13, 1660-61; he had nine or more children. (See "A Sketch of William Beardsley," New York, 1887, by E. E. Beardsley.)

Rev. AARON BLAKEMAN (b.   , 1578; d. Sept. 7, 1665) was born in Staffordshire; was matriculated May 28, 1617, at Christs' College, Oxford, in his 19th year; he preached in the Counties of Leicester and Derby before he came to New England about 1638; he was at Guilford, but in 1640 he became the first minister of Pequannocke (Stratford); he had a daughter Mary (1635-1709), who married Joshua Atwater (1612-1676), and five sons. Bishop Phillips Brooks (1835-1893), was a descendant of this emigrant through his daughter Mary. (For a list of her descendants to the fifth generation see the Atwater Family History, 1901, pages 425-430.)

RICHARD BOOTH (1607-169) was in Stratford in 1640; he married Elizabeth (?) Hawley, a sister of Joseph Hawley (16 - 169); he had eight or more children. In 1688 he testifies that he was 81 years old. (See Genealogy of Richard Booth, Minneapolis, Minn., 1892, pages 12, by W. S. Booth. Also "Report of the Booth Family Association," Burlington, Vt., 1868, 64 pages, by Columbus Smith.)

42

STRATFORD.

DEACON JOHN BIRDSEYE (16 –1690) came from Milford in 1649. (See the chapter " Personnel of Milford Colony.") He died April 4, 1690; made his will August 29, 1689; his second wife was Alice Tomlinson.

ARTHUR BOSTWICK (16 –16) came from Chester County, England, with his son John and other children of his first wife. The sons Joseph, Arthur and Zechariah may have been children of the second wife, Ellen   (16 –1678). (See Bostwick's Genealogy, 1902, by   Bostwick, New York.)

JOHN BRINSMADE (Brinsmeade) (16 –1673) with his wife, Mary Carter (16 –16), whom he had probably married about 1639 in Charlestown, Mass., came from that town to Stratford; he was in Charletown in 1636. At his death in 1673, he left widow Mary, four sons and two daughters. His son Zachariah was drowned in August, 1667.

WILLIAM BURRITT (16 –1651), who died in Stratford, 1651, left a widow Elizabeth (16 –1681); in her will of September 2, 1681, she mentions sons Stephen and John and daughter Mary Smith.

THOMAS FAIRCHILD (16 –1670) at Stratford in 1646; was a representative in 1659, 1660 and afterwards; by his wife, Faith (?) Seabrook (16 –16), he had seven or more children; five of them are named in his will of December 7, 1670. He went to London about 1672, and there married Mrs. Catharine Cragg (contract of marriage December 22, 1662); by her he had three children. His will was made Dec. 7, 1670, and he died at Stratford shortly after.

PHILIP GRAVES (16 ; d. Feb. 11, 1675).

HENRY GREGORY (16 –16) was in Springfield in 1637; removed in a few years to Stratford, and perhaps after 1650 removed elsewhere.

RICHARD HARVEY (16 -16) by wife Elizabeth (?) had Elizabeth, b. July 25, 1644; Mary, b. Sept. 15, 1647; Sarah, b. Feb. 13, 1650. Elizabeth married   , 166 , John Hyde (16 -17); Mary married   , 16 , Thomas Jeffreys.

JOSEPH HAWLEY (1603-1690) was in Stratford in 1649, or before; by his first wife, Catharine (16 -16), he had eight children; of the three daughters, Elizabeth (b. Dec. 17, 1651; d. May 10, 1696) married June 7, 1670, John Chapman (16 -16); Hannah (b. May 26, 1657; d.   , 17) married   , 16 , Joseph Nichols (1656-17); and Mary (b. July 16, 1663; d.   , 17) married December 20, 1682, John Coe (1658-1741). He was a prominent man in Stratford, a Representative, &c. His tombstone is still in existence, an uncommon instance in the case of emigrant settlers. An engraving of it is to be found in the Hawley Memorial, by Dr. Elias Hawley, Buffalo, N. Y., 1890, pp. 608.

JOHN HURD (1614-1682) was in Windsor among the first settlers, and removed from there to Stratford; he was a Representative in 1649, '56 and '57; his first wife died before 1662, and was probably the mother of his daughters, Mrs. Mary Bennett (16 -17) and Abigail Bissell (16 -17). He married December 15, 1662, Sarah Thompson (1642-16), daughter of John Thompson (16 -1678), of Stratford, and had by her six or more children.

WILLIAM JUDSON (15 -1662) was in Concord in 1635; he came to New England in 1634 with his wife Grace (15 -1659), and sons Joseph (b. 1619; d. Oct. 8, 1690), Jeremiah (b. 1621; d. May 15, 1701), and Joshua (b. 162 ; d.   , 166); removed to Hartford in 1639, and was in Stratford in 1644, and in that year was engaged in obtaining aid for the infant college at Cambridge. Some years later he went to New Haven, where his wife Grace died Sept. 29, 1659; he married February 8, 1659-60, Mrs. Elizabeth (   ) Wilmot (16 -16), widow of Benjamin Wilmot, Jr. (162 -1651) of New Haven, and died July 29, 1662.

MR. NICHOLAS KNELL (16 -1675) at Stratford in 1650 or before, married Mrs. Elizabeth (Newman) Knowles (16 -16), daughter of Gov. Francis **Newman** (15 -1660) and widow of Thomas Knowles (16 -1647) of New Haven; she bore him four or more children and survived him; he died April , 1675; the will only mentions his wife and two sons. He was a man of importance, had Mr. prefixed to his name, and the mention in the town records of his death calls him " that aged benefactor of the country." In the History of Stratford it is stated that he had John, b. 1651; d. 1652; Elizabeth, b. May 5, 1653; Isaac, b. Feb. , 1655; John, b. May 17, 1654.

SERGT. FRANCIS NICHOLLS (15 -1650) brought with him from England three sons, Isaac (16 -1695), Caleb (16 -1696), and John (16 -16); he married after 1640, Anne Wines (16 -16), daughter of Barnabas Wines (16 -16) of Southold, L. I.; he had two daughters, the youngest one, Anne, was a daughter of the second wife; his estate was small, and neither will nor inventory is of record in the probate office. (See Nicolls Family, 1888, by W. J. Nicolls.)

JOHN PEACOCKE (16 -1670) was in Milford before 1646, and in Stratford before 1650, where he died in 1670. In his will is mentioned his wife Joyce, daughters Phebe, wife of Richard Burgess; Mary, who married in 1673, Benjamin Beach, and Deborah, wife of James Clark (16 -16), who removed from New Haven to Stratford.

JOHN PEAKE (or Peat) (1597-1678) came in the *Hopewell* in 1635, aged 38, from Duffield Parish, County Derby, England; was in Stratford before 1650 with his son John (b. 1638; d. 17 6), who was probably the John Peake recorded in list of freemen of 1669. He had a wife, Sarah Osborn, and daughter Mary, born in 1620, John, b, 1638, Benjamin, b. 1640, and probably other children.

JOHN READER (16 -16) was in Springfield, Mass., in 1636; had a grant of land there, but did not remain long in

Springfield. He is undoubtedly the same person who was in New Haven in 1638, and is there recorded as having a family of two persons and an estate of £140. In 1656 he is recorded at Newtown, L. I.

ROBERT RICE (16 –16) was a freeman in 1664 in New London; he was at Stratford in or before 1648; on Feb. 8, 1660, he sold "one house lot, one dwelling house upon it, and barn to Thomas Wheeler, now of Paugusit," and removed to New London. (See "Rice Family Gen.", 1858, Boston, pp. 385, by A. H. Ward.)

ROBERT SEABROOK (1566–163) of Stratford, had several daughters, one of them , married in 16 , William Preston (15 –1647) of New Haven; another daughter, , (16 –166), married Thomas Fairchild (16 –1671), and Alice (b. in 1587; d. , 16), married Thomas Sherwood (1586–1656).

THOMAS SHERWOOD (1586–1656) came to Boston in 1634, on the ship *Francis*, from Ipswich, aged 48 years, with wife, Alice Seabrook (1587-16), aged 47 years, and children, Ann, aged 14; Rose, 11; Thomas, 10; Rebecca, 9. Of the eight remaining children, several of them were born in New England; they were Stephen, Matthew, b. 1643, Isaac, Tamsen, Margery, Ruth, Abigail and Mary. (For an account of Sherwood Family, see "Wetmore Family," Albany, 1861, pp. 870.)

THOMAS SKIDMORE (16 –1684) was in Cambridge, Mass., in 1642; in 1636 he had been engaged by John Winthrop in his preparation for planting at Saybrook. He was early in Stratford with son-in-law Edward Higby; soon after 1659 he removed to Fairfield. His will made April 20, 1684, was proved soon after; he had a first wife Ellen, and second wife Sarah, who is mentioned in his will, and left two sons and several daughters.

JOHN THOMPSON (1613-1678) married in England, Mirabel (16 –1690), and had six children, two sons and four daughters. He came to New England for the first time, it is believed, about 1635, then returned to England to dispose of his property there, and before returning to New England married his wife there. (For a romantic account of his courtship see Stratford History, pages 115–116; also see Cothren's History of Woodbury, Vol. I and II, for an account of his descendants.)

DANIEL TITTERTON (16 –1661) was probably the person of that name who was in Boston in 1643; he was in Stratford before 1647; was a Representative in 1647, '49, '52, and '54; he died in 1661, probably in June, as his will was probated July 6, 1661. In the will are named three sons, Daniel (16 –1709), Samuel (16 –1711), and Timothy (1651-17); also three daughters, Elizabeth, Mary (16 –169), who married, 1665, Samuel Sherman (1641-1717), and Johanna Wilcoxson (16 –1662 (?)), probably the first wife of John Wilcoxson (1633–1690). His wife Jane survived him; he gave an estate and lands in England to his children; possibly Samuel and Timothy went to England to procure the property there belonging to them, but if so they both returned to New England and died here.

THOMAS UFFORT (or Offitt) (15 –1660) came to Boston in 1632 in the ship *Lyon*, with his wife Isabel and children Thomas, John and a daughter who married Roger Terrill (16 –16) of Milford.

THOMAS UFFORT, Jr. (16 –1683) married in 16 , in Wethersfield, Frances Kilbourne (16 –1683). They left no children; she outlived her husband only a few weeks, and her estate in January, 1683-84, was divided among her brothers and sisters. The inventory of his property taken Dec. 26, 1683, amounting to £1,-834 according to his will of May 17, 1683, was given to his brothers, sisters and their heirs.

HENRY WALKERLEE (or Wakelee) (16 –16) was in Stratford before 1650; in 1663 he had a son James, and was "attorney before the General Court in behalf of his son James, but the matter was withdrawn from court."

JOHN WELLS (16 -166) was probably the eldest son of Gov. Thomas Wells (15 -16) of Hartford. He was made a freeman at   in 1645; married about 1647, Elizabeth Bourne, who came to New England under the care of Henry Tomlinson and Ellen, wife of Arthur Bostwick. (See History of New Milford, pp. 787; also History of Welles Family, N. Y., 1876, pp. 312, by Albert Welles.)

WILLIAM WILKINSON (or Wilcoxson) came from England in April, 1635, in the ship *Planter*, in company with Richard Harvey (16 -166) and William Beardsley (1604-1660), both of whom settled in Stratford. He was a freeman in Massachusetts in 1636; came from Concord, Mass., to Stratford about 1639; he was a man of prominence in Stratford. In his will dated May, 1651, he gave £40 to the church at Concord; he left a widow and five sons. The name in some localities has been contracted to Wilcox. (For a short account of the Wilkinson family see "Barlow Genealogy," Brooklyn, N. Y., 1895, pp. 508, by Geo. Barlow.)

PERSONNEL OF FAIRFIELD.

JOHN BANKS (16 -1685) was in Windsor previous to 1643, where he married Mary (?) Taintor (16 -16), daughter of Charles Taintor (15 -16) of Wethersfield. He was a town clerk in Windsor in 1643; removed to Fairfield, and was a Representative several years between 1651 and 1666. He removed to Rye from that town 1670-73. He left a good estate; made his will Dec. 12, 1684, and died January, 1685. In the will he mentions wife Mary (possibly not his first wife), sons John (16 - 1699), Samuel (16 -1), Obadiah (16 -1691), Benjamin (16 - 1692), and daughters Susannah Sturges, Harriet Burr and Mary Taylor. A son, Joseph, died in 1682, probably unmarried, as he gave his estate to his four brothers and sister Mary Taylor.

JOHN BARLOW (16 -1674), in his will of March 28, 1674, mentions his wife Ann, sons John, and daughters Elizabeth Frost, wife of Daniel F.; Martha, wife of James Beers; Deborah, wife of John Sturges; Ruth, wife of Francis Bradlee (16 -1689), and Isabella Clapham, wife of Peter Clapham. The poet and diplomat Joel Barlow (1754-1812) was a descendant.

THOMAS BARLOW (16 -165), by wife Rose had Phebe, who married Francis Olmstead (16 -16) of Norwalk; Deborah, who married John Burritt (16 -16) of Stratford, and Mary. He made his will Sept. 8, 1658. The widow Rose married Edward Nash (16 -16) of Norwalk. See Barlow Genealogy (1893) Brooklyn, N. Y., pp. 508, by George Barlow.

FAIRFIELD. 665

JEHUE BURR, Sr. (15 -1672), came to Boston in 1630; was made a freeman in 1632 in Roxbury; removed to Agawam (or Springfield) in 1636, and from there he removed in 1644 to Fairfield, where he died in 1672, leaving four sons, Jehu, John, Daniel (16 -16) and Nathaniel (16 -16).

CAPTAIN JEHU BURR (1625-1692), eldest son of Jehue Burr, Sr. (15 -1672), married in Fairfield , 164 , Mary Ward (16 -16), daughter of Andrew Ward (15 -1659). He married , 16 , Mrs. Esther ( ) Boosey (16 -169), widow of Joseph Boosey (16 -16) of Fairfield. In his will are mentioned his widow and nine children,— Daniel, Peter, Samuel, Mary Wakeman, Esther , Elizabeth, Sarah, Jonana and Abigail.

COLONEL JOHN BURR (16 -1694) came with his father, Jehue, to Fairfield. He married , 16 , Sarah Fitch (16 -16), daughter of Captain Thomas Fitch (1612-1704) of Norwalk. He had nine or more children; two sons died before their father. He was a Representative in 1666, and an officer of various grades in the militia. His wife is not mentioned in his will of March 19, 1694, and had undoubtedly died before that date. The children named were John, Samuel, Jonathan, David and daughters Sarah , Mary and Deborah. Colonel Aaron Burr (1756-1836), Vice-President of the U. S. 1801-1805, was a great-grandson of Col. John Burr. For further information of the Burr family see "The Burr Family" (1891), pp. 535, New York, by Charles Burr Todd.

DANIEL FROST (16 -16), son of William Frost (16 - 1645) of Fairfield, had by his wife, Elizabeth Barlow (16 -16), three sons and five daughters. He was living in 1670. The first child, Rebecca, born in 1640, married Simeon Booth, Sarah married Samuel Smith (16 -16), Rachel married Robert Rumsey, Hannah married John Thorp and Esther married

FAIRFIELD.

WILLIAM FROST (15 -1645) had sons Daniel and Abraham. He came from Northamptonshire and died in Fairfield in 1645. Will made Jan. 6, 1645, names sons Daniel and Abraham, daughters Elizabeth, wife of John Grey; Mary Riley; Lydia, wife of Henry Grey; mentions estate and "all his goods" in England, which he devises to Mary Riley who lived in England.

OBADIAH GILBERT (16 -1674), brother of John Gilbert (16 -1690), and possibly son of William Gilbert (16 -16) of Windsor, married   , 165 , Mrs. Elizabeth (   ) Olmstead, widow of Nathaniel Olmstead (16 -16), who had one daughter, Sarah Olmstead. He had three sons, Obadiah, Benjamin and Joseph. See Memoir of Gilbert Family (1850), pp. 23, by J. W. Thornton.

GEORGE GOODWIN (16 -16).

JOHN GREEN (16 -1703), made a freeman in 1662, left a good estate. He had a wife Hannah and son John. In his will he gives his negro slave Harry his freedom, and a horse, and "the violin he calleth his."

JOHN GREY (16 -16), the person mentioned above as husband of Mrs. Elizabeth (Frost) Watson, widow of John Watson and daughter of William Frost (15 -1645). He removed to Long Island and is probably the John Grey mentioned in Thompson's History of Long Island. He had a son Henry and probably other children. See Gray Genealogy (1887), Tarrytown, N. Y., pp. 316, by M. D. Raymond.

EDMUND HARVEY (15 -1648). See account of this settler in Milford list of emigrants.

ROBERT HAWKINS (16 -16). A Robert Hawkins (1610–16) was at Charlestown. He came in 1635 in the *Elizabeth and Ann*, aged 25 years, with wife Mary, aged 24. He had three children born after 1635 and possibly more.

HUMPHREY HIDE, or Hyde (16 -1679), in his will of Nov. 12, 1679, mentions wife Ann, son John, daughters Sarah, wife of Peter Coley, and Hannah, wife of William Sprague.

WILLIAM HILL, SR. (15 -1649), came to New England June 5, 1632, on the ship *William and Francis* with wife Sarah and probably most of the children mentioned in his will of Sept. 9, 1649, probated May 15, 1650, whose names were Sarah, William, Joseph, Ignatius, James and Elizabeth. Sarah married Sept. 17, 1646, Joseph Loomis (16 -16) of

WILLIAM HILL, JR. (16 -1684), son of William Hill (15 -1649) of Fairfield, was a Representative in 16 , and left a good estate. The inventory was taken Dec. 25, 1684. He left a widow Esther and five children.

SIMON HOYT (16 -1659) was living in Charlestown in 1629; made a freeman there in May, 1631. He was in Scituate 1633–36, and about 1639 he removed to Windsor. While living in Windsor his son Benjamin was born in 1644. About 1650 he removed to Fairfield and died 1659 in Stamford. A son Joshua (16 -17) married Mary Bell, daughter of Lt. Francis Bell (16 -1690) of Stamford.

PETER JOHNSON (16 -16), called a Dutchman, sold his house in Boston in 1638 to Richard Rawlings. He was in Fairfield in 1649 or before. His wife Elizabeth had a child, Moses, born in prison where she had been confined for some time. It is conjectured by Savage that she was imprisoned because she was or had been insane; that the son Moses was a posthumous child, and that John Johnson (16 –1659) and Col. Ebenezer Johnson (16 –17) were also his sons.

THOMAS JOHNSON (16 –16).

REV. JOHN JONES (159 –1665) lived for a time in Concord, where he was ordained pastor April 6, 1637. He arrived at Boston Oct. 3, 1633, coming in the ship *Defence* from London. His name and that of a fellow-passenger, Rev. Thomas Shepard (1605–1649), do not appear on the "list at the custom house, probably for certain good and sufficient reasons. His wife Sarah, aged 34, and children,—Samuel, aged 15, John 11, Ruth 7, Theophilus 3, Rebecca 2, and Elizabeth 1½,—" are all set forth in the document." At Concord he had one son Eliphalet, b. Jan. 9, 1641, and probably his wife Sarah and son Theophilas died at Concord. His will was made Jan. 17, 1665, and inventory taken Feb. 7, 1665. The will mentions the widow, Susanna, and all the children except Theophilus, viz.: the four daughters, Sarah Wilson, Ruth James, Rebecca Hall and Elizabeth Hill, and the sons John and Eliphalet (1643–1731).

THOMAS JONES (16 –16) was first at Concord and removed to Fairfield. He was a freeman there in 1669, and a Representative in 1685. It is suggested by Savage that he might have been a brother of Rev. John Jones.

ALEXANDER KNOWLES (16 –1663), was a freeman in Massachusetts Bay Colony Dec. 7, 1636; the town not stated. He sold land on the Piscataqua River Oct. 14, 1651, and appears in Fairfield in 1653 or before. Jan. 17, 1653, he bought a house and lot of Henry Whelpley. He was chosen an Assistant of the Colony of Connecticut in 1658. He died Dec.   , 1663. In the will is mentioned sons John (16 –1673), Joshua (16 –16), daughter Elizabeth Ford (16 –167), widow of Thomas Ford (16 –1662), and possibly another daughter living in Milford.

DEPUTY-GOVERNOR ROGER LUDLOW (15 –16 was first at Dorchester, Mass. He came in the *Mary and John* from Plymouth, England, in May, 1630, was chosen an Assistant soon after, and in August, 1634, made a Deputy-Governor. In 1635, he removed to Windsor, Conn.; was chosen as Deputy-Governor in Connecticut Colony; about 1639 he removed to Fairfield. The people of Connecticut Colony were very desirous of grabbing all the excellent locations, although they were unable to occupy them for lack of people to settle on them, but still wished to keep them out of the hands of the New Haven, Milford and Stamford colonists, instructed Ludlow and others to possess as much land as possible along the coast west of New Haven and Milford Colonies. It was land that rightfully belonged to the settlers of New Haven, who located in that section of country first in 1637, and who with the Milford and Stamford settlers would soon have spread out all along the coast from Quinnipiac to the Dutch possessions. These instructions Ludlow carried out to the best of his ability, and so Stratford, Fairfield and Norwalk were considered to be a part of Connecticut Colony politically, but geographically they belonged to the New Haven Colony and their business intercourse was with New Haven, and to some extent New Haven Colony people settled among them and the young men married the daughters of the New Haven and Milford colonists. Deputy-Governor Ludlow had a daughter Sarah (16 – 16) who married Rev. Nathaniel Brewster (16 –1690) of Brookhaven, L. I. He removed from Fairfield in 1654 to Virginia and died there.

LIEUT. SAMUEL MOREHOUSE (16 –1733), son of Thomas Morehouse (15 –1658), married Rebecca Odell (16 –17), daughter of William Odell (16 –1676). He had Samuel, Jonathan, Thomas, John and probably others. He was marshal of Fairfield in 1673, and "held offices of trust and usefulness."

THOMAS NEWTON (16 –16), one of the first five settlers; was chosen Representative in 1645. In 1653 he removed from Fairfield. In 1656 he was in Newtown, Long Island. While living there was a captain under Governor Stuyvesant.

JOHN NICHOLS (16 –1655), son of Francis Nicholls of Stratford (15 –1650), was in Watertown in 1636 or 1637. He may have resided at Wethersfield before settling in Fairfield. By wife Grace (16 –16) he had Isaac, Sarah, John and Samuel; probably the children Esther, Elizabeth and Hannah, mentioned in the inventory of June 19, 1655, were the children of a former wife. The widow Grace married about 1655 Richard Perry (16 –1658).

RICHARD PERRY (16 –1658) was in New Haven in 1638 with his wife Mary Malbon (16 –165), daughter of Richard Malbon (15 –16), whom he married in England. He had recorded in the New Haven list an estate of £260 and a family of three. His name ceases in the New Haven records in 1649. He married about 1655 Mrs. Grace Nichols (16 –16), widow of John Nichols (16 –1655), and died in 1658. In New Haven he had Mary, baptized Oct. 4, 1640; Micajah, b. Oct. 31, 1641; Samuel, b. June 8, 1643; John, b. July 11, 1647; Grace, b. Sept. 2, 1649.

FRANCIS PURDY (16 –16) and his wife Mary were in Fairfield in 1644. On January 6, 1645, they are witnesses to the will of William Frost.

GEORGE SQUIRES (16 –1691) was in Concord in 1642; he removed after that year to Fairfield. In his will of Aug. 7, 1691, he gives his estate to his sons Thomas, John, Jonathan, Samuel, a grandson George, a child of his son George (16 –1674), and John Seely, husband of his daughter Sarah.

THOMAS STAPLES (16 -168) had by wife Mary (16 -16) Thomas; Mary, who married Josiah Harvey (16 -1698); another daughter who married John Beach; Mehitable and John; the order of succession is not known. "He was a man of importance, and of spirit enough to prosecute Deputy-Governor Ludlow (15 -165) for defamation in reporting that his wife was a witch. The trial for satisfaction of both parties was in the neighboring Colony of New Haven, where the court wisely held, 'that there was no proof that Goodwife Staples was a witch,' and mulcted Ludlow to pay £10 to the husband for reparation of his wife's name, and £5 for his trouble and cost."

JOHN THOMPSON (16 -1657) had a wife, Elizabeth Sherman (16 -16), and children, Elizabeth, b. 1644; Mary, b. 1649; John, b. 1651; Esther, b. 1654. The widow made a contract of marriage on December 25, 1657, with Daniel Finch (16 -1667) of Fairfield.

CAPTAIN ROBERT TURNEY (1633-1690), eldest son of Benjamin Turney (15 -1648), of whom by his will of Dec. 31, 1689, and inventory taken Jan. 17, 1690, we learn that he had a wife Elizabeth and seven daughters, viz.: Elizabeth, Mary, Ruth, Martha, Rebecca, and the wives of Joseph Jennings (16 -16) and of Ephraim Wheeler (16 -16), called sons-in-law, while their wives were not mentioned, but undoubtedly these wives were daughters and probably were dead.

R. WESTCOAT (16 -16).

MRS. SARAH (JONES) WILSON (16 -167), probably the widow of Thomas Buckley (16 -1658), and who married about 1659 Anthony Wilson (16 -1662). She had sons John and Joseph Buckley, and daughters Sarah, wife of Eleazer Brown, and Rebecca, wife of Joseph Whelpley (16 -16).

HENRY WHELPLEY (16 -16) was at Stratford in 1645, and removed soon after that year to Fairfield. In 1653 he sold his house and lot to Alexander Knowles (16 -1663), and possibly removed to some other town. His widow Sarah married 16 , Ralph Keeler (1613-1672) of Norwalk. He had Joseph, Rebecca, and probably other children.

PERSONNEL OF SOUTHOLD.

THE list of inhabitants of Yennicot (called Southold after 1644) mentioned on page 173 of this history, comprises the names of some who did not come to Southold until many years after the settlement of Yennicot was made from and by residents of New Haven in 1639 and 1640. The first alphabetical list given below is that of names of men who are not mentioned in Savage's Historical Dictionary (1865) as being in any other town previous to 1639, neither are they mentioned in Pope's "Pioneers of Massachusetts" (1900). The probability is that they were the men who with their families came in Rev. Mr. Young's company from England to New Haven direct in the summer of 1639. In numbers it just about equals the number of men who came to New Haven on the first ship and signed the compact of June 1, 1639, and for the very reason that there is no mention of them except at Yennicot (Southold) it is very reasonable to assume that they *did* come direct to New Haven in 1639 in the third ship, and went from there to Yennicot. It is true that Rev. E. Whittaker, in the History of Southold, and the editor of the "Town Records of Southold," scout the idea of the Southold company sailing from England to Quinnipiac (New Haven), as suggested by Mr. Atwater, the author of this history, but they do not furnish the slightest proof that they did *not* do so. As stated in the footnote on page 163, who else could the occupants of that third ship have been if they were not the company that went to Yennicot under the authority of the New Haven Colony? It is an established fact that Rev. John Youngs and his company were in New Haven during that year.

As so little has been found in Savage, Pope, or any history, concerning the persons on this first list, with a few exceptions very little can be said about them. Of those on the second list, considerable information has been found, but as they were not the settlers of 1640, it is not thought best to devote any space to them here. If the readers wish further information concerning them, by consulting the books above mentioned they will be able to find it.

FIRST LIST.

Robert Akerley,
John Booth,
Richard Brown,
John Budd,
Henry Case,
Thomas Cooper,
John Corey,
Caleb Curtis,
Thomas Dimon,
John Elton,
Ralph Goldsmith,
Simon Grover,

James Haines,
Peter Hallock,
Samuel King,
Thomas Mapes,
Peter Paine,
James Reeve,
Richard Skidmore,
John Swazey,
Robert Smyth,
John Tucker,
William Wells,
Rev. John Youngs.

24 men.

SECOND LIST.

Richard Benjamin,
Thomas Benedict,
Matthias Corwin,
John Conklyne,
Philemon Dickerson,
Charles Glover,
John Herbert,

Barnabas Horton,
Thomas Moore,
William Purrier,
Richard Terry,
John Tuttle,
Jeremiah Vaill,
Barnabas Wines.

14 men.

ROBERT AKERLY.

JOHN BOOTH (16 –16), of Southold, in 1659 refused to take the oath of allegiance to the Connecticut Colony, he being one of those who wished to remain faithful to their agreement with the projectors of the New Haven Colony. He would not yield to the bribes and other dishonorable overtures of the residents of Northern Connecticut,—a people, who, ever since their settlement on the Connecticut River, have been grasping and avaricious in their dealings with their neighbors. They were a set of robbers from the start. The Dutch were on the ground first, but these English settlers forced them off, as their English brothers and cousins and their descendants by the force of arms robbed the Dutch of their lands in South Africa, and as the English people are doing in the same country at the present time. They were also dishonest in their relations with their neighbours of the Massachusetts towns from whence they came to Hartford. The pages of this history shows up thoroughly their unfair dealings with the people of New Haven Colony, and they have ever since carried out the same policy. A notable illustration is the manner in which they bribed and cajoled the voters of the remote parts of the State of Connecticut to vote that Hartford should be the sole capital of the State, when upwards of three-fifths of the residents and a still larger proportion of the manufacturing and business people of the State could travel to New Haven at that time by railroads much quicker and at less expense than they could reach Hartford. The insurance and other corporations in that city that have failed and defrauded their confiding patrons and stockholders fully illustrates the business methods of the "smart men" of some of our American cities, methods that were so thoroughly and truthfully characterized and condemned by Charles Dickens in his "American Notes."

RICHARD BROWN.

LIEUT. JOHN BUDD with his wife Katherine was in New Haven in 1639. He is recorded in the New Haven list as having a family of six persons and an estate of £450. He lived for some years in Southold, but in 1664 he was a Representative from Greenwich, Conn., and in 1677 a Representative from Milford. It is very possible that he was one of those who came in the third ship but did not immediately remove to Southold, as he had a large home-lot in New Haven. It is now the land that is bounded on the west by Church street, on the south by Crown street and on the east by Orange street, and it extended to the north some little distance beyond Center street.

HENRY CASE.

JOHN COREY (16 -1680) was a weaver by trade. He with his wife Ann lived in Southold. He died about 1680 at Hashamonack, leaving four sons,—John, Abraham, Isaac and Jacob,—all of whom were married and "raised families. Only a few of the descendants still reside in Southold." (Southold Town Records.)

THOMAS COOPER (16 -1658) died in 1658, leaving no sons. His widow Margaret died about 1687. His "large landed estate" was then divided between his daughters, Abigail (Mrs. Stephen Bailey) and Maria (Mrs. Elnathan Tapping).

CALEB CURTIS (16 -16) with wife Elizabeth Rider, on Feb. 16, 1677, bought land of her father, Thomas Rider. (See Southold Town Records, Vol. 1, pages 236–8.)

THOMAS DIMON may be the same person who died in Fairfield, Conn., in 1658. (See Dimon Genealogy, 8vo, pp. 179, Albany, 1891.)

JOHN ELTON, of Southold, was made a freeman in Connecticut Colony in 1662. He may have been the father of John Elton of Middletown, Conn. He had a second wife, Ann, and died before April 6, 1675. (Southold Town Records, Vol. 1, page 239.)

RALPH GOLDSMITH was a captain of a merchant trading ship. It is not certain that he "ever had a house, or a family in Southold." (See Town Records, Vol. 1, page 236.)

SIMON GROVER.

JAMES HAINES.

PETER HALLOCK (16 –1684) (Halliock, Hallock), through his son William, had descendants, who were prominent in their day. Fitz-Greene Halleck (1790–1867), of Guilford, Conn., and New York City, the poet, was of the 7th generation, and General Henry W. Halleck, U. S. A. (1815–1872), was of the 9th generation. Peter Hallock of Southold died Sept. 30, 1684. (See Halleck Genealogy, by Rev. W. A. Halleck, D.D.)

SAMUEL KING.

THOMAS MAPES (1628–1687) was in Southold in 1657 and probably earlier. It is possible that he was in Ipswich previously. He married Sarah Purrier, daughter of William Purrier (16 –16), of Ipswich, Mass., and Southold. He made his will in 1686. It was proved the next year. He left a family of four sons and five daughters. (See Southold Town Records, Vol 1.)

PETER PAINE (b. March 14, 1617; d. in or before 1658) left a son Peter and some daughters. (See Southold Town Records.)

JAMES REEVES (16 –1697) came from Wales with wife Mary Purrier (16 –16) daughter of William Purrier (16 –1659), of Ipswich and Southold. He died in Southold May 7, 1697. He had five or six sons and four daughters; possibly some of these children were by a second wife.

RICHARD SKIDMORE.

ROBERT SMYTH (16 –1697), of Southold, had a wife or daughter named Prudence.

JOHN SWAZEY (16 –168) died probably before 1686. He had possibly two sons, John and Joseph; perhaps other children.

SOUTHOLD.

CAPT. JOHN TUCKER (16 –16) married first, Mary Johnson of Hingham; second, Mrs. Hannah (   ) Elton, widow of John Elton (16 –16). He had "sons Charles, John and Joseph, daughters Hannah, Ruth and three or four other daughters." (See Southold Town Records.)

WILLIAM WELLS (1618–1671) married in 1656, Mrs. Bridget Tuttle, the widow of Henry Tuttle (1612–164) of Southold. He married   , 16 , Mary   (1619-1709), and had by both wives sons William, Joshua; daughters Mary, Bethia and Mehitable. (See Wm. Wells of Southold and His Descendants, pp. 300, Buffalo, 1878, by Rev. Chas. Wells Hayes.)

REV. JOHN YOUNGS (1598–16), a minister (but probably not the rector) of St. Margarets in Suffolk, aged 35 years, with his wife Joan (1599–163) and six children, viz: John, Thomas, Anna, Rachel, Mary and Joseph, attempted to take a ship for Salem, New England, in 1633, from Yarmouth, and was "forbyden passage by the Commissioners and went not from Yarmouth." Before he arrived at New Haven in 1639, his wife Joan had died and he had married a "widow whose christian name was Mary." It is altogether probable, as suggested by the author of this history on page 163, that he came with a large portion of the Southold settlers of 1640 to New Haven direct from England, and that, as was the case with Rev. John Davenport and other prominent New England ministers, he was obliged to get away from England without the knowledge of the authorities. By his second wife he had Benjamin, Christopher, possibly other children. His descendants have been prominent in the affairs of Long Island and elsewhere wherever they have lived.

PERSONNEL OF NORWALK.

ALTHOUGH Norwalk was not settled until about 1650, and to a considerable extent by persons from Connecticut Colony, yet it belonged geographically, if not politically, to New Haven Colony. Undoubtedly the intercourse of the residents of Norwalk with the residents of Milford and New Haven was much greater than with the residents of the more distant towns of Wethersfield, Hartford and Windsor. For this reason, therefore, the first settlers of Norwalk are recorded in this history.

DEACON EDWARD CHURCH (1628-16), son of Richard Church (16 -1667) and Ann   (1601-1684) of Hartford, probably lived in New Haven for a time before coming to Norwalk. He removed in 16   to Hatfield, Mass., where he was chosen as a deacon. He left some eight or more children. (See Church Family Genealogy.)

NATHANIEL ELY (16 -1675) was in Cambridge in 1632; removed to Hartford in 1636, and from there to Norwalk before 1650. He was a Representative from Norwalk in 1657. About 1660 he removed to Springfield where he died December 25, 1675. His widow Martha died Oct. 23, 1688, leaving children Samuel and Ruth and perhaps others. (Consult Ely Family Genealogy, by Hiram Ely, Cleveland, 1885, 4to, pp. 315.)

ISAAC GRAVES.

THOMAS HALE (Hales) was in Roxbury in 1634, removed soon after to Hartford, but returned to Roxbury, where he married Feb. , 1640, Jane Lord (16 –16); went from there to Norwalk but did not remain long in Norwalk. He probably returned to Massachusetts, living and dying in Charlestown. (See Hale Genealogy, by G. R. Howell, 1889, 8vo, pp. 427, Albany, N. Y.)

JOHN HOLLOWAY.

RALPH KEELER (1613–1672) while living in Norwalk had a wife, Mrs. Sarah ( ) Whelpley (16 –16), widow of Henry Whelpley (16 –16). She was a second wife and possibly not the mother of any of his seven children recorded by Savage. He died between Aug. 20 and Sept. 10, 1672, the date of the drawing up of his will and the date of probating. He was in Hartford in 1635 and in Fairfield in 1645.

MATTHEW MARVIN (1600–1680) came to Massachusetts Colony in "the ship *Increase* from London in 1635, aged 35, a husbandman, with wife Elizabeth, aged 31, and children Elizabeth, 11; Matthew, 8; Mary, 6; Sarah, 3, and Hannah, 6 months." He had at Hartford Abigail, Samuel, and Rachel, the youngest. He was a Representative from Norwalk in 1654. (Marvin Family Genealogy, sketch by T. R. Marvin, 1848, Boston, pp. 36.)

Lieut RICHARD OLMSTEAD (16 –1686) was in Hartford in 1639. He was chosen as Representative for Norwalk in the May session of 1653, and for several other sessions up to 1679. He left sons James and John and possibly some daughters. (See Olmstead Genealogy, by E. J. Thomas, 1869, pp. 30, Albany.)

JOHN RUSCOE (16 –16), the Huguenot, son of William Ruscoe (1594–16), who came from Bellericay, in County Essex, in the ship *Increase* in 1635, aged 41, with wife Rebecca, aged 40, and four children. He was married at Hartford Jan. 2, 1651, to

Rebecca Beebe (16 –16), and had sons Thomas and John and five daughters. Thomas died unmarried; five of the other children were married.

NATHANIEL RUSCOE.

RICHARD SEYMOUR (16 –1655) was in Hartford in 1639. From there he removed to Farmington, and then to Norwalk; was a selectman in Norwalk 1655, and died there Nov. 25, 1655, leaving four sons and two daughters. His widow Mercy (or Mary) (16 –16) married Nov. 22, 1656, John Steele (16 –1664 or '65) of Farmington.

THOMAS SPENCER.

RICHARD WELL.

SETTLERS OF 1651.

SAMUEL BECKWITH (16 –16) removed from Norwalk after 1654, but returned to Norwalk in 1671 or soon after, (See the Beckwith Genealogy, by Paul Beckwith, 1891, pp. 284, Albany.)

SAMUEL ELY.

JOSEPH FITCH (16 –17), brother of Thomas Fitch, was in Hartford before 1640, and in Norwalk a short time only; removed from Norwalk in 1655 to Northampton; in 1660 to Hartford, and finally in 16 to Windsor, where he died, 17 . He was a Representative at Hartford 1662–68.

THOMAS FITCH (1612–1704), the eldest son of Thomas Fitch (15 –1632) of Bocking, Essex County, England, with his mother, Ann Pyne (15 –16), and four brothers, Rev. James (161 –1702),

Samuel (16 –1659), Joseph (16 –17), and John (16 –1676), came to New England in 1637 (?) His children were born before he came to Norwalk probably. He was a very prominent man in the town. His great-grandson, Thomas Fitch (1699–1774), was Governor of the Connecticut Colony (17 –17).

NATHANIEL HAYES (16 –169) had in 1672 seven children living; he was living in 1694. Probably he married (for a second wife) Mary Kimberley, daughter of Thomas Kimberley (16 –1673) of Stamford, for he names in his will of 1673 his grandchildren Nathaniel, Elizabeth and Mary Hayes. (See the Hayes Genealogy, by Rev. C. W. Hayes, 1884, pp. 354, Buffalo.)

SAMUEL LUMIS (Loomis).

Sergt. ISAAC MOORE (1622 (?)–17) was in Farmington before 1650. He married in Hartford December 5, 1645, Ruth Stanley (16 –16), dau. of John Stanley (16 16); was a sergeant in 1649; a Representative for Norwalk in 1657. In 1660 he returned to Farmington; was made deacon and married for second wife Dorothy Smith (16 –17), dau. of Rev. Henry Smith (16 –16) of   .

Rev. THOMAS HANAFORD (162 –1693) was in Norwalk in 1652, and in that same year married Hannah Newberry (16 –1660), who died without children. He married Oct. 22, 1661, Mrs. Mary (Miles) Ince, widow of Jonathan Ince (16 –16) and daughter of Richard Miles (16 –16) of New Haven. By her he had several children.

SETTLERS OF 1854.

ALEXANDER BRYANT was probably only a land owner in Norwalk but never a resident of that town but of Milford, where his name is now to be found on the stone "Memorial Bridge."

NORWALK. 683

EDWARD NASH (16 –16), the Tanner, was possibly the son of Edward Nash (1592–16) of Lancashire, England. By his first wife Hannah he had John, b. 1652, and Hannah, b. 165 , who married Dec. 3, 1678, Deliverance Wakeley (16 –1697), son of Henry Wakeley (16 –16) of Stratford. He married , 16 , Mrs.   (Sherwood) Barber (16 –16), who had three or more children by her former husbands, Thomas Rumble (16 –16) and Thomas Barber (16 –16). She had no children by this, her third husband. John Nash (1652–17) married May 4, 1684, her daughter Mary Barber (b.   , 16 ; d. Sept. 2, 1711.)

CAPT. RICHARD RAIMENT (or Raymond) (16 –1692) was in Salem in 1634. He was a mariner and "did a coasting trade along the Sound and East River as far south as Manhattan Island." In 1664 he removed to Saybrook. His son John (1637–16) married in 1664 Mary Betts (16 –16), daughter of Thomas Betts (16 –16), and remained in Norwalk, where five or more children were born to them. Hon. Henry Raymond (1820–1869), founder of the New York *Times*, was a descendant, also General W. T. and his brother John Sherman, formerly Secretary of the Treasury and Secretary of State. (See Raymond Family Genealogy, by Samuel Raymond, 1886, pp. 286, New York.)

MATTHEW CAMFIELD (16 –1673), with his wife Sarah Treat (16 –16), removed from New Haven to Norwalk in 1652. He had nine or more children; was a prominent man in the town until 1666, when he with a number of others from the coast towns removed to Newark, N. J. His wife was a daughter of Richard Treat of Wethersfield and sister of Governor Robert Treat (1622–1710) of Milford. (See the Canfield Family Book, 1897, pp. 200, Dover, N. J.)

GILES WHITING (16 –1) was in Hartford in 1643.

PERSONNEL OF STAMFORD (Rippowams).

ROBERT BATES (16 -1675) was in Wethersfield in 1640, and removed to Rippowams (or Stamford) during or soon after that year. He was one of the first purchasers at Stamford Oct. 30, 1640. He died at Stamford June 11, 1675, leaving a son John (16 -1   ), daughter Mary (16 -169), wife of Abraham Ambler (16 -1699), and a daughter (name not stated) who had married John Cross (16 -16). They are mentioned in his will of June 11, 1675. He bequeathes "certain negroes who are to be made free at 40 years of age."

LIEUT. FRANCIS BELL (16 -1690) had been at Wethersfield before settling at Stamford; was admitted as freeman in New Haven Colony in 1641. His wife Rebecca (16 -1684) had several children. His will was made May 24, 1689, and he died January 8, 1690. In the will are mentioned a son, Capt. Jonathan Bell (1641-1699), daughter Mary Hoyt, wife of Joshua Hoyt (16 -17), and Rebecca Tuttle (b. Aug., 1643; d. May 2, 1676), wife of Jonathan Tuttle (1637-1705) of New Haven. (For descendants of Rebecca, see Tuttle Family Genealogy, page 192, 1884, pp. 754, Rutland, Vt., by Geo. F. Tuttle of New Haven. Also see Bell Genealogy, 1867, pp. 368, New York, by Ledyard Bell.")

SAMUEL CLARK (16 -16), in Wethersfield before 1640, is probably the same person who was early at Stamford. He was in Milford in 1669; went from there to Hempstead, L. I. He married 16 , Hannah Fordham (16 -16), daughter of Rev. Robert Fordham (16 -1674) of Hempstead and Southampton,

STAMFORD.

L. I. He is possibly the Samuel Clark who was in New Haven in 1685. (See Tuttle Family Book, page 2; also "History of Samuel Clark," St. Louis, 1892, pp. 122, by Rev. E. W. Clark.)

ROBERT COE (Cooe) (1596-1672) was in Watertown in 1634. In that year he came on the ship *Francis*, aged 38, with wife Ann, aged 43, and children: John, 8 years; Robert, 7 years; Benjamin, 5 years. He was made freeman Sept. 3, 1634. He removed to Wethersfield in 1636 and then to Stamford about 1640. From there in 1644, along with Rev. Mr. Denton and others, he removed to Hempstead, L. I.; was made a sheriff there in 1669. His son Robert (1627-165) married Susannah Mitchell (162 -16), daughter of Maj. Matthew Mitchell (1590-1645), and lived and died in Stratford.

RICHARD CRABB (16 -16) was a Representative from Wethersfield 1639-41. In 1643 he sold his land in that town and went to Stamford; in 1654 he was in Greenwich. He had a leaning towards the Quakers, harbored them and possessed Quaker books, and was disciplined and fined £30 by the church and town authorities.

Rev. RICHARD DENTON (1586-1662) was in Wethersfield in 1640; removed from that town to Stamford; about 1644, with several of his friends, he went to Hempstead, L. I., where he died. He was "bred at the University of Cambridge where he had his A.B. 1623, being of Catherine Hall." He had a son Daniel, married April 24, 1676, Hannah Leonard (16 -17) daughter of John Leonard (16 -1676), and probably had other children.

JEFFREY FERRIS (16 -1666), in Watertown in 1635 or before, was a freeman May 6, 1635; one of the first settlers of Wethersfield, from which town he removed to Stamford. In his will, dated Jan. 6, 1664, are mentioned James, Peter, Joseph and Mary Lockwood (possibly a step-daughter) and his wife Judy

Bowers. He had married in 1661 Mrs. Susannah (   ) Lockwood (16 -166), the widow of Robert Lockwood (16 -165).

ROBERT FISKE (or Fisher) was among the first settlers of Stamford. He had land assigned to him by the town, as appears from the testimony of Thomas Morehouse (15 -1658) March 17, 1649, in which he says that John Whitmore sold to his son John the land which *was* Robert Fisher's by gift of the town.

DANIEL FINCH (16 -1667) was in Watertown (perhaps he came with Winthrop) May 18, 1630. He removed to Wethersfield; was a constable in 1636 in that town. From there he removed to Stamford where he was one of the original proprietors, and in 1653 went to Fairfield, where he made Dec. 25, 1657, a contract of marriage with Mrs. Elizabeth (   ) Thompson (16 -16), widow of John Thompson (16 -165), and he died March   , 1667. In his will are mentioned a son Nathaniel and three daughters.

RICHARD GILDERSLEEVE (16 -16), in Stamford in 1641, had previously lived about five years in Wethersfield, and possibly before that was in Watertown. He was a Representative in 1643. About 1646 he removed to Hempstead, L. I.; was living there in 1663; probably had a son Richard.

JEREMY JAGGER (16 -1658) came from Wethersfield to Stamford in 1641; he may have lived also in Watertown. He was a master of a trading vessel and went to the West Indies about 1654. He died abroad Aug. 14, 1658; inventory of estate taken Dec. 11, 1658. He served in the Pequot War of 1637, and grants of land for his services in that war were made to his sons John, Jeremiah and Jonathan in 1671. His widow Elizabeth (16 -16) married May 12, 1659, Robert Usher (16 -1669) of   .

JOSEPH or JOHN JESSOP (16 -16), an early settler at Wethersfield, united with others in 1640 to go and settle in Stamford; removed from that town to Greenwich; was a Representa-

STAMFORD. 687

tive from Greenwich in 1664; in 1673 he was living in Southampton, L. I. (See Jessup Genealogy, Cambridge, Mass., 1887, pp. 453, by Rev. H. G. Jesup.)

RICHARD LAW (16 –16), in Wethersfield in 1638; he may have come from Watertown to Connecticut Colony. He removed to Stamford; was a Representative from Stamford to New Haven Colony and after (1665) to Connecticut Colony. He married Margaret Kilbourne (1607–16), daughter of Thomas Kilbourne (1580–1639), and had Abigail, Jonathan, Sarah (16 – 1732), and probably other children. Abigail married Maj. Jonathan Sellick (1641–1713), and Sarah married a brother, John Sellick (1643–16), a mariner, who was lost at sea.

MAJOR MATTHEW MITCHELL (1590–1645) came to New England in 1633 on the ship *Francis*, from Bristol, bringing with him his wife Susan Butterfield (15 –16) and children David (1619–16), Sarah (1621–16), Jonathan (1624–1668), Susan (1627–16), and Hannah (1631–1702). He settled at Charlestown; removed from there to Concord, and again to Springfield, where he signed a contract in May, 1636; was for a time in Saybrook and took part in the Pequot War. In 1639 he was at Wethersfield; from there went to Stamford. He heads the list of the twenty-eight men who settled at Stamford; he is mentioned first in several lists; paid "nearly three times as much towards the purchase and survey of the land as the next largest purchaser;" was a Representative and a very prominent man. The author of this history and the compiler of the appendix are both descendants. (For fuller information of this family see Cothren's History of Ancient Woodbury, pages 633–42 and 1319–32. A Mitchell Family History is in process of compilation by Dr. Mitchell of New York City.)

THOMAS MOREHOUSE (16 –16) removed to Fairfield; very little more has been learned concerning him. A slight sketch of his son, Lieut. Samuel, is to be found in the pages devoted to Fairfield.

JOHN NORTHEND (16 –16) was one of the first settlers of Wethersfield; from there he removed to Stamford.

THURSTON RAINOR (Rayner) (1594-1667), of Watertown, came in the ship *Elizabeth*, 1634, from Ipswich, England, aged 40, with wife Elizabeth, aged 36; Thurston, 13; Joseph, 11; Elizabeth, 9; Sarah, 7, and Lydia, 1. He removed to Wethersfield and was a Representative from that town in 1638, '39 and '40; in 1641 he went to Stamford, but in a few years removed to Southampton, L. I. There under the Connecticut Colony he was an Assistant in 1661 and '63; made his will July 6, 1667, and it was probated the same year. In the will he names his wife Martha (a second wife), two sons, Joseph (1623-16) and Jonathan (164 – 17), who was not of age in 1667. Four other children are alluded to but no names are given.

JOHN REYNOLDS (16 –16) was in Watertown in 1634; made a freeman May 6, 1635; he removed to Wethersfield about 1636, and from there to Stamford before 1644. He may be the father of Jonathan and John Reynolds who were freemen in 1669 in Greenwich. His wife Sarah died at Stamford in 1657.

JOHN SEAMAN (16 –16) was in Wethersfield before 1641; in that year he went to Stamford, and in later years he removed from Stamford.

SAMUEL SHERMAN (1618-1710) was born in Dedham, England; was baptized July 12, 1618; he came to New England about 1636; settled first at Wethersfield and from there he went to Stamford. He married, probably in 1640, Sarah Mitchell (1621-16), a daughter of Matthew Mitchell (1590-1645), and had nine or more children. In 1654, or before, he had removed to Stratford, where he died. (See Cothren's History of Woodbury, pages 679 and 1544-49.)

VINCENT SIMKINS (or Simpkins) (16 -166) was in Stamford in 1641; he married Mary Ackerly (16 -16), a daughter of Henry Ackerly (15 -1658) and Ann (1587-166) of Stamford. He had sons John and Daniel (16 -1699) and probably other children, and died before 1671. Daniel lived in the adjoining town of Bedford and died there in 1699. John soon after the death of his father sold his estate and removed from Stamford; his widow Mary married William Olliver.

HENRY SMITH (16 -1687) went from Wethersfield to Stamford in 1641; was one of the first settlers. In his will he names only a son Joseph, but he had a daughter Rebecca (16 -16), who married July 2, 1672, Edward Wilkinson (16 -1698) of Milford, and Hannah who married a Lawrence, and perhaps other children.

ANDREW WARD (15 -1659) was a freeman May 14, 1634, at Watertown; he removed in 1635 to Wethersfield; was a Representative in 1636 and '37; in 1641 he went to Stamford. He died in Fairfield in 1659; his will was dated June 8, 1659. By wife Esther (15 -1665) he had Edmund, William, Mary, Andrew (1647-1691), Samuel, Abigail, John and Sarah. Mary (164 -16) married Lieut. Jehu Burr (1623-1692); Ann married Caleb Nicholls (16 -16), and Sarah married Nathaniel Burr (16 -1712), all of Fairfield.

THOMAS WEEKS (or Weekes) (15 -1671), an original settler of 1641; before 1654 removed to Oyster Bay, Long Island, and died in 1671, leaving a widow Rebecca (?), and children,—Thomas, John, Rebecca, Martha, Elizabeth, Mary and Sarah. In 1664 he was in Huntington, L. I. The name has been changed to Wicks.

JOHN WHITMORE (15 -1648) was in Wethersfield in 1639; he brought from England five children,—Thomas, b. about 1615; Ann, b. 1621; Mary, b. 1623; Frances, b. 1625, and John, 1627.

At Stamford he married Mrs. ———— Jessup (16 –16), widow of ———— Jessup (16 –16). He was chosen a Representative to New Haven Colony Assembly in 1647, and was killed by Indians in 1648.

EDWARD WOOD (16 –16) was in Springfield in 1636; he removed that year to Wethersfield, and in 1641 went from Wethersfield to Stamford. In 1644 he removed to Hempstead, L. I.

JEREMIAH WOOD (16 –16) went to Hempstead from Stamford. He was possibly a brother of Edward; he was accepted as a freeman of Connecticut Colony at Hempstead in 1664. (See Wood Family Genealogy, 1898, Worcester, Mass., by W. S. Woods, pages 292.)

JONAS WOOD (16 –16), at Springfield in 1636, removed soon after to Wethersfield; settled at Stamford in 1641, and in a few years after went to Hempstead, L. I., probably under the patent of 1644; before 1654 he was in Southampton, L. I., and a few years later was a Commissioner under the jurisdiction of Connecticut Colony.

NEW LONDON (or Pequot.)

CAPTAIN JAMES AVERY (1620-169) was born in England about 1620, and was a son of Christopher Avery (15 -166), a weaver, who came from Salisbury in County Hants. He married Nov. 10, 1643, Jane Greenstack of Boston. Had Hannah, b. Oct. 12, 1644; James, Dec. 16, 1646; Mary, Feb. 19, 1648; removed that year to New London and there had Thomas, b. May 6, 1651; John, Feb. 10, 1654; Rebecca, b. Oct. 6, 1656; Jonathan, b. Jan. 5, 1657; Christopher, b. April 30, 1661; Samuel, b. Aug. 14, 1664, and Joanna, b. , 1669. He was a Representative in 1659; served in King Phillip's war, when he commanded the Pequot allied forces; he was living in 1694.

WILLIAM BARTLETT (16 -1657) was in New London in 1647; he died about 1657, leaving a widow Susannah but no children.

PETER BLATCHFORD (16 -1671) had served in 1637 in the Pequot war when very young, for which he had a grant of land; was a constable, and in 1669 he removed to Haddam, from which town he was a Representative in 1669 and 1670. He left a widow Hannah (1642-16), daughter of Isaac Wiley (16 -1685), who married after 1671 Samuel Spencer (16 -17), son of Ensign Jared Spencer (16 -1685) of Haddam.

REV. RICHARD BLINMAN (16 -16), at Gloucester in 1641, came from Chipstow, in County Monmouth, on the river Wye, in England. He was made a freeman at Gloucester Oct. 7,

1641. By wife Mary he had Jeremiah, b. July 20, 1642; Ezekiel, b. Nov. 11, 1645, and Azrikam, b. Jan. 2, 164 . He removed October, 1650, to New London "and drew thither many of his Gloucester friends." From New London he removed to New Haven, "whence after a short residence and selling some of his library to the Colony in May, 1659, he went home, carrying all of his children except Jeremiah, who was at New London as late as 1663." His wife is thought to have been a sister of Deacon Wm. Parke (16 –1685) of Roxbury. He died at Bristol, England, "in a good old age."

JONATHAN BREWSTER.

ROBERT BROOKS.

OBADIAH BRUEN (1606-168) was the youngest son of John Bruen (15 –16), of Bruen Stapleford, Cheshire, England He was baptized Dec. 25, 1606, at Taves, near Chester; became a draper at Shrewsbury in the adjoining county of Shalop; had a wife Sarah and daughter Mary (163 –16), and had here Rebecca, b. , 164 ; Hannah, b. Jan. 9, 1644, and John, b. June 2, 1646. He came over in 1640, probably with Rev. Richard Blinman. He was made a freeman May 19, 1642, at Gloucester; selectman in 1642, and Representative in 1647, '48, '49, and in 1651. In 1651 he removed to New London in company with his pastor, Rev. Mr. Blinman; was a town clerk there for 15 years. In 1667, having purchased land at Newark, N. J., in company with several others he removed there. On Oct. 11, 1679, he wrote a letter to his daughter (probably Hannah) and her husband at New London and signed himself Ob. Brewen, while his wife signed herself Sarah Bruen. His daughter Mary (163 –16) married in 1653 John Baldwin (16 –16), of Milford, as his second wife. Rebecca (164 –16) married Sept. 2, 1663, Thomas Post (16 –1701), of New London and Norwich, as his second wife. Hannah (1644–16) married John Baldwin (16 –16), of Milford, a son of the husband of her sister Mary. All descendants of this settler can trace their ancestry through a line of English lords and kings to William the Conqueror (1025–1089).

NEW LONDON.

HENRY CAUKIN, probably Hugh Calkins (1600-1690), was possibly a Welshman. He was in Gloucester in 1640; was made a freeman at Gloucester Dec. 27, 1642; was a selectman 1643-'48, a Representative 1650-'52, and removed to New London after 1650; was a selectman and Representative in that town; was also a town clerk for many years. He removed in 1662 to Norwich and was the first deacon of the Norwich church; also a Representative in 1663-'64, and died in 1690, aged ninety years. From England he came with wife Ann, children John, Sarah, Mary and possibly others. He had at Gloucester, David; Deborah, b. March 18, 1645; Rebecca, who died March 14, 1651. Sarah (162 - 16) married Oct. 28, 1645, Deacon William Hough (16 -1683); Mary married Nov. 8, 1649, Hugh Roberts, and removed to Newark, N. J.; Deborah (1645-16) married June   , 1660, Jonathan Royce. (The historian of Norwich and New London, Miss F. Caulkins, is a descendant of this settler.)

JOHN COITE (16 -1659), a shipwright, was at Salem in 1638 with wife Mary (1596-1676); he removed in 1644 to Gloucester; was a selectman there in 1648, and removed to New London in 1650. He died August 25, 1659, leaving a widow and children John, Joseph, Mary and Martha; a son and two daughters are referred to in his will but no names are given. Mary married John Stevens, who with four children removed to New Haven in 1676; Martha (1644-1737) married Hugh Mould (16 -1692), a shipbuilder, and in 1693 (?) she married Capt. Nathaniel White (1629-1711) of Middletown. (See the Coit Family Genealogy, 1874, Hartford, pp. 341, by F. M. Chapman.)

JOHN ELDERKIN (1616-1687) was in Lynn in 1657; in Dedham in 1641; in Reading 1646. In 1648 he was in Providence, and in New London in 1650, where he built the first church and the first mill. In 1664 he settled in Norwich where he also built the first church and the first mill, and there he died June 23, 1687, aged 71 years. He had by his first wife a daughter Abigail, born Sept. 13, 1641, and probably also Pelatiah, who married Daniel Comstock (1630-1683) of New London. He married about 1669 for a second wife Mrs. Elizabeth (Drake) Gaylord (1621-1716),

widow of William Gaylord (16 –1653), and had Ann, b. Jan.   ,
1661; John, b. April   , 1664; Bathshea, Nov.   , 1665; James,
March   , 1671; Joseph, Dec.   , 1672. His widow died June 18,
1716, aged 95 years. (See Elderkin Genealogy, 1888, Pittsburgh,
pp. 245, by D. W. Elderkin.)

JOHN GAGER (16 –1703), son of Surgeon William Gager
(15 –1630), came with his father in the fleet with Winthrop in
1630. He was in New London in 1650, and in 1660 went to Norwich. He had John, b. Sept.   , 1647; Elizabeth, 1649; Sarah,
1651; Hannah, 1653, died young; Samuel, 1654; Bethia; William,
1662, died young; Lydia, 1663; Hannah, 1666; Mary, 1671. He
died Dec. 10, 1703. The will mentions widow Elizabeth (she may
have been a second wife and not the mother of any of the children), Samuel and "my six sons that married my daughters,"
none of the daughters' names being given. These "sons" were
John Allyn, husband of Elizabeth; Daniel Brewster, Jeremiah
Ripley, Simon Huntington, Joshua Abel and Caleb Forbes.

ROBERT HEMPSTEAD (16 –1655) was in New London in
1645, "one of the four who assisted Winthrop in settling that
place." By his wife Ann (16 –16) he had Mary, b. March 26,
1647, the first child born at New London; Joshua, b. June 16,
1649; Hannah, b. April 11, 1652. He died June   , 1655, and his
widow married soon after Andrew Lister (16 –1669), whose first
wife Barbara had died Feb. 2, 1654. The daughter Mary married
in 1665 Robert Douglass and Hannah married Abel Moore.

ROBERT ISBELL (16 –16) had a son Isaac (16 –1677)
whose record is given in Savage; his children in 1677 were given
to the care of their grandmother, possibly meaning his mother, the
wife of Robert Isbell, or it may have been the grandmother on
the mother's side of the family. Nothing further concerning
Robert is found in Savage. (See Isbell Family Genealogy, 1889,
Oswego, N. Y., pp. 30, by L. W. Kingman.)

NEW LONDON. 695

ANDREW LESTER, or Lister (16 -1669), was an early settler in Gloucester; made a freeman in 1643. By wife Barbara (16 -1654) he had Daniel, Andrew, Mary and Ann. He removed to New London where his wife died Feb. 2, 1653-'54. He married after 1655, Mrs. Ann Hempstead (16 -16), widow of Robert Hempstead (16 -1655), and had Timothy, born July 4, 1662; Joseph, July 15, 1664, and Benjamin. He died after Oct. 14, 1669.

JOHN LEWIS (16 -1676) was in New London in 1648; he had a son John and probably other children, and died Dec. 8, 1676.

SAMUEL LOTHROP (1620-1700), son of Rev. John Lothrop (15 -1653), of Scituate and Barnstable, was born in England and came with his father in 1634. He married at Barnstable Nov. 28, 1644, Elizabeth Scudder (162 -16) and had John, b. Dec. 9, 1645, and eight more children: Samuel, Israel, Joseph, and daughters Elizabeth, Ann, and three daughters whose names are not found in Savage. He removed to Norwich in 1668; died Feb. 29, 1700, leaving a widow Abigail Doane (1631-1735) whom he had married in 1692 and who lived to be 104 years old. An engraving of her tombstone is to be found in the History of Norwich. (See Lathrop Genealogy, 1884, Ridgefield, Conn., pp. 457, by Rev. E. B. Huntington.)

WILLIAM MORTON (16 -1668), one of the first settlers of New London, was a constable in 1658 and after that year. No children are recorded as surviving him.

WILLIAM NICHOLS (16 -1673) was in Salem in 1638. He removed to New London and married after 1655 Mrs. Ann ( ) Isbell (16 -1689), the widow of Robert Isbell (16 -1655). He was a prominent business man in the town. He died Sept. 4, 1673, leaving no children, and his widow died Sept. 15, 1689. (See the Nicolls Family, 1888, by W. J. Nicolls.)

Mr. ROBERT PARKE (15 -1665) was in Wethersfield in 1639, and may have come to New England in 1630 and returned to England, for Savage claimed to have in his possession "what may be the first bill of exchange drawn on our side of the water," which was made here by Robert Parke in 1630. His oldest son William came in the *Lion* to Boston February, 1631, with Roger Williams. It is presumed that he was sent over by his father to select a home and he would follow later on. He was a Representative from Wethersfield in 1642; in 1649 he removed to New London, where his barn was the first place of worship. He was a selectman in 1651; a Representative in 1652; was called an aged man in 1662. He made his will May 14, 1660, which was probated in March, 1665. The will only names William, Samuel and Thomas, but possibly a daughter Ann had accompanied her brother William to Roxbury and there married August 20, 1640, Edward Payson (16 -16), of Roxbury, and died Sept. 10, 1641. A curious order of May 30, 1644, is recorded in which Robert Parke might " proceed in marriage with Alice Tompson, without further publishment." This Mrs. Alice Tompson (15 -165) was the widow of John Tompson (15 -163), of Little Compton, Northumberlandshire, England, and possibly the mother or stepmother of Anthony, John and William Tompson of New Haven Colony.

ROBERT PARKER (16 -1683) was living in Gloucester in 1647; he removed to New London in 1651; had a daughter Mary by his first wife. By his second wife, Susannah Keeny (16 -16), daughter of William Keeny (16 -16), he had Susannah, Jonathan, Ralph (b. Aug. 29, 1670), Thomas, Hannah, Mehitable and Rebecca. He was a " master mariner " and merchant and died in 1688. His eldest daughter Mary (164 -16) married about 1663 William Condy; Susannah (164 -16) married March 27, 1666, Thomas Forster; Hannah married Richard Wyatt; Mehitable married William Pendall; Rebecca (166 -17) married in 1685 John Prentiss (16 -1691) as his second wife. (See Parker Genealogy, Worcester, Mass., 1893, pp. 528, by T. Parker.)

HUGH ROBERTS (16 -16) was first at Gloucester. He married Nov. 1, 1649, Mary Calkins (16 -16), daughter of Hugh

Calkins (1600-1690), at Gloucester. He was a tanner and removed to New London soon after his marriage, where he had Mary, b. Dec. 9, 1652; Samuel, b. April 25, 1656; Mehitable, b. April 15, 1658. In 1667, with several other of the oldest settlers, he went to Newark, N. J.

THOMAS STANTON (1615-1678) came in 1633 from London to Virginia, but was soon after in Hartford as one of the original proprietors; he resided there many years and probably his nine or more children were born there. About 1658 he went to New London or Stonington. He had learned the Indian language and became on that account a very valuable man to the colonists; he was employed in that capacity in the Pequot war of 1637. He died in the spring of 1678; his will was probated in June, 1678. His widow, Ann Lord (1621-1688), daughter of Thomas Lord (1585-16) of Hartford, survived him for ten years and died in 1688. (See Stanton Genealogy, 1891, Albany, pp. 613, by Rev. W. A. Stanton.)

WILLIAM WELLMAN (16 -1671) was in Gloucester in 1649. He married, 1649, Elizabeth Spencer (162 -1718), daughter of William Spencer (15 -1640) of Hartford. He had some eight or more children, several of whom died young. His eldest child Mary (1650-1700) married January, 1667, Thomas Howand (16 - 1676) of Norwich; in August, 1677, she married William Moore (16 -1729) of Westerly. Martha, b. 1652; d. July 5, 1681; she married after 1672 Clement Minor (1640-1700) of New London. Elizabeth, b. 1657; d. Feb. 5, 1718; she married Jan. 9, 1679, John Shethar (16 -1) of Killingworth. He died at Killingworth Aug. 9, 16 ; his widow married May 23, 16 , Jacob Joy of Killingworth. (See the Driver Family Genealogy, 1889.)

GOVERNOR JOHN WINTHROP (1606-1676) son of Gov. John Winthrop (1588-1649) and Mary Forth (15 -1615) came over to New England in the ship *Lion* with his wife Marth Fines (16 - 1634) and bringing also his step-mother and the rest of the family who had not come over at an earlier period with his father, the first Gov. Winthrop of Massachusetts Colony. His first wife died leaving no children. He married a second wife in England in 1635 and had Fitz-John, b. March 14, 1638; Lucy, b. Jan. 28, 1640; Mehitable, b. Feb. 27, 1642; Mary, bap. Sept. 15, 1644; all at Boston. He went to New London in 1645, and in 1646 brought his family (according to Savage) to the shore of Long Island Sound where he had Martha, b. 1649; Margaret, b. 165 ; and Ann, b. 165 . He was chosen as Governor of Connecticut Colony in 1657 and continued in office until his death.

PERSONNEL OF SAYBROOK.

WILLIAM BACKUS (16 -1664) was at Saybrook in 1638; he had there William and Stephen; about 1660 he removed to Norwich; was a freeman there in 1663, and died June, 1664, leaving a second wife Ann, who died May, 1660. (See Backus Family Genealogy, Norwich, Conn., 1889, by Wm. W. Backus, pp. 371.)

THOMAS BLISS (16 -1688), son of Thomas (15 -164) of Hartford, removed from Hartford to Saybrook. In October, 1644, he married Elizabeth (16 -169), and had six children born in Saybrook and two daughters born in Norwich, where he removed in 1660. In his will made April 13, 1688, he mentions wife Elizabeth, six daughters and one son Samuel. He died April 15, 1688.

DEACON FRANCIS BUSHNELL (1600–1681), son of Francis Bushnell (15 -1644), who came to Guilford in 1639 with his son Francis and daughter Rebecca (16 -1647), who married John Lord (16 -16) of Hartford. Deacon Bushnell had a son Samuel and five daughters, and died December 4, 1681.

WILLIAM BUSHNELL (16 -1684), probably a brother of John Bushnell (1614–16) of Boston, had at Saybrook Joshua, b. May 6, 1644; Samuel, Sept. , 1645; Rebecca, Oct. 5, 1646; William, Feb. 15, 1648; Francis, Jan. 6, 1650; Stephen, , 165 ; Thomas, Jan. 4, 1654; Judith, Jan. , 1658; and Abigail, Feb. , 1660. He died August, 31, 1684.

CAPT. ROBT. CHAPMAN (1617-1687) m. April 29, 1642, Ann Bliss (162 -1685), daughter of Thomas Bliss (15 -164), and had seven or more children, three sons and four daughters. He was a Captain, Representative between 1652 and 1673, an Assistant, 1681-5, and died Oct. 13, 1687; his wife died Nov. 20, 1685. His daughter Hannah, b. Oct. 4, 1650, married Feb. 27, 1677, David Bull (1651-17   ) of Saybrook; Mary, b. April 15, 1655, married May 2, 1676, Samuel Bates (16 -1699); and Sarah, b. Sept. 25, 1657, married Sept,   , 1680, Joseph Pratt (1648-170) as his second wife. (See Chapman Gen., 1854, Hartford, by Rev. F. W. Chapman, pp. 413.)

HENRY CHAMPION (16 -1709) married August   , 1647, Sarah (?)   (16 -1697) and had Sarah, b. 1649; Mary, b. 1651; Henry, b. 1654; Thomas, b. April   , 1656; Stephen, b. 1658, died, 1660. He married March 21, 1698, Deborah   (16 -17).

JOHN CLARK (16 -16). See account of his family under Milford.

COLONEL GEORGE FENWICK (15 -1657) came in May, 1636 to Boston, went back home in 1636 or 1637, and returned with wife and children in the first ship of the three that sailed from England to New Haven direct in 1639. This first ship possibly arrived in New Haven in June. (See pages 161-62.) He returned to England in 1647 or 1648 (before May, 1648), taking his daughters, Elizabeth, Dorothy and Mary with him. His wife Mrs. Alice (Apsley) Boteler (15 -164), widow of   Boteler, and daughter of Sir Edmund Apsley, died at Saybrook, where the monument of Lady Fenwick can now be found. On his return to England he married Catherine Haslerigg (16 -16), eldest daughter of Sir Arthur H. (15 -16). In his will of March 8, 1656-7, probated April 27, 1657, he mentions wife Catherine and daughters Elizabeth and Dorothy; probably Mary had died before that year. A sister Elizabeth Fenwick married at Saybrook or Hartford May 20, 1648, Capt. John Cullick (16 -1663) of Hartford, probably as a second wife; she had two children, John and Elizabeth, and married in 1664, Richard Ely (16 -1684), and died Nov. 12, 1683, at Saybrook or Boston.

SAYBROOK.

REV. JAMES FITCH (1622-1702), son of Thomas Fitch (1590-1632-3), was born Dec. 22, 1622, at Bocking, Essex Co., England; he came over to New England with his mother, Widow Anne (Pew) Fitch (159 -1645) and four brothers, about 1638, two or more sisters being left in England unless they had died between 1632 and 1638. He may have been a student in Cambridge University before coming over, as by his father's will made Dec. 11, 1632, and probated Feb. 12, 1632-3 (see New Eng. Hist. Reg. of 1892, page 323), money is left to pay for his tuition at Cambridge. He probably studied theology under Rev. Thomas Hooker (1585-1647) at Hartford, according to an inscription on his tombstone at Lebanon, Conn.; he studied for seven years and was ordained in 1646, as narrated by that somewhat of a romancer, Rev. Cotton Mather (16 -17); he married , 164 , Abigail Whitfield (b. 16 ; d. Sept. 9, 1659), daughter of Rev. Henry Whitfield (1597-16) of Guilford. By his first wife Abigail he had James, Abigail, Elizabeth, Hannah, Samuel, Dorothy. He removed to Norwich in 1660, and there married Oct. 2, 1664, Priscilla Mason (b. Oct. , 1641; d. , 16), daughter of Major John Mason (1601-1672) and Isabella Peck (16 -16), and had John, Jeremiah, Jabez, Ann, Nathanie, Joseph and Eleazer, all of whom were living in 1696, when his will was made; he removed to Lebanon in 1692, and died there Nov. 18, 1702; his older brother Thomas (1612-1704) survived him for two years, and died at Norwalk in 1704. (See Personnel of Norwalk Settlers; also Fitch Family Gen., now being compiled by Attorney Fitch of New York City.)

LT. LION GARDINER (1599-1663) arrived at Boston on Nov. 28, 1635, aged 36 years, with wife Mary Williamson (16 -16), aged 34 years, daughter of Dericke Williamson (15 -16) of Worden in Holland, coming in the ship *Bachelor*. He was soon at Saybrook where he built a fort, and there had David, b. April 29, 1636; Mary, b. Aug. 30, 1638 (both of them born at Saybrook fort); and Elizabeth, b. Sept. 14, 1641, on Gardiner's Island, as it is now called; by him it was called Isle of Wight. He was prominent in the Pequot war; after 1642 he lived on his island and on Long Island, where he died late in 1663. His widow died in

SAYBROOK.

1665, and her will is recorded in New York City. (See Gardiner Genealogy by Curtiss C. Gardiner, 1890, St. Louis, pp. 195.)

LT. MATTHEW GRISWOLD (1620-1698) came from Kenilworth, Warwickshire, Eng.; he was a your..er brother of Edward (1607-1691) of Windsor, and after 1664 of Killingworth. At Saybrook he had five or more children, Elizabeth (b.   , 164 ; d. July   , 1727); married Oct. 17, 1670, John Rogers (16 -1672) of New London, the founder of the sect of the Rogerenes; she was divorced from him and married Aug. 5, 1679, Peter Pratt (16 - 1688), and again in 1691 she married Matthew Beckwith (16 - 1727); Ann, b.   , 165 , married Sept. 2, 1674, Abraham Bronson (1647-17) of Lyme; Sarah married Capt. Thomas Colton of Springfield; Matthew was born at Saybrook in 1633, married and had children, while the remaining son, John, died young, (See Griswold Gen., 1884.)

CHRISTOPHER HUNTINGTON (16 -1691) was at Saybrook and Norwich; he was son of Simon Huntington (15 -1633), "who died of small pox on his passage from England to Boston in 1633"; he with his brother Simon (1629-1706) and Joseph (?) were with their mother, Mrs. Margaret Huntington, at Roxbury until 1635 or 1636, when, she having married Lieut. Thomas Stoughton (16 -1642), the whole family removed to Windsor. Before 1650 he was probably at Saybrook, but married at Windsor Oct. 7, Ruth Rockwell (16 -16), daughter of William Rockwell (16 -16), and had at Windsor Christopher, b. Jan.   , 1653, who died young at Saybrook; Ruth, b. April , 1658, who married Samuel Pratt of Saybrook, and died in 1683; Christopher, b. Nov. 1, 1660, in Norwich, to which town the father had removed shortly before; Thomas, b. March 18, 1664; John; Susanna, b. Aug.   , 1668; married Dec. 10, 1685, Samuel Griswold; Lydia and Ann. (See Huntington Gen., 1863, Stamford, Conn., by Rev. E. B. Huntington, pp. 428.)

WILLIAM HYDE (16 -16), an original proprietor at Hartford, removed to Saybrook, and in 1659 or 1660 went to Norwich; he had a son Samuel, b.   , 1637, who married at Saybrook in

SAYBROOK. 698e

June, 1659, Jane Lee (16 –16), daughter of Thomas Lee (15 – 1641). A daughter Esther married in 166 , John Post (16 –16). (See the Hyde Genealogy, Albany, 1864, two vols., 8vo, 1446 pages, by R. H. Walworth.)

GREENFIELD LARRABEE (16 –16) had by his first wife Elizabeth (?), who is believed to have been an Elizabeth Brown of Providence, Greenfield, b. April 20, 1648; John, b. Feb. 23, 1650; Elizabeth, b. Jan. 25, 1653; Joseph, b. March , 1655, died young; and Sarah, b. March 3, 1658.

JOHN LAY (16 –1675) was in Saybrook in 1648; in his will of January 16 or 18, 1674-5, two days before his death, he names sons John (1633-1706) and James (16 –1683), children by a former wife; Peter, Abigail, Susanna and Elizabeth, children of his present wife Abigail, who died in 1686. Some of the descendants of this settler have changed their names to Laigh and Lee. (See Salisbury's Gen. & Biog. Monographs, 7 vols., New Haven, Conn., 1892.)

LIEUT. THOMAS LEFFINGWELL (1622-1710) was at Saybrook in 1637; he had Rachel, Thomas, Jonathan, Joseph, Mary and Nathaniel. He was one of the purchasers of Norwich, and removed there among the first settlers; was a representative from Norwich in 1662, and a lieutenant in King Philip's War.

REYNOLD (Reginald or Reinold) MARVIN (16 –1662), probably a younger brother of Matthew Marvin (1603-1687) of Hartford and Norwich, was living in Hartford in 1639, removed from there to Farmington and soon after to Saybrook; he was made a freeman in 1658. His will, made May 13, 1662, and probated Oct. 28, 1662, gives a good estate to his son Reynold and daughter Mary, who were probably born in England. (See Marvin Genealogy, Boston, 1848, by T. R. Marvin, 8vo, pp. 36; also the Salisbury Memorial, New Haven, Conn., 1892.)

MAJOR JOHN MASON (1601-1672) of Dorchester, either came over in 1630 with Winthrop, or in 1632. In 1636 he removed to

SAYBROOK.

Windsor, and was prominent in the Pequot Indian War of 1637. He was at different times a Chief Commissioner, Representative, Assistant, and a Deputy-Governor 1660–1668. In 1647 he removed from Windsor to Saybrook, and in 1659 he went to Norwich. His first wife died at Windsor; no children are recorded. He married July   , 1639, Isabel (or Priscilla) Peck (16 –16), and by her had eight or more children. (See Sparks American Biography, vol. 3, second series, for a biography of this warrior and statesman.)

MATTHEW MITCHELL (1590–1645). (See account of this settler under Norwalk.)

WILLIAM PARKER (16 –1686) was an original proprietor of Hartford in 1636, and removed later to Saybrook. He had Sarah, b. Oct.   , 1637; Joseph, died young; John, Ruth, William, Joseph, Margaret, Jonathan, David, Rebecca, b. March   , 1658. He was a Representative in 1662; his wife Margery died Dec. 3, 1680, and he died Dec. 21, 1686.

STEPHEN POST (15 –1659) was in Cambridge, Mass., in 1634; he removed in 1636 to Hartford as one of the original proprietors, and by 1649 or before he was living in Saybrook, where he died Aug. 16, 1659. He had John (16 –1710), Thomas (16 –1701), Abraham (16 –1690) and Catherine (16 –16) who married Sept. 29, 1649, Alexander Chalker (16 –167); she married Sept. 23, 1673, John Hills (16 –1689).

LIEUT. WILLIAM PRATT (16 –1678) was an original proprietor in Hartford; he married 1641, Elizabeth Clark (16 –16), daughter of John Clark (16 –167) of Milford, and had Elizabeth, b. Feb. 1, 1640–41; John, Joseph, Sarah, William, Mary, Samuel, Nathaniel and Lydia, b. Jan. 1, 1659–60; he was a Lieut. in 1661, a Representative in 1666 and several years after. (Consult Pratt Family Genealogy, 1864, Hartford, by Rev. F. W. Chapman, 8vo, pp. 420.)

RESIDENTS OF NEW HAVEN

From 1640 to 1650, who were not recorded in the list on pages 109–111, with the year of the first mention of their name in the Records of New Haven Colony, the year of their death when known, occupation, etc.

1642	Robert Abbott, rem. to Branford, d. 1647.
1640	Edward Adams, rem. to Milford, d. 1671.
1640	Henry Akerlye, rem. to Stamford 1641, d. 1671.
1641	Robert Allen, ret. to England.
1639	David Anderson.
1640	Thomas Ashley, d. 1640.
1641	William Aspenwall, rem. to Boston and ret. to England.
1644	Nicholas Auger, physician, d. 1677.
1638	John Baldwin, rem. to Milford, d. 1681.
	Thomas Badger, d. 1664.
	Timothy Baldwin, 1078-1112 Chapel St., rem. to Milford, d. 1665.
1643	Capt. Allen Ball.
1643	William Ball, rem. to Virginia (?), d. 1648 (?).
1644	Nicholas Baly.
1641	Obadiah Barnes, brickmaker.
1643	Thomas Barnes, rem. to Middletown, d. 1693.
1644	John Bassett, carpenter, 43-63 George St., d. 1653.
1644	Robert Bassett, shoemaker, town drummer, rem. to Stamford.
1642	William Bassett, 72-164 Congress Ave., d. 1684.
1646	Thomas Beamont, d. 1686.
1643	John Beech, rem. in 1649.
1646	Thomas Beech, rem. to Milford, d. 1662.
1638	Isaac Beecher.
1644	James Bell.
1644	Roger Betts, rem. to Branford 1648, d. 1658.
1644	James Bishop, Governor in 16 , 1-19 Elm St., d. 1691.
1644	Henry Bishop, farmer in employ of Rev. J. Davenport.
1647	Adam Blackman.
1643	Thomas Blakeley (1615-16).
1644	John Bracey, d. 1700.

RESIDENTS OF NEW HAVEN.

1644 William Bradley, d. 1691.
1644 Henry Bristow, d. 1695.
1638 William Bromfield, servant to Rich. Malbon.
1644 John Brown, mason.
1642 Francis Brown, d. 1668.
1643 Nathan Burchall.
1646 Samuel Cabells.
1649 Samuel Caffinch.
1643 Thomas Caffinch, d. 1647.
1642 Matthew Camfield, rem. to Stamford, d. 1675.
1643 Edward Campion, d. 1639.
1638 Robert Campion.
1649 Henry Carter, d. 1671.
1640 Thomas Chambers, rem. 1640 to Scituate.
1647 John Chidsey, 1621-1688.
1639 Edward Chipperfield, brickmaker, d. 1648.
1642 Francis Church.
1644 Thomas Clark, d. 1647.
1649 James Clements.
1639 John Cockerill, 1035-73 Chapel St., rem. after 1641.
1644 Thomas Coefield.
1639 John Cogswell.
1640 Matthew Crowder.
1639 John Davenport, Jr., minister, 2-26 Elm St., rem. to Boston, d. 1686.
1642 William Davis, 14-24 College St., d. 1659.
     Ralph Dayton, rem. to Long Island.
1639 Samuel Dayton, rem. to Long Island.
1639 Abraham Doolittle, 1620-1690.
1644 John Dillingham.
1646 Tobias Dimmock, mariner.
1642 Thomas Dickinson, d. 1658.
1644 George Downing.
1640 John Duer.
1639 Roger Duhurst.
1647 Thomas Dunk, rem. to Guilford, d. 1683.
1643 Rice Edwards.
1639 Thomas Ellery.
1643 Robert Emery, rem. to Stamford, d. 1656.
1645 John England, rem. to Branford, d. 1655.
1643 David Evance.
1643 William Fancy.
1638 John Fowler, rem. to Guilford, d. 1677.
1640 Thomas Frankland.
1642 Thomas French.
1642 Lancelot Fuller, d. 1651.
1646 Philip Galpin, rem. to Fairfield, d. 1657.
1646 Thomas Games.
1643 Nicholas Gennings, 1612-1673.

RESIDENTS OF NEW HAVEN. 701

1647 Joseph Gernsye.
1642 William Gibbard, d. 1662.
1640 John Gibbs, d. 1690.
     Henry Gibbons, d. 1686.
1639 William Gibbons, carpenter, d. 1689.
1644 Henry Glover, 1610-1689.
1647 Samuel Goodenhouse, merchant, 75-97 Elm St.
1645 John Gregory.
1647 Henry Gregory, shoemaker.
1642 John Griffin.
1644 James Guillam.
1647 Job Hall, 136-148 Elm St., rem. to Stratford.
1646 John Hall, d. 1676.
1640 William Harding.
1644 John Harriman, d. 1683.
     Arthur Halbish, d. 1648.
1644 Richard Harrison, d. 1653.
1646 John Hart, rem. to Farmington, d. 1666.
1641 Edward Harwood.
1643 James Heywood.
1638 Charles Higginson, mariner, d. 1677.
1638 Samuel Higginson.
1638 Theophilus Higginson, 1620-1657.
1646 Benjamin Hill, rem. after 1649.
1638 John Hill, d. 1647.
     Mark Himes.
1643 Edward Hitchcock, d. 1659.
1643 Luke Hitchcock, rem. to Wethersfield, d. 1659.
1646 Samuel Hodgkins (Hotchkiss), d. 1663.
     John Hodson, d. 1690.
1637 Thomas Hogg.
1642 Samuel Hopkins.
1644 Henry Hummerton, d. 1663.
1644 John Hunter, d. 1648.
1644 John Hutchinson.
1641 —— Huitt.
1645 Jeremiah How, d. 1690.
1645 William Hooke, teacher, ret. to England, d. 1678 or '88.
1643 Thomas Iles.
1643 William Iles, d. 1646.
1647 John Jackson, d. 1683.
1639 Thomas James, Jr., 820-876 Chapel St., d. 1696.
     Richard Jewell, d. 1642.
1638 Robert Johnson, 251-265 York St., d. 1661.
1638 Thomas Johnson.
1644 John Jones, d. 1657.
1647 William Judson, 147-153 College St., d. 1661.
1647 Edward Keylye.

1644 John Kimber.
    Zuriel Kimberly.
1638 Roger Knapp, rem. to Fairfield, d. 1683.
1648 John Knight.
    Thomas Knowles, d. 1647.
1644 Richard Lambert.
1643 Thomas Lamson, d. 1663.
1650 George Lawremore, carpenter.
1643 John Lawrence.
1641 Thomas Leaver, d. 1683.
1647 Edmund Leach, brickmaker.
1643 Robert Lee.
1644 Phillip Leek.
1644 Dea. Henry Lindall, d. 1676.
1645 Francis Linley, d. 1660.
1644 John Linley.
    Henry Lines, d. 1663.
1638 James Love, d. 1684.
1642 John Love, miller.
1647 Richard Lovell.
    ——— Lucking, d. 1641.
1644 Thomas Lupton, rem. to Norwalk, d. 1688.
1639 Thomas Manchester, servant to Mr. Perry.
1644 Peter Mallery.
1646 Richard Marden.
1643 Jonathan Marsh, rem. to Norwalk.
1646 Samuel Marsh.
1647 Thomas Marshall.
1644 Robert Martin, d. 1673.
1640 Samuel Martin, d. 1683.
1644 John Massam.
1644 Robert Meeker, rem. to Fairfield.
1640 John Mason.
1643 William Meeker.
1643 Thomas Meekes, d. 1691.
1643 John Meigs, shoemaker, 820-876 Chapel St., rem. to Guilford, d. 1678.
1646 Mark Meggs, d. 1658.
1646 Vincent Meggs, d. 1658.
1641 Capt. Nathaniel Merriman, d. 1694.
1638 Richard Merriman.
1643 John Metcalf, brickmaker.
1639 Stephen Metcalf, brickmaker.
1638 Andrew Messenger.
1645 Thomas Mitchell.
1640 John Moody.
    Henry Morall.
1638 Thomas Morris, ship carpenter.
1644 Isaac Mould.

1640	Capt. Thomas Munson, carpenter, 1612-1685.
1639	Thomas Mullyner.
1639	John Nash, d. 1687.
1639	Joseph Nash, d. 1678.
1639	Richard Newman.
1644	Edward Newton.
1640	Adam Nichols, d. 1682.
1644	Thomas North.
1644	Jeremiah Osborne, tanner, d. 1676.
1642	John Owens.
	William Paine, d. 1683.
1643	Michael Palmer, rem. to Branford.
1644	George Pardy (Pardee), tailor, d. 1700.
1644	Edward Parker, d. 1662.
1644	Robert Parsons, merchant, d. 1646.
	Thomas Paul.
1639	Benjamin Pauling.
1644	Henry Peck, d. 1651.
1643	Joseph Peck, rem. to Milford 1650, d. 1703.
1639	Thomas Pell, physician, d. 1669.
1644	Ephraim Pennington, d. 1660.
1637	Robert Pigg, d. 1660.
1638	John Pocock, 120-128 College St., rem. to Milford.
1639	William Powell, 1099-1109 Chapel St., d. 1681.
1643	Thomas Robinson, rem. to Guilford.
1643	Mathew Rowe, d. 1662.
1639	William Russell, ship carpenter, Water St., d. 1665.
1642	Jonathan Rudd, d. 1668.
1641	John Sackett, carpenter, d. 1684.
1639	Thomas Saule.
1646	Caleb Seaman.
1638	Capt. Nathaniel Seeley, rem. to Fairfield, d. 1675.
1649	Nicholas Slooper.
1644	William Slow, rem. to Milford 1645, d. 1652.
1639	John Smith. farmer, rem. to Milford 1640, d. 1684.
1645	Nehemiah Smith, shepherd, rem. to Norwich, d. 1686.
1641	Abraham Smyth.
1643	Francis Smyth.
1646	Richard Smoolt, servant.
1645	Obadiah Southwood.
1646	John Speede.
1643	Richard Sperry, farmer to Gov. Goodyear.
1639	Humphrey Spinning, d. 1656.
1642	Antony Stevens.
1639	James Stewart.
1644	Abraham Stolyon.
1648	Robert Talmadge, d. 1662.
1637	Thomas Tibbals, 1615-1703.

1639	Nicholas Tanner.
	John Thomas, d. 1671.
1638	John Thompson, d. 1675.
	John Thompson, d. 1656.
1639	William Thompson, d. 1683.
1645	James Till.
1644	Martin Tichenor.
1642	Thomas Toby, ship carpenter.
1643	Edmund Tooley, d. 1685.
1639	Christopher Todd, 232-252 Grove St., d. 1686.
1647	Daniel Turner.
1648	James Turner.
1639	John Tuttle, 570-614 State St., d. 1683.
1639	Captain John Underhill, d. 1674.
1644	Robert Usher, rem. to Stamford.
1638	John Vincent, d. 1659.
1644	John Wakefield, d. 1660.
1639	Dea. John Wakeman, d. 1667.
1645	George Walker.
1639	John Walker, d. 1652.
	Edward Watson, d. 1660.
1647	Edmund Watters.
1649	Joseph Watters, rem. to Milford.
1646	Jeremiah Watts.
1642	Lawrence Watts, d. 1643.
	Richard Webb, d. 1665.
1647	William Westerhouse, merchant, rem. to New York.
1640	Thomas Wheeler, Sr., d. 1656.
1644	William White, rem. 1666.
1642	Isaac Whitehead, rem. to New Jersey.
1642	Thomas Whitway, Chapel St., d. 1651.
1641	John Wilford, d. 1678.
	John Wilkes, d. 1647.
1639	Benjamin Wilmot, d. 1651.
1642	Matthew Wilson.
1643	Samuel Wilson.
1647	John Winston, d. 1697.
1640	Edward Woodcliff.
1642	John Woolen.
1642	William Woodin, d. 1684.
1643	Ralph Worry.

A CATALOGUE OF YE BOOKS OF YE LATE REVD. MR. ROGER NEWTON DECEASED.

(New Haven Probate Records, Vol. I, part 2, page 107.)

As a matter of historical interest it has been thought that a list of the books of the library of a clergyman of the 17th century would be a valuable contribution; therefore a copy of the inventory of the library of Rev. Roger Newton (16 –1683) of Milford has been copied from the Probate Records of New Haven, Connecticut, and is herewith presented to the readers of this history.

	£	s	d
Hamond on psalms	00	02	00
Jones on ye epistles	00	08	00
Day on Isaiah	00	06	00
Jermin on Eclesiastes	00	07	00
Cottons first epist: John	00	09	00
Rogers on 1st epist peter	00	10	00
Bisield on Colloss	00	06	00
parsons on Revelations	00	08	00

(page 65)

	£	s	d
Dr. Sibbs family cordialls	00	06	00
B. Babington on ye five books of Moses	00	10	00
Durham on Revelations	00	11	00
Downams christian warfare	00	14	00
Strigelious in psalms	00	05	00
Cartwright Rhomish Testmt	00	15	00

	£	s	d
Shepards ten virgins	00	05	00
Calvin's institutions	00	09	00
Cowpers works	00	10	00
Julius Trem biblia	00	10	00
Diodates Annotations	00	10	00

QUARTOS.

	£	s	d
Riders dictionary: old	00	08	00
Zabarella It: reb: natural	00	03	00
2 great English bibles	05	00	00
Bridge his works	00	04	00
Weemse on ye law of Moses, 2 vol	00	12	00
Carill on 34 chaps of Job, 6 vol	03	14	00
Wilsons christian dictionary	00	08	00
Burroughs on ye beatitudes	00	09	00
Montens biblia intelinear, 6 parts	02	00	00
Mayers Cathechisme	00	05	00
Broughtons consent of scripture	00	02	00
jackson on ye 5 books of moses	00	06	00
Cartwright in proverb: Solomon	00	07	00
Two books of Dr. preston	00	14	00
Burrough on Matthew 11th	00	10	00
Burrough on Hosea's, 2 vol	05	10	00
Mr. Hooker on Chts prayer, jno 14	00	07	00
Lawrence his commen & war with angells	00	01	06
Dr. Ames marrow of divinity	00	02	00

Mr. Newtons books remainder not being room in its own place.

OCTAVOS.

	£	s	d
Dr. Sibbs his light from heaven	00	02	06
Dr. Twiss on ye morality of ye gospels	00	03	00
lloyds marrow of history	00	02	00
Gouges gods three arrows	00	03	00
Rogers on ye Sacramts	00	03	00
Cleaver on ye proverbs	00	03	00
Dixon epistolas apostolicas	00	06	00

A CATALOGUE OF BOOKS.

	£	s	d
Amesius in psalms	00	04	00
Bradshaw on 2 epist: Thess	00	01	00
Burroughs gospell worship	00	02	06
Bolton on happiness	00	06	00
Gouges domesticall duties	00	04	06
Greenhill on Ezekiel, 1 part	00	04	06
Rogers practicall cathechisme	00	03	06
Sibbs his bowells opened	00	03	00
Burroughs Moses choise	00	05	06
Sibbs on 3d chap: phillypians	00	02	00
Mayers Treasury	00	03	06
Hewitt upon Daniell	00	02	00
Ursius Cathechisme English	00	08	00
Willetts sinopsis papism	00	08	00
Airay on phillipians	00	05	00
Dod & Cleaver on ye comandmts	00	03	00
Barlow on 2d Tim	00	01	06
Boltons 3 fold Treatise	00	05	00
Ames cases of conscience	00	01	00
Randall on ye Sacramts	00	02	06
perkins Chts sermon on ye mount	00	03	00
Reinolds 3 treatises	00	01	00
jun: Hebr: Gram	00	01	00
Burroughs irenicum	00	03	00
Gilds throne of David	00	02	00
Burroughs gospell reconciliation	00	03	00
Taylor of lives	00	02	06
History of the Waldenses	00	02	00
Boltons 4 last things	00	01	00
Reynolds on psalm 110th	00	03	00
Dyke on conscience	00	01	00
Buchans institutions	00	04	06
pridous Lectiones	00	01	00
pemble on Zachary	00	01	06
The parable of the sower	00	01	00
perkins cases of conscience	00	01	00
Barrows method of phisicke	00	01	06
Burroughs contentmt	00	01	06

	£	S	D
Dod & Cleaver on ye sacramt	00	00	06
Terrence english	00	00	06
Romish forgeries	00	00	06
Forbs on revelations	00	00	06
Brownisme confuted	00	00	04
Kings Lectures on jonas	00	03	00
Hookers survey	00	02	06
Taylor on Rev: 12th	C0	05	00
Brightman on Rev.	00	04	00
Dyke on philemon	00	01	00
parr on ye Romans	00	01	00
Haven of health	00	00	06
Cottons singing psalms	00	00	04
Cotton Reges	00	00	04
Clarkes examples	00	03	00
passons Lexicon	00	03	00
janua Linguarum	00	01	00
Dykes righteous manstower	00	01	00
Stokes on small prophets	00	02	00
Rollock on John	00	04	00
Dod & Cleaver household govermt	00	01	00
Dickson on psalms	00	05	00
Ruatchhills animadversiones	00	03	00
Richardson Logicke	00	02	00
Cotton on Canticles	00	01	00
Dickson on Math	00	01	06
Cotton on Eclesiastes	00	01	00
Calvins institutiones	00	04	00
Bucans institutiones Theol	00	01	00
Martins Heb: gram	00	02	00
Blarminus enerratus	00	04	00
Burgersdissi Lexicon	00	01	06
Bruusuus Lexicon	00	02	00
Mayers physiologie	00	02	00
Areti loci comunes. 2 vol	00	04	00
polari simphonia	00	02	00
Erasmus	00	00	06
Kechermans Logicke	00	01	00

	£	s	d
Downams Logicke	00	00	06
janua Linguarum	00	01	00
Montanus psalter inter	00	02	00
Calliopeia	00	01	00
Amosis Medulla	00	01	00
Balls catechisme	00	00	08
Daneus Hagoge. 2 parts	00	02	06
Wheatleys gods husbandry	00	01	00
junius in genesis	00	01	00
Cottons grounds & end of Bapt.	00	00	06
Owens cathechisme	00	01	06
Newton in Apolonium	00	01	00
Lookyer on ye Chh militant	00	00	08
Gilds Moses unveiled	00	00	06
Golii ethica	00	01	00
Sedgwicks burdened spirit	00	01	00
Trelcatius institutiones	00	01	00
Strigelous in Hagai	00	05	00
Two english bibles	00	04	00
practisse of christianity	00	00	06
Zacheus converted	00	01	00
Ovids metamorph: english	00	01	06
Brookes remedies	00	02	00
Golius ethicks	00	00	06
Strigelius in Ezr: neh	00	01	00
Fenners Theology	00	00	06
piscater in Johanneum	00	00	06
Ovids Heroicall: epistles	00	01	00
Bisields marrow	00	01	00
Donaldsons synopsis	00	00	06
Virgil in English	00	01	00
Justus in Lipsius	00	00	06
practice of piety	00	01	00
Harmony of confession	00	01	00
Lillies Gram	00	01	00
Virgill	00	01	00
Lucan english	00	01	00

DUOCECIMOS.

	£	s	d
Amesii casus conscientiae	00	01	00
Rami Dialectica	00	01	00
Zanchii Chtian Religion	00	01	00
Amesius on peter	00	00	09
Amesius animadversiones	00	01	00
Flores poetaru	00	00	06
psalme booke	00	00	06
A small parcel of old books	00	04	00
Totall of all ye bookes	50	11	07

these books in ye other side with ye rest in ye other part of ye inventory were appraised June 11, 1683,
> By Zachariah Walker,
> Is Chauncey,

In concurrence with John Stream at ye desire of ye rest of ye selectmen in ye towne of Milford.

FOLIOS.

	£	s	d
English anotations. 2 vols	02	10	00
Dutch annot: 2 vols	01	15	00
Musculi opera 6 vols	02	10	00
parea opera 2 vols	01	12	00
piscator in vet: nov: Test: 3 vols	03	00	00
Willets Hexaphla in gen: & exo: 5 vols	00	15	00
Beca in test: nov: 1 vol	00	18	00
Calvini harmonia, 1 vol	00	08	00
Aynsworths anotations, 1 vol	00	10	00
Gualter in prophet minor	00	07	00
Mulleras in psalms	00	05	00
Calvin on Job	00	05	00
Cottons concordance	00	10	00
Leighs critica sacra	00	10	00
Erons paraphrase on ye bible	00	08	00
Willets Heraphla on Daniel	00	06	00
Hutcheson on John	00	08	00

Commencing with folios, on page 12, these are on page 107.

AN ALPHABETICAL LIST

of the persons mentioned on pages 542-554 of this history, together with the year of birth, death, and the maiden name of the wife when known; whether their names are to be found in all three lists of "The Seating of the Meeting-house," or only in one or two of these lists.

15 -1659	Mr. Isaac Allerton, 1, 2		
	Mrs. " " 1, 2, 3		
16 -1684	(Joanna.)		
1647-1717	John Alling, 2, 3		
	Mrs. " " 3		
1653-1746	(Susanna Coe.)		
16 -1674	Roger Alling, 1, 2, 3		
	Mrs. " " 1, 2, 3		
1 -1685	(Mary Nash.)		
1621-1698	Joseph Alsop, 2, 3		
	Mrs. " " 2, 3		
	(Elizabeth Preston.)		
16 -1664	Bro. Wm. Andrews, 1, 2, 3		
	Mrs. " " 2, 3		
16 -1677	Luke Atkinson, 1		
	Mrs. " " 2		
	(Mary Platt.)		
1615-1692	David Atwater, 1, 2, 3		
	Mrs. " " 1, 2, 3		
16 -1691	(Damaris Sayre.)		
1609-16	Sister Ann Atwater, 1		
1612-1676	Bro. Joshua Atwater, 1		
16 -1676	Dr. Nicholas Augur, 2, 3		
	Allen Ball, 2, 3		
	Mrs. " " 2, 3		
16 -1690	(Dorothy)		
16 -1649	Edw'd Banister, 1		
	Mrs. " " 1		
	(Ellen.)		
16 -1693	Thomas Barnes, 2, 3		
	Mrs. " " 2, 3		
16 -1676	(Mary.)		
15 -1653	John Basset, 1		
	Mrs. " " 1		
16 -1684	William Basset, 2, 3		
	Mrs. " " 2, 3		
	(Mrs. William Ives.)		
	(Hannah (?))		
	Richard Beach 1		
	Mrs. " " 1		
	(Mrs. Andrew Hull.)		
	(Mary (?))		
	Thos. Beamont, 2, 3		
	Mrs. " " 2, 3		
16 -1690	Rich. Beckley, 1, 2		
	Mrs. " " 1, 2		
16 -1690	Isaac Beecher, 2, 3		
	Mrs. " " 3		
	(Mary.)		
	Mrs. John (Potter)		
	Beecher, 2		
15 -1659	(Mrs. Hannah ( )		
	Potter.)		
	Abraham Bell, 1		
15 -1661	Bro John Benham, 1, 2		
15 -165	Mrs. " " 1, 2		
163 -17	John Benham, jr., 3		
1645-16	Mrs. " " 2, 3		
	(Mercy Smith.)		
	Joseph Benham, 2, 3		
	Mrs. " " 2, 3		
163 -16	(Winifred King.)		
16 -1691	James Bishop, 2, 3		
16 -1703	Mrs. " " 2, 3		
16 -1672	Samuel Blackley, 3		
	(Hannah Potter.)		

AN ALPHABETICAL LIST.

16 -1661	Wm. Blayden,	2
1630-1687	Rev. John Bowers,	2
	Mrs. " "	2
16 -165	(Rebecca Gregson.)	
1 -1662	Jarvis Boykin,	1, 2
	Mrs. " "	1, 2, 3
16 -1673	(Isabel.)	
16 -1691	William Bradley,	2, 3
	Mrs. " "	2, 3
1610-16	(Alice Pritchard.)	
16 -1707	Mr. John Bracey,	1
	Mrs " "	1
	(Phebe Martin.)	
	Mrs. Francis Brewster,	1
16 -1669	(Lucy.)	
16 -1695	Henry Bristow,	2, 3
	Mrs. " "	3
	(Lydia Brown.)	
1610-1690	John Brocket,	1, 2, 3
	Mrs. " "	1, 2, 3
16 -16	James Brooks,	3
16 -1668	Francis Brown,	1, 2, 3
	Mrs. " "	1, 2, 3
	(Mary.)	
1640-17	John Brown,	3
	Mrs. " "	3
	(Mary Walker.)	
	She was divorced from John Brown.	
16 -1658	Peter Brown,	1
	Mrs. " "	1
16 -1657	(Elizabeth.)	
	Mr. Henry Browning,	1
	Mrs. " "	
	(Mary.)	
	Mr. John Caffinch,	1, 2
	Mrs. " "	1, 2
	(Mary Fowler.)	
16 -1659	Edward Camp,	2
	Mrs. " "	2
16 -1671	(Mary.)	
	Mrs. Nicholas Camp,	2
	(Mrs. Anthony Thompson.)	
	(Kattern.)	
16 -1673	Bro. Mat. Campfield,	1
	Mrs. " "	1
	(Sarah Treat.)	
	Wm. Chatterton,	
	Mrs. " "	3
	(Mary.)	
1615-1708	Ezekiel Cheever,	1
16 -1649	Mrs. " "	1
1621-1688	John Chidsey,	2, 3
	Mrs. " "	2, 3
16 -1688	(Elizabeth.)	
	James Clark,	2, 3
	Mrs. " "	1
	(Mrs. Ann Wakefield mar. in '61 a James Clark.)	
1612-16	John Clarke,	1, 3
	Mrs. " "	1, 2, 3
	(Mary.)	
	Goodwife Clarke,	2
	Sister Clark,	1
	Geo. Constable,	2
16 -1689	John Cooper,	1, 2, 3
	Mrs. " "	1, 2, 3
16 -167	Bro. Jasper Crane,	1
	Mrs. " "	1
	Mr. Stephen Daniel,	2
	Mrs. " "	2, 3
163 -1709	(Ann Gregson.)	
16 -1670	Rev. J'n Davenport,	1, 2, 3
	Mrs. " "	1, 3
1603-1676	(Elizabeth.)	
16 -1686	Mr. J'n Davenport, jr.,	2, 3
16 -1659	Bro. William Davis,	1, 2
	Mrs. " "	1, 2, 3
16 -1663	(Martha Wakeman.)	
1631-1719	Jas. Dennison,	3
	Mrs. " "	
1643-16	(Bethia Boykin.)	
1634-1711	Abra'm Dickerman,	3
	Mrs. " "	3
1631-1796	(Mary Cooper.)	
	Ralph Dayton,	1
16 -1690	Abra'm Doolittle,	2, 3
	Mrs. " "	2, 3
16 -1662	(Mary (?))	
16 -1712	Jas. Eaton or Heaton,	2, 3
	Mrs. James Eaton.	
	(Sarah Street.)	
15 -165	Mrs. Richard Eaton,	1
1592-1651	Gov. Theoph. Eaton,	1, 2
	Mrs. " "	1, 2
	(Mrs. David (Lloyd) Yale.)	
15 -1659	(Ann Lloyd.)	

AN ALPHABETICAL LIST. 713

16 -1672	Anthony Ellicott,	3
16 -1690	Nicholas Elsey,	1, 2, 3
	Mrs. " "	1, 2
	" " "	
	the second wife, formerly Mrs. Robert Coe,	
1631-1702	(Hannah Mitchell.)	3
	Mr. John Evance,	1
	Mrs. " "	1
	(Anne Young.)	
	Mar. in May, 1624.	
16 -1666	Mr. Alexander Field,	3
	Mrs. " "	3
16 -1670	(Mrs. Rich. Mansfield)	
	Mar. Alex. Field after 1655.	
1621-1681	Robert Foot,	3
	Mrs. " "	3
16 -1684	Timothy Ford,	1, 2, 3
16 -1681	Mrs. " "	1, 2, 3
16 -1661	Bro. Wm. Fowler,	1, 2
	Mrs. " "	1, 2
16 -16	(Mary Tapp.)	
16 -1662	Mr. Wm. Gibbard,	1, 2, 3
	Mrs. " "	1, 2, 3
	(Ann Tapp.)	
16 -1686	Henry Gibbons,	1, 2, 3
16 -1689	Wm. Gibbons,	1, 2, 3
	Mrs. " "	2, 3
16 -1680	Bro. John Gibbs,	1, 2, 3
	Mrs. " "	1, 2, 3
16 -1673	John Gilbert,	3
1599-1679	Matthew Gilbert,	2, 3
	Mrs. " "	1, 2, 3
	( )	
16 -1689	Henry Glover,	1, 2, 3
	Mrs. " "	2, 3
	Mr. Sam.Goodenhouse,	2, 3
	Mrs. " "	2
16 -165	(Mrs. Nath'l Turner.)	
	(Mary (?))	
1603-1657	Dep. Gov. Stephen Goodyear,	1, 2
	Mrs. Stephen Goodyear.	
	(Mrs. Geo. Lamberton.)	3
1614-167	(Margaret.)	
	Mr. Goodyear's daughters,	2
	John Gregory,	1
	Mrs. " "	1

162 -17	Rich. Gregson,	1
16 -1703	Mrs. Thos. Gregson,	1, 3
	(Jane.)	
16 -1648	Arthur Halbidge,	1
	Mrs. " "	2
16 -1676	John Hall,	2, 3
	Mrs. " "	2, 3
	( )	
16 -1683	John Harriman,	1, 2, 3
	Mrs. " "	1, 2, 3
	( )	
162 -168	Thos. Harrison,	3
	Mrs. " "	3
	(Mrs. John Thompson),	2
16 -166	(Eleanor)	
15 -1641	Mrs. Francis Higginson,	1
16 -1657	Mr. Theophilus Higginson,	1
1 -1661	Robert Hill,	1, 2, 3
	Mrs. " "	1, 2, 3
	(Mrs. Robert Johnson, second wife),	3
	(Adeline.)	
16 -1659	Ed. Hitchcock,	2
	Mrs. " "	2
1610-1669	Mat. Hitchcock,	1, 2, 3
	Mrs. " "	1, 3
	( )	
16 -1663	Sam'l Hodskins,	2, 3
	Mrs. " "	2, 3
16 -1681	(Elizabeth Cloverly.)	
16 -1690	Mr. John Hodson,	2, 3
	Mrs. " "	2, 3
	(Abigail Turner.)	
	William Holt,	2, 3
	Mrs. " "	3
	(Sarah.)	
16 -1667	Rev. William Hooke,	
	Mrs. " "	1
16 -1680	Ephraim Howe,	3
	Mrs. " "	3
	( )	
16 -1690	Jeremy Howe,	2, 3
	Mrs. " "	2, 3
	( )	
	Sister Howe,	3
	Jeremiah Hull,	3
	Mrs. " "	2, 3
	(Hannah Baldwin.)	

714 AN ALPHABETICAL LIST.

16 -1662	Richard Hull,	2, 3	
	Mrs. " "	1, 2	
	(Hannah (?))		
	Henry Humiston,	3	
	Mrs. " "	3	
	(Joan Walker.)		
	Goodwife Humiston,	3	
1607-1648	William Ives,	1	
	Mrs. " "	1	
16 -167	(Hannah.)		
	See William Basset.		
16 -1683	John Jackson,	3	
	Mrs. " "	3	
16 -1665	(Mary Hull.)		
1583-168	Mr. Thos. James, sr.,	1	
	Mrs. " "	1	
	Ret. to England.		
16 -1696	Thos. James, jr.,	1	
16 -1661	Thos. Jeffreys,	1, 2	
	Mrs. " "	1, 2	
1609-1	John Johnson,	2, 3	
	Mrs. " "	3	
	(Susan.)		
16 -1679	Rich. Johnson,	2, 3	
	Mrs. " "	2, 3	
16 -1661	Robt. Johnson,	1, 2	
	Mrs. " "	1, 2	
16 -166	(Adeline)		
	Thos. Johnson,	2, 3	
	Mrs. " "	2, 3	
	( )		
16 -1657	John Jones,	2	
	Sister Jones,	3	
16 -1706	Dep. Gov. Wm. Jones,	3	
	Mrs. " "	3	
16 -1707	(Hannah Eaton.)		
16 -1661	William Judson,	2, 3	
	Mrs. " "	2	
16 -1659	(Grace.)		
16 -1664	Mrs. Eliz. Wilmot,		
	second wife,	3	
	(Mary.)		
	Abraham Kimberly,	2	
16 -1673	Thos. Kimberly,	1, 2, 3	
	Mrs. " "	1, 2, 3	
16 -1659	(Alice.)		
	Mary, second wife,	3	
	Thos. Kimberly, jr.,	3	
	Mrs. " "		
15 -1647	(Hannah.)		

	Thos. Knowles,	1	
	Mrs. " "	1	
	(Elizabeth.)		
	Hannah Lamberton,	3	
1614-16	Mrs. Geo. Lamberton	1	
	(Margaret.)		
16 -1663	Thos. Lamson,	1, 2, 3	
16 -1676	Philip Leeke,	1, 2, 3	
	Mrs. " "	2, 3	
	(Mary (?))		
1 -1660	Bro. Henry Lindon,		
	or Lindall,	1, 2	
	Mrs. " "	1, 2, 3	
	(Mary (?))		
1 -1663	Henry Lines,	3	
	Mrs. " "	3	
	(Joanna.)		
	Ralph Lines,	2, 3	
	Mrs. " "	3	
	( )		
16 -1673	Mr. Benjamin Ling,	1	
	Mrs. " "	1	
16 -1675	(Joanna.)		
16 -1684	John Livermore,	1	
	Mrs. " "	1	
16 -1690	(Grace.)		
16 -1670	Andrew Low,	1, 2, 3	
	Mrs. " "	1, 2, 3	
	(Mrs. Henry Peck.)		
	(Joan.)		
16 -1660	Mr. Richard Malbon,	1	
	Mrs. " "	1	
	(Martha (?))		
	Peter Mallory,	2, 3	
	Mrs. " "	2, 3	
	( )		
	Jos. Mansfield,	3	
16 -1655	Rich. Mansfield,	1	
	Mrs. " "	1, 2, 3	
16 -1670	(Gillian.)		
	Samuel Marsh,	2, 3	
	Mrs. " "	2, 3	
	(Mary (?))		
16 -1683	Bro. Robert Martin,	1	
	Mrs. " "	1	
	(Mary (?))		
	Wm. Meeker,	3	
	Mrs. " "	3	
	( )		
16 -1681	Ellis Mew,	2	
	Mrs. " "		
16 -1704	(Ann Gibbons.)		

AN ALPHABETICAL LIST. 715

16 -1678	John Meigs,	1	
	Mrs. " "	1	
	(Mary.)		
1614-1694	Nath'l Merriman,	2, 3	
	Mrs. " "	2, 3	
	(Hannah.)		
16 -1667	Bro. Richard Miles,	1	
	Mrs. " "	1, 2, 3	
	( )		
	Mrs. ( ) Constable, second wife, (Catherine.)	3	
	Rich. Miles, jr.,	2	
16 -1659	Thos. Mitchell,	2	
	Mrs. " "	2, 3	
	(Elizabeth.)		
16 -1691	Thomas Mix,	2, 3	
	Mrs. ' "	2, 3	
165 -1731	(Rebecca Turner.)		
16 -1665	Henry Morrell,	2, 3	
	Mrs. " "		
	(Sarah.)		
16 -1673	Thomas Morris,	2, 3	
	Mrs. " "	2, 3	
16 -1668	(Elizabeth.)		
1604-1707	John Moss,	1, 2, 3	
	Mrs. " "	1, 2, 3	
	(Abigail.)		
16 -1668	Mat. Moulthrop,	2, 3	
	Mrs. " "	2, 3	
16 -1672	(Jane.)		
16 -1685	Ens. Thos. Munson,	1, 2, 3	
	Mrs. " "	1, 2, 3	
1610-1678	(Joanna.)		
16 -1690	Thos. Mullener,	2	
16 -1685	Mr. Thos. Mullener,	2, 3	
	Mrs. " "	2, 3	
16 -1687	John Nash,	1, 2, 3	
	Mrs. " "	1, 2, 3	
16 -1676	(Elizabeth Tapp.)	3	
16 -1678	Joseph Nash,	1, 2	
	Mrs. " "	1	
16 -1654	(Mary.)		
	(Margaret, 2d wife),	3	
15 -1658	Thomas Nash,	1	
	Mrs. " "	2	
15 -1656	(Margaret Baker.)		
16 -1660	Mr. Francis Newman,	1, 2	
	Mrs. " "	1, 2	
	(She mar. after '60, Rev. N. Street.)		
	Rich. Newman,	3	
	Mrs. " "	3	
	Ret. to England.		
	Elder Robt. Newman,	1	
	Mrs. " "	1	
	( )		
16 -1682	Adam Nichols,	1	
	Mrs. " "	1	
	(Ann Wakeman.)		
	Rem. to Mass.		
	John Osbill.	3	
16 -1676	Jerem'h Osborne,	2, 3	
	Mrs. " "	2, 3	
	(Mary (?))		
	Rich. Osborne,	1	
	Mrs. " "	1, 3	
	(Elizabeth.)		
	Thos. Osborne,	1	
16 -1673	William Paine,	2, 3	
	Mrs. " "	2, 3	
	( )		
1629-1700	George Pardee,	2, 3	
	Mrs. " "	2, 3	
163 -16	(Martha Miles.)		
16 -1662	Edward Parker,	2, 3	
	Mrs. " "	2, 3	
	(Mrs. John ( ) Potter.)		
16 -1677	(Elizabeth.)		
	Mrs. Eliz. Parmelee,	3	
	(She mar. 166 , John Evarts.)		
	Edw. Patteson,	1, 2, 3	
	Mrs. " "	1, 2	
	(Eliz.)		
	Daniel Paul,	1	
16 -1659	John Peakin,	2	
	Mark Pearce,	1	
15 -1651	Henry Peck,	2	
	Widow Peck,	2	
	(Joan.)		
1601-1693	William Peck,	1, 2, 3	
	Mrs. " "	1, 2, 3	
16 -1683	(Elizabeth.)		
1613-1669	Mr. Thomas Pell,	1	
	Mrs. " "	1	
	(Mrs. Francis Brewster, m. 1647.)		
16 -1669	(Lucy.)		
16 -1660	Eph. Pennington,	2	
	Mrs. " "	2, 3	
	(Mary (?))		

AN ALPHABETICAL LIST.

	Edward Perkins, Mrs. " " (Eliz. Butcher.)	2, 3 2, 3	16 -1684 16 -1707	John Sacket, Mrs. " " (Agnes Tincome.)	2, 3
16 -1658	Richard Perry, Mrs. " " (Mary Malbon.)	1 1	16 -1668	Bro. Robert Seeley, Mrs. " " (Mary.)	1, 2 1, 2
16 -1660	Robert Pigg, Mrs. " " (Margaret.)	2 2	16 -1662	George Smith, Mrs. " " (Sarah.)	1, 2, 3 1, 2, 3
	Goodwife Potter, ( )	2, 3		Richard Sperry, Mrs. " " ( )	3 3
	John Potter, Mrs. " " ( )	3 3		Humph'y Spinnage, Mrs. " " ( )	3 3
	Joseph Potter, Mrs. " " (Hannah.)	3 3		Mr. Nathanael Street, Mrs. " " ( )	3 3
	Sister Potter, the midwife,	1		Rev. Nicholas Street, Mrs. " " (Mrs. Francis Newman, 2d wife.)	3 3
1612-1663 1613-1	Wm. Potter, Mrs. " " (Frances.)	1, 2, 3 1			
16 -1681	Thomas Powell, Mrs. " " (Priscilla.)	1, 2, 3 1, 2, 3	16 -1662	Robt. Talmadge, Mrs. " " (Sarah Nash.)	2 2, 3
	Edw'd Preston, Mrs. " " (Margaret.)	2, 3 3	16 -1671	John Thomas, Mrs. " " (Tabitha.)	1, 2, 3 1, 2, 3
16 -1648	Robt. Preston,	1	16 -1648	Anth'y Thompson, Mrs. " "	1 1
1591-1647 1601-16	Wm. Preston, Mrs. " " (Mary.)	1 1, 2	16 -166	(Kattern.)	
			16 -167 16 -169	John Thompson, Mrs. " " (Ellen.)	2, 3 2, 3
	Wm. Pringle,	3			
16 -1680	John Punderson, Mrs. " " (Margaret.)	1, 2, 3 1, 2, 3	1631-1707	John Thompson, jr.,	2
	George Ross, Mrs. " " Mar. in 1658. (Constance Little.)	3	16 -1683	Wm. Thompson, Mrs. " " ( )	1, 2, 3
			16 -1679 16 -165	William Thorpe, Mrs. " " (Mrs. Margaret Pigge, 2d wife.)	1, 2, 3 2 3
16 -1662	Matthew Rowe, Mrs. " " (Elizabeth.)	2, 3 2, 3			
16 -1673 16 -1674	Serg. James Russell, Mrs. " " (Mary.)	1, 2, 3 1, 2, 3		Martin Tichenor, Mrs. " " (Mary Charles.)	2, 3 2, 3
1612-1665 16 -1664	Wm. Russell, Mrs. " " (Sarah Davis.)	2, 3 2, 3	1617-1686	Christop'r Todd, Mrs. " " (Grace Middlebrook.)	1, 2, 3 1, 2, 3
16 -1668 16 -1674	H'y Rutherford, Mrs. " " (Sarah.)	1, 2, 3 1, 2, 3	1632-1702 1641-1687	Thos. Trowbridge, Mrs. " " (Sarah Rutherford.)	3 3

AN ALPHABETICAL LIST. 717

1634-1690	Wm. Trowbridge,	3	
	Mrs. " "	3	
	(Mrs. Eliz. (Lamberton) Silevant.)		
	(Eliz. Lamberton.)		
	Isaac Turner,	3	
15 -1646	Capt. Nath'l Turner,		
	Mrs. " "	1	
	( )		
	(She mar. 164 , Sam'l Goodenhouse.)		
1631-1683	John Tuttle,	2, 3	
	Mrs. " "	2, 3	
	(Kattareen Lane.)		
1637-1705	Jonathan Tuttle,	3	
	Mrs. " "		
1645-1676	(Rebecca Bell.)		
1634-1710	Thomas Tuttle,		
	Mrs. " "	3	
1641-1710	(Hannah Powell.)		
16 -1675	Mr. William Tuttle,	1, 2, 3	
	Mrs. " "	1, 2, 3	
16 -1684	(Elizabeth.)		
16 -1659	John Vincent,	1, 2, 3	
	Mrs. " "		
16 -1679	(Rebecca.)		
16 -1660	John Wakefield,	1, 2	
	Mrs. " "	1, 2	
16 -1695	(Ann.)		
	She mar. 1661, Jas. Clark.		
15 -1661	Mr. John Wakeman,	1	
	Mrs. " "	1, 2	
15 -165	(Elizabeth.)		
	John Ware,	3	
	Edw'd Watson,	2	
	Mrs. " "	2	
	(Mrs. John ( ) Walker.)		
	(Grace.)		
15 -1656	Thos. Wheeler,	1, 2, 3	
	Mrs. " "	1, 2	
	( )		
	IsaacWhitehead,	2	
	Rem. in '66 to N. J.		
	Mrs. " "		
	(Susanna.)		
16 -1690	Serg. Samuel Whitehead,	1, 2, 3	
	Mrs. Samuel Whitehead,	1, 2, 3	
	( )		
16 -1682	Jere. Whitnell,	1, 2, 3	
	Mrs. " "	1, 2	
	( )		
16 -1654	Edw. Wigglesworth,	1	
	Mrs. " "	1	
	(Hester Middlebrook.)		
1589-1669	Benj. Wilmot,	1, 2, 3	
	Mrs. " "	1, 2, 3	
	( )		
	Goodwife Wilmot, jr.,	2	
	(Mrs. James ( ) Heaton.)		
	(Elizabeth.)		
1632-1689	Wm. Wilmot,		
	Mrs. " "	3	
	(Sarah Thomas.)		
16 -1697	John Winston,	2, 3	
	Mrs. " "	2	
16 -1685	Wm. Wooden,	3	
	Mrs. " "	3	
16 -1695	(Sarah Clark.)		
16 -1678	John Wilford,	1	
	Mrs. " "		
	(Lydia.)		
	After 1678 she mar. Capt. Thos. Tappan of Milford.		
162 -1683	Mr. Thomas Yale,	1, 2, 3	
	Mrs. " "	1, 2, 3	
16 -1704	(Mary Turner.)		

A LIST OF THE OFFICERS OF MILITIA COMPANIES

in the Seventeenth Century in Southern Connecticut, giving their residence, lowest and highest rank, the volume and page of the Colonial Records of New Haven Colony and of Connecticut Colony, where the record can be found.

Name.	Year of Birth and Death.	Lowest Rank.	Reference Page in the Colonial Records.	Highest Rank.	Reference Page in the Colonial Records.	Place of Residence.
Lt. Preserved Abell	1668—1724	Ensign, 1690		Lieut., 17		Stonington.
Sergt. Roger Alling	16 —1674	Sergt., 1665				New Haven.
Capt. Nathan Andrews	1639—17	Ensign, 16		Captain, 17	C. 4, p. 320	New Haven.
Ens. Samuel Andrews	1635—1704	Ensign, 1653	C. 3, p. 118			Wallingford.
Lt. William Andrews	16 —1676	Sergt., 1642	N. 1, p. 76	Lieut., 1648		New Haven.
Ens. John Arnold	16 —17	Ensign, 1698	C. 4, p. 225			Haddam.
Lt. Peter Aspinwall	16 —17			Lieut., 1704	C. 4, p. 465	New London Co.
Dr. Nicolas Augur	16 —1676			Surgeon, 1654	N. 2, p. 108	New Haven.
Capt. James Avery	1620—1694	Ensign, 1663		Captain, 1681	C. 3, p. 80	New London.
Capt. James Avery	1646—1732			Captain, 1692	C. 4, p. 74	New London.
Capt. John Avery	1654—1715	Ensign, 1692		Captain, 1697		New London.
Ens. Samuel Avery	1664—17	Ensign, 1705	C. 4, p. 507			New London.
Capt. Thomas Avery	1651—17	Sergt., 1658		Captain, 1693	C. 4, p. 93	Milford.
Sergt. John Baldwin	16 —1681	Ensign, 1654	N. 2, p. 108			Milford.
Ens. Richard Baldwin	16 —1665			Lieut., 1690	C. 4, p. 21	New Haven.
Lt. Sylvanus Baldwin	16 —17			Lieut., 1693	C. 4, p. 93	Norwich.
Capt. William Backus	1640—1721	Ensign, 1680	C. 3, p. 60	Lieut., 1705	C. 4, p. 507	Fairfield.
Lt. John Barlow	16 —17			Lieut., 1665	C. 2, p. 22	Guilford.
Lt. Geo. Bartlett	16 —1669	Sergt., 1654	N. 2, p. 108	Captain, 1706	C. 5, p. 143	New Haven.
Capt. John Bassett	1652—1714	Ensign, 1700	C. 3, p.	Ch. Drm.,1654	N. 2, p. 108	New Haven.
Robert Bassett	16 —1670			Captain, 1675	C. 2, p. 400	Milford.
Capt. John Beard	16 —16			Captain, 1704	C. 4, p. 476	Stratford.
Sergt. John Beardsley	16 —17	Sergt.,				New Haven.
Lt. John Beldin	16 —1690			Lieut., 1705	C. 4, p. 507	Norwalk.
Capt. James Beebe	1658—17	Lieut., 1606	C. 4, p. 182	Captain, 1710		Danbury.
Lt. John Beebe	16 —1728	Ensign, 1676	C. 2, p. 279	Lieut., 1690		New London.
Lt. Francis Bell	16 —1690			Lieut., 1655	N. 2, p. 145	Stamford.
Capt. Jonathan Bell	1641—1699			Captain, 1698	C. 4, p. 53	Stamford.
Lt. Daniel Benedict	1652—1723			Lieut., 16		Norwalk.

LIST OF OFFICERS. 719

NAME.	Year of Birth and Death.	Lowest Rank.	Reference Page in the Colonial Records.	Highest Rank.	Reference Page in the Colonial Records.	Place of Residence.
Lt. Thomas Benedict	1617—1690			Lieut., 1665		Norwalk.
Lt. James Bennett	16 —1691			Lieut., 1692		Stratford.
Dep. G. James Bishop	1655—17	Sergt., 1665	C. 2, p. 23		C. 4, p. 88	New Haven.
Ens. Stephen Bishop	1653—1728	Ensign, 1705	C. 4, p. 526			Guilford.
Sgt. John Booth	1667—1747	Sergt., 16				Stratford.
Major John Bostwick	1638—1694			Major, 1737		New Milford.
Lt. John Bowers	16 —17			Lieut., 1690	C. 4, p. 17	Greenwich.
Lt. Joseph Bradford	1669—1742	Ensign, 1702	C. 4, p. 386	Lieut.		Lebanon.
Capt. James Brainard	16 —1702	Ensign, 1705	C. 4, p. 507	Captain, 17	C. 4, p. 252	Haddam.
Capt. Stephen Bradley	16 —1710	Ensign, 1690	C. 4, p. 21	Captain, 1698	C. 4, p. 93	Guilford.
Capt. Benjamin Brewster	16 —17			Captain, 1693	C. 4, p. 460	Norwich.
Lt. Daniel Brewster	1610—1690			Lieut., 1704	N. 2, p. 108	Preston.
Surg. John Brockett	1647—69			Surgeon, 1654	C. 3, p. 11	New Haven.
Lt. Abram Bronson	16 —1679	Ensign, 1665	C. 2, p. 21	Lieut., 1678		Lyme.
Ens. Alexander Bryan	1659—1698					Milford.
Capt. Samuel Bryan	16 —17	Ensign, 1702	C. 4, p. 401	Captain, 1692	C. 4, p. 69	Milford.
Ens. Thos. Buckingham	1636—1713			Chaplain, 1675		Saybrook.
Rev. Gershom Bulkeley	1679—1753			Captain, 1726		Fairfield.
Capt. Gershom Bulkeley	16 —1727			Com'ary 16		Fairfield.
Daniel Burr	1625—1692			Captain, 167		Fairfield.
Capt. Jehu Burr	16 —17			Major, 1694	C. 4, p. 134	Fairfield.
Major John Burr	1667—1724			Major, 1694		Fairfield.
Major Peter Burr	16 —1698			Captain, 1692	C. 4, p. 69	Stratford.
Capt. Stephen Burrett	16 —16	Ensign, 1676	C. 2, p. 279			N. Hav. or Milf'd
Ens. Samuel Burrill	16 —1727	Ensign, 1693	C. 4, p. 93	Lieut., 1683	C. 3, p. 116	Milford.
Lt. Samuel Burwell	1648—17			Captain, 1701	C. 4, p. 350	Norwich.
Capt. Richard Bushnell	1673—1755	Ensign, 1746		Lieut., 1679	C. 3, p. 28	Saybrook.
Lt. William Bushnell	16 —17					Milford.
Ens. Benjamin Butler	16 —1689	Sergt. 1669	C. 2, p. 107	Lieut., 1698	C. 4, p. 270	Milford.
Lt. Samuel Camp	1616—1689			Captain, 1675		Saybrook.
Sergt. Thomas Canfield	16 —1705	Ensign, 1677	C. 2, p. 304	Captain, 1705	C. 2, p. 269	Middletown.
Capt. Robert Chapman	1593—1660			Major, 16	C. 4, p. 507	Stonington.
Ens. William Cheney						Guilford.
Capt. Nath'l Chesebrough						
Major Wm. Chittenden						

LIST OF OFFICERS.

NAME.	Year of Birth and Death.	Lowest Rank.	Reference Page in the Colonial Records.	Highest Rank.	Reference Page in the Colonial Records.	Place of Residence.
Com. Rich. Christopher..	16 —17	....	....	Comis'ry, 1692	....	New London Co.
Maj. John Clark..........	16 —17	Lieut., 1699...	C. 4, p. 289.	Major, 17	....	Saybrook.
Ens. George Clark........	16 —17	Ensign, 1693...	C. 4, p. 93..	....	....	Milford.
Lt. Thomas Clark.........	16 —16	....	....	Lieut, 1697...	C. 4, p. 228..	Haddam.
Sergt. John Clarke........	16 —16	Sergt., 1642 ..	N. 1, p. 76 ..	....	....	New Haven.
Lt. John Coe.............	1658—1740	....	....	Lieut., 1706...	C. 4, p. 534..	Stratford.
Ens. Samuel Collins......	1668—17	Ensign, 1690...	C. 4, p. 17 ..	....	....	Middletown.
Capt. Henry Crane.......	16 —17	....	....	Captain, 1704.	C. 4, p. 491..	Killingworth.
Ens. Ebenezer Curtis.....	16 —17	Ensign, 1706..	C. 4, p. 534..	....	....	Stratford.
Lt. Israel Curtis..........	1644—1704	....	....	Lieut., 1690...	C. 4, p. 35 ..	Woodbury.
Ens. Joseph Curtis........	16 —17	Ensign, 1693...	C. 4, p. 89..	....	....	Stratford.
Capt. William Curtis.....	16 —16	....	....	Captain, 1672.	C. 4, p. 101..	Woodbury.
Ens. Thomas Curtis	1648—1736	Ensign, 1704...	....	....	....	Strat'f'd & Wall'd
Capt. George Denison....	1620—1694	....	....	Captain, 1689.	C. 4, p. 5 ..	Stonington.
Ens. John Denison.......	16 —16	Ensign, 1673...	....	....	....	Stonington.
Capt. John Denison......	1646—1698	....	....	Lieut., 1705...	C. 4, p. 507..	Stonington.
Lt. William Denison......	1655—1715	....	....	Lieut., 1683...	C. 3, p. 127..	New Haven.
Lt. Abram Dickerman....	1634—169	....	....	Captain, 1711.	....	Fairfield.
Capt. Moses Dimon......	1672—1748	....	....	....	....	
Sergt. Abraham Doolittle	1620—1690	Sergt., 16	....	....	....	
Sergt. William East......	16 —1681	Sergt., 16	....	....	....	Milford.
Capt. Samuel Eels........	1639—1709	Sergt., 1669...	....	Captain, 1699.	C. 4, p. 288..	Milford.
Anthony Elcot............	16 —1672	....	....	Drum'er, 1654	N. 2, p. 108 ..	New Haven.
Capt. William Ely........	16 —17	....	....	Captain, 1697.	C. 4, p. 205..	Lyme.
Corn. Ben. Fayerweather	1670—1725	Cornet, 16 .	....	....	....	Fairfield.
Lt. Benjamin Fenn........	16 —1672	Captain, 1680.	C. 3, p. 80..	Lieut., 16	....	Milford.
Major James Fitch	1649—1727	....	....	Major, 16	....	Norwich.
Rev. James Fitch	1622—170	....	....	Chaplain, 1676	C. 2, p. 279..	Norwich.
Capt. Jeremiah Fitch	1670—1736	....	....	Captain, 1704.	C. 4, p. 465..	New London.
Capt. Thomas Fitch......	1612—1704	....	....	Captain, 1673.	C. 2, p. 206..	Norwalk.
Ens. James Ferris........	16 —17	Ensign, 1665..	C. 2, p. 14 ..	....	....	Greenwich.
Capt. Joseph Foote	1666—1751	Ensign, 1690..	C. 4, p. 17 ..	Capt. 1715	....	Branford.
Quar. Nathaniel Foote....	1647—1703	....	....	Q'rmastr. 167	....	Branford.
Lt. Robert Foote	1629—1681	....	....	Lieut., 1677...	C. 2, p. 384..	Branford.
Capt. Abraham Fowler..	1652—1719	....	....	Captain, 1704.	C. 4, p. 427..	Guilford.

LIST OF OFFICERS. 721

NAME.	Year of Birth and Death.	Lowest Rank.	Reference Page in the Colonial Records.	Highest Rank.	Reference Page in the Colonial Records.	Place of Residence.
Capt. William Fowler	162 —1683	Lieut., 1666	C. 2, p. 32	Captain, 1676	C. 2, p. 292	Milford.
Ens. John Fowler	162 —1677	Ensign, 1665	C. 2, p. 14			Guilford.
Capt. John Gallop	16 —1675					New London.
Ens. William Gallop	16 —17	Ensign, 1705	C. 4, p. 507			Stonington.
Lt. Lion Gardiner	1599–1663					
Capt. George Gates	1635–1724			Captain, 1692	C. 4, p. 74	Haddam.
Ens. Thomas Gates	1665–1734	Ensign, 1701	C. 4, p. 350			Haddam.
Cornet Jonathan Gilbert	.6 —1683	Cornet, 1668	C. 2, p. 101			Hartford County
Lt. Charles Glover	1610–1670					Southold.
Maj. Nathan Gold	16 —1694	Ensign, 1650	C. 1, p. 281	Lieut., 1653		Fairfield.
Capt. Nathan Gold, Jr.	1663–1723			Major, 1673	C. 2, p. 206	Fairfield.
Lt. Bartholom. Goodrich				Captain, 1695	C. 4, p. 150	Branford.
Capt. Daniel Gookin	1612–1687			Lieut., 1695	C. 4, p. 149	Stonington.
Capt. John Graves	16 —17	Ensign, 1665	C. 2, p. 74	Captain, 1674	Men.C. 2,p.227	Guilford.
Lt. Matthew Griswold	1620–1698			Captain, 1690	C. 4, p. 25	Lyme.
Ens. Abel Gunn	16 —169	Ensign, 1685	C. 3, p. 170	Lieut., 16		Derby.
Ens. Jobama Gunn	16 —17	Ensign, 1698	C. 4, p. 270			Milford.
Surg. John Hall	16 —17			Surgeon, 1675	C. 2, p. 268	Fairfield.
Capt. John Hall	16 —17			Captain, 1699	C. 4, p. 303	Middletown.
Capt. Samuel Hall	1648–1723			Captain, 1704	C. 4, p. 491	Wallingford.
Capt. William Hallett	16 —1729			Captain, 17		Newtown, L. I.
Ens. Gabriel Harris	16 —1684	Ensign, 1665	C. 2, p. 21			New London.
Ens. Daniel Harris	1653–1735			Captain, 1688	C. 3, p. 451	Middletown.
Ens. Thomas Harris	16 —17	Ensign, 1677	C. 2, p. 304			Branford.
Ens. Thomas Harrison	1657–17	Ensign, 1686	C. 3, p. 216			Branford.
Lt. Hawkins Hart	1677–1735			Lieut., 1720		Wallingford.
Capt. John Hart	1655–1714			Captain, 1707		New Haven.
Capt. Nathaniel Harrison	1658–17			Captain, 1706	C. 4, p. 533	Wallingford.
Surg. Josiah Harvey	16 —16			Surgeon, 1665	C. 2, p. 268	Fairfield County
Lt. John Hawley	16 —17			Lieut., 1704	C. 4, p. 465	Fairfield
Capt. Joseph Hawley	1675–1752			Captain, 17		Stratford
Ens. James Heaton	1633–1712	Ensign, 16				New Haven.
Sergt. Samuel Hickox	16 —1705	Sergt., 1686				Waterbury.
Sergt. Samuel Hickox, Jr.	1669–17	Sergt., 17	C. 2, p. 63			Waterbury.
Ens. Hill	16 —16	Ensign, 1667				Stamford.

46

LIST OF OFFICERS.

NAME.	Year of Birth and Death.	Lowest Rank.	Reference Page in the Colonial Records.	Highest Rank.	Reference Page in the Colonial Records.	Place of Residence.
Capt. Edward Hinman..	1670—17			Captain, 1714.		Stratford.
Capt. Titus Hinman...	1656—1736			Captain, 1714.		Woodbury.
Ens. Joshua Holmes ...	16 —17	Ensign, 1729.				Stonington.
Lt. Stephen Hollister ..	16 —17			Lieut., 1692	C. 4, p. 89.	Stratford.
Ens. Increase Holly....	16 —17	Ensign, 1699.	C. 4, p. 300			Stamford.
Ens. Eleazer Holt......	16 —17	Ensign, 1704.	C. 4, p. 460			New Haven.
Lt. John Hopkins	1665—1732	Ensign, 1715.		Lieut., 1716.		Stratford.
Capt. Jonathan Horton.	16 —17			Captain, 1700.		Southold.
Lt. Joseph Horton......	16 —17			Lieut., 1667.	C. 2, p. 63.	Rye.
Lt. John Hough........	16 —17			Lieut., 1703.	C. 4, p. 427.	New London.
Lt. Hezekiah Howell ...	1677—1744			Lieut., 17		Southampt'n, L.I.
Maj. John Howell	1625—1695	Captain, 1674.	Men. C. 2, p. 229	Major, 1684...		Southampt'n, L.I.
Ens. Samuel Hoyt......	16 —17	Sergt, 16		Ensign, 1698..	C. 4, p. 254	Stamford.
Sergt. Walter Hoyt.....	16 —17	Sergt., 1659	C. 1, p. 336.			Rye.
Lt. Jos. Horton or Orton.	1653—1690			Lieut., 1667	C. 2, p. 63	Stratford.
Lt. John Hubbell.......	1654—1738	Sergt., 1677		Lieut., 1690		Fairfield.
Sergt. Richard Hubbell.	1626—1695			Lieut., 167		Fairfield.
Lt. Cornelius Hull	16 —16			Lieut., 1666	C. 2, p. 50	Killingworth.
Lt. Josias Hull	16 —17	Ensign, 1705.	C. 4, p. 507	Captain, 1709.		Fairfield.
Capt. Theophilus Hull .	1640—1727	Ensign, 1704.	C. 4, p. 491			Killingworth.
Ens. John Hull.........	1640—1677			Lieut., 1665		Newtown, L. I.
Lt. Ralph Hunt........	1680—1767	Ensign, 1720.				Wallingford.
Ens. Gideon Ives.......	1673—1751					North Haven.
Capt. Joseph Ives	16 —1735	Sergt., 1642.	N. 1, p. 76	Colonel, 17		Hempstead, L. I.
Col. John Jackson......	16	Lieut., 1685.	C. 3, p. 170	Captain, 1690.	C. 4, p. 16	New Haven.
Sergt. Thomas Jeffries..	16	Lieut., 1684.	C. 3, p. 141	Captain, 1699.	C. 4, p. 288	Derby.
Capt. Ebenezer Johnson.	16 —17	Ensign, 1703.	C. 4, p. 427	Lieut., 1695	C. 4, p. 150	Saybrook.
Capt. Samuel Jones	16 —17					Waterbury.
Lt. Thomas Judd, Sr...	16 —17			Captain, 1698.	C. 4, p. 252	Waterbury.
Ens. Thomas Judd.....	1624—1706			Lieut., 1684.	C. 3, p. 141	New Haven.
Dep. Gov. Wm. Jones ..	16 —17					Stratford.
Capt. James Judson....	16 —17	Ensign, 16		Captain, 1676.	C. 2, p. 279	Woodbury.
Lt. Joseph Judson......	16 —16	Sergt., 1665	C. 2, p. 72			Stratford.
Capt. Joseph Judson ...	16 —16					Guilford.
Sergt. Wm. Johnson ...						

LIST OF OFFICERS. 723

NAME.	Year of Birth and Death.	Lowest Rank.	Reference Page in the Colonial Records.	Highest Rank.	Reference Page in the Colonial Records.	Place of Residence.
Capt. Joseph Judson	16 —16			Captain, 1676	C. 2, p. 279	Stratford.
Lt. Joseph Judson	16 —17			Lieut., 1684	C. 3, p. 141	Woodbury.
Lt. Samuel Keeler	16 —17			Lieut., 1710		Norwalk.
Lt. John Kelsey	16 —17	Ensign, 1686		Lieut., 1704	C. 4, p. 491	Killingworth.
Lt. John Ketcham	16 —1697		C. 3, p. 215	Lieut., 16		Huntington, L. I.
Corpl. Thomas Kimberly	16 —1693	Corpl., 1642	N. 1, p. 76			New Haven.
Lt. John Kirkland	16 —17			Lieut., 1702	C. 4, p. 401	Saybrook.
Ens. Samuel Kitchell	16 —16	Ensign, 1665	C. 2, p. 22			Guilford.
Lt. Thomas Knowles	16 —17			Lieut., 1698	C. 4, p. 252	Stratford.
Lt. Thomas Knowlton	16 —17			Lieut., 1706	C. 4, p. 533	Haddam.
Ens. Robert Lattimer	16 —17	Ensign, 1704	C. 4, p. 491			New London.
Gov. Jonathan Law	1674—17					Stamford.
Capt. John Lawrence	16 —1729			Captain, 1689		Newtown, L. I.
Major Thomas Lawrence	16 —1703			Major, 1689		Newtown, L. I.
Ens. Thomas Lee	16 —1705	Ensign, 1701	C. 4, p. 350			Lyme.
Capt. Andrew Leete	16 —16			Captain, 1686	C. 3, p. 209	Guilford.
Gov. William Leete	1613—1683			Gov., 1676		Guilford.
Lt. Thos. Leffingwell	1632—1710			Lieut., 1676	C. 2, p. 279	Norwich.
Ens. Thos. Leffingwell, Jr	1649—1724	Ensign, 16				
Capt. James Lewis	16 —17	Ensign, 1709		Captain, 1714		Stratford.
Sergt. John Lewis	1655—1777	Sergt., 167				New London.
Capt. William Lewis	16 —1690			Captain, 1674	C. 2, p. 238	Farmington.
Corpl. John Livermore	16 —1684	Corpl., 1647				New Haven.
Lt. John Livermore	1638—1718			Lieut., 16		New Haven.
Lt. Jonathan Lockwood	1639—1688	Ensign, 16		Lieut., 1674	M. C. 2, p. 242	Norwalk.
Capt. Richard Lord	1611—1662			Captain, 16		Lyme.
Lt. Richard Lord, Jr.	1647—1727	Ensign, 1703	C. 4, p. 445	Lieut., 1708		Lyme.
Dep. Gov. Roger Ludlow	1590—1665			Com.-in-chief Conn. forces.		Fairfield.
Cornet William Maltby	16 —1710	Cornet, 1673	C. 2, p. 199	Ensign, 1690	C. 4, p. 35	Branford.
Capt. Richard Malbon	16 —1661			Captain, 1645	N. 1, p. 158	New Haven.
Maj. Moses Mansfield	1639—1703		C. 3, p. 127	Major, 1694	C. 4, p. 134	New Haven.
Capt. John Marsh	1668—1744	Captain, 1683		Captain, 1722		Litchfield.
(?) Capt. Samuel Marshall	16 —1675					
Lt. Reinold Marvin	1633—1676	Sergt., 1661		Lieut, 166		Saybrook.

LIST OF OFFICERS.

NAME.	Year of Birth and Death.	Lowest Rank.	Reference Page in the Colonial Records.	Highest Rank.	Reference Page in the Colonial Records.	Place of Residence.
Quar. Daniel Mason	16 —17			Quar., 1673	C. 2, p. 214	New London.
Maj. John Mason, Jr.	1600—1672					New London.
Lt. Samuel Mason	16 —17					Lebanon.
Capt. Janna Meigs	16 —16	Lieut., 1676		Captain, 1702	C, 4, p. 385	Stonington.
Capt. John Merriman	1672—1739			Captain, 1685	C. 3, p. 170	Guilford.
Capt. Nath'l Merriman	1659—1742	Lieut., 1704	C. 4, P. 465	Captain, 1717		Wallingford.
Capt. John Miles	1614—1694	Sergt., 1665	C. 2, p. 23	Captain, 1712	C. 2, p. 379	Wallingford.
Lt. Ephraim Minor	1644—1704	Ensign, 1673	C. 2, p. 214	Captain, 1675	C. 4, p. 88	New Haven.
Ens. Clement Minor	16 —17			Captain, 1693	C. 4, p. 465	Wallingford.
Capt. John Minor	1640—1700	Ensign, 1692		Lieut., 1704		New London.
Ens. Manasseh Minor	1634—1719			Captain, 1684	C. 3, p. 141	Woodbury.
Capt. Thomas Minor	16 —17	Ensign, 1693	C. 4, p. 88			Stonington.
Maj. Matthew Mitchell	1608—1690	Sergt., 1649		Captain, 1665	C. ?, p. 22	Stonington.
Capt. Samuel Moore	1590—1645			Major, 164		Stamford.
Ens. John Morehouse	16 —16	Ensign, 1689		Captain,		Newtown, L. I.
Lt. James Morgan	16 —17	Ensign, 1676	C. 2, p. 279			Norwich.
Capt. John Morgan	1667—1746	Lieut., 1693	C. 4, P. 93	Lieut., 1692	C. 4, p. 74	New London.
Corpl. John Moss	1604—1707	Corp'l, 1642	N. 1, p. 76	Captain, 1714		Groton.
Lt. John Munson	16 —17			Lieut., 1704	C. 4, p. 460	N. H. & Wall'd.
Ens. Samuel Munson	1643—1693	Ensign, 1675		Captain, 1676	C. 2, p. 279	New Haven.
Capt. Thomas Munson	1612—1685	Sergt., 1642	N. 1, p. 76	Major, 1683	C. 3, P. 119	Wallingford.
Maj. John Nash	16 —1687	Corp'l, 1649	N. 2, p. 76	Captain, 1716		New Haven.
Capt. James Newton	16 —1735			Colonel, 1709		New Haven.
Col. Roger Newton	1685—1777			Captain, 1698	C. 4, p. 270	Colchester.
Capt. Samuel Newton	1646—1708	Ensign, 1675		Lieut., 1645	N. 1, p. 158	Milford.
Lt. Francis Newman	15 —1660			Chaplain, 1676		Milford.
Rev. James Noyes	1640—1719			Captain, 1723		New Haven.
Capt. Thomas Noyes	1679—1755	Lieut., 1680	C. 3, p. 67	Captain, 1691	C. 4, p. 44	Stonington.
Capt. James Olmstead	16 —17	Ensign, 1674	C. 2, p. 223	Lieut., 1691	C. 4, p. 44	Norwalk.
Lt. John Olmstead	16 —16	Sergt., 1653	C. 1, p. 243	Lieut., 1650	C. 1, p. 336	Norwalk.
Lt. Richard Olmstead	16 —1686			Captain, 1704	C. 4, p. 465	Fairfield.
Capt. John Osborn	16 —1709			Captain, 1680	C. 3, p. 67	Norwalk.
Capt. Richard Osborn	1606—1682	Captain, 1672	C. 2, p. 186	Major, 167		New London.
Maj. Edward Palmer	1638—1715					

LIST OF OFFICERS.

Name.	Year of Birth and Death.	Lowest Rank.	Reference Page in the Colonial Records.	Highest Rank.	Reference Page in the Colonial Records.	Place of Residence.
Lt. Ephraim Palmer	16 —			Lieut., 1690	C. 4, p. 21	New London.
Sergt. William Parker	16 —16	Sergt., 1673	M. 3, 2, p. 196			New Haven.
Lt. Joseph Peck	1653—17	Ensign, 1702	C. 4, p. 386	Lieut., 1709		Milford.
Ens. Joseph Peck	1641—1718	Ensign, 1678	C. 3, p. 11			Lyme.
Rev. Abraham Pierson	16 —1678			Chaplain, 1654	N. 2, p. 108	Norwalk.
Capt. Joseph Platt	1672—17	Lieut., 1698	C. 4, p. 270	Captain, 1710		Branford.
Lt. Samuel Pond	1648—1718	Ensign, 1689		Lieut., 1695	C. 4, p. 203	Saybrook.
Lt. Abraham Post	16 —1690	Ensign, 1667	C. 2, p. 60	Lieut., 1680		Saybrook.
Ens. John Pratt	1644—1726	Ensign, 1684	C. 3, p. 141			Saybrook.
Capt. William Pratt	1633—1728	Ensign, 1684		Captain, 1679		Saybrook.
Lt. William Pratt	1622—1628					
Capt. Stephen Prentis	1666—1758			Captain, 1714	M. C. 2, p. 251	New London.
Capt. Thomas Prentice	16 —16			Captain, 1675		New London.
Lt. Samuel Preston	16 —16			Lieut., 1696	C. 4, p. 160	
Cornet Josiah Raymond		Cornet, 1672	C. 2, p. 186			New London.
Ens. Samuel Riggs		Ensign, 1690	C. 4, p. 24			Derby.
Capt. Wm. Rosewell	1630—1694			Captain, 1675	C. 2, p. 256	New Haven.
Gov. Gurdon Saltonstall	1666—1724		Gov. of Conn.	Colonel, 1708		East Haven.
Lt. John Sackett	1653—17			Lieut., 1700	C. 4, p. 321	New Haven.
Lt. Joseph Sackett	1660—17			Lieut., 1704	C. 4, p. 465	New Haven.
Ens. John Scott	16 —16			Captain, 1664	M. C. 4, p. 441	Southold.
Capt. Daniel Sayre	1666—1746			Captain, 1671		Southold.
Capt. John Seaman	1610—1695			Captain, 167		Southampton, L.I
Capt. Nathaniel Seelye	162 —1675			Captain, 16		Stamford.
Capt. Robert Seelye	16 —1668	Lieut., 1642	N. 1, p. 76	Major, 1696	N. 2, p. 108	New Haven.
Maj. Jonathan Selleck	1641—1712			Lieut., 1704	C. 4, p. 168	Stamford.
Lt. John Seward	16 —17			Captain, 16	C. 4, p. 427	Guilford.
Capt. William Seward	1627—1689	Sergt., 1665	C. 2, p. 22	Captain, 1700		Guilford.
Capt. Daniel Sherman	16 —17	Ensign, 1686	C. 3, p. 196	Captain, 1708		New Haven.
Capt. David Sherman	1665—1753	Ensign, 1703	C. 4, p. 445			Stratford.
Ens. David Sherman	16 —16	Ensign, 1667	C. 2, p. 63	Captain, 1711		Stamford.
Capt. John Sherman	1650—1730			Lieut., 1697	C. 4, p. 217	Woodbury.
Lt. Samuel Sherman	1641—17			Captain, 16		New Haven.
Capt. Matthew Sherwood	1643—1715	Ensign, 1685	C. 3, p. 183	Captain, 1692	C. 4, p. 69	Fairfield.
Capt. Joseph Sill	1636—1696					Lyme.

LIST OF OFFICERS.

Name.	Year of Birth and Death.	Lowest Rank.	Reference Page in the Colonial Records.	Highest Rank.	Reference Page in the Colonial Records.	Place of Residence.
Capt. Thomas Smith, 2d	1673—17	Ensign, 1716		Captain, 1723		East Haven.
Sergt. John Smith	1646—1732	Sergt., 16				Milford.
Lt. Samuel Smith	16 —16	Sergt., 16		Lieut., 1659	C. 1, p. 292	New London.
Ens. Jared Spencer	16 —1685	Ensign, 1675	C. 2, p. 365			Haddam.
Ens. John Sprague	16 —17	Ensign, 1703	C. 4, p. 427			Lebanon.
Ens. Samuel Squire	16 —17	Ensign, 1705	C. 4, p. 507			Fairfield.
Lt. Timothy Stanley	16 —17			Lieut., 1703	C. 4, p. 427	Waterbury.
Lt. John Stanley	1616—1677			Lieut., 1689	C. 4, p. 11	Waterbury.
Capt. Thomas Stanton, Jr	1639—1715			Captain, 16		Stonington.
Capt. Josiah Standish	16 —1690			Captain, 1669	C. 3, p. 252	Stonington.
Lt. Thomas Stebbins	1620—1683			Lieut., 1675		Preston.
Lt. Eliezur Stent	1645—1700			Lieut., 1683	C. 3, p. 127	Branford.
Lt. Nathaniel Stevens	16 —17			Lieut., 1705	C. 4, p. 526	Guilford.
Lt. Samuel Stiles	16 —1683	Sergt., 1677	C. 2, p. 304	Lieut., 1705	C. 4, p. 507	Woodbury.
Sergt. Samuel Stocking	1621—1685	Ensign, 1669	C. 2, p. 107			Middletown.
Ens. John Stream	1643—1691					Milford.
Lt. Wm. Sumner	1610—1682	Ensign, 16		Lieut., 1700	C. 4, p. 340	Middletown.
Ens. John Sutton	16 —17	Lieut., 1665	M. C. 2, p. 18	Captain, 167		Branford.
(?) Capt. Samuel Swaine	16 —17			Lieut., 1700	C. 4, p. 321	New Haven.
Lt. Thomas Talmage	1669—1749	Ensign, 1696	C. 4, p. 183			Danbury.
Ens. Thomas Taylor	1615—1703	Sergt., 1671		Captain, 1716		New Haven.
Capt. Samuel Thompson	1658—1703	Ensign, 1690				Milford.
Sergt. Thomas Tibbals	16 —1667			Lieut., 17		Stratford.
Lt. Agur Tomlinson	16 —16	Captain, 1673	C. 2, p. 199	Captain, 1651		Southampton, L.I
Capt. Thomas Topping	1610—1685	Ensign, 1666	C. 2, p. 49	Major, 1674	C. 2, p. 231	New Haven.
Major Thomas Topping	1650—1721			Lieut., 1673	C. 2, p. 306	Norwich.
Lt. Thomas Tracy	1662—1721	Sergt., 16		Major, 1675	C. 2, p. 256	Milford.
Major John Treat	1642—1710	Captain, 1661	N. 2, p. 410	Captain, 1708		Milford.
Capt. Joseph Treat	16 —17			Colonel, 1687	C. 3, p. 391	Milford.
Col. Robert Treat	15 —1647			Lieut., 1675	C. 2, p. 256	New Haven.
Capt. Nathaniel Turner	16 —16			Captain, 1634		New Haven.
Lt. Jonathan Tracy	16 —17			Lieut., 1690	C. 4, p. 24	Preston.
Lt. Solomon Tracy				Lieut., 1701	C. 4, p. 351	Norwich.

LIST OF OFFICERS.

NAME.	Year of Birth and Death.	Lowest Rank.	Reference Page in the Colonial Records.	Highest Rank.	Reference Page in the Colonial Records.	Place of Residence.
Capt. Robert Turney	1633—1689			Captain, 1685	C. 3, p. 183	Fairfield.
Capt. John Wakeman	16 —17			Captain, 1704	C. 4, p. 476	Fairfield.
Capt. Joseph Wakeman	16 —17	Lieut., 1705	C. 4, p. 507	Captain, 1708		Fairfield.
Ens. Wm. Waller	16 —17	Ensign, 1661	C. 1, p. 375	Lieut., 1671	C. 3, p. 166	Saybrook.
Ens. James Ward	16 —17	Ensign, 1703	C. 4, p. 335	Ensign, 1703	C. 4, p. 445	Middletown.
Lt. Thomas Ward	16 —17			Lieut., 1699	C. 4, p. 303	Middletown.
Ens. William Ward	16 —17	Ensign, 1682	C. 3, p. 100			Middletown.
Lt. David Waterbury	16 —17			Lieut., 1668	C. 4, p. 253	Stamford.
Lt. Robert Webster	161 —1677			Lieut., 1654		Middletown.
Capt. Nathaniel Webster	1629—1711			Captain, 1690		Middletown.
Lt. James Wells	16 —17	Lieut., 1686	C. 3, p. 215	Captain, 1697	C. 4, p. 228	Haddam.
Capt. Daniel Wetherell	16 —17	Ensign, 1703	C. 4, p. 427	Captain, 1695	C. 4, p. 144	New London.
Ens. Noah Wells	16 —17	Ensign, 1697	C. 4, p. 203			New London.
Ens. Isaac Wheeler	16 —16	Ensign, 1653	C. 1, p. 243			Fairfield.
Lt. Thomas Wheeler	1629—1711	Lieut., 1677	C. 2, p. 304	Captain, 1699	C. 4, p. 303	Middletown.
Capt. Nathaniel White	16 —16	Sergt., 1654	N. 2, p. 108			Milford.
Sergt. Sam'l Whitehead	16 —17			Lieut., 1699	C. 4, p. 202	Milford.
Lt. Francis Whitmore	16 —17			Captain, 1705	C. 4, p. 507	Saybrook.
Capt. Samuel Willard	16 —17			Captain, 1690	C. 4, p. 27	New Haven Co.
Capt. Samuel Williams	1683—1707	Captain, 1658		Colonel, 1691	C. 4, p. 51	New London.
Col. Fitz John Winthrop	1641—1717			Captain, 1665	C. 2, p. 14	New London.
Capt. Waitstill Winthrop	16 —17					Southampton, L.I
Lt. Jonas Wood	16 —16	Sergt., 1675	C. 2, p. 365			Haddam.
Sergt. William Ventrus				Captain, 1662	M. C. 1, p. 386	Southold.
Capt. John Young						

ALPHABETICAL LIST OF THE NAMES OF PERSONS IN NEW HAVEN

before 1640, as printed on pages 109 to 111 of this history, together with some additional data, such as the present boundaries of their lots, year of death, amount of their property as inventoried, etc.

NOTE.—The names of the wives are given only when they died before 1647, or their names are not recorded in the alphabetical list of the "Seating the Meeting House." Where no year of arrival is given the year of 1638 is believed to be the correct one. No attempt has been made to define the lots of those who lived outside of the nine squares.

Year of Arrival	NAME.	No. of persons in family.	No. of children born before 1638.	Occupation.	Street.	Remarks.	Year of Birth and Death.	Amount Estate in 1638.	Inventory of Estate.
1638	Dea. Roger Alling	Un m			65-141 George		16 -1674	£40	£394 17 0
164	Isaac Allerton			Merchant.	41-69 Union	Came on Mayflower.	15 -1659		118 5 0
	William Andrews	8	3	Joiner and Inn-keep'r	96-120 Grove		16 -1676	150	367 17 0
1639	Luke Atkinson	4			Meadow		16 -1677	50	
	David Atwater	Un m		Farmer	120-28 College		1615-1692	500	551 18 2
1637	Joshua Atwater	Un m		Merchant	52-6 College	Rem. to Mil.	1612-1676	300	
	Nathaniel Axtell	Un m			161-67 George	Rem. to Mil.	16 -1640	500	
	Mrs. Sylvester Baldwin	5	4		1098-124 Chapel		16 -16	800	
1639	Samuel Bailey	Un m			14-24 College			250	
1639	Edward Bannister	3			Meadow		16 -1649	10	65 16 0
1639	Richard Beach	Un m			Meadow		16 -1663	20	
	Thomas Beamont				East Water				
1639	Abraham Bell	Un m			136-60 Elm	Rem. to Mass.	16 -1663	10	
	Sergt. Richard Beckley	4	2		218-48 Church		16 -1690	20	80 18 0
	John Benham	5	2	Br'km'k'r	745-71 Chapel		16 -1662	70	
1637	John Beecher								
	Jarvis Boykin	2		Carpenter.	137-43 College		15 -1637	40	173 2 2
	Francis Brewster	9		Merchant.	75-97 Elm		15 -1646	1000	316 16 0
	Dr. John Brockett	Un m		Surveyor.	5-21 Church		1610-1690	15	

PERSONS IN NEW HAVEN.

Year of Arrival	Name	No. of persons in family	No. of children born before 1638	Occupation	Street	Remarks	Year of Birth and Death	Amount Estate in 1638	Inventory of Estate
1639	Peter Brown	3		Baker	West Water		16 -1658	£30	
	Francis Brown	8			East Water			340	
	Henry Browning	6			146-52 College	R. to Eng		450	
	John Budd	4	2		1-13 College	R. to South'd		60	
1639	Thomas Buckingham	4			130-38 College	R. to Milford	15 -1657	500	
	John Caffinch	2	2	Mariner	Meadow			50	
	John Charles	3	1	Teacher	771-803 Chapel	R. to Branf'd	16 -1673	300	
	John Chapman	4	1	Ind. Int.	249-62 College	R. to Fair. '47	16 -1665	20	
1639	Ezekiel Cheever	3			Meadow	R. to Ipswich	1615-1708	240	£144 8 3
	John Clark	4			Hill		15 -1648	50	
	James Clark	4			Hill			60	
	Robert Cogswell	3			Hill			150	222 6 5
	Mrs. Cath. Constable	3	1	Fence Ins.	68-72 College	R. to Branf'd	16 -1684	30	
	John Cooper	3			248-74 Church	R. after 1666		480	
1638	Jasper Crane	Un m.		Minister	28-48 Elm	R. before 1648	15 -1670	1000	
	Rev. John Davenport	Un m.			2-26 Elm	Non-resident		300	
	Jeremiah Dixon				295-313 York			300	
	Mr. Dearmer	2			110-18 College			150	
	Mrs. Richard Eaton	6	3	Minister	18-30 Grove		15 -1663	800	1513 12 0
1637	Rev. Samuel Eaton	5	4		1-19 Elm		16 -1666	3000	
	Gov. Theophilus Eaton	2			21-41 Elm		1592-1658	1000	
	Mrs. Eldred	Un m.		Cooper	65-73 Elm			30	
	Nicholas Elsey	2		Merchant	800-818 Chapel	Ret. to Eng	16 -1690	500	
	John Evance	6		Farmer	84-96 College	Rem. to Mil.	16 -1672	80	166 70 0
	Benjamin Fenn	2			21-41 George			10	0 0
	Timothy Ford	3	2	Miller	Meadow		16 -1684	800	701 0
	William Fowler	2		Secretary	2-12 College	Ret. to Eng	15 -1661	400	
	Thomas Fugill				223-31 York			600	502 13 0
	William Gibbons	3	2		East Water		16 -1679		
164	Gov. Matthew Gilbert				831-875 Chapel				

730   PERSONS IN NEW HAVEN

Year of Arrival.	NAME.	No. of persons in family.	No. of children born before 1638.	Occupation.	Street.	Remarks.	Year of Birth and Death.	Amount Estate in 1638.	Inventory of Estate.
	Dep. Gov. S. Goodyear..	9	2	Merchant	894-996 Chapel....	Ret. to Eng..	1603-1657	£1000	£804 9 0
	Mrs. Mary Goodyear....	6	4			Lost at sea..	160 -1646	600	364 3 0
	Thomas Gregson.......	3		Merchant	46-120 Church...	Lost at sea..	15 -1646	80	80 15 5
1639	Mrs. Arthur Halbidge.....	4	2		189-99 York......		16 -1643	20	43
	Francis Hall...........	3	1		Meadow...	R. to Stratf'd	16 -1690	10	
	William Hawkins.......			..Never liv	ed in Quinnipiac				
	Mrs. F. Higginson......	8	5		230-52 Grove....		15 -1640	250	469 15 8
	Matthias Hitchcock.....	5	1		Hill............		1610-1669	50	107 15 5
	Robert Hill............	3	Un m		191-235 Elm.....	R. to Hartf'd	16 -1663	10	
	Edward Hopkins.......	2			570-614 State....	Ret.to Eng.'52	1600-1657	40	
	Andrew Hull..........	4	2		Hill............		15 -1640	19	98 6 6
	Richard Hull..........	4	2		788-806 Chapel..		1607-1648	25	
	William Ives...........	2			72-160 Congress	Ret. to Eng..	1583-167	200	
1638	Rev. Thomas James.....	5	3	Minister..	181-87 York.....		16 -1691	150	154 10 3
	William Jeanes........	5		Tanner....	Church.........		16 -1661	10c	
	Thomas Jeffries........	2	3		240-80 State....	Rem. to Mass	16 -16	150	
	John Johnson.........	5	3	Marshal..	251-65 York.....		16 -1675	150	
	Thomas Kimberly......	7			807-29 Chapel...	R. to Fairf'd..	16 -1675	12	
	Roger Knapp..........								
	Mr. Lucas.............	6	4	Mariner...	98-118 College			400	1202 12 4
	George Lamberton.....	6	4		196-238 State...		15 -1646	1000	939 0 5
	Benjamin Ling.........	2			145-149 College		16 -1673	320	53 7 0
	Andrew Low...........	3	1		135-159 Elm....		16 -1670	10	
	John Livermore........	4	2		Fleet..........	R. to Water- town, Mass...		100	
	Richard Malbon........	7	5	Merchant	410-448 State....	Ret. to Eng...	15 -1660	500	
	Richard Mansfield.....	4		Steward..	55-63 Elm......		16 -1655	400	393 11 6
1645	John Meggs...........			Shoem'kr	820-876 Chapel..		16 -1678		
	Matthew Moulthrop....				Hill...........				

PERSONS IN NEW HAVEN.

Year of Arrival.	Name.	No. of persons in family.	No. of children born before 1638.	Occupation.	Street.	Remarks.	Year of Birth and Death.	Amount Estate in 1638.	Inventory of Estate.
164	Nathaniel Merriman	3			East Water	Rem. to Wall.	1604-1707	£ 10	
	John Moss	7	1		Meadow		16 -1666	400	£ 285 16 10
	Richard Miles		4	Ship Car.	189-231 George		16 -1673		391 16 10
164	Thomas Morris			Carpenter	East Water		16 -1685	110	279 4 2
	Capt. Thos. Munson	7	5		George & W. River		15 -1656	160	110 16 0
	Thomas Nash	2			375-409 State		16 -1669	700	430 2 7
	Francis Newman	2			138-144 College				
165	Robert Newman				122-146 Grove	Ret. to Eng			
	Jeremiah Osborne	3	1	Tanner	George & W. River		16 -1670	10	
	Richard Osborne	6	4	Tanner	Hill			300	
	Thomas Osborne	Un m.		Tanner	Hill	Rem. to L. I.	16 -167	40	
1638	Edward Patteson	Un m.			14-22 College			100	
	Daniel Paul	2		Ship Car.	Fleet			150	170 11 4
	Mark Pearce			Teacher	121-35 College		1604-1694	12	
1646	Dea. William Peck	4	2	Merchant	Meadow	R. to Milford	1613-1669	260	176 12 5
	Dr. Thos. Pell			Physician	75-97 Elm	R. to Fairf'd			
	Richard Perry	3	1		43-53 Elm				
1637	Robert Pigg				East Water		16 -1660	200	547 5 7
	Richard Platt	6	4		1036-74 Chapel	R. to Milford	1603-1684	40	
	John Pocock				120-28 College	R. to Milford		40	
	William Potter	4	2		Hill		16 -1662	30	
	Widow Potter	4	1		Fleet			25	
	John Potter	4	2		Fleet			100	
	Thomas Powell	Un m.			1099-1105 Chapel		16 -1681	10	
	James Prudden	3	2		337-51 George	R. to Milford	15 -1648	500	
	Rev. Peter Prudden	4	2	Minister	307-55 George	R. to Milford	160 -1656	40	
	William Preston	10	8		740-86 Chapel		15 -1647	180	527 11 3
	Dea. John Punderson	2			233-47 York		16 -1680	140	
	John Reeder	2			Hill	R. to Strat'd	16 -165		

PERSONS IN NEW HAVEN.

Year of Arrival	Name	No. of persons in family	No. of children born before 1638	Occupation	Street	Remarks	Year of Birth and Death	Amount Estate in 1638	Inventory of Estate
	James Russell	2		Ship Car.	East Water		16 –1673	£ 20	£ 205 3 8
	William Russell	2		Ship Car.	East Water		16 –1665	100	586 0 9
	Henry Rutherford	4	2	Shoem'kr	Fleet	R. to Stamf'd	16 –166	179	
	Capt. Robert Seeley	3	1		43–63 George		16 –1668		
	John Sherman	Un m			Hill		15 –1641	50	
	Widow Sherman	Un m			Hill		15 –16	50	
	George Smith	7	5		Hill		16 –166	300	
	Henry Stonhill	3	1		2–46 Church	R. to Milford	15 –1655	800	
	Edmund Tapp	4	2	Farmer	101–35 York	R. to Milford	16 –1640	400	
	Edward Tench	3	1		317–59 York		16 –1648	150	
	Anthony Thompson				Hill		16 –1679	10	102 19 10
	William Thompson	Un m			271–33 York		16 –1675		
	John Thompson				East Water		16 –1686		989 3 8
1638	Christopher Todd	5	3	Merchant	Fleet	Ret. to Eng.	16 –1672	500	457 7 8
	Thomas Trowbridge	7	5	Farmer	232–52 Grove		15 –1646	800	499 8 6
164	Capt. Nath. Turner	4		Farmer	227–47 Church	Rem. to Bran.	16 –1673	450	
	William Tuttle	6	4	Ship Car.	570–514 State	R. to Bran.	16 –1653	10	
1639	George Ward	2		Ship Car.	East Water		16 –1671	30	
	Lawrence Ward	Un m			East Water	R. to Milford	16 –1681	250	922 1 1
	Thomas Welch	2			245–5 George	R. to Stratf'd	16 –1690	50	
	Moses Wheeler	2			East Water		16 –166	60	
	Samuel Whitehead	2			66–104 George	R. to Milford	16 –1666	800	359 12 8
	Zachariah Whitman	2	1		24–50 College		16 –1682	50	212 18 2
	Jeremiah Whitnell	3			233–43 George		16 –1654	300	401 14 2
	Edward Wigglesworth	2	1		1075–99 Chapel	Ret. to Eng	16 –1657	150	
	William Wilkes	2			170–194 State			60	
	Widow Williams	Un m			161–89 Elm			300	
	David Yale	Un m			32–58 Grove	R. to Boston	16 –	100	
	Thomas Yale				201–219 York		162 –1683		479 5 3

INDEX
TO
NEW HAVEN COLONY HISTORY
PAGES 1 TO 592.

A.

Abbot, George, Archbishop of Canterbury, 19, 20, 26, 35, 41, 160.
Abbot, Sir Maurice, 35.
Ahaddon, *alias* Joshua, 333.
Akerly, Robert, 173.
Allerton, Isaac, 135, 204, 435, 543, 546.
Allerton, Isaac, Mrs., 435, 544, 548, 552.
Allerton, Isaac, jun., 370.
Alling, John, 547, 550.
Alling's, John, wife, 552.
Alling, Roger, 109, 133, 290, 291, 543, 545, 550, 556.
Alling, Sister, 544, 548, 553.
Allyn, John, 477, 478, 485, 486, 491, 500, 502, 503, 506, 507, 513, 514, 515, 518, 521, 522, 523, 524.
Allyn, Matthew, 465, 467, 477, 478.
Alsop, Joseph, 419, 546, 550.
Alsop, Goodwife, 548, 553.
Andrews, Nathan, 142.
Andrews, Samuel, 381.
Andrews, William, 101, 102, 111, 147, 218, 297, 446, 542, 545, 550.
Andrews, Goodwife, 549, 554.
Ansantaway, 91, 318.
Arbella, Eaton owned one-sixteenth of, 51.
Armor, defensive, 298.
Arms, persons subject to military duty must furnish themselves with, 294, 297. Inspection of, 295, 296, 297, 303.
Arrival at Quinnipiac of its first planters, 69.
Artillery Company, 296, 304.
Ashford in Kent, 42, 48.
Astwood, John, 156, 157, 389.
Athletic games, 306.
Atkinson, Luke, 110, 148, 543.
Atkinson, Goodwife, 549.
Atwater, David, 43, 47, 111, 144, 213, 290, 543, 546, 550.
Atwater's, David, wife, 544, 547, 552.
Atwater, Joshua, 43, 47, 63, 111, 141, 208, 211, 220, 265, 542.
Atwater, Sister, 544.
Atwater, Thomas, 47.
Augur, Nicholas, 128, 190, 204, 290, 311, 322, 367, 369, 546, 550.
Austin, Francis, 167.
Average time of voyages from London to Boston in the seventeenth century, 54.
Axtell, Nathanael, 109, 136.
Aylmer, John, 53, 54.

B.

Bacon, Francis, 10.
Bacon, Leonard, 60, 101, 206, 208, 212, 239, 428, 435.
Bailey, Samuel, 109, 135.

Baker, Thomas, 159.
Baldwin, John, 155.
Baldwin, Joseph, 155.
Baldwin, Nathanael, 155.
Baldwin, Richard, 155.
Baldwin, Timothy, 137, 155.
Baldwin, Widow, 110, 137, 155, 229.
Ball, Allen, 142, 150, 546, 550.
Ball, Goodwife, 548, 553.
Bannister, Edward, 97, 110, 148, 542.
Bannister, Goody, 544.
Baptists at New Haven, 232.
Barker, Mr., 207.
Barn, Mr. Newman's, meetings in, 95, 99, 147, 163, 164,
Barnes, Obadiah, 153.
Barnes, Thomas, 546, 550.
Barnes, Goodwife, 549, 552.
Bartlett, George, 166, 311.
Bassett, John, 132, 218, 543.
Bassett, Sister, 544, 548, 553.
Bassett, Robert, 219, 311, 376, 405, 406, 407.
Bassett, William, 150, 546, 550.
Beach, Richard, 97, 110, 149, 152, 543.
Beach, Goody, 545.
Beamont, Thomas, 152, 153, 547, 552.
Beamont, Goodwife, 549, 553.
Beckley, Richard, 111, 147, 543, 546.
Beckley, Sister, 544, 548.
Beecher, the elder, Goodwife, 549, 553.
Beecher, Isaac, 63, 547, 551
Beecher, John, 63.
Beecher, Lyman, 63.
Bell, Abraham, 110, 140, 543.
Bell, Francis, 175, 176.
Bellingham, William, 84, 442, 535.
Benedict, Thomas, 173.
Benham, John, 109, 125, 429, 542, 545, 546, 551.
Benham, Sister, 544, 548.
Benham's, John, wife, 549, 553.
Benham, Joseph, 547, 551.
Benham's, Joseph, wife, 553.
Benjamin, Richard, 173.
Benton, Edward, 166.
Besthup, Mr., 322.

Betts, Thomas, 166, 167.
Bishop, James, 118, 291, 472, 496, 500, 513, 520, 522, 525, 545, 550, 556, 560, 564, 580.
Bishop, Goodwife, 548, 552.
Bishop, John (of Guilford), 161, 164, 167, 168, 500.
Bishop, John, Rev. (of Stamford), 242.
Bishop, Stephen, 167.
Blackley, Samuel, 167, 551.
Blayden, William, 547.
Blinman, Richard, 275, 346.
Booth, John, 173.
Boreman, William, 167.
Botsford, Henry, 311.
Bowers, John, 266, 267, 546.
Bowers, Mrs., 548.
Boykin, Jarvis, 111, 146, 218, 311, 542, 545.
Boykin, Sister, 544, 549, 554.
Boynton, Sir Matthew, 53.
Brace, Joab, 120.
Bracey, John, 542.
Bracey, Mrs., 544.
Bradley, William, 211, 213, 546, 550.
Bradley, Goody, 548, 552.
Bradstreet, Simon, 388, 494.
Branford, settled, 385 ; in one jurisdiction with New Haven, 385.
Bread, bad, carried to Virginia and Barbadoes, 204 ; assize of, 223 ; inspector of, 224.
Breedon, Thomas, 421, 423.
Brewster, Francis, 111, 145, 213.
Brewster, Mrs. Francis, 233, 253, 544.
Bristow, Henry, 547, 552.
Bristow, Sister, 553.
Bristow, Richard, 166.
Brockett, John, 77, 97, 109, 133, 215, 311, 324, 447, 543, 546, 550.
Brockett, Sister, 544, 548, 552.
Brook, Lord, 445.
Brooks, James, 551.
Brown, Constable, 577, 580.
Brown, Francis, 63, 152, 153, 543, 546, 551.
Brown, Sister, 545, 548, 552.

Brown, John, 551.
Brown's, John, wife, 553.
Brown, Peter, 110, 149, 542.
Brown's, Peter, wife, 545.
Brown, Richard, 173.
Browning, Henry, 111, 143, 542.
Bryan, Alexander, 204.
Buckingham, Thomas, 109, 136, 155, 156.
Budd, John, 109, 133, 173, 206.
Bull, Lieut., 510.
Busheage, 330.
Bushnell, Francis, 161, 167.

C.

Caffinch, John, 111, 144, 164, 167, 168, 542, 546.
Caffinch, Mrs., 544, 547.
Camp, Edward, 322, 546.
Camp, Goodwife, 548, 549.
Camp, Nicholas, 151, 159, 433.
Canary Islands, commerce with, 210.
Canfield, Matthew, 150, 542.
Canfield, Goody, 544.
Card-playing, 381.
Carman, Mr., 210.
Carpentry at New Haven, 218.
Carr, Robert, 509.
Carroughood, 84, 88, 328.
Cartwright, George, 509.
Caryl, Mr., 207.
Case, Henry, 173.
Cellars as temporary habitations, 71.
Chais, Dr., 368.
Chalker, Alexander, 166.
Chambers, Richard, 24.
Chapin, John, 424.
Chapman, John, 102, 109, 125.
Charles, John, 110, 149.
Charles the First, 6, 15, 17, 20, 21, 22, 127, 445.
Charles the Second, 386, 418, 421, 442, 569.
Chatfield, Francis, 161.
Chatfield, George, 167.

Chatfield, Thomas, 167.
Chatterton, William, 551.
Chauncey, Charles, 232.
Cheever, Ezekiel, 41, 100, 102, 109, 120, 121, 122, 146, 262, 263, 532.
Cheever, Sister, 544.
Chidsey, John, 546, 550.
Chidsey, Goodwife, 548, 553.
Chittenden, William, 161, 164, 166, 168, 304.
Church, the, is not established by the State; but itself institutes civil authority, 227.
Church gathered in New Haven, 101.
Churches, were Congregational, 228, 237.
Church-members, only, shall be free burgesses, 99, 157, 170.
Church, officers of a, 238.
Clapboards for the Canary Islands, 210.
Clark, Capt., 225.
Clark, Daniel, 485, 486, 491.
Clark, Goodwife, 548.
Clark, James, 110, 151, 152, 546, 551.
Clark's, James, wife, 545.
Clark, John, 97, 102, 110, 148, 297, 543, 551.
Clarke, Sister, 544, 545, 554.
Cloth, manufacture of, 364.
Coats quilted with cotton-wool for defensive armor, 298.
Cockerill, John, 141, 142.
Codman, Goodman, 271.
Coe, Robert, 173, 175, 179.
Cogswell, Robert, 110, 151.
College at New Haven projected from the beginning, 271; Mr. Hopkins's bequests in aid of, 275.
Colonial government, Constitution of, 185.
Confederation of the four colonies, 169, 176, 179, 181.
Conklyne, John, 173.
Connecticut lays claim to the territory of New Haven, 447; sends Winthrop to procure a charter, 448; receives the charter, 462; begins to

treat with New Haven for a comfortable and happy union, 466.
Constable, George, 546.
Constable, Mrs., 110.
Constable, Sir William, 141.
Contributions for the maintenance of the elders, 242.
Conway, Sir Richard, 28, 29, 30.
Cook, Thomas, 161, 166.
Cooking-utensils, 357.
Cooper, John, 111, 147, 198, 284, 311, 446, 542, 545, 550.
Cooper, Sister, 544, 549, 554.
Cooper, Thomas, 173.
Corey, John, 173.
Corwin, Matthias, 173.
Cotton, John, 34, 411, 539.
Crampton, Dennis, 425.
Crane, Jasper, 108, 109, 128, 208, 220, 285, 322, 377, 421, 427, 432, 433, 466, 468, 490, 506, 513, 542.
Crane, Sister, 544.
Crittenden, Isaac, 500.
Cromwell, Oliver, 200, 202, 310, 377.
Cruttenden, Abraham, 161, 166.
Cruttenden, Abraham, jun., 167.
Cullick, John, 278, 555.
Curtis, Caleb, 173.

D.

Dana, Rev. James, 63.
Danforth, Thomas, 494.
Daniel, Stephen, 546.
Daniel, Mrs., 548, 552.
Darley, Sir Richard, 138.
Davenport, A. B., 356.
Davenport, John, 28, 29, 30, 32, 33, 34, 35, 36, 39, 40, 41, 43, 44, 45, 46, 47, 52, 53, 54, 58, 59, 60, 63, 67, 68, 69, 70, 72, 73, 76, 81, 82, 84, 85, 90, 91, 93, 95, 96, 98, 99, 100, 109, 113, 123, 127, 128, 129, 135, 140, 141, 148, 160, 162, 163, 171, 172, 196, 208, 214, 232, 238, 239, 240, 241, 270, 271, 272, 273, 275, 276, 277, 280, 281, 282, 283, 284, 285, 287, 288, 289, 290, 291, 294, 317, 318, 344, 352, 354, 355, 356, 365, 367, 368, 369, 370, 371, 372, 374, 415, 417, 419, 423, 424, 425, 429, 430, 433, 434, 440, 442, 449, 468, 469, 473, 474, 481, 483, 485, 494, 504, 507, 526, 528, 535, 539, 540, 541, 555, 556, 557, 559, 560.
Davenport, Mrs., 31, 354, 369, 544, 552.
Davenport, John, jun., 291, 546, 549, 556.
Davenport, Rev. John, of Stamford, 214.
Davids, James, 146.
Davis, John, 435.
Davis, William, 136, 153, 196, 266, 542, 545.
Davis, Sister, 544, 547, 552
Day, Horace, 531.
Day of extraordinary humiliation, 74.
Dayton, Ralph, 153, 543.
Dearmer, Mr., 111, 145.
De Forest, John W., 318, 331, 336.
Delaware Bay, purchase of land at, 193; attempts to settle a plantation at, 193, 195, 196.
Dennison, James, 551.
Denton, Richard, 175.
Desborough, Samuel, 166, 169.
Dexter, Franklin B., 138.
Dickerman, Abraham, 551.
Dickerman, Goodwife, 553.
Dickerson, Philemon, 173.
Diet, 357, 358, 359.
Dillingham, John, 211.
Dimon, Thomas, 173.
Division of land at New Haven, 103.
Dixon, Jeremiah, 100, 101, 111, 145.
Dixwell, John, 146.
Doolittle, Abraham, 546, 550.
Doolittle, Goodwife, 548, 552.
Dowd, Henry, 161, 167.
Dudley, William, 161, 166.
Dunk, Thomas, 167.
Dunster, Henry, 231, 273, 536.
Dutch, the trade with, 191; seize a vessel in New Haven harbor, 192; ask aid in their war with the Indians, 308; a quarrel with, 309.

E.

Eaton or Heaton, James, 381, 382, 547, 551.
Eaton, Mrs. Richard, 109, 120, 250, 544.
Eaton, Nathanael, 127, 535.
Eaton, (Rev.), Samuel, 37, 38, 39, 54, 90, 95, 99, 102, 109, 117, 118, 120, 127, 143, 302.
Eaton, Samuel, 197.
Eaton, Theophilus, 39, 40, 46, 47, 51, 61, 62, 63, 65, 67, 73, 76, 81, 82, 84, 85, 98, 100, 101, 102, 104, 109, 114, 115, 119, 120, 123, 127, 131, 135, 136, 138, 141, 143, 154, 172, 180, 183, 192, 195, 197, 208, 212, 213, 232, 278, 294, 302, 317, 318, 326, 327, 334, 344, 348, 354, 355, 356, 360, 370, 377, 382, 384, 386, 398, 411, 414, 415, 416, 422, 423, 535, 555, 566, 567, 568, 569, 570, 571. 582.
Eaton, Mrs. Theophilus, 115, 117, 233, 234, 250, 356, 382.
Eaton, Theophilus, jun., 382.
Edwards, Timothy, 120.
Egerton in Kent, 42, 43.
Elcott, Anthony, 311, 551.
Eldred, Mr., 140, 145.
Eldred, Mrs., 111, 145, 275, 291, 559.
Election days, 379.
Elective franchise limited to church-members, 99.
Eliot, John, 345.
Elizabeth, Queen, 3, 4, 5, 7, 25, 244.
Elizabeth the washer, 153.
Ellis, Henry, 200.
Elsey, Nicholas, 109, 134, 542, 545, 550.
Elsey, Sister, 545, 549, 552.
Elton, John, 173.
Emigration to New England occasioned by troubles in England, 1; restrained by royal proclamation, 51.
Endicott and his company emigrate, 22.
Endicott, John, 293, 428, 498, 575.
England, contest between arbitrary and constitutional government in, 3; condition of, when the founders of New Haven resolved to emigrate, 23.
English people, contest between the, and the Stuarts, 6.
English Puritans, how they received James the First, 7.
Evance, John, 40, 76, 110, 129, 140, 193, 199, 211, 221, 542.
Evance, Mrs., 544.
Evarts, John, 166.
Eyers, Simon, 435.
Eyers, Mrs. Simon, 434, 435.

F.

Fairbanks, Richard, 191.
Family worship, 360.
Feaks, Robert, 320, 413.
Fences, cost of, at Quinnipiac, 77.
Fenn, Benjamin, 109, 131, 155, 234, 420, 443, 466, 468, 490, 492, 493, 506, 513.
Fenner and Turner, 42.
Fenwick, George, 162, 333, 334, 341, 342, 446, 448, 449, 584.
Fernes, William, 47, 49.
Field, Mr., 550.
Field, Sister, 554.
Fiennes, Charles, 445.
Finch, Abraham, 328, 329.
Fitch, James, 337, 338, 346.
Fitch, Joseph, 467.
Fletcher, John, 159.
Foot, Robert, 551.
Foot, Goodwife, 553.
Footway across fields in Milford, 159.
Ford, Timothy, 110, 149, 150, 543, 546, 550.
Ford, Goody, 545, 549, 553.
Fowler, John, 155, 166, 167.
Fowler, William, 76, 109, 137, 155, 156, 157, 158, 543, 546.
Fowler, Sister, 544, 548.
Foxon, 333, 337.
French, Thomas, 167.
Fugill, John, 142, 263.
Fugill, Thomas, 100, 101, 102, 110, 111, 122, 138, 139, 140, 142, 147.
Fuller, Thomas, 25, 54.
Fundamental law, 386, 408, 409, 410.

G.

Gardiner, Lion, 69.
Garret, Mr., 412.
Gibbard, William, 322, 420, 542, 545, 549.
Gibbard, Sister, 544, 547, 552.
Gibbons, Goodwife, 548, 553.
Gibbons, Henry, 543, 547, 550.
Gibbons, William, 152, 153, 218, 543, 546, 550.
Gibbs, John, 542, 545, 550.
Gibbs, Sister, 544, 547, 552.
Gilbert, John, 550.
Gilbert, Jonathan, 503.
Gilbert, Matthew, 100, 101, 102, 109, 126, 127, 128, 179, 239, 248, 284, 285, 291, 421, 425, 426, 427, 433, 434, 437, 440, 441, 468, 473, 490, 494, 506, 513, 549, 556.
Gilbert, Sister, 544, 547, 552.
Gildersleeve, Richard, 175.
Glover, Charles, 173.
Glover, Henry, 290, 543, 546, 550.
Glover, Goodwife, 549, 553.
Goffe, Stephen, 35.
Goffe, William, 126, 127, 365, 418, 421, 422, 423, 424, 428, 430, 431, 432, 433, 435, 436, 440, 443, 444.
Goldsmith, Ralph, 173.
Goodenhouse, Samuel, 146, 192, 545, 550.
Goodenhouse, Mrs., 547.
Goodwin, William, 278, 555.
Goodyear, Stephen, 41, 109, 135, 136, 192, 198, 205, 206, 208, 209, 211, 212, 214, 224, 250, 264, 272, 344, 377, 403, 415, 416, 537.
Goodyear, Mrs., 552.
Goodyear's, Mr., daughters, 548.
Gookin, Daniel, 201, 202, 337, 338, 421.
Government at New Haven instituted, 101.
Government at Milford instituted, 156.
Government, provisional, at Guilford, 168; institution of, at Guilford, 169.
Greene, widow, 110, 138.

Greenwich, 412, 413, 414, 465.
Gregory, Henry, 220, 221, 222.
Gregory, John, 542.
Gregory, Sister, 544.
Gregson, Richard, 546.
Gregson, Thomas, 41, 76, 105, 109, 112, 135, 179, 180, 208, 209, 214, 334, 537, 539, 568, 583, 584.
Gregson, Mrs., 544, 552.
Grover, Simon, 173.
Guilford, covenant of its planters not to forsake one another, 161; proprietors of, in 1652, list of, 166; church instituted, 169; limits suffrage to church-members, 170; enlarges its territory, 452; disaffected persons at, received by Connecticut, 465.
Gunn, Jasper, 269.
Gutridge, Richard, 161, 166.

H.

Haines, James, 173.
Halbidge, Arthur, 97, 110, 149, 542.
Halbidge, Goodwife, 549.
Hall, Francis, 110, 151.
Hall, Job, 140.
Hall, John, 153, 546, 552.
Hall, Goodwife, 548, 553.
Hall, William, 161, 166.
Hallock, Peter, 173.
Halstead, Mr., 481.
Hames, Goodman, 153.
Hampden, John, 23, 445.
Hampton Court Conference, 8.
Handicrafts, variety of at New Haven, 216.
Hanford, John, 265, 266, 267.
Harding, Will, 258.
Harriman, John, 544, 545, 550.
Harriman, Goodwife, 549, 553.
Harrison, Thomas, 550.
Harrison, Goodwife, 552.
Hawkins, William, 109, 136.
Haynes, John, 179.
Health of New Haven colony as compared with Old England, 365.

INDEX.   739

Hector, the, 45, 47, 48, 49, 50, 51, 52, 53, 54, 55.
Henry the Seventh, 3, 6.
Henry the Eighth, 33.
Herbert, John, 173.
Hereford, emigration from, to New Haven, 43.
Heresy law against, 231.
Hickock, Mr., 108, 109, 133.
Higginson, Francis, 23, 46, 54, 56, 143.
Higginson, Mrs. Francis, 111, 143, 544.
Higginson, John, 165, 166, 167, 169, 241, 269, 363.
Higginson, Theophilus, 143, 542.
High Commission, 25.
Highland, George, 167.
Hill, Robert, 97, 111, 145, 543, 546, 550.
Hill, Sister, 545, 549.
Hitchcock, Edward, 546.
Hitchcock, Goodwife, 548.
Hitchcock, Matthias, 110, 151, 543, 546, 551.
Hitchcock's, Matthias, wife, 544, 552.
Hoadley, John, 161, 166, 169.
Hodskins, Samuel, 547, 551.
Hodskins, Goodwife, 549, 553.
Hodson, John, 149, 290, 546, 550, 560.
Hodson, Mrs., 548, 552.
Hogg, Thomas, 63.
Hollister, Gideon H., 504.
Holt, William, 546, 550.
Holt, Sister, 553.
Hood, Timothy, 31, 33.
Hooke, William, 196, 207, 239, 240, 273, 275, 377, 440, 441.
Hooke, Mrs. William, 422, 423, 544.
Hooker, Samuel, 465, 467.
Hooker, Thomas, 179, 255, 539.
Hopkins, Edward, 40, 53, 114, 118, 119, 120, 271, 275, 276, 277, 279, 280, 281, 283, 289, 290, 334, 412, 555, 556, 558.
Hopkins, Mrs., 114, 115, 555.
Horton, Barnabas, 163.
House, interior of Gov. Eaton's, 116.
Houses, four in New Haven which excelled in stateliness, 135; a general description of the in New Haven colony, 352, 353.

Household furniture, 354, 355.
Householders at New Haven who in 1641 were not free-planters, 153.
Howe, Ephraim, 190, 550.
Howe's, Ephraim wife, 552.
Howe, Jeremy, 545, 550.
Howe's, Jeremy, wife, 548.
Howe, Sister, 552.
Hubbard, George, 166, 167.
Hubbard, William, 172, 321, 366, 370, 373, 387, 414, 538, 540.
Hughes, John, 161, 162.
Hughes, Richard, 167.
Hull, Andrew, 110, 151, 152.
Hull, Jeremiah, 552.
Hull, Goody, 545, 548.
Hull, John, 527.
Hull, Richard, 102, 109, 134, 547, 551.
Humiliation, days of extraordinary, 377.
Humiston, Henry, 551.
Humiston, Goodwife, 553.
Humiston, Sister, 553.
Humphrey, John, 445.
Hutchinson, Ann, 59.
Hutchinson, Richard, 48.
Hutchinson, Samuel, 48.
Hutchinson, Thomas, 200, 255, 435.

I.

Indian conspiracy, 334, 344, 388.
Indians, Mohegan, 331, 333; Quinnipiac, 73, 74, 317, 318, 328, 329, Wepowaug, 318, 319.
Indians, treated with justice and kindness, 321, 322, 323, 324, 325; endeavors to Christianize, 345, 346, 347.
Iron-ore brought from North Haven, 224.
Iron-works, 224.
Ives, William, 110, 112, 150, 543.
Ives, Sister, 544.

J.

Jackson, John, 551.
Jackson, Sister, 553.

INDEX.

James the First, 6, 7, 9, 10, 29, 41, 244, 445.
James, Thomas, 110, 137, 138, 263, 302, 542.
James, Mrs., 545.
James, Thomas, jun., 543.
Jeanes, William, 109, 134, 263, 264, 266, 268.
Jeffrey, Thomas, 102, 109, 130, 131, 196, 198, 220, 284, 297, 314, 324, 543, 546.
Jeffrey, Sister, 544, 548.
Jenningson, William, 293.
John, King, 3.
Johnson, Old Goodwife, 549, 552.
Johnson, John, 97, 110, 167, 546, 550.
Johnson's, John, wife, 552.
Johnson, Richard, 547, 551.
Johnson, Robert, 353, 543, 547.
Johnson, Goody, 544, 548.
Johnson, Thomas, 546, 550.
Johnson's, Thomas, wife, 548, 552.
Jones, John, 322, 546.
Jones, Sister, 553.
Jones, Thomas, 161, 166.
Jones, William, 291, 422, 425, 428, 429, 430, 466, 468, 478, 485, 486, 490, 502, 506, 510, 512, 513, 514, 515, 549, 556.
Jones, Mrs. William, 422, 423, 552.
Jordan, John, 161, 167.
Jordan, Thomas, 166, 390, 396, 397, 399.
Judson, William, 143, 545, 550.
Judson, Goodwife, 549, 552.
Juries, no, in New Haven, 386.

K.

Kellond, Thomas, 424, 427, 428, 430, 434, 443.
Kent, Surrey, and Sussex, a company from, settle at Guilford, 160.
Kieft, Governor, 568.
Kimberley, Abraham, 547.
Kimberley, Eleazar, 126.
Kimberley, John, jun., 551.
Kimberley, Thomas, 109, 123, 125, 126, 153, 267, 297, 435, 543, 546, 550.
Kimberley, Sister, 544, 548, 552.

Kimberley, Zuriel, 134.
King, Samuel, 173.
Kingsley, Professor, 380.
Kingsworth, Henry, 161, 166.
Kirk, Thomas, 424, 427, 428, 430, 434, 443.
Kitchel, Robert, 161, 164, 166, 168, 286.
Knightly, Richard, 445.
Knowles, Thomas, 543.
Knowles, Goody, 545.

L.

Lambert, Edward R., 63, 73, 159, 269.
Lamberton, George, 76, 83, 84, 105, 109, 129, 131, 133, 135, 194, 209, 537, 540.
Lamberton, Mrs., 254, 544.
Lamberton, Hannah, 552.
Lamberton's ship, 208, 537.
Lamson, Jonathan, 112.
Lamson, Thomas, 543, 546, 550.
Land at New Haven, purchased from the Indians, 84; first division of, 103, second division of, 107.
Larrymore, George, 153, 219.
Lathrop, John, 37, 38.
Laud, Archbishop, 19, 20, 26, 30, 31, 32, 33, 34, 36, 41, 42, 43, 160, 226.
Law, Richard, 470, 473, 513, 514.
Lawrencson, John, 193.
Laws of the colony, 411, 412.
Leather to be sealed, 223.
Leaver, Thomas, 153.
Lechford, Thomas, 252.
Leeke, Philip, 220, 322, 543, 546, 551.
Leeke, Goodwife, 549, 553.
Leete, William, 150, 161, 164, 166, 168, 169, 234, 237, 238, 276, 285, 313, 389, 390, 396, 397, 399, 403, 409, 415, 416, 421, 424, 425, 426, 427, 433, 434, 435, 439, 440, 441, 443, 468, 476, 479, 481, 482, 483, 484, 485, 487, 490, 492, 493, 500, 502, 503, 506, 507, 510, 512, 513, 573.
Leigh, Lord, 52.
Leighton, Alexander, 24.
Letter, of Davenport and Eaton to the governor and council of Mas-

sachusetts, 65; of Davenport to Lady Vere, 162; of Davenport to John Winthrop, jun., 415; ditto, 417; of the Council of Massachusetts to Gov. Leete, 436; of the General Court of New Haven to the Council of Massachusetts, 438; of John Norton to Richard Baxter, 443; of Connecticut to New Haven, 447; of Lord Say and Seal to John Winthrop, jun., 450; of George Fenwick to William Leete, 452; of William Leete to John Winthrop, jun., 457; ditto, 458; of Connecticut Committee to their much honored and reverend friends at New Haven, Milford, &c., 467; of New Haven Committee in reply to the foregoing, 467; of the freemen of New Haven to the General Assembly of Connecticut, 470; of John Winthrop, jun., to Major Mason, Deputy-Governor of Connecticut Colony, and the rest of the Court there at Hartford, 475; of Davenport to John Winthrop, jun., 481; of William Leete to John Winthrop, jun., 484; of New Haven Committee to Connecticut Committee, 486; of Connecticut Committee in reply to the foregoing, 488; of New Haven Committee to the General Assembly of Connecticut, 495; of Connecticut Committee to Gov. Leette, 502; of Gov. Leete to Connecticut Committee, 503; of New Haven Committee to Connecticut Committee, 505; of Connecticut Committee in reply to the foregoing, 506; of New Haven Committee to Connecticut Committee, 507; of Connecticut Committee in reply to the foregoing, 507; of New Haven Committee to the Council of Connecticut, 519; of the Council of Connecticut in reply to the foregoing, 522; of New Haven Committee to the Council of Connecticut, 523; of Nathanal Rowe to John Winthrop, 535; of James Pierpont to Cotton Mather, 540; of remonstrance from New Haven to the General Assembly of Connecticut Colony, 561; entitled "New Haven's Case Stated," from the New Haven Committee to the General Assembly of Connecticut Colony, 565.

Leveret, Capt., 438.
Liberty, religious, the planters of New Haven not advocates of, 226.
Lindon, Henry, 542, 545.
Lindon, Goody, 545, 547, 552.
Lines, Henry, 552.
Lines', Henry, wife, 553.
Lines, Ralph, 547, 550.
Lines', Ralph, wife, 552.
Ling, Benjamin, 111, 146, 147, 482, 542, 560.
Ling, Sister, 544.
Linsley, John, 167.
Livermore, John, 110, 149, 543.
Livermore, Sister, 544.
Lord, Robert, 322.
Lord's day, the, began at sunset, 361.
Low, Andrew, 97, 110, 145, 543, 546, 551.
Low, Goodwife, 549, 553.
Lucas, Mr., 111, 145.
Ludlow, Roger, 344, 404, 405.
Lumber, price of, at Quinnipiac, 79.

M.

Malaria at New Haven, 366.
Malbon, Mary, 122.
Malbon, Richard, 41, 100, 109, 122, 123, 124, 129, 130, 135, 179, 208, 295, 369, 542.
Malbon, Mrs., 544.
Mallory, Peter, 546,
Mallory, Goodwife, 549, 553.
Manchester, Earl of, 560.
Mansfield, Joseph, 550.
Mansfield, Richard, 109, 129, 130, 144, 145, 213, 543.
Mansfield, Sister, 544, 549, 552.

Mapes, Thomas, 173.
Market-place at New Haven, 105.
Marriages, how solemnized, 363.
Marshall, Mr., 111, 129, 130, 145, 147.
Marsh, Jonathan, 219.
Marsh, Samuel, 547, 551.
Marsh, Goodwife, 549, 553.
Martin, Capt., 202.
Martin, Robert, 542.
Martin, Sister, 544.
Mary, Queen of Scots, 5.
Mason, John, 132, 295, 313, 332, 338, 339, 475, 476, 480, 481, 482, 496, 565, 571, 586.
Massachusetts, desirous to retain Davenport and his company, 58; reasons why Davenport and his company were not content to settle in, 61; requires Mr. Eaton to pay taxes, 65; refuses to join in a war against the Dutch, 389.
Massachusetts Bay Company, transfer the government of their plantations to New England, 22; Davenport a director of, 36; Eaton a patentee of, 39.
Mather, Cotton, 99, 101, 116, 121, 141, 155, 200, 540.
Mather, Richard, 232.
Maverick, Samuel, 509.
Mayer or Mayres, Mr., 100, 110.
Medal, commemorating the settlement of New Haven, 74.
Meeker, William, 550.
Meeker, Goodwife, 553.
Meeting-house at Guilford, 246; at Milford, 246; at New Haven, 247; seating the, at New Haven, 250.
Meigs, John, 134, 220, 221, 222, 426, 501, 542.
Meigs, Goody, 544.
Mepham, John, 161, 167, 169.
Merriman, Nathanael, 152, 153, 447, 546, 550.
Merriman, Goodwife, 549, 552.
Metcalf, Stephen, 152, 376.
Mew, Ellis, 551.
Mewhebato, 328.
Miantinomoh, 333, 334, 335, 336, 344.

Miles, Richard, 109, 136, 141, 155, 157, 202, 203, 208, 248, 419, 542.
Miles, Mrs., 544, 547, 552.
Miles, Richard, jun., 546.
Milford, land bought for a settlement at, 91; church at, organized, 155; first general court at, 156; town seal of, 157; limits suffrage to church-members, 157; name given to, 159; original name of, 159; first division of land at, 160; obstacle which delayed the reception of, into the colony of New Haven, 183.
Military duty, exemption from, 303.
Military officer, chief at Quinnipiac, 294; only a church member could be a, 311.
Mill, the first in New Haven colony, 198.
Miller, Thomas, 47.
Mills, Thomas, 167.
Mitchel, Mathew, 175.
Mitchel, Thomas, 153, 547.
Mitchel, Goodwife, 548, 553.
Mix, Thomas, 290, 546, 550.
Mix, Goodwife, 548, 552.
Mohawks, 316, 317, 331.
Momaugin, 84, 88, 89, 318, 339.
Montauk Indians, 313, 320.
Montowese, 89, 318, 327, 339, 447.
Moore, Thomas, 173.
Morality in New Haven colony, 255.
Morrell, Henry, 547, 551.
Morris, Thomas, 152, 153, 219, 546, 551.
Morris, Goodwife, 548, 553.
Moss, John, 110, 148, 149, 297, 543, 546, 550.
Moss, Goody, 545, 548, 552.
Moss, Joseph, 148.
Mould, Isaac, 211.
Moulthrop, Matthew, 110, 151, 545, 550.
Moulthrop, Goodwife, 548, 552.
Mullener, Mr., 545, 550.
Mullener, Mrs., 548, 552.
Mullener, Thomas, 546.
Munson, Thomas, 130, 153, 196, 218, 284, 297, 298, 311, 543, 545, 550.
Munson, Sister, 545, 549, 553.

N.

Nash, John, 153, 202, 284, 297, 311, 474, 543, 545, 550.
Nash's, John, wife, 544, 547.
Nash, Joseph, 543, 546.
Nash's, Joseph, wife, 545.
Nash, Thomas, 109, 124, 125, 126, 161, 162, 167, 215, 543.
Nash, Sister, 544, 548, 552.
Naylor, James, 236.
Neighborhood meetings, 100, 255, 378.
Neighborly helpfulness, 374.
Neighborly intercourse, 379.
Nepaupuck, 102, 327, 328, 329, 330.
New England, occasion of the Puritan emigration to, 1; connection between the history of, and the history of the mother country, 2.
New Haven, its planters leave Boston for Quinnipiac, 68; its planters who were not proprietors supplied with house-lots, 103; the name of when given to that plantation, 113; its planters endeavored to make it a commercial town, 189; receives a proposal to remove to Ireland, 200; receives a proposal to remove to Jamaica, 201; town on Sunday morning, 376.
Newman, Francis, 41, 111, 118, 144, 197, 211, 285, 297, 322, 397, 398, 403, 412, 415, 416, 417, 424, 542, 545.
Newman's, Francis, wife, 544, 547.
Newman, Richard, 153, 551.
Newman, Goodwife, 553.
Newman, Robert, 41, 76, 95, 99, 100, 101, 102, 104, 111, 147, 162, 163, 164, 165, 207, 239, 441.
Newman's barn, 95, 99, 147, 163, 164.
Newman's, Elder, wife, 544.
Newton, Roger, 241, 468.
Nicolls, Adam, 152, 543.
Nicolls, Sister, 545.
Nicolls, Richard, 509, 517.
Ninigret, 310, 313, 315, 321, 338, 400, 403, 404, 406, 408.
Norton, Humphrey, 234, 235.
Norton, John, 232, 443.
Norton, Thomas, 161, 167.

O.

Obechiquod, 337.
Osbill, John, 551.
Osborne, Goodman, 178.
Osborne, Jeremiah, 546, 550.
Osborne, Richard, 110, 151, 152, 543.
Osborne, Goody, 545, 548.
Osborne, Thomas, 110, 137, 152, 542.
Osborne, Sister, 544, 552.
Ourance, 322, 323.
Overton, 311.
Oyster Point, 75.
Oyster-shell Field, 106.

P.

Paine, Peter, 173.
Paine, William, 546, 551.
Paine, Goodwife, 548, 552.
Palfrey, John G., 276, 345, 349, 350, 509.
Pardee, George, 289, 546, 550.
Pardee, Goodwife, 549, 553.
Parker, Edward, 546, 550.
Parker, Goodwife, 548, 553.
Parmelee, Sister, 553.
Parmelin, John, 161, 166.
Parmelin, John, jun., 166.
Parrot, Francis, 137.
Patrick, Daniel, 320, 413.
Patteson, Edward, 110, 151, 152, 543, 546, 551.
Patteson, Sister, 545, 548.
Paul, Daniel, 110, 149, 219, 543.
Paulding, Benjamin, 153.
Payne, Mr., 225.
Peakin, John, 545.
Pearce, Mark, 111, 146, 214, 268, 298, 543.
Peck, Goodman, 153.
Peck, Jeremiah, 269, 270, 285, 286, 287, 378.

INDEX

Peck, Widow, 548.
Peck, William, 41, 110, 149, 291, 359, 542, 546, 556.
Peck, Sister, 545, 548, 552.
Pelham, Herbert, 445.
Pell, Thomas, 146, 367, 543.
Pennington, Ephraim, 547.
Pennington, Goodwife, 549, 553.
Perkins, Edward, 547, 552.
Perry, Richard, 109, 120, 122, 377, 543.
Perry, Mrs., 544.
Peters, Hugh, 69.
Philip of Spain, 5.
Pierce, Capt., 417, 419.
Pierpont, James, 219, 540, 541.
Pierson, Abraham, 242, 275, 285, 287, 311, 325, 346, 347, 385, 468, 484, 525.
Pigg, Robert, 63, 152, 153, 547.
Pigg, Goodwife, 548.
Pikes to be provided at the town's charge, 298, 305.
Plane, William, 161, 167.
Plastowe, Josias, 375.
Platt, Richard, 110, 137, 155, 210.
Pocock, John, 145, 155.
Ponus, 319, 320, 331.
Population of New Haven in 1641, 153.
Portrait of Davenport, 123.
Portrait which belonged to the Eaton family, 115.
Post-office, germ of, 191.
Potter, Goody, 548, 552.
Potter, John, 97, 110, 150, 551.
Potter's, John, wife, 552.
Potter, Joseph, 551.
Potter's, Joseph, wife, 553.
Potter, Sister, the midwife, 544.
Potter, Widow, 110, 150.
Potter, William, 110, 144, 213, 543, 545, 550.
Potter's, William, wife, 544.
Powell, Thomas, 111, 142, 474, 543, 546, 551.
Powell, Sister, 545, 548, 553.
Preston, Edward, 546, 550.
Preston's, Edward, wife, 553.
Preston, Robert, 543.

Preston, William, 109, 129, 134, 151, 152, 543.
Preston, Sister, 178, 544, 548.
Prices at New Haven, 77, 79, 211, 217.
Prince, Thomas, 494.
Pringle, William, 351.
Privy Council, notes of its proceedings in January, 1637, 42.
Proprietors of Guilford in 1652, 166.
Proprietors of Milford in 1646, map opposite p. 155.
Proprietors of New Haven in 1641, a list of, 109.
Prudden, James, 109, 137, 155.
Prudden, Peter, 44, 53, 68, 73, 90, 93, 99, 109, 137, 155, 156, 241.
Prynne, William, 24.
Punderson, Ebenezer, 140.
Punderson, John, 100, 101, 110, 140, 543, 546, 550.
Punderson, Sister, 544, 548, 552.
Purchase of lands from the Indians, 84, 89, 91, 164, 172, 174, 319, 320, 321.
Puritan emigration commences in the time of the third parliament of Charles the First, 22.
Puritans and Separatists at New Haven, 93.
Puritans, English, reasons why they emigrated to New England, 1.
Purrier, William, 173.
Pym, John, 445.

Q.

Quakers, 234.
Quarters in the town-plot at New Haven, 76.
Quarters, outland, at New Haven, boundaries of, 104.
Quesaquash, 84, 88.
Quinnipiac, the Pequot war made the English acquainted with, 61; seven men spend the winter at, 63; arrival at, of its first planters, 69; name of, changed to New Haven, 112.
Quinnipiac Indians, 73, 74, 317, 318.

INDEX.   745

R.

Rates, Theophilus Eaton pays, in Massachusetts, 65.
Rawson, Edward, 434, 436, 442.
Raynor, Thurston, 175.
Reeder, John, 110, 151.
Reekes, Stephen, 205.
Reeve, James, 173.
Regicides, the, Whalley and Goffe, arrive at Boston, 418; at New Haven, 423; are concealed in the mill, 428; at Judges' cave, 431, 434; at Milford, 435; at Hadley, 444.
Relf, Thomas, 167.
Restraint which the Puritans put upon their feelings, 370.
Rich, Lord, 445.
Rich, Sir Nathanael, 445.
Richards, James, 501, 502, 503, 506, 514.
Richardson, Edward, 421.
Robinson, John, 125.
Robinson, Thomas, 211.
Rogers, Ezekiel, 81, 82, 83, 84, 131, 137, 141, 364.
Ross, George, 551.
Rosseter, Bray, 500, 501, 503, 504, 577, 578, 579, 580.
Rosseter, John, 500.
Rowe, Matthew, 546, 550.
Rowe, Goodwife, 549, 553.
Rowe, Nathanael, 127, 535, 536.
Rowe, Owen, 109, 127, 128, 377.
Rowlandson, Mr., 266.
Ruggles, Thomas, 241.
Russell, James, 111, 129, 219, 543, 546, 550.
Russell, Sister, 548, 549, 553.
Russell, John, 444.
Russell, Sir William, 49.
Russell, William, 152, 153, 219, 290, 546, 550.
Russell's, William, wife, 548, 552.
Rutherford, Henry, 110, 150, 419, 542, 546, 550.
Rutherford, Sister, 544, 547, 552.

S.

Sabbath worship, at Quinnipiac under an oak-tree, 72; in the meeting-houses, 252, 375.
Sacket, John, 547, 551.
Saltonstall, Sir Richard, 445.
Sanford, Thomas, 433.
Sassacus, 328, 332.
Saul, Thomas, 218.
Savage, James, 127.
Sawing lumber, 79, 217.
Sawseunck, 89.
Say and Seal, Lord, 445, 449, 569.
Schedule for taxation at New Haven, 109.
School, colony grammar, 275; Mr. Peck, master of, 285; Mr. Peck's propositions concerning, 286.
School, town, at Guilford, Mr. Higginson, master of, 269; Mr. Peck master of, 269.
School, town, at Milford, Mr. Gunn, master of, 270.
School, town, at New Haven, Mr. Cheever, master of, 262; Mr. Jeanes, master of, 264; Mr. Hanford, master of, 265; Mr. Bowers, master of, 266; Mr. Pardee, master of, 289.
Schools, early established, 261.
Scott, John, 481, 484, 485.
Scranton, Dennis, 425.
Scranton, John, 166.
Searl, Mr., 528.
Sebequanash, 332.
Secretary Fugill put out of office, 139.
Sedgwick, Robert, 201, 202.
Seeley, Robert, 102, 109, 126, 130, 132, 196, 211, 295, 311, 313, 314, 542, 547.
Seeley, Sister, 544, 548.
Sellevant, David, 322.
Separatists and Puritans at New Haven, 93.
Seven men, chosen for the foundation-work of a church and a government, 101.
Seward, Edward, 167.

Shaumpishuh, 85, 88, 164, 318.
Sheader, John, 167.
Sheafe, Jacob, 169.
Shearman, Samuel, 513, 514, 515, 518, 521, 525.
Shepard, Thomas, 138, 255, 342.
Sherman, John, 241.
Sherman, Old Father, 150.
Sherman, Widow, 110, 112, 150.
Ship-carpenters, at New Haven, 219.
Ship-money, 23.
Shoe-making, unworkmanlike, 220.
Sickness at New Haven in 1658 and 1659, 366.
Signature of Davenport, 67; of Eaton, 67; of Momaugin, and other Quinnipiacs, 88; of Montowese, 89; of Sawseunck, 89.
Skidmore, Richard, 173.
Smart, Peter, 25.
Smith, George, 110, 112, 150, 543, 546, 550.
Smith, Sister, 545, 548, 552.
Smith, Judge, 380.
Smith, Ralph D., 162, 276, 350.
Smith, Thomas, 214.
Smyth, Robert, 173.
Social compact at Quinnipiac, 74.
Social life, influenced by religion, 372; and by residence in a new country, 373.
Social inequality, manifestations of, 374.
Soldiers sent to defend Uncas, 307, sent against the Dutch, 310; rations for, 312, 314; sent against Ninigret, 314.
Somers, William, 167.
Southold, settled, 171; church of gathered, 171; purchased in the name of New Haven, 172; under one jurisdiction with New Haven, 172; some of its planters, 173; sedition at, 406; revolts from New Haven to Connecticut, 463.
Sowheag, 325, 326, 327, 582.
Sperry, Richard, 430, 431, 434, 551.
Sperry, Goodwife, 554.

Spinage, Humphrey, 551.
Spinage, Goodwife, 381, 552.
Spinning, 364.
Stamford, purchased, 174; settled, 175; admitted to membership in the colony, 175; named, 175; in favor of war, 309, 404, 405; sedition at, 405, 406; some of its inhabitants received under the protection of Connecticut, 465.
Standish, Miles, 293.
Stanton, Thomas, 84, 89, 347.
Star Chamber, 23, 24.
Stephenson, William, 421.
Stevens, Thomas, 167, 311.
Stiles, Ezra, 81, 121, 126, 135, 241, 348, 434, 447.
Stillwell, Jasper, 166.
Stolyon, Mrs., 210, 211.
Stone, John, 161, 166.
Stone, Samuel, 237, 465, 467, 482, 571.
Stone, William, 161, 167.
Stonehill, Henry, 136, 155.
Stoughton, Israel, 61, 343.
Stoughton, William, 27.
Street, Nathanael, 550.
Street, Nicholas, 239, 275, 285, 287, 291, 419, 440, 441, 468, 474, 504, 556.
Street, Mrs., 552.
Street, Samuel, 289, 290.
Stuyvesant, Peter, 195, 205.
Sugcogisin, 84, 88.
Sumptuary laws, none in New Haven, 382.
Sunday evening, spent in social intercourse, 550.
Swain, William, 329, 385.
Swazey, John, 173.
Swinerton, Mrs., 153.

T.

Table furniture, 356.
Talcott, John, 477, 493.
Talmadge, Robert, 324, 545.
Talmadge, Goodwife, 548, 552.
Taphanse, 331.
Tapp, Edmund, 110, 137, 155, 156, 157.

INDEX. 747

Tappan, Capt., 408.
Tapping, James, 433.
Target-shooting, 297.
Taynter, Michael, 322.
Temple, Sir Thomas, 430, 433, 442.
Tench, Edward, 76, 104, 105, 111, 140, 145.
Terry, Richard, 173.
Thanksgiving, the annual, 360; postponed, 416.
Thomas, John, 543, 546, 551.
Thomas's, John, wife, 545, 548, 553.
Thompson, Anthony, 110, 150, 151, 542.
Thompson, Sister, 544, 547, 552.
Thompson, John, 149, 153, 545, 550.
Thompson, John, jun., 546.
Thompson, Major Robert, 481, 484, 485, 555.
Thompson, William, 542, 545, 550.
Thorp, William, 111, 145, 543, 547, 551.
Thorp, Goodwife, 548, 552.
Thorpe, Nathanael, 322, 323, 324.
Tibbals, Thomas, 155.
Tichener, Martin, 546, 551.
Tichener, Goodwife, 549, 553.
Todd, John, 142.
Todd, Christopher, 143, 153, 543, 545, 550.
Todd, Sister, 544, 548, 552.
Toquatoes, 331.
Town plot at New Haven laid out, 75.
Trade of New Haven with Boston, 190; with Manhattan, 191; with Delaware Bay, 203; with Virginia, 204; with Barbadoes, 205; with England, 207.
Trainings, military, 296, 378.
Treat, Robert, 285, 421, 433, 466, 468, 490, 506, 513.
Troopers, a company of, 304.
Trowbridge, Thomas, 110, 150, 290, 550.
Trowbridge's, Thomas, wife, 552.
Trowbridge, William, 550.
Trowbridge's, William, wife, 552.
Trumbull, Benjamin, 59, 64, 68, 73, 90, 165, 171, 173, 174, 175, 194, 195, 212, 316, 318, 326, 346, 388, 404, 525.

Tucker, Francis, 37.
Tucker, John, 173.
Turkish pirate, 210.
Turner and Fenner, 42.
Turner, Isaac, 551.
Turner, Nathanael, 100, 102, 109, 121, 122, 124, 138, 144, 146, 174, 209, 210, 213, 293, 294, 295, 296, 298, 319, 537.
Turner, Mrs., 544.
Tuthill, John, 173, 176.
Tuttle, Elizabeth, 120.
Tuttle, John, 546, 551.
Tuttle's, John, wife, 553.
Tuttle, Jonathan, 550.
Tuttle, Sister, 544, 547, 552.
Tuttle's, Thomas, wife, 553.
Tuttle, William, 109, 119, 324, 474, 543, 546, 550.

U.

Uncas, 307, 331, 332, 333, 334, 335, 336, 337, 338, 339, 343, 344.
Underhill, John, 62, 178, 293, 308, 320, 330.

V.

Vail, Jeremiah, 173.
Vane, Harry, 52.
Vere, Lady Mary, 29, 31, 113, 172.
Vincent, John, 153, 543, 547.

W.

Wakefield, John, 151, 543, 546.
Wakefield, Sister, 545, 548.
Wakeman, John, 179, 208, 220, 229, 230, 420, 545.
Wakeman, Sister, 544, 547.
Walker, John, 153.
Wampum, 212, 259.
Ward, Andrew, 174, 175, 176, 179.
Ward, George, 111, 129, 219.
Ward, Goodman, 214.
Ward, Lawrence, 111, 129, 219, 433.
Ware, John, 551.
Warwick, Earl of, 445, 446, 448, 449, 569.
Wascussue, 319.
Wash, 322.
Watch-house, 301.
Watch, night, 299.

INDEX.

Watch to be kept on days of worship, 302.
Waters, Joseph, 514.
Watson, Edward, 547.
Watson, Goodwife, 549.
Wattoone, 328, 329.
Wawequa, 335, 336, 337.
Weaving, 364.
Welch, Thomas, 136, 155, 156.
Wells, William, 173.
Wepowaug, land at, bought by Prudden and his company, 91.
Wepowaug Indians, 318, 319.
Wequash, 332, 338, 339, 340, 341, 342, 343, 344, 345.
Wesaucunck, 84, 88.
Westerhouse, William, 149, 192, 193, 367.
Westminster confession of faith, 243.
Whalley, Edward, 142, 365, 421, 422, 423, 424, 428, 430, 431, 432, 433, 435, 436, 440, 443, 444.
Wheeler, Thomas, 543, 546, 547, 551.
Wheeler, Goody, 545, 548.
Wheeler, Moses, 111, 129.
Whitaker, Ephraim, 172, 173.
White, Henry, 112, 134.
Whitehead, Isaac, 546.
Whitehead, Samuel, 110, 148, 297, 311, 543, 545, 550.
Whitehead, Sister, 545, 548, 553.
Whitfield, Henry, 43, 125, 144, 160, 161, 162, 164, 165, 166, 167, 168, 169, 240, 241, 269, 275, 318, 423, 481.
Whitfield's house, 349, 350, 351, 352.
Whiting, Mr., 510.
Whitman, Zachariah, 137, 155, 156, 157, 241, 377.
Whitmore, John, 175, 331.
Whitnell, Jeremiah, 109, 136, 543, 547, 551.
Whitnell, Sister, 544, 549.
Whitway, Thomas, 333.
Wigglesworth, Edward, 111, 142, 376, 377, 542.
Wigglesworth, Sister, 544.
Wigglesworth, Michael, 72, 142, 262, 531.
Wilford, John, 543.

Wilkes, William, 131.
Willard, Major, 314, 404.
Williams, Roger, 64, 342.
Williams, Widow, 111, 145.
Willis, Mr., 535, 536.
Willoughby, Francis, 555.
Wilmot, Benjamin, 153, 542, 546, 551.
Wilmot, Goodwife, 544, 548, 552.
Wilmot, Goodwife, jun., 548.
Wilmot, William, 551.
Wines, Barnabas, 173.
Winslow, Edward, 46.
Winslow, Josiah, 494.
Winston, John, 290, 546, 550.
Winston, Goodwife, 549.
Winthrop, John, 52, 54, 56, 60, 61, 63, 68, 78, 83, 91, 114, 127, 131, 190, 208, 210, 219, 231, 321, 330, 341, 358, 382, 383, 535, 537, 540, 566, 572.
Winthrop, John, jun., 53, 224, 239, 354, 368, 369, 415, 417, 419, 422, 423, 424, 443, 449, 464, 467, 469, 471, 473, 475, 476, 477, 481, 482, 483, 484, 485, 493, 494, 496, 497, 505, 506, 517, 526, 527, 563, 565, 566, 569, 570, 571, 573, 574, 575.
Winthrop, Mrs. John, jun., 354.
Winthrop, Waitstill, 500, 502, 503.
Wolcott, Henry, 506.
Wooden, Will, 551.
Wooden, Goodwife, 553.
Woodgreen, Mr., 437.
Worship, public, on the Lord's day, 252.
Wyllys, Samuel, 463, 465, 467, 477, 478, 485, 486, 491, 495, 500, 502, 503, 506, 510, 513.

Y.

Yale, David, 40, 109, 120, 138.
Yale, Elihu, 120, 138.
Yale, Thomas, 40, 110, 138, 213, 446, 543, 546, 549.
Yale, Mrs., 544, 548, 552.
Yorkshire company of emigrants at Quinnipiac, 81.
Young, Anne, 40.
Youngs, John, 171, 172, 173, 174, 234.
Youngs, John, jun., 315, 406, 407, 408, 409, 463, 464.

INDEX TO SUPPLEMENTARY HISTORY.

NOTE.—As the names in the lists beginning on pages 699, 711, 718 and 728 are arranged alphabetically, and thus easy for reference, it has been thought best to omit adding those pages to the names in this index.

A.

Abbott, Abigail, 613.
Abbott, Benjamin, 613.
Abbott, Daniel, 613.
Abbott, Deborah, 613.
Abbott, Hannah, 630.
Abbott, John, 613.
Abbott, Marie, 613.
Abbott, Mary, 613.
Abbott, Peter, 613, 630.
Abbott, Robert, 598, 613.
Abbott, Sarah, 613.
Abel, Joshua, 694.
Abut, Robert, 607.
Ackerly, Henry, 689.
Ackerly, Mary, 689.
Adams, George, 621.
Adams, John, 621.
Akerly, Robert, 674.
Allcote, Thomas, 624.
Allyn, John, 694.
Alsop, Elizabeth, 642.
Alsop, Joseph, 642.
Ambler, Abraham, 684.
Apsley, Sir Edmund, 698*b*.
Arnold, John, 599.
Astwood, John, 639, 640.
Astwood, Martha, 640.
Atwater, David, 624.
Atwater, Joshua, 631, 657.
Atwater, Mary B., 631.
Atwood, Capt., 648.
Atwood, Hannah, 648.
Atwood, John, 639, 640.
Austin, Francis, 626.
Austin, Joshua, 613.
Avery, Christopher, 691.
Avery, Hannah, 691.
Avery, James, 691.
Avery, Capt. James, 691.
Avery, Joanna, 691.
Avery, John, 691.
Avery, Jonathan, 691.
Avery, Mary, 691.
Avery, Rebecca, 691.
Avery, Samuel, 691.
Avery, Thomas, 691.

B.

Backus, Ann, 698*a*.
Backus, Elizabeth, 698*a*.
Backus, Stephen, 698*a*.
Backus, William, 698*a*.
Backus, Wm. W., 698*a*.
Bailey, Mrs. Stephen, 676.
Baker, Thomas, 639, 640.
Baldwin, Anna, 643.
Baldwin, Benjamin, 620.
Baldwin, Elizabeth A., 647.
Baldwin, Hannah, 641.
Baldwin, Joanna, 643.

Baldwin, John, 639, 640, 692.
Baldwin, Jonathan, 617.
Baldwin, Joseph, 639, 641.
Baldwin, Martha, 642.
Baldwin, Mary, 640, 641, 642, 650, 654, 655.
Baldwin, Nathaniel, 639, 641, 644.
Baldwin, Richard, 639, 641, 642, 648.
Baldwin, Robert, 643.
Baldwin, Ruth, 642.
Baldwin, Samuel, 640.
Baldwin, Sarah, 640, 642.
Baldwin, Sylvester, 640, 642, 650.
Baldwin, Timothy, 634, 639, 641, 655.
Ball, Ed., 614, 625.
Ball, John, 604.
Banks, Benjamin, 664.
Banks, John, 664.
Banks, Joseph, 664.
Banks, Mary, 664.
Banks, Obadiah, 664.
Banks, Samuel, 664.
Barber, Mary, 683.
Barber, Mrs. Sherwood, 683.
Barber, Thomas, 683.
Barker, William, 620.
Barlow, Ann, 664.
Barlow, Deborah, 664.
Barlow, Elizabeth, 665.
Barlow, George, 663, 664.
Barlow, Joel, 664.
Barlow, John, 664.
Barlow, Martha, 664.
Barlow, Mary, 664.
Barlow, Phebe, 664.
Barlow, Rose, 664.
Barlow, Ruth, 664.
Barlow, Thomas, 664.
Barnard, Samuel, 606.
Bartlett, George, 626, 627.
Bartlett, Levi, 627.
Bartlett, Susannah, 691.
Bartlett, William, 691.
Bateman, William, 650.
Bates, John, 684.
Bates, Mary, 684.
Bates, Robert, 684.
Bates, Samuel, 698*b*.

Beach, Benjamin, 660.
Beach, Bessie B., 593.
Beach, John, 671.
Beard, James, 641, 654.
Beard, Jeremy, 641.
Beard, John, 641.
Beard, Mrs. Martha, 639, 641, 654.
Beard, Sarah, 642.
Beardsley, E. E., 657.
Beardsley, John, 657.
Beardsley, Joseph, 657.
Beardsley, Mary, 657.
Beardsley, William, 657, 663.
Beckwith, Matthew, 698*d*.
Beckwith, Paul, 681.
Beckwith, Samuel, 681.
Beebe, Rebecca, 681.
Beers, James, 664.
Bell, Lieut. Francis, 667, 684.
Bell, Capt. Jonathan, 684.
Bell, Ledyard, 684.
Bell, Mary, 667.
Bell, Rebecca, 684.
Benedict, Thomas, 674.
Benjamin, Richard, 674.
Bennett, Mary, 659.
Benton, Andrew, 639, 642.
Benton, Ann, 642.
Benton, Edward, 626, 627.
Betts, Ann, 614.
Betts, Hannah, 614.
Betts, Mary, 614, 683.
Betts, Mercy, 614.
Betts, Peter, 614.
Betts, Roger, 614.
Betts, Samuel, 614.
Betts, Thomas, 614, 627, 628, 683.
Biscoe, Nathaniel, 656.
Biscoe, Sarah, 656.
Birdseye, Joanna, 642.
Birdseye, John, 639, 642, 658.
Bishop, Ann, 627, 628, 632.
Bishop, Anna, 632.
Bishop, John, 626, 627, 629, 632.
Bishop, Rev. John, 651.
Bishop, Sarah, 629, 637.
Bishop, Stephen, 627.
Bishop, Susannah, 614.

SUPPLEMENTARY INDEX. 751

Bissell, Abigail, 659.
Blackley, Samuel, 626, 628.
Blakeman, Rev. Aaron, 657.
Blakeman, Mary, 657.
Blakesley, Samuel, 628.
Blatchford, Hannah, 691.
Blatchford, Peter, 691.
Blatchly, Aaron, 607, 608, 614.
Blatchly, Abigail, 614.
Blatchly, Miriam, 614, 615.
Blatchly, Moses, 613, 614.
Blatchly, Susanna, 614.
Blatchly, Thomas, 598, 602, 613, 614, 625.
Blinman, Azrikam, 692.
Blinman, Ezekiel, 692.
Blinman, Jeremiah, 692.
Blinman, Mary, 692.
Blinman, Rev. Richard, 691, 692.
Bliss, Ann, 698*a*.
Bliss, Samuel, 698*a*.
Bliss, Thomas, 698*a*.
Bolt, Francis, 639, 642.
Bolt, Philip, 642.
Bolt, Susanna, 642.
Boosey, Esther, 665.
Boosey, Joseph, 665.
Booth, John, 674.
Booth, Richard, 657.
Booth, Simeon, 665.
Booth, W. S., 657.
Boreman, William, 627, 628.
Bostwick, Arthur, 658, 663.
Bostwick, Ellen, 658, 663.
Bostwick, John, 658.
Bostwick, Joseph, 658.
Bostwick, Zechariah, 658.
Boteler, Alice Apsley, 698*b*.
Botsford, Elizabeth, 642.
Botsford, Henry, 639, 642.
Bourne, Elizabeth, 663.
Bowers, John, 601.
Bowers, Rev. John, 612.
Bowers, Judy, 686.
Bowers, Ruth, 612.
Boyse, Joanna, 651.
Bradfield, Lesly, 620, 624.
Bradfield, Luther, 598, 620.

Bradfield, Maria, 621.
Bradfield, Mary, 621.
Bradfield, Samuel, 621.
Bradlee, Francis, 664.
Bradley, Elizabeth, 635.
Brewster, Daniel, 694.
Brewster, Jonathan, 692.
Brewster, Rev. Nathaniel, 669.
Brinsmade, John, 658.
Brinsmade, Zachariah, 658.
Brinsmade, John, 658.
Briscoe, Abigail, 643.
Briscoe, Elizabeth, 643.
Briscoe, James, 643.
Briscoe, Mehitable, 642.
Briscoe, Nathaniel, 639, 642, 643.
Bristow, Richard, 614, 627.
Bronson, Abraham, 698*d*.
Brooks, Phillips, 657.
Brooks, Robert, 692.
Brooks, William, 639, 643.
Brown, Eleazer, 671.
Brown, Elizabeth, 698*e*.
Brown, John, 643.
Brown, Mary, 643.
Brown, Richard, 674, 675.
Brown, Sarah, 671.
Bruen, Hannah, 692.
Bruen, John, 692.
Bruen, Mary, 640, 692.
Bruen, Obadiah, 640, 692.
Bruen, Rebecca, 692.
Bruen, Sarah, 692.
Bryan, Alexander, 639, 643.
Bryan, Thomas, 643.
Bryant, Alexander, 643, 682.
Buckingham, Hannah, 656.
Buckingham, Rev. Stephen, 644.
Buckingham, Thomas, 639, 643, 656.
Buckingham, Gov. William H., 644.
Buckley, John, 671.
Buckley, Joseph, 671.
Buckley, Thomas, 671.
Budd, John, 674, 675.
Budd, Katherine, 675.
Bull, David, 698*b*.
Bundocke, Captain, 640.
Burgess, Richard, 660.

SUPPLEMENTARY INDEX.

Burr, Aaron, 665.
Burr, Abigail, 665.
Burr, Daniel, 665.
Burr, David, 665.
Burr, Deborah, 665.
Burr, Elizabeth, 665.
Burr, Esther, 665.
Burr, Harriet, 664.
Burr, Capt. Jehu, 665.
Burr, Jehue, 665.
Burr, John, 689.
Burr, Col. John, 665.
Burr, Jonana, 665.
Burr, Jonathan, 665.
Burr, Mary, 665.
Burr, Nathaniel, 665, 689.
Burr, Peter, 665.
Burr, Samuel, 665.
Burr, Sarah, 665.
Burritt, Elizabeth, 658.
Burritt, John, 658, 664.
Burritt, Stephen, 658.
Burritt, William, 658.
Burwell, Alice, 644.
Burwell, Elizabeth, 644.
Burwell, John, 639, 644.
Bushnell, Abigail, 698*a*.
Bushnell, Cornelius S., 628.
Bushnell, David, 628.
Bushnell, Francis, 626, 628, 632, 698*a*.
Bushnell, John, 698*a*.
Bushnell, Joshua, 698*a*.
Bushnell, Judith, 698*a*.
Bushnell, Rebecca, 628, 698*a*.
Bushnell, Samuel, 698*a*.
Bushnell, Sarah, 628, 632.
Bushnell, Stephen, 698*a*.
Bushnell, Thomas, 698*a*.
Bushnell, William, 698*a*.
Butler, Elizabeth, 615.
Butler, Mabel, 622.
Butterfield, Susan, 687.

C.

Cabell, John, 614.
Caffinch, John, 627.
Calkin, Ann, 693.

Calkin, David, 693.
Calkin, Deborah, 693.
Calkin, John, 693.
Calkin, Mary, 693.
Calkin, Rebecca, 693.
Calkin, Sarah, 693.
Calkins, Hugh, 693, 697.
Calkins, Mary, 696.
Camfield, Matthew, 683.
Camp, Abigail, 641, 644.
Camp, Edward, 649.
Camp, Mary, 649.
Camp, Nicholas, 639, 641, 644.
Camp, Nicholas, Jr., 642.
Camp, Samuel, 649.
Camp, Sarah, 644.
Camp, William, 644.
Campe, John, 644.
Canfield, Fred, 645.
Canfield, Thomas, 639, 644, 645.
Carter, Mary, 658.
Carter, Widow, 633.
Case, Henry, 674, 676.
Catlin, John, 641.
Caukin, Henry, 693.
Caulkins, Miss F., 693.
Chalker, Alexander, 627, 628, 698*f*.
Champion, Deborah, 698*b*.
Champion, Henry, 698*b*.
Champion, Mary, 698*b*.
Champion, Sarah, 698*b*.
Champion, Stephen, 698*b*.
Champion, Thomas, 698*b*.
Chapman, F. M., 693.
Chapman, Rev. F. W., 644, 698*b*, 698*f*.
Chapman, Hannah, 698*b*.
Chapman, John, 659.
Chapman, Mary, 698*b*.
Chapman, Robert, 698*a*.
Chapman, Sarah, 698*b*.
Chatfield, Francis, 626, 629.
Chatfield, George, 627, 629, 637.
Chatfield, John, 637.
Chatfield, Mercy, 637.
Chatfield, Thomas, 627, 629, 637.
Chittenden, Johanna, 629.
Chittenden, William, 626, 629.
Church, Ann, 679.

SUPPLEMENTARY INDEX. 753

Church, Edward, 679.
Church, Richard, 679.
Clapham, Isabella, 664.
Clapham, Peter, 664.
Clark, Abigail, 604, 645.
Clark, Hon. Daniel, 645.
Clark, Elizabeth, 618, 698*f*.
Clark, Rev. E. W., 685.
Clark, George, 639, 645.
Clark, George, Jr., 639, 645.
Clark, James, 660.
Clark, John, 596, 645, 646, 698*b*, 698*f*.
Clark, Mary, 645.
Clark, Ruth, 645.
Clark, Samuel, 645, 684, 685.
Clark, Sara, 645.
Clark, Sarah, 645.
Coe, Ann, 685.
Coe, Benjamin, 685.
Coe, John, 659, 685.
Coe, Robert, 685.
Coite, John, 693.
Coite, Joseph, 693.
Coite, Martha, 693.
Coite, Mary, 693.
Coley, Peter, 667.
Collins, John, 602, 609, 633.
Comstock, Daniel, 693.
Condy, William, 696.
Conklyne, John, 674.
Cooe, Robert, 685.
Cook, Thomas, 626.
Cooke, Sarah, 629.
Cooke, Thomas, 629.
Cooley, Martha, 654.
Cooley, Samuel, 639, 645.
Cooper, Abigail, 676.
Cooper, John, 617.
Cooper, Margaret, 676.
Cooper, Maria, 676.
Cooper, Thomas, 674, 676.
Corey, Abraham, 676.
Corey, Ann, 676.
Corey, Isaac, 676.
Corey, Jacob, 676.
Corey, John, 674, 676.
Corwin, Matthias, 674.
Cotton, Capt. Thomas, 698*d*.

Crabb, Richard, 685.
Cragg, Catharine, 658.
Crance, Phebe, 645.
Crane, Azariah, 612.
Crane, Benjamin, 645.
Crane, Delivered, 612.
Crane, Hannah, 612.
Crane, Henry, 645.
Crane, Jasper, 598, 611, 612, 624.
Crane, Jasper, Jr., 611, 612, 619.
Crane, John, 612.
Crane, Mercy, 612.
Crane, Micah, 612.
Croft, Moses, 623.
Cross, John, 684.
Cruttenden, Abraham, 626, 627, 629.
Cruttenden, Abraham, Jr., 627.
Cruttenden, Mary, 627, 629.
Culpepper, Susannah, 616.
Cullick, Elizabeth, 698*b*.
Cullick, John, 698*b*.
Cullick, Capt. John, 698*b*.
Curtis, Caleb, 674, 676.

D.

Dalglish, Robert, 646.
Darcy, Thomas, 605.
Davenport, Grace, 604.
Davenport, Rev. John, 595, 678.
Davenport, John, Jr., 604.
Dennison, Esther, 645.
Dennison, Hannah, 645.
Dennison, James, 646.
Dennison, John, 645.
Dennison, Mary, 646.
Dennison, Robert, 639, 645.
Dennison, Samuel, 645.
Denton, Daniel, 685.
Denton, Rev. Richard, 685.
Desborough, Samuel, 627, 629.
Dickerson, Philemon, 674.
Dimon, Thomas, 674, 676.
Doane, Abigail, 695.
Dod, Daniel, 598, 607, 608, 614.
Dod, Ebenezer, 608.
Dod, Hannah, 608.
Dod, Mary, 607, 608, 614.

48

Dod, Samuel, 608.
Dod, Stephen, 607, 608.
Douglass, Robert, 646, 694.
Dowd, Elizabeth, 630.
Dowd, Henry, 626, 630.
Dudley, Dean, 630.
Dudley, William, 626, 630.
Dudley, Hon. Wm. W., 630.
Dunk, Thomas, 626, 638.

E.

East, Solomon, 646.
East, William, 640, 646, 650.
Eaton, Gov., 602, 652.
Eaton, Samuel, 596.
Eaton, Theophilus, 595, 596.
Edwards, John, 598, 623.
Edwards, Thomas, 623.
Elderkin, Abigail, 693.
Elderkin, Ann, 694.
Elderkin, Bathshea, 694.
Elderkin, D. W., 694.
Elderkin, James, 694.
Elderkin, John, 693, 694.
Elderkin, Joseph, 694.
Elderkin, Pelatiah, 693.
Elton, Ann, 676.
Elton, Hannah, 678.
Elton, John, 674, 676, 678.
Ely, Hiram, 679.
Ely, Martha, 679.
Ely, Nathaniel, 679.
Ely, Richard, 698*b*.
Ely, Ruth, 679.
Ely, Samuel, 679, 681.
England, John, 617.
England, Jonathan, 598.
Evarts, Daniel, 630.
Evarts, Elizabeth, 630.
Evarts, James, 630.
Evarts, John, 627, 630, 631, 635.
Evarts, Judah, 630.

F.

Fairchild, Thomas, 658, 661.
Farnam, Chas. H., 656.

Fenn, Benjamin, 640, 646.
Fenn, Mehitable, 648.
Fenner, Thomas, 598, 618.
Fenwick, Catherine, 698*b*.
Fenwick, Dorothy, 698*b*.
Fenwick, Elizabeth, 698*b*.
Fenwick, Col. George, 698*b*.
Fenwick, Lady, 698*b*.
Fenwick, Mary, 698*b*.
Ferris, James, 685.
Ferris, Jeffrey, 685.
Ferris, Joseph, 685.
Ferris, Peter, 685.
Ferry, Orrin S., 653.
Finch, Daniel, 671, 686.
Finch, Nathaniel, 686.
Fines, Martha, 697.
Fisher, Robert, 686.
Fiske, John, 686.
Fiske, Robert, 686.
Fitch, Ann, 698*c*.
Fitch, Anne Pew, 698*c*.
Fitch, Attorney, 698*c*.
Fitch, Dorothy, 698*c*.
Fitch, Eleazer, 698*c*.
Fitch, Elizabeth, 698*c*.
Fitch, Hannah, 698*c*.
Fitch, Jabez, 698*c*.
Fitch, Rev. James, 637, 681, 698*c*.
Fitch, Jeremiah, 698*c*.
Fitch, John, 682, 698*c*.
Fitch, Joseph, 681, 698*c*.
Fitch, Nathanie, 698*c*.
Fitch, Samuel, 643, 682, 698*c*.
Fitch, Mrs. Samuel, 643.
Fitch, Sarah, 665.
Fitch, Thomas, 645, 681, 682, 698*c*.
Fitch, Capt. Thomas, 665.
Fletcher, E. H., 646.
Fletcher, John, 640, 646.
Fletcher, Samuel, 646.
Foot, Stephen, 622.
Forbes, Caleb, 694.
Ford, Elizabeth, 669.
Ford, Lydia, 647.
Ford, Thomas, 640, 647, 669.
Fordham, Hannah, 684.
Fordham, Rev. Robert, 684.

SUPPLEMENTARY INDEX. 755

Forster, Thomas, 696.
Forth, Mary, 697.
Fowler, Abraham, 631.
Fowler, John, 627, 630, 631, 639, 647, 649.
Fowler, Mehitable, 630, 647.
Fowler, Sarah, 654.
Fowler, Lieut. William, 640, 647, 654, 655.
Fowler, William, Jr., 640, 647.
Freeman, Hannah, 648.
Freeman, Martha, 648.
Freeman, Mary, 648.
Freeman, Samuel, 648.
Freeman, Sarah, 648.
Freeman, Stephen, 648.
French, Ebenezer, 631.
French, John, 631.
French, Mary, 631.
French, Thomas, 626, 631.
Frior, Thomas, 650.
Frisbie, Abigail, 612.
Frisbie, Benoni, 612.
Frisbie, Caleb, 613.
Frisbie, Ebenezer, 613.
Frisbie, Edward, 598, 612.
Frisbie, Hannah, 612, 613.
Frisbie, John, 612, 623.
Frisbie, Jonathan, 612.
Frisbie, Josiah, 613.
Frisbie, Samuel, 612.
Frisbie, Silence, 613.
Frost, Abraham, 666.
Frost, Daniel, 664, 665, 666.
Frost, Elizabeth, 664, 666.
Frost, Esther, 665.
Frost, Hannah, 665.
Frost, Lydia, 666.
Frost, Rachel, 665.
Frost, Rebecca, 665.
Frost, Sarah, 665.
Frost, William, 665, 666, 670.

G.

Gager, Bethia, 694.
Gager, Elizabeth, 694.
Gager, Hannah, 694.
Gager, John, 694.
Gager, Lydia, 694.
Gager, Mary, 694.
Gager, Samuel, 694.
Gager, Sarah, 694.
Gager, William, 694.
Gardiner, Curtiss C., 698*d*.
Gardiner, David, 698*c*.
Gardiner, Elizabeth, 698*c*.
Gardiner, Lion, 610, 698*c*.
Gardiner, Mary, 698*c*.
Gaylord, Elizabeth D., 693.
Gaylord, William, 694.
Gibbard, William, 655.
Gilbert, Benjamin, 666.
Gilbert, John, 666.
Gilbert, Joseph, 666.
Gilbert, Obadiah, 666.
Gilbert, William, 666.
Gildersleeve, Richard, 686.
Gillet, Josiah, 622.
Gillett, Rev. T. P., 602.
Glover, Charles, 674.
Gold, Nathan, 649.
Goldsmith, Ralph, 674, 676.
Goodrich, Richard, 631.
Goodwin, George, 666.
Goodwin, Thomas, 654.
Goodyear, Margaret L., 638.
Graves, Isaac, 679.
Graves, Philip, 658.
Green, Hannah, 666.
Green, John, 666.
Greenstack, Jane, 691.
Gregory, Henry, 658.
Gregson, Thomas, 602.
Grey, Henry, 666.
Grey, John, 666.
Griswold, Ann, 698*d*.
Griswold, Edward, 698*d*.
Griswold, Elizabeth, 698*d*.
Griswold, John, 698*d*.
Griswold, Lt. Matthew, 698*d*.
Griswold, Samuel, 698*d*.
Griswold, Sarah, 698*d*.
Grover, Simon, 674, 676.
Gunn, Abel, 648.
Gunn, Ann, 648.

756 SUPPLEMENTARY INDEX.

Gunn, Daniel, 648.
Gunn, Dr. Jasper, 639, 648.
Gunn, Jobama, 648.
Gunn, Samuel, 648.
Gutridge, Richard, 626, 631.

H.

Haines, James, 674, 677.
Hale, Thomas, 680.
Hales, Thomas, 680.
Hall, Esther, 631.
Hall, Highland, 631.
Hall, John, 631, 632.
Hall, Rebecca, 668.
Hall, Samuel, 632.
Hall, Thomas, 629.
Hall, Capt. Thomas, 631.
Hall, William, 626, 631.
Halle, Francis, 624.
Halleck, Fitz-Greene, 677.
Halleck, Gen. H. W., 677.
Halleck, Rev. W. A., 677.
Halliock, Peter, 677.
Hallock, Peter, 674, 677.
Hallock, William, 677.
Hanaford, Rev. Thomas, 682.
Harrison, Ann, 620.
Harrison, Benjamin, 619, 620.
Harrison, Elizabeth, 620.
Harrison, George, 620.
Harrison, Henry Baldwin, 619.
Harrison, John, 620.
Harrison, Joseph, 617.
Harrison, Maria, 605, 619.
Harrison, Mary, 620.
Harrison, Nathaniel, 613, 619, 620.
Harrison, Richard, 598, 602, 605, 619.
Harrison, Richard, Jr., 619, 620.
Harrison, Samuel, 617, 620.
Harrison, Sarah, 619.
Harrison, Thomas, 619, 620.
Harvey, Edmund, 639, 648, 666.
Harvey, Edward, 648.
Harvey, Elizabeth, 659.
Harvey, Hannah, 649.
Harvey, Josiah, 648, 671.
Harvey, Martha, 648.

Harvey, Mary, 659.
Harvey, Richard, 659, 663.
Harvey, Sarah, 659.
Haslerigg, Sir Arthur, 698*b*.
Haslerigg, Catherine, 698*b*.
Hatley, Philip, 639, 649.
Hawkins, Hannah, 644.
Hawkins, Mary, 667.
Hawkins, Robert, 667.
Hawley, Catharine, 659.
Hawley, Dr. Elias, 659.
Hawley, Elizabeth, 657, 659.
Hawley, Grace, 648, 653.
Hawley, Hannah, 659.
Hawley, Joseph, 648, 653, 657, 659.
Hawley, Mary, 659.
Hayes, Chas. Wells, 678.
Hayes, Rev. C. W., 682.
Hayes, Elizabeth, 682.
Hayes, Mary, 682.
Hayes, Nathaniel, 682.
Hempstead, Ann, 694, 695.
Hempstead, Hannah, 694.
Hempstead, Joshua, 694.
Hempstead, Mary, 694.
Hempstead, Robert, 694, 695.
Herbert, John, 674.
Herrick, Martha T., 656.
Hewitt, Lucy M., 593.
Hide, Ann, 667.
Hide, Hannah, 667.
Hide, Humphrey, 667.
Hide, John, 667.
Hide, Sarah, 667.
Higby, Edward, 661.
Higginson, Ann, 629, 637.
Higginson, Rev. Francis, 629, 631, 637.
Higginson, Rev. John, 627, 631, 637.
Highland, George, 626, 631.
Highland, Mary, 631.
Hill, Adeline, 635.
Hill, Elizabeth, 667, 668.
Hill, Esther, 667.
Hill, Frances, 623.
Hill, Ignatius, 667.
Hill, James, 667.
Hill, John, 598, 623, 628.

SUPPLEMENTARY INDEX. 757

Hill, Joseph, 667.
Hill, Robert, 635.
Hill, Sarah, 667.
Hill, William, Sr., 667.
Hill, William, Jr., 667.
Hills, John, 698*f*.
Hine, Robert C., 649.
Hine, Thomas, 649.
Hitchcocke, Mathias, 624.
Hoadley, John, 626, 632.
Hoadley, Rev. John, 628.
Hoadley, William, Jr., 612.
Holloway, John, 680.
Hooker, Rev. Thomas, 698*c*.
Hopkins, Edward, 605.
Horton, Barnabas, 674.
Hosmer, Thomas, 654.
Hough, William, 693.
Howand, Thomas, 697.
Howell, G. R., 680.
Hoyt, Benjamin, 667.
Hoyt, Joshua, 667, 684.
Hoyt, Mary, 684.
Hoyt, Simon, 667.
Hubbard, George, 627, 630, 632, 639, 647, 649.
Hubbard, Mary, 630, 632, 647.
Hughes, John, 626, 632.
Hughes, Mary, 632, 636.
Hughes, Richard, 627, 632, 636.
Hughes, Samuel, 632.
Hunt, Mrs. Clement H., 654.
Hunt, Jonathan, 654.
Huntington, Ann, 698*d*.
Huntington, Christopher, 698*d*.
Huntington, Rev. E. B., 695, 698*d*.
Huntington, John, 698*d*.
Huntington, Joseph, 698*d*.
Huntington, Lydia, 698*d*.
Huntington, Mrs. Margaret, 698*d*.
Huntington, Ruth, 698*d*.
Huntington, Simon, 694, 698*d*.
Huntington, Susanna, 698*d*.
Huntington, Thomas, 612, 698*d*.
Hurd, John, 659.
Hyde, Esther, 698*e*.
Hyde, Humphrey, 667.
Hyde, John, 659.

Hyde, Samuel, 698*d*.
Hyde, William, 698*d*.
Hyland, George, 631.

I.

Ince, Jonathan, 682.
Ince, Mary Miles, 682.
Isbell, Ann, 695.
Isbell, Isaac, 694.
Isbell, Robert, 694, 695.

J.

Jagger, Captain, 621.
Jagger, Elizabeth, 686.
Jagger, John, 686.
Jagger, Jonathan, 686.
Jagger, Jeremiah, 686.
Jagger, Jeremy, 686.
James, Ruth, 668.
Jeffreys, Thomas, 659.
Jennings, Joseph, 671.
Jessop, John, 686.
Jessop, Joseph, 686.
Jessup, Rev. H. G., 687.
Johnson, Abigail, 633.
Johnson, Eliphalet, 617.
Johnson, Elizabeth, 667.
Johnson, Col. Ebenezer, 668.
Johnson, Isaac, 633.
Johnson, John, 626, 633, 635, 668.
Johnson, Joseph, 604.
Johnson. Mary, 678.
Johnson, Moses, 667, 668.
Johnson, Nathaniel, 606.
Johnson, Peter, 667.
Johnson, Ruth, 633.
Johnson, Thomas, 611, 668.
Jones, Eliphalet, 668.
Jones, Elizabeth, 668.
Jones, John, 668.
Jones, Rev. John, 668.
Jones, Mary, 633.
Jones, Nathaniel, 633.
Jones, Rebecca, 668.
Jones, Ruth, 668.
Jones, Samuel, 668.

SUPPLEMENTARY INDEX.

Jones, Sarah, 633, 668.
Jones, Susanna, 668.
Jones, Theophilus, 668.
Jones, Thomas, 626, 633, 668.
Jordan, Elizabeth, 633.
Jordan, John, 626, 632, 633.
Jordan, Thomas, 627, 633.
Joy, Jacob, 697.
Judd, Thomas, 648.
Judson, Grace, 659.
Judson, Jeremiah, 659.
Judson, Joseph, 659.
Judson, Joshua, 659.
Judson, William, 659.

K.

Keller, Ralph, 671, 680.
Keeney, Susannah, 696.
Keeney, William, 696.
Kilbourne, Frances, 662.
Kilbourne, Margaret, 687.
Kilbourne, Thomas, 687.
Kimberley, Mary, 682.
Kimberley, Thomas, 682.
King, Samuel, 674, 677.
Kingman, L. W., 694.
Kingsworth, Henry, 626, 633.
Kitchell, Abigail, 617.
Kitchell, Robert, 626, 633.
Kitchell, Samuel, 604, 633.
Knell, Isaac, 660.
Knell, John, 660.
Knell, Nicholas, 659.
Knowles, Alexander, 647, 668, 671.
Knowles, Elizabeth, 647, 660.
Knowles, Elizabeth N., 659.
Knowles, John, 660.
Knowles, Joshua, 669.
Knowles, Thomas, 660.

L.

Lamberton, Mrs. George, 638.
Lampson, Eleazar, 611.
Lane, Isaac, 649.
Lane, John, 639, 649.
Lane, Kattareen, 649.

Larrabee, Elizabeth, 698*e*.
Larrabee, Greenfield, 698*e*.
Larrabee, John, 698*e*.
Larrabee, Joseph, 698*e*.
Larrabee, Sarah, 698*e*.
Launce, Mary, 605, 652.
Law, Abigail, 687.
Law, Jonathan, 687.
Law, Gov. Jonathan, 645.
Law, Richard, 687.
Law, Sarah, 687.
Lawrence, Bothia, 623.
Lawrence, Ebenezer, 623.
Lawrence, Edward, 623.
Lawrence, Esther, 623.
Lawrence, Richard, 598, 607, 623.
Lawrence, Sarah, 623.
Lawrence, Thomas, 639, 649.
Lay, Abigail, 698*e*.
Lay, Elizabeth, 698*e*.
Lay, James, 698*e*.
Lay, John, 698*e*.
Lay, Peter, 698*e*.
Lay, Susanna, 698*e*.
Lee, Jane, 698*e*.
Lee, Thomas, 698*e*.
Leete, Andrew, 633.
Leete, Ann, 634.
Leete, Governor, 612.
Leete, John, 634.
Leete, William, 626, 633, 634.
Leffingwell, Jonathan, 698*e*.
Leffingwell, Joseph, 698*e*.
Leffingwell, Mary, 698*e*.
Leffingwell, Nathaniel, 698*e*.
Leffingwell, Rachel, 698*e*.
Leffingwell, Lt. Thomas, 698*e*.
Leonard, Hannah, 685.
Leonard, John, 685.
Lester, Andrew, 695.
Lester, Ann, 695.
Lester, Barbara, 695.
Lester, Benjamin, 695.
Lester, Daniel, 695.
Lester, Joseph, 695.
Lester, Mary, 695.
Lester, Timothy, 695.
Lewis, John, 695.

SUPPLEMENTARY INDEX. 759

Limon, John, 607.
Lindon, Hannah, 629.
Linsley, Benjamin, 616.
Linsley, Bethia, 616.
Linsley, Debora, 616.
Linsley, Ellen, 615.
Linsley, Francis, 598, 615, 616.
Linsley, John, 598, 615, 616, 620, 627, 634.
Linsley, John, Jr., 615.
Linsley, Ruth, 616.
Linsley, Thomas, 625.
Lister, Andrew, 694, 695.
Lister, Barbara, 694.
Lockwood, Mary, 685.
Lockwood, Robert, 686.
Lockwood, Susannah, 686.
Loomis, Joseph, 667.
Loomis, Mary, 622.
Loomis, Samuel, 682.
Lord, Ann, 697.
Lord, Jane, 680.
Lord, John, 698a.
Lord, Thomas, 697.
Lothrop, Ann, 695.
Lothrop, Elizabeth, 695.
Lothrop, Israel, 695.
Lothrop, John, 695.
Lothrop, Rev. John, 695.
Lothrop, Joseph, 695.
Lothrop, Samuel, 695.
Ludlow, Dep.-Gov., 671.
Ludlow, Roger, 610, 669.
Ludlow, Sarah, 669.
Lumis, Samuel, 682.
Lupton, Thomas, 598, 625.
Lutman, Jane, 630.
Lyon, Henry, 617, 639, 650.

M.

Malbon, Mary, 670,
Malbon, Richard, 670.
Mapes, Thomas, 674, 677.
Marvin, Abigail, 680.
Marvin, Elizabeth, 680.
Marvin, Hannah, 680.
Marvin, Mary, 680, 698e.

Marvin, Matthew, 680, 698e.
Marvin, Rachel, 680.
Marvin, Reynold, 698e.
Marvin, Capt. Reynold, 645.
Marvin, Samuel, 680.
Marvin, Sarah, 680.
Marvin, T. R., 680, 698e.
Mason, Major John, 698c, 698e.
Mason, Priscilla, 698c.
Mather, Rev. Cotton, 698c.
Mather, Richard, 598, 625.
Meeker, Robert, 598, 624.
Megs, Goodman, 624, 625.
Mepham, John, 626, 634, 641.
Mepham, Mary, 641.
Merchant, William, 598, 625.
Miles, Richard, 682.
Mills, Thomas, 627.
Minor, Clement, 697.
Mitchell, David, 687.
Mitchell, Dr., 687.
Mitchell, Hannah, 687.
Mitchell, Jonathan, 687.
Mitchell, Matthew, 698f.
Mitchell, Maj. Matthew, 685, 687, 688.
Mitchell, Sarah, 687, 688.
Mitchell, Susan, 687.
Mitchell, Susannah, 685.
Moore, Abel, 694.
Moore, Sergt. Isaac, 682.
Moore, Thomas, 674.
Moore, William, 697.
More, Ruth, 618.
Morehouse, John, 669.
Morehouse, Jonathan, 669.
Morehouse, Lieut. Samuel, 669, 687.
Morehouse, Thomas, 669, 686, 687.
Morris, Thomas, 598, 625.
Morton, William, 695.
Mould, Hugh, 693.
Mulliner, Elizabeth, 606.
Mulliner, Thomas, 606.

N.

Nash, Edward, 664, 683.
Nash, Hannah, 683.
Nash, John, 600, 683.

Nash, Lt. John, 655.
Nash, Thomas, 626, 634.
Nettleton, Hannah, 625.
Nettleton, Isabel, 629, 637.
Nettleton, Maria, 625.
Nettleton, Samuel, 598, 624, 629, 637.
Newberry, Hannah, 682.
Newman, Francis, 634.
Newman, Gov. Francis, 660.
Newton, John, 647.
Newton, Rev. Roger, 647.
Newton, Thomas, 670.
Nicolls, W. J., 660, 695.
Nichols, Elizabeth, 670.
Nichols, Esther, 670.
Nichols, Francis, 670.
Nichols, Hannah, 670.
Nichols, Isaac, 670.
Nichols, John, 670.
Nichols, Joseph, 659.
Nichols, Samuel, 670.
Nichols, Sarah, 670.
Nichols, William, 695.
Nicholls, Anne, 660.
Nicholls, Caleb, 660, 689.
Nicholls, Francis, 660.
Nicholls, Grace, 670.
Nicholls, Isaac, 660.
Nicholls, John, 660.
North, Samuel, 618.
North, Thomas, 638.
Northam, Isabel, 641.
Northam, James, 641.
Northend, John, 688.
Norton, Abigail, 635.
Norton, Ann, 635.
Norton, Dorothy, 618.
Norton, Elizabeth, 618.
Norton, Grace, 635.
Norton, Hannah, 618.
Norton, John, 598, 618, 634.
Norton, Mary, 635.
Norton, Richard, 618.
Norton, Samuel, 618.
Norton, Thomas, 618, 626, 634.

O.

Odell, Rebecca, 669.
Odell, William, 669.
Offitt, Thomas, 662.
Ogden, David, 611.
Olliver, William, 689.
Olmstead, Elizabeth, 656.
Olmstead, Francis, 664.
Olmstead, James, 680.
Olmstead, John, 680.
Olmstead, Nathaniel, 666.
Olmstead, Lt. Richard, 680.
Olmstead, Sarah, 666.
Osborn, Sarah, 660.

P.

Paine, Peter, 674, 677.
Palmer, Daniel, 615.
Palmer, Elizabeth, 615.
Palmer, John, 615.
Palmer, Joshua, 615.
Palmer, Mary, 615.
Palmer, Micah, 615.
Palmer, Michael, 615.
Palmer, William, 598, 614, 615.
Parke, Ann, 696.
Parke, Robert, 696.
Parke, Samuel, 696.
Parke, Thomas, 696.
Parke, William, 692, 696.
Parker, David, 698*f*.
Parker, Edward, 609.
Parker, Hannah, 696.
Parker, John, 609, 698*f*.
Parker, Jonathan, 696, 698*f*.
Parker, Joseph, 698*f*.
Parker, Margaret, 698*f*.
Parker, Margery, 698*f*.
Parker, Mary, 696.
Parker, Mehitable, 696.
Parker, Ralph, 696.
Parker, Rebecca, 696, 698*f*.
Parker, Robert, 696.
Parker, Ruth, 698*f*.
Parker, Sarah, 698*f*.
Parker, Susannah, 696.

SUPPLEMENTARY INDEX. 761

Parker, T., 696.
Parker, Thomas, 696.
Parker, William, 698*f.*
Parmalee, John, 635.
Parmalee, Spencer T., 635.
Parmelee, Elizabeth, 630, 635.
Parmelee, Hannah, 635.
Parmelee, John, 630, 635.
Parmelin, John, 626, 635.
Parmelin, John, Jr., 627, 635.
Parmily, John, 635.
Patterson, Albert Clark, 645.
Payson, Edward, 696.
Peacocke, Deborah, 660.
Peacocke, John, 650, 660.
Peacocke, Joyce, 660.
Peacocke, Mary, 660.
Peacocke, Phebe, 660.
Peake, Benjamin, 660.
Peake, John, 660.
Peake, Mary, 660.
Peat, John, 660.
Peck, Hannah, 633.
Peck, Isabel, 698*f.*
Peck, Isabella, 698*c.*
Peck, Joseph, 648.
Peck, Priscilla, 698*f.*
Pendall, William, 696.
Permely, John, 635.
Perry, Grace, 670.
Perry, John, 670.
Perry, Mary, 670.
Perry, Micajah, 670.
Perry, Richard, 670.
Perry, Samuel, 670.
Petersfield, Philip, 638.
Phipper, Dorcas, 616.
Philips, Rev. George, 605.
Pierson, Abigail, 604.
Pierson, Rev. Abraham, 599, 601, 603, 604, 619, 622, 645.
Pierson, Rev. Abraham, Jr., 604.
Pierson, Grace, 604.
Pierson, Isaac, 604.
Pierson, John, 604.
Pierson, Mary, 604.
Pierson, Rebecca, 604.
Pierson, Susanna, 604.

Pierson, Theophilus, 604.
Pierson, Thomas, 604, 619, 622.
Plane, William, 626, 635.
Platt, Isaac, 650.
Platt, John, 650.
Platt, Lewis, 650.
Platt, Mary, 650.
Platt, Richard, 639, 650.
Platt, Sarah, 650.
Platt, Thomas C., 650.
Plum, Dorcas, 607.
Plum, John, 597, 607, 622.
Plum, Robert, 639.
Plumb, H. B., 650.
Plumb, John, 618, 650.
Plumb, P. B., 650.
Plumb, Mary, 646, 650.
Plumb, Robert, 646, 650.
Pocock, John, 639, 650.
Pond, Benjamin, 616.
Pond, Elizabeth, 616.
Pond, Hannah, 616.
Pond, Jonathan, 616.
Pond, Lt.-Gov., 614.
Pond, Mary, 616.
Pond, N. G., 648.
Pond, Samuel, 614, 615.
Pond, Sarah, 615, 616.
Porter, Robert, 648.
Post, Abraham, 698*f.*
Post, Catherine, 628, 698*f.*
Post, John, 698*e*, 698*f.*
Post, Stephen, 628, 698*f.*
Post, Thomas, 692, 698*f.*
Potter, Elizabeth, 609.
Potter, Hannah, 628.
Potter, John, 609.
Pratt, Elizabeth, 698*f.*
Pratt, John, 633, 698*f.*
Pratt, Joseph, 698*b*, 698*f.*
Pratt, Lydia, 698*f.*
Pratt, Mary, 698*f.*
Pratt, Nathaniel, 698*f.*
Pratt, Peter, 698*d.*
Pratt, Samuel, 698*d*, 698*f.*
Pratt, Sarah, 698*f.*
Pratt, Lt. William, 698*f.*
Prentiss, John, 696.

Preston, William, 661.
Price, Mary, 638.
Price, William, 638.
Prichard, Roger, 653.
Prime, E. D. G., 650.
Prime, James, 650.
Prime, Rebecca, 650.
Prime, Sarah, 650.
Prudden, Ann, 651.
Prudden, Elizabeth, 651, 653.
Prudden, James, 639, 650, 653.
Prudden, Rev. John, 651.
Prudden, Rev. Peter, 643, 646, 650, 651, 653.
Prudden, Rev. Roger, 639,
Prudden, Samuel, 651.
Purdy, Francis, 670.
Purdy, Mary, 670,
Purrier, Sarah, 677.
Purrier, William, 674, 677.
Pyne, Ann, 681.

Q.

Quinny, Mary T., 656.

R.

Raiment, John, 683.
Raiment, Capt. Richard, 683.
Rainor, Elizabeth, 688.
Rainor, Jonathan, 688.
Rainor, Joseph, 688.
Rainor, Lydia, 688.
Rainor, Martha, 688.
Rainor, Sarah, 688.
Rainor, Thurston, 688.
Rawlings, Richard, 667.
Raymond, Henry, 683.
Raymond, M. D., 666.
Raymond, Richard, 683.
Raymond, Samuel, 683.
Rayner, Thurston, 688.
Reader, John, 660.
Reed, Thomas, 651.
Reeve, James, 674, 677.
Reif, Thomas, 627.
Relfe, Elizabeth, 633.

Relfe, Thomas, 633.
Reynolds, John, 688.
Reynolds, Jonathan, 688.
Reynolds, Sarah, 688.
Rice, Robert, 661.
Richalls, Sigismond, 698, 624.
Richards, Thomas, 598.
Rider, Elizabeth, 676.
Rider, Thomas, 676.
Riggs, Edward, 639, 651.
Riggs, Elizabeth, 651.
Riggs, Joseph, 651.
Riggs, Mary, 651.
Riggs, Samuel, 651.
Riley, Mary, 660.
Ripley, Jeremiah, 694.
Roberts, Hugh, 693, 696.
Roberts, Mary, 697.
Roberts, Mehitable, 697.
Roberts, Samuel, 697.
Roberts, William, 651.
Robins, John, 613.
Rockwell, Ruth, 698*d*.
Rockwell, William, 698*d*.
Rogers, Eliezer, 647.
Rogers, Henry, 601.
Rogers, James, 652.
Rogers, John, 617, 639, 652, 698*d*.
Rogers, Noah, 621, 622.
Roosa, Elizabeth, 651.
Rose, Daniel, 609.
Rose, Dorcas, 609.
Rose, Elizabeth, 609, 621, 622.
Rose, Hannah, 608, 609, 618.
Rose, John, 609.
Rose, Jonathan, 608, 609.
Rose, Margery, 608.
Rose, Mary, 609.
Rose, Robert, 598, 607, 608, 609, 611, 621.
Rose, Samuel, 609.
Rose, Sarah, 609.
Rowe, Matthew, 613.
Rowland, Elizabeth, 652.
Rowland, Henry, 652.
Rowley, Ellen, 618.
Royce, Jonathan, 693.
Rumble, Thomas, 683.

SUPPLEMENTARY INDEX.

Rumsey, Robert, 665.
Ruscoe, John, 680, 681.
Ruscoe, Nathaniel, 681.
Ruscoe, Rebecca, 680.
Ruscoe, Thomas, 681.
Ruscoe, William, 680.
Russell, Capt., 626.
Rutherford, Henry, 634.
Rutherford, Sarah, 634.

S.

Sanford, Edward, 652.
Sanford, Elizabeth, 652.
Sanford, Ephraim, 652.
Sanford, Ezekiel, 652.
Sanford, Mary, 652.
Sanford, Samuel, 652.
Sanford, Sarah, 652.
Sanford, Thomas, 639, 652.
Sargent, Jonathan, 617.
Sargent, Thomas, 598.
Scranton, Joanna, 635.
Scranton, John, 627, 635.
Scranton, Sarah, 635.
Scranton, Thomas, 635.
Scudder, Elizabeth, 695.
Seabrook, Alice, 661.
Seabrook, Faith, 658.
Seabrook, Robert, 661.
Seaman, John, 688.
Seargent, Hannah, 620.
Seargent, John, 620.
Seargent, Jonathan, 620.
Seargent, Thomas, 620.
Seely, John, 670.
Sellick, Jonathan, 687.
Sellick, Maj. Jonathan, 687.
Sevearsmith, Nicholas S., 655.
Seward, Edward, 627, 635.
Seward, Lieut. William, 635.
Seymour, Mary, 681.
Seymour, Mercy, 681.
Seymour, Richard, 681.
Sill, Capt. Joseph, 645.
Simkins, Daniel, 689.
Simkins, John, 689.
Simkins, Vincent, 689.

Simpkins, Vincent, 689.
Sheader, John, 627, 636.
Sheader, Samuel, 635.
Sheafe, Jacob, 627, 636.
Sheaffe, Joan, 629.
Sheaffe, Joanna, 636.
Sheaffe, Margaret, 633.
Sheather, John, 635.
Shepard, Rev. Thomas, 668.
Sherman, Abiah, 600.
Sherman, Abigail, 606.
Sherman, Barren, 606.
Sherman, Bezaleel, 606.
Sherman, Daniel, 606.
Sherman, Edmund, 605.
Sherman, Elizabeth, 606, 671.
Sherman, Grace, 606.
Sherman, Hester, 606.
Sherman, James, 606.
Sherman, John, 606, 683.
Sherman, Rev. John, 598, 599, 605, 606, 639, 652.
Sherman, Mary, 606, 652.
Sherman, Mercy, 606.
Sherman, Samuel, 606, 662, 688.
Sherman, Gen. W. T., 683.
Sherwood, Abigail, 661.
Sherwood, Ann, 661.
Sherwood, Isaac, 661.
Sherwood, Margery, 661.
Sherwood, Mary, 661.
Sherwood, Matthew, 661.
Sherwood, Rebecca, 661.
Sherwood, Rose, 661.
Sherwood, Ruth, 661.
Sherwood, Stephen, 661.
Sherwood, Tamsen, 661.
Sherwood, Thomas, 661.
Shethar, John, 697.
Skidmore, Ellen, 661.
Skidmore, Richard, 674, 677.
Skidmore, Sarah, 661.
Skidmore, Thomas, 661.
Slough, Hadidiah, 653.
Slough, James, 653.
Slough, William, 637, 653.
Smith, Charles S., 636.
Smith, Columbus, 657.

Smith, Dorothy, 682.
Smith, Ephraim, 653.
Smith, Hannah, 689.
Smith, Henry, 689.
Smith, Rev. Henry, 682.
Smith, John, 648, 653.
Smith, John, Sr., 639, 653.
Smith, Joseph, 689.
Smith, Mary, 658.
Smith, Rebecca, 689.
Smith, Robt. A., 593.
Smith, Samuel, 665.
Smith, Walter, 650.
Smith, Winthrop B., 653.
Smith, Mrs. John, 648.
Smyth, Prudence, 677.
Smyth, Robert, 674, 677.
Somers, William, 627, 636.
Spencer, Elizabeth, 697.
Spencer, Jared, 691.
Spencer, Samuel, 691.
Spencer, Thomas, 681.
Spencer, William, 697.
Sprague, William, 667.
Squires, George, 670.
Squires, John, 670.
Squires, Jonathan, 670.
Squires, Samuel, 670.
Squires, Sarah, 670.
Squires, Thomas, 670.
Stanley, John, 682.
Stanley, Ruth, 682.
Stanton, Thomas, 697.
Stanton, W. A., 697.
Staples, John, 671.
Staples, Mary, 671.
Staples, Mehitable, 671.
Staples, Thomas, 671.
Stedman, Elizabeth, 638.
Steele, John, 681.
Stent, Eleazar, 621.
Stent, Elizabeth, 620.
Stevens, John, 627, 633, 693.
Stevens, Mary, 633.
Stevens, Sarah, 608.
Stevens, Thomas, 627.
Stillwell, Jasper, 627.
Stone, Hannah, 636.

Stone, John, 626, 636.
Stone, Mary, 636.
Stone, William, 626, 632, 636.
Stonhill, Henry, 639, 654.
Stoughton, Lt. Thomas, 698*d*.
Stream, John, 639, 642, 654.
Street, Mary, 634.
Street, Rev. Nicholas, 634.
Sturgess, John, 664.
Sturgess, Susannah, 664.
Stuyvesant, Gov., 670.
Swaine, Abigail, 611.
Swaine, Christiana, 611, 617.
Swaine, Daniel, 597, 609, 611.
Swaine, Debora, 611.
Swaine, Dorcas, 611, 622.
Swaine, Elizabeth, 611.
Swaine, Joanna, 611, 612.
Swaine, John, 611.
Swaine, Jonathan, 611.
Swaine, Phebe, 611.
Swaine, Mary, 610, 611.
Swaine, Samuel, 597, 599, 600, 609, 610, 611.
Swaine, Sarah, 611.
Swaine, William, 597, 610.
Swayne, Samuel, 606.
Swazey, Joseph, 677.
Swazey, Richard, 674, 677.

T.

Taintor, Charles, 621, 622, 664.
Taintor, Charles, Jr., 622.
Taintor, Elizabeth, 622.
Taintor, Johanna, 622.
Taintor, John, 611, 621, 622.
Taintor, Joseph, 622.
Taintor, Marie, 622.
Taintor, Mary, 664.
Taintor, Michael, 602, 609, 621, 622.
Taintor, Sarie, 622.
Talcott, Dr. Alvan, 629.
Tapp, Ann, 655.
Tapp, Edmund, 639, 647, 655.
Tapp, Elizabeth, 655.
Tapp, Mary, 647, 655.
Tapping, Elnathan, 655.

SUPPLEMENTARY INDEX.

Tapping, Mrs. Elnathan, 676.
Tapping, Emma, 655.
Tapping, James, 655.
Tapping, Lydia Wilford, 623.
Tapping, Thomas, 634.
Tapping, Capt. Thomas, 639, 655.
Taylor, Mary, 664.
Terrill, Roger, 640, 662.
Terry, Richard, 674.
Thomas, E. J., 680.
Thompson, Anthony, 644.
Thompson, Elizabeth, 671, 686.
Thompson, Esther, 671.
Thompson, John, 620, 659, 661, 671, 686.
Thompson, Kattern, 644.
Thompson, Mary, 620, 671.
Thompson, Mirabel, 661.
Thompson, Sarah, 659.
Thornton, J. W., 666.
Thorp, John, 665.
Tibballs, Abigail, 654.
Tibballs, John, 655.
Tibballs, Mary, 654, 655.
Tibballs, Mercy, 654.
Tibballs, Samuel, 654.
Tibballs, Thomas, 640, 654.
Tilley, Edith, 644.
Tilley, John, 644.
Titterton, Daniel, 661.
Titterton, Elizabeth, 662.
Titterton, Jane, 662.
Titterton, Mary, 662.
Titterton, Samuel, 662.
Titterton, Timothy, 662.
Todd, Charles B., 665.
Tomkins, Micah, 640, 656.
Tomlinson, Alice, 642, 658.
Tomlinson, Henry, 642, 663.
Tompkins, Mary, 655.
Tompson, Alice, 696.
Tompson, Anthony, 696.
Tompson, John, 696.
Tompson, William, 696.
Topping, Thomas, 623.
Treat, John H., 655.
Treat, Mary, 612.
Treat, Richard, 683.
Treat, Robert, 612.

Treat, Gov. Robert, 612, 655.
Treat, Sarah, 683.
Treadwell, Edward, 598.
Tredwell, Edward, 618.
Tredwell, Samuel, 618.
Tuberfield, Susan, 624.
Tucker, Charles, 678.
Tucker, Hannah, 678.
Tucker, John, 674, 678.
Tucker, Joseph, 678.
Tucker, Ruth, 678.
Turney, Benjamin, 671.
Turney, Elizabeth, 671.
Turney, Martha, 671.
Turney, Mary, 671.
Turney, Rebecca, 671.
Turney, Capt. Robert, 671.
Turney, Ruth, 671.
Tuttle, Bridget, 678.
Tuttle, George F., 684.
Tuttle, Henry, 678.
Tuttle, John, 649, 674.
Tuttle, Jonathan, 684.
Tuttle, Rebecca, 684.
Tyler, Peter, 624.
Tyrrell, Roger, 656.

U.

Uffort, Isabel, 662.
Uffort, John, 662.
Uffort, Thomas, 662.
Uffort, Thomas, Jr., 662.
Uncas, 607.
Usher, Robert, 686.

V.

Vaill, Jeremiah, 674.

W.

Walworth, R. H., 698e.
Ward, A. H., 661.
Ward, Abigail, 689.
Ward, Andrew, 610, 665, 689.
Ward, Ann, 689.

Ward, Deborah, 617.
Ward, Dorcas, 617.
Ward, Edmund, 689.
Ward, Elizabeth, 617.
Ward, Esther, 689.
Ward, George, 598, 616, 617.
Ward, Hannah, 617.
Ward, John, 598, 617, 689.
Ward, Josiah, 611, 617.
Ward, Joyce, 617.
Ward, Lawrence, 598, 600, 607, 609, 616, 617.
Ward, Phebe, 617.
Ward, Mary, 617, 646, 665, 689.
Ward, Nathaniel, 611, 617.
Ward, Samuel, 617, 689.
Ward, Sarah, 617, 689.
Ward, William, 689.
Wakelee, Henry, 662.
Wakeley, Deliverance, 683.
Wakeley, Henry, 683.
Wakeman, Mary, 665.
Walkerlee, James, 662.
Walkerlee, Henry, 662.
Warriner, Elizabeth, 641.
Warriner, William, 641.
Watson, Elizabeth F., 666.
Watson, John, 666.
Webb, Henry, 636.
Webb, Margaret, 636.
Weekes, Thomas, 689.
Weeks, Elizabeth, 689.
Weeks, John, 689.
Weeks, Martha, 689.
Weeks, Mary, 689.
Weeks, Rebecca, 689.
Weeks, Sarah, 689.
Weeks, Thomas, 689.
Welch, Thomas, 640, 656.
Well, Richard, 681.
Welles, Albert, 663.
Wellman, Elizabeth, 697.
Wellman, Martha, 697.
Wellman, Mary, 697.
Wellman, William, 697.
Wells, Bethia, 678.
Wells, Grace, 634.
Wells, John, 663.

Wells, Mary, 678.
Wells, Mehitable, 678.
Wells, Thomas, 663.
Wells, William, 674, 678.
Westcoat, R., 671.
Wheeler, Elizabeth, 652.
Wheeler, Ephraim, 671.
Wheeler, Gen. Joseph, 651, 655.
Wheeler, Sarah, 643.
Wheeler, Thomas, 640, 656, 661.
Wheeler, William, 643.
Wheelwright, Abigail, 603, 604.
Wheelwright, Rev. Jonathan, 603.
Whelpley, Henry, 668, 672, 680.
Whelpley, Joseph, 671, 672.
Whelpley, Rebecca, 671. 672.
Whelpley, Sarah, 671, 680.
White, Capt. Nathaniel, 693.
Whitehead, Damaris, 624.
Whitehead, Eliphalet, 624.
Whitehead, Elizabeth, 624.
Whitehead, Hannah, 624.
Whitehead, John, 621, 624.
Whitehead, Samuel, 624.
Whitehead, Thomas, 598, 624.
Whitfield, Abigail, 637, 698c.
Whitfield, Rev. Henry, 626, 630, 631, 634, 636, 637, 698c.
Whitfield, Sarah, 631.
Whiting, Giles, 683.
Whitman, John, 656.
Whitman, Zachariah, 640, 654, 656.
Whitmore, Ann, 689.
Whitmore, Frances, 689.
Whitmore, John, 686, 689.
Whitmore, Mary, 689.
Whitmore, Thomas, 689.
Whitney, Eli, 647.
Whittaker, Rev. E., 673.
Whitway, Thomas, 606.
Wilcockson, Timothy, 642.
Wilcoxson, Johanna, 662.
Wilcoxson, John, 662.
Wilcoxson, William, 663.
Wiley, Isaac, 691.
Wilford, John, 600, 622, 623, 655.
Wilford, Lydia, 655.
Wilford, Richard, 623.

SUPPLEMENTARY INDEX.

Wilkinson, Edward, 689.
Wilkinson, William, 663.
Willard, Samuel, 606.
Willett, Capt. Thomas, 651.
Williams, Daniel, 623.
Williams, Richard, 623.
Williams, Roger, 696.
Williams, Samuel, 623.
Williamson, Dericke, 698c.
Williamson, Mary, 698c.
Wilmot, Benjamin, 659.
Wilmot, Elizabeth, 659.
Wilson, Anthony, 671.
Wilson, Sarah, 668.
Wilson, Sarah Jones, 671.
Wines, Anne, 660.
Wines, Barnabas, 660, 674.
Winthrop, Ann, 698.
Winthrop, Fitz-John, 698.
Winthrop, John, 601, 602, 661.
Winthrop, Gov. John, 652, 697.
Winthrop, Lucy, 698.
Winthrop, Margaret, 698.
Winthrop, Martha, 698.
Winthrop, Mary, 698.
Winthrop, Mehitable, 698.
Wood, Edward, 690.
Wood, Jeremiah, 690.
Wood, Jonas, 690.
Woods, W. S., 690.
Wright, Benjamin, 627, 637.
Wright, Jane, 637.
Wyatt, Richard, 696.

Y.

Youngs, Anna, 678.
Youngs, Benjamin, 678.
Youngs, Christopher, 678.
Youngs, Joan, 678.
Youngs, Rev. John, 673, 674, 678.
Youngs, Joseph, 678.
Youngs, Mary, 678.
Youngs, Rachel, 678.
Youngs, Thomas, 678.

www.ingramcontent.com/pod-product-compliance
Lightning Source LLC
Chambersburg PA
CBHW052107010526
44111CB00036B/1489